INFINITE PHENOMENOLOGY

INFINITE PHENOMENOLOGY

The Lessons of Hegel's Science of Experience

John Russon

Northwestern University Press
Evanston, Illinois

Northwestern University Press
www.nupress.northwestern.edu

Printed in the United States of America

10 9 8 7 6 5 4 3 2 1

Library of Congress Cataloging-in-Publication Data

Russon, John, 1960– author.
Infinite phenomenology : the lessons of Hegel's science of experience / John Russon.
pages cm
Includes bibliographical references and index.
ISBN 978-0-8101-3190-3 (cloth : alk. paper) — ISBN 978-0-8101-3191-0 (pbk. : alk. paper) — ISBN 978-0-8101-3192-7 (ebook)
1. Hegel, Georg Wilhelm Friedrich, 1770–1831. Phénomenologie des Geistes. 2. Hegel, Georg Wilhelm Friedrich, 1770–1831. I. Title.
B2929.R858 2015
193—dc22

2015025261

Dedicated to Jay Lampert, my friend for more than thirty years, and the guy who introduced me to Hegel.

’Tis the good reader that makes the good book.
—Emerson, *Society and Solitude*

Contents

Acknowledgments

Writing acknowledgments is a particularly pleasant task, because it gives one the opportunity to make clear the personal level of meaning and indebtedness that is purposely effaced from scientific writing. This book is a major personal accomplishment for me, and so it has a reality that reverberates with all the major intersubjective dimensions of my life. First and most obviously, I am eager to acknowledge my incalculable debt to Shannon Hoff, who daily supplied me with the emotional and intellectual support that kept me motivated to do this work. Indeed, much of the writing of this book was done while sitting across from Shannon at Ideal Coffee as she wrote *The Laws of the Spirit,* her first book on Hegel, and much of the writing of this book channels the energy and insights generated in our conversations in that setting. Throughout the time of the writing of this book I also drew heavily on the resources of my dear friends Patricia Fagan from the University of Windsor (to whom I dedicated my first book on Hegel) and Kirsten Jacobson from the University of Maine, both of whom have proved themselves over many years to be intellectual interlocutors of the first order, as well as excellent companions. I have also benefited greatly from the inspiration and insights offered by many other friends and colleagues, some of the most prominent of whom are Kym Maclaren, David Ciavatta, Maria Talero, Luis Jacob, Greg Kirk, Whitney Howell, Laura McMahon, John Lysaker, Len Lawlor, Pravesh Jung, Siby George, John Hacker-Wright, Pete Costello, Tim Brownlee, Réal Fillion, Karen Robertson, Brian Rogers, Joe Arel, Bryan Richard, Jacob Singer, Jeff Morrisey, Jill Gilbert, Emily Jaklic, Cherilyn Keall, Fred Guerin, Jing Long, Scott Marratto, Alexandra Morrison, Thom Campbell, Adam Loughnane, Tim Fitzjohn, Jared Babin, Jenn Friis, and Adam Schneider. I am also extremely grateful to all those who have participated, over the last ten years, in my annual Toronto Summer Seminar in Philosophy: this has proved to be the most stimulating and rewarding arena for philosophical exchange that I have known, and I am grateful to you all for your contributions to this intellectual community.

Many of the chapters of this book were initially delivered as public lectures. I am grateful to all those who participated in sessions at Emory

University, the Institute for Christian Studies, IIT-Bombay, Boston University, King's College University, Ryerson University, McGill University, Bishop's University, York University, and Brock University, and at the Society for German Idealism and the Hegel Society of America for their kind reception of my work. Finally, I am very happy to thank specially Henry Carrigan of Northwestern University Press. It was Henry's idea that I write this book, and I have found the professional and philosophical relationship that we have developed since that time very gratifying.

An earlier version of the prologue was published as "The Project of Hegel's Phenomenology," in Stephen Houlgate and Michael Baur (eds.), *A Companion to Hegel* (London: Wiley-Blackwell, 2011), pp. 47–67.

Earlier versions of chapters 1 and 5 were published respectively as "Temporality and the Future of Philosophy in Hegel," *International Philosophical Quarterly* 48 (2008): 59–68, and "Emotional Subjects: Mood and Articulation in Hegel's *Philosophy of Mind*," *International Philosophical Quarterly* 49 (2009): 41–52.

An earlier version of chapter 3 was published as "Reading: Derrida in Hegel's Understanding," *Research in Phenomenology* 36 (2006): 181–200. I am grateful to Brill Academic Publishers for permission to publish a revised version of the chapter here.

An earlier version of chapter 4 was published as "Desiring Production and Spirit: On *Anti-Oedipus* and German Idealism," in Karen Houle and Jim Vernon (eds.), *Hegel and Deleuze: Together Again for the First Time* (Evanston: Northwestern University Press, 2013).

An earlier version of the epilogue was published as "Subjectivity and Objectivity in Hegel's *Science of Logic*," in Michael Baur and Robert Wood (eds.), *Person, Being and History: Essays in Honour of Kenneth L. Schmitz* (Washington: Catholic University of America Press, 2011). I am grateful to Catholic University Press for permission to publish a revised version here.

An earlier version of the appendix was published as "Dialectic, Difference and the Other: The Hegelianizing of French Philosophy" in Alan Schrift and Leonard Lawlor (eds.), *Responses to Phenomenology* (Dublin: Acumen, 2009), pp. 17–41.

A Note on Citations

All references to Hegel's *Phenomenology of Spirit* will be to *Phänomenologie des Geistes,* edited by H.-F. Wessels and H. Clairmont (Hamburg: Felix Meiner Verlag, 1988), translated into English by A. V. Miller as *Phenomenology of Spirit* (Oxford: Oxford University Press, 1977). Textual references will be given to the paragraph number of the English translation (M) and to the pagination of the German text (W/C). Roman numerals will be used to refer to chapters of the *Phenomenology of Spirit,* whereas Arabic numerals will be used to refer to my own chapters. All translations of this work are taken from Miller's text, unless otherwise indicated. I have consistently changed Miller's "notion" (as a translation of *der Begriff*) to "concept," and I have silently corrected instances in which the emphasis in Miller's translation does not match that of the German text.

References to Hegel's *Science of Logic* will be to *Wissenschaft der Logik,* volumes 1 and 2 (*Werke* 5 and 6), ed. Eva Moldenhauer and Karl Markus Michel (Frankfurt am Main: Suhrkamp, 1986), translated into English by A. V. Miller as *Science of Logic* (New York: Humanities Press, 1976). References will be to Miller's English translation (E) followed by reference to the German text (G).

References to Hegel's *Encyclopaedia of the Philosophical Sciences* will be to *Enzyklopädie der philosophischen Wissenschaften,* volumes 1, 2, and 3 (*Werke* 8, 9, and 10), ed. Eva Moldenhauer and Karl Markus Michel (Frankfurt am Main: Suhrkamp, 1970), and to the English translations: *The Encyclopaedia Logic, with the Zusätze,* translated by T. F. Geraets, W. A. Suchting, and H. S. Harris (Indianapolis/Cambridge: Hackett, 1991); *Philosophy of Nature,* translated by A. V. Miller (Oxford: Clarendon, 1970); and *Philosophy of Mind,* translated by William Wallace and A. V. Miller (Oxford: Clarendon, 1971). Unless otherwise indicated, all translations will be quoted from these texts. When page references are necessary, the page in the English translation will be followed by a reference to the page of the relevant volume of the *Enzyklopädie* (*Enz* 1, 2, or 3).

References to Hegel's *Philosophy of Right* will be to *Grundlinien der Philosophie des Rechts* (*Werke* 7), ed. Eva Moldenhauer and Karl Markus Michel (Frankfurt am Main: Suhrkamp, 1986), translated into English as *Elements of the Philosophy of Right* by Allen W. Wood (Cambridge: Cambridge University Press, 1991). Reference will be to the pagination of the *Philosophy of Right* followed by pagination in the *Grundlinien.* I also periodically refer to the *Zusätze* translated in Wood from Gans's selections from Hotho's and Grisheim's transcription of lectures. I have repeated Wood's identification of these as (H) and (G) to identify the relevant manuscript. On the nature of these texts, see Wood's "Translator's Preface" to *Elements of the Philosophy of Right,* pp. xxxv–xxxvi.

Throughout the text, I will generally alternate between the masculine and the feminine when personal pronouns are required.

Introduction

Reading Hegel's Phenomenology

It is easy, living in a world in which the works of a great philosopher have already been written, to see those works as containers of easily graspable ideas, as works that are readily available for our interpretation of judgment. Once they are written, such books become "facts" in our world, and learning what the author said is accomplished in much the same way one finds out about other facts: by listening to teachers, by looking up reference works, and so on. This way in which these works exist for us, however, is not—not at all—the way those works existed for their authors, and the recognition of this is essential to understanding such works truly.

For the authors of the great philosophical works, the ideas with which they grappled were new, and the theses they put forward were unprecedented and revolutionary. Having not been articulated prior to their expression in these novel words, the ideas involved were also such that the authors had to wrest those ideas into existence through grappling with them in writing. Those of us who write regularly ourselves are familiar with this idea that it is only through the process of writing that we bring our own ideas to clarity; how much more profound and creative is the importance of expression for the articulation of the original and world-transforming ideas that the great philosophers have brought forward for us.

There is a fundamental way, in other words, in which the writing of any of the great works of philosophy is closely akin to the creation of a great work of art, and we need to bear this in mind when reading the works of the great philosophers. Generally speaking, the great works of philosophy transform our thinking and, indeed, create new forms of expression in order to do this. Plato's dialogues, Augustine's *Confessions,* Descartes's *Meditations on First Philosophy,* Kant's *Critique of Pure Reason,* Heidegger's *Being and Time,* Derrida's *Voice and Phenomenon*: these works each inaugurated a new genre of philosophical expression, and we need to be attentive to the unique interpretive demands that the *form* of such writing puts upon us as we try to apprehend its content.

Hegel's *Phenomenology of Spirit,* similarly, is a revolutionary book of philosophy, both for the content of the ideas it communicates and for its inauguration of a new form of philosophical writing. Some aspects of the novelty of this form are regularly recognized by the familiar acknowledgement that Hegel's writing is opaque, by the questions raised about the use of the "we" and the "for us" to articulate Hegel's philosophical voice, by puzzlement about "how we get from" this stage to that stage of his argument, and so on. To describe this novel form well would be a significant (and worthwhile) task in its own right, and it would include recognizing the uniquely dynamic character of Hegel's writing, such that what is being studied is *actually in motion*, whereas typically we study a fixed object; it would include recognizing the unique intertwining of rigorous systematicity with this articulation of a "moving target"; it would include recognizing Hegel's development of an original technical vocabulary to express the essential conceptual parameters of this systematic expression; it would include recognizing the stylized way in which Hegel integrates cultural reference and allusion into his account. It is not my intention to undertake the full description of the unique character of Hegel's writing, but simply to note that this novel form puts upon us significant interpretive demands, and an approach to the text that assumes that reading the text is as simple as, and follows the same rules as, reading, for example, the standard examples of academic prose produced by contemporary philosophy professors will fail in fundamental ways to appreciate what Hegel's book communicates. Just as Hegel had to learn what his ideas were through writing them, we who read Hegel's book must learn how to read it through the process of trying to read it. We must let the book itself teach us what it requires of us, rather than approaching it with pre-fabricated demands and expectations about how such a philosophical text "must" work.

Throughout the preface and the introduction of the *Phenomenology of Spirit,* Hegel attempts to make clear what the project of a "phenomenology of spirit" is. He calls this project "the science of the experience of consciousness," and he describes it as the presuppositionless method that "just looks on" at experience, to witness how, behind its own back, that experience is critically judging and transforming itself.[1] Just as I have said that in our reading we must turn to the work itself and allow it to teach us how to read it, so must a phenomenology turn to the happening of experience, and allow experience itself to teach it (phenomenology) what experience is and how it needs to be understood. Most basically, the project of phenomenology is the project of approaching the happening of experience that for each of us is our own, living reality, right here, right now, with a responsiveness, an educated passivity, sufficiently attuned to this happening—the phenomenon—to witness its own determinacy and dynamism. This is Hegel's project—in his language, the "concept" of phenomenology—and reading his book aright will be reading it *as* the attempt to carry out this project: what is actually written—in his language, the "actuality" of phenomenology that is the *Phenomenology of Spirit*—is only understood when it is understood as the enactment of this project. This project, the generative "silence" that is heard throughout what is actually written—what Hegel calls "the creative secret of its birth"[2]—is the immanent standard by which this actuality is to be judged. We can conclude from this that adequately reading the *Phenomenology of Spirit,* then, requires three things of the reader.

First, each section of the book must be read against this silence, this definitive project of phenomenology, that is the motivation and justification for each section. Hegel's text is not reducible to the finite set of ordered words that define its determinate actuality. Beyond these words, Hegel's text is *what they mean to say.* It is, indeed, only in and through these exact words that Hegel says anything at all, and, indeed, those words have the capacity to reveal a sense that Hegel himself never anticipated.[3] Nonetheless, reading the text is not a simple "calculus" in which one establishes the meaning of each of the components independently and then derives the overall meaning of their conjunction; rather, those words themselves have their meaning only insofar as they adopt their status as participating in the expressing of what Hegel is trying to communicate, and reading is recognizing how the resources that these words make available allow a meaning to become available that is uniquely realized through their cooperative venture. Reading the text is not calculating the sense of the words, but is seeing how they express Hegel's effort to communicate the witnessing of experience in which he is (was) engaged.

Second, each section must be read in relationship to the specific phenomenon—the specific event of experience—of which it is the phenomenological description. What Hegel's text offers is brilliant insight in its description of familiar experiences. If the reader does not know, however, what the phenomenon is that is being described, there is no way even to know whether what Hegel says is correct or not, let alone to learn from his insight. If one is not familiar with the experience of understanding, scepticism, or conscience, for example, then Hegel's discerning of the definitive characteristics and logic of those experiences will be no more meaningful to the reader than an essay differentiating the tonal qualities of different orchestral instruments will be to someone born deaf. To appreciate such discussions of understanding or conscience, the reader (I presume) already conveniently has access to the phenomenon in question at his disposal, and needs only to "turn around" and observe his own experience (rigorously and insightfully, of course) to be able to recognize the features Hegel describes. When Hegel discusses ancient Greek funerary practices, views of women, and political organization, when he discusses the principles, phases, and structures of the French revolution, or when he discusses the differences between mechanical, chemical, and organic processes in nature, though, the reader will need to do more than turn to herself to understand and assess his claims, but will, in fact, need to study those empirical matters in order to be able to appreciate what Hegel is saying. One cannot practice phenomenology except by turning to the phenomenon.

Reading the book well, then, will always require that the reader be asking two questions: "how is this a description of a basic event of experience?" and "how is this Hegel's attempt to carry out this project?" The text, in other words, must be *seen in its striving*, must be seen in terms of its constitutive endeavor. Legitimate judgment of the success of the work will be made by thus measuring the actuality of Hegel's accomplishment against the "subjective" standard of his project/concept and the "objective" standard of the phenomenon to be described. Hegel's work is unsatisfactory by its own standards to the extent that it does not do justice to these "subjective" and "objective" poles, and the task of the reader is to read the text critically, measuring the adequacy of Hegel's actual writing to these its definitive, constitutive norms. In fact, in my own judgment, when one does read the book in this way, one finds it to be a remarkably rigorous and compelling carrying out of its project.

Finally, third, beyond these demands of correct "observation"—correctly holding on to the overall project and correctly identifying the relevant specific object—Hegel's phenomenology puts upon the reader the demand of *participation*. We are accustomed to reading books in which an author expresses her own view—"I think that . . ."—or describes something in the world—"It is . . ."—and this first-person and this third-person situation each presents us with an object, an "other," that we observe. Hegel's project, however, is to describe the living happening of experience *from the inside*, and, for us to appreciate this, we, too, must be on the inside of this experience, which means the experience under description must be our own. In other words, Hegel's phenomenology *speaks in the second person*, that is, it calls to *you* to enact the experience under discussion in order to be able to notice in your own experience the features it describes. Identifying the phenomenon under discussion means, in fact, identifying the phenomenon *of your own* experience that is under discussion, and, without thus turning to reflect upon one's own experience, one is not reading Hegel's *Phenomenology*. From the start, then, one must *do* something to engage with this work, and, indeed, the lessons of the work must thus become lessons for oneself, the transformations of the experience under discussion must become transformations within one's own experience. Rilke's poem "Archaic Torso of Apollo" expresses well the central message of Hegel's phenomenology: "You must change your life."[4]

While various claims regarding the failure of Hegel's philosophical project circulate widely, my own attempt to follow these three principles in reading Hegel's text has left me unconvinced by the familiar criticisms of Hegel's work. My own assessment of critical writing on Hegel is that in general it does not operate with sufficient plasticity and openness in responding to Hegel's writing, that is, it precisely fails to appreciate the demands upon the reader to situate Hegel's writing in relation to the project of phenomenology and the phenomena of experience and this, generally, because it fails to appreciate the uniqueness and originality of Hegel's form of writing, insisting instead that Hegel's writing follow the "rules" that one might impose upon oneself when submitting a term paper for evaluation by a professor or an article for publication in a journal. My task in this work, however, is not at all to defend this claim about the characteristics of critical scholarship on Hegel. My goal, instead, is the more positive one of actually showing how Hegel's writing does successfully carry out the phenomenological description of the event(s) of experience that it purports to accomplish.

Hegel's writing is the actualization of a concept, the rendering determinate of an intention. This rendering determinate, this actualizing, is a realization of the project, but it is not its exhaustive—and therefore terminative—enactment. The project is "ideal" in the sense that it defines a sense, an endeavor, that can always be realized again, beyond any realization it has so far had. This inexhaustibility of the project is, in part, what is reflected in my title *Infinite Phenomenology*, and my own goal in reading and writing about Hegel is to grasp the ideality in his claims, that is, to see his writing as the realization of a project that has the capacity to educate one into the ability to enact that project oneself. My own discussions of Hegel are thus reiterations of his phenomenology: I do not treat Hegel's *words* as the ultimate—"the absolute"—but as its "traces," as Derrida would say; that is, I read the text as exhorting me to notice something, and my own writing is an attempt to deliver that same exhortation to the reader.

My own reading, then, operates with (1) the phenomenon under question, (2) the project of phenomenology, and (3) the insight that I have learned/grasped through my own study of Hegel's phenomenology of the phenomenon, and my project in writing about Hegel's text is to carry out a phenomenology of the phenomenon in a way that reveals to the reader the insight that I apprehended through my engagement with

Hegel's text. In my chapters, then, the reader will find more focus on the phenomenon and on the enactment of the method than on the repetition and dissection of the details of Hegel's writing.

At the same time, however, because there is no way to Hegel's meaning—the "ideal"—except through the reality, the finite "traces," through which it is articulated, my own apprehension of *the sense of his text* could come from nothing other than the text itself—that reality *of which* the ideal is the ideal. For that reason, my approach to Hegel is nonetheless what it has become a common cliché to call "a close reading": my own study has developed through years of poring over the intricacies of Hegel's text, and my writing is an attempt to articulate Hegel's insights in a way that is highly responsive to the details of his text. To demonstrate in detail how I understand each sentence of Hegel's text, or how each of my sentences is responsive to precise details of Hegel's text, would require a book thousands of pages longer than this, and carrying out such a project of demonstration would undermine other goals that define this book, which include clarity of focus on the central experiential and conceptual issues and, especially, ease of use. My writing thus makes a compromise between the projects of original reiteration and textual commentary. In addition to teaching Hegel's insight to the reader through the phenomenological description of the phenomenon, my goal in each chapter is to tie my analysis closely enough to the determinacies of Hegel's text to allow the reader to see how my claims are in fact the claims *of* the text. To accomplish this, I typically try to identify the pivotal point in the text at which the crucial phenomenological observation or conceptual argument is made, and discuss these passages explicitly; I also choose my language overall to resonate with the language of the text such that, though I do not cite textual passages, the reader working with both Hegel's text and my own will recognize the passages I am drawing upon; finally, I document my claims in the footnotes with references to textual passages such that the reader who is prepared to do the work of following out my references will indeed find that what I am offering is, indeed, a very "close reading."

I describe my own project as "reading," but this reading, though singular in its purpose, is in fact enacted through a multiplicity of specific "readings." These are the "lessons" (from Old French *leçon,* itself from the Latio *lectio,* "a reading") of Hegel's science of experience, to which the subtitle of the book refers. Hegel's text is structured as a systematic series of studies of different aspects of human experience, each of which investigates how the fundamental nature of experience and the fundamental nature of reality is revealed through that experience. My own text is a series of "readings" of these studies, a series of "lessons," in which I draw out what is to be learned from these studies. My approach to reading Hegel's *Phenomenology*, in other words, does not take the form of a continuous textual commentary, but aims to extract from the book a set of teachings that can inform—indeed, transform—one's life. Because these discrete "readings" are also generally geared to the successive sections of Hegel's text, they also, I hope, will be suitable supplements to university courses on Hegel's *Phenomenology*, each offering something like the weekly "lesson" for each class of a one-semester course.

In this structure of successive, independent studies of the successive segments of Hegel's book, this volume echoes my earlier book, *Reading Hegel's Phenomenology*, and, indeed, in addition to being a self-standing work in its own right, this volume is also intended as a complement to that earlier book. In an effort to demonstrate the richness and plasticity of Hegel's text, I have here offered a second "reading" of Hegel's *Phenomenology* that generally differs in focus and theme (but not in its fundamental theses) from *Reading Hegel's Phenomenology*; I have done this to demonstrate to the student of Hegel how to be simultaneously rigorous and creative—philosophical—in interpreting Hegel's text, and to demonstrate how powerfully Hegel's philosophy can speak to, essentially, whatever questions we bring to it. In addition to offering a different focus and thematic emphasis, this new volume also differs from *Reading Hegel's Phenomenology* by including discussions of other texts by Hegel that themselves complement the *Phenomenology*, namely, the *Philosophy of Spirit*, the *Philosophy of Right*, and the *Science of Logic*. While this new volume is still very much intended as a self-contained study of the *Phenomenology* as a whole, suitable for introducing that work to the new reader, it is less oriented than *Reading Hegel's Phenomenology* is to the introduction and explanation of all the basic "moves" of Hegel's text, and more oriented to moving from these basic teachings of Hegel's text to an interpretation of their broader implications.

This new "reading" of Hegel's *Phenomenology* proceeds through three main sections: "Reality," "Personality," and "Freedom." These three sections parallel roughly sections A, "Consciousness," B, "Self-Consciousness," and C (untitled) of Hegel's *Phenomenology*. This material is preceded by one chapter that studies the project of Hegel's *Phenomenology* as that is laid out in his preface and introduction. It is succeeded by a chapter that offers in outline an interpretation of Hegel's *Science of Logic*, and considers the relationship between that book and the *Phenomenology*, and an appendix that discusses the reception and appropriation of Hegel's *Phenomenology* in twentieth-century French philosophy. Let me briefly explain the individual steps—the "lessons"—through which this reading of the *Phenomenology* will proceed.

In the preface and introduction to the *Phenomenology*, Hegel describes the philosophical project he will undertake in the work, and my prologue, "The Project of Hegel's Phenomenology of Spirit," studies the distinctive character of this undertaking, which is, simply, to describe experience as it is experienced. One of the most distinctive—and challenging—aspects of this project is that *it can only be understood through enacting it,* that is, one must *do* phenomenology in order to *know* what is being described. The prefatory description, in other words, is something like a promise, a glimpse in advance of what one would come to recognize were one to undertake the project oneself. Further, inasmuch as this phenomenology is the description of experience, one must *engage in the experience under description* in order to *engage in description.* The main thrust of this chapter is thus to show that the method of phenomenology cannot truly be enacted except by enacting a progressively more responsible engagement with one's own experience: phenomenology is not the detached observation of a finished object, but is the embrace of the internal imperatives of experience itself, and can itself ultimately be realized only in and as cognitive, ethical, and spiritual practice. The prologue thus introduces in outline the central steps through which the phenomenology actually proceeds in order to show how those steps, in their determinacy, uniquely enact and define the phenomenological project and to show how the reader herself can be said truly to be reading the book only if she is herself experientially implicated in the subject-matter—*die Sache selbst*—under description. This chapter also shows how Hegel's *Phenomenology* is a taking up of the philosophical project pioneered by Kant, namely, the recognition of the infinite within the finite, and this theme of the recognition of the indwelling infinite that is realized in, but not exhausted by, finitude provides one of the main conceptual touchstones for the studies undertaken in subsequent chapters. Just as the book overall aims to reveal the infinitude of Hegel's phenomenology through its finite articulation, so do the separate studies generally reveal specific "infinites" that are at play in different facets of experience; as our studies progress we will become more and more attuned to this theme, ultimately, in chapters 12 and 13, addressing the logic and the phenomenon of "the infinite" directly.

Section A of Hegel's *Phenomenology*, "Consciousness," describes the forms of experience that take themselves to be recognizing an independent reality: "knowing." The task of phenomenology is to describe accurately this experience of an independent reality, and we can correctly describe this experience in three ways, which are the subjects, respectively, of Hegel's three chapters "Sense-Certainty," "Perception," and "Understanding." If you ask me what I see when I look in front of me, I can correctly say that I see colors, that I see things, and that I see the world. What is important to note is that each of these designations—"colors," "things," and "world"—refers to the same situation: *through* the colors, I see things, and *through* the things, I see a world. The former term is, in each case, the "front end" or the "show" of the latter term, which is the "truth" or the "essence" of that appearing. What Hegel's phenomenology of consciousness shows is that an attitude that takes any one of these terms as the "absolute" while denying the irreducible essentiality of the other two will implicitly reveal the equal essentiality of those others through its own natural process. In other words, there is no temporal priority here, no moving from a more basic to a more derived; rather, our sensory experience is always the experience of a world of things, things always and only exist as sensory presences situated in a contextualizing world, and the world is only experienced as sensorily present things. The three chapters of part 1, "Reality," investigate this mutual embeddedness of quality, thing, and world.

Chapter 1, "The Lessons of Sense-Certainty: Temporality and Ontology," distills from Hegel's chapter "Sense-Certainty" the central lesson that experiential significance is always given as contextualized and, indeed, temporally contextualized. Hegel's "Sense-Certainty" chapter begins by describing the experience that takes itself to be exclusively absorbed in sensory immediacy and shows that this experience, contrary to its own self-interpretation, is always implicitly mediated, always implicitly related to a constitutive non-presence as much as it is explicitly oriented to immediate presence. Chapter 1 extracts this central lesson of the constitutive, mediating temporality of experience, and shows how this conception of mediating temporality is essentially of a piece with the distinction between "primary actuality" and "secondary actuality" that is central to Aristotle's ontology of natural beings and, indeed, is the distinctive logic of a *thing*. The perception of things is always implicit in the experience of sensory qualities, and this chapter works out the implications of this, and of the correlating of temporality and ontology in general, for the more advanced forms of experience that Hegel will go on to describe throughout the *Phenomenology*.

Chapter 2, "The Logic of Perception: On Things, Persons, and the Nature of Love," follows Hegel's study in his "Perception" chapter of the distinctive character of the individual thing. In "Perception," Hegel describes our everyday experience of perceiving individual things, a perception we take to be simple and immediate. What Hegel's description of the experience of perception reveals, however, is that, contrary to its own self-interpretation, perception is neither simple nor immediate but is, rather, a process of shifting between contradictory interpretive theses regarding the nature of the object. This mediating interpretation reveals that perception is always implicitly reliant upon a practice of interpretation, and the perceived thing always implicitly dependent upon its place in a coherent, intelligible world. Drawing on the resonances of Hegel's argument with the philosophies of both Descartes and Sartre, chapter 2 works through this implicit logic of perception and draws out the implications for interpersonal experience of this implicit complexity and implicit dependency upon understanding. In particular, we can see that our familiar experiences of love rely upon the logic of perception and, indeed, evince the same contradictions; the natural propulsion of perception toward understanding offers a lesson in love, showing how we must approach each other in order not to suffer the contradictions of perceptual life in our relations with each other.

Whereas "Sense-Certainty" and "Perception" each demonstrate the embeddedness of specific individuals (qualities or things) in a presupposed context of universality (the thing or the coherent world), Hegel's third chapter, "Understanding," reveals the ontological dependence of universality upon the particularities in and through which it is realized. Chapter 3, "Understanding: Reading and *Différance*," follows the basic dialectic of understanding, contrasting in particular (1) the "understanding" that applies the abstract universality of independently defined rules to specific instances to which the rules are in principle indifferent to (2) the understanding that learns from particularity its own immanent sense. This latter is the apprehension of a concrete universality from which neither particularity nor, indeed, the practice of understanding itself can be detached. Chapter 3 concludes by showing that this conception of the concrete intelligibility of reality is of a piece with Jacques Derrida's notion of "*différance*."

The transition from the stance of perception to the stance of understanding is the recognition that what we, in everyday perception, take to be independent realities—things—are really so many manifestations of a single reality. Through each, that is, reality as such is showing itself. This stance of understanding is the familiar stance of the (modern) scientist who sees all the putative realities of perceptual life as in fact the expression of the ultimate forces that shape reality, and those things are known in their truth when they are understood as such expressions.[5] When we *understand reality* we treat it as, ultimately, a single force: what we encounter (and, indeed, what we are) is reality expressing itself, reality realizing itself. For a force to express itself, however, there must be difference: it must *ex*press itself, realize itself in otherness, and thus make a difference. If reality is one, then, that one must be two, that is, force can only realize itself as a relation to other, and so force must enact itself as an opposition, as a relation of soliciting and solicited, as a "negative self-relation."[6] This structure of "relating to itself as relating to another" or "relating to another as relating to itself" is a structure we experience from the inside in our experience of self-consciousness, and section B of Hegel's *Phenomenology*, "Self-Consciousness," studies the different forms of self-conscious experience.

Just as objectivity was simultaneously sensory, thingly, and worldly, so is subjectivity immediate, independent, and answerable to an immanent universality. Hegel's study of self-consciousness progresses through the description of these three dimensions of desire, interpersonal independence, and free thinking, and the four chapters of part 2, "Personality," extract the lessons of these studies for our developing of an adequate self-understanding.

In "theoretical" consciousness—the familiar stance of wanting to *know* our surroundings—we experience reality as the self-defining force that is responsible for itself and for our experience of it. In desire, the subject of chapter 4, "Desiring-Production and Spirit," we live from a denial of the "absoluteness" of reality, and instead treat ourselves—our desire—as the "absolute," the ultimate force for which the "soliciting" world is only the occasion for its—desire's—own practical self-expression. Drawing upon Kant's *Critique of Pure Reason* and Deleuze and Guattari's *Anti-Oedipus*, chapter 4 draws out this fundamental contrast between the stance of knowing—"objectivity"—and the life of desire in order to show how it is that desire occupies a logical/ontological space irreducible to and, indeed, transcendent of, the logic of consciousness. A careful reading of Hegel's description of desire then demonstrates how it is that desire itself always has intersubjective relations on its horizon: desire, that is, is implicitly "of" independent persons, just as sensory qualities are implicitly "of" things. The lesson of desire, then, is that what we implicitly seek in our desiring relationship to the world is the recognition—the endorsement—of others.

The idea that our self-conscious life is fundamentally defined by our dependence upon the recognition of others is perhaps Hegel's most famous—and most important—thesis. In the *Phenomenology of Spirit*, Hegel documents the experiential emergence of this need within the life of (putatively) immediate desire. In the "Anthropology" section of his *Encyclopaedia of the Philosophical Sciences*, and in a fashion resonant with Heidegger's discussion of *Dasein* in *Being and Time*, Hegel offers a complementary study of the implicit role of intersubjective recognition within the immediacy of affective life, and chapter 5, "Mood and Articulation," works through the material on "mood" from the *Encyclopaedia* in order to bring further depth to this notion that our most immediate "personal" life is inherently "spiritual," that is, inherently answerable to the demands of intersubjective recognition. We saw with desire that it can be the "force" that is definitive of "reality" only by having a soliciting other upon and within which it expresses and realizes itself. Hegel's description of mood reveals that it, similarly, is an impulsion toward—a desire for—expression. Hegel documents different forms that this "outering" takes, but it is ultimately in language that this desire for expression is satisfied. To express ourselves in language we must define ourselves in relationship to an outside that is *constitutively* outside, that is, we must acknowledge that we are dealing with an other-for-itself, with another self-consciousness. Our desire for emotional self-expression can only find satisfaction through participation in the world of co-subjectivity, of "spirit." Spirit is the reality that is realized only in this situation of self-expression accommodated by a self-consciously supporting other, a force that expresses itself only in and as the mutually recognized equality of "solicited" and "soliciting" forces.

In his study of "The Independence of Dependence of Self-Consciousness," Hegel presents this concept of equality of recognition and describes patterns of interpersonal behavior that engage dishonestly and inadequately with this domain of mutual recognition. Rather than working through in detail the problems evinced by these insufficient forms of self-consciousness (a working through that I have done elsewhere[7]), chapter 6, "Recognition and Religious Narrative," draws out the central positive lesson of this section by comparison with R. D. Laing's notion of "ontological insecurity." Laing, following Hegel, shows that our very experience of ourselves *as* coherent selves is something that is only accomplished cooperatively, only achieved, that is, through the support of others. Carrying forward the theme of language from chapter 5, chapter 6 focuses on the essential role of *narrative* in our establishing of an identity in a shared interpersonal space. This notion of the essentiality of recognition to identity and the essentiality of narrative to identity in turn provides the key to understanding the nature of religion, and chapter 6 ends by showing the essential connection between Hegel's study of the dialectic of recognition and his phenomenology of religion.

Religion is both a cultural phenomenon—the communal sharing of a narrative about the ultimate nature of reality—and a personal experience of answerability to an infinite beyond. This latter stance of experiencing a "calling" is the stance Hegel calls "unhappy consciousness," and it is the final stance in Hegel's description of self-consciousness. Chapter 7, "The Call of the Beyond: Unhappy Consciousness and the Structure of Hegel's Argument," takes up the study of unhappy consciousness as the culmination of the dialectic of the "freedom" of self-consciousness.

Desire revealed itself to be something that occurs within the world of interpersonal and social interaction, and this world of recognition is itself composed of individuals who experience within themselves their own contextualization by an intelligible reality—what Hegel here calls the world of "thinking"[8]—beyond their singularity, a world of sense that is not defined by the contingent, historical terms of intersubjective life, but that carries an independent and compelling force within itself—indeed, a force normative *for* intersubjective life. This revelation of sense, reducible neither to desire nor to intersubjective recognition, is the experience of "the absolute." Chapter 7 considers how, just as the universal upon which sensory qualities and perceptible things revealed their own dependence itself revealed its inseparability from the singularity and particularity of sensuous, perceptible reality, so does this universal truth to which desire and recognition show themselves answerable reveal itself to be inseparable from its realization within the singularity and particularity of the self-conscious lives of individuals within communities. Chapter 7 then shows in outline how the remainder of Hegel's *Phenomenology* is dedicated to the description of the experiences in which this reciprocal dependence of the finitude and the infinitude of self-consciousness is explicitly acknowledged.

The six essays in section C, "Freedom," study the forms of social experience in which "spirit," the intersubjective reality of simultaneously answering to and realizing the absolute, is enacted. As chapter 7 indicated, the untitled part C of Hegel's *Phenomenology* proceeds through four chapters: "Reason," "Spirit," "Religion," and "Absolute Knowing." The essays of section C focus exclusively on the "Spirit" and "Religion" chapters, having as their goal the understanding of what Hegel's *Phenomenology* specifically reveals about the nature of human social life, in light of the characteristics of sense and intersubjectivity that have been developed through the earlier studies in the *Phenomenology*.[9] Whereas *Reading Hegel's Phenomenology* emphasized the earlier chapters of Hegel's *Phenomenology*, and focused largely on discerning the *logic* of his later chapters, the focus here is much more on the *politics* of these later chapters.

Chapter 8, "Spirit and Method," introduces Hegel's concept of *Geist*—"spirit"—in relationship to the themes developed in the preceding chapters. We concluded our study of "Consciousness" by describing the metaphysical world entailed by the experience of understanding, a world of force and of dynamic tension between being and beings; we concluded our study of "Self-Consciousness" by describing the subjective situation entailed by the experience of unhappy consciousness, a domain in which freedom is not separable from an experience of answerability to a beyond. Through his description of the exemplary experience of Antigone in Greek mythology (specifically, in Sophocles' tragedy *Antigone*), Hegel introduces the notion of spirit as a distinct metaphysical domain—a distinct kind of reality—that carries forward these metaphysical and experiential parameters that have proven to be definitive of conscious and self-conscious life. We have already seen desire and intersubjective recognition carry forward the notion of "force" that understanding recognizes as definitive of the nature of reality. Spirit is, essentially, the "ultimate" name for the force that is reality, is, that is, the true context of human action: "the real thing," *die Sache selbst.* Spirit, the defining context of human life, is first and foremost "ethicality" (*Sittlichkeit*), the shared sense of cohabitation that characterizes a community's experience of being at home in the world. Chapter 8 uses Hegel's discussion of Antigone's ethicality to discern the way in which spirit carries forward the metaphysical and experiential demands we have so far studied. Ethicality alone, however, is insufficient to realize the nature of spirit, because it does not adequately recognize the autonomy of individual, self-conscious life. Chapter 8 uses Hegel's discussion of the experience of the slave to show how spirit must be self-critical and self-transformative—must be *self-conscious*—in order to fulfill its own mandate which is, ultimately, to be the realization of freedom.

"Freedom" is the fullest realization of reality, and Hegel's study of spirit is the study of freedom realizing itself. In part A, "Ethicality," and part B, "Culture," of chapter VI of the *Phenomenology*, "Spirit," Hegel studies the transformations of Western history from the city-state system of ancient Greece to the universal democracy of the French Revolution, and chapter 9, "Freedom as Nature, Revolution, and Event," distills the essential lesson from this study of the history of freedom. Hegel's description shows that Western history has been the political enactment of two different—and equally essential—interpretations of the nature of human freedom, each of which has been a profound realization of human liberation and fulfillment, but each of which has also exhausted its promise and thus become oppressive in its continued definition of the political domain. This history of the emergence, mutual opposition, and exhaustion of these two interpretations points to and defines the need for a new interpretation of human freedom, and, consequently, a new politics. Drawing on Aristotle, St. Paul, and Foucault to complement Hegel's study of Western political history, chapter 9 provides the basic "map" of the history and nature of human freedom that chapters 10 through 12 study in greater detail.

Chapter 10, "Freedom and Institutions: Perception, Spirit, and the Time of Right," draws on Hegel's parallel study of political institutions in the *Philosophy of Right* to complement the analysis of freedom that chapter 9 distilled from the "Spirit" chapter of the *Phenomenology of Spirit.* By considering the nature of everyday experience, we can see that political life is not a separate domain of experience but is the pervasive context for enacting a free life, and the successful carrying out of our everyday perceptual life thus rests upon the establishment of the appropriately supportive political institutions. By studying the nature of freedom as such, it is possible to establish the forms of political—institutional—life that are required to support the needs of freedom, and chapter 10 distills from the *Philosophy of Right* the essential character of the necessary institutions of freedom. Paralleling the interpretations of freedom that characterize the ancient "ethical" polity and the modern "cultural" polity, the forms of freedom realized in the family and civil society similarly present equally necessary but mutually opposed institutions of human sociality. A third institution, the state (i.e., government), is necessary to support, mediate, and organize the relations of family and civil society. Free perceptual life thus depends upon the establishing of a polity in which the reciprocal necessity of these three institutions is recognized. Further, however, the simple fact of establishing these institutions is not itself the complete accomplishment of freedom; instead, it is incumbent upon perceptual life itself to realize explicitly its inherently political character and to become the site for enacting this institutional life as a site for establishing with others a shared experience of freedom in the living practice of conscientious action and multicultural dialogue.

Whereas chapters 9 and 10 establish the overall logical terrain of freedom, chapter 11, "Democratic Regime and Democratic Practice: The Politics of Modernity," draws out the lesson of this analysis for the understanding of the distinct problems and needs of our modern political world. Drawing upon Hegel's description of the political transformations of the French Revolution, chapter 11 studies how, specifically, the modern politics of individualistic democracy is both a necessary and an insufficient interpretation of human freedom. As we saw in the phenomenology of self-consciousness, we are essentially embodied, and essentially dependent upon the recognition of others, a recognition essentially embedded in the cultural and religious narratives that provide the matrix within which our individuality grows. While individualist democracy and its attendant notion of universal human rights is essential to recognizing the inherent singularity of the experience of self-conscious freedom, the institutions of the political society that bases itself exclusively on this individual interpretation of freedom fail to appreciate and support the material, interpersonal, and social preconditions that are presupposed by that individual freedom. Hegel studies the "Terror" that developed in the later phases of the French Revolution as something like the *reductio ad absurdum* of the principle of individualist democracy, the exemplary demonstration of the anti-humanism that is implicit in this attempt to develop a political humanism. Chapter 11 demonstrates how Hegel's analysis of the Terror has as its lesson a critique of the politics of modernity that is of a piece with Marx's critique of capitalism and with Derrida's analysis of the aporias of democracy. Just as chapter 10 showed that the domain of human freedom will never be reducible to the set of political institutions but will always exist only in a performance that engages with the emergent needs of the present situation, chapter 11 similarly shows why the sphere of *Moralität*—"Morality"—is the proper completion of Hegel's "Spirit" chapter, pointing to the experience of conscience as the "absolute form" of self-conscious freedom.

Chapter 12, "Conscience and the Unity of Being," returns us to the question of the *metaphysical* character of self-consciousness: we saw above that spirit is *a particular kind of reality*, and chapter 12 considers how self-consciousness introduces a unique problem for, and raises unique possibilities for, what it is to *be*. Drawing upon the logic of "infinitude and finitude" from Hegel's *Science of Logic*, chapter 11 investigates the way in which it is integral to the nature of being to be a multiplicity of irreducibly unique beings that exist exactly to the extent that they are mutually integrated into a single fabric of "reality." The reality that is self-consciousness poses a unique metaphysical challenge, because, inasmuch as it is self-determining *for itself*, self-consciousness is precisely *resistance* to integration. Chapter 12 considers how the imperative to integration is uniquely and constitutively felt within self-conscious singularity, and what "integration" means in the context of self-consciousness. Law is the fundamental enactment of self-conscious integration, and chapter 12 develops a metaphysics of law from Hegel's description of the dialectic of spirit in the *Phenomenology*. Conscience is the culmination of the dialectic of spirit because it is the stance of self-consciousness that simultaneously and coherently maintains the singular and irreducibly self-defined nature of self-conscious individuality and maintains the necessity of the mutual integration of self-consciousnesses. In holding itself singularly responsible to enact an integration of self-consciousness within the domain of spirit made available by law, conscience realizes most fully the logic of finite and infinite studied in Hegel's logic, that is, it is the finite that, in its recognition of its ownmost finitude, experiences the emergence of the infinite within itself.

In his study of unhappy consciousness as the completed form of free self-consciousness, Hegel showed that freedom always exists as a dynamic relationship between the finite, individual self-consciousness and the definitive beyond—the "infinite"—to which that individual finds itself answerable. The "Spirit" chapter studied the concrete experience of the development of freedom (from ethicality, through culture, to conscience) from the side of the finite self-consciousness; the "Religion" chapter studies the concrete experience of the development of freedom (from the religions of nature, through the religion of art, to the religion of revelation) from within the terms of the "beyond" to which self-consciousness finds itself answerable. Chapter 13, "The Phenomenology of Religion: Freedom as Exposure to the Absolute," follows Hegel's phenomenological description of the history of world-religions to show how the dialectic of religion parallels, and ultimately comes to the same conclusion as, the dialectic of spirit. Different forms of religious life correspond to different political regimes, the religion of art being the religion of the "ethical" society and the religion of revelation being the religion of the society of "culture." And, just as politics as such ultimately pointed to its own limitations and the need that it be superseded by morality, so does religion ultimately point to the need for the transcending of its own alienated and exclusionary characteristics in a freedom that is most fully realized in the conscientious taking up of one's determinate cultural heritage in the singular act of enacting a reconciliation with other self-consciousnesses in the practice of conscientious action and multicultural dialogue.

With these parallel stories of spirit and religion and in the conclusion that both stories share, the *Phenomenology of Spirit* is completed. Hegel's chapter VIII, "Absolute Knowing" (as we saw in our discussion of unhappy consciousness in my chapter 7), describes the character of this stance of experience that both spirit and religion point to as the fullest enactment of freedom. This stance is precisely the stance of the phenomenologist, which was the subject of our opening chapter on the project of phenomenology. "Absolute knowing" is the stance of the one who, in her experience of singularity, finds herself called to take responsibility for the reality of her situation, and our various discussions of phenomenology, love, understanding, recognition, unhappy consciousness, politics, conscience, and religion have all been investigations into the parameters of such a "taking responsibility."[10] Our own studies—like all the studies in Hegel's *Phenomenology*—have been studies of experience, but we have repeatedly seen that our studies of experience are interwoven with interpretations of the nature of reality. One form of experience that is distinctly opened up by the stance of taking responsibility for one's situation is the stance, unique to and distinctive of the philosopher, of investigating the nature of reality as such. Metaphysics—the study of the nature of reality—is itself a distinctive, a definitive, and a necessary dimension of the experience of absolute knowing, and Hegel ends his discussion of absolute knowing by pointing to the necessity of enacting this stance by carrying out a study of reality, the study that is itself carried out in his *Science of Logic*.[11] The Epilogue, "Subjectivity and Objectivity in Hegel's *Science of Logic*," offers a schematic interpretation of Hegel's argument in the *Science of Logic* to show how its results parallel and complement those of the *Phenomenology of Spirit*, both works ultimately reaching the same conclusion.

Finally, the appendix, "The Reception of Hegel in French Philosophy," studies the way in which Hegel's philosophy was discovered and taken up by French philosophers from the 1920s to the 1960s. The chapters of this book have frequently demonstrated the resonance of Hegel's thinking with that of the great figures of twentieth-century European philosophy, and the appendix traces the historical ways in which Hegel's philosophy was in fact formative for the work of these thinkers. For most of the thinkers in the period I discuss, Hegel's text was recognized as a rich and exciting resource for original philosophical thinking. In this same period, however, many false perceptions of Hegel's work developed and, through the last generation of French thinkers (in the 1960s) especially, these have unfortunately been passed on to contemporary readers as part of the general "received view" of Hegel's philosophy.[12] My hope is that, from the study of that history, the reader will learn to appreciate the interpretive dynamism that characterized this whole tradition of Hegel-appropriation and appreciate the superiority of this dynamism to the static dullness of the familiar clichés about Hegel, thereby learning the lesson not to be simplistic or reductionistic in the interpretation of Hegel's philosophy.

This recognition of the need to appreciate the compelling and demanding character of Hegel's philosophy is, too, the overall lesson that I have tried to reinforce through the writing of this book. I have tried always to approach Hegel's text with the expectation that it would communicate to me its sense, rather than approaching it with a sense that I already knew what I would find, and the text has never let down this expectation. In my experience, Hegel's text is very successful at communicating its meaning, provided one approaches it with openness, with rigor, and with an appropriately educated background into the issues under discussion in the text. The reading of Hegel's text demands from the reader great care and considerable patience, but it is always profoundly rewarding. Hegel's text is a great teacher, and what follows is my attempt to pass on to others the lessons of Hegel's science of experience.

INFINITE PHENOMENOLOGY

Prologue

The Project of Hegel's *Phenomenology of Spirit*

> You would never discover the limits of soul, should you travel every road, so deep a *logos* does it have.
>
> —Heraclitus, fragment 45

Hegel's *Phenomenology of Spirit* was and remains a revolutionary book in the history of philosophy. It continued and developed what Kant called his own "Copernican Revolution" in philosophy, simultaneously speaking authoritatively to the questions that animated the tradition of philosophy that it inherited and opening up the lines of analysis and inquiry that continue to fuel the tradition of philosophy that developed after it.[1] I want here to describe the distinctive project of this book: the project of phenomenology. A unique characteristic of Hegel's project is that the method of phenomenology is itself shaped by what it reveals. Understanding Hegel's project will thus require a consideration of both the methodological principle that animates the book and, in broad outline, the central results of that method insofar as they shed light on the concrete significance of that principle. I will begin by describing the basic principle of Hegel's phenomenology—the principle of scientific passivity—and the beginning of the project of phenomenology. I will then turn to considering how that method is shaped by what it reveals. Hegel's project is a development of the project Kant pioneered and, in discussing what the method reveals, I will draw on Kant's *Critique of Pure Reason* to establish the most fundamental point about experience, namely, that it is inherently characterized by the experience of infinity. From here, and broadly in continuing dialogue with Kant, I will consider the dimensions of infinity that Hegel reveals within experience, identifying the distinctive way in which Hegel shows experience to be inherently characterized by a conflict of infinities, most especially the conflict of the infinity of substance and the infinity of subjectivity. Investigating the infinity of subjectivity will allow us to see that the phenomenological method demands that one be a participant and not simply an observer, and that this in turn entails that one's embrace of the project of phenomenological description be as much practical as theoretical. In conclusion we will see that the project and method of phenomenology is ultimately to bear witness in vigilant openness to the unacknowledged absolutes that leave their trace in finite experience, a project realized in conscience, absolute knowing, and the project of phenomenology itself.

Hegel's Project of Phenomenology

Hegel describes the *Phenomenology of Spirit* as "the science of the experience of consciousness."[2] This work is a description of the form(s) experience takes, and the special project of the work is to let experience itself dictate the form in which the description unfolds. Hegel's objective is to be simply the medium through which the form of experience is able to present itself: his philosophy aims, that is, to be a philosophy without an author.[3]

In this desire to give voice to reality rather than to his own private perspective, Hegel's objective—the objective of philosophy—is basically the same as the objective of the artist or the religious person. The religious person aims to make herself open to being led by the divine, and to remove her own agency from the central position in her experience: "not my will, Lord, but thine be done" (Luke 22:42; cf. John 5:30).[4] The artist, similarly, wants her artwork to be a revelation of truth, a new form in and through which human experience can be articulated, rather than merely a presentation of her private interests: as Michelangelo is famously reputed to have said, "Every block of stone has a statue inside it and it is the task of the sculptor to discover it."[5] The philosopher, likewise, aims not to present mere "opinions," but to articulate for others a compelling revelation of the nature of things. As Hegel says in the preface,

> It is customary to preface a work with an explanation of the author's aim, why he wrote the book, and the relationship in which he believes it to stand to other earlier or contemporary treatises on the same subject. In the case of a philosophical work, however, such an explanation seems not only superfluous but, in view of the nature of the subject-matter, even inappropriate and misleading.[6]

Like the artistic and the religious person, the philosopher is not putting forth her "own" ideas, and the book is not strictly her "own" work, but is more like an act of devotion, inviting the truth itself—"the absolute"—to show itself.[7] In short, all—the artist, the religious person, and the philosopher—aspire to a stance of passivity, and Hegel's *Phenomenology of Spirit* is thus a project of passivity. To let experience show itself, then, the philosopher must approach experience simply with the question, "what is the immediate given form of experience?" or, perhaps more clearly, "what appears?" The task, that is, is simply to describe the immediate form, simply to describe the appearing as it appears.[8]

How might we describe the immediate form of experience? If we just open ourselves to the observation of the fact of our own experiencing, what can we say? Shall we simply say "there is" or "now"? Will that simple term—"now" or "is"—be sufficient to articulate the character of our experience? This is where Hegel's phenomenology begins, namely, with the attempt simply to announce the fact of experience—"now." As Hegel explains,

> The knowing which is first or immediately our object can be nothing other than that which is itself immediate knowing, *knowing of the immediate* or *of being*. We must ourselves also be immediate or receptive, and alter nothing in it as it presents itself and, in apprehending, hold ourselves back from conceptualizing.[9]

In fact, however, what the *Phenomenology* demonstrates in its actual enactment of this project of description is that the immediate form of experience is not so easy to describe. Let us see how this is so.

Hegel's work is a work of phenomenology: a description of the happening of experience. Just as one must have sight in order to appreciate a discussion of colors, so in general must one have the experience under discussion if the phenomenological description Hegel gives is to be meaningful. For that reason, one must oneself *enact* the experience he is describing in order to recognize the sense and the force of his claims. One must be a participant in this work, not just an observer. To understand and appreciate Hegel's claims about the experience of "now," one must oneself have that experience in front of one, and so, to begin, the reader must herself attend to experiencing simply this moment, now. If one does this, one should recognize what Hegel notes in his description of this experience, namely, that the now is itself not experienced as an isolated instant, but is experienced as a passage: it is experienced as coming into being and passing away in a temporal flow.[10] But the notion of "passage" is more complex than the notion of "is"—it is becoming, a motion defined as "from . . . to . . ," and not just an unqualified immediacy of being. What we see here is that, if we try to describe experience simply in the terms of unqualified immediacy—if we use a simple term such as "is" or "now" or "here"—we under-represent the character of that experience, and *the experience of the "now" itself reveals this.* Our approach to receptiveness—our attempt to describe the experience without introducing an intervening interpretation—allows our object to reveal itself to us in such a way that *it* demonstrates the insufficiency of our own initial approach to it, demonstrating that it is *becoming* and not simply *being* as our initial apprehension implies. The project of phenomenology seems initially to demand an interpretively "hands off" approach but, in enacting that project, we find out *from the object* that this attitude is inadequate to it. The "hands off" approach is in fact a tacit presumption that the object must be simple "being," and does not allow the object to appear on its own terms as becoming: apprehending the object as becoming goes hand in hand with a transformation of perspective, a transformation in what one is prepared to recognize. From this, we learn two important lessons about the method and project of the phenomenology.

The first lesson we learn from our attempt to describe the experience of "now" is that the project of phenomenology itself comes to be defined through its enactment. In other words, it is only through its realization that the real meaning of the originating intention can be determined. Thus Hegel remarks in the preface:

> For the real issue [*die Sache selbst*] is not exhausted by stating it as an aim, but by carrying it out, nor is the result the actual whole, but rather the result together with the process through which it came about. The aim by itself is a lifeless universal, just as the guiding tendency is a mere drive that as yet lacks an actual existence; and the bare result is the corpse which has left the guiding tendency behind it.[11]

Just as experience itself cannot be understood except through participating in the happening of experience, so the project of phenomenology cannot be understood except through working through its actual unfolding.

The second lesson from our description of the "now" is that, in order to relate to experience so as to "let it be," one must make oneself *appropriately* receptive, and this is not the same as the removal of perspective. The object, in other words, demands of us that we be active in certain ways in order to receive it, in order to be passive. This passivity, however, is not an abandonment of intelligence, effort, or learning, but is rather a passivity enabled by the most rigorous engagement.[12] The project is to allow experience to show itself, but this "letting show," this releasing of the inherent form, is not itself immediately within one's power. One must learn how to apprehend what shows itself. Though it is indeed one's own experience that is to be described—and thus in principle one *has access to* the object, obviating the sceptical concerns that typically accompany projects of knowledge—it is not the case that one automatically *has insight into* one's own experience, into oneself.[13] For this reason, being passive is the same project as developing the rigorously answerable attitude of the scientist, for one is called upon to make one's perception conform to the demands made by the object under study. This is Hegel's stance as the "author" of the *Phenomenology of Spirit*: "[t]o help bring philosophy closer to the form of science . . .—that is what I have tried to do."[14] Holding himself to the highest scientific standards of comprehensiveness and rigor, he endeavors to make manifest the self-presentation and self-movement—the dialectic—of experience itself.[15] This scientific passivity amounts to an acceptance of the givenness of experience: "scientific cognition . . . demands surrender to the life of the object."[16] The philosopher, that is, must be open to what experience itself presents, whether it meets her expectations or not.[17] Based on what we have already learned through the first enactment of the method in relationship to the "now," we can say something in outline of what this adequate receptivity involves.

The form of our experience is not adequately captured by a simple term like "is" or "now" because our experience is always inherently complex. What we experience is not just an indeterminate, immediate field of being, but a world of diverse things. That world is complex, for it comprises many things in their complex relations with each other;[18] those things, too, are themselves inherently complex, being simultaneously discrete, autonomous individuals, differentiated from each other, and assemblages of different properties.[19] The world of our experience is not adequately captured by a single, simple term like "is"—by what Hegel calls a "logic of immediacy"—but requires more complex terms that name relations, terms like "thing" (which implies a relation of thinghood and properties) or "appearance" (which implies a relation of inner essence and outer show)—what Hegel calls a "logic of reflection."[20] And there is a further complexity to experience, in that the world of our experience is always *appearing to* us, it is there *for* us. Though explicitly an experience of consciousness—the awareness of an other, of an object—our experience is always implicitly an experience of self-consciousness—an awareness of ourselves as experiencers in our awareness of the object.[21] "What appears" in appearance is simultaneously the world and our awareness of it. Adequately describing what appears, then, requires a logic of reflection to adequately characterize the nature of the object—"*substance*" in the language of the preface—but, beyond that, it requires what Hegel calls a "logic of the concept" to characterize this way in which the fabric of experience is *subjectivity* itself, that is, it will require terms that express a relationship in which something relates to itself in relating to what is opposite to it.[22] Experience is simultaneously the explicit appearing of an object and an implicit appearing of a subject, a simultaneity of substance and subject, the significance of which we will go on to pursue in greater detail below.

The immediate form of experience, then, only shows itself to one who is prepared to recognize relations of "reflection" and of "the concept," and not just situations of immediacy. The immediate form of experience, then, does not itself appear immediately, but shows itself only to a developed onlooker. What this project of receptivity seems most immediately to require is a stance of non-intervention, a stance of non-interpretation in which one "clears one's mind" of any structures, plans, or expectations, but such a stance is in fact a stance without intelligence, a stance *unable to recognize* intelligence when it sees it. To see the world in its rationality, one must look at it rationally.[23] The ongoing process of the *Phenomenology of Spirit* describes experiences in which these logics of reflection and concept are inherently at play (what the experience is "in itself") but are not acknowledged as such (not what the experience is "for itself"). The description notices how this disparity that characterizes the experience (the disparity between what it is in itself and what it is for itself or, as Hegel sometimes says, the disparity between its concept and its actuality) manifests itself within the process of experience itself. In other words, the phenomenology bears witness to the ways in which particular forms of experience themselves demonstrate, through their own process, the inadequacies internal to their own make-up. The simple description of experience thus offers the phenomenological observer an education into the nature of experience to the point at which the immediate form of experience can be adequately described. This education into the proper description of experience itself comes through the progressive attempt to describe the immediate form of experience and the discovery within experience that the form of experience exceeds the terms of the description. In other words, it is through the *attempt* made by a given form of consciousness to describe experience that one is taught by experience how one *needs* to describe experience. The *Phenomenology of Spirit* offers an education into how to describe experience by allowing its reader the opportunity to learn the lesson enacted by each shape of consciousness, and thus to see the rationale for the development of different shapes of consciousness, even if that realization is not explicitly made within those shapes of consciousness themselves (a project completed when the phenomenological experience itself becomes the experience under description).[24]

The project of phenomenology as Hegel understands it is a handing of oneself over to experience in order to learn from it what its nature is. This project of phenomenology had already been pioneered by Kant. Though Kant's work does not follow this same route of allowing the process of describing experience to educate itself, he had in fact already made the phenomenological description of experience the core to his argument in the *Critique of Pure Reason*, especially in his study of the role of "intuition" in experience. Through a brief consideration of Kant's study we can see particularly clearly that the simple description "now" hides within itself a complexity—a richness of "mediation," in Hegel's language—that the simplicity of the mere term "now" does not adequately express. As with Hegel, so with Kant we will see that the fabric of experience is the co-occurrence of substance and subject. More specifically, what we will learn from Kant is that "what appears" is always infinite, a lesson that Hegel's phenomenology in turn will take up and develop more fully.

Kant and the Infinite Within-and-Without Experience

Kant's philosophy emerges naturally from a simple phenomenological observation: the object of our experience is given in experience *as* something not defined by our experience. To understand this, let us engage in a simple exercise in thinking: let us distinguish between what we mean when we say that something is "real" and what we mean when we say that something is "imaginary."

When we merely imagine ourselves to be at the beach, we experience ourselves as having the power to modify at will the character of our imagined beach-experience. At will, I can change the beach in my imagination from sandy to rocky, the atmosphere from sunny and dry to cloudy and humid, the time from late evening to early morning, and so on. Also, the beach in my imagined experience will have only as much of its sensuous character filled in as I in fact imagine—I may not, for example, imagine the scent of the water, the temperature of the air or the color of the clothes I am wearing. Further, the relation of the beach-situation to the "rest of the world" is left unspecified. I focus on it in isolation, and there is no answer to the question "and what's over there?" unless I have in fact specified it to myself. These characteristics are sufficient to allow us to distinguish what we experience as "imaginary" from what we experience as "real."

When we experience ourselves as *really* at the beach, it is not up to us to decide whether it is hot or cold, sunny or cloudy, early or late. On the contrary, these characteristics of the situation are forced upon us. Again, the real object has all of its sensuous features filled in without gaps, regardless of whether we happen to be attending to them.[25] Further, unlike the imagined object for which its relationship to the rest of the world is left undefined, the real object is seamlessly integrated with all other things in reality.[26] The real object is sensuously saturated, and has definite characteristics that answer to its own internal reasons, without reference to our will, and stands in definite relation to all other things, again according to reasons internal to "the nature of things" in general, without reference to our will. In short, the form of the imaginary object answers to our will, whereas the form of the real object is something to which our will must answer: it is something that must be *known*, something that is the proper object of *science*, whereas the object of imagination is a matter of fantasy.

We can now ask, "How do we experience the world that is the normal object of our experience?" The answer is that we experience it *as* something real, not *as* something imaginary. Whether or not the world ultimately *is* an independent reality or, instead, is a figment of our imagination is not here at issue. The question is simply *how we experience it.* We *experience* it *as* something real. The object of our experience is given in experience *as* something not defined by our experience. Empirically, the object of our experience is *real.* This *description of our experience* is the sole fact from which Kant's philosophy (in the *Critique of Pure Reason,* at least) emerges. His philosophy is only the rigorous description and analysis of various aspects of this fact. Let us pursue a few of these aspects.

We noted above that something we experience as "real" is something we experience as seamlessly integrated with everything else that is real, such that they form a single fabric: "the" real, "reality." Perceptually this is manifest in the fact that whatever part of the world we experience here and now is experienced *as* participating within a space and time that go on infinitely beyond the determinate specificity that we are presently experiencing. Space, as Kant notes, is experienced as "an infinite, given magnitude."[27] Again, whether or not space *ultimately is* such, *within our experience* space is *given as* infinite: we experience space *as* going on forever (and the same for time).

Here, in this observation about space, we see again a way in which the object of our experience is experienced *as* not defined by our experience. Indeed, the object of our experience is experienced precisely as exceeding our experience. We experience space *as* real and *as* infinite, and therefore as something not defined or exhausted by our finite experience of it. We find ourselves exposed in principle to the infinite space in which we are situated. From this observation about the form of our experience, Kant draws an important epistemological point.

Since the very form of the object of experience is that it exceeds our experiences of it, that object cannot be simply the sum of those finite experiences. If our finite experiences were the sole source of our knowledge then we would know the object to be exactly defined by the sum of those experiences. In that case, we would never experience the object *as* infinite. We *do* thus experience the object, however, and therefore that experience must have some source other than the finite history of our specific experiences. Said otherwise, this openness to the experience of space could not have been *learned*: it must be *inherent to* our experience to experience the object in this way, for otherwise we could never come upon the experience we actually do have. This Kant describes by saying that the form of our experience of space—the fact that any *specific* experience of space (and all our experiences are that) is always given as contextualized by participation in the infinitude of space—is an *a priori* rather than an *a posteriori* dimension of our experience.[28] It is a *condition* of our finite experience of space, not a *result* of it, that it be situated in infinite space. Space, Kant says, is a "transcendental"—that is, pervasive and inherent—condition of our experience.

To call this knowledge of space as infinite "transcendental" is simply to say in different words what we already said above: to say that the infinitude of space is *empirically real* is *only* to describe the form of our experience, and not to say anything about the "ultimate nature" of reality as such, of reality beyond any possible experience or "in itself." As well as being empirically real, then, space is "transcendentally ideal"; that is, we are describing structures *internal to the happening of experience*, not "transcendent" realities beyond experience.[29]

This distinction between real "within experience" and real "in itself" pertains to our approach to ourselves as subjects of experience as well as to the objects of experience. Our reality is the ("first-person") reality of *experiencing*: we are not objects but subjects, those *for whom* experience is happening. We also experience ourselves as bodies, as things of a piece with the world, in space. As Kant says, describing the *a priori* character of the experience of space,

> the presentation of space must already lie at the basis in order for certain sensations to be referred to something *outside me* (i.e., referred to something in a location of space *other than the location in which I am*).[30]

The space of which I have an *a priori* experience is a space *that contains me. Empirically*, we are situated *within the world*: I am one thing among many. At the same time, however, we are subjects *for whom* the appearing of reality is happening. In that sense the world—the *real* that is the object of our experience—is *in us* inasmuch as we are the act of experience, the fact of the happening of appearing. "I," then, names simultaneously and equivocally the form of the whole of our experience and one thing within our experience. "I" is the very *form* of all our experience in that there is experience only as it is experienced as "my experience," that is, I experience the appearing *as* appearing, that is, *as* for me, and "I" is thus the *transcendental*—pervasive and inherent—form of the unity of *all* experience.[31] For this reason, this transcendental "I" can only be found by *thinking*, since it could never be identified with any determinate object of experience.[32] But "I" is also the name for a specific thing in the world. "I" is always experienced as both in the world and the form of the world. Though "I" is always experienced as a finite specificity—this empirical self, here and now in this world—that experience is itself necessarily contextualized by its being defined by a sense of "I"—*itself*—that is the form of experience as such. Like space, however, this *transcendental* "I" is not a *transcendent* reality—an independently existing reality beyond experience that fabricates experience—but is only the form of meaningfulness *inherent within* all experience.[33]

In sum, our experience is always a finite situatedness—a "being in the world," as Heidegger describes it—that inherently involves an infinity of substance (reality) and subject that is its form.[34] There are two important points here. First I exist *as* an inherently finite crystallization of what is inherently infinite. Second, the form of this finite enactment of the infinite is that I always experience myself as one thing among others located here *in* a real spatial world, while simultaneously experiencing that world as *in* my experience. In neither case, though—neither in the case of the containing real nor of the containing I—are we considering a causal thing-in-itself beyond experience. Instead, these are forms *inherent to experience*, and *they are forms that must be acknowledged in any accurate description* of experience. We can only describe, not account for the constitution of, experience. It is *given* as this happening of meaning and we can describe its form, but we can never get beyond this.

We began with the project of describing the form of experience—"what's happening?" or "what appears?" With Kant, we have seen that our experience always takes the form of a specific, finite experience within which a deeper, *a priori* character manifests itself. That deeper form is itself the appearance of the infinite. That infinite is both *within* finite experience, inasmuch as it is inherent to it as a form *of* experience, and it is *outside* experience, in that the very sense with which it is given—to intuition in the case of space, to thought in the case of the "I"—is "beyond." In fact, the specific experience is the site for the co-occurrence of—our inherent exposure to—two such infinites "within-and-without": the infinite beyond of the real, the spatial, causal "is" within which we are contained, and the infinite beyond of the "I," which is the form of all appearing, that within which the very experience of the real is contained. Hegel's *Phenomenology of Spirit* began by asking whether "now" adequately describes the form of experience. What we saw already is that "now" always appears as the site of co-occurrence of substance and subject, and now, with Kant, we have seen that these are infinites and that the method of phenomenology, therefore, is a witnessing to infinity. What we will now explore is how each of these infinites contests with the other for the claim of ultimacy.[35] This infinite contestation is the form of experience, and describing this properly is the project of Hegel's *Phenomenology of Spirit.*

The Phenomenology of Infinite Conflict

It is the very character of experience to present us with a "real," and this is precisely experienced as an imperative within experience. Within our experience we are claimed—held answerable to—the demands of an object that does not itself answer to the terms of our subjectivity: *within* experience it is *given as* infinite in itself, both in its spatial extension and in its causal interiority: the object is *given as "without,"* as infinitely exceeding us in its providing on its own both the domain of its existence (the spatial domain in which, indeed, we too are contained) and the causal principles of its existence. The very nature of the object, then, as it is *given,* challenges any attempt we might make to treat it as "merely mine": *it* calls us to science, to answerability to it, whether we explicitly acknowledge this or not. Like Kant's analysis in the *Critique of Pure Reason,* Hegel's analysis in the "Consciousness" section of the *Phenomenology of Spirit* similarly culminates in the description of the inherent infinity of the real and its imperative force.[36]

At the same time, however, Kant's correct description of the infinite claim of the object does not end the question of the nature of what appears. With Kant, we have seen that the "I" is necessarily already insinuated within any appearance as its overarching form. We are called, that is to say, to recognize ourselves as what is *really* appearing in any appearance. Though the given nature of the real calls us to knowledge of its infinite, independent nature, we are also claimed by the nature of the "I," and the claim of the "I" is in tension with the claim of the real object. Kant himself recognized this tension. It is the central concern of the "Third Antinomy" from his study of the "Dialectic of Pure Reason," and it is the organizing principle behind the larger articulation of his philosophy in the relationship between the *Critique of Pure Reason* and the *Critique of Practical Reason*.[37] It is the force of this claim that is worked out through the section called "Self-Consciousness" in Hegel's *Phenomenology of Spirit*.

Appearance, by its nature, is *for* me, and I feel the imperative force of this as desire, as the sense that the real is the site for the satisfaction of my subjectivity.[38] In acting from desire, the significance of experience comes from me: my desire is expressed in the world, and thus I impinge upon the real as much as the real impinges upon me. In opposition to the stance of knowing in which my subjectivity is answerable to taking its determination—its form—from the object, in answering to desire I experience the object as rightly receiving its determination from my subjectivity.[39] Just as the character of the real is given in experience, so too is this sense of "mineness" given: it is not something I "make," but is rather the experiential precondition for there being any "I," any "making." It is thus just as much a given form—indeed an infinite form—by which I am claimed as is the form of space or the form of causality. And yet, even though these desires are "me," it is nonetheless the case that I *find out* the nature of my desires, the nature of my singular subjective perspective, by being exposed to it.

We exist in a state of exposure: this is the basic form of experience recognized by both Kant and Hegel. By exposure, I mean the way that we are unprotectedly in contact with an outside that defines us but that exceeds our grasp, an infinity that claims us without our having the option to refuse, a constitutive imperative to which our experience is answerable. With Kant, we notice that we are always spatial, always wrapped up in a space that in magnitude infinitely exceeds us—we could never "gather this experience up," so to speak—and that in essence is inherently opaque to us, that is, it is an intuition, an immediate given determinateness that is impenetrable to our insight. We are always exposed in space. With Hegel, we notice that we are exposed in further ways, and, furthermore, the dimensions of our exposure are in tension with each other. Desire—the experience of our singular subjectivity—is one such dimension, one such domain of opaque, alien determination. We find ourselves compelled by desires as imperatives to which we are internally answerable, having neither insight into their source nor the ability to control their emergence: the "heteronomy" of the will, as Kant describes it, "it" [*das Es*] as Freud describes it. In desire, we experience ourselves as subjected to an alien authority, even as that authority is given as our very self. The "I," our most intimate "self," is itself, in other words, something to which we are beholden, something with which we find ourselves confronted. It is in exploring the claims of desire that constitute the "I" that further dimensions of our exposure reveal themselves.[40]

The progress of the phenomenological method is the progressive unearthing of more and more fundamental "infinities," more fundamental "absolutes," that characterize, contextualize, or constitute our experience. As we shall see in chapters 1 through 3, such an unearthing occurs throughout the "Consciousness" section of the *Phenomenology of Spirit.* Hegel's phenomenology here is, in fact, somewhat richer than Kant's, witnessing within-and-without the infinitude of sensuous multiplicity the emergence of the infinitude of the thing, as well as witnessing within-and-without the domain of things the emergence of the infinitude of the real as such that Kant acknowledged. Within the domain of meaning opened up by desire, which will be our concern in this section, Hegel witnesses within-and-without the infinitude of sensual multiplicity the emergence of the infinitude of other self-consciousnesses and, further, he witnesses within-and-without the domain of others the emergence of the infinitude of the "Other" as such. With any infinite (as Kant showed in the *Critique of Pure Reason*), our experience of it is an *exposure* and not something *learned.* In other words, it is something that can be described and discussed only by someone who actually participates in the experience. Thus, with the "now," the "thing," and the "real," and also with "others" and "the Other," we can understand Hegel's phenomenology only if we first recognize within our own experience the exposures he is describing. In this domain of desire the conflict of these infinites is not merely a conceptual matter, but a matter of the most intimate, living practicality, and the phenomenological acknowledgment of this conflict—the phenomenological method itself—becomes as much a practical as a theoretical affair.

In the discussion that is perhaps most definitive of the *Phenomenology of Spirit,* Hegel first considers a particular way in which we are exposed, a particular desire that claims us: we are exposed to others, and we desire to be acknowledged by them. Appearance has an inherently intersubjective form. We experience ourselves as already in a world, already subject to the perspectives of others. Experience is "for" us in the sense that we are the subjects of our own experience—we are having our experience—but we precisely experience this world that is for us (and, furthermore, ourselves) as "for" others: we are perceived as much as we are perceiving. For this reason, *our own* identity is from the start dual—*we* are both subject and object, perspective on the world and thing within the perspectives of others. We experience ourselves, in other words, as insufficient on our own to account for our own identity: we experience ourselves as dependent upon others to let us know who we are. Our experience is characterized by a *constitutive* desire for recognition by others, itself a desire that conflicts with other desires.

This desire for recognition is the primary imperative that drives the development of our identities, and the bulk of the *Phenomenology of Spirit* is devoted to describing this development.[41] At the most personal level, we seek the recognition of our immediate companions in order to establish a sense of our self-worth. Our basic sense of self is established only in dialogue, only in a negotiation between our own immediate sense of our primacy—we are, after all, always at the center of our own experience—and the sense of our secondariness in the eyes of others (who, of course, experience themselves at the center of their own experience). The sense of ourselves as equal participants in a shared world—the sense with which we normally live—is itself a developed view, a view accomplished through this negotiation. Indeed, this is perhaps Hegel's most distinctive contribution to our philosophical heritage: the *Phenomenology of Spirit* demonstrates that the sense of ourselves that we typically live with—a coherent sense of ourselves as independent agents, coherently integrated with the human and natural world—is an achievement (indeed, a complex negotiation with the conflicting infinities of reality, desire, and others) and not our "given" state.[42] The achieving of this coherent, integrated sense of self is accomplished only through interpersonal negotiation, and Hegel demonstrates, in his descriptions of the "Struggle to the Death" and "Lordship and Bondage," the ways in which we can fail to cooperate in allowing each other to live as equal selves. Hegel's book reveals that violence and power struggles do not exclusively obtain in the relations between fully developed selves—between "egos"—but that such violence and struggles for power are inherent to and constitutive of the very concept of self-conscious experience. In describing these power struggles that characterize the dialectic of recognition by which we cooperatively establish our sense of ourselves, Hegel's *Phenomenology of Spirit* also demonstrates (in keeping with the demand of phenomenology that it bear witness to the intrinsic dialectic of the experience under observation) that such situations of unequal recognition reveal their own inadequacy and point, from within themselves, to the need to establish a situation of equal recognition.

Our experience is inherently intersubjective, that is, "what appears" is "other people." We saw above that what it takes to recognize "now" was a perspective attuned to a more sophisticated rationality than simply the "logic of immediacy." Analogously, Hegel's description here points to the complex demands of recognizing another person. Recognizing another person *as such* requires understanding, compassion, and respect, and these attitudes themselves can be meaningfully enacted only in a shared context of communication (language) and cooperative living (law): if, for example, we do not understand language, we cannot appreciate what another person presents; if we do not establish a context of law, another person cannot come into her being as a person. There are, in other words, perceptual, behavioral, and material conditions that must be met in order for the other person to be able to appear as such. With this recognition we see that the project of phenomenology itself comes to impinge upon us practically as well as theoretically. What the object prescribes for its adequate recognition—what it takes for us to carry out our project of description—is our practical acceptance of our answerability to the demands of other persons.

This situation of equal recognition—the situation of a cooperative enactment of a situation in which we each recognize ourselves and others as an integrated community of equals—is what Hegel calls "*Geist*," "spirit," "the I that is we and the we that is I."[43] It is this domain of "spirit," "infinity realizing itself in self-consciousness," that provides the fundamental context for the bulk of our experience—it is our basic "home"—and, as the title "Phenomenology of Spirit" suggests, it is the primary project of the book to describe this reality of "spirit," this definitive character of our experience.[44] The *Phenomenology of Spirit* is as much the recognition of an ongoing imperative to realize this community as it is a description of its already accomplished form.

The dialectic of recognition establishes the fundamental parameters of our identity. Identity, however, is always something "reflected" in Hegel's language, that is, it is always something turned back on itself, something defined as a kind of response or interpretation. The identity may be the "truth" of something, but precisely by being the truth "of something" that truth points to a something of which it is the truth, that is, it points to the immediacy of which it is the truth, of which it is the essence.[45] It is indeed in inhabiting an identity that we first experience ourselves as someone specific and determinate in relation to others. Yet, in inhabiting this identity, we can also experience a sense that "this is not enough," that something in us has been betrayed. We can precisely experience ourselves as living from an immediacy that is lost in our established identities, the immediacy of our singularity as a desiring being.

There is, then, within identity, always a voice calling that very identity into question, and calling us to an originating source beyond the neatly resolved, systematic character of our social identity. The experience of the challenge to the limits of our established identity can also take the form of an experience of a "higher calling," a sense of the possibility of a meaning beyond even desire and community. This sense that the identity established in the dialectic of recognition is circumscribed by a higher calling is described by Hegel in the dialectic of what he calls "the Unhappy Consciousness."[46]

A community—spirit—is always realized in a determinate and therefore limited form. It is through the collective embrace of a particular language and the historical establishing of laws and other institutions that a system of equal recognition is realized, but such laws and language are always determinate, always the specific institutions of *this* community, and therefore inherently finite, that is, inherently exclusive of other communities and other individuals.[47] As developed, integrated members of such a community, we can experience the limitations of this finitude, and, though our community is itself a way of answering to our exposure to others—it is a way of being open to others and thus a fulfillment of the project of equal recognition—we can, like Socrates, Mohammed, or Luther, recognize that in establishing a settled way of doing things it also encourages a complacency and a closedness to other possibilities. Within our identities, we can precisely experience a call from beyond our identities, that is, we can recognize an exposure to an infinite not adequately realized by our finite identities.[48] What Hegel calls "Unhappy Consciousness" is the recognition of this exposure to a source of meaning that in principle will never be addressed adequately by any finite system of identity: beyond the other that is the infinite real object, beyond the other that is the infinity of desire, beyond the other that is another infinite self-consciousness, we are exposed to the other "as such," the other that is the infinite giving power behind experience as such.

These different imperative infinites—the infinity of the real, of singular subjectivity, of others, and of the Other—all conflict, that is, practices of recognizing one are not automatically practices of recognizing the others, and our experience is the space of contestation between these different principles. The lives of individuals testify to the fact that these demands do not automatically speak with a single voice but instead invite us—tempt us, perhaps—to various ways in which we can commit ourselves one-sidedly to one or the other of these definitive dimensions of meaning; such one-sided lives are found in the rational agents of "Pleasure and Necessity," "Virtue and the Way of the World," "The Spiritual Animal Kingdom," in "Ethical" agents such as Antigone and Creon, in

"Cultured" agents such as the "Noble Consciousness," the "Wit" and the "believing consciousness," in moral agents such as the "Hard-Hearted Judging Consciousness," and in other figures described throughout the *Phenomenology of Spirit.*[49] The imperative the phenomenology puts upon us is to enact in our experience a reconciliation of these imperatives. The later sections of the *Phenomenology of Spirit*—Reason, Spirit, Religion, Absolute Knowing—deal with various experiences that are precisely attempts to acknowledge the necessity of the reconciliation of the infinities of consciousness with the infinities of self-consciousness and to enact this reconciliation. Ultimately, the demand will be realized in an experience that, operating within the terms of the real, realizes the imperative to community while also answering to the imperative of "the Good as such"—the divine, the Other—and this within the imperative to be a finite, desiring, singular self.

Finally, with this experience of Unhappy Consciousness, we have returned to the standpoint with which the project of the *Phenomenology of Spirit* begins. Phenomenology is the project of bearing witness to the given dimensions of meaning, the parameters of experience that can only be described, not deduced, a project that itself produces the recognition that our nature as self-conscious subjects—as experiencers in a real world of other people—is only fulfilled in giving ourselves over to the project of giving voice to the self-presentation of the absolute.

Hegel, and Witnessing to the Traces of Unacknowledged Absolutes

So let us return, now, to Hegel's phenomenology, and to the simple question "what is the immediate form of experience?" or "what appears?" What is the given form of experience? On the one hand, we undergo our experience as knowers, that is, we experience the world as presented to us as an object. This world floods our senses, is itself articulated into a manifold of independently existing things, and holds itself together as a single unity. This is the world to which our cognition answers—our consciousness is to be determined by it. On the other hand, we are subjects, and our subjectivity floods our experience, articulated into the manifold desires that give meaning to the things of the world, defining the terms of the unity of our experience. Within this world of desire, the gaze of the other floods in upon us, and we are constitutively drawn to answer to it and to participate in a world of language, companionship, community, tradition, and law. Within our experience as members of the community, we are called beyond the finite determinateness of our established human world to realize the possibilities that exceed that world, an experience often identified as the flooding in of the divine. Our experience is shaped by the contestation of these inexhaustible, infinite dimensions of experience to which we are inherently exposed, these irreducible dimensions of meaning within our experience.

The world is the setting in which we are torn by the imperative force of all these many directions—called to objective knowledge, drawn to self-interested action, commanded to answer to the needs of others, and summoned to bear witness to the Other—and these different imperatives conflict, each claiming absolute authority. Our experience is the ongoing negotiation with these multiple, given absolutes to which we are intrinsically exposed. Kant's *Critique of Pure Reason* focuses on the infinity that is constitutive of the imperative of objectivity that operates within our experience of ourselves as knowers. And, as Kant began to acknowledge in his *Critique of Practical Reason*, in all these other dimensions as well, in our experience of ourselves, of others, and of the Other, we experience comparable infinites—irreducible and unsurpassable dimensions of our experience that are given in experience as exceeding our experience—and Hegel's *Phenomenology of Spirit*, in describing the self-showing of experience, particularly reveals, displays, and demonstrates the overlaying of these mutually conflicting infinites, these mutually conflicting imperatives.

Our experience always takes the form of answering to the commanding force of an absolute, of an infinite that gives itself as self-authoritative, and the various experiential stances we adopt—now studying the object, now satisfying our desires, now caring for others, now worshipping the divine—are necessarily selective, one-sided enactments of a reconciliation of these conflicting demands that necessarily relativizes and contradicts these absolutes qua absolute. Inasmuch as these absolutes are given as intrinsic and pervasive to all experience ("transcendental"), they make their "presence" felt even in those experiences that do not adequately answer to them. *Within* any one-sided enactment of reconciliation, then, a voice of dissatisfaction will express itself: a one-sided experience carries within itself the challenge to its own form, a self-critique in which an indwelling infinite leaves a trace of its insufficient acknowledgment. Thus the thing of perception, which, in its negativity and determinacy is not acknowledged by sense-certainty, shows itself to be implied in the very fact that sense-certainty can recognize passage, that is, can recognize the "of" of the property;[50] or again the "One" of reality as such betrays its essentiality in the unacknowledged but presupposed holding of the many things together in a common field;[51] or the authority and autonomy of another self-consciousness shows itself in the very fact that the master seeks the recognition of the slave in the first place.[52] Hegel's description brings to light the presence within experience of the traces of unacknowledged absolutes that bespeak the insufficiency of the stance of experience to live up to its own intrinsic demands. The success of Hegel's method is its recognition that it is the nature of experience to be this texture of self-opposition:[53] this is not a situation to be *corrected* but is rather the very character of the situation within which we must make meaningful lives.

Our own experience, ultimately, is a finite embrace of these conflicting infinites. Our experience will always be the determinate form of holding them together in an attempted reconciliation. The project of the *Phenomenology of Spirit* is to unearth the ways in which different determinate forms of experience are one-sided, and do not adequately acknowledge one or another of these essential dimensions of meaning.[54] Where does the phenomenology conclude? We have already anticipated the answer to this question in our discussion of the imperative to the reconciliation of the contesting infinites. The phenomenology concludes in the experience that is the acceptance that we are always one-sided appropriations of an infinity that exceeds us and claims us. This acceptance is described in the *Phenomenology of Spirit* as the moral stance of conscience and the philosophical stance of absolute knowing.

The project of the *Phenomenology of Spirit* points, ultimately, to the stance of conscience, as the self-conscious embrace of the stance of finite answerability to these infinite claims. It is the conscientious agent who recognizes what we have recognized in this analysis, namely, that what is without is within—we are *intrinsically* called to an answerability to the outside. The conscientious agent knows herself to be a singular desiring self, irreducible to any other, but knows herself to be answerable to others. The conscientious agent knows herself to be a member of a community and answerable to it, but also knows this membership to be finite, and therefore to be guilty of realizing inadequately the imperatives of the other and of the Other. The conscientious agent knows that her conscience must be enacted within the demands of the real. In short, the conscientious agent recognizes herself in her others and makes her finite situatedness a site of hospitality to her others within-and-without, while simultaneously forgiving herself for the necessity of her limitations and forgiving her others for their own.[55]

An enactment of conscientious commitment, "absolute knowing" is the ultimate methodological acknowledgment of answerability to the given, and the methodical enactment of this is dialectical, phenomenological method itself. Absolute knowing is this experiencing of ourselves as the agents of the real, as the ones who speak on behalf of the absolute: we are "certain of being all reality" in the sense of recognizing our infinite indebtedness, and recognizing that the absolute must speak here and now.[56]

Conclusion

In the "Transcendental Dialectic" of the *Critique of Pure Reason,* Kant demonstrated that reason unaided by intuition produces conclusions about the nature of reality that do not carry cognitive weight despite their seemingly compelling argumentative force. In his discussion of the "Antinomies of Pure Reason" in particular, he demonstrates the insufficiency of purely discursive constructions—trying to "reason" to ultimate conclusions about the nature of reality—by showing the contradictions these rational arguments produce. Equally compelling arguments can be made, for example, to defend the necessity of free will and the necessity of determinism. Though each side taken by itself seems compelling, seeing the equally compelling character of the argument for the opposed side reveals that reason cannot settle the matter.

In these cases of purely rational argument, we try to *deduce* what reality *must* be like, without any intuitive support for the conclusions we reach. In this way, these rational constructions differ fundamentally from Kant's own method in the "Transcendental Aesthetic" or the "Analytic of Principles," in which he follows the essentially phenomenological method discussed earlier. This phenomenological method does not speculate about a reality beyond the limits of intuition—it does not *construct* a model of experience—but instead *starts from* the given form of experience, with the imperative to discern its intuitive character, and then to describe the logic *inherent to* it. This is surely a method that requires a great deployment of thought, but it is thought aimed not at fabricating a model, but at recognizing what is already at play within experience. In this way, the indubitability of what is revealed is assured by the given intuitive ground of those revelations, in contrast to the dubitability that attaches to the contradictory results of purely rational argumentation.

Kant rightly demonstrates that, so to speak, intuition "trumps" discursive *construction* here. Sound philosophical method must think *from* the "found" meaningful forms within experience. That is why Hegel's own method can only be a method of exhortation, and never deduction: Hegel can describe experiences, but it is only the reader's own recognition that she is participating in such an experience that gives her access to the phenomenon that is the sole source of meaning here.[57] And this is the form Hegel's writing typically takes: he initially describes the phenomenon in question, and only then proceeds to investigate what is revealed in the characteristic process of development of that experience.[58] Like Kant, then, Hegel rejects the method of deduction, and, like Edmund Husserl after him, his "method" is at root a method of "intuition":[59] it is a method that requires the most rigorous thought, but it is thought that holds itself answerable to the ways in which experience *reveals its own determinate forms*, ways that can never be predicted but must be experienced. Beyond Kant, however, what Hegel shows is that it is not merely unaided reason that produces contradictions. On the contrary, these indubitable intuitions themselves conflict.

Kant argued that attempting to use reason alone to reach metaphysical conclusions produces contradictory results. In the case of the conclusions of merely rational construction we can dispense with them as mere temptations. What Hegel shows, however, is that these intuitions that are constitutive of our experience—the infinites to which we are exposed—themselves conflict. In the case of conflicting intuitions we are not free to reject the contradictory results, for *they claim us*. The conflict of intuitions is not evidence of an error in method; rather, it is evidence of a conflict—a contestation—that is definitive of the very nature of meaning, the very nature of experience. The conflict of intuitions is not an error, but is the lived imperative to enact a reconciliation between them within experience.[60] Such a reconciliation, however, is not a removal of the tension, but an embrace of the tension that does not one-sidedly disavow one aspect of the tension. The tension is final—it is constitutive of the nature of experience—and our imperative is to enact forms of experience that acknowledge the equal claim of each side. So, finally, the tension between the call of knowing and the call of acting. So, finally, the tension between the call of the I and the call of the we. So, finally, the tension between the infinite call of the beyond and the specific call of this community. We exist as these tensions, as the mutual contestation of these infinities, these absolutes.

Part 1

Reality

1

The Lessons of Sense-Certainty: Temporality and Ontology

Some time ago, I saw a documentary about young drug addicts in Britain. One scene featured a young woman who wanted to quit using, but was not worried about it. As she put it in the documentary, "I'm young; I've got time." This remark was very interesting to me, for two reasons. First, it was interesting because I thought she was right. She was young, and she did have time. Many of us, perhaps all of us, have imagined large projects we want to engage in, and have rightly recognized that, though we cannot turn to them immediately, we need not fear their loss, because we will have time eventually. I experienced just such an eventuation myself recently. Ever since I was a teenager, I had imagined learning to play jazz guitar. I always said to myself, "someday." It turns out I was right: that "someday" happened over the last dozen years, and I have now realized that young fantasy of becoming a jazz guitarist. So this young woman's remarks were interesting because, in contrast to the hysteria with which we typically approach our discourses about drug addiction, this woman evinced a more mature perspective on her future, rightly recognizing that she could get around to kicking the habit later, and that she need not panic about the urgency of getting it done right now.

The second reason I found this remark interesting runs in the opposite direction. I suspect that most viewers of this documentary heard much more naïveté than maturity in her remarks. "Kicking a drug addiction is not like learning jazz guitar," they might think to themselves. Why? Not least because taking the drugs will kill you: you, as a living body, will deteriorate and die, so that there is no "later," no "someday," when you are finally able to get around to it. Now in fact, the literature I have non-systematically reviewed does support the claim that many heroin users who live do stop using by the age of 30; the proviso though is important—those who live give it up. There is no age of 30 for the others.

These two reflections on drug addiction will orient us in a temporal interpretation of Hegel's phenomenology. The first reflection shows that time is something oriented, intelligible and personally relevant; in short, time carries within it the structure of a project, and *my* project at that. The second reflection shows that the living body is itself the possibility of such time. As we shall see, the relation between these two aspects of time is central to both the development and the conclusion of Hegel's *Phenomenology of Spirit.*

It is the dialectic of chapter I, "Sense-Certainty," that will provide us with our primary orientation to the nature of temporality, and we will begin by looking in more detail at the analysis of the "now" that we introduced in the prologue. What we will discover is that presence is possible only when contextualized by the absences of past and future; equally, however, past and future themselves can "be" only if there is presence. Hegel's analysis reveals this "now that is many nows" as the form of all experience, and this allows us to interpret subsequent experiences studied in the *Phenomenology of Spirit* as forms of this "now that is many nows."[1] That is, rather as Kant reinterprets metaphysical categories as temporal schemata, the *Phenomenology of Spirit* is readable as an investigation into the different forms of *concrete* temporality.[2] After extracting the basic lesson from the dialectic of the "now," and the transition from this to the perception of things in chapter II, "Perception," we will indeed develop this lesson through reflections on the inherent temporal dimensions of further forms of experience studied in the *Phenomenology of Spirit* to see how this reciprocal contextualizing of present and non-present can take importantly different forms. Specifically, we will consider the experiences of life, *Sittlichkeit,* and phenomenological philosophy itself in terms of the distinctive relations of past, present, and future definitive of each. As well as revealing the inherent richness of the dialectic of "Sense-Certainty" and giving us a basic orientation to the path of the *Phenomenology of Spirit* as a whole, this analysis will also allow us to establish the ultimate status of the future in Hegel's philosophy.

Sense-Certainty and the Temporal Matrix of Experience

Hegel's phenomenology is to describe experience as such, without prejudice to this or that form of experience.

> Our approach to the object must . . . be *immediate* or *receptive*; we must alter nothing in the object as it presents itself. In apprehending it, we must refrain from trying to comprehend it.[3]

Hegel's phenomenology is to *describe* experience, rather than offer a theory of experience, and is to describe experience *as it happens,* rather than select a privileged form of experience (such as, for example, the experience of the "cogito") as normative for all experience. The phenomenology, then, must begin with the bare fact, the basic form, of experience. What is this basic form of experience? "There is": experience is the fact of immediate presence, the happening of appearing.

> The knowledge or knowing which is at the start or is immediately our object cannot be anything else but immediate knowledge itself, a knowledge of the immediate or of what simply *is*.[4]

As Kant notes in the *Critique of Pure Reason*, there is no experience without intuition, that is, experience is happening if and only if I am being struck by something, impinged upon by a given determinacy that I am aware of and that impinges upon me without my having an option about it.[5] Hegel's phenomenology of experience, then, in turning to the basic form of experience as such, turns to the experience of immediate presence, the experience that Hegel calls "sensuous certainty" (*die sinnliche Gewißheit*). Hegel's phenomenology begins by describing the "now" of immediate presence. What we discover through the description is that immediacy is never simply immediacy, and that what is present is never simply immediately present. Sense-certainty teaches us a different way to construe presence.

The present has two fundamental forms in which it occurs: here and now.[6] Hegel's description of the dialectic of the "now" is the easiest to follow. Simply, the "now" is experienced as passing. But a passage can only be experienced as such if it is experienced in relation to difference: the difference between from . . . and to . . . . The phenomenological description Hegel gives of this is found in paragraphs 106 and 107 in Miller's translation.[7] Let me quote from paragraph 107:

> (1) I point out the 'Now,' and it is asserted to be the truth. I point it out, however, as something that *has been*, or as something that has been superseded; I set aside the first truth, and (2) I now assert as the second truth that it *has been*, that it is superseded. (3) But what has been *is not*; I set aside the second truth, its *having been*, its supersession, and thereby negate the negation of the 'Now,' and thus return to the first assertion, that the *'Now' is* . . . . However, this first, as thus reflected into itself, is not exactly the same as it was to begin with, viz. something *immediate*; on the contrary, it is *something that is reflected into itself*, or a *simple* entity which, in its otherness, remains [*bleibt*] what it is: a Now which is an absolute plurality of Nows.[8]

I try to grasp this moment now as an immediate isolated moment. In grasping it, it has already passed. The moment that *was* "now" *is* no longer "now": it is past. But the recognition of that moment *as* past *is happening now.* This new "now"—the "now" that recognizes the passage—is different from the "now" construed as an immediate, isolated moment, for this "now" inherently defines itself in terms of the (former) "now" that it is not.

This description allows us to formulate more accurately the character of the "now." Rather than being an immediate, isolated instant, the "now" endures [*bleibt*]. To be experienced as passing, a "now" must have a future—a future in which it will be recognized as past—and the "now" must have a past—the past it differentiates itself from as it looks back.[9] The "now" is thus not an isolated moment, but a duration, a temporal whole. The "now" is not *only* "the present," but *simultaneously* past and future. The "now"—what is present—is, in other words, never present all at once. The present is never simply present.

Though it takes considerable technicality and intelligence to work through the argument that the present is never simply present, the basic truth of this lesson is, in fact, very familiar to us in our everyday experience. The experience of music is one of our most familiar experiences of this structure. While all that is "present" in any moment of hearing a melody, for example, is a single note, what one actually hears is that note *in the context* of the meaningful, ongoing flow of the melody. *In and through* the single, "present" note, the (absent) past and future of the melody are also presented as the response and anticipation that are the very structure—the "mediation"—of this immediate presence. The melody as a whole is "what one hears": the melody is the essence of what is heard *in,* what "shows through," the immediate. Similarly, to perceive rhythm is to feel an ongoing pulse with our moving bodies. Though at any moment there is only a single beat of the drum present, what is *made present through* the individual beat of the drum is a rhythmic pattern, a form *of* which the individual beat is the representative: the individual beat is an avatar or a messenger of the deeper identity that cannot itself ever simply be directly presented but can instead only be presented through a multiplicity of immediate moments. In these ways, our experiences of music powerfully attest to the way in which the present is inherently informed and contextualized by the non-present.[10]

This way in which the rhythm or melody as a whole is what is presented through the immediate is, in fact, the structure of our experience in general: through the sound you utter I hear a word, a sentence, a story, a continuation of our conversation; in the visual tableau I see a face, my friend, an answer to my request for help. Because we are experientially so familiar with the recognition of these deeper identities, we typically do not notice theoretically the difference between the immediately present and what is presented, between the immediate sensory moment and the deeper ongoing identity of which it is the presentation. "What" is present is always a temporal whole rather than a temporal moment, a "now" that exists only in definitive relationship to other actual or possible "nows."

The now, as Hegel says, is many nows, as likewise the here is many heres.[11] As a temporal or spatial whole—this day, our afternoon walk, the job interview—the now or the here is internally differentiated, and thus divisible. The various internal divisions—the many nows or heres—are, further, the nows and heres *of* the whole. That present reality—the here and now—endures: it has begun, and it is in process, but it is not wholly present in any isolated moment. Indeed, we can meaningfully ask when an event really takes place: is it in the immediacy of my first recognition of it as when I am first confronted with a confession of love, is it in its lingering presence of that experience as I find myself living in its warm but disconcerting glow later in the day, or is it in the sedimentation of that experience into my identity in the life I have built with my partner on its basis?[12] Here and now you are reading this chapter. But my first remarks may only truly become present to you when you see their fulfillment in the end of the chapter, or perhaps years from now when their real wisdom or foolishness becomes apparent to you. There is no isolated moment when the event happens. Nonetheless this moment now is a moment *of* the reading of my chapter. As Hegel goes on to note in the transition into the next section of the *Phenomenology of Spirit,* the now cannot be construed adequately without introducing "reflected" determinations, without approaching it with the distinction between thing and property: the determinacy of this moment is a property *of* this reading.[13]

> Immediate certainty does not take over [*nimmt sich nicht*] the truth [*die Wahre*], for its truth is the universal, whereas certainty wants to apprehend the *this* . . . . Since the principle of the object, the universal, is in its simplicity a *mediated* universal, the object must express this its nature in its own self. This it does by showing itself to be *the thing of many properties.* The wealth of sense-knowledge belongs to perception [*Wahrnehmung*], not to immediate certainty, . . . for only perception contains negation, that is, difference or manifoldness, within its own essence.[14]

We have thus reached the concept of thinghood: we have seen, in other words, why perception—the apprehension of things—properly follows the dialectic of sense-certainty, for we have seen why the now as a presence that cannot be captured in an isolated moment is the metaphysical domain of identity—of being a "what," a thing.

In light of this talk of the relation of thing and property, let us notice, finally, one characteristic of the many nows in this "now that is many nows." Let us notice specifically that the past and the future, as they have emerged in our phenomenological description of presence—and, remember that, from the perspective of Hegel's project, our phenomenological description and its inherent dialectic is the only legitimate court of appeal—are inherently *of* the present. The future is how this now has its possibilities opened up for it, just as the past is what opened up the possibilities this now fulfills.

Body as Time

What Hegel has introduced through his analysis of the now falls essentially within the domain of Aristotelian metaphysics—not in all respects, but in the sense that it demands the distinction between potentiality and actuality. In terms of presence (the present) we need a notion of a presence that is not *simply* immediate presence, a presence that is mediated—specifically, mediated by absence. The now, we have seen, is a present that carries within it past and future. In terms of potentiality and actuality, we would say that the present actualizes (fulfills) certain potentialities (anticipations) of the past, as it opens new horizons, new potentialities for the future.[15]

Aristotle's philosophy helps us to think further about the complexities of the metaphysics of potentiality and actuality. In *On the Soul*, in particular, he distinguishes two senses of actuality.[16] Actuality in the first sense is, roughly, a power actually possessed. Actuality in the second sense is that power in use. I am actually a driver, though I am not actually driving. I have accomplished that identity—first actuality—but am not actively deploying it—second actuality. In this example of the nondriving driver we see something important about presence: what I actually, presently am is a driver, though that reality does not show itself in action. My driver-identity is my reality—my "first actuality"—so *what* is present is a driver, but that presence is not present in a moment.[17] It is present *only as* an enduring identity. My first actuality, my identity, is something that is present, and something that can only be present if time is not a passing instant.

This notion of first actuality can help us to understand better the temporality with which we are engaged. When Aristotle speaks of first actuality, he primarily means the soul, that is, the identity of a living body. Further, the analogical examples he uses to clarify his distinction are such things as "to cut" (in the axe), "to see" (in the eye), literacy (*he grammatikē*), and sleeping.[18] All of these examples are precisely *powers*, that is, each is a potentiality to act in a specific way: to cut, to see, to read, to be awake. The primary definition of what is present as the body—the soul—is precisely the power of living. Hegel's description of the organism in chapter V, "Reason," similarly implies that the reality that is the soul is not simply statically present but is present only in and as a temporal process:

> But the being-for-self of the living organism does not stand on one side in this way over against its outer [as does the determinateness of the inorganic]; on the contrary, it has in its own self the principle of *otherness*. If we define being-for-self as *simple, self-preserving relation-to-self*, then its otherness is simple *negativity*; and organic unity is the unity of a self-identical relating-to-self and pure negativity.[19]

The organic being does not exist by itself in isolation from what is other to it, but exists instead as a body in dynamic relationship with its outside: it exists precisely as *the power to live*, which is a power only realized in and as engagement with the world, only in and as action. The identity of the living body—its "first actuality"—is this "to live." Primarily, first actuality names *an established power*, and a power is something that portends a future: an action. Let us linger with this point a moment longer.

It is *as* having this actuality—*as* having this power—that there is for *me*, or for the subject in question, a possible future. Until I became a driver, a quick trip to the grocery store in the mall was not a possibility, but it is now, in any situation in which I run short on kitchen supplies. Being a driver does not make it be the case that going to the mall will happen; rather, it makes it the case that that future is on my horizon. *That ability being present*—being my actuality—is *the same reality as that future being on my horizon.*

Let me return now to the young drug addict with whom I began. The troubling aspect of her vision that she will quit later is that she may not have a "later": she may die. This reminds us of our mortality, of our need to be living bodies. Hegel remarks of self-consciousness that "life is as essential to it as self-consciousness," and that is the point we are recognizing here.[20] It is only my body, as the enactment of my most basic "first actuality," that is my fundamental ability to live, and for that reason it is the irremovable context for all my possibilities. Without my living body, there is no now, and without the now, no future.

Said otherwise, time is a bodily phenomenon, or, again, time is what body essentially is. The body is an oriented determinateness, a potentiality for action, and that means it is a kind of congealed time, a living, present identity that makes futures—specific futures—possible (and, as we shall see in chapter 3, Hegel emphasizes that only the specific is not nothing).[21] If, then, we want to get in front of ourselves the phenomenon of time, we should stop looking at the clock, and look instead at life, at nature, at bodies.[22] The clock constructs the illusion that time is isolated instants, whereas the body enacts the reality that time is the bringing into possibility of futures by virtue of being an established identity.

As we noted above, the dialectic of the now pointed us to the notion of the thing and its properties. With these ideas about body and time now in mind, let us consider the temporality of thinghood as such. Specifically, let us now turn to a contrast of the temporality of thinghood with the temporality of a cultural *ethos* or *Sittlichkeit.*

Thinghood and Ethicality

In the dialectic of sense-certainty, we have seen that the simplicity of the now and the here is not to be found in an isolated moment. In the phenomenology of perception that follows, Hegel identifies thinghood as the "simple here" of the properties, and what I have been suggesting is that thinghood is equally a "simple now."[23] What we have been seeing is that identity—a "reflected" determination or a "determination of reflection"—can never be simply immediate because it is the whatness, the essence, *of* some determinacy, a pervasive characterization in which the thing is, as it were, doubled: the thing is both its multiple determinacies, and its unitary identity. This metaphysical doubling that is thinghood is a temporal determination because it is a projective determination: the pervasive identity, the thinghood, entails that, at whatever actual point we pick, there is a beyond to that point in which its identity remains self-same. Whatever isolated moment we pick, we need to recognize that, though the thing actually is "this," it is *also* "this" more beyond and *also* "this" more, and so on.[24] The self-same presence entails a future, a beyond, to whatever actual moment of its presence is isolated.

At the same time, however, our everyday concept of thinghood is pointedly non-dynamic. We conceive of the thinghood as a fixed identity that is itself unaffected by its own history. Though the thinghood is inherently temporal, it is conceived in a non-temporal fashion as the eternal, unchanging essence of the thing—what Aristotle calls *ousia.*[25] If we now consider the experience of living from a traditionally handed-down and habitually adopted cultural attitude, an experience, that is, of embracing an *ethos,* we find a similar identity—a similar congealed temporality, or non-immediate presence—that is, on the contrary, itself pointedly temporal.

An *ethos*, like thinghood, is a pervasive, enduring identity. In his phenomenological description of the experience of *ethos* in chapter VI, "Spirit," Hegel draws upon the portrait of Antigone in Sophocles' *Antigone* to present the "ethical" consciousness.[26] Antigone confronts the situation in which her brother has been killed in battle and denied burial because he was declared a traitor. Antigone believes that it is a law of the gods that each individual is to be buried, and she, in her singular identity, takes upon herself the responsibility for upholding this divine law: in the name of the gods and of the deepest commitments of her society, she opposes the edict and buries her brother (a decision that precipitates disastrous conflict in herself, her family, and her community). In this intimate, lived commitment to the "unwritten laws" of proper action, Antigone is exemplary of what Hegel calls an "ethical" consciousness.[27] Let us consider Antigone's identity. When Antigone is present, the identity that is present is not a simple immediacy, but a reflected identity, and not just the identity of an isolated person, but a communal (familial, civil, societal) identity: in Antigone's action, the self-conscious individual "Antigone" is present, but, inasmuch as she exists as a member of society and has, through her upbringing, been shaped by this society, in Antigone's action Thebes (her immediate community) is present, and Hellas (the broader religious, linguistic, and cultural "nation") is present.

> By acknowledging the *absoluteness* of the right, I am within the ethical substance; and this substance is thus the *essence* of self-consciousness. . . . [T]his self-consciousness is the *actuality* and the *existence* of the substance, its *self* and *will*.[28]

Indeed, Antigone proudly acts as the defender of her religious-cultural identity, and she thus self-consciously views herself as the agent of the making present of the community and the gods: "This [ethical] consciousness," Hegel writes, "has put its merely individual aspect behind it."[29] In short, in Antigone's action, what Hegel calls "spirit" is present.

This identity that is present in Antigone's action is, again, a kind of congealed time, in that it is a first actuality, present as the promise of possible futures, as we saw above. But what is especially interesting about *ethos*, as opposed to simple thinghood as *ousia*, is that an *ethos* is historically accomplished. "Ethicality" (*Sittlichkeit*) does not occur naturally, but is something cultivated, a kind of culture (*Bildung*). An *ethos* is a habit: it is something accomplished through a process of repetition (the repetition of the rituals of cultural membership) to the point that the practices become what someone *is*.[30] This is the nature of any habit. The drug addict, again, *is* now "an addict," not because she is using drugs at this moment, but because she repeated certain actions to the point that she accomplished a specific identity with a specific future. As well as a present that portends a future, the presence of *ethos*—or of any habit—is also the enduring presence of a specific history.

One more interesting feature of an *ethos*: it is not a computer program. While it involves a set of norms and practices, it is precisely a way of *responding* to events, that is, to emergent situations.[31] An *ethos*—or, again, any habit—is like a hand or an eye: though it has a determinate (historically accomplished) form, it is precisely a power to respond to the unanticipatable character of what comes, a way of *grasping* what is available.[32] Personal and cultural habits, that is, are not matters of rote repetition, but are forms of intelligent discrimination that occur without the need of explicitly self-conscious deliberation and direction. Inasmuch as their very nature is to be responsive to uniquely new situations, their character is precisely a form of *openness*. I want to consider briefly one—perhaps the most essential—dimension of an *ethos* to see this openness more clearly. I want to consider language.

As I indicated above, literacy (if that is a fair translation of *hē grammatikē*) is one of Aristotle's own primary examples of first actuality.[33] To become a proper member of society is to develop a basic literacy in that culture, which, though we use the expression metaphorically to refer to broad cultural competence, first and foremost means learning the language.[34] Acquiring language is an exemplary case of first actuality, and an exemplary dimension of ethical life.

If we consider what it is like to acquire a language, we can see very clearly how much an *ethos* is not a computer program. It is precisely in acquiring a language that we develop the capacity to say new things (poetry), to engage with others (conversation), and to transform ourselves (education). Language is precisely the medium in which we become open to being affected from without, we become open to what is beyond our horizons. And surely what is evident to any teacher from all the student papers she has read is that it is incompetence with the language—with the rules of grammar, the knowledge of definitions, and so on—that inhibits the ability of students to advance in their studies. In other words, becoming more competent with the rules of language is not limiting one's capacity for expression, but enhancing it, allowing one access to a world of things and of thoughts (including one's own thoughts) that one could not otherwise grasp.[35] Language, then, is particularly helpful for letting us see how the rigidity of an habitual identity—an addiction or an *ethos*—can *be* an openness to innovation and growth.

What I have been outlining in this section, then, is the different *temporalities* of, basically, *ousia* and *ethos* (or perhaps, considering my particular focus on languge, *ousia* and *logos*). Both a thing and an *ethos* are forms—pervasive identities—that are inherently temporal actualities. They differ in how they are enactments of a past, the thing being construed as that which has no past but is eternal in character, and *ethos* being that which is inherently historical. This difference with respect to their inherent pastness is also a difference with respect to the future: whereas the future of the thing is as unchanging as the past—it is utterly indifferent to what emerges—the future of *ethos* is undecided—it is open to what comes. But, finally, this openness of *ethos* is not at odds with a certain rigidity and closedness to its past: any habit is the *fixing* of a form, and, as we saw with language in particular, the openness is precisely enhanced by the rigorousness of the closure.

Non-Synchronous Temporalities

We have been using Hegel's dialectic of sense-certainty to show a way in which being can be reinterpreted as time: we have interpreted different metaphysical types—thing, *ethos*—as different temporalities. The notion of first actuality that we drew upon to develop this temporal interpretation was introduced by considering the living body as an enactment of temporality. Having distinguished the temporality of things from the temporality of ethicality, let us now return to the temporality of the organic body and consider something about the different temporalities of body and *ethos*, or, more broadly, of nature and spirit.

My main point is simply this: the two temporalities of nature and spirit are at the same time, we might say, simultaneous and not simultaneous. What I mean is that, in an important sense, I *am* a living body and I *am* spirit, but these two times run, so to speak, on different schedules. This is essentially the point with which we began when we considered the British drug addict. For this young woman, *her* time is a time of spirit *and* a time of nature, that is, the meaning of her actions is simultaneously the working out of her self-defined human projects and the enactment of her given, natural vitality. Our concern about her is that the time of nature, which is the founding precondition for the time of spirit, will be exhausted in a way that is premature from the point of view of the time of spirit. While it is true that the time of spirit—the time of her ability to define her own life—leaves room for her to kick the habit later, this temporality is itself predicated on the time of nature. Each, in different ways, has precedence over the other, the time of spirit because it *defines* her temporality, the time of nature because it is the *condition sine qua non* of her temporality: they are different, but co-dependent. Let us look a bit further into this difference as a way of conceptualizing the difference between nature (life) and spirit in Hegel's philosophy.

Once again, the definitive mark of the temporality of spirit is how it incorporates the past. The identity of the body is dynamic, unlike the simple concept of the thing, but it is still essentially *ousia*-like, in that the forms of natural life are fundamentally given rather than accomplished. Though species may change over time (which is something not itself acknowledged by either Hegel or Aristotle), this does not change the fact that the living individual lives out a temporality that its own actions do not transform. "Life," Hegel writes, "consists rather in being the self-developing whole which dissolves its development and in this movement simply preserves itself."[36] In this sense, nature is not historical: the natural individual does not record its past in its own substance.[37] This recording, on the contrary, is what is definitive of spirit: spirit is inherently historical. Again, a fundamental metaphysical difference—this time the basic difference between nature and spirit—is a difference of temporality.

Let us consider what this lets us say about history. History is not a simple passage of discrete events as a series of now points successively substituted for each other. That is already shown to us by the simple dialectic of the now. But it is also not a series of facts construed as things, and, indeed, even the temporality of the living body—the temporality of nature—does not accommodate the reality of history. It is only when we step beyond instants, beyond things and beyond nature, that we enter a realm where the reality "history" enters the scene. History is history only insofar as it is what spirit holds onto as its own identity.[38] Our reflection on temporality, then, allows us to recognize the necessity for the distinction Hegel draws between nature and spirit.

But if it is the case that history is spirit holding onto its own identity, history can no more be removed from the identity of, so to speak, the historian (spirit as the subject constituted by this history) than the instantaneous now can be removed from the context of past and future. This point can help us understand something further about temporality.

The past and the future are not "out there" as existent, alien realities that we somehow have to get to. The past and the future are always "of" the present, that is, they are the indissociable dimensions of the identity of the subject, of spirit. What we have seen from looking at spirit is that history is that identity *as accomplishment,* and what we have seen from looking at the thing and the body is that the future is precisely what those identities *make possible.* The question of the future, then, is not how some identity answers to some existent other, but is instead what that identity opens up.

Conclusion: Phenomenology, Closure, and the Future of Philosophy

The understanding of temporality that we have here developed allows us, finally, to understand the distinctive character of Hegel's philosophical project, specifically with respect to familiar concerns about the closure of his system and the "end of history." Just as thinghood, the natural body, and *ethos* can be interpreted fundamentally as different temporalities, different forms of "now," we can also ask, "What is philosophy itself as a now, and how is it a different now from these others?" What we can see is that Hegel's philosophy is precisely and definitively a philosophy of the future.

At different points in his writing, Hegel characterizes his own method as "phenomenological," "dialectical," and "presuppositionless." Phenomenology "has as its object only knowing as it appears," ["nur das erscheinende Wissen zum Gegenstande hat"], experience as it is experienced;[39] it is a method of description, a method of letting experience show itself:

> Consciousness provides its own criterion from within itself, so that the investigation becomes a comparison of consciousness with itself. . . . Consequently, we do not need to import criteria, or to make use of our own bright ideas and thoughts during the course of the inquiry; it is precisely when we leave these aside that we succeed in contemplating the matter and hand as it is *in and for itself*.[40]

Dialectical philosophy bears witness to the self-transformation of its object, "this *dialectical* movement which consciousness exercises on itself" ["Diese *dialektische* Bewegung, welche das Bewußtsein an ihm selbst ausübt"], letting the object itself dictate what form the "method" must take.[41] A presuppositionless philosophy cannot dictate in advance any rules to its subject-matter, but must precisely take all existing certainties not as guides, but as *explananda*:

> All . . . presuppositions or assumptions must equally be given up when we enter into the science, . . . for it is this science in which all determinations of this sort must be investigated. . . . Science should be pre-

> ceded by *universal doubt,* i.e., by total *presuppositionlessness* [*die gänzliche Voraussetzungslosigkeit*].[42]

Such a "method" is simply the resolve to witness, and is thus equally an abandonment of any determinate method.[43] "The power of spirit," Hegel writes, "is only as great as its expression, its depth only as deep as it dares to spread out and lose itself in its exposition";[44] like spirit itself, "[s]cientific cognition demands surrender to the life of the object."[45] What we must recognize in all these characterizations is that philosophy as Hegel understands it is precisely the commitment to the project to be *open.* If, for example, it could be shown that Hegel in his writing carries forward his own prejudices or builds presuppositions into his analyses, this would show that he had failed to live up to the definitive philosophical/ phenomenological imperative to presuppositionless openness.[46] In other words, it is the constitutive and inherent demand of this project that it be enacted as a letting-go of prejudices; indeed, this philosophy is, Hegel says, a "pathway of despair" which is the very "loss of one's own self":

> But since [natural consciousness] directly takes itself to be real knowledge, this path has a negative significance for it, and what is in fact the realization of its concept counts for it rather as the loss of its own self; for it does lose its truth on this path. It can therefore be regarded as the pathway of *doubt,* or more precisely as the way of despair.[47]

It is thus the project to be determined by the future, to be transformed by what eventuates.

The history that Hegel studies is the history *of* this openness, the history *as which* a subject is accomplished that *is* this openness. In an Aristotelian way, we might ask a question about hypothetical necessity:[48] "Assuming this openness is to be realized, what would be the historical conditions that would be presupposed for its accomplishment?" This is a meaningful question, and this is what Hegel is answering when he studies the philosophy of history and when he announces its completion. Far from closing *off* the future, the end of history is precisely the accomplishment for the first time of the radical openness to the future.

Let us review our earlier discussion of temporality. After seeing how thinghood or identity should be understood as a realization of the notion of a "now that is many nows," we saw that the inherent temporality of such identities is only properly accomplished in spiritual identities, that is, in *ethos,* for only here are the identities truly shaped by history and futurity. We saw in particular that there is true futurity in *ethos,* and that this is precisely correlated with its character as a historical accomplishment—a habit, essentially. But though *ethos,* unlike life or simple thinghood, does have a kind of openness, *ethos does not itself exist for the sake of openness.* On the contrary, *ethos* is inherently conservative, as we see in *Antigone*: though an ethical identity is always enacted as a creative response to a novel situation, it is a "firm trust" in "staid custom," and its goal and its self-interpretation is to be a re-enactment of an established, traditional identity.[49] Antigone herself enacts her identity by taking a stand on the authority of the "divine laws," laws which do, indeed, perpetuate the power of a traditionally established cultural identity, but do so in a conservative insistence upon opacity and ignorance, enforcing rigid sex-role stereotypes and rejecting the self-defining power of self-conscious human rationality.[50] Indeed, such a conservative, tradition-minded "ethicality" is what condemned Socrates to death in 399 B.C., on the grounds that his rigorous, philosophical open-mindedness corrupted the "moral fiber" of Athens by rejecting its established religion. Though an ethical identity is *in fact* (is "in itself") historical and futural, it explicitly interprets itself (is "for itself") as a given, immutable, and eternal identity. *Ethos,* in other words, models itself on something like the *ousia* of simple thinghood, or on natural life.

What is unique and different about *philosophy* as a temporality is not just that it happens to be futural, but that this is its *raison d'etre.* The openness of dialectical phenomenology is thus a metaphysical innovation, a reality that is not reducible to thinghood, nature, or *ethos.* Like *ethos,* it is an historical accomplishment—indeed, the openness is only the inherent futurity *of* this history. It is only as a specific accomplishment that this stance can be realized, and the closure or completion of history is nothing more than the fact of the eventuation of this stance.

2

The Logic of Perception: On Things, Persons, and the Nature of Love

> Our perception ends in objects, and the object once constituted appears as the reason for all the experiences of it which we have had or could have.
>
> —Maurice Merleau-Ponty, *Phenomenology of Perception*

> Love does not consist in gazing at each other but in looking together in the same direction.
>
> —Antoine de Saint-Exupéry

In the first of his *Meditations on First Philosophy,* Descartes seeks a criterion for knowledge, and the meditation proceeds by proposing possible criteria and then demonstrating their dubitability.[1] The first candidate he proposes is immediate sensation, but this proves unreliable as even our simple sensations can mislead us about their objective qualities. His second candidate is a response to the doubt produced by challenging the ability of sensation to reliably reveal the nature of reality. Even if, he argues, I might be mistaken under extreme circumstances about sensory details, still it seems that I could not be mistaken about the bodies—the things—of my immediately surrounding situation:

> But it may be that although the senses sometimes deceive us concerning things which are hardly perceptible, or very far away, there are yet many others to be met with as to which we cannot reasonably have any doubt, although we recognize them by their means. For example, there is a fact that I am here, seated by the fire, attired in a dressing gown, having this paper in my hands and other similar matters.[2]

In fact, the experience of dreams does present a challenge to this everyday certainty, and this leads him to propose a third criterion, namely principles that are understood by the mind, a criterion that is itself subsequently cast into doubt by the idea of an all-powerful god (a theme the significance of which we will confront directly when we consider religion in chapter 13) and resolved finally in his indubitable experience of himself as a thinking thing. These last stages of the argument are not my interest here, however. Instead, my interest is in the distinct domain of experience that Descartes has marked out as the second possible criterion for knowledge, namely, our everyday certainty of the familiar things of our surrounding world.

Like Descartes, Hegel maintains that philosophy begins with universal doubt—"the scepticism that is directed against the whole range of phenomenal consciousness . . . renders the spirit for the first time competent to examine what truth is"[3]—but this "pathway of *doubt*" ["Weg des *Zweifels*"] is not an abstract dismissing of what it doubts, but is a tarrying with its specificity, a commitment to the thing itself by which it on its own demonstrates its unique problems, its own unique "dubitability" or "*determinate* negation" ["*bestimmte* Negation"].[4] In thus learning *from the experience itself* how it is able to be doubted—"consciousness suffers this violence at its own hands," Hegel writes[5]—we simultaneously are educated into what form experience must take if it is to overcome these problems: "the new true object issues from it."[6] Like Descartes, Hegel situates the experience of things between immediate sensory awareness and understanding as a possible criterion for knowledge. In this chapter, we shall follow Hegel's description of the everyday experience of things, and, with him, witness the unique ways in which the distinctive characteristics of this experience reveal both the limitations of that experience and the possibilities for richer forms of experience.

"Perception" [*Wahrnehmung*] is the name Hegel gives to the everyday recognition of things.[7] In our everyday perceptual experience, it seems to us obvious that reality exists in the form of a multiplicity of things, a multiplicity of individual, self-defined beings—*ousiai,* Aristotle calls them[8]—that maintain their self-identity in and through a multiplicity of properties. Such things share certain features with each other—being colored, being situated in place, having a mass, etc.—but each nonetheless retains its own metaphysical autonomy and independence.[9] About these things, "we could not reasonably have any doubt," Descartes initially remarks, and it is true that, though logical doubts might be introduced into our belief in the existence of things, it does not seem optional for us to recognize—to "posit"—their existence.

Note that I use the language of both "recognition" and "positing."

"Recognition" suggests the apprehension of what is independently and truly there. "Positing" suggests subjective stipulation, the assertion of one's personal choice. The perceptual attitude itself operates with the presumption that it is simply passively recognizing:

> [Consciousness] has only to *take* it, to confine itself to the pure apprehension of it, and what is thus yielded is the True. If consciousness itself did anything in taking what is given, it would by such adding or subtraction alter the truth.[10]

Part of the strength of Hegel's description of experience, however, is that he shows that, though we in fact take it simply to be a given truth that reality takes the form of things such that our own stance toward them is just passive reception, just a "recognition," in fact the notion that reality takes the form of things is a thesis, something that one "posits," that one might affirm or deny—and, indeed, it is an internally incoherent thesis at that. Perception—the apprehension of things—is indeed an irreducible form of our experience, but it is not the absolute form and we can see this by investigating more precisely what we mean by "thing," and considering how well this notion, this "thesis," captures the dimensions of meaning that are in fact in play in our experience.

In what follows, I will articulate the distinctive logic of perception—the logic of "the thing"—in order to demonstrate both its opposition to other contending theses about the nature of knowledge and reality and its internally self-opposed character. Though the notion of the thing is essential to our experience, it actually stands in conflict both with other essential notions and with itself. After clarifying what the problems are with reducing the interpretation of our experience to the apprehension of things, and identifying the further dimensions of experience that must be acknowledged in order to correct the one-sidedness of this interpretation, we can see the interesting and important way in which this same perceptual logic—with the same problems—is at play in the most intimate domain of our interpersonal life, namely, in the domain of love; investigating this last experience will allow us to anticipate the themes of the phenomenology of self-consciousness, which is the heart of Hegel's philosophical project.

The Tacit Thesis of Perception

It is our everyday attitude to take reality to be a vast assemblage of individual things. We take things to be independently and intrinsically real—to be "absolute." Our study of the experience of the "now" in the previous chapter already revealed why the notion of "the thing and its properties" is essential to apprehending the nature of our situation, and, as we have indicated above, the experience of things is an irreducible dimension of our experience of the world. Perception is the attitude that recognizes the thing as what is "absolute," that is, it takes the thing with its properties to be the ultimate nature of reality. This positing of the absoluteness of the thing is not, however, our unequivocal attitude in everyday experience. We regularly adopt another attitude in which we treat things as merely relative—relative to each other and to a more basic reality. Before focusing on the internal logic of perception, let us look first at this way that, within our everyday experience, we already adopt an attitude that relegates the perception of things to a position relative to a more fundamental "absolute": let us consider the everyday stance of *understanding*.

We treat things as merely relatively real when we try to *explain* them, when we try to understand them by seeking their cause(s) in some more basic reality.

> [The] true essence of things has now the character of not being immediately for consciousness; on the contrary, consciousness has a mediated relation to the inner being and, as the understanding, *looks through this mediating play . . . into the true background of things.*[11]

Whether we treat things as caused by the vicissitudes of the changing states of matter and energy or as creations of an all-powerful god, we are, in either case, positing the existence of something more truly real than the things, and we see them as the way in which that more basic reality, that more basic power, shows itself. To apprehend things is to say "that," and to have our consciousness come to a halt at this, its ultimate term. When we ask "why?" however, we undercut the ultimacy of the thing and posit—either presume or recognize—some other ultimate reality that causes the thing, and by seeing the thing in relation to this cause—relative to this absolute—we *understand* it.[12]

> [T]here now opens up above the *sensuous* world, which is the world of *appearance*, a *supersensible* world which henceforth is the *true* world, above the vanishing *present* [*Diesseits*] world there opens up a permanent *beyond* [*Jenseits*].[13]

In understanding, both the ultimate nature of reality and our cognizing subjectivity exceed the grip of the thing and deny it the status that we attribute to it in everyday perception.

Indeed, the presumption that things can be coherently related with other things into a unified, understandable world is an unacknowledged presupposition of perception. As Merleau-Ponty writes,

> the tacit thesis of perception is that at every instant experience can be co-ordinated with that of the previous instant and that of the following, and my perspective with that of other consciousnesses.[14]

It is inherent to the very way one perceives things that one takes them to belong to the same world as other things, and one has thus already tacitly posited an ultimate domain—the domain of "the real"—that is not itself a further perceptible thing but is the always already assumed sharedness of ontological "fabric" of all things *and oneself* as perceiver. By the time we perceive things, they have already been "illuminated" for us, but this common field that houses them and our perception of them itself escapes the logic of perception. We experience things *as co-constitutive (with us and with each other) of the real,* and this is something we *understand*—it is how we *interpret* our experience—not as an optional attitude we might or might not adopt, but as the constitutive, already understood nature of the real that makes possible the perception of things in the first place.[15] Perception thus rests on what Kant would call a "transcendental" act of understanding, or what Heidegger would call the event of being-in-the-world. The absoluteness of the logic of perception is thus always already undermined in principle, and we "live" this experientially whenever we ask "why?" and draw upon this already presumed ontological and epistemological answerability of things to our understanding of the ultimate nature of reality.

Perception as a whole, then, naturally points to its own supersession in understanding, its own inherent subordination to a domain of meaning that it depends upon but that exceeds its terms, and this immanent dialectic is what is described phenomenologically in the transition between chapters II and III of the *Phenomenology of Spirit.*[16] Perception, however, is also internally contradictory, that is, it vacillates between positing two different theses about the nature of the thing. We saw the contradiction between perception and understanding by considering the difference between the recognition "that" and the question "why?"; we can see the contradiction within perception by considering the difference between the recognition "that" and the question "which?" Hegel gives a phenomenological description of the experience of perceiving a thing that brings out the significance of this difference;[17] as we, similarly, consider the characteristic pattern of perception, we shall see that perception is in fact not a single, instantaneous act, but a process that goes through self-contradictory phases.

The Process of Perception

When I notice a thing, I notice its metaphysical autonomy: it is something real unto itself, something responsible for its own identity, for its own character. That my experiential field is articulated into things is not a matter of choice, but is the way I experience the very nature of "what is" to be imposing its form upon us. The thing presents itself within experience as an identity in its own right that must be recognized in its autonomy and integrity. It is *a thing*—a unitary whole, a "one" in Hegel's language—that shows itself to me, and I say to you "look at that."[18]

You, too, are experientially compelled by the weight of the thing, but your field of experience contains many things. Though my attention has focused on the single thing, and I can know to what I point when I say "that," your experience does not immediately have the same focus. Hence you ask, "what?" To answer this question, I will have to enter into *specific* language, language that picks out one thing from another. I say "the bird." Yet even this language, though more specific, may be insufficient to identify for you the thing to which I am attending, and you may have to ask, "which bird?" It is when I say "the small blue one, sitting on the branch of that tree with the reddish leaves over there by the tall hedge" that you are able to identify the object of my perception.

But notice, now, what has happened to make it possible for us to share in the perception of the thing. Whereas my initial response was to the thing in its singularity—the thing as "one"—the demands of our communication led us to focus on those aspects of the thing—its "properties"—by virtue of which it participates in a common domain, a domain of repeatable, universal significances. Explaining the ontological tension between the thing in its ontological singularity and the thing as a manifold of properties, Hegel writes,

> The One is the *moment of negation*; it is itself quite simply a relation of self to self and it excludes an other; and it is that by which "thinghood" is determined as a Thing. Negation is inherent in a property as a *determinateness* which is immediately one with the immediacy of being, an immediacy which, through the unity with negation, is universality. As a One, however, the determinateness is set free from this unity with its opposite, and exists in and for itself.[19]

To take what is before me as "one," in other words, is ontologically at odds with taking what is before me as "properties," because properties have a reality that inherently exceeds the domain of the singular thing.[20] Color, for example, is a feature of every thing, and red a particular species of that genus—a determinate color that has its determinacy, its definitive specificity, by its standing in relation to other colors (e.g., green) which it definitively excludes—similarly present in many different things.[21] While color, as Aristotle notes, could not exist on its own apart from things, but "is" only insofar as it is present in things that exist independently—indeed, it is the thing's very immediacy, the very quality of its presence—it is nonetheless true that the ontological character of color is not reducible to the reality of the individual thing "in" which it is; if it were, *it* could not also be present in others. To the extent that color—which is inherently "public," inherently a reality shared by many—is real, there is a domain of reality that exceeds the reality of singular things, exists in a way not reducible to or explicable in terms of an absolute singularity that is defined only in relation to itself. Indeed, it is precisely because properties are a common reality that it is by reference to them that we can communicate about *which* thing I am noticing.

In other words, whereas when I am initially struck by the perception of the thing I immerse myself in an absorbed fascination with the singularity of the thing as an ontological absolute, when I specify to you *which* one I shift my perceptual stance to an ontological commitment to realities that exist in a supra-singular domain of sharedness, communal "matters" that define and determine things.[22] The thing itself is here no longer construed as an ontological original, a self-defined, absolute "one," but is a derivative reality that exists as the coalescence of a multiplicity of properties: it is the simple fact of being-together of the independently existing matters, their "also."[23] What is crucial to recognize is that our sense of a thing inherently involves *both* of these significances—"one" and "also"—that is, we have no sense of a thing about which we could not specify to another "which" one it is, and, equally, we have no sense of a thing that does not involve its actually *being* a thing, that is, being a reality unto itself. Indeed, this is precisely Hegel's point when he writes,

> [I]f the many determinate properties were strictly indifferent to one another, if they were simply and solely self-related, they would not be determinate; for they are only determinate in so far as they *differentiate* themselves from one another, and *relate* themselves *to others* as to their opposites. Yet; as thus opposed to one another they cannot be together in the simple unity of their medium, which is just as essential to them as negation; the differentiation of the properties, in so far as it is not an indifferent differentiation but is exclusive, each property negating the others, thus falls outside of this simple medium; and the medium, therefore, is not merely an Also, an indifferent unity, but a *One* as well, a unity which *excludes* another.[24]

The thing *is not* other things, and this means *both* that it communicates with the reality of others *and* that it has a reality unto itself. If it did not communicate with others it could not even be differentiated from them, that is, it could not even be recognized *as* exclusively itself; if it did not have a reality unto itself, the properties would not be "properties," that is, they would not be "of" anything but would simply be unattached qualities unrelated to each other such that this sweet taste and this rough texture would not both *belong to* the honeycomb, to use Descartes's example.[25] Our very sense of "thing," then, is inherently contradictory, vacillating between conflicting but equally necessary senses of the thing as original and derivative, metaphysically absolute and metaphysically relative.[26] The experience of perception is neither the simple, nor the passive, one that we take it to be, but is in fact a process—an unacknowledged process—of shifting ontological commitments.

And notice, too, that our commitment to the equal essentiality of recognizing "that" and specifying "which" points to something further: the way we perceive things is *as* realities that can be pointed out to others. I say "look at that" because I see the thing as already belonging to a reality shot through with intersubjectivity: I see from a context in which I already recognize myself to be involved in a world with others—others with whom I can communicate—and I see the thing "objectively," that is, I see it as something that should be available to others in the same way that it is available to me. Indeed, I see the thing as something that, in drawing my attention, should also draw your attention, or, more exactly, should draw *our* attention, and my perceptual experience is only fulfilled though my participation in language by which I turn my experience of the thing into a shared experience, an experience of "joint attention," an experience of what Hegel calls "spirit."[27]

In these further observations, we see other ways in which the experience of the thing depends on reality having a character that is not acknowledged in the perceptual attitude that explicitly takes "thinghood" to define the nature of reality. The putative "absoluteness" of thinghood is implicitly challenged by these unacknowledged aspects of the perceptual experience; by drawing out those other dimensions, we can see that, in fact, thinghood is relative to a coherent domain into which it is integrated ("reality," the domain reflective of ultimate ontological principles only open to understanding), itself a reality inherently open to the communication between perceivers (the intersubjective domain of language, shared attention, "spirit"). These deeper contextualizing realities do not, however, eliminate the significance of "thinghood"; they reveal, rather, that "thinghood" is not the absolute character of reality, but is rather ontologically relative to these deeper dimensions of reality. Indeed, the flip-side of the truth that thinghood inherently reveals these deeper realities is that these deeper realities only exist in and through, and are only revealed in and through, things. It is precisely in and through things, that is, that reality is enacted, only in and through things that our intersubjectivity is accomplished.[28]

We have thus understood the ontological significance of thinghood: both its problematic character when taken to define the absolute and its essentiality as a relative dimension of reality. This primary enactment of this logic of thinghood is in its definitive role in our everyday perceptual experience, but we do also rely upon this logic in other domains. Let us now consider in particular its significance in our interpersonal experience.[29]

Perceiving Spirit

The contradiction between the "one" and the "also" is very familiar to us from our interpersonal lives. It is especially definitive of our familiar attitudes in experiences of love. We typically speak both of the familial love of parents for children (which we will consider below, in chapter 10) and of the romantic love that involves one person "falling in love" with another. While both sorts of love are, as Hegel writes, "the disposition of individual persons whereby they have their essential self-consciousness in this unity," it is specifically romantic love that is my focus here.[30] Such romantic "falling in love" we typically understand to be a situation in which another person has been uniquely captivated by our unique singularity. This aspect of the experience of love is well described by Sartre in *Being and Nothingness*:

> [I]f the Other loves me then I become the *unsurpassable*, which means that I am the absolute end. In this sense I am saved from *instrumentality* . . . . [T]he Other must make me be . . . an absolute center of reference around which all other instrumental-things of the world are ordered as pure *means*. At the same time . . . I am the absolute value. . . . Thus to want to be loved is to want to be placed beyond the whole system of values posited by the Other and to be the condition of all valorization and the objective foundation of all values.[31]

Whereas our normal experiences involve our struggling to fit in and measure up to standards and to persons who do not particularly care about us, love promises to be the situation in which I am valued precisely because *I am I*. Love, we think, is unconditional acceptance and devotion. If another claims to have fallen in love with me, that other has been taken by me *as such*. If the other says, on the contrary, that she loves me *because of* my long legs or my beautiful blue eyes, or if the other says "I really love brunettes," I will be offended: I do not want to be treated as a sum of parts, as the successful resolution to a shopping list, and one who approaches me guided by her sense of such "desirable parts" is not *in love with* me, has not been *smitten* by *me*. It is not love if I am appreciated because of my possession of independently defined parts; it is love only if my "parts" are appreciated *because they are me*. "I must," as Sartre says, "no longer be seen on the ground of the world as a "this" among "thises," but the world must be revealed in terms of me."[32] In love, we demand to be taken as a "one," not as an "also."

On the other hand, however, we also expect to be treated as an "also" by a lover. When it is my birthday—"my" place within the independently defined calendar—I expect you to remember that and I expect you to give me a gift that is appropriate to me: I wear size 8 shoes and hate plaids, and I expect you to know that. If you give me size 7 shoes and a plaid shirt on the wrong day, I will be offended; more specifically, I will deem it inconsistent with your claim to love me if you comfortably remain in ignorance of my specific "properties"—my shoe size, birth date, and fashion preferences. If you respond, "It was a pure gift from me to you, and I only see you in your uniqueness," I will not experience that as an expression of appreciation but as an experience of ignorance and disrespect: it is precisely a failure of you to appreciate *me* as the me that I actually am; it is a failure for you to appreciate *my* determinateness. As Hegel says in another context (in his discussion of the "Spiritual Animal Kingdom"), love is not just a passive feeling, but requires an active commitment, and that requires *knowledge*: it requires a commitment to the specificity of the others.

> Active love—for love that does not act has no existence and is therefore hardly intended here [in the commandment to "love thy neighbour as thyself"]—aims at removing an evil from someone and being good to him. For this purpose I have to distinguish what is bad for him, what is the appropriate good to counter this evil, and what in general is good for him, i.e., I must love him *intelligently*.[33]

It is precisely a mark of your failure to really love me if you do not love me in my specificity, and that means I demand of you that you appreciate me as an "also," and not as a strictly incomparable and immeasurable "one."

From these familiar experiences, we know what it is like to be on the "inside" of the metaphysical problem of the "one" and the "also." From our own self-experience, that is, we know the difference between "one" and "also," we know their opposition—that is, we know in each case the necessity for one that is equally the necessity for *not* the other—and we know the necessity for both. It is not difficult, in other words, to appreciate the compelling weight of both sides of the love-scenario just described and to recognize that there is a contradiction between them and, thus, a contradiction within each side. In love, then, we have a living familiarity with the dialectic of the thing. And just as the contradiction of the thing illuminates the conflicting stances we take to our love relationships, so in the further development of the dialectic of the thing can we see a route to clarifying the nature of our interpersonal life.

What we should notice in this familiar story of our desires surrounding love is that in each situation—wanting to be recognized as a "one" and wanting to be recognized as an "also"—we *want to be recognized* by the other person. Even as I insist upon my "oneness," I want that "oneness" to *register meaningfully* in the eyes of the other. Indeed, my pleasure or displeasure at your behavior is my interpretation of your actions as *gestures*, as expressions of language (and, indeed, language that I then return to you in my expressions of satisfaction or dissatisfaction). My very desire, then, is premised upon the contextualization of my "oneness" by a situation of communication, a situation in which you and I inhabit the same space of meaningful exchange. By my own standards, in other words, my "thinghood" is shown not to be absolute, but to be relative to a more basic domain of interpersonal communication. Indeed, my very desire that *you* recognize me involves my singling you out from a field of actual and possible others, and so my putatively singular significance in fact depends on your individual significance, both of which depend upon a more basic domain of shared intersubjectivity within which you and I stand out as the important ones. The very desire for recognition, in other words, implies not a desire for status as a singularity, but a desire for the status of a particular—a species—within a field of shared universality.[34] Love, in other words, is inherently a form of *spirit*, a *relationship* inherently conditioned by language (and, ultimately, by law, tradition, and all the other structures presupposed in the establishing of meaningful relationships between people).[35]

In the attitude that we often adopt toward our love relationships, we interpret ourselves according to an inadequate logic of "thinghood," an interpretation that conceals the context of shared intersubjectivity—the context of language or "spirit"—that makes the very elements of our faulty interpretation available to us. We purport to demand from the other a kind of "unconditional welcoming," but, though we name our desire thus, this is in fact not what we desire, for we desire from a particular individual recognizable gestures that speak meaningfully to our own determinacies: what we seek, in other words, is an acceptance and endorsement that is highly conditioned by the terms of our own participation in a system of recognition and interpretation of the nature of human situations. Our desire for love, in other words, is a desire *within* our established system of social intercourse, rather than a desire to escape the terms of intersubjective communication, which would be a desire for a singularity beyond articulation that would disallow any form of possible realization and would not even by recognizable by me.[36]

On the one hand, then, these familiar experiences of love point to their embeddedness in the dialectic of recognition (which we shall consider more directly in chapter 6), and they reveal that it is in fact shared communication that will ultimately satisfy our intersubjective desire, rather than the magical devotion by an under-recognized other to our incoherently articulated self-interpretation. On the other hand, however, our placement within a dialectic of recognition—an interaction between lovers that embraces the particular identities each has established with the shared space of spirit—by itself is insufficient to explain the full demands of love. Beyond the system of interdependence that defines the domain of intersubjective recognition in which we are both able to have meaningful identities for ourselves and for each other, there remains a further dimension to each of our identities. While the opposition of "one" and "also" is insufficient to capture the logic of a person, primarily because it fails to acknowledge the embeddedness of persons in intersubjective relations of communication, that opposition does point to the logical difference between singularity and determinateness. But whereas the logic of thinghood construes each of these logical terms as present actualities, this opposition in fact needs to be construed precisely as the opposition between actuality and possibility.

Beyond those which we have already considered, there is a further way in which we can be dissatisfied with the way we are treated in situations of love. We can find that the way we are recognized by our partner feels limiting, holding us to ways of behaving or ways of being that are indeed familiar routes between us, but that do not liberate us for who we might be. Often, we seek the companionship of others—others who are not our official partners—because around those others we can "be someone else." Others bring out from us possibilities of ourselves that we cannot realize on our own and to which we cannot have access in the company of our partners. Unlike the "one or also" construal of love, this familiar situation reveals that our own identity is intertwined with that of our companion in a dialogue of mutual recognition; it also shows, however, that those situations of recognition—which, as we saw above, are necessarily always conditioned/conditional, rather than "unconditional"—are always one-sided, always limit us to an actual identity whereas we *could* be otherwise. This subjunctive mood of language—the "could"—precisely indicates the domain of *possibility*.

In our relationships of recognition, it is our possibilities that are realized. But these realizations are always finite and determinate, whereas our possibility in principle always exceeds these actualizations. The final, and perhaps most important, requirement in our love relationships is that we be recognized *as free*. The free will, Hegel writes in the *Philosophy of Right*,

> contains (α) the element of *pure indeterminacy* or of the 'I''s pure reflection into itself, in which every limitation . . . is dissolved; the limitless infinity of *absolute abstraction*; . . . [and] (β) . . . the transition from undifferentiated indeterminacy to . . . the *positing* of a determinacy as a content and object . . . the absolute moment of the *finitude* or *particularization* of the 'I.'[37]

As free, we are precisely beings that exist beyond our determinacies. Our "being beyond our determinacy" is not, however, a non-determinate existence, nor is this "beyond" another determinacy elsewhere: our "being beyond determinacy" rather, is the possibility of self-transformation.

When we learn, when we develop relationships with new people, or when we embrace our moral responsibilities, we commit ourselves to situations in which we cannot determinately anticipate where we will be led: we can anticipate that we will change, but we cannot say how. To be committed to these situations—learning, interpersonal life, morality—is to embrace this sense that we must follow where we are led, and we must thus be open to the openness of our own futures, open, indeed, to the sense that we do not know who we shall become. These are situations in which we embrace our own selves as beings of possibility, as beings who are open.

Though these situations of committing ourselves to following where we are led are in fact situations of giving up our sense of self-control and giving up the established terms of our identities, it is nonetheless in these experiences of commitment to a determining "beyond" that we typically most find ourselves realized, most experience "ourselves": it is here that I, most truly, am I; that is, paradoxically, I "know myself"—I am "self-conscious"—most truly in these experiences of committing myself to a "calling" such that I do not know who I shall become.[38] This is what Hegel draws our attention to in identifying the completion of self-consciousness—the culmination of "freedom"—in the "unhappy consciousness" (which we will study in chapter 7), in the self-consciousness that finds its reality in following its "higher calling." I experience my freedom most fully in my freedom to follow my calling, my vocation, and, if you are to support me *as me*, it is *as* such an I, *as* such a one who is called, *as* such a one who cannot yet know who she is, that you must support me.

In our desire to be loved, we desire to be recognized as persons, and that means as persons who will become otherwise, will become someone new, and not determinately anticipatable in the present situation. We experience our personal fulfillment in answering to our calling, and we want to be followed as such, we want to be supported in our sense of the urgency of our calling. Without such support, a conflict develops: either a conflict that one will resolve by abandoning one's aspirations and resigning oneself to the familiar sense of oneself that is already established in the relationship, or that one will resolve by following one's conscience and thereby challenging one's established situation of mutual recognition. In other words, if one is to love another, one must be prepared to love someone one does not yet know, one who is not—and cannot be—simply "present," and in place of the security of established identities, one must trust in the form the other's future will take.

This, then, is the ultimate "truth" of the one and the also in the context of love. The truth of my singularity—my identity as "one"—is that I must respond to the call of conscience, my "higher self." I will do this, however, from a base of recognition, a sharedness of identity—my identity as "also"—that provides the platform for my pursuit of my higher calling. Indeed, we, as free beings, always live our determinacy as a capacity for self-transcendence: my body is my capacity to "do," to engage with and to transform the world beyond myself; my language is my capacity to surpass the limits of my personal life; whatever I determinately "am" is a *power*, something whose meaning is not fixed in itself, but waits upon my determination of its significance. The same is true of the determinacy of our interpersonal relationships: the determinate "who" I have become is the established capacity I have for engaging with my future possibilities, possibilities that themselves are most fully realized in my singular answering to what I experience as my higher calling. Our love as the situation of shared recognition has its ultimate justification, in other words, in supporting us in our self-transcendence, our answering to our callings. The "one" and the "also" are reconciled, that is, in a mutual relationship that is *for* the singular embrace of self-transcendence.

Conclusion

In his *Phenomenology of Spirit,* Hegel confirms both Descartes's recognition of the compelling and irreducible character of "things" within experience and his claim that the experience of things is nonetheless dubitable. Unlike Descartes, however, Hegel demonstrates this dubitability concretely, showing that the very logic of thinghood (a) is contradictory in itself and (b) depends upon a further shared realm of reality that it does not itself acknowledge. We have seen that this same (onto-)logical structure applies both within the world of objects (the domain of "Consciousness"), where it points to the need to acknowledge domains of knowledge and interpretation—"understanding"—beyond the level of the immediate recognition of what it presents, and within the world of subjects (the domain of "Self-Consciousness"), where it points to the necessity for (ethical) modes of behavior that recognize forms of social participation that exceed individuals, and the aspirations and potentialities that exceed the given determinacies of the individual. It is these further forms of experience that we will study in the ensuing chapters.

3

Understanding: Reading and *Différance*

Our study in the previous chapter has led us to see the essential way in which our perceptual experience is dependent upon and contextualized by the experience of understanding. "Understanding," Hegel writes in the preface to the *Phenomenology of Spirit,* is "the most astonishing and mightiest of powers, or rather the absolute power."[1] Understanding is the ability to analyze and the power of asking "why?"; it is the ability to recognize the shared identity of separate individuals; it is our capacity for insight. To live in the world understandingly is to be able to have things *make sense.* At the same time, understanding can be a power that alienates us from our immediate engagement with things and tries to force things to conform to our concepts of them. Hegel also writes in the preface about this darker side of understanding in which it imposes its constructions on situations without regard to the sense of the situation:

> The understanding, in its pigeon-holing process, keeps the necessity and concept of the content to itself—all that constitutes the concreteness, the actuality, the living movement of the reality which it arranges. Or rather, it does not keep it to itself, since it does not recognize it; for if it had this insight [*Einsicht*], it would surely give some sign of it. It does not even recognize the need for it, else it would drop its schematizing, or at least realize that it can never hope to learn more in this fashion than one can learn from a table of contents. A table of contents is all that it offers, the content itself it does not offer at all.[2]

The understanding, our very power to be open to the sense of things, can equally be that which interposes its own sense between us and the sense of things—can be precisely that which keeps us from understanding the situation in which we are involved. Chapter III of Hegel's *Phenomenology of Spirit,* "Force and the Understanding: Appearance and the Supersensible World," concludes Hegel's study of "Consciousness" by presenting a phenomenological description of the experience of understanding that precisely shows why understanding naturally takes these two opposed forms. We will use the theme of reading to follow this basic dialectic of understanding. In so doing, we will also establish the way in which Hegel's Idealist philosophy is itself the flowering of this project of understanding, and the way in which Jacques Derrida's "method" of "deconstruction" is itself a continuation of Hegel's phenomenology.

All Consciousness Is Understanding

I have referred to this book as "lessons"—"readings"—and to grasp the nature of understanding, let us reflect on what it is to read. A language is not just a set of nouns, and reading is not merely the assembling of a list of words. Indeed, think of the difference between the *experience* of reading and the *fact* of a dictionary. The dictionary is a list of words without a subject, without couplings between the words, without comprehension, and so on, and it expresses no meaning: indeed, on its own, it does not "express" at all. These characteristics, alien to the dictionary, are all essential to reading. Reading, beyond the list, is an *understanding*, by a subject, of the *sense* manifest only in and as the determinate bondings of words; the words, the components of the "list," are the expression of a force of meaning, a *sense* that is precisely what is (to be) understood.[3]

To read is always to understand and, indeed, to understand is always to read, to discern the sense expressed through some manifold determinacy. "Understanding," in Hegel's *Phenomenology of Spirit* is, in this sense, the stance of reading, the stance that approaches its object as something to be understood, as a reality that has the character of a force expressing itself as the immediate determinacies of experience. Reality, for understanding, is not the determinacy immediately sensed, but the sense expressed in and as this determinacy. The immediately encountered determinacy, then, is not "the real" as such, but how the real appears, and the immediate determinacy is thus to be *explained by* the *intelligible* sense that is its ground, source, or cause. Indeed, this is how we read: we *understand the sentence* when we have recognized the *sense* that caused this list of words to be here in this order, that is, the sense that *expressed itself in these terms.* By these characteristics, "understanding" shows itself to be a fundamentally different attitude than "perception" or "sense-certainty."

Perception is a stance that accepts something like the dictionary as its model for reality. Perception effectively identifies the world as a list of positivities: "this" one thing, "that" one thing, property *a*, property *b*, property *c*, etc. In perception—our normal, everyday attitude—we construe the world as populated by a multiplicity of independent, self-contained realities ("ones" in Hegel's language; compare Aristotle's "*ousia*"),[4] and we further construe those things to be assemblages of determinate properties (thus the thing is an "also" in Hegel's language: this property *and also* this property *and also* this property, and so on; compare Locke's "substance").[5] As we saw in chapter 2, in our perceptual life, we note the *separation* of things, their *independence* from each other, but we do not note that this independence itself rests on their *integration* into a single, coherent texture of reality; that is, we do not recognize their ontological (causal) *dependence* upon one another. (Indeed, we might here recall Hume's argument that dependence—necessary connection—is not a *perceptible* reality, not a positivity.[6]) Similarly in our daily perceptual attitude we note the list of positive properties of a thing as if they could be identified each on its own, without noting the puzzling feature of their twofold non-independence: (i) the properties are always "of" a thing, and this "of-ness" is not itself another perceptual property alongside the others, but an immanent, definitive *relation of dependence* (recall Hume again) between each property and the thing it is "of";[7] (ii) each property itself is also intrinsically defined by its relations of sameness and difference both to the other properties of the thing (color to shape to texture to weight, and so on) and to the properties of other things (this is blue, which is also the color of that thing, and which is not the green of that other).[8] In the second case, again, these are immanent *relations of dependence*, not separable from the very positive identity of the property we recognize. Just as a dictionary only exists in a world of reading, the reality of which exceeds and explains the dictionary, so does the world of perception presuppose the reality of a coherent world of relations of dependence that exceeds and explains its existence. The stance of perception, in other words, always lives on the basis of a tacit attitude of understanding, which it does not acknowledge. Something similar is true of the stance of sense-certainty.

Sense-certainty is the attitude that presumes itself to be fully present to itself in the unique moment. This is the stance we often typically presume in our self-interpretation, for we take ourselves to be *immediately self-possessing*. We resort to this when our words are challenged, for example, and we say, "I know what I meant," authoritatively attributing to our own positive self-identity an authoritative self-grasp. We treat the "me" now as immediately identifiable with the "me" then who spoke, and we treat ourselves as possessing our "meaning" independently of any articulation that would need interpretation (that is, the sentence in which one expressed oneself). In our sense-certain stance, we take ourselves to grasp immediately the reality present to us and to grasp ourselves immediately: we know who we are and what is present. As we saw in chapter 1, though, this attitude fails to acknowledge the substantial mediation that is presupposed in its having a sense of "self" and "world."

The self I mean to put forward is one I recognize to be different from other selves—me, not you—and the reality that is (was) present to me is a determinate one I pointedly wish to distinguish from others—you had to be *there* to know what I expressed and it is not what I experienced another time or what you experienced—hence my ability to *correct* your *mis*apprehension of my meaning in the first place. But this means my meaning is *articulate*: it is based on a recognition and a coordination of meaningful parts—a dictionary—that is, it is a sense that is *expressed (to me!) in terms,* and thus not separable from mediating processes of recognition, differentiation, and interpretation—in short, reading. I am not wholly present in (or to) the moment: if I were, I could never *notice* its passing (or, indeed, its differentiation from any others) for that would require me—the *self-same me*—comparing the two moments, which means I could not be wholly identifiable with just one: I must be in this moment *and* absent from it, in the other, in order to compare.[9] To assert the *distinctive, determinate* identity of this present or this me requires that I be fully identifiable with neither, and that I *remember* each while comparing it with my present me: I must implicitly remember, compare, and, ultimately, *conclude* that they are the same or different.[10] In other words, there can be no recognition of determinacy, no "being present" (to "it" or to "myself") that is not *inherently* mediated by tacit processes of interpretation. ("Synthesis" in the language of Kant and Husserl, "reading" in the language I am using here.[11])

Sense-certainty, then, insists about itself that it needs no language, that its experience / its meaning is *immediately determinate* with no mediating structures of articulation or reading; in fact, though, it can be an experience only as a determinate *articulation,* an expressing (writing) and an interpreting (reading). Its very distinctive assertion of its own self-possessed authority betrays its character as always at a distance from itself, able to possess a world or itself only by presupposing a "dictionary" of differentiated, determinate identities, and an activity of reading.

Both "perception" and "sense-certainty," then, are stances that depend upon implicit epistemic processes that they do not themselves avow. Understanding, in particular, is necessarily implicitly alive in these attitudes. Let us now look at understanding in its own right.

Reading Is the Proper Model for Understanding

As we saw in chapter 2, understanding—the perspective that looks for the originary force responsible for the manifold determinacy that expresses it—is an orientation to the world that emerges in answer to the question, "why?" We encounter a particular setting and want to know what accounts for it.[12] I ask, "why is that cup there?" and my friend answers, "Mary put it there," and I then feel satisfied that I understand what formerly puzzled me. I ask, "why is my car no longer running?" and my friend answers, "because it's out of gasoline," and I feel satisfied. These are typical experiences of understanding: a "why" is answered by a "because." I may, however, not be fully satisfied by the answer. I may, for example, ask my friend, "why does the absence of gasoline make the car stop running?" My friend may then explain to me the role of fuel in an internal combustion engine. Again, this may satisfy me, or I may ask "why?" again, this time asking what it is that makes gasoline combustible. Here it is an explanation in terms of the chemical properties of gasoline that will satisfy me. The answer may be, "gasoline is composed of hydrocarbon molecules, and hydrocarbons act in the following way." There are a number of important things to notice in these examples.

First, it is important to notice that we *do* say in cases such as these, "ah, now I understand." These ways of answering our "why" questions demonstrate the normal phenomenon of understanding in our experience. Notice, second, that these answers most typically take the form of saying, "because when (if) *x* is the case, then *y* follows." The answer that satisfies our understanding is typically *a rule.* Indeed, my example of the car is good for reminding us what we typically do when we face a puzzle: we know that we do not understand the why, so we turn to an *expert* who *does* understand. We turn to the mechanic or the doctor. In these cases, the one who understands is the one who has learned the rules that "explain" the circumstances. If we then ask where *ultimately* we turn for these answers, it is to the "scientists," chemists, and—even more ultimately—the physicists who investigate the ultimate rules of reality. Typically, then, we understand understanding to be the possession of the rule under which the relevant circumstances are subsumed and thereby explained, and we understand this to be a multi-layered process of answering "why" that ultimately stops with the ultimate rules of reality as studied by the natural scientist (the physicist in particular).[13]

This is the attitude that Hegel studies in chapter III of the *Phenomenology of Spirit* when he considers the "first supersensible world":

> This difference is expressed in the *law,* which is the *stable* image of unstable appearance. Consequently, the *supersensible* world is an inert *realm of laws* which, though beyond the perceived world—for this exhibits law only through incessant change—is equally *present* in it and is its direct tranquil image.[14]

In our normal attitude of understanding, we look "beyond" the immediately perceived to the mediating rules—the laws—that "explain" the perceived. These rules take the situation in question and re-describe it in (putatively) more basic, "causal" terms: "Why does this situation appear as it does?" "Because *it is* hydrocarbons and a hydrocarbon is something that does this in these circumstances." The ongoing flux of experience is explained by redescribing it in the terms of an unchanging set of relations.

There is a problem with this immediate mode of understanding, though, and we can see that problem both conceptually and experientially. Let us consider first the conceptual problem, that is, the way that this stance of understanding does not live up to its own immanent logic.

The mandate of understanding is to move beyond the givenness of a determinate particular, and to situate this givenness in terms of its cause. The charter principle of understanding is never to rest content with the given, but always to insist that the opacity of a given determinateness be clarified in terms of its inner intelligibility, to mediate any immediacy.[15] "The true essence of things," Hegel writes in his description of understanding, "has now the character of not being immediately for consciousness; on the contrary, consciousness has a mediated relation to the inner being."[16] But notice that this is precisely what the model of understanding as "subsuming under a rule" *fails* to do. In place of a given immediacy, this immediate mode of understanding offers a *rule*, that is, it offers another given determinacy, without in any way penetrating to the inner intelligibility of the given.[17] This is clearer if we consider again our questioner's advance to the many layers of "because" answers in the car scenario. In each case, the questioner is entitled—indeed *impelled* by the desire to understand—to ask, "but why?" and in each case, the answer that is given is precisely a determinacy that leaves this basic desire unsatisfied. This is clearest when we get to the ultimate point in our explanation. If we ask, "but why is there matter and energy?" or, indeed, "but why is there something at all?" there is no answer available. This "why" question is not the *type* of question that the physicist can answer. In our typical mode of understanding, then, we betray the very project of understanding in that, in the use of the "rule," we simply supply another opaque (non-understood), given determinacy in response to our desire precisely to go beyond givenness as such.

This recognition of logical incoherence in the immediate mode of understanding is also familiar experientially. In our daily life, we are already familiar with the unsatisfactory situation of possessing a rule *rather than* understanding. This is especially clear in "practical" matters. Consider, again, the car, this time from the point of view of driving. When one begins to *learn how* to drive, one is told many rules: depress this pedal when the red octagonal sign appears, pull this lever when this meter says 3000 rpm, etc. Sitting in a car for the first time as a driver introduces a qualitatively new dimension to one's formerly theoretical comprehension of driving, and the initial efforts one makes to deal with this new situation will be reliant upon the pre-learned "rules." When one only operates in this way, though, we say that one *has not yet learned how* to drive: merely to have the rule is precisely *not* to understand. One learns how to drive—becomes a driver—precisely at that moment when one no longer approaches the driving situation as an alien material upon which rules are to be applied, but instead *lives from* the driving situation, finding within one's *immanent comprehension of the experience* the *reasons why the rules make sense*, rather than (as the student does) turning to the rules to make sense of the situation.

This transition from the use of rules *in lieu of* understanding to the insight that is living from the understanding of the situation is the familiar path of an apprenticeship, and it is the path of understanding so insightfully described by Aristotle.[18] It is an experience especially familiar to us in the learning of music and in our chosen model for understanding, reading. Let us consider these two experiences.

While the student learning music must typically acquire many rules, the successful musical education is only completed when one passes beyond the rules. In jazz improvisation, for example, the student will begin by learning which scales can be played with which chords, which tones are more consonant and which more dissonant, how to structure a solo to reach a climax three-quarters of the way through, and so on. Learning to play jazz will typically mean applying these rules to various song-structures repeatedly, until the student becomes familiar with them. What the student plays, though, will sound formulaic and, indeed, student-like. The student becomes a musician when the playing comes *not* from the application of rules, but from the musical demands the player feels in the musical moment. The transition from student to musician is something like the transition to fluency in a language. At a certain point, one no longer applies rules to an alien situation, but rather inhabits the situation and lives from its demands, such that one's playing or speaking is now an *expression* of oneself, that is, of oneself *as* living in and from the situation (the *archē, die Sache selbst*).[19] While the learning of the rules—in music or speaking—is the necessary discipline of the apprentice, operating from the rules actually keeps the creative self-expression—the music—from happening. The transition is the transition from my being *governed by* an alien necessity—the given, opaque rules that I apply to an alien matter—to a situation of free self-expression in which the "rationality" for my choices comes from my living insight into the "inner" of the situation.[20] What this example of musical experience reveals, then, is that in insight—in understanding proper—my self-expression is the same as the expression of the demands of the object, for the object and its rationality no longer have the status as aliens. This overcoming of the dualism (not to say the effacing of the difference) of subject and object is equally the transition from a kind of servitude to an alien necessity to a situation of freedom. Let us now look to the experience of reading to discover more about the characteristics of understanding proper.

Notice how in reading we "make sense," as we say, of a page of text. Typically, we do not "make" sense at all, but experience ourselves as simply being informed by the sense the text itself makes clear to us. Sometimes, though, a text is difficult and so we do struggle to "make" sense of it. Here, we may apply various "rules": we revert to the practices we adopted as we initially learned to read and again work through the grammar carefully, and we think explicitly, perhaps, about what we might expect *has to be* said here. Yet we do not confuse these processes with reading proper.[21] They are precisely substitute practices that stand in when the normal/proper "sense-making" does not happen. And, indeed, if these stand-in practices do what we want them to do, we will suddenly discard them as the sense of the text itself becomes manifest and we "get it." The applying of rules is not the actual practice of reading, but only a preparation in which we hope to make a suitable environment in which the "sense-making" proper to reading suddenly happens. What I want to note here is that the form of our grasp of the understood sense in reading is *intuitive*:[22] it exceeds whatever grasp we can "manufacture" through our discursive (rule-following) procedure. We must *wait* for the sense of the given to *manifest itself*, to *give* itself.

Note, then, that, in this situation of insight, we have returned to something like a stance of perception, but this time in the sense of recognizing a given other that is not alien to the world of intelligibility but that is self-interpreting; in other words, its rationality is its own *immanent* logic. In reading, we do not "apply a rule," but wait for the given other to *show us how it is rational.* Its rationality—its sense—in turn is not a universally applicable rationality that makes sense in independence of its particular "instantiation" in these words, but is precisely *the meaning of these particular words.* While there are many day-to-day senses for which we have no concern beyond their "universal" character (e.g., the level of commonness of meaning between "where is my room" and "dov'é la mia sala" is sufficient *for my purposes* at the moment), in fact the sense of words—of language—can never be stripped from the uniqueness of the particularization of its expression, as is made especially clear in works of literature, which would precisely *lose their identity* were they to be "said in different words."[23] So in reading (as a model of understanding proper) we turn to the object itself to give us its immanent sense. Let us take this point further, by relating it back to the theme of the overcoming of the subject-object dualism that we considered in the music example.

We saw above that if we follow rules in reading, they are only preparatory practices. What they are preparatory for is precisely a *self-transformation* in which the parameters under which they were launched are toppled and the situation is defined anew in a way that rejects the alienation of subject and object (as well as the alienation of given object [matter] and its rule) that characterized the space of the procedure.

The overcoming of the subject-object dualism is not the loss of the otherness of the object in the sense of an imposition upon that other of a pre-established subjective identity. On the contrary, understanding is precisely the destruction of who the reader was prior to reading, for reading is precisely giving oneself over *to the object.*[24] This is not just a hyperbolic statement of the logical relationship, but is, again, a description of a familiar experience. It is *by opening* ourselves to the works of philosophers, artists, or even prophets, for example, that we have our lives radically changed. As Derrida notes in *Glas,* Genet fears that in reading the gospel of John, he will never come out again, and surely this is precisely how one is "supposed to" read the bible, or, indeed, Descartes's *Meditations.*[25] It is the very nature of these expressions (language, art), in other words, to be the call to us to change our lives. This, again, is how Rilke reads the message in ancient art: "You must change your life."[26] Reading—understanding—is inseparable from existential change.

So reading, which is to say understanding, is "giving oneself to the object" in a twofold sense. First, we only understand when we get beyond the stance of discursive "reasoning" and become intuitive of the *particular* rationality that is the sense the object itself makes manifest (even if, especially, it *breaks* our pre-conceived rules and expectations about the limits of sense). And, second, this giving oneself over to what is "making sense" for us is inseparable from our giving up of our own pre-established identities in order to allow ourselves to be re-defined by the object. Our own identities must be, as it were, "at play" if there is to be reading.

The world—the object—as thus construed in understanding proper is what Hegel refers to as the "second supersensible world," the "inverted world," or the "simple infinite":

> Through this principle, the first supersensible world, the tranquil kingdom of laws, the immediate copy of the perceived world, is changed into its opposite. The law was, in general, like its differences, that which

> remained self-same; now, however, it is posited that each of the two worlds is really the opposite of itself. . . . *This second supersensible world* is in this way *the inverted world* . . . . With this, the inner world is completed as appearance.[27]

In understanding, we face a world in which rationality is immanent to determinacy. This is a world in which our stance is one of observing how things move through their own immanent logic, working themselves out through their own internal oppositions, according to their own internal norms. For that reason, this second supersensible world is the world in which our typical presumptions are inverted: the very ground of the possibility of the distinction between the sensible and the intelligible is itself shown to be founded in a reality that cannot be comprehended in terms of that opposition, for this is a reality that answers only to its own immanent, concrete logic.[28]

As thus a self-interpreting reality, this world is a negative self-relation, an original self-differing—"simple difference," in Hegel's language[29]—a world that opposes itself to itself in the sense that it, qua actuality, answers to itself, qua norm. Reality thus has the form of an originary negativity whose nature is to give form, to give the articulations/oppositions we live by, without itself being contained by them.[30] Our act of understanding, though intensely active in the sense of needing to work with the utmost rigour to attend to the determinacies themselves in their innermost self-activity, is ultimately a stance of passivity, a stance of opening one's sense of oneself and of the real to transformation through the life of the object (a process for which Hegel's *Phenomenology of Spirit* is exemplary). Understanding thus completes itself in understanding itself as founded in an original giving power that exceeds the opposition of sensibility and intelligibility, the presumption of which is the immediate/original shape of understanding.[31] This original giving beyond/behind the opposition of sensible and intelligible is exactly what Derrida refers to as *différance.*

Différance

By "*différance,*" Derrida intends the following:

> Now if *différance* [is] . . . what makes possible the presentation of the being-present, it is never presented as such. It is never offered to the present. Or to anyone. Reserving itself, not exposing itself, in regular fashion it exceeds the order of truth at a certain precise point, but

> without dissimulating itself as something, as a mysterious being, in the occult of a non-knowledge or in a hole with indeterminate borders (for example in a topology of castration). In every exposition it would be exposed to disappearing as disappearance. It would risk appearing: disappearing.[32]

Différance is the very possibility of determinacy; it is the negative as such, of which actual differentiations within the real are so many realizations, so many "traces."[33] *Différance*, the originary negation, never appears "as such" in that it is the unexceedable giving power that manifests itself precisely *as* specific particularities ("differences").[34] It is only these differences themselves that reveal this power, in that it is only through them that the power is. And yet it is not exhausted in those articulations. It is thus "betrayed" by actuality in the double sense that they—the actualized articulations of it—allow it to be seen through them, hence they present it as more than it is, while they also present it as less than it is.[35]

We can understand this conception of power if we return again to familiar experiences. As we saw in chapter 1, Aristotle, in *On the Soul*, distinguishes two sorts of actuality. He considers, for example, a scientist.[36] The scientist *is* a scientist even when not exercising his knowledge. In a different sense, he *is being* a scientist specifically when he does exercise his knowledge. In the first case, he is a scientist in the sense that he is characterized by the positive capacity (*hexis*) to practice science; this is his "first actuality" as a scientist. In the second case (exercising his knowledge) he is *actualizing* that *potential* that is his first actuality. The power precisely is the power to practice, and it is not actualized in any other way; but this second actuality "betrays" the first in the same double sense we just considered. It is only through the actualization that the power appears, but it never appears as such—as power—but only in a limiting actuality that never equals or exhausts the power. This is especially clear if we turn back again to our example of the musician.

The improvising musician has developed the *positive capacity* (the *hexis*) of musical self-expression: the musician "has something to say." This "having something," however, is not in the form of a determinate possession, but in the sense of a power and an urge that is itself only realized as expression.[37] The power is not exhausted in an act of "saying," nor is it fully captured qua power even in the whole history of its acts. Hence we can meaningfully wonder what Clifford Brown or John Coltrane would have played had they not both died young, or, again, what Hegel or Merleau-Ponty would have gone on to write, given time. Of course, that power was extinguished with death, but it was not exhausted, that is, it did not, at the point of death, reach its own immanent fulfillment.[38] That power can only be in the context of its actualization, and in that sense it is less than what is realized—made present—but it is equally not exhausted or fully comprehended in that realization and hence is more than what it realized. It is a power revealed—betrayed—in and through those acts, but not fully captured by them. Now, beyond these powers of science or music, consider the very power *to be.*

What is it to be? By virtue of what do we call beings "beings"? This is the question with which Hegel's *Science of Logic* begins. Of being, Hegel writes:

> In its indeterminate immediacy it is equal only to itself. It is also not unequal relatively to another; it has no diversity within itself nor any with a reference outwards. It would not be held fast in its purity if it contained any determination or content which could be distinguished in it or by which it could be distinguished from an other.[39]

By "being" as such we mean, so to speak, the "beingness" that must be present in anything such that that thing *is.* And yet it cannot be "present in it" as one determinate quality among many, for it must be the very reality of whatever is: nothing else could "be" an aspect of the thing were it not itself "being." Being must be present universally—it must be present in everything: it must be the very thing that makes a being be, and it must make every being be. In seeking being, we are thus seeking the very ground of reality, that without which there can be no further qualitative determinateness, no further anything. We are asking, in other words, what it is without which there would be nothing. What is it, we might ask, that differentiates whatever is from nothing? What is it to hold off nothing, to oppose it, and instead to be? To be is to have immediacy. This is the quality of being by which it takes hold—we might almost say, "takes hold of being"—and by which it emerges beyond nothing, beyond utter nothingness, beyond complete emptiness. Yet this character of immediacy, if it is to be universal, would appear to have to be strictly indeterminate, for if it were some determinate immediacy—if it were this rather than that—it would have failed in its mandate to be the very nature of what it is "to be" at all.[40] Being as such, then, would be indeterminate immediacy. But as such—as the utter absence of any determination—it cannot be, that is, as such it is no different from nothing. As Hegel writes: "Being, the indeterminate immediate, is in fact nothing, and neither more nor less than nothing." "Indeterminate immediacy" does not exist on its own; indeed, it is the very definition of not being anything at all.

What, then, is it to be not-nothing? It is to be something, a determinate being. If being were not enacted as beings but were just being as such, it would be precisely nothing. Being, in other words, only exists as determinate beings.[41] Yet, what it is "to be" is not exhausted in any being or in any multiplicity of beings. As we just saw, being cannot be equated with "what is," for this equation ignores the *real* possibility for what will, or even more, what could be. And, indeed, being, beyond what is, is precisely infinitely emergent as ever more beings. Being, then, must always be this *relation* of actual being *and its possibility*. Here, at the level of being itself, we are seeing replayed the same logic of reality-as-betrayal that we considered above in the cases of grammar and music. Being is always, in Hegel's language, a "bad infinite," that is, there is always another being and then another and then another, *ad infinitum*, beyond (spatially and temporally) any realized determinacy. Yet the "infinity" of being is not merely this unending sequentiality. Being is also always a coherent totality. Being is always seamlessly self-identical, holding itself together as a coherent whole; being is, in Hegel's language, also always a "good infinite."[42] Let us consider further the ways in which being exceeds the finitude of determinate beings.

The very nature of a determinate being is to be limited, which means it is defined by the very point at which it contacts a beyond. A being, in other words, cannot be determinate on its own, but can be such only in a context of other possibilities that it actively "is not." By its very nature, then, determinate being points beyond itself to its contextualizing others. Indeed, we saw this in our initial consideration of consciousness as understanding/reading: we recognize determinacy only by its integration in a meaning-giving context of interaction and integration. We are conscious of determinacy only insofar as it has a beyond—a co-implication in/with others. But the others implied in a determinate being are not themselves "in" it as determinate beings; rather, its others are implied in it as the possibilities to which it points. Others, in other words, are always on the horizon of a determinacy, such that the determinacy itself implies its own character is to-be-integrated with a beyond that it simultaneously depends upon but precisely does not contain (or that beyond would not be beyond, and itself would not be determinate).[43]

In order to be, then, there must always be determinate beings, which themselves point beyond themselves to the necessity of their integration with the others that lie on their horizon. To be, then, is to be different from all others—actual or possible—but to be integrated with them in principle. This "integration in principle," this horizon that is definitive of being as such, can never appear *as such*: all that appears are determinate beings. This horizon of possibility is only a trace in the figure that betrays it. This is the character of being that allows being to appear only by never itself being such as can appear. It—the immanent horizon of being within all beings—can never appear as such: "there is" only the intimation of its founding disappearance within what appears. Like the possibility of the musician, the possibility of being is always actualized as an actual and therefore not actualized as such, and thus never exhausted, never finished. This is why being is always novel, always newly and uniquely expressive as what it is to be, while it is equally necessarily always already integrated in . . . in, precisely, being. To be is always to be a novel redefinition of the real that exists precisely as the inscription of itself within the real. This is being as *différance.*

As Aristotle argued, being cannot be a genus, for, though it is the "absolute concept" in the sense of being what everything *universally* and necessarily is, it is also the most absolutely substantial, that is, it is not one of a type, but is rather the absolutely *singular,* the one and only. The *Homeric Hymn to Earth* begins,

> I will sing of the well-founded Earth, mother of all, eldest of all beings. She feeds all creatures that are in the world, all that go upon the goodly land, and all that are in the paths of the seas, and all that fly; all these are fed of her store.[44]

We might thus metaphorically call being as *différance*—this generative matrix of all, that is realized and expressed only in and as the totality of determinate beings, but is never exhausted therein—"earth," to indicate this status as the absolutely singular, giving power.[45]

Deconstruction as Presuppositionless Science

Derrida reads like Hegel. He typically opens a text and reads through it to the point that it manifests an original giving power that simultaneously founds and exceeds the terms of sense-making employed in the text: "deconstruction." He gives himself over, in other words, to the dialectic of the text itself.[46] This giving oneself over, however, is not an erasing of one's own agency and determinacy, but rather their maximally rigorous employment for the sake of allowing the text to do its work of self-expression (and thence transformation of oneself qua reader). Derrida describes such an opening of the text:

> The *incision* of deconstruction, which is not a voluntary decision or an absolute beginning, does not take place just anywhere, or in an absolute

> elsewhere. An incision, precisely, it can be made only according to the lines of force and forces of rupture that are localizable in the discourse to be deconstructed.[47]

"Deconstruction," in other words, is giving oneself over to the logic of the text itself in a process whereby the text reveals its own *limits* and also how it has already (illicitly) lived beyond those limits.[48] Deconstruction, then—that is, reading proper—is not a method in the sense of a rule, but is precisely that surpassing of rules that we identified in our study of understanding.[49] Indeed, such deconstruction is, as we have seen in our dialectic of understanding, in this sense, the very deconstruction of method itself.[50]

Method, construed as a map or as rules possessed in advance that offer a secure manner for apprehending the object, will always be inadequate to the object, for such rules have not allowed for the unique rationality of the particularity under study; as Adorno aptly writes in this regard, "the name of dialectics says no more, to begin with, than that objects do not go into their concepts without remainder."[51] Dialectic and deconstruction must precisely let go of such methodological presumptions. Such "letting go" is precisely what is accomplished through Hegel's great scientific works, the *Phenomenology of Spirit* and the *Science of Logic*. These works, in their respective realms of, roughly, epistemology and metaphysics, let go of methodological presuppositions precisely by embracing them for the sake of going through their own dialectical self-overcoming. Hegel observes their self-movement as they reveal their logical dependence upon further principles that in fact undermine their own (the original stance's) viability; their conditions of possibility are, in other words, shown to be equally their conditions of impossibility. Each book ends, in absolute knowing or the absolute idea, with the imperative to turn to the particular in its immanent self-movement. This means that this "truth" of absolute knowing is not a *possession*: it is only the infinite imperative to turn to "the things themselves." This means, then, that what is "finally settled" in absolute knowing is that the meaning of the situation can never be settled in advance: particularities must be allowed their own dialectic, which means their own redefinition of our very sense of rationality.[52]

Derrida is often taken (perhaps even by himself) to be a critic of Hegel.[53] This is usually based on a view of what Hegel means by "absolute knowing." By offering a "presuppositionless science," Hegel appears to his critics to claim that he now possesses the "inner" of all reality in such a manner that all reality is now understood in advance, and such that the philosopher has effectively made himself the ultimate reality: the one whose act of knowing is now the ground of the real.[54] While there are no doubt many aspects of this picture that are subject to criticism, one of the most central is based on the issue of the "giving power" of *différance* that we have been considering.

Absolute knowing is accused of mistaking (present) actuality for being, and not acknowledging the unpresentable withdrawing power that gives. Reality is then construed as the working out of the logical games of getting our reasoning straight, and all reality is seen to be forced to conform to a model of difference as dialectical opposition in need of a synthesis that happily secures our self-possession from threatening differences.[55] As I have shown through my analysis of understanding, however, this is far from Hegel's position. Indeed, his notion of "absolute knowing" is precisely an embrace of the originary giving power of being—of *différance*—and far from thus revealing the impossibility of presuppositionless science; this is precisely *why* absolute knowing is presuppositionless science.

The presuppositionlessness of science is not the *removal* of the presupposed, but rather the *identification with* it: it is *as unacknowledged premise* that a presupposition needs to have its status changed. Hegel's phenomenology—like Derrida's deconstructive incision—starts with the logic of the *Sache* and allows it to reveal its dependence on giving powers it has not acknowledged. Precisely what the dialectic allows to be seen is the inescapable dependence of all experience—all meaning, all being—on the "sense" of given particularity. Our experience is always mediated by language (shown in the analysis of "sense-certainty"), by the body and death (shown in the analysis of "self-certainty"), by the "light-shy power" of emotion and family life (shown in the analysis of "ethicality"), and so on. Absolute knowing does not somehow remove these conditions of our existence, but rather *gives them absolute status.* We can never escape their originary primacy. Experience can be "explained" by nothing other than itself: there is nowhere else to turn.[56] The presuppositionless science is the *acknowledgment* of our irreducible dependence on the given; the science is the way that *other claims prove from within themselves* their dependence on this giving. *They* show that the conditions of their possibility are their conditions of impossibility. The "texts" themselves deconstruct themselves and reveal "the deconstructive imperative" as the presuppositionless science of absolute knowing as their truth.

Derrida's reading, then, begins from the perspective of absolute knowing, that is, he reads through/from Hegel, showing in each case how the particularities of a text deconstruct themselves. Derrida is thus beyond and not beyond "the system." The very nature of "the system" is the recognition that the sense—the "reason"—of reality is only self-given, and hence always a re-inscribing/re-reading of what has gone before. *Every* particularity then *by definition* is "beyond the system," in that it can never be settled in advance. Yet equally "the system" is just the recognition that the beyond always is the reinscription of the system itself.[57] Derrida's deconstruction, then, is really just reading Hegel's phenomenology.[58]

Conclusion

By focusing on the distinctive nature of understanding, we have thus been able to see both how this "shape of consciousness" makes a unique contribution to our experience, not reducible to the (equally essential) contributions of sense-certainty and perception. By focusing on its own internal dialectic, further, we have been able to see why the very logic of understanding ultimately demands the very project that Hegel undertakes in the *Phenomenology of Spirit*, itself the enactment of the "non-method" of deconstruction. With this study, Hegel's description and analysis of "Consciousness," that is, his study of the forms of experience that take themselves to be encountering an alien reality, is complete. Accordingly, we turn now, in part 2, to Hegel's description and analysis of "Self-Consciousness," that is, his study of the forms of experience in which we take ourselves to be encountering ourselves.

Part 2

Personality

4

Desiring-Production and Spirit

Hegel introduces the study of desire at the beginning of part B of the *Phenomenology of Spirit*, "Self-Consciousness." Its immediate import is that it reveals that, behind the attitude that presumes itself to be a detached subject trying to comprehend an independently existing real object (the attitude of "Consciousness," studied in part A of the *Phenomenology of Spirit*), there is a more fundamental stance of subjectivity: we have a real object only on condition that we have a more fundamental desiring attitude toward the world that is not articulated in these terms. (It is thus the most immediate demonstration that we are conscious only on condition that we are self-conscious.) Hegel's phenomenological description of desire takes us first into this unacknowledged pre-condition of objective consciousness, and then reveals how, on its own terms, desire gives rise from out of itself to a world of intersubjectivity and objectivity. This latter point involves one of the most distinctive and definitive lessons of Hegel's *Phenomenology of Spirit*, namely, that, as explicitly self-conscious beings, the desire to be recognized by another is inherent to our experience of desire. In order to appreciate the force of this ultimate lesson that we desire the recognition of others, we will first establish the context of the challenge that desire poses to objectivity by looking at the exemplary working out of that challenge in the critique of Kant posed by *Anti-Oedipus*, the collaborative work of Gilles Deleuze and Félix Guattari.

Though written in France in 1971, *Anti-Oedipus* in many respects follows the typical form of a book of German Idealist philosophy. Like Fichte, Schelling, and Hegel, Deleuze and Guattari model their work in *Anti-Oedipus* on the form of Kant's *Critique of Pure Reason*, and then use the form of Kant's own project to develop a critique of Kant. By taking up this critique of Kant, we will precisely see why the dialectic of desire "supersedes" the dialectic of consciousness; *Anti-Oedipus*, that is, fundamentally articulates the logic of the position of desire with which Hegel's chapter on "Self-Consciousness" begins. I will argue, however, that, although the critique of Kant in *Anti-Oedipus* is in general compelling, there remains a fundamental way in which the "schizoanalysis" that Deleuze and Guattari offer is ultimately unsatisfactory. Specifically, I will argue that Deleuze and Guattari presume the phenomenon of "mineness" and its attendent sense of the "mine" of someone else without being able to account adequately for either. Developing this critique of *Anti-Oedipus* will allow us to appreciate the force of Hegel's introduction of the dialectic of recognition in is his description of desiring self-consciousness.

Kant on Understanding and Reason

Kant's critical project in the *Critique of Pure Reason* serves two purposes. On the one hand, Kant establishes how there can be objective knowledge within experience. On the other hand, Kant rules out the possibility of an unconditioned knowledge of things-in-themselves. These two results are both rooted in the same aspect of experience, namely, the categories of subjective synthesis that provide unity to experience.

Kant's epistemology is a kind of phenomenology. Kant argues backward from meanings with which we do in fact engage to the subjective conditions that must be in place in order for such experiences of meaning to be possible. Kant ends up discovering that there are three essential powers that must be in play in order for us to have experiences of objects. These are the powers of sensibility, imagination, and understanding, and these powers make meaning possible through enabling, respectively, the synthesis of apprehension in intuition, the synthesis of reproduction in imagination, and the synthesis of recognition in a concept.[1] I will discuss each of these briefly.

Roughly, Kant's point is as follows. We must be ontologically active in our openness to experience or there would be, between ourselves and our world, no encounter, no being-aware-of. It is only because, by our very nature as subjects, we pose a specific question to our world—because we look from within a particular framework—that we can experience a world in answer. Experience must begin with a reception, with a being-struck, an intuition. This intuition, however, can only happen to a being that is open to being struck. It is only because we constitutively ask, effectively, "is there something striking us?" that we can be aware of anything. Space and time are the forms of our openness to being struck—we ask, "where?" and "when?", and it is only because these fields of space and time are in principle meaningful to us that we are capable of discerning an impact, capable of intuition, sensitive.[2] Thus even at our most passive, we are active—being struck/affected requires a capacity to be affected. Thus, "to sense" is a power, a function of enabling meaning, specifically in the form of intuition.

Furthermore, however, our experience has a lasting character and a coherent character. We are not just struck and then struck again and then struck again with no encounter between these experiences. Rather, as we saw in our discussion of "Sense-Certainty" in chapter 1 and in our discussion of "Understanding" in chapter 3, we experience these intuitions as coordinated with each other, spatially and temporally, in such a way that we experience the significance of one *in relation to* the experience of another—this one is before that, beside that. This again requires of us that we have an ability. We must be able still to be engaged with the significance of an intuition even as we are no longer—or not yet—actively intuiting it. This power—the power to engage with an absent intuition as if it were present—is the power of imagination.[3] An experience of coordination, in which we navigate significances that are not immediately present, rests upon our imaginative power. "To imagine"—the ability to present the absent—is the second constitutive power involved in enabling meaning.

The third essential power is the power of understanding (also described as "apperception," that is, the perception of perception, or self-perception). This is essentially the power of self-reflexivity or self-commentary within experience—the power to say of one's experience, "this is that." Kant refers to this power as "the synthesis of recognition in a concept," or the ability to deal with "representations of other representations," meanings about our other meanings.[4] As we noted in chapter 3, we are familiar with this power of understanding in our daily life when we learn that many particular items within our experiences are instances of some more universal identity—"oh, these are all members of the same family." Kant's point is that this power not only operates *within* the world of our experience, but is a power that must already be at play for us ever to have a world of experience. The power of understanding is the power to recognize coherent identities that extend through multiplicities. Any meaningful relationship of different experiential elements rests on such a recognition. We might equally call it the power of interpretation. Thus, along with intuiting and imagining, interpreting must always be at play in the enabling of meaning: it is from these three powers that the very tissue of experience is woven.

Now what is the form this tissue of experience takes? What is the familiar meaning for which Kant is discerning the necessary preconditions? As we saw in the prologue, it is specifically the experience of "objective reality." Normally, we have the experience of a world composed of things—substances with discernible identities and measurable properties—that enter into causal interaction with other things in such a way as to present a coherent world open to scientific investigation. This is the experience for which Kant is determining the necessary preconditions. In order that a subject might be conscious of such a world, that subject's experience must be organized from the start according to expectations of substantiality, causality, and systematic community: only a subject who lives with such *a priori* demands upon its experience could ever encounter an *object*, an independently defined reality that is open to our subjective investigation but not causally affected by our subjectivity.[5] What Kant, then, goes on to specify in greater detail is the specific set of "categories" or *a priori* concepts—the specific schemata for conceptual recognition—that together make up the scheme of an object. It is because we all operate with such universal and necessary categories that we are able to recognize the kind of world in which we can perform science, that is, that we operate in a domain in which we are able to make judgments about objective reality. These syntheses of intuition, imagination, and interpretation together make a coherent world, accessible to all similar cognitive subjects. The syntheses define the coherence of the tissue of experience.

"The categories" are the specific, necessary functions of interpretation that together allow a sensible manifold to appear in the form of coherent objectivity, the functions that allow us to experience, that is, a community of substances integrated according to causal relations and manifest through coherent patterns of sensation.[6] These categories allow us to interpret our sensation in such a fashion as to experience our world objectively and this is indeed what allows for a science of things as they appear to us. It is our tendency, however, to use these same interpretive powers in an effort to move beyond the practical coherence they lend our scientific endeavors in order to develop a coherent, compelling theoretical account of being as it is in itself, and it is the real force of Kant's critique to demonstrate that this practice is not, in fact, cognitively legitimate. Kant's overall project in the *Critique of Pure Reason* is to show that our attempts to use conceptual reasoning to establish a presuppositionless metaphysics are based upon using powers that lend coherence within experience beyond the terrain of their legitimate employment: we make *transcendent* use of what are legitimately only *transcendental* (i.e., immanent) principles of meaning.[7] Causality, for example, is an essential dimension *of coherent experience*; we abstract the concept of causality from its role as a dimension of the meaning *of experience*, however, and presume that we can demand *of experience as a whole* that it be explicable in terms of "causality," that is, we *argue* that experience *must* have a first cause, explaining either our experience as caused by a self "in itself" (a position whose untenability is exposed in the "Paralogisms of Pure Reason"), or that there must be a causal reality-in-itself that lies behind the object of our experience (a position whose untenability is exposed in the "Antinomies of Pure Reason"). We try to hold the happening of experience itself answerable to a meaningfulness that experience itself makes available, a version of the "experience error" that Merleau-Ponty diagnoses in his *Phenomenology of Perception.*[8] Essentially, we want our experience to make sense *in an ultimate sense,* but our efforts necessarily draw upon meanings that are necessarily internal to experience and Kant demonstrates that our efforts to produce such an ultimately satisfying theoretical account fail and lead to incoherence and contradiction, rather than to science.

I have begun with this sketch of the main outlines of Kant's critical project in the *Critique of Pure Reason* for two reasons. On the one hand, Kant is the explicit focus of criticism in *Anti-Oedipus;* indeed, Deleuze says of his book on Kant, "I wrote it as a book on an enemy."[9] On the other hand, though, this Kantian program of critique is strongly parallel in format to the program of *Anti-Oedipus.* Let us see now how Deleuze and Guattari carry out a critique of the Kantian philosophy by employing the very form of the Kantian critique.

Anti-Oedipus and Schizoanalysis

Like Kant's *Critique of Pure Reason,* Deleuze and Guattari's *Anti-Oedipus* focuses on the syntheses that are constitutive of meaning—indeed, the syntheses that constitute the fabric of *reality.* This synthetic generation of meaning goes by the name of "desiring production." The synthetic fabric Deleuze and Guattari identify is threefold, as is the fabric discerned by Kant. Furthermore, the specific three syntheses are remarkably reminiscent of the three syntheses Kant identifies: "production" replaces Kant's "intuition," "recording" replaces Kant's "imagination," and "consumption" replaces Kant's "apperception." Further, Deleuze and Guattari, like Kant, identify a legitimate and an illegitimate use of these syntheses, and they specifically distinguish these two as the immanent (transcendental) and transcendent uses, exactly as does Kant.[10] The project in *Anti-Oedipus* mirrors the project of the *Critique of Pure Reason* with, however, two central differences. The first is that it is the very objectivity that Kant interprets as the legitimate use of the syntheses of experience that Deleuze and Guattari argue is the product of the illegitimate use of the syntheses. The second is the different relation that Deleuze and Guattari recognize between desire and sense, compared to that which Kant recognizes. Let us review the three syntheses identified by Deleuze and Guattari.

The original of all sense—indeed, of all reality—is desiring production. Desire, originary contact, is the multiplicity of machines establishing and interrupting flows, making connections and breaking them off, coupling and separating. Desire is enacted as the "and . . . and . . . and . . ." of the non-premeditated, partial couplings of (what we would normally call) "self" and "world" that are the generative parameters of all of our experience. Like the intuition recognized by Kant, desire is thus the immediate, that behind which there is nothing further. Desire is the starting point and the element of everything further, and all more developed meaning must answer back to desiring production as it source and motor.[11]

The flows and interruptions pass. They are not, however, simply lost. Their happening is inseparable from an inscription, a recording taken of them. As soon as they are produced, productions also become "of . . .": of what? Of a body without organs, the giant egg of a recording surface that is no entity over and above the productions it records but is precisely their entry into a log book in relation to all the others. The body without organs is roughly the lived readiness to engage that is the virtual identity of the network of flows and interruptions. Like imagination in Kant's analysis, then, the synthesis of recording is the tissue of remembrance and expectation into which productions are immediately entered upon being produced.[12]

And finally, there is the synthesis of consumption. The product is enjoyed and consumed, and in its consumption a subject takes pleasure, a subject is consummated. The consumption of the product in the experience of pleasure is the production of a consummated subject, that is, the subject is itself the last product—the residue—of the whole production line of desire. The subject is not a pre-existent substance but is rather an identity generated only in its consummation and thus only able to say, in a backward-reference, "so that's who I was." Like apperceptive understanding in Kant, then, the third synthesis in Deleuze and Guattari is the self-referential moment of recognition within meaning.[13]

The gist of the analysis of Deleuze and Guattari is that subjectivity—the very sort of subjectivity that Kant takes as his starting point—is never realized: we never are such coherent subjects, but are, rather, multiple partial selves, regionally coherent but never fully, systematically orchestrated. Let me say a bit more now about this issue of subjectivity in Kant, in order to be clearer about the critique of this notion in Deleuze and Guattari. To do this, I want to return to Kant's notion of the "synthesis of recognition in a concept" and discuss two further notions he develops in explicating this synthesis, namely, the "transcendental object = x" and the "transcendental unity of apperception."

Deleuze asks, regarding his interpretation of Kant,

> Can we say with complete accuracy . . . that synthesis is sufficient to constitute knowledge? In fact, knowledge implies two things which go beyond synthesis itself: it implies consciousness, or more precisely the belonging of representations to a single consciousness within which they must be linked. . . . On the other hand, knowledge implies a necessary relation to an object. . . . [T]he manifold would never be referred to an object if we did not have at our disposal objectivity as a form in general ("object in general," "object = x"). Where does this form come from? The *object in general* is the correlate of the unity of consciousness. . . . Therefore, the real (synthetic) formula of the *cogito* is: I think myself and in thinking myself, I think the object in general to which I relate a represented diversity.[14]

This is a helpful discussion of Kant's argument: the meaningfulness of experience rests on the ability of a subject to interpret its experience as "about" an object, and the presumption of a unitary object to which it refers its experience is itself premised upon the ability of the subject to be present to itself throughout all of its experiences, that is, the object to which it refers its experiences must itself be referred back to a self-same subject. Ultimately, then, the coherence within experience is just the articulation of the demand that I be myself—coherence is my holding together of a consistent identity throughout the full range of the history of my consciousness. This is the ultimate ground and significance of objectivity.

Now, as I said, the analysis of *Anti-Oedipus* leads to the claim that the subject is unrealized in experience and remains multiply diverse and residual, and this is the very nature of the production of meaningfulness. Kant's *Critique of Pure Reason,* on the other hand, makes the unity of the subject the ground of meaningfulness. Indeed, even if the argument is not that that unity is a permanent acquisition, at the very least that unity of the subject must be the invariant *telos* of all experience, the infinite striving to be itself that provides the very arena for meaning. I want to pursue this opposition between the two works a little further.

In *Anti-Oedipus,* what we typically think of as the normal, individuated subject is understood as a product of the Oedipal take-over of desire. This normal subject is imposed upon desire, and, indeed, it emerges only in the familial triangulation "daddy-mommy-me," which is itself the "3 + 1" that depends on a definitive relation of lack to the phallus. In other words, *Anti-Oedipus* argues for two claims that are very relevant to assessing the force of Kant's argument, namely, (a) that the individual ego Kant identifies is itself only a member of a trinity of selves, and

(b) that this self, and indeed the whole trinity, is further dependent on another identity to which it is referred, namely, the perfect self-possession of the phallus. Thus, we could see *Anti-Oedipus* in part as expanding upon Kant's five layers of synthesis (sense-imagination-concept-object-ego) to produce layers 6 and 7 (family-phallus). But the point of *Anti-Oedipus* is not to advance this Kantian story through its analysis of the organizing role of Oedipus. Rather, the point is to show that already in what Kant deems the legitimate use of synthesis, the proper terrain of desiring production has been exceeded. That is, the illegitimate transcendent use of the syntheses that Kant sees in reason is already at play in his own approach to understanding. Kant understands experience to be by nature the experience of objectivity—the experience by a well-formed, normal individual of a detached, well-formed, independently real object—whereas, Deleuze and Guattari maintain, experience that takes this form is experience that has already been "normalized": it is a derived rather than the original form of experience. Kant, they contend, has confused something established *within experience*—namely, the norms of objectivity and normalized subjectivity—with something that is *normative for experience,* thus himself committing a form of the "experience error" he exposes in the dialectic of pure reason. In the language of psychoanalysis, we could say that Kant has not recognized that the experience organized around the "reality principle" is not original, but is a development within and transformation of experience organized around the "pleasure principle," where experience governed by the pleasure principle is not a well-organized network of clear and systematic relationships between well-defined identities, but is a patchwork of processes of localized sense-making that link partial subjects to partial objects by the relations of condensation and displacement that constitute the "logic" of affective, desiring life.[15] Let me quote a passage from *Anti-Oedipus.*

> Partial objects now seem to be taken from people, rather than from the nonpersonal flows that pass from one person to another. . . . Oedipus has as its formula 3 + 1, the One of the transcendent phallus without which the terms considered would not take the form of a triangle. It is as if the so-called signifying chain, made up of elements that are themselves non-signifying—of polyvocal writing and detachable fragments—were the object of a special treatment, a crushing operation that extracted a detached object from the chain, a despotic signifier from whose law the entire chain seems consequently to be suspended, each link triangulated. There we have a curious paralogism implying a transcendent use of the syntheses of the unconscious: *we pass from detachable*

> *partial objects to the detached complete object, from which global persons derive by an assigning of lack.*[16]

What has happened is that the subject that is the *residuum of* production has been treated as production's ground, with the result that desiring production is seen to *belong to* the subject (where it, too, now, is further understood as dependent on the complete object it lacks). The world of desire, on its own quite satisfied with its own *regional* sense-making, is now re-interpreted as participating in a reality governed by the demand for *universal* sense. The multiple desires are seen as expressions of the total person (whose identity is their *telos*), and therefore seen as secondary and incomplete on their own, whereas they are in fact originary, and on their own terms not at all incomplete, not at all defined in terms of any lack.

What this entails is that the very notion of objectivity is inseparable from the notion of the Oedipal subject—Kant's analysis of objectivity depends on his ability to refer the sense within experience to the sense of a coherent subject/substance of experience, but Deleuze and Guattari show that this subject is the Oedipal subject of psychoanalysis (the subject itself made one only as its lack of the phallus). Kant has thus wrongly imported the demands of meaning within the Oedipal world—an aspect of empirical life—into the realm of transcendental synthesis; or, we could say that he has taken the notion of subject, which properly is only the passing synthesis of consummation, and hypostasized it into a transcendent substance which is then used as the basis for analyzing the original synthesis. In this way, then, Deleuze and Guattari follow out Kant's project to the point of showing Kant himself to be guilty of the very offense he attributes to rationalist metaphysics.

> A consciousness is nothing without the synthesis of unification, but there is no synthesis of unification of consciousness without the form of the I, or the point of view of the self. . . . Only when the world, teeming with anonymous and nomadic, impersonal and pre-individual singularities, opens up, do we tread at last the field of the transcendental.[17]

Let me turn now to describing what I take to be the other revision to Kant, namely, the transformation of the relation of desire and sense that comes with this critique of objectivity.

Drawing on Heidegger's distinction between the "readiness to hand" of the inconspicuous equipment with which we work and the "presence at hand" of the objects we explicitly notice, we could argue that Kant's analysis of experience is flawed from the start because it takes the experience of objects to be original, whereas objects are derived from the breakdowns of the experience of readiness, and it is something like this that is going on in *Anti-Oedipus*.[18] The modeling of experience on the recognition of an object is inherently Oedipal, and we need to re-describe the logic of sense.

In fact, Kant's portrayal of experience as objective goes hand in hand with his separation of the story of sense from the story of desire. The primacy of the detached, self-sufficient, indifferent object—the ideal of his theoretical philosophy—entails that the object has a significance of its own that it imparts to us. We can see that, virtually by definition, its sense is not in any way determined by our desire. This is indeed how Kant views experience. We recognize things theoretically, and we apply our desires to them, but the realm of recognition and the realm of desire are entirely separate.

What Deleuze and Guattari recognize, however, is that we cannot begin by presuming an ontologically independent world of things from which we would then derive an explanation for our experience: the sense "independent things" is precisely a sense that emerges within our experience, that is, our having that sense is to be *explained by* our experience, rather than being something that can *explain* our experience. Desire, then, is not the "subjective" contact of an ontologically independent subject with an ontologically independent object, but is, instead, the enactment of the domain within which "there is." Desire is itself precisely the production of reality. The immediacy of sense—intuition—is no different from the immediacy of desire, and, inasmuch as this is the one and only arena, that happening of sense within which any further sense emerges, the immediacy of sense and desire is no different from the immediacy of the real. Thus, in what is perhaps the most extreme phenomenology, knowledge of reality simply amounts to a description of the flows and interruptions that characterize our desire. The ever-changing multiplicity of desiring-production is the only phenomenological "subject"—it is to the parameters of desire that we must turn to determine the parameters of the real. Consequently (a) the analysis of practical life cannot be separated from the analysis of theoretical life, as Kant apparently does in the first two Critiques, and (b) desire cannot be subordinated to or regulated by any other source of meaning, since all meaning is simply desiring production. Thus with the critique of objectivity comes the installation of desire at the very heart of meaning (rather than its Kantian location as a separate force applied to the world of sense).

In sum, then, the rigorous adherence to the Kantian demand that we reveal phenomenologically the immanent bases of sense amounts to a radical critique of the Kantian philosophy that both abandons the primacy of the ideal of objectivity within meaningful experience and installs desire at the foundation of all sense. Deleuze and Guattari have attempted to radicalize Kant's project, articulating the implications of staying true to the limits of immanence (the "transcendental," in Kant's language), rejecting any attempt to explain experience—"sense"—on the basis of alien, "transcendent" standards. Rejecting the importation of alien norms and standards, however, does not by itself entail that norms and standards as such are inherently alien to sense, inherently alien to immanence. Indeed, turning now to Hegel, we will now see precisely that desire *immanently* gives rise to a certain *telos* of normalization and objectivity. We will see this specifically by describing the experience of other subjects, an experience, I will argue, that is insufficiently comprehended by the conceptual tools that Deleuze and Guattari provide.

Desiring-Production and Other People

In the *Phenomenology of Spirit,* Hegel begins his study of self-consciousness by considering the experience of desire.[19] Desire has as its manifest "object" the thing desired. Desire is not lived as a strategic "planning" by an already formed self, but is an experience of the compelling "magnetism" of the various determinate matters that draw one's attention. Nonetheless, implicit in this attractive object is the experience of the desiring subjectivity: what desire "harvests" from its object is what satisfies its terms. Even if "its terms" are not self-consciously recognized or strategically deployed by the desiring subject, that desiring subjectivity is nonetheless co-constitutive of the "attraction": desire is not an inert passivity with no character of its own, but is precisely *desire,* is precisely a determinate openness and desire to be attracted. Desire is the lived, practical presumption that being is "for me," that is, when I operate out of desire, I appropriate the world as if my reality—my desire—superseded the object's right to independence.[20]

> [S]elf-consciousness is *desire* in general . . . [and] has a double object: one is the immediate object, that of sense-certainty and perception, which however *for self-consciousness* has the character of a *negative*; and the second, namely, *itself,* which is the true *essence,* and is present in the first instance only as opposed to the first object. Self-consciousness here exhibits itself as the movement in which this antithesis is removed, and the identity of itself with itself becomes explicit for it.[21]

Desire is thus, in Hegel's language, an experience of "self-certainty," a lived conviction of the legitimacy of one's claim to centrality:

> Certain of the nothingness of this other, it [desire] explicitly affirms that this nothingness is *for it* the truth of the other; it destroys the independent object and thereby gives itself the certainty of itself.[22]

While being explicitly object-oriented, desire is thus implicitly an experience of itself, an experience of self-consciousness.

To this point, there is no conflict between the interpretation of desire in Hegel and in *Anti-Oedipus.* Both recognize desire to be a level of engagement that operates "below" the level of the normalized articulation of subjects and objects, a non-thetic embrace of part-objects, a non-strategic coupling that gives rise to an experience of self as the sense of an enjoyment whose subjective and objective terms could not be defined in advance of their co-enactment.[23] But, as Hegel writes,

> Self-consciousness which is simply *for itself* and directly characterizes its object as a negative element, or is primarily *desire,* will . . . learn through experience that the object is independent.[24]

These terms we have so far laid out, in other words, are not sufficient for the understanding of desire. Let us look further at Hegel's analysis of desire to see how desire's object reveals the insufficiency of desire's own terms, ultimately demonstrating that desire is implicated in relationships of intersubjectivity and objectivity. (The logic of Hegel's argument is quite clear and simple, but it is awkward to articulate, and these next three paragraphs in particular must be read slowly and carefully.)

Desire is the lived experience of being as "for me." Being, here, is not recognized as "reality," that is, not construed as "for itself" (which is, indeed, why Freud describes desire as operating on the "pleasure principle" rather than the "reality principle").[25] To live from this perspective is to live from the sense that there is a surplus of desire over determinacy: determinacy—"it"—is not real "in-itself," not an exclusively self-related, independent reality that deterministically governs all behavior including our own, but exists in the context of what Hegel calls a "negative self-relation," that is, determinacy is experienced *in relation to* my desire.[26] "The simple 'I' [desire]," Hegel writes, "is this genus or the simple universal, for which the differences are *not* differences only by its being the *negative essence* of the shaped independent moments."[27] Like the thing in relation to *its* properties, which we considered in chapter 2, desire is a negative self-relation in that desire *is* its determinacy, but desire is determinacy "in the mode of not-being it," as Sartre might put it: "I" am taken with determinacy, immersed in it, but also detached from it, related to it. To experience desire is to experience the excess, the negativity—the lived space of possibility, the "virtuality"—that exceeds any positivity, any determinacy.

But to live with the recognition that determinacy is never the last word but that it is always, rather, the "surface" or the "front end" of desire entails that determinacy always carries within it the implicit question "of what desire are you the front end?" In other words, if the very premise of desire is that determinacy never simply is itself but is always in principle superseded by desire, is always the way "a certainty has become explicit for self-consciousness in an objective manner,"[28] then when desire relates to a determinacy, it is relating to something *already defined as* defined by another desire: determinacy is never simply present, but is the presence of an absence, and thus desire, in relating to a present determinacy, is always in principle—by its own constitutive premise—relating to that which has an absence at its core.

> [T]he truth of this certainty is really a double reflection, the duplication of self-consciousness. Consciousness has for its object one which, of its own self, posits its otherness or difference as a nothingness, and in so doing is independent. . . . The object of self-consciousness is . . . independent in this negativity of itself; and thus it is *for itself* a genus, a universal fluid element in the peculiarity of its own separate being; it is a living self-consciousness.[29]

To live from desire is to be open in principle to the possibility of other desires, and to live from the recognition of one's desire is to live from the recognition in principle of other desires. In other words, to be a self-consciousness is to be open in principle to other self-consciousnesses: "It is a *self-consciousness for a self-consciousness*."[30] To be the kind of being who can recognize itself is to be the kind of being who can recognize others.

But what is it to *recognize* others? The other, as the desire that exceeds determinacy, the negativity that contextualizes positivity, is *precisely what cannot be present*, and, thus, to be open to others is precisely to be open to what cannot be present. Desire's own constitutive premise, however, is that this "what cannot be present" is the essential and independent reality that defines the sense of determinacy: "A self-consciousness, in being an object, is just as much 'I' as 'object.'"[31] Being an explicit self-consciousness thus opens one to the realm of negativity-for-itself—"absolute negation"[32]—as the reality beyond immediate determinacy, and thus, even as desire is the experience of self-certainty, even as desire experiences its own negativity as what is determinative of the sense of the determinacy in which it is absorbed, desire is equally the experience of itself as held—through this determinacy—in essential relation to a defining reality that eludes its grasp: it is held by the negativity that is the other self-consciousness, the other possible self-certainties that equally enact themselves in this same determinacy.

> Self-consciousness is faced by another self-consciousness; it has come *out of itself*. . . . [I]t has lost itself, for it finds itself as an *other* being.[33]

Now, one can live one's "mineness," one's self-certainty, without having to notice it as such: desire, precisely, is an orientation toward the object. This relationship to the object is definitive of desire:

> Desire and the self-certainty obtained in its gratification are conditioned by the object, for self-certainty comes from superseding this other: in order that this supersession can take place, there must be this other.[34]

In encountering the object, however, one encounters the site that is the fulfillment of the trajectory of someone else's desire, someone else's self-certainty. To act from desire is implicitly to enter into the "mine-field" of other self-consciousnesses.

Hegel's point is that, inasmuch as desire experiences itself as the "truth" of its object, its own activity naturally involves it in asserting itself over the exactly parallel claims of other desires—other "self-certainties"—that assert themselves in and through precisely the same determinacies that are the objects of the first desire. The attitude of desire thus always has competition with other desires on its horizon. Let me complete the above quotation:

> Self-consciousness is faced by another self-consciousness; it has come *out of itself*. This has a twofold significance: first, it has lost itself, for it finds itself as an *other* being; secondly, in doing so it has superseded the other, for it does not see the other as an essential being, but in the other sees its own self.[35]

Because desire always exists in this context of implicit competition with the desire of the other, its desire to establish itself as the truth of its object is the desire to be recognized as the truth by the other desire. It is ultimately the other's desire that is thus the object of the desire, and desire is thus inherently the desire of the other. The life of desire thus naturally ushers in an engagement between desires in which each one has its immediate sense of self-certainty challenged by the conflicting assertion of the other. The life of desire thus inherently puts upon us the need to establish a viable sense of self through negotiation with those other desires, parallel to our own, that are engaged with the same lived imperative to carry out such a negotiation:

> Each sees the *other* do the same as it does; each does itself what it demands of the other, and therefore also does what it does only in so far as the other does the same. Action by one side only would be useless because what is to happen can only be brought about by both.[36]

This mutual negotiation is what Hegel calls "recognition" [*Anerkennung*]: "They *recognize* themselves as *mutually recognizing* one another."[37]

The further details of Hegel's analysis of recognition do not need here to be taken up—we will discuss them in more detail in the ensuing chapters. What is essential here is to notice that there is a distinctive sense, "other self"—a sense by definition not reducible to the terms of any determinacy, any presence—that is inherent to our experience of desire. Furthermore, this sense itself has an imperative force, in that it is lived as the demand—a demand ushering from the internal constitution of desire itself—to negotiate a viable sense of self with the other. There is, in other words, an immanent imperative to *communicate,* which entails the establishing of a shared language, shared terms of reference for identifying each other and the things of the world. In short, there is an immanent imperative to establish what is ultimately a normalized identity in a system of social relations.

This analysis reflects no "preference" on Hegel's part for "normalization," nor is there any sleight-of-hand by which some metaphysical notion of "subject" or "spirit" is illicitly installed prior to the analysis. Rather, it is desire itself that by its own nature must be open in principle to the appearance of another desire on its own horizon and, for that reason, is already *internally* or *immanently* defined by the imperative to answer to the unpresentable absence of the other. This distinct, irreducible, imperative sense of "autonomous other" is presumed, but not accounted for, in the schizoanalysis of Deleuze and Guattari. Let us see how that is so.

Let us now think again about desiring machines. Imagine the machine that connects the flow of milk from the breast to the mouth onto the floor. Experientially, this is not a story of two subject bodies—that of the child and that of the mother—coming into contact and having a liquid pass between them and then onto a third thing, namely the floor (though it looks that way to our "objective" adult perception). Rather, the mouth, breast, milk, and floor together realize a machine, itself the locus and realization of a passing, temporary identity. This assemblage, stuck together as the flashing of a certain locally coherent intensity, provides the "who" of the "experience." It is such collages, such disparate assemblages of fleeting intensities, that populate the world of desiring production.[38]

But let us consider the elements grafted together in such machines. From the point of view of the world of Oedipal subjectivity, the elements that are united in the milking machine just described belong to different people: *the child's* mouth, *the mother's* breast. Let us consider what this entails "phenomenologically," that is, from the point of view of desiring production. What we will see is that these descriptions are not just alien Oedipal importations, but that, on the contrary, the recognition of such "personal ownership" is immanent to the experience of desire itself.

What we recognize as the separation of the child's and the mother's bodies entails that the very elements of desire's realization themselves have contested identities. The child-as-milking-machine enjoying itself in the breast is enjoying itself in a domain in which the mother also enjoys herself, and such counter-enjoyment shows itself in desire as resistance. The mother, for example, does not want to continue feeding the child and applies force to remove the breast from the child's mouth; the child, for example, does not want the breast removed and strains to keep its lips connected to the nipple. One and the same determinacy—the breast—is the site in which two opposed desires, two opposed self-certainties, are enacted: each desire is struggling to realize itself *within the domain of the other's (opposed) desire.* The breast, the mouth, the floor are so many sites for proprietary claims, sites for conflict—*but specifically* conflict that takes the form of one "mine" versus another "mine." The resistance the child faces, then, is not just the recalcitrance of the material, but precisely *the opposition of another desire, and the resistance can indeed be experienced as such by the child.*

Children (and, of course, parents) are not unaware of the subjectivity—the absence "for itself"—of the other. The absent other who offers resistance is not experienced simply as an instrumental impediment to the project of suckling or not-feeding. On the contrary, the experience of breast-feeding—both from the side of the child and from the side of the mother—can itself be *a way of engaging with the other's subjectivity,* that is, breast-feeding can precisely be a site of communication, of intersubjective contact: the child can suckle at the breast *precisely out of a desire to engage with the mother as subject,* and the enjoyment of suckling can be an enjoyment of community as much as it is sensually gratifying:

as Brian Massumi, describing the baby's behavior, notes, "[t]he joy of eye-to-eye contact with its mother resonates through its body and comes out the far end in a kick."[39] The child, in other words, is responding to whatever determinacy it is encountering in the world *as the presence of the mother: the absence that is the other self* is precisely *one of the elements* of the assemblage, of the "machine." But such an assemblage can no longer be accounted for without invoking the language of subjectivity and intersubjectivity—that is, a language that acknowledges the irreducible ontological autonomy of the self-defined absences that constitute desiring subjectivity.

But because the other is precisely an absence—that is, because it is precisely that which can never be explained on the basis of present actualities—there would be no possibility of experiencing such an other if one were only open to apprehending determinacy. Only a being—a desire—that is already constitutively open to the sense "other person" could come to recognize another person. This sense "other person" is precisely the sense of a self-defined absence that exceeds any possible determinacy and is thus not reducible to the syntheses of production, recording, and consumption; nor can it be explained by an Oedipal imposition.[40] If desire were not always already open to the sense "other self," no such sense could ever arise within its experience.

For this reason, the sense of "I" or "me" *is* thus "destined" to emerge within desiring production. What Hegel describes in his analysis of desire in the *Phenomenology of Spirit* is precisely this situation in which desire, open in principle to the desire of the other, is destined to encounter that other as an *immanently motivated* experience of transcendence, a sense of other "for itself" emerging within the domain of the "for me." This other for itself first emerges as *that which opposes me*; in other words, "me" is originally the sense with which *the other* challenges my desire, demanding of me that I reciprocate with my own sense of "me."[41] The relevant "self" within desire, then, is not so much the "residue" that is the synthesis of consumption, but is, rather, the self to whom I must answer, the self whose autonomy and irreducibility is already woven into the very sense of the elements fused together into the assemblages of the desiring machines themselves, a self that demands of me that I similarly be an autonomous and irreducible subjectivity.

In this sense, then, the sense of "I" *is* something very much like the *telos* of desire, for it is the natural response to the natural emerging sense of "someone else's" that is forced upon me by the immanent logic of desiring production itself, inasmuch as desire already sets flows in motion that cross boundaries of the "mine." It is precisely in such "mine" fields that desire operates. Once desire takes the form of a challenge to one desire by another, the question cannot fail to be an opposition of "mine" vs. "mine," so the *demand for* coherent self-identity is already *immanent* in the very logic of desire, the very logic of sense. This "*telos*," though, is an *immanent* telos. In other words, it is not something someone "planted" there, and it is not something that pre-exists as a desired goal. It is a *telos*, rather, in the sense that it arises as the natural consequence of the internal dynamism—in Hegel's language, the "dialectic"—of desire.

Desire, in other words, is inherently defined by answerability to the other and thus by the immanent demand that its own self-certainty be reconciled to the self-certainty of the other. Desire, then, is not satisfactory to itself in its immediacy, but immanently projects for itself a standard to which it must answer by transforming itself: desire itself has a natural trajectory of growth toward a reconciled experience of intersubjectivity, or what Hegel calls "mutual recognition" or "spirit" [*Geist*], which is itself an experience of a shared, objective world.[42] In other words, the very aspects of Kant's portrayal of experience that Deleuze and Guattari criticize as the result of illegitimate, "transcendent" uses of synthesis are, on the contrary, immanent to the self-development of desiring production itself.

Conclusion

There is a tremendous parallel between the arguments of *Anti-Oedipus* and those of the *Critique of Pure Reason*, and in general, the schizoanalytic revision of Kant covers the ground of bodily, prepersonal experience initially laid out by the German Idealists. What is lacking in Deleuze and Guattari, though, is the acknowledgment that desire implicates us in the domain of intersubjective conflict and thereby inaugurates the dialectics of intersubjective recognition. This points to a general deficiency in the way in which Deleuze and Guattari discuss desire, giving insufficient ontological weight to the other as an autonomous realm of sense. Hegel's analysis of the desire for recognition, on the contrary, precisely shows how the autonomous, unpresentable other is always on the horizon of desiring production, and that therefore the dialectic of intersubjective recognition—"spirit"—is the immanent *telos* of desire.

Discovering this "*telos*" of desire does not, however, eliminate desire, nor does it challenge its characterization as the non-egoic enmeshment in part-objects we analyzed above. It shows, rather, that desire is not the whole of sense, and that its terms, therefore, are insufficient as such to analyze and interpret—to understand—the whole realm of experience and reality. Desire *points beyond itself* and *reveals itself* to be implicated in the domain of interpersonal answerability, the domain of intersubjectivity, objectivity, morality, "spirit." We have seen in earlier chapters that "sense-certainty"—the singular immediacy of sensory life—is the fabric *within which* things and, indeed, a world of reality, make their appearance, and sensuous immediacy is "of" the particular things, which are themselves "of" the universal world in which they participate. Analogously, "self-certainty"—the singular immediacy of desiring life—is the fabric within which higher subjective realities come into being: desire is ultimately only fulfilled in being the desire "of" the particular personal subjects who are themselves "of" the spiritual community—the universal—to which they belong.

Like sensuous certainty, desire will always remain an irreducible domain of immediacy that, in its singularity and givenness, remains opaque to understanding; like sensuous certainty, desire will always operate with a logic that does not acknowledge the terms of the normalized opposition of subject and object; but also like sensuous certainty, desire is a dimension of sense that reveals itself to be always already contextualized by further dimensions of sense that are not reducible in their significance to its terms. Specifically, desire is an originary matrix of sense that is already inherently open to the sense "other person," and thus destined to experience in terms of that. Finally, though this sense has the dialectic of recognition on its horizon, there is no guarantee that desire will be enacted such as to answer adequately to the demands of recognition; indeed, Hegel's most famous analyses (of the "Struggle to the Death" and "Lordship and Bondage") precisely show how we can fail to live up to the terms of recognition. What is true, though, is that the demand to live up to the terms of recognition is a meaning that beckons from within the experience of desire, and is not an alien imposition.

5

Mood and Articulation

As we have already begun to see through the analysis of desire in chapter 4, one of the great contributions of German Idealism to the history of philosophy is its investigation of the layers of subjectivity that do not have the form of the ego, but upon which the ego's experience of itself depends. Such investigations constitute a major challenge to many of the most central assumptions and practices of the earlier history of philosophy, and the carrying forward of these analyses in contemporary Continental philosophy has been one of the most valuable dimensions of the legacy of German Idealism. In addition to the well-known analysis of desire in the *Phenomenology of Spirit,* Hegel offers an exciting but understudied contribution to this history through his analysis of ourselves as emotional beings. Indeed, his analysis of the essential moodiness of subjectivity anticipates much of Heidegger's famous analysis of this topic in *Being and Time.* My goal in this chapter is not specifically to map this relation between Hegel and Heidegger, but simply to articulate what I understand to be this basic story of mood that can be found in the pages of Hegel's *Philosophy of Mind,* and to use the rich material from this parallel text to supplement the study of the core themes of the *Phenomenology of Spirit.*[1]

"Sensibility" and "feeling" are the technical terms through which Hegel's analysis of mood is articulated. I will begin by situating "mood" within the context of "sensibility," and then focus on the inherently "outwardizing" or self-externalizing character of mood. I will then consider the different modes of moody self-externalization, especially for the sake of asking why we express ourselves in language. Hegel's analyses here are an especially helpful complement to the phenomenology of desire and recognition in the *Phenomenology of Spirit,* and my goal here will be to show how the *Phenomenology of Spirit*'s central notion of "spirit" is essentially linked to the notion of mood. Along the way, we will see the essential place of the body, intersubjectivity, and language in the making possible of the subject-object relations we typically take for granted.

What Is Mood?

Hegel defines mood [*Stimmung*] as a form of sensibility [*Empfindung*] and so to understand mood we must first understand what sensibility is. The distinction we might observe from the outside of someone sleeping and waking is roughly what, from the inside, is sensibility. Sensibility is finding oneself, being awake to one's own being. In writing about *Empfindung*, Hegel is trying to characterize that most basic reality of what it is to be aware, and that is primarily to be alive *to*, to be awake *to*, oneself.[2]

We are accustomed to think of ourselves as being aware of *something*, as having an object. This structure—basically, intentional consciousness—already, however, describes a higher level of experience than what we find in sensibility. Prior to noticing some specific thing outside me, I must in a more basic way be a self-sensitive being. It is only against the background of my awareness of myself as that upon whom or within whom something can register that something can stand out. This is not to say, however, that I have an encounter with myself *as object* prior to experiencing something else as an object. On the contrary, analogously to our consideration of desire in chapter 4, we are here considering my self-awakeness as a field of sensibility that precedes the distinction of subject and object.

Hegel's own example of what it is like to wake up is helpful here. When we initially wake up from sleep we are often still in a rather dreamy state in which we are sensing, but we are not relating to the world as an alien thing.[3] We are alive only to something like the fact of our own experience, without recognizing a separation of subject and object. Merleau-Ponty says something analogous in the opening of his *Phenomenology of Perception*. What, he asks, could we mean when we speak of "pure sensation"? He says,

> I might in the first place understand by sensation the way in which I am affected and the experiencing of a state of myself. The greyness which, when I close my eyes, surrounds me, leaving no distance between me and it, the sounds that encroach on my drowsiness and hum "in my head" perhaps give some indication of what pure sensation might be. I might be said to have sense-experience (*sentir*) precisely to the extent that I coincide with the sensed, that the latter ceases to have any place in the objective world, and that it signifies nothing for me.[4]

Sensing in this sense means something like feeling, living in a wakedness within one's own experience.

In his analysis of life, Hegel distinguishes "*Sensibilität*"—another term that might also properly be translated as "sensibility"—from "irritability," and this distinction would be helpful to keep in mind here.[5] What in our everyday philosophical discourse we call sensing is more akin to irritability than to this "sensibility." Irritability is my ability to be affected by something else—to be irritated, to have my tranquil self-possession interrupted or disturbed. This self-possession that might be disturbed is *Sensibilität*: the dwelling within its own inwardness of the organism, the feeling of the organism for itself as a whole. No matter where you touch my body—no matter at which different part—you touch me, the same me. That self-same-self-that-can-be-touched that runs throughout me as a whole is *Sensibilität*.[6] It is the organism in its universality, its self-sameness as a subject, a "soul."[7]

In imagining this example from life, one likely pictures an animal body from the outside, and imagines a sensibility somehow overlain on that bodily form. To understand sensibility [*Empfindung*] as Hegel uses it in the *Philosophy of Mind*, that image of the determinate bodily figure must be removed, and this experience simply imagined *from the inside*. This aliveness to or being-awake-to oneself as a whole is indeed an aliveness *within* one's determinateness, but it is not an awareness *of* one's determinateness. We, looking on, might say that it is the inwardness of that body as opposed to some other body, but from the inside that differentiation of one from another is not explicitly posited. Sensibility is an awareness of oneself within one's determinateness that is prior to the positing of an object. We might (following Sartre) call it a non-positional consciousness (of) self, with the "of" put in parentheses to indicate that this is an aliveness to oneself and not the taking of oneself as an object.[8]

This self-aliveness is what Hegel calls "negativity." Negativity is like intentionality, in that it is always negativity of . . . , but the relation of the negative to what it is "of" is one of immanence, rather than one of separation as we often presume with intentionality. The "of" of negativity is possessive rather than objective, as we might speak of the grasping power "of" a hand: such a power is the pervasive and defining reality that emerges as the truth of the hand's determinacy, rather than being an independent force brought to bear upon it. It is, as Hegel says of *Empfindung*, the "subjectivizing" of a "substantiality."[9] Negativity, like the power of the hand, is always thus "from" a substantiality, but, inasmuch as this negative "subjectivizing" is immanent to it, the substantiality does not precede its negation any more than the substance of the hand precedes the power to grasp.[10]

Sensibility, then, is not yet the awareness of an alien object, and similarly, it is not an experience of an alienated ego. This second point is important. This original form of experience is itself embodied; it is not the *tabula rasa* as a kind of as-yet-empty mental container, but is rather the self-awareness *of* (again, possessive, not objective, genitive) this very corporeality, this very determinacy. Sensibility is awareness that precedes the opposition of self and other, but for that reason it is, as it were, consciousness entangled with corporeality.[11] It is being awake—being awake to oneself—within one's determinacy.

Mood is a species of this sensibility, this being-awake-within-one's-determinacy.[12] Mood is living within a non-differentiation of self and other. Mood is my immediate at-home-ness in determinateness; it is how I find myself.[13] It is a grasp (of) being, but a grasp (of) being that is identically a grasp (of) oneself. Let us consider this experientially for a moment.

In the logical sequence according to which Hegel is analyzing spirit, mood precedes ego-based consciousness. Mood, however, is not something simply done with once one reaches egohood. On the contrary, mood is a continuingly necessary dimension of all experiential life. *We*—those of us who are reading and who, thus, function already at the level of the ego—are already conscious. Let us consider mood as it functions within ourselves. Mood is the way in which our conscious experience is always grounded in a fundamental, affective being-at-home in determinacy.[14] Mood is the way we live in *a world that reflects our subjectivity back to us.* When we indulge our moodiness (when we are "emotional") we treat the world as if its reality were simply how it feels for ourselves. This is the main feature that Hegel emphasizes about mood. Mood is inherently subjective in the sense of being singularized, non-shared, non-objective. It is the taking up of reality as if my take on it were its sole truth. In mood, my being-in-the-world and my being-for-self (my self-consciousness) are not distinguished.

Though from the outside we might say of someone that his subjectivity is something occurring within the world, and something added on to an already existent reality, *for* that someone there is no such pre-existent reality. *For* each of us, reality and ourselves are co-emergent: our original experience of being and our original experience of ourselves are the same experience. This is mood. Merleau-Ponty, again, says something that is very close to expressing Hegel's point:

> If, then, we want to bring to light the birth of being for us, we must finally look at that area of our experience which clearly has reality and significance only for us, and that is our affective life.[15]

Our affectivity, our moodiness, is our original aliveness to being. But this moodiness is inherently subjective—it precisely fails to answer to the demands of "reality" as such. We are familiar with something like this point in Freud.

According to Freud, the child initially acts only according to desire or the "pleasure principle," according to which things are only how they appeal to me. It is the destiny of the child's growth of development to learn the "reality principle," that is, to learn that there is a reality to the world that is not defined in terms of my desires, and that I am answerable to.[16] Though mood is defined by its not operating with this "reality principle," it is nonetheless the field within which all further experience emerges. Whatever else there is to be for us—an ego, reality, knowledge—must exist as a dialectical development of our affectivity. Let us continue the quote from Merleau-Ponty above:

> Let us try to see how a thing or a being begins to exist for us . . . [in emotion] . . . and we shall thereby come to understand better how things and beings can exist in general.

Let us now turn to that emergence of a significance of *being in general* that is not merely singular.

Mood Requires Expression

From the inside, sensibility does not distinguish subject from object. All of us, however, recognize this distinction (because we function at a much higher level than mere sensibility). We can thus recognize within sensibility a distinction that is not itself posited there. Sensibility is being awake within one's determinacy, and this has two sides: there is what Hegel calls the "substantial" side, which is the determinacy, and there is what Hegel calls the "subjective" side, or the "negative self-relation," which is the side of the self-awakeness. Inasmuch as sensibility is the awakeness of this determinacy to itself, the *identity* of these two sides is posited, but this identity itself implicitly has two directions. Sensibility, the identity of the substantial and the subjective, can be understood both as the subjectivizing of the substantial and as the substantializing of the subjective.[17]

The former—the subjectivizing of the substantial, what Hegel calls "outer sensibility"—is relevant, but need not concern us much at this point. It is the way, Hegel says, that we live our experiences of colors, for example, not simply in disinterested objectivity, but rather as charged with subjective meaning, as exciting, depressing, etc.[18] It is the latter—the substantializing of the subjective, or "inner sensibility"—that is the proper terrain of mood.

Mood is *how* we are awake to ourselves—cheerful, sad, etc.—and this "how" is *lived*, not as a thought, but *as a corporeality*.[19] The way of being of the inwardizing is the way of being of the determinacy. Rather than having a *how* of inwardizing *called up by* the determinacy (as in "outer sensibility"), this "inner sensibility" is the way a *how* of the determinacy is *called forth by* the inwardizing. In outer sensibility, I experience a color as exciting. In inner sensibility my happiness immediately realizes itself as a smile. It is this outer directedness that now concerns us.

From our discussion of the two sides of *Empfindung*—outer sensibility and inner sensibility—we can see that both are trajectories or directions. *Empfindung*, in other words, is inherently characterized by negation (a distinction and direction *from* here *to* there), and as such is a sphere of impulsion, motivation. *Empfindung* is my being awake within my determinacy (being subjective in my substantiality) and the how or form of this awakeness is always a kind of "call," a beckoning toward, which itself calls for a kind of resolution or satisfaction. In outer sensibility, the form of determinacy calls us to feel a certain way. In inner sensibility, more importantly for us, the form of our feeling calls us *to make determinate.*

This making determinate takes three fundamental forms. The first is the form I mentioned above in the example of happiness as smiling. I will call this mode of making determinate "realization": happiness is realized as a smile, excitement in a fast-beating heart. We might also call this first an "immediate corporealization" or a simple substantializing.

Hegel emphasizes the importance of a second form. In a fundamental way, he says, moods call for *externalization* (*Entäußerung*).[20] Beyond placid realization (and thereby a kind of cementation), moods need to be got beyond, and we live our mood as the need to get it out. Laughter and crying are good examples of this further externalizing of emotion. In these practices, we realize the emotion and simultaneously work through it. We might call this second form a dynamic and self-alienating corporealization. Let me make two observations about this point, before moving on to the third form of making determinate.

Let us first make an observation about the impulsion to making determinate. The basic idea here is that *it is only as making determinate* that we successfully enact the mood. It is *by smiling* and *by laughing* that I am able to be happy. Without these realizations, I am only an as yet indeterminate impulsion toward. . . . The realization is not a super-added after-thought to an already accomplished emotion, but is its actual accomplishment, or its embodiment. It is *in the realization* that we live the emotion.[21]

Let us make a second observation about externalizing and getting beyond. When Hegel discusses this point, he often refers to Aristotle's notion of dramatic catharsis and to Goethe's literary work. In Greek tragedy as Aristotle understood it, or in Goethe's *Sorrows of Young Werther* and similar works, emotions are made objective to us; that is, we can *be explicitly conscious of* the states that normally implicitly embody us. In having these states as objects, we put our own consciousness beyond them, and thereby make them controllable. It is by this making of ourselves objective to ourselves that we become free.[22] Note here that the satisfaction of our mood depends on our being able to differentiate ourselves as subjects from our object.

What we are already beginning to see in these two points is that it is the very nature of mood to call for the making of itself into an object for itself, and by so doing to transcend itself from a kind of inarticulate bondage into freedom. Before continuing with this theme, let me introduce the third form of making determinate that Hegel identifies.

The third form of making determinate is *gesture*, which is itself completed in *language*. Hegel marks the important distinction between this and the second form of making determinate ("externalization") as the *voluntariness* of gesture.[23] In voluntary action, my subjectivity is explicitly posited: I say, "that choice was *mine*, and mine alone." In the voluntary, the "me"-ness that originates in mood is not merely lived, but asserted. We will be occupied with this notion explicitly in the next section, so for now let us only note the voluntary gesture as the third form of making determinate, about which Hegel says, "articulate speech is thus the highest mode in which man rids himself of his inner sensations."[24]

Language

Before turning to the consideration of language directly, it is helpful to consider briefly Hegel's analysis of one particular mood. At one point, Hegel explains why it is that we become bored.[25] Boredom can happen in two ways. On the one hand, if something is too monotonous and undifferentiated, we become bored with it. On the other hand, if something is too varied and arbitrary, we become bored with it. Why is this? It is because our very nature as subjects is to be self-differentiated unities. Something too monotonous does not address our impulsion to differentiation, and forces our consciousness into too uniform a mode to reflect its own nature. Something too arbitrarily varied does not address our centralized selfhood, and draws our consciousness into too dispersed a mode to reflect its own nature. What is interesting in this analysis is that it shows that we seek something in the form of an object, namely, we find satisfaction only in an object that adequately reflects back to us our own form. We will consider this theme again in the course of our analysis of language.

We just saw that the soul by its nature is impelled to "out" itself.[26] There is a problem here, though. The very nature of the moody soul is that it is thoroughly subjective, that is, the outside is, for it, only *for it.* The very propulsion of mood is toward externalization, but there is, for it, no external. Though the very nature of the soul is to put itself outside itself, it is equally the nature of the soul to overreach that outside and, in the outside, to find only itself. The soul thus needs to, and cannot, get beyond itself.

This problem is logically analogous to the founding tension of experience as Fichte describes it. Fichte identifies two fundamental principles of conscious life. The first principle is that "the ego posits itself," and the second that "the ego opposes to itself a not-self." It is the irreconcilable conflict of these two principles and the need to reconcile them (which is the third principle) that defines experience. Let me explain.

All of my experience is *my* experience; as Kant says, the "I think" must be able to accompany any of my representations.[27] This is Fichte's first principle: in all experience, the ego is positing herself; that is, to the extent that anything is recognized, the recognizer must tacitly be recognizing itself: to say that the rose is a self-identical reality is to assert that it is itself—generically, A = A—and to assert that A = A requires that I who assert the first A am the same and know myself to be the same as the I who asserts the second; thus the assertion A = A (and, therefore, the recognition of any self-identical reality) implies or presupposes the recognition that I am I. Thus, all experience has, as its most general form, the self-positing of the ego.[28]

If this were all, though, there would in fact be no experience. Experience also requires difference and determination. Experience thus rests also on a second principle, namely, the recognition of difference; but since all experience is in principle the ego recognizing itself, the only thing that could count at this level as difference would be the ego opposing itself to a not-self. There can be no experience, in other words, that does not take the form of a recognition that "that is not me."[29]

There is a problem here, though. The need for all experience to be self-experience and the need for all experience to be experience of a not-self are equally necessary and yet diametrically opposed. The basic logical problem here can be put this way: to the extent that *I experience* an other, it is an other *for me,* but in that case it is a facet of my experience, and not other.[30] This logical problem is also a lived significance in all our experience. In all our experience we find ourselves called upon to *struggle with* the given, alien form of experience, but, for all our struggle, we can always ask ourselves whether we are just living in our own private perspective. Experience is defined by this problem. The fact that the ultimate form of experience is the self-positing of the ego means that every other that I experience is, because I experience it, already mine, and thus the ego must constantly be in search of a check [*Anstoss*], a limit to itself.[31] And yet, every such limit, inasmuch as it is experienced, is always absorbed back into the self. The problem is that the other is always an other that is other *for the self.* What we need is an other that we experience as other *for itself.*

Though the exact details of Hegel's analysis differ in some respects from Fichte's, this same basic tension, it seems to me, is the problem of the moody soul, which propels the move to language. It is this need to find an adequate externality in which the soul can be external to itself that brings us to the theme of language.

The soul needs to express itself. We have already seen that this is the very nature of moods, namely, that they only exist insofar as they are realized. Hegel refers to gesture, the third mode of making determinate, as voluntary, and this, indeed, reveals even more the urgency of self-externalization: as self-possessed, explicitly self-conscious egos, we *want* to express ourselves. Gesture is the point at which we actually own up to the urgency of expression, acknowledge its propriety for us, or make it our property, as it were. And in our gestures, then, inasmuch as they are voluntary, what we are giving voice to is ourselves as voluntary egos, ourselves as self-conscious agents. At the level of gesture, the two sides of the tension we have been considering are both present, and both more pronounced. We here more pointedly portray our desire for an outside, and, by the higher degree of our self-agency, also demonstrate a higher level of inwardness, a greater privacy to our world. It is for such a self that language is a reality.

A gesture is unsuccessful if it is not recognized.[32] To the extent that the meaning of the gesture is solely my own, the gesture fails as a gesture. In a gesture, then, I express my desire to pass beyond my isolated subjectivity to a world of otherness. But the otherness in which I express myself is not a mere natural being—for this would never maintain its independence of meaning against my subjectivizing interpretation. The otherness of the natural thing is merely *for me*, for I can overreach it and set its significance for myself; the otherness I need is an otherness *for itself*, and this is an otherness that, like me, can set the terms of significance for *it*self. In language, I seek to externalize myself in an otherness I cannot overreach, *and that otherness I cannot overreach is the otherness of other self-conscious selves like myself.* In recognizing an other as another voluntary, self-conscious agent like myself, I recognize an inwardness, a subjectivity, a soul for whom being is *for it.* In an other self, I find one whose claim to contain my reality within her experience is equal to my own claim to contain her reality in mine. In another self like me, I encounter a "second principle" (in Fichte's language) that is itself a "first principle" like me. Here I have an object that adequately reflects my own reality to me. In gesture, then, we see the culmination of the logic of moody expressiveness, for here we find an expression that has recognized a domain of *otherness-for-itself*, within which it can come upon an outside that by its nature cannot be comprehended by my isolated subjectivity. It is in the recognition of our gestures by others that the tension inherent to emotion—the tension we explored through discussion of Fichte's first two principles—is resolved. This logical structure of the solution can also then tell us something about the nature of language.[33]

The very nature of gesture, and of articulate speech, which Hegel identifies as the highest form of gesture, is that it must be public. A gesture then must be publicly meaningful: it must be simultaneously the expression of my mineness, of my inner, *and* a meaning we all share. In language, my inner is expressed in a corporeality that is public: not just a putatively universally accessible "thing" upon which each of us projects his own meaning, but a thing whose very nature is publicness, is sharedness of meaning.[34]

This thing that has as its reality to be a sharedness of public meaning is what Hegel calls a "word."[35] A word is a "thing"—a sensible determinacy—that is experienced precisely as *not* itself qua occurrent determinacy, but is itself only as a showing forth of something beyond itself. A word is a signifier, a determinacy that is only as the showing of another. And the "beyond" that it shows, the signified, is necessarily not private. The meaning of the word *as word* is inseparable from the demand that in it I answer to the perspectives of others—not to their arbitrary perspectives, however, but to their perspectives as equally constrained by the demand for sharedness of meaning. A word is a sensible determinacy experienced as a demand for intersubjectivity. It is because emotion needs to express itself in order to be fulfilled, and because that fulfillment can only be realized in the domain of intersubjective recognition, that we have words. Words are the material conditions, so to speak, of such expression.

It is only in words—in a sensible determinacy whose determinacy denies its own significance and shows forth instead an intersubjective meaning—that moods can be adequately realized. But in expressing myself in words, I thus express a self *already beholden to others*. In expressing myself in words, I affirm that my "I" is a "we."[36] Whatever more specific content I give voice to, most fundamentally what I articulate, is my reality as an intersubjective being. This is most basically what we need to communicate, what we need to affirm through our gestures. The subjectivity of emotion fulfills itself when it sublates itself and expresses itself as intersubjectivity. Our reality is spirit, and it is this nature that we most urgently feel the need to express.

With that remark, let us return to the discussion of boredom with which we began this section. Boredom was interpreted as an emotional expression of the inadequacy of the object to be an outside for us, that is, boredom is emotion itself attesting to our need for an adequate other. (Expressive) participation in an intersubjective world is what our emotional life needs to complete itself. Hegel's discussion of boredom reminded us that in our object we seek a mirror of ourselves, and only the intersubjective world can adequately reflect our own inherently intersubjective nature back to ourselves. Only in such a reality can I adequately fulfill myself, for only in such a reality can the power of my inwardness find an outside capable of withstanding it. It is only in the realm of spirit that spiritual beings are fulfilled.

Conclusion

Normally, we think of emotions and objectivity as opposites. What is exciting in Hegel's analysis is the argument that the emergence of the world of objectivity and intersubjectivity is itself an emotional demand. Emotion is the subjective non-differentiation of subject and object that seeks an adequate externalization. It accomplishes itself only in its expression of itself as an intersubjective reality. Here, our subjectivity again finds itself in the object, but now as an experience of a we.

With this discussion of Hegel we have given ourselves a basic map of the terrain of Hegel's idealism; that is, we have something like the basic "map" of experience as that is understood in Hegel's philosophy. In particular, we have seen that the easy relations of subject and object that characterize our everyday experience are themselves rooted in dynamic sources that do not have that same form, and our experiences of subjectivity and objectivity are thus products of more basic powers. We have seen in particular that those more basic sources of our experience are essentially bodily, essentially self-transcending, and essentially intersubjective. This, in short, is what it means to say that "spirit" is the fundamental fabric of our experience.

6

Recognition and Religious Narrative

In his brilliant book *The Divided Self*, published in 1960, the Scottish "anti-psychiatrist" R. D. Laing makes a telling observation. Our English expression "self-consciousness" indicates, he notes, two significantly different experiences. On the one hand, we use "self-consciousness" to refer to our knowledge of ourselves, typically meaning something like our introspective insight into our own, private psyches. On the other hand, we describe ourselves as "self-conscious" precisely when we experience ourselves as exposed before the gaze of another: in other words, self-consciousness here names not my view of myself, but my exposure to the view others have of me.[1] In this observation, and in *The Divided Self* overall, Laing, who was himself highly influenced by the interpretation of self-consciousness in post-Hegelian phenomenology, offers one of the clearest and most insightful studies of Hegel's dialectic of recognition. Hegel, like Laing, emphasizes the way in which our sense of ourselves is worked out in and through our negotiation with the perspectives of others. Self-consciousness, in other words, is a collective accomplishment: self-consciousness is, as Hegel writes, an "'I' that is 'We' and 'We' that is 'I,'" or in Hegel's language, "spirit" ("*Geist*").[2]

Laing's focus is on the way our sense of self is accomplished in the relationships between individuals (specifically, in relationships between family members), but the collective accomplishment of self-consciousness is also something that is enacted at a social level. One's "I," that is, is crucially shaped by the terms in which one's culture interprets itself as a "We." It is this larger "'I' that is 'We' and 'We' that is 'I'" that Hegel calls "spirit," and, on Hegel's account, it is religion that provides the primary domain in which a spirit is enacted. Ultimately, then, the dynamics of recognition that subtend our efforts to establish healthy self-consciousness have their basis in *religious* life, which Hegel calls "spirit's consciousness of itself."

In order to understand the force of Hegel's analysis of recognition, I will begin this chapter with a description of Laing's notion of "Ontological (In)security," which he identifies as the fundamental accomplishment of healthy self-consciousness. Here, we will see that a healthy sense of "I" depends on the intersubjective dynamics that operate, so to speak, "before" the "I," in the pre-personal negotiation of formative family bonds. In addition to seeing the crucial intersubjective communication that is definitive for self-consciousness, we will see in particular that our sense of self-identity depends essentially on a kind of intersubjective *narrative.* It is this theme of narrative that will allow us to turn to a study of the essential role of religion in self-consciousness. Here, we will see that a healthy sense of "I" depends on a negotiation with a dynamic social and cultural heritage that exists well beyond the level of any individual "I."

Ontological Security

In *The Divided Self,* Laing argues that it is an essential aspect of human development that we need to accomplish a sense of ourselves as legitimate, functioning members of the world in order to be able to act effectively and to maintain a healthy mental life. Since for most of us this sense of self-worth is well-established and familiar, we tend to think of it as something simply "given," rather than as something that had to be accomplished. Laing's point, however, is that the accomplishing of this sense—what he calls "ontological security"—is in fact the central task of our early development in our family life, and that this development depends upon the support of our significant others (most notably our parents). It is precisely the failure to successfully establish this sense—to live with "ontological insecurity"—that Laing identifies as the source of mental illness.[3]

By "ontological security," Laing literally means "assurance that I am real." Let us think about what it is to be real. Though there are, of course, great subtleties to this notion, which are powerfully explored by Parmenides, Aristotle, Kant, and others, most basically by "real" we mean something like "making a difference in the world," or "being able to have an impact on things," or "mattering." Something that is real, as opposed to something merely imaginary, impinges on all around it: anything real is a site of universal answerability, something that sets determinate limits on anything and everything else. As Bergson says,

> that which distinguishes it as . . . an objective reality . . . is the necessity which obliges it to act through every one of its points upon all the points of all other[s] . . . , to transmit the whole of what it receives, to oppose to every action an equal and contrary reaction, to be, in short,

> merely a road by which pass, in every direction, the modifications propagated throughout the immensity of the universe.[4]

To understand Laing's sense of "ontological security," we must ask, "what is it to *experience oneself* as thus real?"

To experience oneself as real is to experience oneself as making a difference, to experience oneself as an agent whose self-originated action has consequences in the world. Laing's point is that this *self-interpretation* is one we develop and can maintain only through the support of others *because it is primarily others who define the real for us.* If I am surrounded by others, all of whom respect each other and are swayed by the desires of each other but all of whom disregard me and pay no heed to my desires, then, within this intersubjective domain, I am effectively having my reality denied. Those of us who are psychologically healthy adults can no doubt accommodate such treatment in contained circumstances. For the child, however, whose sense of self-identity is just developing, and for whom there is no escape from the domain of familial interaction, such an experience of non-recognition by other family members is not something that can be accommodated but is rather the very medium for her development of self-interpretation:[5] it is the disregard from these all-important others that is the evidence for the child of how she should understand herself. A child who grows up without sufficient endorsement, without sufficient recognition of her autonomous agency and importance from parents and other significant figures, will live with a sense of ontological insecurity, an uncertainty, that is, about her own reality. For the already well-developed adult, such situations amount to passing experiences. For the child for whom they are the basic context of life, however, such experiences are not simply passing "contents" of experience, but become the *form* of experience, the environment to which she becomes habituated and from which she lives, the materials out of which her character is developed.[6]

I will not develop the discussion of Laing's interpretation of mental health further.[7] I draw on it this far only because it does an effective job of showing how what Hegel analyzes as the "dialectic of recognition" [*Anerkennung*] is integral to the most basic formation of ourselves as persons.[8] Living as an autonomous person—living with a sense of oneself as an important and effective agent—is not something simply given and not something that one accomplishes on one's own, but is a self-interpretation developed on the basis of the evidence supplied by others' interpretations of us (as demonstrated, to be sure, primarily through behavior, rather than simply in explicit affirmations) and on the basis of their cooperation and support: "self-consciousness exists in and for itself when, and by the fact that, it so exists for another; that is, it exists only in being acknowledged."[9] Our sense of self, in other words, is a product of dialogue: we do not begin as fully formed selves and subsequently enter into dialogue with others; on the contrary, it is only through a lived process of practical dialogue that it becomes possible for us to live with a sense of ourselves as discrete, fully formed individuals. Let us turn now to Hegel's discussion of intersubjective recognition, and thence to his account of religion.

Practice, Narrative, and Self-Identity

In chapter IV of the *Phenomenology of Spirit,* Hegel undertakes a description of the lived experience of self-consciousness in an effort to determine what are the constitutive structures of "first-person" experience.[10] Beginning from a description of the lived sense of self that is implicit in the experience of desire, Hegel proceeds to investigate the way in which that sense of self is engaged when desire finds itself interacting with the desires of another. Specifically, as we saw in chapter 4, Hegel shows that it is fundamental to our experience of desire *that we desire to be recognized by others*: we desire, that is, to be esteemed, to be desired.[11] In other words, the perspective of the other inherently matters to us, and how we matter to that perspective—how the other recognizes us—is an essential dimension of our self-consciousness, an essential frame of reference by which we define ourselves to ourselves. Self-consciousness, then, before being a matter of the sort of rational self-reflection about which Epictetus or Descartes speaks, is more fundamentally something experienced practically and affectively in passionate attraction, love, or jealousy, in experiences of belonging or being excluded, in relationships of domination or subordination.

In his study of "The Independence and Dependence of Self-Consciousness," Hegel describes experiences in which one deals with one's dependence on others by trying to deny it (in the "Struggle to the Death") or by trying to control the power of the other through domination or submission (in "Lordship and Bondage").[12] His descriptions of these experiences demonstrate the ways in which these strategies undermine themselves, ultimately pointing to the conclusion that inequality of recognition—one party trying to be acknowledged by the other in a way that is not met with an equal recognition by itself of that other—always and in principle produces an incoherent and unsatisfactory situation.[13] It is only in mutual, reciprocal recognition that self-consciousness is satisfied: here, self-consciousness does not strive to be independent of the other, but to be free with and through the other.

> With this, we . . . have before us the concept *of spirit*: . . . this absolute substance which is the unity of the different independent self-consciousnesses which, in their opposition, enjoy perfect freedom and independence: "I" *that is "We" and "We" that is "I."*[14]

Let us look briefly at Hegel's phenomenology of unequal recognition.

What definitively characterizes our self-consciousness—what makes us call it "self-consciousness"—is our awareness *of* ourselves *as* selves. The primary phenomenon of this self-experience is our lived sense of ourselves as free. In fact, "Freedom" ["*Freiheit*"] is itself a technical term that Hegel reserves for the specific forms of self-experience that he calls "Stoicism," "Scepticism," and "Unhappy Consciousness" (which we will study below in chapter 7), but I am using the term here in its familiar non-technical sense. We feel free, roughly speaking, when we encounter our situation as something from which we have sufficient detachment so as not to be determined by it, and we experience ourselves as having sufficient initiative to independently shape that situation. Other people fit uncomfortably into this experience.

In an eminently practical way, other people—who are "free" like us—can make choices that conflict with our own choices, and can thus inhibit our ability to carry out our plans. You, for example, might shut the window that I had just opened, thereby frustrating my efforts to cool off in the breeze. Notice, then, that your choice to shut the window was not just a choice about the window—it was also a choice about me. In explicitly choosing to close the window, you implicitly chose to oppose me. Your opposition to me may well have been unintentional—indeed, you may not have known that I just opened the window—but *for me* your action has the significance of an act of opposition. Indeed, whereas in feeling myself to be free I feel myself able to dictate to my situation, here my situation dictates to me, and my very sense of freedom—my self-consciousness—is challenged. Though most of us can cope with this most of the time, we all surely have witnessed others or ourselves responding to such opposition with a range of counter-actions, running from mild emotional resentment to extreme anger. Sometimes, indeed, such "conflicts of will" lead to fist-fights or worse. Let us reflect upon this range of possible responses.

Note, first, that this is a range of *responses*. Our counter-action is in each case an enactment of the freedom we identified above inasmuch as it is not necessitated by the situation but is rather how we express our own attitude toward that situation. Indeed, it is precisely because these are enactments of freedom that we can learn to respond differently. If we reflect upon the differences between the different responses, especially between the extremes of "dealing with it" and fist-fighting, we can see that they reflect different *interpretations* of the situation, and, specifically, different interpretations *of the nature of self-consciousness.* Consider first a familiar portrayal of the fist-fight: one person opposes another—intentionally or unintentionally—and the other says "Oh yeah?" and then punches the first. The expression "Oh yeah?"—or the similar and equally familiar "I'll show you"—is telling here, because it conveys the definitive idea that this gesture—punching—somehow answers effectively to the initial experience of opposition, as if to *prove* that opposition wrong. The fighting response imagines that bodily force can force upon the other will the recognition of its error. Consider, in contrast, the attitude of "dealing with it," which acknowledges—either resignedly or cooperatively—that the other is something to which one must accommodate oneself. The accommodating response recognizes the other's will to be (at least) the equal of one's own, whereas the fighting response denies that the will of the other is a reality that one must accept. These two responses, then, are different stances on the nature of (the other's) self-consciousness, one interpreting it as subject to bodily force (which is itself a reflection of one's own will), one interpreting it as something to which one's own will is answerable. Each response is an expression of freedom, and this in the form of interpretation of the nature of self-consciousness. Hegel's study "The Independence and Dependence of Self-Consciousness" describes and analyzes different variants on the "fighting" response in order to identify a problem intrinsic to the interpretation of self-consciousness implied in this response.

The "Stuggle to the Death" is the stance in which one person responds to the will of the other with a fighting "Oh yeah?" and the other responds in kind. When two free individuals each interpret their situation of dealing with the other as one in which the other's opposition must be proven false by force, a life and death struggle ensues: this logic of the forceful denial of the other will not end until either the participants change their responses or one of them dies. Notice that as long as both are fighting, each says to the other "Oh yeah?" with equal weight: each through the blows he lands says, effectively, "You think it's you who matters, but I'll show you that you're wrong." What Hegel invites us to notice here is that, even with the blow that ultimately ends the life of the other, the intended "showing," the "proof," is not accomplished. The resistant will of the other has been stopped, but that will *as such* was never defeated: such a defeat would only happen were *that will,* that freedom, to *acknowledge* its defeat, to *be shown*, as the "I'll show you" promised. In death, life ended, but the will never relented. Indeed, we anticipated this in referring to the blows as "saying": though the blows take the form of bodily force—that is, they are one body making an impact on another body—the *intention* of the agent is to *express* something *to the other will*: they are *gestures*. The stuggle to the death reflects a confused interpretation of the situation, in which the self-conscious agent simultaneously (and self-contradictorily) treats its own action as imposing bodily force on a body (a matter of mechanics) and as expressing its self-conscious desire to another self-conscious desire (a matter of language). Further, this confusion points to the inherent failure of fighting as a strategy: to respond to the other with bodily force is to imply that the other is a body—that is, to deny the reality of the other's will—yet it was only and precisely the other's will—the other's opposition—that motivated the struggle. What one wants is for the other's will to relent, but this is not a result that bodily force as such can cause. The very fact that one participates in a struggle to the death implicitly reveals that one seeks the *recognition* of one's own will by the will of the other, even as one incoherently responds to the evidence of that other will by denying its reality as such.

Another variant on the "fighting" response is the use of force, not to cause the elimination of the other will, but to cause the capitulation of the other will. In struggling to the death, one fails to acknowledge that it is really the recognition of one's will by the other that one seeks; one can use force, however, precisely in order to win such recognition. In the most literal situation of slavery (the situation Hegel describes), in which one threatens force in order to win from the other the other's compliance with one's will, or in more figurative "enslavements" in which one uses analogous threats (of humiliation, abandonment, and so on) to achieve a position of domination over another, we acknowledge that the other's will is important to us, but we try to manipulate that will by indirect means: we want that will to recognize the authority of our own will without ourselves having to acknowledge the authority of that other will. Such strategies are, again, self-contradictory in principle, since our very desire of that will has already implicitly acknowledged its authority, which is what we explicitly deny. Such strategies are also practical failures as well, in that the "authority" we win for ourselves can never be the authority we desire, and this for two reasons. Practically, we rely upon the compliant efforts of the other in carrying out our desires, which indicates that we are dependent upon those others, even as we claim for ourselves independent authority. Emotionally or existentially, the failure is even greater: when we hold slaves and demand of them that they say "You are strong, sexy, and powerful, and I love you," we have not thereby won the love and admiration for which we had hoped precisely because this recognition is not given freely, but is coerced. We seek to have our status elevated by the other's recognition, but since the premise of our strategy is the non-authority of the other's will, such recognition is *ipso facto* unsatisfactory. Like the struggle to the death, the strategy of enslavement is an interpersonal failure in principle, because it simultaneously depends upon and denies the equality of the other's will with one's own (a point we will revisit in chapter 8). As with the struggle to the death, so with the strategy of domination, the attempt to win recognition through the use or threat of violent bodily force lives in denial of the intersubjective equality that is presupposed in the gestural weight that such violence actually depends upon to be effective.

These problems of inequality of recognition that Hegel studies are precisely what characterize the sorts of interpersonal relationships that Laing identifies as giving rise to an ontologically insecure character, and the study of Hegel's argument here can shed much light on the conditions in which healthy human development is possible. My goal here, however, is not to study the dialectic of these forms of recognition or to attend to the problems involved in healthy character formation that arise from the encountering of such interpersonal strategies in the course of childhood development. Instead, I am interested in Hegel's idea that, as Laing argues with respect to ontological security, healthy psychological life depends on becoming habituated to a sense of self that is defined by relationships of mutual, equal recognition: well-formed, self-conscious personhood is thus a matter of character, and character developed precisely through habituation to patterns of interpersonal exchange. In discussing Hegel's analyses of the struggle to the death and the relationship of master and slave, I have emphasized that, under the guise of bodily interaction, what is actually being enacted is a system of communication. What I specifically want to consider here is the form of communication that provides the context for this interpersonal negotiation and personal formation. I noted above that this negotiation is primarily affective and practical, rather than conceptual and theoretical (and this was the subject of chapter 5). What I want to consider in particular is the idea, further, that this affective and practical medium of self-articulation is also fundamentally a *narrative* medium. Let us consider this sense in which our healthy, self-conscious identity is fundamentally a narrative identity.

As well-developed adults, we are accustomed to establishing our judgments about the world by gathering evidence and assessing it conceptually. We also parse out our activity, differentiating one area of concern from another, and practice a kind of personal division of labor, exercising our skills in dealing with one topic when we have time but patiently "putting it on hold" while we deal with other, more pressing issues. In short, we have, in general, a very orderly and self-controlled approach to life-interpretation and management. From this adult perspective, learning and interpretation seems like very well-defined and self-directed activities.

For the child, however, the clear sense of herself is not yet well-developed; how she will come to differentiate herself from the world and from others is precisely *what is to be developed* through her growth and learning. Similarly, the skills for collecting, sorting, categorizing, and judging information are the skills she will be working at developing as she grows.[15] In other words, all of the given structures we rely upon in our adult situations of interpretation are for the child, on the contrary, precisely the structures she has to develop through the process of interpretation. If the process of childhood learning does not take the form of adult "scientific" investigation, what form does it take? What is the form that its meaningful and formative dialogue with others takes?

The engagement with intersubjective meaning *out of which* well-defined conceptuality emerges is, as I suggested above, an affective and practical participation in *narrative.* Our learning begins in *stories,* and stories in which we *participate.*[16] It is from out of these stories that precisely delineated, systematic identities gradually percolate up. To grasp this model of learning, imagine yourself moving to a large new city. I will describe my own experience of moving to Toronto, an experience that many others have confirmed to be typical of such a move.

When I initially moved to Toronto, the city felt like a fertile, vibrant space, alive with activities and identities with which I was not familiar, but which seemed exciting and alluring. As I traveled through the city spaces, they seemed alive with lines of force and meaning, an intrinsic orientation that I could recognize (or imagine) to be there, but whose delineations I could not clearly discern. Through my own practices of engaging with city life, typically with the guidance of others who were experienced, longer-term residents of the city, I gradually became familiar with certain activities—going out for dinner in the Greek area (which involved riding the subway, walking down the avenue on which the older Greek people typically took their evening promenade, smelling the aromas of olives, grilled lamb, and strong cheeses, and participating with the specific community of strangers and friends that this activity typically involved), strolling down Queen Street (which involved looking in shop windows, observing with interest the activities of "downtown people" as they conducted their lives on the street, navigating traffic and traffic lights at intersections, periodically buying books, records, or street food, and listening to the snippets of music coming from stores, apartment windows, or passing cars), shopping in Kensington Market (which involved hearing a mélange of different languages—Italian, Cantonese, Gujarati, Portuguese, Yiddish, English—and seeing a range of different dressing styles, ranging from the Hasidic Jewish earlocks and hats to the North American "punk" studded leather jackets and safety-pin-pierced cheeks, navigating through pedestrians, delivery persons, and shop-keepers, all of whom competed for use of the sidewalk, brushing past "hawkers" calling one to buy goods or donate money, smelling the scents of butcher shops, bakeries, and cheese shops, mixed with the aroma of roasting coffee and the incense of "head shops," listening to the live music of buskers, and dropping in and out of used clothing stores), and so on. My familiarity with these activities led to a familiarity with particular locations—the big park far out on Queen Street, the Italian restaurant near the university, the bakery in Chinatown, and so on. It was from this context that I then had some surprising discoveries.

As I spent more time with the city, and gradually became more familiar with some areas and engaged in more and more different activities around town, I had a number of experiences of coming to recognize, unexpectedly, that "this is right beside that!" What I discovered was that, for example, a location I had come to notice in my activities in the Italian area on College Street (which I thought of as quite close to the university where I studied) was situated on the same cross-street as a location I frequented on Queen Street (which I thought of as very far away from the university). My lived sense of the space of one set of activities was formerly not systematically integrated with my lived sense of the space of another set of activities except by the very limited sense that, if I went back over there and took a bus to that spot, then I could walk to that other place: only through very specific and localized activities did I have a way of connecting one spatial domain with another. I was, consequently, frequently surprised when I discovered connections between these spatial domains that I formerly lived as self-contained domains, heterogeneous to each other. I would frequently comment, "It never occurred to me that this place was right beside that place," and, indeed, discovering the spatial contiguity of two locations that were otherwise dissociated in my experience often led me to recognize that I would often have been factually wrong if I had assessed how close or far such locations were to each other based upon my lived sense of their placement. Over time, this last experience of learning the spatial co-ordination of different locations led into my developing a knowledge of the objective "map" of the city, and this became my primary frame of reference for thinking about the space of the city.

In this history of my relationship to the space of Toronto (a history

I believe to be typical of the way people relate to new spaces), I identify three distinct stages. Initially, the space was a mysterious and amorphous environment, alluring but opaque, oriented by lines of force with which I could not identify and pregnant with possibilities for involvement. Next I came to know it in determinate, localized ways: I knew situations, not things, and those situations had an inherent narrative to them, a story of when we go there, how we get there, what we do there, whom I see there, and, ultimately, who I am there. Finally, I developed a universal map of the grid of the unified space of the city, a space indifferent to the specificities of local narrative from which my initial experience of the locations developed.

I have told this story because I think it demonstrates well the way in which identities percolate up from situations of practical, affective immersion in narrative situations. The situations I dealt with were first, roughly, wholes, and it was only through a history of practical engagement with these wholes that I gradually developed a sense of the more specific identities—this storefront and that, this clerk, the difficulties at this intersection, how many streets one passes before the lights, and so on—contained within those wholes. Further, the characteristics of these situations called for certain ways of engaging, and so who I was to be was articulated by them in the same process by which they articulated their own character: I am, apparently, a customer, a tourist, a white guy, a target, a local who can give directions, someone who gets in the way on the busy sidewalk, a young hipster, etc. The different situations—situations that are human, thingly, spatial, and sensuous all at once—recognize me in various ways, beckoning me, shunning me, affirming me, and ignoring me according to what turn out to be my relevant and salient features. As my practical involvement with the situation develops, and the determinate features of its identity gradually percolate up to the surface of my experience, so too does a sense of my own identity in that situation percolate up to me. It is, in short, through my coming to participate affectively and practically in the narrative of the situation that my situationally and intersubjectively defined sense of self-identity comes to be formed.

This story of my becoming a Torontonian can help us to understand how a child comes to have its sense of self-identity emerge. The child is thrown into a situation of which he has no former experience, and, though he has, no doubt, great innate resources for perception, reasoning, morality, and language—the resources of *logos*, as Aristotle says[17]—he nonetheless must learn everything about the significance of these resources and about how to enact and deploy these resources through participation in this situation into which he is born. This situation will precisely be defined for the child by his affectivity, his practice, and by the narrativity of the situation as that is presented to him by his parents or whoever else defines the intersubjective context of his formative home environment.

Through their behavior—the way they set up a living environment, the way they interact with it, and, within this context, the way they interact with the child—parents (or whoever is in the parental role) will effectively articulate their "story," they will express their narrative sense of their world, themselves, and the child. Just as the child is learning his own sense of self below the level of explicit theoretical perception, so are the parents expressing themselves below the level of explicit language and behind their own explicitly reflective self-interpretation. This is why, as psychoanalysis and existential psychology show, it is their neuroses that parents pass on to their children; that is, they pass on the affective, practical "take" on things that they themselves habitually developed as the matrix for their own sense-making.[18]

We live in language—that is, we establish the basic parameters of our sense of ourselves and our relation to the world in and through the dialogue we enact with our significant others. This language, however, is not the language of grammar textbooks, but is the figured, oriented, and charged language of story. We develop a sense of ourselves by "feeling out" how our received narratives articulate us, how we can find ourselves in those stories. Hegel marks out a parallel structure when he discusses the development of the forms of ancient Greek literature. Greek literature—the shared stories in which the ancient Greeks recognized themselves as a community—began as the epic, the narrative of the Greek nation: Hegel here refers to "the earliest language, the *epic* as such."[19] It is only subsequently that this literature developed into tragedy, in which the drama of personal *pathos* becomes thematic: the "first-person" position, in other words, *comes into being within* the context of narrative.

> This higher language, that of tragedy, gathers closer together the dispersed moments of the inner essential world and the world of action. . . . In regard to form, the language ceases to be narrative because it enters into the content [the language is now content, i.e., it becomes dialogue], just as the content ceases to be one that is imaginatively presented. The hero is himself the speaker, and the performance displays . . . *self-conscious* human beings.[20]

Here, in these stages of the development of a cultural literature, we see the process by which a self-conscious subject emerges and assumes its self-active position within, and within the figured and oriented terms of, a founding narrative. In an analogous way, it is the stories passed on to us by our significant others that are formative for our identities. Who are these significant others? Most immediately, it is the family that provides the significant others for our most basic processes of self-formation.[21] These families themselves, however, do not exist in a vacuum. Though we, as children, may have little perception of it, our families are in fact situated in a larger social world. Our "family story" is itself typically situated in a larger cultural narrative, and, through initiation into our family's narrative, we are also initiated into cultural membership. Let us consider now this supra-familial cultural narrativity that provides the context for our intra-familial formation.

Religion and Language

"Ethicality" is the name Hegel uses to describe the way in which we live from an embeddedness in a social fabric that has a shape and orientation given by values that have been handed down and taken up practically: our "ethical" life is the "home base" of beliefs and values that command our perception rather than being objects of our theoretical cognition. Describing our relationship to such "ethical" values, Hegel writes,

> The *relationship* of self-consciousness to them is equally simple and clear. They *are*, and nothing more; this is what constitutes the awareness of its relationship to them. . . . They *are*. If I inquire after their origin and confine them to the point whence they arose, then I have transcended them; for now it is I who am the universal, and *they* are the conditioned and limited. If they are supposed to be validated by *my* insight, then I have already denied their unshakeable, intrinsic being, and regard them as something which, for me, is perhaps true, but also is perhaps not true. Ethical disposition consists just in sticking steadfastly to what is right, and abstaining from all attempts to move or shake it, or derive it. . . . [I]t is right because it is what is right. . . . By acknowledging the *absoluteness* of the right, I am within the ethical substance; and this substance is thus the *essence* of self-consciousness.[22]

Whereas we normally experience ourselves as reflective, self-conscious beings who are free to evaluate different perspectives—we can take up a theoretical attitude toward proposals others might make about what is right or wrong, and so on—*our very ability to have this perspective is rooted in an embrace of values that is not thus theoretical.* It is only on the basis of a living embrace of a value-laden, socially shared perspective that we are able to adopt a meaningful, interpretive stance upon the world. We think *from* an original participation in a social "interpretation" of the world, and this participation is not itself an enactment of the detached, theoretical stance it enables.

What is the character of this pre-theoretical stance? What is the character of this lived perspective that precedes our experience of existing as separate, self-conscious individuals? What is the nature of this inhabitation of the world that precedes the alienation of subject and object, that precedes the separation of self from others? Like the experience of the child, this original ethical existence is the experience of finding oneself in a narrative, and this narrative that forms the foundation of our social life is the basic phenomenon of religion.

Just as the well-formed individual self does not precede its recognition of itself in and through intersubjective narrative, so a well-formed community does not precede its enactment as the carrying on of a narrative. A community exists, that is (as we have already anticipated in referring to Hegel's discussion of Greek epic and tragedy), as the handing down of stories, articulated in word and deed, in tale and in ritual practice: "we" is originally "the people of the story," "the people of the myth." In our well-developed twenty-first century world, the term "religion" carries with it a complex array of associations, ranging from animal sacrifice, to priests, to mosques, to confession, to "saying grace," and so on. The fundamental phenomenon of religion, however, is this collective embrace of a story in and through which a community finds itself: "Religion," Hegel writes in the introduction to his lectures on the *Philosophy of History*, "is the sphere where a people gives itself the definition of what it regards as the True."[23] Religious practices and stories are handed down ritually over time as "what must be handed down." Their origins and their motivations are opaque and the reasons for the urgency of their perpetuation are not known beyond the sense that they *are* true. Attempts will be made within a culture to make sense of those practices, and these theoretical justifications, too, will be handed down, but the myths and rituals themselves do not derive from those theoretical stances. These un-understood, "uncaused" determinacies of myth and ritual—a kind of cross-generational gossip, essentially—are the rich narrative context within which our sense of world and sense of self percolates up.[24] These practices, these opaque, non-conceptual fabrics of social life, are in fact articulating the identity of self and world, self and society, self and others: they are the narrative fabric telling us who we are.[25] These opaque religious practices are the original form of a community's self-consciousness, and thus the original matrix of our own, individual self-consciousness.

Chapter VII, "Religion," in Hegel's *Phenomenology of Spirit,* is the attempt to read the sense implied in these determinacies of myth and ritual, to see how a communal self-consciousness is enacted within these non-conceptual fabrics of social life. I will not pursue the details of that interpretation here—that will be the subject for chapter 13—but I want instead to note only the basic experiential role of religion.[26] We are accustomed to thinking of society as a world with courts, schools, trade centers, and sports clubs, but these are all developments *within* societies established through and around traditions of burial practice, sacrifice, song, and dance. These established institutions—many of them "secular"—are not an alternative to, but are developments within, this original religious matrix, developments in and through which our very sense of our humanity—our self-consciousness—and our establishing of the means for its satisfaction are gradually introduced and refined. In his *Encyclopaedia of the Philosophical Sciences,* Hegel writes:

> Thus for self-consciousness religion is the "basis" of moral life and of the state. It has been the monstrous blunder of our times to try to look upon these inseparables as separable from one another, and even as mutually indifferent. The view taken of the relationship of religion and the state has been that, whereas the state had an independent existence of its own, springing from some force and power, religion was a later addition, something desirable perhaps for strengthening the political bulwarks, but purely subjective in individuals:—or it may be, religion is treated as something without effect on the moral life of the state, i.e., its reasonable law and constitution which are based on a ground of their own.[27]

The phenomenological interpretation of religion we are developing, however, reveals on the contrary that "the secular" is not an alternative to, but a development of, "the religious":

> The Philosophy of Religion has to discover the logical necessity in the progress by which [1] the Being, known as the Absolute, assumes fuller and firmer features; [2] it has to note to what particular feature the kind of cultus corresponds—and then [3] to see how the secular self-consciousness, the consciousness of what is the supreme vocation in man—in short how the nature of a nation's moral life, the principle of its law, of its actual liberty, and of its constitution, as well as of its art and

> science, corresponds to the principle which constitutes the substance of a religion. That all these elements of a nation's actuality constitute one systematic totality, that one spirit creates and informs them, is a truth on which follows the further truth that the history of religions coincides with the world-history.[28]

Religion, in short, is not an optional dimension of life, and religious faith is not a matter of "Do you believe in this theory of reality or not?" (which is how religion is often understood from *within* the theoretical consciousness to which it gives rise); on the contrary, religion is the fundamental context of sharing a world within which the possibility for things like reflective choice become possible, and faith, properly speaking, is the commitment to these original shared terms—the ritual, practical narrative—within which cohabitation is first enacted.

Before law and before science, religion is the framework and fabric of social communication, of our cohabitation.[29] We saw above that it is our inherent trajectory to seek the recognition of others, and that we are satisfied only in situations of equal recognition. Religion is the medium within which this happens: religion is the joint embrace of the terms of shared living, the embrace of the terms in which we will articulate to ourselves and to each other our mutuality of recognition. Both socially and personally, therefore, freedom and self-defining self-identity emerge from these religious narratives. We can imagine this according to the threefold pattern I identified above in my relation to the spatiality of life in Toronto.

As a child, one is born into a matrix of cultural behavior into which one is to be initiated, a rich, determinate mix of ritual practices and stories that promise meaning but are initially opaque. Without ever having an overarching theory—indeed, one is a child and is precisely developing the resources for having abilities such as "espousing a theory"—one "learns the ropes," making sense of oneself in the terms offered, gradually having a localized sense of self "percolate up" in tandem with the emerging sense of the terms of the world. This second stage—the stage in which we unquestioningly understand ourselves in the terms of our cultural, religious heritage, living *from* that heritage, without thereby having deep insight *into* that heritage—is the stage at which most of us live, most of the time.

Through our religious, cultural narratives, we establish the context for mutual recognition, that is, the medium within which we can establish our own freedom with respect to the freedom of others and with respect to the determinate parameters of the natural world: our religious culture is our language, our shared terms, and the terms of our sharedness. It is by growing up into our religious traditions—"learning the ropes" of our cultural modes of shared communication—that we come to establish a sense of ourselves as community members and self-responsible individuals, as *persons*. A fundamental part of this growing up is precisely learning to be "theoretical," that is, learning to be someone who develops the sort of "map" I identified above as "stage 3" of my initiation into inhabiting Toronto. Our religions function as the medium for our establishing a situation of mutual recognition—a situation in which we can realize our freedom—and it is the natural trajectory of these religions to call for thinking: to call for individuals to take responsibility for understanding themselves and their situations.

Learning to function as a free individual—a self-responsible person, recognized as such by others (whom Hegel calls the "stoic"[30])—is not, however, the end of the story either of personal development or of religion. It is characteristic of all the great world religions—Islam, Hinduism, Christianity, Judaism, Buddhism—that they offer the resources for and cultivate the development of free, rational individuals. To embrace the stance of "thinking individual" is not the same, however, as in fact establishing the universal "map" of one's environment; in other words, the religious analogue to the third stage I identified in my inhabitation of Toronto has not been sufficiently established simply in the establishing of the stance of self-reflective individuality. This is because such a stance of self-reflective individuality can exist precisely without understanding its own foundations in religious life.

Our religions are the materials *from* which we enact our rational individuality but our religions are not automatically the object *of* our rational insight. We can, and typically do, live as rational individuals without having understood the opaque, religious foundations of that very rationality. Indeed, it is typical of our attitude as rational individuals to misinterpret both our rationality and our religion. Putatively speaking on behalf of reason, we typically portray it as something independent of and opposed to religion—the stance of "enlightenment" or "pure insight" that Hegel discusses in his analysis of "Culture"—and, putatively speaking on behalf of religion, we misinterpret religion—the stance of "faith."[31] In fact, however, our reason is itself the flowering of the resources *for being free* that are our religions. There is a fundamental difference, in other words, between how a religion in fact fosters our growing up and how either secular or theological reflection theoretically interprets its meaning.

As the matrix for recognition and freedom—the matrix for the fulfilling of our nature as self-conscious beings—religion, in sponsoring our self-interpretive self-insight, should ultimately usher in a stance in which we understand religion itself as this very sponsoring, that is, the religious impulse is ultimately fulfilled in our understanding the foundations of our own rationality to be the opacities of religious narrative and our understanding our rationality to be the fulfillment of these narratives.[32] But to understand the relation of one's reason and one's religion in this way has consequences for one's understanding of reason and religion in general.

Religions will always be the specific practices of specific communities—the very practices whereby they enact themselves *as* communities. For that reason, religion, the very matrix of the equality of recognition, will always be multiple, that is, religion will always exist as a multiplicity of determinate, and therefore *exclusive,* systems of cohabitation. The imperative of religion—the requirement incumbent upon religion precisely by virtue of its nature as religion—is to recognize that its necessarily determinate and exclusive narratives provide different localized contexts for the emergence of a cohabitation that is *to-be-universal.* Though our participation in a religious culture initially takes the form of a commitment to the essentiality of its terms of reference for establishing equality of recognition, the enacting of that project of equal recognition ultimately demands that we transcend our commitment to the ultimacy of those terms and recognize the comparable legitimacy of the terms of other religious cultures for enacting the same project of enabling our freeedom. In the terms of my example of inhabiting Toronto, we must recognize that our religion and the other's religion are "on the same grid." It is only in recognizing the way these different local religious communities are constituent members of the same shared space of freedom that we enact what I identified above as the third stage of self-consciousness.

Conclusion

Our self-consciousness is rooted in a dialectic of recognition in and through which we need to establish a secure sense of what it means to be "I." It is fundamentally through coming to find ourselves within social narratives that we accomplish this self-consciousness, and our enactment of self-consciousness within this narrative context is not completed until we understand our environment as *for sharing,* which means until we establish the terms of *co*-habiting. We will never lose our narrative roots, however, and our "transcendence" of our finite roots will therefore not be their disappearance: our roots are the very terms *from which* we engage, and they are therefore our only route to universality, our only route to sharing. For this reason, the ultimate "map" of our shared world will not be a Cartesian grid of indifferent space in which all particularities are effaced but will be, rather, a multi-cultural dialogue—a dialogue in which our ineffaceable particularities remain, but are constantly challenged to be open to the unanticipated demands of creating a home for freedom, the unanticipated demands of recognizing the other. Accomplishing this dialogue requires that we must find within our own religious-cultural terms a plasticity that allows them to articulate *the same world* that is articulated within the others' terms; and, indeed, it requires that the others' terms evince a comparable plasticity. In short, the imperative of equal recognition is ultimately the imperative to establish a co-inhabitation of a shared world through a multi-cultural dialogue in which what is fundamentally taken up within each cultural heritage is the inherent plasticity by which its terms can be resources for sponsoring the freedom of self-consciousness. "It is the nature of humanity," Hegel writes, "to press onward to agreement with others; human nature only really exists in an achieved community of consciousness."[33]

7

The Call of the Beyond: Unhappy Consciousness and the Structure of Hegel's Argument

Section B of the *Phenomenology of Spirit,* "Self-Consciousness," occupies a distinct logical space in the structure of the book that also makes it distinctively important for us as readers. It comes between section A, "Consciousness," which addresses those attitudes that ignore subjectivity in favor of an apprehension of a universal—an absolute—reality, taken as object, and the untitled section C, which addresses those attitudes in which the standpoint of the singular self has been in some way transcended. The single chapter of "Self-Consciousness" on the other hand is the one that explicitly addresses our own situation as finite; that is, it addresses those experiences in which we recognize ourselves as on the "hither" side of reality. Section B, "Self-Consciousness" addresses those attitudes—from which we cannot escape—in which we grapple with our *in*ability to be fully "present to" meaning and reality, whereas the other sections either presume it or have accomplished it somehow.

The single chapter of "Self-Consciousness" has two main parts. Chapter IV, part A, "Independence and Dependence of Self-Consciousness," addresses ways in which we try to assert our dominance over our other in order to deny the reality of our finitude, to deny our limitation by its power. The attitude of desire in general (discussed in the introductory section of chapter IV that precedes part A) is one of treating oneself as the truth of reality, living only to conceal the difference between oneself and the other.[1] As we saw in chapters 4 and 5, living from this attitude meets its limit in the encounter with a reality—an other—that likewise (i.e., reciprocally) denies the autonomy of its other, that is, denies oneself.[2] As we noted in chapter 6, the stances discussed in chapter IV, part A (the "Struggle to the Death" and "Lordship and Bondage") are the practices that try to efface the significance of the experience of a reality that explicitly lives as a denial of one's own exclusive reality.[3] Chapter IV, part B, "Freedom of Self-Consciousness," addresses ways in which we grapple with the question of how we can be real and how there can be meaningfulness given that we are defined by and answerable to a beyond. The first attitude, "Stoicism," affirms the beyond but denies its relevance, and aims to isolate itself in its own hermetically sealed reality.[4] The second attitude, "Scepticism," denies the possibility of a coherent experience of that beyond.[5] The third and final attitude, "the Unhappy Consciousness," is the stance that honestly grapples with the existential problem of meaning, that is, the problem—definitive of our existence—that is raised by our being a "here" in relation to a reality "there."[6]

Section B, "Self-Consciousness," is important as a whole for its role in the argument of the *Phenomenology of Spirit,* and the figure of "The Unhappy Consciousness" is particularly important because it is the completed form of self-consciousness, the form that provides the logical context for all further developments of self-consciousness.[7] In what follows, we will see what the basic experience of "unhappy consciousness" is, and see how it both completes the study of individual self-consciousness and provides the logical matrix for the remainder of the *Phenomenology of Spirit.* We will see (in outline), in other words, how the shapes of section C—"Reason," "Spirit," "Religion," and "Absolute Knowing"—are all forms of unhappy consciousness; how it is, in other words, that what might first appear to be a turn to the irrational and an abrogation of self-consciousness is in fact the very form of truth, the very form of the fulfillment of self-consciousness.

Unhappy Consciousness: Freedom as Faith

We are explicitly self-conscious beings and, as such, are inherently free. We fulfill our self-conscious nature—we become for ourselves what we are in ourselves—when we assume our freedom: when we recognize our free nature and embrace the powers, responsibilities, and realities it makes available to us, and in "Freedom of Self-Consciousness" Hegel studies the three forms—"Stoicism, Scepticism, and the Unhappy Consciousness"—in which we carry out this self-conscious appropriation of ourselves as free beings.[8]

Our most immediate experience of being self-conscious in our freedom is the experience of ourselves as being in control of our own will and of being able to determine for ourselves and on our own what things mean to us. This stance, the stance of "stoicism," is one's experience of oneself as self-defining, "a consciousness which, as the infinitude of consciousness or as its own pure movement, is aware of itself as essential being."[9]

> I *am free,* because I am not in an *other,* but remain simply and solely in communion with myself, and the object, which is for me the *essential* being, is in undivided unity my being-for-myself.[10]

The stoic finds her own sense of self-determination to be the foundation of meaning, the criterion by reference to which the significance of appearances can be judged.

The sceptic, on the contrary, recognizes that this self-experience upon which the stoic relies is as much an "appearance" as are putative experiences of the "non-self," with the result that self-experience is no more sure than anything else.

> Scepticism causes to vanish . . . not only objective reality as such, but its own relationship to it. . . . What vanishes is the determinate element, or the moment of difference, which, whatever its mode of being and whatever its source, sets itself up as something fixed and immutable. . . . But it is just in this process that this consciousness, instead of being self-identical, is in fact nothing but a purely casual, confused medley, the dizziness of a perpetually self-engendered disorder.[11]

Our deeper experience of freeedom, in other words, is an anxiety of meaninglessness and uncertainty, rather than a confident self-possession:

> It is itself aware of this; for itself maintains and creates this restless confusion. Hence it also admits to it, it owns to being a wholly contingent, single, and separate consciousness—a consciousness which is *empirical,* which takes its guidance from what has no reality for it, which obeys what is for it not an *essential* being, which does those things and brings to realization what it knows has no truth for it.[12]

In scepticism, in other words, freedom is recognized not as the source of meaning, but as the source of meaninglessness. As Jean Wahl notes, such scepticism is deeper than the academic, epistemological doubt we often associate with the term "scepticism," and is rather exemplified in the attitude of existential disbelief of Ecclesiastes, who claims that "all is vanity."[13]

But beyond these stances of stoicism and scepticism, there is yet a further stance of freedom, a further stance of meaning, and that is the stance in which one *finds oneself* implicated in a meaning of which one is not the author. This is a stance that retains an experience of free selfhood, but that neither considers itself to be self-defining, nor finds meaning to be inherently non-compelling, but finds instead a unique experience *within its free selfhood* of compelling and authoritative meaning. This is the stance of unhappy consciousness.

The stance of unhappy consciousness is that of the individual who recognizes that the compellingly authoritative meaning and significance of its own reality is found in its answerability to a beyond, and that the call of that beyond is already constitutively present within itself. The stoic had imagined that the call of the beyond could be ignored through hermetic self-enclosure, while the sceptic found this self-enclosure to be vacant. The unhappy consciousness, however, finds that the call of the beyond is there in the innermost depths of itself: the most beyond, in other words, is equally the most intimate. This stance—the stance that completes the development of self-consciousness—is familiar to us: as H. S. Harris writes, "[t]he ordinary name for this . . . is 'faith.'"[14]

The stance of self-consciousness in this its completed form is that it experiences itself as ineluctably called by its authoritative beyond, to which it must acknowledge its subordination. It is subordinate in that it cannot master that which calls it, and in that it cannot escape from the imperative of answerability. This self-consciousness looks to a reality beyond that it cannot master, but upon which it must wait: "The Unhappy Consciousness," says Harris,

> finds itself looking into a thought-world whose content can only become known to it if the supersensible Other freely elects to *give* knowledge. . . . The revelation must be *given*; it must come from the absolute Self as an act of grace.[15]

This subordination, however, is not oppression or a failure of recognition of the sort experienced by the slave. For the unhappy consciousness, the call comes from within itself, and it is a call to itself to be maximally devoted to answering—it is not an effacing of its agency, but an imperative to action. The basic situation here is that one experiences an imperative to a meaningfulness that is beyond the self, and yet one *is* only this self; but equally this "beyond" *is the reality of* the self itself. As Wahl says, explaining the "unhappiness" of consciousness, "consciousness is too small for itself, because greater than itself";[16] as Harris puts it, "[t]he 'unhappiness' of finite self-consciousness consists first, therefore, in being conscious that real freedom belongs to an inner self which is . . . unknown."[17] Hegel writes:

> This *unhappy, inwardly disrupted* consciousness, since its essentially contradictory nature is for it *one* consciousness, must for ever have present in the one consciousness the other also. . . . One of them, viz. the Un-

> changeable, it takes to be the *essential* Being; but the other, the protean Changeable, it takes to be the unessential. . . . [I]t identifies itself with the changeable consciousness, and takes itself to be the unessential Being. . . . and the Unchangeable is, for it, an alien Being.[18]

The unhappy consciousness, that is, relates to its own true self as to an alien.[19]

In unhappy consciousness the self in its singularity experiences itself as defined by the absolute—the ultimate truth or reality, hence "the universal," that is, the unchanging truth or reality of all. The experience of "being defined by" is the imperative to identify with that universal: inasmuch as the unhappy consciousness experiences the "alien" absolute to be its own true self, "it cannot itself be indifferent towards the Unchangeable."[20] The singular self, however, cannot be that universal—its very singularity (by definition exclusive) holds it apart.[21] The singular self is a finite, living individual. As the early parts of the analysis of self-consciousness showed, self-consciousness is only realized in living individuals, and the first crucial "lesson" learned by the single self-consciousness (in the "struggle to the death") is that "life is as essential to it as self-consciousness."[22] This life supplies the "bonds" by which the slave is held by the master, and it sets the limits to accomplishing an identity with "the universal."[23] As Harris notes, "death, (the finitude of life generally)," is the mark of the single self-consciousness.[24] The living individual will die. It is the experience of this its mortal finitude that marks, for the unhappy consciousness, its non-identity with the absolute that is its true self.

The unhappy consciousness is our experience of our mortality, but it is the experience of mortality *as the demand to be meaningful.* Our mortality is, as Derrida might say, both the condition of the possibility and of the impossibility of meaning in that it is our mortal exclusion from the "universal" that makes for us the imperative to *realize* its significance in ourselves while simultaneously making it impossible that this imperative could ever be satisfied (i.e., eliminated). It is *as this finite individual* that the unhappy consciousness is "called," and it is precisely called to recognize itself as *inherently in communication with the absolute,* that is, as open to a universal meaning beyond itself. What Hegel is addressing is, in Harris's words,

> how there can be (as there evidently is) an "eternal" . . . standpoint within time. We *know* intuitively that this "absolute" standpoint exists.[25]

The unhappy consciousness knows—by experiencing it immediately, as the imperative of its being, not by deducing it or arguing to it—that "it matters," that is, that there "is such a thing as" "the real," "the true," or "the good." Hegel calls this stance "consciousness" to emphasize the "intuitive" character of this recognition, to highlight the way in which the unhappy consciousness is characterized by a fundamental passivity, a fundamental *in*ability to be its own ground. The unhappy consciousness is the experience of *its own reality* as something deeper than itself to which it can never be adequate.

This unhappiness of (self-)consciousness, moreover, is not penultimate to some happiness. On the contrary, the "happiness" of consciousness is the *prior* state. The ancient Greek ethical world, for example, is characterized by "happiness."[26] The "happy" consciousness of the communal spirit of the "true spirit" (in Hegel's language) is precisely shattered by the demands of singular self-consciousness for autonomy and independence from communal definition, and the singularity of self-consciousness is ineffaceable.[27]

> But from this happy state of having realized its essential character and of living in it, self-consciousness, what at first is Spirit only *immediately* and in *principle*, has withdrawn. . . . Reason *must* withdraw from this happy state. . . . [T]he single, individual consciousness as it exists immediately in the real ethical order . . . is not aware of himself as a pure individuality on his own account. But once he has arrived at this idea, as he must, then this *immediate* unity with Spirit . . . is lost.[28]

This happy "true spirit" is superseded by the merely "self-certain spirit," that is, the spirit that can never happily live in its comfortable identity with the absolute, but that must always have that identity as a question, a proposition in need of confirmation from without.[29]

Unhappy consciousness, in other words, is the final form of self-consciousness, for it is the stance in which our self-consciousness finds its own limits: it knows itself as something that ultimately exceeds its knowledge. In self-consciousness as unhappy consciousness, we *own up to* our answerability to what inherently defines us, and thereby enact our freedom in a form that corresponds to the truth about what form the nature of our freedom actually takes. As thus the true form of freedom, unhappy consciousness provides the logical matrix in which the richer developments of human life—richer than the single lives of self-conscious individuals—take place. Let us turn now to the later sections of the *Phenomenology of Spirit*—the four parts of the untitled section C—to see how these later forms realize this logic of "unhappy consciousness." Indeed, in describing unhappy consciousness above, I used a quotation from Harris, but in that quotation Harris is actually describing the *Phenomenology of Spirit* as a whole. Let me repeat that full quotation in its proper context:

> [The *Phenomenology*] is the logic of time—the explanation of how there can be (as there evidently is) an "eternal" (i.e., logical) standpoint within time. We *know* intuitively that this "absolute" standpoint exists. . . . [W]e must . . . ask *how time comprehends eternity*."[30]

In his interpretation of Hegel in *Logic and Existence,* Jean Hyppolite says something similar: "Man is the house of the Logos, of the being which reflects on itself and thinks itself," or again,

> Through this freedom, which Hegel says is the absolute Idea of history . . . man does not conquer himself as man, but becomes the house of the Universal, of the Logos of Being, and becomes capable of Truth.[31]

Harris and Hyppolite here identify the self-consciousness of single individuals as the site for the self-showing of the absolute, and this is precisely the definitive structure of unhappy consciousness. Let us now consider how, as Harris says, the "eternal" exists within time—the ways, that is, in which "the absolute is with us all along."[32]

Unhappy Consciousness and the Structure of the *Phenomenology of Spirit*

I emphasized above the ineffaceability of the standpoint of the single consciousness—"the absolute form"[33]—and the ultimacy of unhappy consciousness as an attitude of single self-consciousness. With his phenomenological description of the unhappy consciousness, Hegel has shown that self-consciousness is always defined in response to a meaning-giving reality that exceeds it. So just as much as this phenomenology is about the limits of singularity, in truly describing the experience of that singularity it is equally about what exceeds those limits, or, we might say, those limits' "own" excess. This "own excess" is the essential otherness, the essential beyond that is definitive for the single self.[34] The remaining chapters of the *Phenomenology of Spirit,* under the headings "Reason," "Spirit," and "Religion," point to further facets of this reality beyond.

In his discussion of Unhappy Consciousness, Hegel identifies three ways ("a threefold way") in which this relationship of the singular and the universal is enacted:

> There is thus a threefold way available to consciousness for how the singular is connected with the unchangeable. *Firstly* it comes to itself again

> as opposite to the unchangeable essence, and it is thrown back to the beginning of the struggle, which remains the element of the whole relation. *Secondly*, however, for it the *unchangeable* itself has *singularity in it*, so that singularity is the shape of the unchangeable in which herewith passes the whole way of existence. *Thirdly* it finds itself as this singular in the unchangeable.[35]

The "religious" form of unhappy consciousness that we most immediately picture corresponds primarily to the first two of these ways. These two are ways that construe the universal to be an independent and indifferent reality, and the singular to be inessential.[36] Within these passages Hegel primarily discusses the second of these ways, in which the call to "answering" is taken as an imperative to unite with the absolute by effacing the particularity of the single ego (a strategy that, as the case of "Absolute Freedom and Terror" will later show, is inherently contradictory, for the singularity that loses its particularity equally loses itself).[37] The third way is that in which the unhappy consciousness recognizes the mutual participation of singular and universal, that is, the way in which the universal is actually *realized in and through* the particularities of the practices of the single self. We know this third form from a number of familiar, "secular" experiences; the experience of moral duty or conscientious action is an exemplary case of this, and a consideration of this experience will be helpful for understanding how this seemingly "religious" structure of unhappy consciousness is in fact the structure of the most definitive experiences of our "secularity."

When we act out of a sense of moral duty, we feel inwardly compelled to bring into being a reality that is good in itself. In morality, I, as an individual free being, find myself called upon to "do what is right." If either my individual freedom or the worthiness-in-itself of this situation were removed, it would no longer be a situation of moral action: removing the freedom would result in the production of a good result, but not *someone's* moral *action*; removing the inherent worth of the deed would result in an action that is an expression of my personal preference, an act of subjective self-affirmation, but not something inherently and universally recognizable as "right." And what is striking in this experience is that we find this ability to act *from an experience of necessity* to be a profound experience *of freedom*; indeed, it is here, Kant argues, in this moral action in which our action is in fact commanded by a good-in-itself that is not of our making, that we experience ourselves as *autonomous*, as released to our own freedom in a way that we do not otherwise experience in our "merely subjective" behavior.[38] As we shall see below, we experience something analogous in our experiences of reasoning, of cultural belonging, and, indeed, of philosophizing. What all of these situations really share is that they are experiences of *participation in reality*. I experience myself as truly free in experiences of being commanded by necessity because *my action is what I take it to be*; reality, that is, confirms my "self-certainty," or, in the language of Kant's *Critique of Pure Reason*, subjectivity is objectivity. Freedom is surely not found in my absorption in reality, but, equally, it is not truly found in my break with reality; freedom, ultimately, is found in my experience of myself *as the agent of reality*, in my experience of reality as something within which I meaningfully participate. From another angle, then, we are seeing again what we saw in the preceding chapter through our discussion of Laing's notion of "ontological security": freedom, ultimately, is my experience of my subjectivity *as real*. This experience of my subjectivity as real, this experience of my singularity as intrinsic to "the absolute," is precisely the third form of unhappy consciousness, and it is this third way of enacting the stance of unhappy consciousness that provides the logical structure for the phenomena described in the remaining chapters of the *Phenomenology of Spirit*.

In the third enactment of unhappy consciousness, the single self-consciousness is conscious of herself *as* the legitimate agent of the absolute; that is, she recognizes that "the *single* consciousness is *in itself* the absolute essence."[39] According to the syllogistic logic of the unhappy consciousness, which involves the two extremes of the universal and the singular and the relationship that is their mediation,

> its truth is that which, in the syllogism, where the extremes appeared absolutely held apart, appears as the middle term, expressing to the unchangeable consciousness that the singular has renounced itself, and to the singular that the unchangeable is no longer for it an extreme, but is reconciled with it. This middle term is the unity directly knowing both, and relating them to one another, and the consciousness of their unity, which it expresses to consciousness and thereby to itself, to be the certainty of being all truth.[40]

The third form of unhappy consciousness, in other words, is the experience of oneself as actually speaking on behalf of the universal. This experience of "the middle," which does not efface the difference of universal and singular, but in which the self-consciousness knows herself to be "all truth," this experience of being empowered to speak on behalf of reality, is most immediately recognizable to us in reasoning, the defining experience of chapter V, "Reason."

As Harris wrote, "evidently there is" an "'eternal' standpoint within time." Whenever you ask me for the sum of 7 and 5, I can answer without hesitation, "12," *and know that I am speaking a universal and necessary truth.*

In this exemplary experience of reason, my sense of my own singularity is not lost—it is clearly I who am speaking—but I am also aware of the autonomy of the universal—what I am speaking is my own knowledge, but it is not of my own making. I am aware of myself as speaking on behalf of—with the authority of—the absolute.

This stance of reason is logically a stance of unhappy consciousness because my true self—here reason itself—remains different from me, even as I share an identity with it. I *receive* rational insight: I do not make it. I do speak on its behalf, and in that sense it is "my" ability, but it is equally an *in*ability inasmuch as it is an incomprehensible mystery to me how it works and how I receive it. This is the experience of reason, and Hegel's chapter on reason investigates in detail the breadth of ways in which one can try to comprehend reality from within this rational imperative.[41]

The power of reason is immense. It is, precisely, an ability *to know a truth absolutely*. This is what Hegel describes when he writes, "Reason is the certainty of being all *reality*."[42] Hegel continues, however, "[t]his *in-itself* or this *reality* is, however, a universal pure and simple, the pure *abstraction* of reality."[43] In legitimately invoking myself as the voice of reason, I speak on behalf of the universal and necessary truths to which all of reality is answerable. At the same time, however, reason suffers from a fundamental kind of sterility, because it is based on a notion of formal truth that is indifferent to content: when we reason, we rely on structures of necessity (laws of logic or mathematics) that are true of everything precisely because they pay no heed to the empirical specificity of anything. Reason is *entirely* and *exclusively* necessity, *entirely* and *exclusively* structures of mediation that depend upon a givenness of data that is itself inexplicable to reason. Reason depends upon, but stands outside of, empirical genesis. The expression of rational truth is absolute—absolutely true—but it is not *the* absolute truth, for it is conditioned by what it excludes, namely, empirical genesis, history, the realm, precisely, of contingency.

Recalling Wahl's remark about unhappy consciousness that it is "too small for itself, because greater than itself," we can say that reason is a way in which the single self is able to be greater than itself. Reason is the ability of the self to know and do more than it can take credit for—it can act on the basis of an agency to which it, in its singularity, is not adequate. This same structure is also true of the domain Hegel calls "Spirit," the realm of history, culture, and education.

We, as single individuals—those of us with language, anyway—all live in a context of humanity that is an accomplishment that exceeds the power and the ken of any individual (or, for that matter, any generation, or even any culture). We live in and draw upon the resources of a historical, communal, cultural world, and it is through the processes of education by which this history is passed on to us that we assume our humanity and our "individual" identities.[44] We undergo our experience *as* representatives of this traditional, cultural reality. It is a universal that calls us, and within which we as single selves participate. This, again, is logically a structure of the third form of unhappy consciousness.

The primary experience of spirit is what Hegel calls "ethicality." As we saw already in chapter 6, ethicality is the state of educated, cultural existence in which the way we have assimilated cultural traditions leads us to perceive reality as having a normative force. Sophocles' character Antigone is used by Hegel as an exemplary representative of ethicality.[45] In Sophocles' tragedy, Antigone feels herself duty-bound to bury her brother Polyneices, despite an edict by Creon, the legitimate ruler of Thebes, that Polyneices is not to be buried because he died a traitor to the city. Antigone is a young woman who is unquestioningly committed to the cultural values into which she grew up. For Antigone, at least in her normal life (prior, that is, to the crisis she faces in her conflict with Creon), the singularity of her self is not experienced as something alienating her from others and from the world (as in the attitude of stoicism), but she feels, instead, an unproblematic, natural community with her fellows and her world. She is "at home" in her world—"an objective, actual world, but a world which has completely lost the meaning for the self of something alien to it, just as the self has completely lost the meaning of being-for-self separated from the world"[46]—and confident that she acts as a representative of the will of the gods:

> [the divine] laws are the thoughts of its own absolute consciousness, thoughts which are immediately its *own*. Also, it does not *believe* in them. . . . Ethical *self*-consciousness is *immediately* one with essential being through the *universality* of the self.[47]

Here again, then, we see the third form of unhappy consciousness enacted: Antigone's self-consciousness—her lived sense of who she is—is her sense of being "real" in the sense we considered above, that is, she experiences herself in her singularity as an agent of "the absolute."

Like the attitude of "Reason," however, the attitude of "Ethicality" is one-sided, and therefore not "the" absolute, not the ultimate enactment of self-consciousness, not the ultimate enactment of freedom. We see this in the unacknowledged way in which Antigone's experience of being at home in fact rests upon a kind of "homelessness"; that is, there is an alienation of the singular from the universal—revealed in the fact that Antigone must rely upon *her own* judgment to decide how to resolve the conflict between her ethical duty as a sister to bury her brother and her ethical duty as a Theban woman to obey the leader Creon—that is presupposed but not acknowledged here.[48] This comfortable "happiness" of the true, ethical spirit that unquestioningly accepts its cultural upbringing as normatively authoritative is in fact in error about its situation and its self, for it wrongly presumes itself to be occurring in a state of natural harmony when its situation is actually a contingent development of historical human practice. While there are indeed fundamental ways in which ethicality is a fundamental and essential dimension of our self-conscious reality, our freedom will not be sufficiently realized except in experiences in which this "self-blindness" of ethicality is overcome. The "happy" ethical consciousness, then, that presumes it can speak directly on behalf of the gods, needs to acknowledge the unhappiness implicit within it. Indeed, it needs to be corrected by precisely the self-critical stance of reason that we just discussed (and it will be the dialectic of the chapter to bring it to this recognition in the notion of self-certain spirit, just as it was the dialectic of the chapter on "Reason" to bring reason to the recognition of its emptiness, and its need to be rooted in history and ethicality).

Though Antigone and the ethical consciousness in general mistake the work of history for the work of the gods, and accordingly mistake cultural particularity for natural universality, there remains something fundamentally right about the deference with which such a singular here treats "its" universal. In Antigone, or in the experience of the ethical consciousness in general, we see the huge weight of cultural accomplishment. Let us think, for a moment, about language, which is exemplary of our ethicality.

Each of us grows up in and into a language that comes to provide for us the (seemingly) obvious articulation of the parameters of the real. Our "mother tongue," our "first langauge," seems to us to be naturally authoritative for how to recognize and acknowledge whatever is. Indeed, it is only *within* the terms and the resources that the language opens up for us that we can even begin to try to understand it. Our language—itself an historical human accomplishment—is "the universal" on behalf of which each particular, singular self speaks. While we may grow beyond this original language, that growth will itself draw on its resources. And this is the character of ethicality in general. We are always embedded in—at home in—a finite cultural particularity that must itself provide us with whatever resources we might use to transcend its limitations.

So, even if the dogmatic ethical attitude is not ultimately an adequate realization of our self-consciousness, it has shown us another "absolute" beside reason, another universal whose self-giving both makes our lives meaningful and, in a sense, undermines meaning, leaving the meaning of our lives resting on a kind of "non-sense," a mysterious, given reality we can never comprehend or master. We belong to a history that makes us who we are. On its basis, we live beyond our own limits, but are therefore equally necessarily not able to live up to ourselves, "greater than ourselves and smaller than ourselves."

So far, we have established two points. We have seen ethicality (history, language, law) and reason to be two "beyonds" in which we participate, two beyonds by which we live, act, and think. Chapter VII, "Religion," investigates this same issue from another angle. Because the unhappy consciousness is a *relation* of the singular and the universal *within the same consciousness*, the story of Unhappy Consciousness must be told from the side of the singular self—the "changeable" consciousness—*and* from the side of the universal—the "unchangeable," the absolute other, the infinite object. This latter is what is accomplished in the "Religion" chapter. We have just been witnessing the reality of "the Unchangeable consciousness" *functioning within* the experience of individuals. Religion is the cultural phenomenon of *affirming that* there is such a universal. We can accept that such an affirmation in general is true, but how that affirmation is made and whether it is made truly is another matter, and the analysis of that is what is accomplished in the chapter on "Religion." In the chapters on "Reason" and "Spirit," then, we witness the playing out of the *experience of* the absolute in which we all live. In chapter VII, "Religion," we witness the playing out of the *story about* this very same absolute. Because our goal here is only to understand the logical structure of section C of the *Phenomenology of Spirit*, and to discern its relationship to the logic of Unhappy Consciousness, we will not pursue this paralleling in any detail, except insofar as it is relevant to the point of the final chapter, "Absolute Knowing," which we will now consider briefly.

The conclusions of both the "Spirit" chapter and the "Religion" chapter are basically the same, developed, respectively, from the side of the "here" and the side of the "beyond" within the experience of unhappy consciousness. The arguments of these two chapters are developed from the two sides of unhappy consciousness, and they both essentially take us back to where we began, namely, to an affirmation of the ultimacy of unhappy consciousness. Let me discuss first the "Spirit" chapter.

We are inextricably bound into an ethical order—we live in a language, in a culture, and in a history, and, inasmuch as these *give* us the very powers by which we can relate to them, they all exceed our powers. We can never remove ourselves from them, we can never comprehend them, we can never master them. We are irremediably defined by our cultural particularities. These particularities, when we relate toward them "happily"—that is, uncritically—are exclusionary and one-sided.

> [T]he ethical order exists merely as something *given*; therefore this universal spirit itself is a separate, individual spirit, and the customs and laws in their entirety are a *specific* ethical substance, which only in the higher stage, viz. in spirit's consciousness of its essence, sheds this limitation and in this knowledge alone has its absolute truth, not directly as it immediately is.[49]

Because they are historically contingent—because they are matters of "genesis," rather than "structure"—they are not universal, and one culture will develop differently from another. Our reason, however, allows us to be self-critical, to demand universality of ourselves, and thus to recognize the insufficiency of these exclusionary particularities to be adequate to the demands of our reality. It is in the attitude of morality—the self-certain spirit—that these two are brought together.[50] Morality is the attitude that sees itself as necessarily defined by its particularities, but it lives those particularities as materials for universality, that is, materials for reconciliation. Morality—specifically in its completed form of conscientious forgiveness—sees all the particularities of its world as language: language not, however, as a medium simply for reaffirming already established lines of communication (as in ethicality), but as the medium through which to establish communication with the other, with the excluded.

> This [consciousness which] . . . makes itself into a superseded *this*, thereby displays itself as in fact universal. . . . The forgiveness which it extends to the other . . . acknowledges that what [it] characterized as bad . . . is good. . . . The word of reconciliation is the *existing* spirit . . .—a reciprocal recognition that is *absolute* spirit.[51]

To be forgiving is *to reconcile onself to the particularities of the other* and so, for the forgiving attitude, particularities are not closed justifications for exclusion, but are inherently open to what is beyond. The forgiving conscience, unlike the self-mortifying second attitude of unhappy consciousness, lives its particularities as the site for realizing the universal. Here we have the singular self that has most fully enacted the logic of the third form of unhappy consciousness.

The chapter on "Religion" comes to the same conclusion from the side of the absolute. In this chapter, Hegel narrates the history of religion as the history of changing portrayals of the nature of God, changing portrayals, that is, of the ultimate nature of reality—"the absolute." Whereas in different cultures and in different contexts, God might be portrayed as light or as a world-manufacturer, in Christianity God is ultimately portrayed as love and forgiveness: as the reconciliation of the absolute with finitude.

> The *reconciliation* of the divine essence with *the other* in general and particularly with *the thought* of it, with *Evil*, is thus here represented.[52]

This Christian portrayal exemplifies the absolute religion—the final form of religion—because it recognizes the necessity that the absolute exist in and as the reconciliation of particularities.[53]

Both from the side of the experiencing, singular self and from the side of the story of the absolute, the result is the same: "[t]his reconciliation of consciousness with self-consciousness thus shows itself as brought about from two sides: on one side, in the religious spirit, and on the other side, in consciousness itself as such":[54]

> This concept fulfilled itself on one side in the self-certain spirit that *acted*, and on the other, in religion: in religion it won for consciousness the absolute content *as content* or, in the form of . . . otherness for consciousness; on the other hand, in the prior shape the form is that of the self itself, for it contains the self-certain spirit that *acts*; the self accomplishes the life of absolute spirit.[55]

Both in the terms of the divine and in the terms of the singular self—both from the side of the absolute content and from the side of the absolute form—the singular self is ultimately recognized as the site of the realization of the divine, a realization enacted as the reconciling of otherwise exclusive particularities.

Ultimately, then, *the logic* of unhappy consciousness, *our experience* of the absolute in our own self-consciousness, and *the history of religion* all point to the same conclusion, namely, that we, as self-consciousnesses, are true to ourselves ("authentic") inasmuch as we enact the project of making the particularities of our singular situation sites for universal reconciliation. Recognizing this explicitly is absolute knowing, the stance of the philosopher.

> Thus, what in religion was *content* or a form for presenting an *other*, is here the *self's* own *act*; the concept requires the *content* to be the *self's* own *act*.—For this concept is, as we see, the knowledge of the self's act

> within itself as all essentiality and all existence, the knowledge of this subject as substance and of the substance as this knowledge of its act.[56]

In this notion of the absolute—the universal—that exists only in its enactment as the opposition and reconciliation of particularities, we thus have "the" concept, the characterization, that is, of the fundamental character of reality: of a reality, indeed, that is simultaneously substance and subject, a reality in which (as we anticipated above), the singular subject participates constitutively.

> This last shape of spirit—the spirit which at the same time gives its complete and true content the form of the self and thereby realizes its concept as remaining in its concept in this realization—this is absolute knowing; it is spirit that knows itself in the shape of spirit or a *comprehensive knowing* [*das begreifende Wissen*]. . . . Spirit, *appearing* in consciousness in this element, . . . *is Science.*[57]

It is the calling of the philosopher to allow particularity to show how it can be a site for reconciliation, that is, how its own nature is to grow into its beyond, and to know reality thus is to know it in its concept [*Begriff*], is "conceptual" or "comprehensive knowing," [*das begreifende Wissen*]—"science." This is exactly what the project of dialectical phenomenology aims to display, and Hegel's *Phenomenology of Spirit* is precisely Hegel's attempt to allow determinacy to show, of its own accord, that it *is* "for the sake of" universal reconciliation. Unhappy consciousness is definitive of the character of experience, the character of reality, and their relation, and absolute knowing is the recognizing of this structure that is simultaneously an enacting of this structure.

Conclusion: The Calling of the Philosopher

"Absolute knowing" is the stance of allowing reality to show itself in its concept and thereby to fulfill itself in its concept. To enable this self-showing of reality is the philosopher's calling, the philosopher's experience of answerability to the absolute; but the philosopher is still a single individual, and absolute knowing—the stance of philosophy—is thus a stance of unhappy consciousness. Hegel's project—the constitutive demand of the project of philosophy—is to have a philosophy that has no author: the "author" (Hegel) is to be only a site through which being speaks for itself. Hegel, however, is, himself, a singular self-consciousness, a man living in Jena in 1807, and this "*Dasein*," this unique and determinate subjective hold on reality, can never be eliminated. The work of philosophy—the work of the philosopher—is thus always doubly the idiosyncratic, historically datable product of an individual agent and the making-present of a self-speaking of being of which the presentation in that book is only one possible instance; indeed, it is a meaning necessarily repeatable by others in their own idiosyncratic terms. And, for that reason, the single self can never claim an adequate perspective from which to evaluate the success of the work—she must wait upon the confirmation of reality. Hence the conclusion of the preface:

> We must hold to the conviction that it is the nature of truth to prevail when its time has come, and that it appears only when this time has come, and therefore never appears prematurely, nor finds a public not ripe to receive it; also we must accept that the individual needs that this should be so in order to verify what is as yet a matter for himself alone, and to experience the conviction, which in the first place belongs only to a particular individual, as something universally held.[58]

To understand Hegel's *Phenomenology of Spirit* as the philosophical work that it is, we must thus read it as an expression of unhappy consciousness, as the effort of a singular philosopher committed to allowing the self-showing of being to speak in his philosophy for the sake of universal reconciliation. Similarly, our own "scholarship" on Hegel must not be a dry antiquarianism, but a similar answering to such a "calling" to release within the particularities of Hegel's words the possibilities they contain for enabling such a reconciliation.

Part 3

Freedom

8

Spirit and Method

Hegel's *Phenomenology of Spirit* joins in its title an epistemological notion ("phenomenology") and an ontological notion ("spirit"), and posits their inherent relationship ("of"). To explore this linkage is to explore the idea that there is a method implied in being. Taking up this theme in relation to Hegel's *Phenomenology of Spirit,* we shall discover that it is precisely "spirit" that is the notion that essentially joins these two themes of method and being. We will begin with a consideration of the "Doctrine of Being" in Hegel's *Science of Logic,* through which we will discern a founding, dynamic tension at the heart of reality. We will then look briefly at how this tension plays out in the domain of nature before turning to our central concern, which will be the relationship of spirit to this founding tension. By considering two central figures from Hegel's *Phenomenology of Spirit*—Antigone's ethicality and the slave's self-consciousness—we will see how spirit offers a method of answering to the nature of being that is true to it *by* accomplishing it. Antigone's recognition of being as an imperative will show us one side of this, but we will see that, as we saw in chapter 1, her attitude under-represents the ontological importance of the future. We will turn to the slave's experience of work to correct this one-sidedness. This will allow us, finally, to conclude with a discussion of Hegel's philosophical method as the stance of openness that closes history by opening it to the future.

Logic: Being Open and Closed

In many ways, the central issue in Hegel is the relationship between something—whatever it might be—and its preconditions. There are two main sides to this relationship as it figures in Hegel's concerns. First, Hegel is occupied with the issue of how a thing draws resources from its preconditions, but does or does not adequately acknowledge that withdrawal. Second, he is occupied with the ways in which things fulfill, develop, or otherwise exceed their preconditions. We can here continue the study we introduced in chapter 1, and notice a kind of temporality to these two themes. The first—drawing on one's preconditions—is roughly the issue of what one owes to one's past (logical or chronological). The second—the development of the preconditions—is roughly the issue of what is owed to the future (logical or chronological). I want to consider these relations as they are at play in a number of different domains of Hegel's thought.

We might first, and perhaps most profoundly, notice that this relationship defines what it is to "be" at all. In general, in other words, "to be" is to rest upon something that one does not live up to, but equally, it is to make that upon which one rests able to be. Let me take this up in relationship to the opening of Hegel's *Science of Logic*.[1]

Let us return to the theme we considered in chapter 3, and think about what we mean by "being." Being is a notion that must be all-encompassing; indeed, it is the notion *of* what must be all-encompassing. Being is the name of the reality of whatever is. By definition, nothing could elude its grasp for whatever might thus elude it would have to, in some sense, be, and would thus not elude being's grasp—it would have to *be*, to *be* outside being, and would thus be inside being.[2] But this also means that being *as such* can never be a simple actuality, can never be fully present. Any actual being will always be one situated among others. It will be a "determinate" being, a specific being characterized by specific features that both connect it with and differentiate it from others. Being as such could never be such a determinate being, for it could never be one among others, could never be characterized by one feature as opposed to its opposite, for those others it would be among, that opposite to which it would be opposed, must equally be. Being could no more be one side than another. Being could thus never be *a* being. Again, whatever *was* and whatever *will be* must also be, and, indeed, the very reality—the very fact of—pastness and the very fact of futurity must be; "there is" such a thing as the future and "there is" such a thing as the past only insofar as being is not exclusively the present. Being as such, then, can never be fully present, can never be an actual, determinate being, but must be the reality of whatever is, in any and every sense of "is."[3] Being as such must, by definition, be utter and infinite openness "as such." There is nothing to which it could be closed, or it would not be being.

At the same time, there must be something, or else there is only nothing. In other words, it is only if there is presence, if there is actuality, if there are determinate beings, that "there is" at all. It is only insofar as being is determinate, insofar as being is actually present, that being is. Being only is *as* determinate beings. It is only, in other words, insofar as being is fixed and settled—finite and closed—that it is. Hegel typically analyzes his chosen subject-matter to disclose within it the definitive contradiction that is its founding dynamism. Here, we have seen the founding dynamism—the definitive contradiction—that is being itself: being is the contradiction of openness and closure, infinitude and finitude, indeterminate immediacy and mediated determinateness, universal possibility and present actuality.[4] Being is neither one nor the other of these two sides, but is their eternal struggle, their mutually irreducible opposition and interdependence, their simultaneous non-synchronicity, if I may so call it.

Let us say this same thing from the side of the specific, finite, determinate being, rather than from the side of being as such. Any being is itself only inasmuch as it participates in the real as such (this latter being something that it itself helps to constitute). To be something is *in principle* and *necessarily* to be open to all others, that is, to be subject to the rules of the real, so to speak. To be is to be integrated with others—with all the others. To be is to participate in reality, which is to be integrated with—answerable to—everything else, and, indeed, to be *automatically*, that is, *constitutively* thus integrated. It is a demand on each thing that it must harmonize with all that is, was, and will be.

"To be" is thus to rest upon something to which one is not equal and, equally, to make that upon which one rests able to be. We might play upon the familiar formula of self-identity which we introduced in chapter 5—"A is A"—to interpret "being." Being is always and only itself—"there is" nothing else it could be—so being is being, A is A. But these two As are significantly different in their sense. Being, the indeterminately immediate, the infinite openness, is being, the closed, mediated determinateness. Being, as possibility, only is as actuality. For this reason then, we can equally say that being is not itself, A is not A, that is, a founding opposition—"simple difference," or "absolute difference" in Hegel's language[5]—is definitive of being. And, indeed, neither the "A is A" nor the "A is not A" can precede the other. It is precisely *insofar as* being is itself that it is not itself, and vice versa.

There is thus, here, something like a joint indebtedness to the past and to the future. Any determinate being relies upon its situatedness with respect to other determinate beings, both actual and possible: it relies, that is, on the seamlessness of "is." This we could call the debt of determinacy to its (logical) past, the debt of determinate being to being as such. But, equally, being, *in order to be,* depends upon determinacy, depends on determinate beings. This we could call the debt of being to its (logical) future. Being needs what comes forth from it in order to be; determinate being needs a context that does not come forth from itself in order to be.[6] Each is itself only in a necessary relation with the other that does not efface the distinctive significance of either. "Pure being" and "determinate being" are equally necessary dimensions of what it is to be—hence equally necessary and irreducible concepts—each of which necessarily depends upon the other. Being proper ("the infinite") is thus itself only as the intertwining of these two necessarily different moments. Being is always itself (qua pure being) in relation to itself (qua determinate beings), where these two are both "itself," but neither can be confused with the other: their difference is necessarily not effaced.

We could say, then, that Being is precisely the realizing of itself that, in so doing, fails to live up to itself.[7] This is not a "failure" in the sense that something better should have happened; it is just a way of saying that there is a real difference in meaning between the concept of pure being and the concept of determinate being, and that this conceptual difference articulates an ontological difference—an ontologically "tragic" character—that is necessarily constitutive of reality as such and, indeed, of anything that is real.[8] Being-proper ("the infinite") is the reciprocal non-identical enabling of being as such, "pure being," and beings, such that each is both more and less than the other, that is, each side is irreducible to the other side, both drawing upon it and furthering it—and this in a single unity.[9]

Now that we have seen the two sides (the debt to past and future) in their essential definitiveness for being as such, we are adequately equipped to consider something of how these issues arise in other, more specific domains. Let us, then, turn away from logic to the domains of nature (briefly) and spirit.

Nature and Science

The logical demands of dependence, self-transcendence, and integration that characterize finitude as such are the structures that define the processes of nature. Hegel writes of being that, "the being as such of finite things is to have the germ of disease as their being-within-self; the hour of their birth is the hour of their death," and he similarly writes of the animal that, "[t]he original disease of the animal, and the inborn germ of death, is being inadequate to universality."[10] The core idea that things draw upon, and are answerable to, resources they do not acknowledge is clear in the things of nature.

In the sense we drew from the opening moves of the *Science of Logic*, we can immediately recognize at a general level that any natural thing rests in a larger natural world, and is determined by its place in relation to wind, season, light, surrounding geography, etc. Of the relationship between organic "individuals" and the surrounding inorganic medium, Hegel writes:

> Neither the individuality, nor the universal element, is absolutely in and for itself; on the contrary though they appear to observation as free and independent, they behave at the same time as essentially connected, but in such a way that their independence and mutual indifference are the predominant feature.[11]

Describing specifically the nature of "life," he writes:

> In the first moment there is the existent shape [the living individual]; as being *for itself* . . . it comes forward in antithesis to the *universal* substance, disowns this fluent continuity with it and asserts that it is not dissolved in this universal element, but on the contrary preserves itself by separating itself from this its inorganic nature, and by consuming it.[12]

The living thing, by its very nature, enacts an ontological denial of the very medium from which it emerges but upon which it simultaneously depends. Hegel, continuing, writes:

> The simple universal fluid medium is the *in-itself*, and the difference of the shapes is the *other*. But this fluid medium itself becomes the *other* through this difference; for now it is *for the difference* which exists in and for itself, and consequently is the ceaseless movement by which this passive medium is consumed.[13]

This essential embeddedness in the very environment from which the individual differentiates itself is a version of the notion of "integration" I used above. We can also see this drawing on unacknowledged resources at more intimate levels. This will be clearest if we take the organism as our example.[14]

The dog depends on the functioning of its digestive system, depends on having a heart, depends on its ability to see, and so on. Every aspect of the dog's activity—its life, its perception, its movement—is subtended by a kind of passivity, a givenness for which the individual dog cannot claim causal responsibility. The dog, in other words, did not make itself. When we are considering, then, the "unacknowledged resources," we are not just considering the larger context within which an individual is situated, but we are also considering the very powers that are definitive of that individual: *its* powers, its very "itself." As Hans Jonas says of organic life:

> Its "can" is a "must," since its execution is identical with its being. It can, but it cannot cease to do what it can without ceasing to be. Thus the sovereignty of form with respect to matter is also its subjection to the need of it.[15]

Both externally and internally, then, we see here a version of what I called above the "debt to the past."

But, though the dog did not make itself, and is thus *inherently* passive, it is nonetheless true that these given capacities are the capacities *for* action, the powers of living as a separate individual.[16] The dog *is* an agent; it is an "itself." In the dog, then, we see the way in which the "inheritance," the powers, are precisely *for* the "future," so to speak, that is, these "given powers" have their proper reality only insofar as their primacy is subordinated to the self-active reality of the individual, that is, the individual that takes responsibility onto itself for its own being: it *does* its own living—it does not merely *receive* it passively.

Let me use these brief remarks on nature to begin to say something about method; we will here revisit briefly the themes of "Perception" and "Understanding" that we took up in chapters 2 and 3. Typically, in our everyday (Aristotelian) approach to affairs, we take the existence of "things"—the normal objects of our perceptual life—for granted in our analyses, and develop our views of causality on their basis. We see the individual animal, for example, as active, as the cause of certain things happening. We model our conception of causality upon the action of individual beings—this one acts on that—without recognizing that the very causality that emanates from those individuals—their very "agency"—is itself rooted in their essential non-agency, that is, the very ability to be active is *given* them, and is not itself explicable *in terms of* their agency. In general, the agency of individuals is explicable only upon the basis of a passivity not itself explicable in terms of that agency. We will have to go on to think further about making our method equal to this reality, but what I want to note is something about the familiar stance of natural science as it relates to this issue.

There is a basic way in which the method of natural science—the stance of "Understanding" that Hegel considers in the *Phenomenology of Spirit*—makes a move in this direction we are considering in its advance from thinking of things to thinking of forces.[17] Understanding comes into its own when it stops operating in the service of perception (trying to answer the question "why?" *in the terms of* the perceptual world of things and their given properties) and sees things themselves as products of deeper forces; understanding becomes science when it takes as its object these ultimate causes, the ultimate forces of nature (which is what Hegel calls the "first supersensible world"[18]).

> This true character of things has now the character of not being immediately for consciousness; on the contrary, consciousness has a mediated relation to the inner being and, as the understanding, *looks through this mediating play of forces into the true background of things.*[19]

Whenever we study causality in the natural world, we are investigating the relations of dependence in which the individual is embedded. There is an important way, then, in which the reductive physicist who looks to "ultimate matter" to explain things has made an advance over everyday perception and the everyday approach to causal understanding, inasmuch as he is close to recognizing the "debt to inheritance" that is constitutive of everything.

> [I]t is in the *inner* world that [infinity] has first freely and clearly shown itself. Appearance, or the play of forces, already displays it, but it is as '*explanation*' that it first freely stands forth.[20]

Such science, however, remains unsatisfactory (indeed, remains "positivistic"), inasmuch as it seeks an original matter or force that has the characteristics in terms of which all else is to be explained. Hegel illustrates this with the attempt to use the force "electricity" as the explanation of why there are the opposed forms of positive and negative electricity, which are themselves the terms used to explain other phenomena ("the law"):

> In this sense, *simple* electricity, e.g., is *force*; but the expression of difference falls with the *law*; this difference is positive and negative electricity. . . . Electricity itself is not difference *per se*, or is not in its essence the dual essence of positive and negative electricity; hence it is usually said that it *has* the law of this mode of *being*, and, too, that it *has the property* of expressing itself in this way. It is true that this property is the essential and sole property of this force, or that it belongs to it *necessarily*. But necessity here is an empty word; force *must*, just *because* it *must*, duplicate itself in this way.[21]

Such science is ultimately unsatisfactory because the ultimate force to which the science appeals will itself be characterized by a given power of which it itself cannot be the explanation. Whatever the original determinate reality is that is posited to explain others, that reality's explanatory force will come from its own given constitutive character, and understanding, thus, will ultimately have failed to get beyond the everyday stance of perception and its acceptance of the ultimacy of a given, determinate being. In sum, then, we can see how the shift from perception to understanding responds in a limited way to the need to recognize the debt to inheritance, but that shift by itself is not equal to the epistemological/methodological task posed by reality. Basically, the reductiveness of that shift overstresses the weight of the debt to the past and loses the sense of the importance of the debt to the future and, by seeking to explain beings solely by reference to other beings, it fails to address truly the passivity that gives determinacy and instead simply replaces one given determinacy with another.

I will not pursue these issues further here. Instead, I want to turn to my primary area of interest, which is the domain of spirit. These reflections on nature and natural science will allow us to see something of the distinctive significance of that domain.

Ethicality and Obedience

Of course, people are participants in the natural world, so, as living individuals, we draw upon powers not of our own making in every action, just as does the dog. We also, however, draw upon a further set of powers, which are those drawn from our cultural situation—both the current institutions and social relationships, and the history behind them. This is true in a very immediate sense—

> It does not occur to someone who walks the streets in safety at night that this might be otherwise, for the habit of safety has become second nature, and we scarcely stop to think that it is solely the effect of particular institutions.[22]

—and in the deeper sense that our characters as persons are formed by taking on our traditions. There is also a second distinctive feature of people, in contrast to the natural world, that pertains to this issue of "unacknowledged resources," namely, that with people we first enter the domain in which "acknowledgement" really becomes a reality. In the other domains, we were considering something about how *we* might take account of *those* things—how we conceive of being, how we employ a notion of cause, etc.—that is, we addressed things that do not take account of themselves, but in the human sphere, we are also considering beings for whom "taking account" is part of their definitive reality, that is, we are beings who take account of ourselves.[23] Let us consider both of these new dimensions in turn: cultural givenness, and the adequacy or lack thereof of our self-representation, our self-accounting.

Our culture is handed down to us as nature is handed down to natural things in the sense that we live out of a developed significance we did not ourselves develop.

> [I]n the child's progress through school, we shall recognize the history of the cultural development of the world traced, as it were, in a silhouette. This past existence is the already acquired property of universal spirit which constitutes the substance of the individual, and hence appears externally to him as his inorganic nature. In this respect formative education, regarded from the side of the individual, consists in his acquiring what thus lies at hand, devouring his inorganic nature, and taking possession of it for himself.[24]

We grow up into traditional ways of seeing, speaking, and acting, and these become the very substance of our lives, but we typically do not notice that or how we are doing this, and the result is that we take on this cultural inheritance—the result of contingent human action—as if it simply were natural. Our cultural inheritance is, as Aristotle said, our "second nature":

> [T]he *habit* of [behaving from cultural custom] appears as a *second nature* which takes the place of the original and purely natural will and is the all-pervading soul, significance, and actuality of individual existence.[25]

The experience of adopting a contingent, historical inheritance as if it were natural is what Hegel calls "ethicality."[26]

Ethicality, as we have seen in earlier chapters, is the way we undergo our experience when we experience it *as a necessity* that we interpret and evaluate our situations according to the norms handed down to us by tradition. When I say, "we experience it as necessary," I mean that we have the experience of an immediate lived imperative, of a duty that we experience *as* inscribed in the very fabric of things, *as*, simply, natural.[27] We find an imperative *given*: indeed, the experience of this givenness *as such* is integral to the experience.

> Thus, Sophocles' Antigone acknowledges them as the unwritten and infallible laws of the gods: "they are not of yesterday or today, but everlasting, / though where they came from, none of us can tell."[28]

Antigone's recognition of her duty to divine law—Hegel's paradigm for ethicality—is thus a kind of acknowledgment of the very passivity we have been talking about, the very beholdenness to the demands of the resources we rely upon but did not ourselves create. Antigone precisely experiences herself as subject to a significance *to* which she is responsible.

What Hegel stresses in his introduction of Antigone's experience is the challenge it offers to morality as portrayed by Kant.[29] Kantian morality, the morality of individual autonomy, emphasizes the ability of the individual to be an agent, to take responsibility for his own agency. Antigone instead demonstrates a kind of "unhappy consciousness," for her experience shows that our ownmost reality is one to which we are answerable, not one we generate from ourselves: we experience our subjectivity as received.[30] In her sense of her answerability to what she calls divine law, Antigone demonstrates an acknowledgment of what I have called our debt to our inheritance, our debt to the past. This basic recognition on her part is correct as far as it goes, but in other respects it, too, is inadequate, and this inadequacy is the second point Hegel stresses in his account of ethicality.

> The [ethical] community, however, can only maintain itself by suppressing th[e] spirit of singularity, and, because it is an essential moment, all the same creates it and, moreover, creates it by its repressive attitude towards it as a hostile principle.[31]

In stressing the autonomous and inexplicable givenness of ethical imperatives, the ethical attitude challenges the autonomous authority of singular, self-conscious agents to engage in moral judgment, even though it inherently depends upon that very initiative within the acting individuals who commit themselves to the laws.

Antigone's obedient action is as essential to giving the traditional values reality as those traditions are to giving her actions value. It is only in the world of the *real living issues* of Antigone and her companions *that there is a question* of value—of the good—at all. The traditional values are *nothing by themselves.* They are a *possibility* for value, a *possibility* for meaning, but only that, only a possibility. It is only in the context of *her actually facing living issues,* and in the circumstance of *her acknowledging* the import of the laws, that the laws have any capacity to be meaningful and compelling. As Kant and Fichte showed, any experience of necessity is necessarily a phenomenon of subjectivity. In Antigone's case, her *seeing the laws as* necessary is the condition of their being binding. Even more importantly (this a point Hegel will make more pointedly in his discussion of the problems in Kantian morality), *it is precisely the context of human actuality that establishes the basic domain of meaningfulness in which the laws can pertain.*[32] In other words, the very *sense* of the laws is derivative of the sense of actuality: *the parameters of the situation* give the *terms* for interpreting the sense of the law, and it is only within this original establishing of a meaningful situation that the laws can speak to that situation meaningfully.

So Antigone's view that they—the laws—one-sidedly inform her and her world is mistaken. Antigone—any ethical agent—construes the laws/values to be independent *actualities,* metaphysically self-sufficient both to hold themselves in being and to be causally forceful on "agents." In fact, the single agent who enacts them (or the community that holds them dear) cannot be thus dismissed as inessential. It is only in and *as experienced and enacted* by living actual subjects that "there is" any law, any ethical substantiality, at all.[33] It is, in other words, the very "to be" of the laws *that they speak to us in the living significance of our present.* They are *for us;* we are not "for them."

Here we see, again, the basic lesson we learned in the *Science of Logic,* but with an added dimension. As in the *Science of Logic,* so here we can see that the grounding possibility is real only *as* the grounded actuality, that is, the ethical law only is insofar as it is realized in the endorsing actions of—the acknowledgment of it by—the agents who interpret themselves as beholden to it. The further dimension here is the way that the law is only *for* them; that is, it is beholden to *their* autonomy, their independent significance. This idea by itself might already be detected in the material we discussed from the *Science of Logic.* Indeed, against the notion of a "night in which all cows are black," Hegel very much is oriented toward the ultimacy of real, singular individuals whose difference is not effaced in an all-comprehending whole.[34] In that sense, we could say that being is "for" beings (ontologically speaking). What is added here, though, is the specific sense of this in relation to us: the laws are *for* freedom, and that means *they* owe a debt to the future. Let me explain.

In Hegel's understanding—against that of Antigone—(and presumably we would agree with him here), the laws are not "god-given," but are the result of historical human interaction. Specifically, they are the means by/in which a community has established for itself an identity and a set of institutional patterns of recognition. Through its ethical ways, the community establishes ways in which we reciprocally endorse each other's sense of who we individually and collectively are, that is, we establish ways in which we can reconcile ("harmonize") or integrate our sense of ourselves and our self-worth as individual, free agents with a recognition of the equal worth of others as such free agents. Very directly, then, the laws are, in Hegel's view, *for* us: they are how the free space of mutual recognition is realized.

It is, in other words, the very *raison d'etre* of the laws to found human freedom. The very law of law, one might say, is "be free." But human freedom is itself transformative: it is precisely the power of the possibility to be otherwise, to move reality beyond itself to its future. Freedom is *inherently* futural, and in this sense the laws *by nature* owe a debt to the future: they are fulfilled only insofar as through them we are fulfilled.[35]

Ethicality makes an advance over nature in that ethical life is a *reality* that is more adequate to itself: referring back to my earlier discussion of "A = A," we can say that its "second A," so to speak, is truer to its "first A," its actuality closer to its possibility than is the case with nature. Why? Because the very form of its actuality *is* a *recognition* of its indebtedness to its given ground. The ontological situation *we* can discern in it is closer to what it itself claims about itself. Nonetheless, while it is an advance over the natural reality that is oblivious to its own ground, the ethical reality is still insufficient as a realization of the demands of being as such. Reality always underrealizes itself in nature: nature is not totally true to what it is to be, because there is a *discernibly definitive* possibility of being that it does not and *cannot* realize. Spirit *in its recognition* of its debt is the domain in which reality can be realized, that is, the very *kind* of reality that spirit is exceeds the kind of reality that nature is. We have, then, spirit as the necessary realm for the realization of being—for the adequate form of being, for something that is really and fully real—but in ethicality we do not yet have the adequate form of spirit. In terms of method, we can say that the adequate method for answering to the nature of the real will be a spiritual response, but simple ethicality is an inadequate method. Let us pursue further this notion of the recognition of debt in the context of spirit.

Slavery and Self-Representation

In ethicality, we have seen as distinctive of the human domain that we *recognize* our indebtedness: though we may well misconstrue the nature of the debt, such recognition, or at least the capacity for it, is a constitutive feature of our kind of reality. We also have as a distinctive characteristic of our reality that we are self-interpreting, in the sense that we explicitly represent ourselves to ourselves (and these self-representations are consequential for our actions). Let us now consider this issue of self-representation.

The question of the adequacy of our acknowledgment of our debt is always, in some sense, a question of our self-representation, for it is a question of what or who we construe ourselves to be in relationship to the terms of "reality." We have already seen with Antigone that we can represent ourselves as "indebted," but still misrepresent the determinate nature of this indebtedness. Now, Hegel's philosophical method is not to impose external models of evaluation, but to discern the animating tensions *within* a given subject to see how, from within its own founding dynamism, it moves itself forward. If, then, we are making claims about self-*mis*representation, then we must be able to find the grounds for recognizing such misrepresentation within the subject we are considering. In his discussion of the experience of the slave, Hegel precisely directs us to the point at which we are confronted, *within our self-recognition*, with the grounds for criticizing and correcting our self-representation.[36]

What we saw above is that natural reality is characterized by a disparity: the individual lives on the basis of powers it does not acknowledge, and, indeed, we could say that nature itself, in what Hegel calls its lack of "history," does not acknowledge the individuals that actualize it.

> But organic nature has no history; it falls from the universal, from life, directly into the singleness of existence . . . . [T]he whole is not present in it, and is not present in it because here it is not qua whole *for* itself.[37]

Both sides of the disparity—of the power to the individual and of the individual to power—are manifest *within* natural reality, but not *to* either side.

> [Life is] the self-developing whole which dissolves its development and in this movement simply preserves itself. . . . It is the simple genus which, in the movement of life itself, does not exist *for itself qua* this *simple* determinateness; on the contrary, . . . life points to something other than itself, viz. to consciousness, for which life exists as this unity, or as genus.[38]

A third must be presumed here—a third that exceeds both—if this disparity that is constitutive of life is itself to "mean," that is, if the fact of the ontological inadequacy—itself an ontological feature—is itself to have any weight in reality. In his analysis of the slave's work, Hegel shows this disparity coming to be *for itself*: the slave, in the experience of the products of his work, is the very one *for whom* the evidence of self exceeds the self-description. There is a way, in other words, in which the experience of the slave opens up a kind of reality that allows reality to complete itself, to be true to its own nature, that is otherwise (at least in the sphere of nature) impossible.

A situation of slavery is premised on a denial of the slave's freedom—a denial of the slave's agency. When a slave is forced to work, however, the products of the slave's work give evidence of the slave's powers, and those evident powers are the powers of freedom—the powers precisely of *agency*—that are explicitly denied in the interpretation of the slave as a slave.

> [I]n fashioning the thing, the slave's own negativity, his being-for-self, becomes an object for him. . . . [He] posits *himself* as a negative in the permanent order of things, and thereby becomes *for himself*, someone existing on his own account.[39]

Indeed, despite the constitutive denial, in slavery, of the slave's freedom, Hegel's phenomenological description shows that slavery in fact depends in principle on the slave's participation in it, inasmuch as the slave accepted to sacrifice freedom for life (rather than, say, to die fighting for freedom).[40]

> [T]his consciousness has been fearful, not of this or that particular thing or just at odd moments, but its whole being has been seized with dread; for it has experienced the fear of death.[41]

"In this experience," Hegel writes, "self-consciousness learns that life is as essential to it as pure self-consciousness," and gives in to the will of the master, accepting to be a slave.[42] In this way, slavery is something done by the slave in conjunction with another—a master—and it is an institution: it is the establishment of a shared situation of mutual interpretation in which the participants mutually agree on how they will interpret each other. Slavery is an (unfair and unjust) institution of *unequal* recognition in that the master and slave share an interpretation according to which one is a free, self-defining, desiring agent, and the other is not. Hegel's argument is that the very capacity of the slave to enter into this institution already shows him to be a self-defining self-consciousness inherently equal to the master,[43] and that this reality that exceeds the terms of their shared co-interpretation is manifest in the products of the slave's labor.[44] What the slave accomplishes gives evidence that the definition of the slave as slave is not equal to the slave's reality.

Master and slave together share a recognition of the slave as slave, and the very products of the slave's labor show this to be an inadequate recognition. *For the slave himself*, the recognition therefore becomes possible—through reflection on/from the products—that "I am (we are) wrong about what I am (we are)," that, "I give evidence of living on the basis of powers I do not acknowledge." The slave, as slave, is required to live in denial of his free agency, in denial of his capacity for independent action. What the products of the slave's labor offer is the opportunity to notice that this denial is false.[45] The slave evinces independent action at every level—action for which his singular initiative is necessary—and so in every deed the slave produces a challenge to the word of his self-definition. Hegel argues that it is in this situation of encountering the products of its own behavior that self-consciousness encounters the opportunity for its own development that is the basis of all the subsequent advances in self-consciousness. Let us make a few points about this recognition of ourselves through the evidence of our powers.

The import of this recognition is itself quite interesting. It might have seemed from our discussion of the need to recognize passivity that we would produce an argument against our being too self-important in our self-interpretation. That is what Antigone sees. Here in the case of the slave, though, the recognition of unacknowledged power is *liberating*—the slave finds himself to be better than he imagined.

Indeed, since the slave's self-perception is itself something like a "spiritual" heritage, that is, it is a view taken on as "natural" from a shared situation, the recognition of himself through his powers is something like a challenge to ethicality. Because master and slave share their co-interpretation, the view of the slave as slave is what their "we" thinks, without acknowledging the origination of the view in the we: the view is taken as a perception of natural reality, not as an agreement; indeed, to acknowledge it as an agreement would be to acknowledge the slave's founding agency in this institution, when that is precisely what the institution denies. Here, then, the recognition available to the slave through its products is a recognition both of *power* and *against* tradition. Unlike the ethical recognition we saw with Antigone, then, the slave's recognition acknowledges the possibility of meaning beyond what tradition has passed down, beyond what seemed "naturally" given. In the products of his labor, the slave precisely has the opportunity to recognize the essentiality of agency *denied* by Antigone. It is through the experience of the slave, then, that we see the possibility of the distinctive recognition of freedom as such, that is, the recognition of what I am calling the debt to the future.

When we spoke of nature, we spoke of the epistemological challenge of properly apprehending things in their causal relations, and so on. In our discussions of spirit—in relation to ethicality and slavery—we have seen our notion of method move into a new domain, a domain that is as much one of participation as it is of observation; in other words, "spirit" and "method" are not notions that can be separated. In ethicality, adequate answering to reality took us into the realm of the imperative. That recognition was insufficient, however, because in effacing the essentiality of the singular agent it failed to recognize, as we said, the law to "be free"; this is analogous to failing to recognize the infinity and openness of being. Now with the slave we have the corrective to this in the recognition of the debt to the future, that is, in the recognition of the imperative to go beyond the received tradition. Let me conclude by taking up this last theme of openness to the future in relation to philosophy.

Conclusion: Philosophy, Spirit, and Method

From the consideration of the *Science of Logic* with which we began, we can see easily enough what our method must be: we must look to realities to see how they are the reciprocal, unequal enabling we spoke of above. In our language of "A = A," we can say that we must look to any self-identity to see precisely how the second A is "A" only by *not* being strictly equal to the first A. In other words, we will look in each case to see how each actuality is a living beyond its means, so to speak, that is, how it is drawing upon a basic inheritance but also taking that inheritance beyond itself. These sentences are all so many formulations of what I think should be recognizably the Hegelian procedure, and we can see why this method is what is mandated by the very nature of reality.

What we have seen in our investigation here, though, that enriches our sense of the meaning of this is that this notion of method cannot be separated from *the reality that is spirit.* This method is a kind of *recognizing*, or, said from the side of the "object," an *appearing* of A in relation to A. The very space of this appearing—itself a particular kind of reality—is spirit, that is, we are the kind of beings who *notice* these things. And, inasmuch as this is a kind of reality, we can ask of this reality how it is with respect to its "A = A," that is, we can ask how successful it is at realizing reality. What we have seen is that, inasmuch as it is establishing the space in which the relation of A and A can be posited, spirit (i.e., method) actually *accomplishes* reality. Spirit is in its nature a kind of method for recognizing reality, a "method" that is or is not equal to the task of answering to reality not by virtue of being something *applied to* reality but by virtue of *realizing* it.

Simultaneously, then, with recognizing that spirit in a fundamental way *allows* reality to be real ("lets being be"), we must also notice that "method" itself cannot be construed as something alien to reality.

> [T]he method has emerged as the *self-knowing concept that has itself* as the absolute, both subjective and objective, *for its subject matter,* conse-

> quently as the pure correspondence of the concept and its reality, as a concrete existence that is the concept itself.[46]

All reality is, in a sense, method: the method of self-adequation, the method of being equal to the task of being oneself.

We might, then, finally ask how philosophy stands with respect to this. Based on what I have said here, we can say the following. Philosophy is the method of acknowledging its debt to its inheritance *precisely as* the accomplishing of the definitive openness of being. Hegel's "system" is the closure of comprehending its own past, its own preconditions, precisely so as to inaugurate a future, and the closure of history is just the recognition of the ultimacy of this stance. Antigone's ethicality is "closed" in the narrow sense of being a hide-bound traditionalism that is blind to freedom and creativity; for that very reason, it is not the end of history, for it has not yet enacted a stance adequate to the nature of reality: it has not acknowledged the debt to the future. Hegel's stance closes history precisely in recognizing that reality must be openness, and his comprehension of his past is just the demonstration that this is the imperative it imposes upon us.

Finally, though, we must remember that such philosophy, such openness, is not something accomplished by an isolated, self-active individual. The individual, with all her powers of free agency, always stands on the ground of a spirit to which she is not adequate, and faces a task to which she is not equal. The philosophic gesture is a creative gesture launching a new reality that is inaugurated by the free individual but that must wait upon the confirmation of reality—of the future. Hegel's method is a commitment to allowing the realization of the self-showing of the object, a task to which the individual contributes, but to which she is never equal.

> Because of this, the individual must all the more forget himself, as the nature of Science implies and requires. Of course, he must make of himself and achieve what he can; but less must be demanded of him, just as he in turn can expect less of himself, and may demand less for himself.[47]

9

Freedom as Nature, Revolution, and Event

> . . . the secular self-consciousness, the consciousness of what is the supreme vocation of man . . .
>
> —*Philosophy of Mind* §562

In the preceding chapter, I argued that comprehending reality ultimately means comprehending (and hence enacting) freedom. In keeping with this insight, Hegel identifies this enacting of freedom as the essence of history, and, through three short sketches, I will look at how he understands the story of Western history to be the story of freedom.[1] Drawing on the *Philosophy of History* and the *Phenomenology of Spirit*, I will argue that there have been two great eras of human freedom, each characterized by a one-sided realization of freedom. To sketch the first—the ancient world—I will draw upon Aristotle and Sophocles. To sketch the second—the modern world—I will draw upon Foucault and St. Paul. Our study of the limitations of these two great accomplishments of freedom, and how they do violence to our nature as free beings, will prepare us for studying the terms under which freedom can be adequately realized. To complete this final stage of our analysis, we will consider briefly Hegel's notion of "the infinite" from the *Science of Logic*, before sketching the dialogical, dialectical nature of a free politics. Our study will take us through three different conceptions of freedom: freedom as nature, freedom as revolution, and freedom as event.

The Ancient World: Aristotle and *Antigone*

Freedom is what history is about. Indeed, it is what history is made of. There is no pre-existent reality to freedom somewhere else: freedom just is history—it just is what it has made itself.

> *[A]ll* the properties of spirit exist only through freedom. All are but means of attaining freedom; all seek and produce this and this alone. . . . [F]reedom is the sole truth of spirit. . . . It is the ultimate purpose toward which all world history has continually aimed.[2]

Though human being is always free in principle, there have been two great actual accomplishments of freedom in practice, namely, the ancient and modern worlds, the worlds (in the language of the *Phenomenology of Spirit*) of "Ethicality" and "Culture."[3] Though each world essentially accomplished—that is, brought into reality—freedom, each was equally premised on a vision of freedom that necessarily hinders the full development of freedom. Let us begin by discussing freedom in the ancient world.

"The consciousness of freedom," Hegel says in his lectures on world history, "first arose among the Greeks."[4] What marks the ancient Hellenic and Hellenistic world as the inauguration of freedom proper is that this is a society governed by the idea that it—that we—should be self-legislating. The Greeks are typically cited as the originators of democracy. The important sense of democracy here is not so much the question of the precise structures of governmental decision-making, but is the fact that the community recognizes itself as responsible for making its own laws:

> The *community*, the superior law whose validity is openly apparent, has its real vitality in the government as that in which it has an individual form. Government is the reality of spirit that is reflected into itself, the simple *self* of the entire ethical substance.[5]

In the *polis*, people come together *as representatives of the community* to deliberate *on behalf of the community*.[6] Though different communities might adopt different means of realizing this ideal, they are all democratic if they build themselves around the idea that, as a human community, they must decide for themselves how to live. Though the Greeks may well have invented this democracy, the form of this Greek-style "politics"—the idea that human community should establish governing bodies with a fundamentally legislative function—is not unique to that small nation, but became the dominant political model for the whole of the ancient Mediterranean world. Hegel's discussion of "ethicality" is his analysis of this distinctive form of the Greek realization of this project of self-legislation, and his analysis reveals both its strengths and its distinctive problems.

The Greek approach to freedom (as embodied in their political institutions, their religion, and their art) is rooted in the recognition of our participation in nature, and Aristotle's philosophy is one of the most helpful articulations of this vision. Aristotle recognizes that we find ourselves members of a world of nature, which is a world of self-moving bodies each of which evinces a definitive species-identity.[7] Each such form of life—each natural species—has its own intrinsic ends, and its life history is the process of its maturation, that is, the process of actualizing its potential. Aristotle's approach to humans is to ask of us, "how are we a natural species?" and "how do we fulfill our intrinsic end?" On the basis of the same methods of observational biology that he employs in other domains of the natural world, Aristotle determines that the human nature is "*zōion logon echon*," that is, we are the "animal having *logos*."[8] Translating the word "*logos*" is notoriously difficult, but for our purposes it is enough to translate his definition as "the animal that takes account of itself," or even the traditional "rational animal."[9] What we see in this definition is a juxtaposition of nature and reason, of the givenness of identity together with self-responsibility. Here we see the tension within this Greek approach to freedom that Hegel studies in his analysis of "ethicality."

In recognizing that we are self-legislating, the Greeks acknowledge that we are self-defining, that we are responsible for who we are (another way of saying "self-accounting," as in Aristotle's definition). At the same time, the Greeks see us as part of nature—that is, as having a given nature. In other words, the Greeks hold us answerable both to the demand to measure up to our given nature—our essence—and to the demand to define ourselves. By recognizing that our nature involves *logos*, the Greeks recognize the necessity to give space to our free creativity, and this is the basis for the emergence of democracy, of the freedom of the self-legislating community. By interpreting our *logos* as a nature, though, the Greeks hold our creativity to a pre-given norm. Freedom is bound by the givenness of a nature to which it must answer.

Hegel uses Sophocles' tragedy *Antigone* to portray this. *Antigone* portrays a Thebes normally characterized by the harmonious functioning of the demands of self-legislation and the demands of answering to nature, that is, the demands of our aspirations and the demands of "how things just are." Whereas life is normally the happy balance of answering to the demands of human law and divine law—"the peaceful organization and movement of the ethical world, . . . [the] order and harmony of its two essences, each of which authenticates and completes the other"[10]—a conflict emerges (in this case, as a consequence of nature not being "rational," and producing twins in the context of hereditary monarchy[11]) and makes manifest the incompatibility of these two demands: the demands of divine and human law.

> On its formal side, it is the conflict of the ethical order and self-consciousness with unconscious nature and the contingency stemming from nature. . . . On the side of content, it is the clash between divine and human law.[12]

The clash is specifically the clash of two competing laws, but ultimately it is the clash of the demands of the givenness of identity and the demands of self-determination.

Hegel's point is that an approach to human society that recognizes us as having a rational "nature" on the one hand allows for the emergence of the institutions of self-legislation, and the proof of this is the amazing flourishing of the ancient world, in which human freedom was first realized, and on the other hand holds that freedom bound to a presumed natural givenness of the defining values of our existence, and for that reason is ultimately repressive of our freedom: "The community, however, can only maintain itself by suppressing the spirit of singularity," the spirit of singular initiative and self-consciousness inherent to the nature of freedom.[13] This repression is exemplified in the trial and death of Socrates, who is condemned by the "free" society because he will not accept the boundedness of his *logos* by the presumed givenness of a natural sense of the good.

This political system, then, simultaneously supports and does violence to our freedom. By operating with a sense that our nature is to be rational and free, the Greeks created political, religious, artistic, and educational institutions that supported the development and flourishing of this free rationality. At the same time, though, the freedom whose growth was thus encouraged was itself held captive by the presumption of a given natural order to which it was answerable. Indeed, I said above that freedom cannot be the following out of a pre-established plan, but that is exactly how it is construed in ethicality.[14]

The ancient world launched a set of institutions that allowed a millennium of human flourishing and self-development, but those institutions were based on a conception of the person that could not reconcile the self-defining singularity of the individual with the substantial definedness of the individual by its "species" identity, that is, the given natural and social roles into which it is born. The ancient world thus produced societies that either held to the presumed givenness of the good, and sacrificed the singularity of the individual to it, or that responded to this problem by abandoning any sense of the substantial good and licensing only insubstantial, isolated singularity.[15] After a millennium, the ancient inspiration had run its course, and left the West to its so-called

"Dark Ages." The first great human accomplishment of freedom exhausted itself.

The Modern World: Foucault and the French Revolution

The modern world is the second great accomplishment of human freedom. The modern West is the second attempt to institutionally realize a world of self-creating humanity. Whereas the ancient world found its approach to freedom through something like the notion of the natural powers through which an organism fulfills itself, the modern world finds its approach to freedom through the recognition that in freedom the individual has *within* herself the intrinsic capacity to reach an absolute truth and a value that is not defined in the terms of the natural world.[16]

> [T]he Germanic peoples came, through Christianity, to realize that man as man is free and that freedom of spirit is the very essence of man's nature. This realization first arose in religion, in the innermost region of spirit; but to introduce it in the secular world was a further task which could only be solved and fulfilled by a long and severe effort of civilization.[17]

It is primarily Christianity that is responsible for this new approach to human freedom; as Paul writes,

> This righteousness from God comes through faith in Jesus Christ to all who believe. There is no difference, for all have sinned and fall short of the glory of God, and are justified as a gift by his grace through the redemption that came by Christ Jesus. (Romans 3:22–24.)

Because of this emphasis on personal faith, Christianity, unlike traditional Jewish or Greek religions which are religions that are co-extensive with particular communities, is equally open to all.[18]

> For we maintain that a man is justified by faith apart from observing the law. Is God the God of Jews only? Is he not the God of Gentiles too? Yes, of Gentiles too, since there is only one God, who will justify the circumcised by faith and the uncircumcised through that same faith. (Romans 3:28–30.)

Faith precisely requires that one recognize the insufficiency of given, external structures, and instead find salvation only in the commitment of one's innermost self to the absolute: salvation requires *conversion.*

The essentiality of conversion is the central point of Paul's epistle to the Romans, in which he identifies our reality as not to be made present through our natural birth, but only through being born again. "It is not the natural children who are God's children, but the children of the promise" (Romans 9:8). We "are" not how we occur naturally, and therefore our givenness—our race, gender, etc., that is, any specific determinacy we have only by birth—is not definitive of ourselves.

> You are all sons of God through faith in Christ Jesus, for all of you who were baptized into Christ have clothed yourself with Christ. There is neither Greek nor Jew, slave nor free, male nor female, for you are all one in Christ Jesus. If you belong to Christ, then you are Abraham's seed, and heirs according to the promise. (Galatians 3:26–29.)

What is definitive is our capacity to convert, that is, to disavow these particularities and define ourselves by the intrinsic ability, possessed by each of us singly, to apprehend the universal truth, the absolute.

> [S]elf-consciousness . . . has *actuality* only in so far as it alienates itself from itself; by so doing, it gives itself the character of a universal, and this its universality is its authentication and actuality. This *equality* with everyone is, therefore, not the . . . immediate recognition and validity of self-consciousness simply because it *is*; on the contrary, to be valid it must have conformed itself to the universal by the mediating process of alienation.[19]

In conversion, we acknowledge the non-naturalness, the non-givenness of our nature, and recognize that, as free beings, we must take responsibility *in our freedom* for realizing our nature.

Our freedom, then, is found in our capacity to subject ourselves individually to judgment by our higher selves: "this consciousness is confronted by the unity of self and essence, *actual* consciousness by *pure* consciousness."[20] Freedom is found in autonomy, for in accepting the rule of the absolute within us, we are not ruled by another; since that higher judge is our own true self, we also cannot escape its gaze, which means we know when we are guilty of violating its rule. Freedom, then, is found in a kind of self-criticism and self-transcendence: "the self is itself actual only as a *transcended* self."[21]

In contrast to the "naturalism" of the ancient embodiment of freedom, modernity thus begins with this explicit anti-naturalism.

> It is therefore through culture that the individual acquires standing and actuality. His true *original nature* and substance is the alienation of himself as spirit from his *natural* being. . . . This individuality *moulds* itself by culture into what it intrinsically is, and only by so doing is it an intrinsic being that has an actual existence.[22]

This modern, Christian, apprehension of freedom precisely demands the recognition that our humanity is not at home in nature—"do not," Paul writes, "conform any longer to the pattern of this world" (Romans 12:2)—and that it is only by defining ourselves in opposition to the terms of nature that we realize ourselves. The modern conception of freedom, in other words, is found in the notion of "cultivation," or "culture."

> What, in relation to the single *individual*, appears as his culture, is the essential moment of the *substance* itself. . . . The process in which the individuality moulds itself by culture is, therefore, at the same time the development of it as the universal, objective essence, i.e. the development of the actual world.[23]

Freedom, that is, is found in answering to the calling to improve ourselves and our world, to make reality over according to the terms of the absolute: "offer yourselves to God . . . and offer the parts of your body to him as instruments of righteousness" (Romans 6:13).

Though this idea begins as a distinctly religious idea, Hegel looks at the development of this insight—that freedom is realized only in conversion—throughout the history of Western political institutions, and it is the French Revolution that is the ultimate emblem for this vision of freedom. Inasmuch as the definitive norm of spirit as culture is to negate its given nature, that is, to transcend itself, "revolution" is here taken as the very definition of spirit. "The revolution" as the form of political life is the institutionalizing of the driving idea of this whole spirit of culture, the whole spirit of the modern world. The French Revolution itself purports to be the realization of freedom against the old order, and, in becoming *the* institution of cultural life, the cultural spirit has, in an important sense, accomplished itself. Revolution, in other words, is the very form of cultural life, and, in the establishing of the revolution, this norm has now achieved political dominance.[24]

In this modern world, we have a new kind of democracy, compared to the self-legislating democracy of the Greek city. This is a democracy of the universal equality of rational individuals. It is not "more" democratic than the ancient model, but it is democracy of a different sort for it is a democracy that licenses one *insofar as one has converted to rationality*. The individual, rather than the community, is the primary locus of moral and political worth, and this is thus a democracy of individual rights, and equally of individual responsibility.

And yet this freedom of the rational individual who is an authority unto himself—the self valorized by liberalism—is no more the perfect realization of human freedom than is the ancient model. Foucault in particular has challenged the teleological self-conception of this modern "liberal" culture, according to which its achievement is humanity's "progress" to the proper recognition of human subjectivity. Foucault shows how the supposed "humanitarianism" of modern systems of discipline that precisely operate on the principle of the individual who is an authority unto himself in fact introduces a new form of oppression, a new form of violence. I will not specifically pursue Foucault's reasons for deeming this system oppressive, but will look only at his analysis of the particular mechanisms by which this regime is accomplished.

In *Discipline and Punish*, Foucault investigates the transition from an older approach to punishment to a more modern, and putatively more "humane," approach to punishment. In place of savage, public abuse of the body of the accused, the modern world witnessed the emergence of systems of incarceration that relied on means of control other than direct bodily violence. This new system of punishment is interwoven with the rise, throughout all sectors of modern culture, of what Foucault calls "disciplines." "Discipline" is a system of power that works through techniques of surveillance, normalization, and examination to distribute coercive power pervasively throughout the forms of everyday life.

By "discipline," Foucault basically means the situation in which individuals come to take into themselves, through the enforcement of myriad regulations for (bodily) behavior, the norm of regularized, orderly uniformity. The most important dimension of this as a system of social power is the use of universal surveillance; indeed, Foucault refers to discipline as relying on a mechanism that "coerces by means of observation."[25] "It is," he says, "the fact of being constantly seen, of being able always to be seen, that maintains the disciplined individual in his subjection."[26] The instituting of practices of constant surveillance—constant examination, living quarters into which a guard or supervisor can see, written documentation of the minutiae of daily affairs—has the effect of making individuals internalize the surveilling glance; that is, we habituate ourselves to practices that answer to the need to be observed. Individuals thus become self-regulating according to the norms of the social institutions; that is, the coercive and controlling power is not exercised upon the individual from an alien, centralized source, but is carried forward by the individual against himself through all his behaviors. In this way, the disciplinary power is enacted in and by the very individuals upon whom it is enacted. Individuals thus make themselves answerable to an inner, "higher" authority.

This self-regulation is indeed explicitly the ideal in modern systems of punishment in particular; that is, this construction of the self-regulating individual is not just the means by which power is enacted, but is explicitly put forward as a human—indeed, a humane—goal. The objective in these modern systems is to get the individual to reform, to convert herself to the proper norms of civil (cultured) life. This new system of the prison, the emergence of which Foucault documents in *Discipline and Punish*, is precisely based on the recognition of the primacy of self-responsible subjectivity: "correction" aims at the prisoner *as a rational individual*, not as a natural body, and speaks to the responsibility of her subjectivity. It is, so to speak, the mind that must be addressed, not the body, the individual qua rational, not the individual in her natural particularities; hence the condemnation of other forms of punishment as "inhumane." We can see in this very structure of the "reforming" prisoner the same logic of "conversion" that Hegel identifies as characterizing the world of culture. This normalized, self-regulating individual is indeed precisely the ideal subject of liberal political theory, the "rational individual," licensed to participate in modern democratic life.

On Foucault's analysis, then, this modern society is precisely a society of universal surveillance. Through the disciplinary practices that shape modern society, everyone is now made subject to the universal gaze. This gaze is not embodied in any particular individual, but is enacted in the behaviors of each individual. Said otherwise, the modern state is one in which everything—even the most minute "private" matters—are public; that is, they are all matters in which the normalizing demands of discipline have entered.[27] In Foucault's analysis of discipline, then, we see precisely the mechanism by which the paradigmatically "free" modern subject is cultivated. Discipline as a cultural system accomplishes the cultural ideal proclaimed in Christianity and emblematically instituted in the French Revolution. Let us now consider Hegel's discussion of the problem of the French Revolution.

The French Revolution is the institutionalization of the challenge to particular privilege. In the democratic, equal society of free, rational individuals, it is only qua rational individual—that is, as an individual who is in principle equal to all others—that one has standing; no privilege is accorded to the particularities of one's position.

> After the various spiritual spheres and the restricted life of the individual have been done away with . . . all that remains . . . is the immanent movement of the universal self-consciousness as a reciprocity of self-consciousness in the form of *universality* and of *personal* consciousness. . . . [T]his singular consciousness is no less directly conscious of itself as universal will. . . . [T]herefore, in passing over into action and in creating objectivity, it is doing nothing individual, but carrying out the laws and functions of the state.[28]

Whereas this universal equality may initially seem liberating in its power to overthrow existing abusive and unfair structures of the distribution of wealth and power, it is in fact ultimately oppressive, for it is impossible for one to exist as such an indifferent, inherently and exclusively universal self:

> It follows from this that it cannot achieve anything positive. . . . The work which *conscious* freedom might accomplish would consist in that freedom . . . making itself into an *object* and into an *enduring being* . . . . [W]hen placed in the element of *being*, personality would have the significance of a specific personality; it would cease to be in truth universal self-consciousness.[29]

The principle of universal equality entails that anything particular to one is, *ipso facto*, something that holds one apart from the universal self one is supposed to be. Insofar as one is particular, one is an enemy of the state, an enemy of the revolution, but every "I" will necessarily always be particular.[30] *One is not entitled* to hold anything private, or exclusive. And, thus, one is not entitled to "be" at all. Hegel himself sees this problem emblematized in the transformation of the institution of the Revolution of 1789 into the Terror of 1793, in which the revolution turns upon itself, and leads to an institution of universal suspicion and death.

> In this its characteristic *work* [the work of the guillotine], absolute freedom becomes explicitly objective to itself, and self-consciousness learns what absolute freedom in effect is. *In itself*, it is just this *abstract self-consciousness*, which effaces all distinction and all continuance of distinction within it. It is as such that it is objective to itself; the *terror* of death is the vision of this negative nature of itself.[31]

Whether in the coercion of "discipline" or in the Terror of the guillotine, the modern realization of freedom results in the subjection of all to a universal surveillance in which one can never make oneself "at home" in a particularity. In all areas, one must constantly be conformed to the judgment of the universal, an imperative in relation to which one will always be guilty.

Whereas the ancient world destroyed the individual by denying legitimacy to its ability to be responsible on its own to ultimate truths, the modern world destroys the individual by denying legitimacy to its need to be partial. Though it has been a great culture of human flourishing and freedom, this modern world, like the ancient, is ultimately a political order that does violence to what it is to be a person.

I want now to look at the nature of freedom itself, and at the political context of its realization.

Being as Event, and Spirit as Freedom: Multiculturalism

What kind of reality is freedom? Most obviously, it is the reality that is the subject matter of Hegel's philosophy of history—freedom is, he implies, the moving, the material, the formal and the final cause of history.[32] In introducing my discussion of the history of freedom, I said that freedom does not realize itself in relationship to some pre-established plan. On the contrary, freedom is precisely the self-emergent. It is not defined in terms of another, and cannot be explained on the basis of some other reality. Said otherwise, freedom is the absolute; that is, it is only in and as freedom that being is most really realized. Let me address this theme by reflecting again on the terms of Hegel's *Science of Logic.*

The *Science of Logic* is "about" being. The simplest, and most immediate description of what that book studies is "being, pure being, without any further determination." Let us think for a moment about what this means. Most simply, this is a description of the absolute. By "the absolute" I mean the ultimate context, that which is relative to no other: "[t]he absolute reality would be but an empty name if in truth there were for it an 'other.'"[33] "The absolute" is simply the same thing we all regularly invoke when we say "reality," and that is what is said in "being." As we noted in chapter 3, "being" is whatever is, whatever is real, the reality of whatever is. Whatever we might refer to—a cause, an idea, a difference—would always "be," that is, it would always necessarily already be contained within the purview of the term "being" and, indeed, would always necessarily already be "of" being. And if we were to break down any being into its constituents—its qualities, its structure, its organization, its actions—these, too, would all "be"—they would all be "beings" of one sort or other. Being itself already contains any and all beings, and, indeed, it is itself only made of being. By definition, there could be nothing else. Being, then, is the absolute: it is that in relation to which there is no other. It is all reality, and the very reality of whatever is real.

I said that being is that in relation to which there is no other. Being, in other words, cannot pertain to this and not that, for in that case there would be no "that" for it to be opposing. But if being cannot be this as opposed to that, it can have no determinacy. And, in the absence of any determinacy, it would be nothing. For there *to be,* in other words, there must be *something.* It is only inasmuch as there is something rather than nothing that there is being. Thus, just as it is true that being must be pure being, the absolute reality of all that is, it is equally true that being, in order to be, must be *something,* must be determinate. There is being—being is—only insofar as there is determinateness, and determinateness is always a particularity, a this-not-that. There is determinateness, then, only if there are determinatenesses. Being is, then, only insofar as there are determinate beings.

Here, in these two descriptions, we have articulated the nature of being. Being, as we argued in chapter 8, is the determinate totality of what actually is, and the infinite openness to whatever might be. But these two descriptions, as we investigated in detail in chapter 8, are opposed. Indeed, being proper precisely is this conflict of these two descriptions; that is, being is the conflict of pure being and determinate being. This is what Hegel calls the infinite. It is precisely determinateness—the actual—as pointing beyond itself as to its own self. Being is determinate being occurring as infinite openness.

Anything that is realizes and exemplifies this logic to some degree. Any being is what it is only by its embeddedness with what is beyond it in the seamless fabric of being. But, qua individual thing, a determinate being does not acknowledge this embeddedness: it is defined by its limit, and opposed to what is beyond it. Indeed, as Hegel shows in the *Phenomenology of Spirit,* the very nature of any living being is to enact this embeddedness in every desire, in every action, but the very nature of desire is to deny this debt to the beyond. All beings implicitly realize this logic of being both limited and beyond the limit, but (as we saw in chapter 8), it is only the reality that Hegel calls spirit—that is, free self-consciousness—that realizes it fully, for it is only spirit that explicitly acknowledges this its nature. It is the free being that recognizes that it itself—this determinacy—is not exhausted by its actuality, but "is" precisely to be open. Said otherwise, it is only *as freedom* that being accomplishes the event of openness.

If we look back now at our discussion of history, we can say that, at root, the problem in each of the two great historical accomplishments of freedom is inadequate metaphysics. In each of those political realizations of freedom, freedom is cultivated according to a conception of the nature of freedom that is inadequate to the nature of freedom. Ancient Greek ethicality construed freedom on the model of nature. Christian-Enlightenment culture construed freedom on the model of revolution. Expressed in the language I have used to discuss the *Science of Logic*, ancient Greek ethicality construes freedom as one existent determinacy among others, and Christian culture construes freedom as the denial of all determinacy in favor of a beyond. We have seen, though, that freedom must be understood as the infinitely open event. Freedom can never simply be a determinacy, nor can it simply not be determinacy. Freedom must be determinacy opening itself to its beyond. Freedom, that is, must be the event of reconciliation, of finding itself in its beyond. What politics construes freedom on the model of event? Is there a third form of democracy beyond the *polis* and the Revolution?[34]

What we have seen from our consideration of being as the infinite is that being itself—the universal—does not exist independently of the determinate beings, but is realized only as the open beyond that they project from themselves. The universal is only constituted in and through the determinate crossing of limits that is accomplished *as*, *by*, and *in* the limited realities themselves. This means that it is the singular and the particular that are the givens, not the universal.[35] The universal exists precisely as the demand for reconciliation that emanates intrinsically from the determinate beings. It is something they must accomplish.

But if the universal is not defined *except in the terms of* the particularities of determinate situations, then there cannot be any other reality to which one can appeal for an answer to how to accomplish freedom. There can be neither a given nature nor an impersonal beyond to legislate relations; rather freedom is accomplished only in the demand that these particularities reconcile. This can only entail a politics of dialogue and multiculturalism.[36]

Each of the other regimes of freedom involved a fundamental sort of violence against the free individual—indeed, against freedom itself. Ethicality recognizes the substantial weight of the particular dimensions of our existence, but by presuming this givenness to be *normative*, it suppresses the self-creative, self-responsible power of human singularity. Culture recognizes the irreducible necessity for truth and value to answer to the demands of this singularity of individual perspective, but in presuming the sufficiency of this in abstraction, it denies legitimacy to our need to be particular, to be local, to make a home for ourselves in the world that is not made in universal terms. Unlike the world of "Culture," the politics of multicultural dialogue recognizes the necessity that freedom is always embodied, that is, individuals and communities will always be irreducibly committed to particular forms of existence; unlike the world of "Ethicality," the politics of multicultural dialogue recognizes the necessity that these particularities be the bases for self-transformation and openness to what is other, rather than as naturally given sources of value.

Now here too, in this call to multicultural dialogue and reconciliation, one might also hear a kind of violence. Freedom as multicultural dialogue is violence in the sense that it is a demand that limits be crossed, and boundaries be overcome. But this is a violence that is internal to the thing itself. It is a not a suppression imposed from without, but is the thing's own indwelling demand for self-transformation, its own intrinsic dialectic, its own need to measure up to the reality it implicitly is. Freedom is only realized as the self-transformative event of openness.

10

Freedom and Institutions: Perception, Spirit, and the Time of Right

Each of us is in principle a free being. Each of us also exists as a finite consciousness. This is the situation of freedom: freedom, itself infinite by definition, is always and only realized in and as free, finite individuals. It is this tension between the infinitude and finitude of freedom—a tension we have explored in relationship to Hegel's interpretation of history—that provides the context and rationale for Hegel's *Philosophy of Right.* I will take up the interpretation of this work first by considering the nature of perception, which, as the definitive condition of finite consciousness, provides the arena within which freedom as such is to be realized. Taking a cue from Merleau-Ponty's argument that perception is a practice, I will consider the distinctive character of the perception of a person, that is, the recognition of a self-consciously free being by a self-consciously free being. I will then turn to a consideration of freedom on its own terms, and investigate the forms of determinacy necessary to the realization of freedom, first discussing the notion of determinateness in general, and then discussing the specific forms of determinateness—family, civil society, and ethical institutions in general—that characterize the intersubjective aspects of our freedom; we will see that the basic forms of institution that are logically demanded by the nature of freedom parallel the basic accomplishments of ancient and modern politics, which we studied in chapter 9. My goal in this analysis is not to penetrate into the details of Hegel's analysis of institutions, but to understand the overall logic and structure of his analysis of these institutions; specifically, we see that freedom can only be embodied in institutions that are in constitutive tension with one another. This analysis will conclude, as did the analysis in chapter 9, by showing that freedom demands ultimately to be realized as a practice of multicultural dialogue in which the institutions of right subordinate the ultimacy of their own determinateness and assume the role of language, the role of being a medium for realizing the freedom of the other. Let us begin with the nature of perception.

Freedom and Perception as Practice

One of the central ideas of Merleau-Ponty's *Phenomenology of Perception* is that perception—which we typically deem to be a passive "being-impressed"—is in fact a practice.[1] The perception of the world outside us is not something that simply happens to us but is something only accomplished with our cooperation. The world, then, is not simply what causes us to notice its form—as appears to be the case in the "finished" work of perception—but is rather a solicitation of our engagement, and perception is thus realized in a dynamic of call and response.

This structure of perception as a response to a call is, not surprisingly, most obviously manifest in what we explicitly designate as "a call": to be called by someone else is to apprehend certain sounds *as* the imperative to turn around and face the one uttering the sounds, and it is precisely *in this impulsion to turn* that I experience the call *as* call. Something like this "hearing by turning" is in fact the normal structure of all our perception. In my everyday experience of walking down the stairs in my office building, I experience the handrail, for example, as soliciting my grasp: there are not two phases—one the recognition that it is a handrail and the second a self-conscious decision to grasp it—but it is in and as grasping it that I accomplish my perception of it. Though I certainly can have the experience of taking the handrail as a thematic object of perception by staring at it, the normal form of my perception is to "live through" it as a non-thematized aspect of the whole network of determinate features that constitutes my perceptual and behavioral field. Merleau-Ponty underscores the way in which this structure of perception-by-action is the normal form of perception by showing its operation at the most basic levels of perceptual life:

> One can discern, at the rudimentary stage of sensibility, a working together on the part of partial stimuli and a collaboration of the sensory with the motor system which, in a variable physiological constellation, keeps sensation constant, and rules out any definition of the nervous system as a simple transmission of a given message.[2]

Even "sensation" itself is a call to the body *to act* in such a way as *to allow* a unitary phenomenon to be perceived. Let us consider how this structure of call and response is operative in the context of the perception of other people: what is the nature of the "call" that characterizes another person, and what is the nature of the performance in which the perception of this other is accomplished?

One can apprehend another person in many ways, but what is it to apprehend another person *as* a person? This is the question that animates Hegel's discussion in part A of Chapter IV of the *Phenomenology of Spirit,* "Self-Consciousness," which we considered in chapters 3 through 6.[3] Fundamentally, the distinctive experience of "another person" is the experience of a freedom: it is the experience of a determinate body as a self-determining site of meaning. Describing this experience, Hegel writes:

> Consciousness has for its object one which, of its own self, posits its otherness or difference as a nothingness, and in so doing is independent. . . . [It] does not have the object before it merely as it exists primarily for desire, but as something that has an independent existence of its own, which, therefore, it cannot utilize for its own purposes, if that object does not of its own accord do what the first does to it.[4]

To experience the other as such a free individual is to experience that other as a source of meaning that exceeds the limits of one's own meaning-giving powers. When other things in the world "call" to me, that call typically takes the form of an invocation of an habitual way of being-in-the-world that I have developed.[5] The handrail, for example, is a piece of "equipment" that has its meaning as "handrail" because that is the interpretation it gets in my worldly projects.[6] In this respect, then, the "meaning" of the things of our world typically reflects back to us our own desires. Precisely what the other person as person reflects, however, is that she is not simply answerable to the terms of my desire. Experiencing the other person as another person is experiencing that other as setting the terms of meaning for herself, that is, it is experiencing her as self-determining: "the other is . . . independent and self-contained, and there is nothing in it of which it is not through it."[7] This self-determining freedom of the other is primarily her freedom to determine the sense of her world. I want to make two points here, first about what this entails in principle, and second about what this entails concretely.

First, inasmuch as the other, qua free, sets the terms for meaning within her world, the sense of that other's world is inherently open to her self-transformative gestures, awaiting her free decision by which its meaning is determined. That the other perceives the meaning of the world as open is what defines her as free, and thus my perceiving the other *as* free entails perceiving the sense of her world as thus open, that is, perceiving her as self-transformatively autonomous.

Second, this experiencing of the other as free is itself inseparable from a perception of the form of the things in the world. Qua free, the other person is one whose desires set the terms for things, as much as I myself in my desire set the terms for meaning in my everyday world. And, inasmuch as the same things populate my world and hers, the experience of the other as another person is the experience of, so to speak, the conflict of loyalties at the heart of things—I experience the other in experiencing the orientation of things in my world away from myself and toward a freedom located there, in a position I cannot occupy.[8]

Let us consider, finally, what one must be like in order to accomplish this perception. Specifically, one must be free oneself in order to apprehend the other as free. We have seen that to apprehend the other as free is to operate in a world where the significance of things is not fixed in advance. Such an experience of things as having an essentially open significance is precisely what defines the experience of a free being. It is only if one is oneself a free being that one is capable of apprehending another free being as such.

In sum, then, the experience of another person *as* a person is accomplished only in an openness to experiencing the very things of the world as reflecting the self-transformative autonomy of that other, and that perception of the freedom of the other can itself only be accomplished in a situation in which the perceiver is himself free. Inasmuch, then, as our experience is inherently intersubjective, the world is a call to us to perceive it as the site of the recognition of freedom by freedom, that is, in Hegel's terms, it is the call to perceive that what really "is there" is "spirit." In Hegel's language, then, we could say that the ultimate "concept" of perception—or, in Hegel's language, "experience" ["*Erfahrung*"]—is spirit recognizing itself as spirit. Perception is thus the arena in which the issue of the adequate respect for freedom—the question of right (*Recht*)—emerges. Let us turn now to consider the conditions under which this concept of perception—spirit recognizing itself as spirit, freedom recognizing freedom—can realize itself.[9]

Freedom and Determinateness

We are born free in principle, but that freedom needs to be developed. As Hegel says,

> the child is *in itself* a human being; it has reason only *in itself*, it is only the potentiality of reason and freedom, and is therefore free only in accordance with its concept.[10]

The development of that freedom rests on "material conditions," as Marx might call them, and also upon intersubjective conditions, for,

Hegel argues, freedom is only realized cooperatively. Let us reflect on what it is to be free.

"Ability" and "initiative" are the most central ideas embedded in the notion of freedom. First and foremost, "freedom" means freedom of action. To be free is to be able to do, and our freedom is thus primarily our experience of "I can . . . ."[11] Action itself is the inauguration of change within reality. For me to be able to act, then, I must be such a thing as can introduce change into the world, and that means I must be of a piece with that world: I must be a determinate reality, a body. To be free, then, I must be something.[12] Specific actions as well depend upon specific competencies. My body must be formed, for example, with joints if I am to be able to walk. The ability to walk, in other words, is not an "abstract," disembodied power but is precisely the freedom possessed *by* the jointed body: freedom is not something alien to determinacy, but is precisely the freedom *of* determinacy.

The first demand upon freedom, then, is that it be realized as something determinate. This is how Hegel begins his analysis of the conditions of freedom with his discussion of "property."

> Through this positing of itself as something *determinate, 'I'* steps into existence [*Dasein*] in general—the absolute moment of the *finitude* or *particularization* of the 'I.'[13]

He continues,

> [t]he person must give himself an external *sphere of freedom* in order to have being as Idea. . . . Not until he has property does the person exist as reason.[14]

We realize ourselves by putting ourselves outside ourselves, by establishing ourselves as a reality in the world, which is to say in the bodily, spatial terms of the world. Freedom is only real insofar as it stakes a claim in the real and exists as a finite, determinate actuality. My freedom will be the freedom *of* this actuality, will be *its* powers of engagement.

This notion that freedom, as "the power to . . . ," is the freedom *of* a determinacy is especially central to the notion of education. With effort, we *learn how* to do various things. That learning typically requires discipline, development, and habituation. We constrain ourselves to operate within certain parameters (discipline) and through so doing we change ourselves, perhaps through the reshaping of our muscles through exercise, or perhaps through the establishing of habits of disciplined behavior in learning to dance, for example. It is precisely by molding ourselves into a new *specificity* that we develop a new power. My ability to enter into conversation with you comes through my constraining myself always to speak according to the demands of the English language; my ability to capture my thoughts on paper comes through my constraining my hands always to move according to the patterns of forming English words, either through the difficult and tedious elementary-school exercises of learning basic penmanship or through the hours of practice on a keyboard in secondary school.[15] The freedom of language use is precisely the ability *of* this *developed* body, and the enhanced freedom comes with an enhancement of determinateness. It is by being educated *into* very specific determinacies that we assume the powers of a free individual, that we release the freedom that is our native potential. In its finitude, however, this determinateness is not adequate to the freedom it thus actualizes.

Hegel discusses the inherent tension of freedom and determinateness particularly clearly in his 1817–18 lectures on *Natural Right and Political Science.*

> The science of right has the free will as its principle and starting point. . . . The will contains (1) the element as absolute negativity—the pure *indeterminacy* [*Unbestimmtheit*] of the ego consisting in its pure reflection into itself, having within itself no limitation, no immediately present content determined by nature, needs, desires and instincts, or in any other way. This is the boundless infinity of the absolute abstraction of pure thinking, of *universality.*

At the same time, however,

> (2) As absolute negativity the ego is at the same time the *passing over to determinacy* and the positing of a determinacy or of a distinction as an inner content. . . . and it is only through positing itself as something determinate that the ego enters into *determinate existence* [*Dasein*]—the *absolute finitude* or infinitude of its *individuality.*[16]

The tension here, then, is that freedom by its nature is the capacity not to be defined by another, but to be "free of" any determinacy. Only insofar as that freedom *is* something specific, however, is it a reality. Freedom, then, inherently exists as a tension with itself, a "negative self-relation," the tension between the infinitude of its universality and the finitude of its determinateness.[17] Freedom "exists" its determinateness *as* defined by what is beyond itself, defined by a reality to which it is not adequate.[18]

This, then, is the challenge that is definitive of the conditions of freedom. Freedom must be realized as a determinacy, must be realized as a fixed identity, but that fixity threatens to reduce the infinitude of freedom to a settled condition. Hegel expresses the crux of the challenge:

> Here either the ego decides to *close itself off* [*Beschliessen*], to posit one determinacy as its essence and exclude everything else, or else it decides to *open itself up* [*Entschliessen*], insofar as all determinacy [is] contained in the ego as *universal*.[19]

Freedom is in essence openness, infinite openness, but its necessarily determinate realization in finitude is a kind of closure. The essential issue then, regarding the conditions of freedom, is whether they are lived as sites of an already established concluded freedom, or as sites of decision, that is, as sites of closure or as sites of openness.

The Institutional Conditions of Freedom

As Aristotle makes clear in the *Nicomachean Ethics* and the *Politics*, humans need to be cultured in order to assume their human nature. More than anything else, this is because our existence is something realized only through sharing, and we thus need to be initiated into the media of sharing, which, primarily, are language and laws, the institutions that embody the constitution of a self-organizing community.[20] Our laws establish a meaningful way to behave *together*, and joining a community is not separate from adopting its laws. This is the social version of the releasing of freedom through the establishing of determinateness that we addressed above.[21] Similarly, in adopting a language (itself in some respects the ultimate law), we commit ourselves to what is to be the very material of communication, the very fabric of intersubjective life.[22] Laws and language do not occur by nature but are precisely the ways that humans *collectively and cooperatively establish* modes of cohabitation.[23] Laws and languages will thus always be historical human accomplishments, and therefore the forms in which they have developed will always be marked by contingency and the (different) determinate forms they take will reflect the (different) specific histories of the (different) communities that accomplished themselves in and through those laws and languages.[24]

More than anything else, this determinacy of shared institutions of communal life is what Hegel means by "ethicality," for this contingent, determinate medium of sharedness is the ground of all humanity.[25] These original sharings are not themselves the work of the explicit positings of reflective egos, but are instead the only context within which such reflective egos can emerge.[26] The *Philosophy of Right* especially focuses on the internal developments that are necessary if this ethicality is to live up to its mandate to be the ground of freedom, but those developments will never usurp the position of originality that the "light-shy powers" of these founding gestures of intersubjective life hold for allowing for or accomplishing the release or realization of freedom.[27]

Our freedom is essentially our freedom to participate in the intersubjective world. We realize our freedom in making ourselves determinate, but determinacy is participation in the real, and that means participation in the world shared with others.[28] We saw above that the freedom of others entails that the meaning of the things of the world cannot be established exclusive of reference to that freedom, and thus, inasmuch as we embed our own identity in the things of the world, we make our identity beholden to the freedom of others. We realize ourselves by putting ourselves outside ourselves, and it is only our realization in this realm of contested authority that is our embodiment: our freedom is the freedom "of" that contested determinacy.[29] For that reason, we always experience our own identities as contested, as a site in which our own self-certainty—our presumptions about ourselves—must be reconciled with who we show ourselves to be in the eyes of others. We must embody our freedom in a natural body and in worldly property, but in doing so we commit ourselves to an intersubjective world, and thus make ourselves dependent on the ways in which our identities can be collectively established and recognized within the world of law and language.[30]

This "ethicality"—the "idea" of the will, or the concept of freedom as actually existing[31]—is fundamentally realized in what Hegel calls *das Volk*, the people or the nation.[32] To the extent that this *Volk* has articulated itself in explicit laws, it is the State, "the self-conscious ethical substance," "the ethical spirit as substantial will, manifest and clear to itself."[33]

> In the existence of a people [*eines Volkes*] the substantial aim is to be a state and preserve itself as such. A people [*Volk*] with no state formation (a *nation* [*eine Nation*] as such) has strictly speaking no history—like the peoples [*die Völker*] that existed before the rise of states and others which still exist in a condition of savagery [*als wilde Nationen*].[34]

This reality that exists as the continuum between nation and state is the fundamental, actual context of human life and the fundamental phenomenon of "spirit" (the cooperative reality accomplished in the domain of contested identities that we saw above). This human reality (spirit) that fundamentally exists as a nation-state is itself enacted through the opposition of the two essential species of human collective existence, the two great institutions of family and civil society [*bürgerliche Gesellschaft*], and it is the definitive challenge of a state to enact itself as a unity through the opposition of these elements.

> The really living totality—that which preserves, in other words continually produces the state in general and its constitution, is the *government.* The organization which natural necessity gives is seen in the rise of the family and of the "estates" of civil society. The government is the universal part of the constitution, i.e. the part which intentionally aims at preserving those parts, but at the same time gets hold of and carries out those general aims of the whole which rise above the function of the family and civil society.[35]

It is this founding and irreducible opposition of family and civil society upon which I will focus before returning at the end of the chapter to a further consideration of the state.

Family and civil society are the two basic intersubjective realizations of our identities, the two great species of the determinate practice of freedom. The family, as Hegel says in the *Phenomenology of Spirit,* is the "element" of spirit: it is where "we" begin, for it is the family that introduces one to the communal world, the world structured by laws and languages.[36] Civil society, in turn, is the arena in which one is liberated from the closure of the sense of "belonging" that the family accomplishes, and allowed to live as a self-defining individual.[37] These institutions, responding respectively to the finitude and the infinitude of freedom, define the parameters within which freedom can be realized.[38] Let us explore their opposition further.

We spoke above of the discipline and development necessary to becoming determinately free. What Hegel's analysis here shows is that it is first and foremost by *the discipline of family membership* that we become free.

> The aim of education is to subjugate the natural, immediate aspect and bring into prominence the aspect of self-determination or freedom. . . . Human beings can only become free through the negativity involved in sublating natural life. Discipline must begin with obedience, for one who has not learned to serve cannot rule; the entire capriciousness of children must be sublated. . . . The child must come to view the free personality of the older members of the family as its own and submit to their will.[39]

It is in the family that the child *learns to be a person.*[40] Family life provides the immediate context in which our personal identities are realized. Let us look at the family.

The family, Hegel says, is characterized by love, "the disposition of individual persons whereby they have their essential self-consciousness in this unity."[41] We have seen that, as free individuals, we are dependent upon others to confirm for us our identities. The family provides this initial matrix of cooperative, mutual recognition, a community through which each finds his identity.[42] Hegel elaborates on this cooperative self-consciousness that is experienced as the feeling of shared identity:

> This consciousness . . . has the shape of love, of the self-consciousness that one has not in oneself but in another, in whom one has one's own self-consciousness in such a way that this knowledge of the identity [of self and other] is the essential matter. Self-consciousness knows itself to be conscious of itself in the other, and is the intuiting, the feeling of this unity.[43]

This shared sense of identity is true both for the relation between the marriage partners and for the relation between children and parents.[44] For our purposes, it is the relation of children and parents that is especially pertinent.

For the children who grow up in the family, the family provides the immediate context of intersubjective trust and intimacy in which they are enabled to assume identities, and the task of the family is that of "educating them to independent personality."[45] "Children," Hegel remarks, "do not yet have actual free will, they are not yet persons; they are consequently . . . made persons, educated [by their parents]."[46] The family is the original matrix within which one becomes "someone." "The initial education of children comes essentially from the character of the parents; it is this that draws them into the actual world."[47] Aristotle notes in the *Poetics* that our love of imitation is central to our learning and, indeed, it is essentially through imitation of the way "personhood" is manifested in the family that the child assumes its identity as a person.[48]

Through participation in a family, one comes to have a sense of oneself as a participant in "our world." Here, as we saw in chapter 6 in our discussion of R. D. Laing's notion of "ontological security," the child develops a secure sense that she *is* someone in the medium of shared human life. This is the crucial *accomplishment of determinacy*, the crucial securing of a finite reality within the world of freedom. Hegel stresses, however, that the ultimate import of the education of the child is to facilitate the child's development of an identity that leaves the family behind.[49] This movement precisely reflects the insufficiency of a finite determinateness to realize a free individuality. The family allows one to be free by establishing for one a determinate identity. That identity will be a *free* identity, however, only if that *determinacy* is recognized to be non-ultimate, which means the family must be recognized as not the ultimate arena of human life.[50]

Civil society is the institution of a social recognition of the insufficiency of the family to supply the conditions for the realization of freedom. Civil society is the social recognition of the need of individuals to realize their free individuality beyond the constraints of the determinate identities of family life.[51] Civil society is precisely the social recognition that the individual needs to be sanctioned in her self-determination. Civil society, then, precisely *refuses* to allow determinateness to enter into its conception of the person, and it is thus the institution of the *abstract* recognition of persons, the institutionalization of the need *not* to allow determinateness a role in defining the person.

There is considerable propriety, then, in the liberal critiques of traditional culture and of "family values," and in the defense of the institutionalization of the "rights" of individuals, for there is an inherent demand of freedom that it be realized in an institutional domain that recognizes the authority of the individual to define herself in independence of her finite determinateness. At the same time, however, we must recognize the one-sidedness of this critique.[52] We have already seen the essential dependency of the individual on her participation in a determinate social "fabric," and, as critics of liberalism rightly note, the discourse of "rights" does not give adequate recognition to our social embeddedness.[53] The domain of civil society is essential, but it is with considerable justice that this domain—the "free market" world of abstract individuals—is accused of being "soulless" and irresponsible.[54] While civil society is a social recognition of something absolutely essential about human freedom, it is insufficient on its own to embody that freedom.

What we can see, then, is, first, that there are reasons *internal to the nature of freedom* for why the institutions of family life and civil society are the appropriate conditions for the realization of freedom. Each institution enacts a collective recognition of the free nature of that very collectivity, the family allowing the accomplishment of determinate identity, civil society allowing the subordination of that determinateness to the self-determining universality of free personality. We can also see, however, that, second, each institution on its own is antagonistic to freedom, family life by enforcing a fixity to human identity that represses the singularity of self-definition, civil society by suppressing an acknowledgment of the essential particularity and social embeddedness of individuals.

We are family members, parts of the "free" world of individual interaction and self-definition (the world of "morality" and "business"), and members of states that themselves operate within a global interaction of states. In our existence as family members and as rational individuals, we treat ourselves as "owning" ourselves (and, indeed, other property). In fact, though, our very identities are premised on an involvement in an ethicality that exceeds us, by which we are ultimately "owned." This ownership is especially clear with language, for, whereas other posited laws can seem to be alien and optional restrictions,[55] it is only *within* our possession by language—"the most spiritual existence of the spiritual"[56]—that we "possess" ourselves at all. The family and civil society provide the domains within which we interpret ourselves as self-possessed persons, but both family and civil society themselves rest within their participation in a self-organizing community of mutual recognition whose terms precede and exceed the terms by which family and civil society operate.[57] Qua *Volk*, we are already *implicitly* "owned" by this spiritual reality; qua *state*, the explicitness of this ownership is "posited." We belong to a self-organizing community (*Volk*) that naturally articulates itself into the contested domains of family and individual identity, and that, as a state, enacts measures to contain the tendencies of families and individuals to define themselves independently of the community.

In the institutions of the family and civil life, and in the collective efforts we make to control their interaction, we have the map of the permanent terrain for the realization of human freedom, and the establishing of these institutions "completes" the story of the conditions of freedom.[58] In the practices of the family, civil society, and the explicit attempts by a people to enact the explicit recognition by the family and civil society of their belonging to a greater reality, we have mapped out the logical terrain of freedom, the conditions for accomplishing the adequate perception of spirit by spirit. These institutions are the "objective conditions" in which freedom embodies itself.

With the institutions of family, civil society, and state we have completed the story of "right" (*Recht*); any social reality that has not developed these institutions will be fundamentally repressive of the needs of human freedom. But, though essential and complete, these institutions nevertheless remain essentially inadequate to the final accomplishment of freedom. As we saw, family and civil society are themselves the embodiment of constitutive resistances to the development of freedom and the state that attempts to "sublate" this opposition will itself only ever be an attempt by finite self-consciousness to be adequate to the inherently "light-shy" ethical powers that enable freedom.[59] But this inadequacy to the ultimate demands of freedom will not be addressed by the development of further institutions, for these will be only so many more objective determinacies, so many more variants on this same terrain. Rather the further demands of freedom consist in determining how these institutions are taken up. We saw above that Hegel identified the ambivalence inherent to the embodiment of freedom as the question of whether determinacy is embraced as a closure or as an opening. That issue of closing and opening is equally the essential issue for these determinacies in which collective freedom is realized. The institutions of family and civil society are the conditions that make possible freedom, but freedom is only accomplished in these finite forms adopting a stance of infinite openness to the other.[60] Let us turn now to consideration of this issue.

Freedom as the Practice of Multicultural Dialogue

In the first section, we considered the nature of perception (or "experience" [*Erfahrung*] in Hegel's vocabulary). We determined (a) that perception is a practice and (b) that the *telos* of perceptual life is the perception of freedom by freedom. We can use that theme, now, to complete our reflection on the family and civil society as the essential, elemental conditions of freedom. Basically, the imperative of freedom is to live these institutions as conditions for accomplishing the perception of freedom by freedom.

In the *Encyclopaedia*, Hegel writes,

> The Objective Mind [i.e., the conditions of right] is the absolute Idea [freedom/spirit], but only existing *in posse*; and, as it is thus on the territory of finitude, its actual rationality retains the aspect of external apparency.[61]

He continues:

> But the purposive action of this will is to realize its concept, Liberty, in these externally objective aspects, making the latter a world moulded by the former, which in it is thus at home with itself.[62]

He reiterates this point later:

> The failure of [objective spirit] consists—partly in having its freedom *immediately* in reality, in something external, therefore in a thing—partly in the abstract universality of its goodness.[63]

In other words, objective spirit, qua finite and determinate, is in principle inadequate as a realization of freedom.[64] What this means is that there can never be a "perfect" society. Just as there is no educational system that could be devised that would eliminate the fact that children need to learn, so there is no system of institutions that can accomplish the enactment of openness that characterizes freedom. "Objective spirit" or the conditions of right will always be like a text that needs to be read: the institutions of right provide the conditions that allow the release of freedom, but they are not themselves the accomplishment of that release. Freedom is *performed*, not instituted.

What is the performance of freedom that these institutions allow? We saw above that freedom is ultimately the perception of freedom by freedom, that is, the experience of the things of the world as the enactment of the openness to the self-determining openness to the other. We have seen that our own freedom in always embedded in a community, first familial and then civil: it is as a community member that one enacts one's own free identity.[65] The *ethical nature* of our freedom entails that our freedom is allowed to mature and develop only by committing itself to determinacies of law, culture, and language, but the *imperative* our freedom puts upon us is to live these determinacies as open rather than closed. We saw above that freedom embodies itself in a determinateness insofar as it makes itself—itself qua free—"at home" in it. We have also seen, however, that our freedom is always a cooperative realization, a shared project. The demand on the determinacies of freedom, then, is that *they be a home for this shared freedom.* To be free in my determinacy is to live it in the spirit of hospitality, to make it a site for the other; this, we might say, is the ultimate law of law.[66] It is only *in perceiving my determinacies as the call of the other* that my freedom qua freedom is embodied. Our freedom is given determinate reality by participation in a local community, and so is the freedom of the other. This means our freedom is realized as such in enacting our cultural membership as the imperative to be open to laws, cultures, and languages other than our own, or, more exactly, to be open to those other laws, cultures, and languages as themselves sites for the realization of freedom.

Freedom, the "truth" of right, then, is found in a spirit of multiculturalism. The "completion" of Right, that is, is not found in further institutions of right, but in the living of those institutions *as* the site of a perception of freedom by freedom, and this means both experiencing one's institutions as the imperative of such a perception and experiencing the institutions of the other as such an imperative. This perceiving of freedom through the other's determinateness means that freedom is properly accomplished in the perception of things and their organization into institutions as ultimately language, that is, in the perception of them as media for accomplishing communication, for accomplishing the perception of freedom by freedom.[67] We began with the idea that perception is a practice, and we can now see that perception itself fulfills its *telos* of being the perception of freedom by freedom in the practice of multicultural dialogue.[68]

Conclusion: The Time of Right

Our freedom requires that we be determinate. This is what laws and all institutions accomplish—they are the discipline and determinateness that makes us something. Though we can rightly recognize the inhibitions to freedom that are entailed by the ambivalence that characterizes the finitude of family and civil society in general, and all the specific details of the institutions of right, we nonetheless should not wish to be free of them for it is only their determinacy that accomplishes the realization of freedom. Freedom demands that we be beholden to our determinacy, which is why the determining of an age of majority, the divisions of electoral districts, punishment, and so on, are just in principle, though always demonstrably inadequate to the justice they make possible.

These institutions are the institutions of justice, but they do not by themselves constitute justice: they are *for* the perception of freedom by freedom, and it is only *as* the conditions of this perception that they are valid. It is, therefore, only in the enactment of these institutions as the media for a multicultural dialogue that these institutions find their truth. This means that the institutions of right find their truth only in the circumstance in which the non-ultimacy of their finitude is enacted through them, that is, in the circumstance in which their exclusive definitiveness of the terms of right is superseded. The conditions of right *are* thus conditions of right only in the performance of a dialogue in which their already-surpassedness-in-principle is acknowledged. The conditions of right are fulfilled only as the conditions of a practice of dialogue in which a stance of openness is performed.[69]

Freedom is thus ultimately not a matter of the past, not a matter of institutions, though this past is constitutive of it inasmuch as freedom must always be realized in a determinacy. Failure to recognize the "pastness" of freedom is the failure to recognize its necessary determinateness, its particularity. In its openness to the other, freedom is also inherently futural, but, again, it is not a matter of the future, not something for which we must wait as if it might eventuate at some time yet to come: it is *always* futural, so there is no time at which that commitment to openness can be overcome.[70] Failure to recognize the futurity of freedom is the failure to recognize its necessary openness, its universality. Though past and future are constitutive of it, freedom is ultimately a matter of the present inasmuch as it is a reality that must be performed.[71] Freedom is not something already accomplished, nor is it something to wait for: it is something to *do*, a practice. Failure to recognize that it is a matter of the present is the failure to recognize its necessary performativity, its singularity. This ultimate performative dimension of freedom is the demand to make *these* institutions here and now the sites of the realization of openness: "Here is your Rhodes—here is your jump."[72]

11

Democratic Regime and Democratic Practice: The Politics of Modernity

The modern world, by which I mean the distinctive culture that emerged in Europe around 1300 and that continues to define the terms of contemporary global politics, is distinctly characterized by an institutional and a broad cultural endorsement of a particular conception of the human person. This conception is most familiarly manifest in the notion of "human rights" that attach to the individual person, and is especially interwoven with the modern conception of democracy. I will outline more clearly what I take this conception to be by drawing on Hegel's analysis of "Culture" in the *Phenomenology of Spirit*, and especially on his analysis, in the section called "Absolute Freedom and Terror," of the inherent problems in this conception made manifest historically in the French Revolution. I will then turn to Marx's analysis of capitalism to bring out some of the implications of this view for modern politics, and end with reflections on democracy that take their lead from Derrida's writings on this topic, especially in his book *Rogues*. As was the case in chapter 10, in this chapter my conclusion will be about the nature of democracy, arguing that the democratic ideal can only be realized as a practice and not as a fixed set of institutions.

Modern Politics and Its Inherent Problem

There is a particular sense of what it is to be a human being that emerges powerfully and definitively in many different areas of early modern thought and culture. This is the conception of the intrinsic worth of the individual person. Roman law, as Hegel makes clear in his analysis of "Legal Status," had already acknowledged the legal priority of the single ego.[1] The modern conception is richer, though, than the essentially "stoic" conception of the person that underlies Roman law. Whereas Roman law acknowledges the ultimacy of the choice and self-responsibility of the single individual, the modern conception—drawing upon the force of the Christian sense of the "higher calling" intrinsic to all persons, as we saw in chapter 9—validates not simply the single, choosing ego as such, but instead the single ego that is inherently characterized by rationality, that is, by the innate ability to speak from the authority of universal and necessary truths. Hegel writes:

> [I]t gives itself the character of a universal, and this its universality is its authentication and actuality. This *equality* with everyone is, therefore, not the equality of the sphere of legal right, not that immediate recognition and validity of self-consciousness simply because it *is*; on the contrary, to be valid it must have conformed itself to the universal by the mediating process of alienation.[2]

It is this individual—the individual, precisely, who lives from a standpoint that supersedes the idiosyncrasy of the singular perspective—that is recognized, legally and otherwise, as being of infinite, that is, intrinsic, worth.

The clearest and most rigorous statement of this Modern view of the intrinsic worth of the rational individual is surely to be found in Kant's *Groundwork for the Metaphysics of Morals*, and this conception of the inherent worth of the individual who has the universal within herself is also the conception of the person implied in the democratic principle according to which all rational individuals are included in principle within the domain of political "rights," and thus the responsibility of politics is to enact a public reality—enact a set of political institutions—that reflects, realizes, and embodies this conception.[3] This politics enacts, as Hegel says, the Christian principle that all are free, a politics of universal inclusion, committed thus to a universal mission, and also to the impossibility of legitimate exclusivity.[4]

This conception is politically liberating, in that it gives a ground for the resistance to situations of political oppression based on models of political access that rely upon exclusionary grounds such as race, birth, gender, or wealth. In early modern Europe, this gave ground for the challenge to traditional prerogatives and privileges, a challenge embodied most famously in the French Revolution. This conception also points to the need to install political institutions that acknowledge the worth of such a rational self, thus licensing the freedom in inquiry of, for example, the Scientific Revolution. This model thus grounds the project of progress, of the individual who represents universal humanity taking up a stance of creative openness toward the world, rather than conservatively maintaining the status quo. The Scientific Revolution won its way into the world through conflict with the conservatism of established institutions, and the political revolutions in America and France brought about the explicit political recognition of the conception of the human person that legitimates these practices (of science and technology). This political liberation of the individual is also thus the legitimation of the capitalist and industrial revolutions.

As we noted in chapter 9, Hegel studies the French Revolution (in the section of the *Phenomenology of Spirit* called "Absolute Freedom and Terror") because it is exemplary of this situation, both as an expression of the pure principle of this view of humanity and as a raw expression of a constitutive problem in this view.[5] The principle of this view is that every individual person is, in herself, a representative of the universal, an agent inherently legitimated to speak on behalf of the rational essence of each of us: "the universal will goes *into itself* and is a *single* will; . . . th[e] singular consciousness is no less directly conscious of itself as universal will."[6] According to the principles of the French Revolution, every person is, qua rational, that is, qua living from the perspective of universality, a representative of the regime and thus legitimated in principle for inclusion in this regime:

> [T]he singular consciousness itself is directly in its own eyes . . . universal consciousness and will. . . . [I]n passing over into action and in creating objectivity, it is doing nothing individual, but carrying out the laws and functions of the state."[7]

The problem is that this view of the person, in validating what is universal within us, denies the definitive weight of what is not universal within us. Every person is thus immediately an *opponent* of the regime insofar as (a) she cannot fail to live from a privileging of the particularities that happen to characterize her life and, (b) qua *such particularity*, she is excluded from "the universal": "when placed in the element of *being*, personality would have the significance of a specific personality; it would cease to be in truth universal self-consciousness."[8] Ultimately, all that makes the self an actual existent is the target of the revolution in its opposition to particularity and exclusivity.

> But the supreme reality and the reality which stands in the greatest antithesis to universal freedom, or rather the sole object that will still exist for that freedom, is the freedom and singularity of actual self-consciousness itself.[9]

The only "legitimate" individual is the individual *without* any determinate characteristics, for all such determinacies are particularities, "properties" one has to the exclusion of others—indeed, even one's distinctness as "this" one makes one logically non-universal and thus excluded in principle from participation in the regime.

> [N]ow . . . this is its sole object, an object that no longer has any content, possession, existence, or outer extension, but is merely this knowledge of itself as an absolutely pure and free individual self.[10]

Whatever resources I have power over, for example, will be expended on my bodily needs and not on everyone's equally, in my community and not everywhere equally, in accordance with my interests and beliefs and not impartially. For that reason, the only individual that can be recognized by the state is not an *actual* individual, but only an *abstract* individual—"all that remains of the object by which it can be laid hold of is solely its *abstract* existence as such"[11]—and thus every actual individual is excluded from the state. In advocating inclusion in opposition to exclusion, then, the principle of rational humanity is opposed to ways in which our identities are realized in *inherently* exclusionary ways. In fact, however, such exclusion is essential to us: it characterizes whatever about us is particular or specific. Each of us is, indeed, rational and therefore a representative of a universality that defines humanity in principle; each of us, however, is also always an individual characterized by a limited perspective, realized one-sidedly in local conditions of space, time, body, community, and so on. Each of us, that is, *necessarily* has "content, possession, existence, and outer extension."

This conflict in principle between universality and particularity in general entails a number of problems for the revolutionary government. The revolutionary government cannot articulate itself into laws or institutions, for in thus particularizing itself and its members it would be returning to the differentiation of powers and privileges that it is opposing.[12] It cannot make a decision, because decision will always be the non-shareable initiative of a "one."[13] Indeed, whatever government does exist will always be one faction, one particular alternative, winning out against others.[14] Ultimately, inasmuch as the conflict in principle between the universality and the particularity of the individual ultimately implies the exclusion of every individual from the state, the functioning of the government is naturally driven to the elimination of individuals, and it is this logical reality that Hegel sees dramatized in the Reign of Terror into which the French Revolution developed:

> The sole work and deed of universal freedom is therefore *death* . . . [wherein] what is negated is the empty point of the absolutely free

> self, . . . the cold, matter-of-fact annihilation of this existent self, from which nothing else can be taken away but its mere being.[15]

This principle of the universal equality of all rational individuals thus has as its ultimate effect the equalizing of all individuals as alien to the universal and hence excluded from participation within the rational community: this principle of universal inclusion thus demonstrates universal exclusion to be its truth.

Hegel's analysis corresponds well to the historical events. The French Revolution itself began in an attempt of the "Third Estate" to undermine the position of political and economic privilege of the French aristocracy. What began as a simple effort to change the terms of voting at the assembly of the Estates-General snowballed through a series of progressively more aggressive and more popular challenges to the established political order. Over a period of about five years, the Revolution moved through a repeated pattern of one progressive group rising to power against the established situation only to be "trumped" shortly thereafter by a more progressive group. At each stage, a revolutionary "party" sought to establish itself, only to be challenged as too conservative and self-interested by a more radical party claiming for itself the purer ability to represent the nation.[16] The revolution thus found itself constantly fighting for its own maintenance against internal tendencies to settle into a new order (and, indeed, against external threats such as war with other European states).[17]

In his speech of February 5, 1794, Maximilien Robespierre, himself widely acknowledged as the voice of the "pure" revolution, defended the need for the Revolution to employ Terror to preserve itself against its enemies in what Carl Schmitt would call a "State of Exception."[18] The corresponding "Reign of Terror" of 1793–4 was a period of vast execution of enemies of the Revolution in which, following the "Law of Suspects" of September 17, 1793, and ultimately the Law of 22 Prairial [June 10, 1794], the revolutionary tribunal had the power to arrest and ultimately execute "all those who, through their conduct, associations, comments or writings have shown themselves partisans of tyranny, or federalism and enemies of liberty."[19] Instead of being an independently articulated code, the system of "law and justice" here became instead the maintenance of the self-defining and self-legitimating revolution, which, by thus establishing itself as answerable to nothing else, became effectively a dictatorship.[20] In this situation, virtually anyone could be determined to be guilty of subverting the revolutionary aims and working in her own self-interest (and, indeed, Robespierre himself eventually fell victim to the Terror). What is important here, though, is that this situation emerged through the attempt to realize the universalist goal of the revolution, and thus reveals something about the founding principles themselves: the Terror is not simply an accidental development in this situation, but is the starkest exemplification of the implicit conflict within the revolution such that anyone, by virtue of her particularity, is always already condemned as a self-interested subverter of the universality of the revolution.

Though the Terror brings into clear political focus the logical contradiction implicit in the modern conception of the person, it is by no means the only political enactment of this contradictory stance. Indeed, the French Revolution itself represents the inauguration of the modern political world, and the political structures of the contemporary world largely reproduce these conflicts already laid bare in the Terror.[21] The contradiction that showed itself in the Terror is already manifest in the defence of property essential to the Revolutionary programs of both France and the United States.[22] Though each embraces in principle the universal equality of free, rational individuals (the principle of universalist anti-exclusionism), each also recognizes the essentiality of establishing the free individual in his own private domain, where he has authority to dispose of his particularity in his own way. While this "right to property" rightly recognizes that the individual must be embodied, enhomed, enpropertied, it also entails the establishment of a differential and exclusionary political domain. Modern regimes, based on this "liberal" principle of the freedom (liberty) and equality of rational and rightfully property-bearing individuals, live with a tenuous—and contradictory—reconciliation of universalist principles with the needs of individual particularity that always enact the stance of the Terror implicitly (and sometimes do it explicitly).

This implicit enactment of the Terror is what Marx diagnoses in his analyses of capitalism. Marx saw the French Revolution as the effective installation of capitalism as the modern political regime.[23] Capitalism itself, Marx shows, is an inhuman (and ultimately anti-human) machine that defends and embodies an abstract conception of the person at the cost of universal alienation.[24] The capitalist thesis of individual economic freedom to compete in an open market leads to the establishment of a class of winners and losers, which amounts to an opposition of owners—those whose successful competition has allowed them to re-invest their profits in their own enterprises by establishing as industrial and technological capital their ownership of the means of production—and workers, who can only effectively enter the marketplace through working for and within the terms of the marketplace that have thus been established.[25] The equality of individual competition that seemed to be the "moral" essence of this economic regime thus becomes replaced by the competition between highly developed economic interests, each of which has its possibility of success in the marketplace determined by its capacity to profit through maximizing productivity while minimizing expenses. Capitalism thus exists as a constant revolutionizing of the means of production—a constant growth in "efficiency"—coupled with a constant diminishing of its paying out of support for its resources: workers and raw materials.[26] Success in capitalism, then, is synonymous with exploitation.

As this system develops, the successful economic interests become more and more massively powerful industrial monopolies that maximize their own capacities for growth (and hence competitive power) by offering less and less support for human individuals. As the class of owners become smaller and richer, the class of those who can compete only as workers grows, with the result that the human equality capitalism offers is only the possibility of being an indifferent labor-resource, equal to all others only in one's ability to be of service to the capitalist economic regime.[27] The "efficient" industrial system, furthermore, offers work situations that are less and less satisfying of human needs. In place of work through which one establishes for oneself a home in the world, establishing through one's engagement a meaningful communication with one's body, nature, and community, and experiencing satisfaction in the enjoyment of the meaningful products of one's labor, the developed capitalist marketplace offers the worker instead an experience of alienation from all the essential dimensions of her particularity—body, locale, community, etc.[28] Like the French Revolution, capitalism is a permanent revolution that feeds itself at the expenses of human individuals. Like the universal equality of the revolution that comes at the price of all particularity, the universal equality of capitalism is the equality to be a resource for the regime, exploited and alienated in one's particularity. This economic regime, advocated as a defence of the freedom—the liberty and equality—of human individuals becomes instead a machine for which human individuals are only resources: means, rather than ends.[29] They are "for" the economic regime, which, like the "Revolution" itself, becomes the solely self-defined value for which all others are simply expendable resources.[30] The "State of Exception," in which the autonomous worth of the individual is subordinated and sacrificed to the self-defined worth of the regime itself, is thus not an exceptional state at all, but is the implicit structure of the entirety of this regime.[31]

Both in an exemplary way in the Reign of Terror, then, and in an ongoing way through the progressive exploitation of human and nonhuman nature in capitalism, we can see the contradiction inherent to the modern conception of the person. In aiming for a universal human equality that does not conceptually recognize the rights of exclusionary particularity, modern politics produces an equality that exists only in a practical denial of human particularity, and thus a denial of humanity. This is a problem inherent to the modern conception of the person that will characterize any political system based on that principle and that cannot be adequately addressed by further political means that are themselves based on that same principle.

Beyond Modernity: The Political Prospect of Freedom

In the *Phenomenology of Spirit*, Hegel's study of "Absolute Freedom and Terror" concludes his discussion of "Self-Alienated Spirit: Culture," which is essentially his study of the logic of the modern world.[32] This study is immediately followed by the section called "Self-Certain Spirit: Morality." By considering the significance of this transition within the argument of the *Phenomenology of Spirit*, we can work out the nature of the political imperative that confronts us and that takes us beyond the politics of modernity.

Though Hegel's study of morality begins with a description of the Kantian moral position—a position that seems to maintain very much the problematic modern conception of the person as definitively characterized by a non-particularized universality—there is nonetheless a significant advance made here over the problem of modernity.[33] The advance is not found in the distinctively Kantian form of the moral view of the world, but in the definitive practical imperative that animates the moral stance in general.[34] Whereas the logic of the regime of the French Revolution is effectively that the conflict of universal and particular makes it in principle unable to act, the experience of morality is the experience of the imperative upon the single individual to enact the reconciliation of the universal and the particular here and now. Whereas what is "given" in the modern conception is the single self with its universal value, while particularity is disregarded, what is "given" to the moral standpoint is the singularity of the self in its particular situation; whereas in the politics of modernity it is the excluded particularity that must somehow find a place for itself with the given parameters of singularity and universality, here in morality it is the universal that must make its way into the given parameters of singularity and particularity.

In Hegel's argument this stance of making the universal emerge within the parameters of singularity and particularity is ultimately worked out in the stance of conscience, in its structure of transgression, confession, and forgiveness.[35] When one acts out of conscience, one does not begin from abstract, universal moral laws and then apply them to a situation as a particular instance, a "case"; rather, one feels the pull of a particular situation of injustice such that one is compelled to rectify the situation through intervention.

> Conscience does not split up the circumstances of the case into a variety of duties. . . . [I]t is simple action in accordance with duty, which fulfills not this or that duty, but knows and does what is *concretely* right.[36]

Here, one acts on one's convictions, confident that they are authoritative—indeed, experiencing them as compelling—but unable to appeal to anything beyond oneself to guarantee their legitimacy: literally, one must singularly take responsibility for one's actions.

> This *immediate* concrete self-certainty is the essence; . . . the content of the moral action is the doer's own immediate *individuality*; and the *form* of that content is just this self as a pure movement, viz . . . his *own conviction*.[37]

Inasmuch as one is unable to turn elsewhere for legitimation, one is, in Hegel's language, merely "self-certain." Indeed, in thus acting, one is intervening in the world and arrogating to oneself the authority to transgress against others. One is not truly acting from conscience if one does not recognize this about oneself, that is, if one is not embracing the risk, the urgency, and the responsibility for "making a difference." Necessarily, then, the conscientious agent is open to the judgment of others who do not see in the realized action simply the pure expression of duty, but the idiosyncratic expression of the judgment of the singular subjectivity of the conscientious agent. Inasmuch as conscience is called to act, it is called to realize its intention in the public world, and thus called to answerability to others.[38] Conscientious action thus entails an owning up to this transgression, a confession of one's sense of responsibility for one's invasiveness. Conscience is compelled to act from an unjustifiable duty, and can only hope for forgiveness from those against whom it trespasses. Conscience is therefore only realized—the intention of the conscientious agent to be the agent of the universal is what comes to pass in the world—in a dialogue in which transgression is admitted, forgiveness is offered, and a shared perspective—the universal—is enacted.[39] Further, inasmuch as the stance of conscience experiences its conscientiousness as the justification for its action—that is, inasmuch as it justifies its behavior by appeal to the claim that it was compelled by conscience—it has implicitly embraced the norm of conscientiousness in general. To point to the compelling character of one's own conscience qua conscience is to point to conscientious compulsion as a justification for anyone's action. Thus, the very forgiveness that the conscientious agent seeks in the context of its own transgressive acts is forgiveness that it in principle owes to other conscientious agents who transgress against it. Thus the stance of conscience is implicitly committed to a situation of reciprocity, that is, a situation of mutual forgiveness in the context of mutual transgression.

What this stance of forgiveness recognizes is the compelling character of the *finite* perspective of itself and the *finite* perspectives of others. Forgiveness recognizes, in other words, that we are only self-certain, and must act as singular agents in particular circumstances compelled by the values and motivations that in fact drive us. In the language we used earlier, we can say, then, that forgiveness recognizes the essentiality of the particularity of our identities, the primacy of our determinateness for setting the terms of our perspective. Indeed, in thus recognizing the ultimacy of perspective, in recognizing, that is, that one must (by definition, so to speak) work within the terms within which one actually sees, the stance of forgiveness embraces the very principle of phenomenology. Forgiveness—the culmination of the stance of conscience—recognizes, in other words, that reconciliation must be accomplished through and within the terms recognized by the other with whom one is engaged and to whom one is answerable. This imperative to reconciliation, furthermore, is thus precisely the imperative to mutual recognition through dialogue that Hegel identifies as the internal demand of self-consciousness as such.[40]

This mutual dialogue in which one embraces the terms of the other is not, however, a simple acquiescing to the ultimate authority of the other as given. Rather, it is holding oneself answerable to the particular other in the context of the ultimacy of the norm of conscience. In other words, one answers to the other, but to the other as herself answerable to the imperatives of conscience. One answers, that is, to an other who is as responsible as oneself to establish a mutually forgiving reconciliation. One does not simply answer, then, to the other as an already established identity, but to another who, like oneself, is characterized by a self-transcending particularity, that is, an other whose particularity itself calls out, like one's own, to be the site for establishing a mutuality of recognition. Like me, the other is merely self-certain, and thus in need of confirmation and legitimation from the others against whom she transgresses: like me, the other is answerable to the demands of dialogue. This dialogue of mutual forgiveness in which we establish a shared community through an embrace of each other's particularities is the culmination of the dialectic of spirit: "the word of reconciliation" enacts "a reciprocal recognition which is *absolute spirit*."[41] Let us now translate this into the domain of politics.

What Hegel's study of the French Revolution in the dialectic of "Absolute Freedom" demonstrated was the essentiality of the dimension of our particularity. Modernity on the one hand liberates us from the *determinism* of particularity, according to which political participation is determined by, for example, race, gender, or religious/ linguistic heritage, but it cannot do justice to the way that we are nonetheless essentially *determined* by particularity, that is, it is only as determinate that we *are* at all, and it is only *as* thus essentially one-sided that we can be free at all. Our identities and our political communities thus will always be and must always be exclusive. It is only on the basis of being something actual—and the actual is always finite and particular—that we can be at all.[42]

Nonetheless, as the stance of morality makes clear, the imperative to universality remains constitutive of our reality as "rational" selves. We are necessarily inherently particular—inherently exclusive—but the exclusivity that defines our particularity is itself inherently characterized by the imperative that it be reconciled with that which it excludes. The exclusivity that is essential to us must thus be characterized by openness. Indeed, it is only as exclusionary that there can be an openness. This is the political imperative to which the determinate institutions of our political life are answerable.

The dialectic of exclusivity and openness that defines Hegel's postmodern politics is at the center of Derrida's discourse on hospitality.[43] Derrida emphasizes the impossibility of the notion of an unconditional hospitality. The simple definition of hospitality would be something like "to be open," unconditionally, but one must *be something* in order to be open, and this characteristic of "being something" necessarily entails closure, conditionality. Unconditional hospitality "as such" would have no significance, that is, it would not be the embrace of anyone specific by anyone specific. Hospitality can itself only be realized conditionally, for to open one's doors to another one must first have doors, so to speak. It is only inasmuch as there is already established an exclusionary boundary that there can be any meaningful gesture of letting what is beyond the boundary—the alien—into one's own proper domain. Yet hospitality as such—unconditional hospitality—remains the definitive norm that any hospitality must enact in order to be hospitality. "Unconditional hospitality" is thus the "impossibility" that is the very possibility of hospitality. "To be hospitable" *simpliciter* is the imperative that any finite hospitality answers to, though the embrace of this norm will always be *within the conditions* of the actual, finite situation. This amounts to the imperative to have one's terms be open to what is beyond one's limits, rather than to simply forcing what is beyond one's limits to conform to one's already established parameters: it is the imperative to be open within our actual terms to what exceeds our terms. We make our homes in our determinate political domains—our determinate cultures—and Derrida's point is that it is of the nature of home to offer hospitality to guests, to those strangers, those foreigners, who are not themselves members of our household. The notion of home, then, can be a model for politics not primarily because of the sense of domestication (though that side is unavoidable) but because of the imperative to hospitality that it involves.[44] Hospitality is the openness to risk within the heart of domestication.

We can see in this notion of hospitality a political and cultural model of the structure of exclusionary openness that we developed from the dialectic of conscience. This political model is the basis for Derrida's prospect of the future of freedom, the freedom of the future, which he describes as "messianicity without messianism."[45] Michael Naas explains this nicely as "a hope that would be rooted in some tradition, history, and language, but that would gesture or call us toward something that must remain heterogeneous to that particular tradition."[46] This notion of hospitality, in other words, points us to a future in which we can retain our identity only by living through its transformation into a new identity reconciled with, and redefined by an engagement with, what it currently excludes.

What this means is that the identity—the universal—that is called for is nowhere given.[47] The unity—the community—will be accomplished in and as a real communication. The enactment of the communication will be transformative of the participants, bringing them to an identity they did not possess—that did not exist—in advance of their shared creation of it. For this reason the terms of the universality can never be specified in advance. We are called to an identity that can only be defined through the process by which we come to it.

Our political imperative, then, is to engage with our *actual* others, those particular others whom we definitively exclude by our own particularity. "Here is your Rhodes, here your jump," Hegel quotes in the preface to the *Philosophy of Right*.[48] The site for justice and universality is not found in the establishment of an ideal regime, but is found in the determinacy of our actual situation of opposition. *Here* is the one who must be included, *here* the one with whom one must establish a mutual hospitality. Let us consider how this might pertain to our contemporary world.

Globalization is accomplishing the "oneness" of the world by the kind of abstract inclusionism characteristic of liberal democracy and capitalism.[49] This is the uniformizing of cultures, the leveling of all into the rationalism of the enlightenment, a kind of Westernizing or Europeanizing of the world through a kind of cultural colonialism, if not a military one. This one world, though, excludes virtually all of the world, in that it is precisely the definitive particularities that are excluded. Derrida describes the exploitative and exclusionary side of globalization:

> Consider the context we've inherited from the Cold War: a so-called globalization or *mondialisation* that is more inegalitarian and violent than ever, a globalization that is, therefore, only simply alleged and actually less global or worldwide than ever, where *the* world, therefore, is not even there, and where we, we who are worldless . . . *form* a world only against the backdrop of a nonworld. . . . It is this so-called globalization that then confiscates to an unprecedented degree and concentrates into a small part of the human world so many natural resources, capitalist riches, technoscientific and even teletechnological powers, reserving also for that small part of the world those two great forms of immunity that go by the names public health and military security.[50]

This universal inclusion is thus in fact a virtually universal exclusion (as was implied by our discussion above of the inhumanism of capitalism). Globalization takes the oneness of the world as a fact, as a *presumption* rather than a *possibility*, and by treating us as "already one," absolves itself in advance of all the hard work of acknowledging and negotiating with essential differences, challenges, and oppositions.

What we need instead is a unity accomplished, rather than a unity presumed, a unity *through* cultural differences, rather than a unity against them, despite them, or prior to them. As Derrida writes,

> Is it not then in the name of these heterogeneous rationalities, in the name of their specificity and their future, their history, and their "enlightenment," that we must call into question the masterly and mastering authority of . . . the unity of the regulative Idea of the world that authorizes that world in advance?[51]

Against the presumption of an already existent unity of the world, we must imagine instead a unity that would be accomplished through identities opening themselves up to what they exclude—through, therefore, a process of self-othering. Inasmuch as some version of European enlightenment rationality—itself the very essence of the French Revolution—is arguably the prime force, ultimately, behind this globalizing it is really the European identity—what Derrida calls "Europe"—that must become other, and, in general, "the" "world" must become such by a universal process of becoming other, of becoming a new world, unanticipatable on the basis of current identities.[52]

What would it be for "Europe"—the world of enlightened democracy—to include those whom it definitively excludes? That is a question that can be answered only historically, only by reference to the determinate, empirical parameters of the present "global" situation. In his book *Rogues* from 2002, Derrida suggests that it is the Islamic world with which contemporary "Europe"—we—must establish (transformative) dialogue. As Derrida emphasizes,

> the only regimes that *do not fashion themselves* to be democratic, the only ones that *do not present themselves* as democratic, unless I am mistaken, are statutorily linked to the Muslim faith or creed.[53]

These regimes are thus the definitively excluded other of Euro-global democracy and the *real particularity* with which our particular political world with its *ethos* of democratic universalism is called to include.

Even if we do limit our focus to this pair of putative aliens, I cannot articulate what such an inclusion—such a dialogue—would entail. The imagined partners in this dialogue are massive cultures, each defining itself against a vast and complex history—including, especially, a very troubled history of interaction in the exploitative and debilitating European colonization of Asia and Africa from the 1500s to the 1900s[54]—each incredibly varied internally, and each situated within a contemporary world shaped by the material and social structures of industrial, economic, and teletechnological systems that are not defined in the terms of religion or nation-state. Such a "dialogue" would be an historical process beyond the scope of what anyone can control or predict. Our earlier discussions, though, nonetheless can helpfully remind us of the logical nature of this dialogue, if it is to be a transformative dialogue of the sort imagined. It is, as Derrida would say, "a certain Islam" with whom dialogue is possible, and that is the Islamic world that must be as open to its own self-transcendence as must be that "certain Europe" that would venture and seek hospitality.[55]

Just as the abstract democracy of modernity has shown itself incapable in principle of answering to the needs of human freedom, so, Hegel argues, has the traditional ethical society to which the modern world was a progressive response.[56] The modern conception of the rational individual has limitations as an interpretation of human freedom, as we have seen, but it nonetheless marks a non-effaceable recognition of the nature of human subjectivity, such that any social system that fails to recognize rational autonomy is *ipso facto* oppressive of human freedom. In fact, much of the traditional culture and religion of Islam points to something like such an "ethical" ideal of a community life that holds itself answerable to the received values of religious tradition, and this tradition has been carried forward in the last two hundred years in myriad ways ranging from political projects of democratic modernism to political projects of fundamentalist theocracy.[57] The dialogue that is called for must be a mutually transformative embrace by which these two different (and sometimes opposed) cultures establish a new, shared reality, and cannot be either a simple acquiescing to the extreme agenda of a fundamentalist theocracy, nor a simple insistence upon the market liberalism of unregulated capitalism. It must be a dialogue that does not revert to either of the exhausted forms of ancient or modern politics.

Indeed, just as the *Phenomenology of Spirit*, by bearing witness to the self-exhaustion of the ancient and the modern forms of political regime, reveals the inadequacy of various systems of institutions to the needs of freedom, the *Philosophy of Right* demonstrates positively the essentiality of various institutions to political life, that is, it translates the historical dialectic into a positive lesson about the institutions without which freedom will always in principle be unfulfilled. Roughly, these institutions are the family (the institution of substantial, communal freedom), and civil society (the institution of individual liberty and voluntary association), themselves both answerable to the nation as embodied in the principled policies of social organization of the state. Whatever form the contemporary dialogue takes, it cannot count as a movement toward a new universality if it does not answer to these institutional demands, inherent to the very nature of freedom.

Such institutional demands, however, fall far short of specifying the determinate policies and institutions to be enacted. These policies, again, must be uniquely determined in accordance with the unique demands of our particular situation. The new unity will be realized through determinate measures and will accomplish its unity—its communication—within the determinate terms of the member identities involved. In "A Europe of Hope" (2004), Derrida, for example, reasonably articulates a few policies that would address real needs in our situation. He suggests for Europe, for example, that it needs

> a military force and a foreign policy capable of supporting a transformed United Nations, one headquartered in Europe and equipped with the means to implement its resolutions without having to yield to the interests or unilateral opportunism of the techno-economic-military power of the United States.[58]

Similarly, he speaks in *Rogues* of the essentiality of reforming the nature of the United Nations Security Council.[59] Such proposals for internal policy, and other specific proposals for the reconciling of "Europe" and "Islam," must, however, always be developed in relation to the specific parameters of the determinate situation.

Since the terms of the reconciliation are always determinate, the universal thus achieved will itself be exclusionary. In other words, there will be no final word in the sense of any final set of institutions that will guarantee justice and freedom for all. As reasonable as specific institutions may be for answering to the imperatives of the day, the accomplishment of these things is no ending of the issue, no guarantee of "democracy." Inasmuch as all institutions are determinate, they are ambivalent—they can be open or closed. As much as they can be resources for freedom, they also can themselves all be inverted and exploited.

No particular institutions, therefore, will ever be adequate on their own to the realization of human freedom, and thus there can be no "universal" community realized in laws. Those laws, those institutions, will always be determinate, and therefore exclusionary. The ideal of a non-transgressive actuality upon which the liberal democratic model of universal inclusion is built is unrealizable in principle. We must, rather, recognize that communities must be self-*determining*, which is to say they will be exclusionarily self-legislating, and that it is always and only *within this context* that issues of oppression and exclusion can be *meaningfully* articulated. The challenge will be, not to remove determinacy, but to bring about a reconciliation between antagonistic determinacies; that is, it requires developing the plasticity inherent within any determinacy to speak in the terms of another determinacy, to establish a new way of being in which the different determinacies can co-inhabit a space/identity.

"Democracy," as the name for political inclusion—the name for hospitality—will always name a *practice*, a universality always "to be done," not to a fixed determinacy, not a *regime*, that would end the need for transformative, communicative engagement.[60] This is the practice of multicultural dialogue, a practice to be enacted here, within these non-effaceable determinacies.[61]

12

Conscience and the Unity of Being

In his *Science of Logic*, Hegel, as we have seen, argues that the relation of finite and infinite defines the character of the unity of being. By looking at the distinctive character of self-consciousness, we will see the particular problems that self-consciousness poses for enacting this unity of being. Specifically, we will see that self-consciousness is realized in free action, and the integration of self-conscious action depends upon the essential mediation of law. Law, however, while offering the unique medium for the fulfillment of self-consciousness in its project of integration, has a number of distinct features that themselves pose problems for the very integration it makes possible. In particular, the ethicality and the historicality that inherently characterize the domain of law reveal ways in which our self-consciousness is always dependent upon unconscious dimensions of meaning which it cannot adequately "own." We will consider in detail how it is that adequately responding to the project of owning these structures in an attempt to produce a situation of integrated self-consciousness ultimately takes the form of acting from conscience, and that the stance of conscience is itself ultimately fulfilled in the attitude of forgiveness that has cosmopolitan politics as its proper realization. It is ultimately the stance of cosmopolitan forgiveness that can enact the relationship of finite and infinite and establish the reality of a shared world.

The Unity of Being

As we have already noted in our earlier studies, it is the nature of the real that any feature of it is answerable to every other.[1] Reality on the one hand is simply all the determinate beings that actually are. On the other hand, however, reality is also the fact of their interdependence and, indeed, their interdependence with whatever other unactualized possibilities there are. To be a real being is to participate in the seamless fabric of all that is, was, will be, and could be.[2] Any particular being has its status *as a being*—that is, *is real*—insofar as it participates in this seamless fabric of being as such that, because of its intrinsic openness to what is beyond the presently actual, in principle could never be exhausted by the beings that constitute it. Being, in other words, is only realized determinately, and therefore in that sense finitely, but is realized precisely *as* not exhausted in that finite determinacy. This relation of finite and infinite is how Hegel understands the nature of being in his *Science of Logic*.[3]

As Hegel describes it in the *Science of Logic*, any finite, determinate being depends on opposition, on what is not itself, in order to be. Its opposition to what lies outside of it is equally, therefore, a reconciliation to and identification with it. The finite carries its relation to what is external to it in itself, or what is external to it is necessary for its very being.[4] What is beyond the finite, however, is not simply more finite beings: the infinite, inexhaustible context of being as such is also the inherent "beyond" of the finite—indeed, of the finite as such.[5] Finite being exists only as the seamlessly self-integrating whole that includes within itself the intrinsic imperative that it be open to reconciling seamlessly with whatever else might be, without thereby effacing its irreducible difference from anything and everything else. Just as the finite can only be as thus in relation to the infinite, so too must the infinite be in relation to the finite. Being is literally nothing (i.e., the very opposite of being) if it is not something determinate, something actual and specific.[6] The inexhaustible infinitude of being is itself only a reality *if there is reality*, if there is something rather than nothing. Thus, though the infinite context is the definitive condition under which finite being can be, it is equally only within the context of the finite that that condition is possible.[7] Infinite and finite are opposite, and yet stand in necessary relation and it is only within and *as* this relation that being is.[8]

In short, for things to be, they must be in relation, their opposition reconciled in their co-dependency and their co-constitution of the real. Each determinate being has unique authority and a unique role in constituting the real, but the condition of this its autonomous particularity is its intrinsic groundedness upon an imperative to universal reconciliation: it is its own unique self only on condition that it integrate itself with all else. With this account of being as the mutual dependence and irreducible difference of infinite and finite, Hegel accomplishes (at least) two things: (1) he justifies for the finite its claim to its own particularity, that is, his elaboration of the nature of the singularly finite derives for it a certain dignity that demands that we elaborate it in its own terms; and (2) he shows, however, that on the basis of its own nature the finite is called to reconciliation and identification with what is "external" to or other than it; that is, the finite both falls short of the infinite and gives it existence. Infinite and finite are thus reconciled to each other in their difference.

The logic of the infinite-finite relation thus makes two demands. First, it demands that we speak from the side of the finite, and work through its determinacy on its own terms, that we take the standpoint of singularity, and not impose upon the finite a universal or an abstract understanding achieved apart from interaction with it. Second, the logic of the finite-infinite relation demands that we recognize the identification of the finite with what is external to it. While the self-defining autonomy of the singular is recognized, in other words, this self-definition must equally be a participation in a shared reality.

This notion of the infinite-finite integration that is the definition of the very nature of reality is relatively easy to grasp abstractly, but what it is for this concept to be enacted—what it is for it to be *real*—is more difficult to grasp. We will see this if we consider in particular the unique demands that the existence of self-consciousness and its enactment in free action puts upon reality.

The Problem of Action

All action is in principle transgressive of the existing order in that it asserts a separation between the self and the world, the self and others. Action is an expression of desire, an affirmation that desire is what determines reality, rather than being determined by reality.[9] Action is a free initiation of self-determined change. If this were not so—if what we call "action" were simply the playing out of the already determined consequences of an already determined actuality—it would not truly be action, it would not be something *done,* but would be something undergone: an effect, not a cause. In this way, action, as such, is always an inauguration of novelty, a spontaneous emergence of what could not be sufficiently determined on the basis of the pre-conditioning actuality.[10] At the same time, however, it is the imperative of action that it integrate itself into the world, integrate itself with its others. *Nothing would be done* if action did not in fact exist as *a change in actuality*. It is the very nature of action—of freedom—then, that it enact itself *as* an integration with actuality. This is Schelling's point when he writes:

> All action can be understood only through an original unification of freedom and necessity. The proof is that every action, alike of the *indi-*

> *vidual* and of the entire *species*, must be conceived of, *qua* action, as free, but *qua* objective consequence, as standing under natural laws.[11]

It is not an *action* if it is not free, but it is not *an* action if it does not take place within the parameters of the natural world.

> Subjectively, therefore, for inner appearance, we act, but objectively, we never act; it is rather that another acts through us, as it were.[12]

We experience the action as our own—this is the condition of its being "our" action, but in fact what makes the inaugurated reality have the character it has is the established order of things: what we experience as our own action exists as an event *in and of the world*. Schelling notes, however, that this opposition of self and other cannot be the last word: "But now this objective agency, which acts through *me*, must again be *myself*."[13] Schelling's point, in other words, is that this can be "my" action *only if* I can identify with the cause of "my" action, if what gives the reason for the event for which I claim responsibility is in fact me. If this identification cannot be made, then I cannot say that I acted, for something else is what caused the change in the world; hence, I am not the agent I imagine myself to be: I am not free.

Free action, then, has two defining characteristics beyond the immediate, subjective feeling for freedom. It is defined, first, by the need to exist as a determinacy integrated with the rest of determinacy according to necessity, that is, according to the alien terms that that domain of determinacy sets out as its own. It is defined, second, however, by the demand that it "own" these alien terms; that is, it must find itself in its "other," in the necessity that governs the logic of its integration.[14] Let us turn first to establishing the distinctive nature of the domain of the integration of self-consciousness. We will then turn to the terms of the "necessity," the logic of integration, that governs the domain of such self-conscious action, and then establish the terms in which the explicitly self-conscious individual can subjectively identify with—can "own"—this "objective" necessity in its action.

When we consider this notion of integration simply in terms of the distribution of bodies within the universe, it seems easy to imagine, inasmuch as we imagine every body to be simply occupying a unique spatial location in conflict-free coordination with all other bodies, and functioning in accordance with a uniform system of causality. This coherent fabric of bodies is, however, only a superficial vision of "the real": with human action, the issue of integration is in fact considerably more complex. It is one thing for my freedom to realize itself in the world of nature, enacting itself *as* a coherent bodily finitude; it is something else for my freedom to realize itself in the domain of intersubjective spirit.

We *are* self-conscious subjects. That self-consciousness is real entails that perspectives and feelings and the first-person phenomena of inner life in general *are essential dimensions of the real.* The issue of integration as it pertains to human action is not just a matter of coordinating bodies in a single space, but is a matter of negotiating the space of conflicting perspectives and establishing a reconciliation between self-conscious subjects.

> An individuality sets about carrying out something; by so doing it seems to be making something into *the real thing* [*etwas zur Sache gemacht zu haben*]; it acts, and in acting becomes involved with others and seems to itself to be concerned with *reality* [*die Wirklichkeit*]. The others therefore take its action to be a sign of its interest in the real thing as such [*an der Sache als solcher*]. . . . [But] it is its *own* action and its *own* effort that constitute its interest in the thing [*bei der Sache*], and when the others become aware that this was *the real thing itself* [*die Sache selbst*], then they feel they have been deceived.[15]

"Actualization is," Hegel writes, "a display of what is one's own in the element of universality whereby it becomes, and should become, the affair [*die Sache*] of everyone."[16] Integration in the domain of self-consciousness, in other words, is a matter of establishing what Hegel calls a situation of mutual recognition (*Anerkennung*).[17]

The self-referentiality of perspective—the fact that all my experience makes definitive reference to "I"—entails that different perspectives are immediately defined by and as different frames of reference, that is, they naturally conflict with respect, precisely, to "perspective," to what each takes to be the truth of the situation. Equal recognition is essentially accomplished when we establish a shared perception, that is, when the harmonization with your perspective is an internal norm of my perspective and vice versa; that is, I live my experience as defined by definitive reference to "you" as much as it is defined by "I." Other perspectives, though, are not just the immediate companions one encounters—family, friends—but also those to whom one is not personally attached. Beyond this coordination of "I" and "you," equal recognition ultimately requires the integration of the first- and second-person perspectives with the third-person perspective of "her," "him," or "anyone." The impetus behind law is the search for principles that will govern action so as to accomplish the integration of actions in the domain of conflicting perspectives—the domain of others—as such, which is simply the domain of self-consciousness.

Law and Its Limits

Law is the domain of shared principles of behavior, the domain where one holds oneself answerable in one's action to the norms others hold for evaluating action. Law can be the rules explicitly posited by a self-conscious government but it can also be the traditionally held and handed-down values that community members adopt without deliberately choosing to do so. Indeed, these latter laws—the traditionally transmitted, shared presumptions about the proper form of communal living—are what establish the primary bond between people that in turn provides the context within which the essentially "contractual" bonds of explicitly posited laws can function effectively. The traditional bonds—what Hegel calls "ethical life"—are not experienced by their members as matters of choice, but as matters of necessity, and they are not therefore treated as optional.

> The law is . . . an eternal law which is grounded not in the will of a particular individual, but is valid in and for itself. . . . [The individual self-consciousness] does not *believe* in them, for although belief does perceive essential being it perceives it as something alien to itself. Ethical *self*-consciousness is *immediately* one with essential being.[18]

Ethical laws constitute "a reality, the being of which is the *action* of the *single* individual and of all individuals":[19]

> As the single individual in his singular work already *unconsciously* performs a *universal* work, so again he also performs a universal work as his *conscious* object; the whole becomes, *as a whole,* his own work, for which he sacrifices himself and precisely in so doing receives back from it his own self. There is nothing here that would not be reciprocal.[20]

These ethical bonds are the determinate ways we *live* our sense of being beholden to each other, our sense of being answerable to the perspectives of others. Without such a founding sense of answerability, the laws of contract—the rules of behavior that one must explicitly "choose"—cannot have a compelling force, but will always in principle remain optional. It is only our prior commitment to our mutual answerability that will make the principle of obeying posited laws itself something to which we find ourselves answerable. Said otherwise, *adherence to* legislation cannot be accomplished *through* legislation. Posited law thus rests upon non-posited law as its foundation.[21]

To live according to law is to participate in a world where action *makes sense.* Law-governed actions essentially *speak,* for they are enactments of the system of values—the systems of meanings—that the participants of the law-governed community hold in common.

> This unity of being-for-another or making oneself a thing, and of being-for-self, this universal substance, speaks its *universal language* in the customs and laws of its nation.[22]

As well as enacting my desires, my law-governed actions also *affirm* you and the others: my action is a way of saying that I respect the fact that I am living in community with others, a way of saying that the world in which I realize my desire—the world in which I affirm/assert myself—is a shared world.[23] Because we are self-conscious beings—because we are intersubjective—our action is always essentially an intersubjective gesture as much as it is a practice of personal fulfillment, whether or not one explicitly acknowledges this. Acting in a law-governed fashion is the acknowledgment of this essential intersubjectivity of all action. It is by the embrace of law as such that one enters the realm of equal recognition, that a "We" is enacted, for this is the embrace of the answerability of the terms of one's own perspective to the terms of shared meaning. In this way, it is law that accomplishes the integration of self-consciousness, as causality accomplishes the integration of bodies in space.

It is in and through law—both in the narrow sense of explicitly posited law and in the broad sense of the institutions of social life in general—that our shared participation in reality is accomplished and, as such, law is "the universal," the medium of our shared identity.[24] The very nature of law, however, poses problems for this notion of integration at the same time as it is the condition that enables that integration. The problems of law are, first, that its roots are in "ethicality," the unconscious, traditional bonds of custom and, second, that its self-conscious enactment is carried out in and carried down through history. Let us consider the problems that ethicality and historicality pose for the integration of self-consciousness(es).

We just noted above that it is a lived sense of a communal bond that gives to law its compelling force. The motivation and justification for law is that it accomplishes the integration of self-conscious life; that is, law is the medium in which the realities of the first-person perspective can be coordinated and shared. The first-person perspective, however, is, precisely, the phenomenon of *self-consciousness*, that is, the experience of "I." The character of the law that allows the integration of "I"s, however, is precisely *unconscious*, that is, it is precisely that with which the "I" *cannot* immediately identify. In abandoning myself to the unwritten law, I am—we are—thus fundamentally abandoning our self-consciousness:

"the single individual in his singular work . . . *unconsciously* performs a *universal* work."[25] Ethicality, in other words, accomplishes the integration of self-consciousness, but *not as self-consciousness*: in accepting tradition as the ultimate norm of our shared life, in other words, we accomplish a shared existence only at the expense of suppressing our very nature as self-conscious beings; that is, we accomplish a shared existence at the expense of the very thing that motivated the need for establishing that sharedness.

> The [ethical] community, however, can only maintain itself by suppressing this spirit of singularity, and, because it is an essential moment, all the same creates it and, moreover, creates it by its repressive attitude towards it as a hostile principle.[26]

Even as ethical law accomplishes the integration of singular self-consciousnesses, it does not acknowledge the rights of the "I."

For this reason—the reason, namely, that customary practices do not address adequately the needs of self-consciousness *as such*—our need for law as the medium for our sharedness is not satisfied with the realities of tradition, with the realities of "unwritten law." On the contrary, the nature of our self-consciousness—namely, the fact this it is *to be self-conscious*—demands for its fulfillment the medium of posited law, that is, laws that have their source in the "I," laws in which human self-consciousness can itself be recognized: "This spirit can be called the human law, because it is essentially in the form of a *reality that is conscious of itself*."[27] Though contract—posited law—cannot be the fundamental phenomenon of law (for it *presupposes* the bond it depends upon for its character *as law*, its character as something compelling, something to be obeyed), it is the necessary form that law must take if it is to fulfill its constitutive task of accomplishing the integration of self-conscious (that is, accomplishing the integration of self-consciousness *as self-consciousness*).

Posited law, however, poses a further problem of its own for the integration of self-consciousness as self-consciousness. Though every given posited law was at some time the product of, and historical act of, self-conscious human deliberation and legislation, the laws that structure our social and political life are laws that we inherit. In other words, though the laws were made by humans, *we* did not make those laws for ourselves. We live, on the contrary, in the context of about three millennia of the gradual development of a complex institutional life, an institutional life that is fundamentally formative of the self-conscious abilities we develop—the very abilities we would draw upon in any efforts we might ourselves make to transform these legal structures. As with ethicality, then, so with posited law do we find self-consciousness dependent upon a structure of meaningfulness that it presupposes but does not develop from out of itself.[28]

Law is what allows our actions *to make sense*: it is what makes our self-expression an act of participation in a shared world. Yet the very nature of this "making sense" is that *the terms in which it is enacted do not make sense to us.* In other words, our law-governed behavior is always inherently shaped by ethicality and historicality, the very nature of each of which is that it is immediately opaque to self-consciousness: it is an inheritance, a given, rather than something understood, something in which I immediately find myself, my "I."

In acting in the world, my freedom is always realized as a change within the determinacy of nature, always an enactment of itself according to the structures of necessity that govern natural existence. These issues of law that we have just been considering are similarly matters of freedom reconciling itself to necessity. Whether with respect to ethical custom or to posited law, the terms in which my action can be integrated with others are *inherited.* I enact my freedom by becoming a member of a world defined by structures opaque to me, structures that specify the necessary form that action must take if it is to be part of this community, structures, that is, of necessity, comparable within the domain of self-consciousness to the structures of physics that define the parameters for participation in the natural world. For both these reasons—ethicality and historicality—then, the realization of self-consciousness in law seems to be thwarted by the very nature of the law that makes it possible. Let us consider what would be required, then, to fulfill self-consciousness within this context of the opacities of law.

On the one hand, our institutions are the institutions of freedom inasmuch as they in fact enable and embody the realization of the inherent demands of freedom. Freedom is substantial as well as subjective, and this means that freedom is not simply a matter of my thinking myself to be free, but is also a matter of actually having the inherent demands of my nature met.[29] In this respect, it is freeing for children to be compelled to participate in practices of education, for these practices release the abilities for bodily competence, linguistic expression, emotional self-possession, social integration, and interpersonal responsibility that are the very substance of freedom.[30] At a political and cultural level, too, we can live in situations that are essentially—substantially—free, without subjectively recognizing how that is so (with the result, indeed, that we can in fact wrongly oppose, in the name of freedom, the very structures and institutions that give us our freedom). When we act on the basis of our inherited laws, then, we are acting without insight into the significance of our own actions, and are thus unfree to the extent that our self-interpretation is at odds with our actual existence, and, further, our own subjective interpretation of our own freedom can be at odds with (and markedly inferior to) the true logic of the freedom that is in fact animating the institutions by and from which we live.[31]

The full development of our freedom requires both the development of the substantial institutions of freedom and, ultimately, the bringing of our subjective consciousness of ourselves as free beings into accord with the actual situation of our freedom; that is, we need to come to identify ourselves with the actual sources of our freedom, our meaning and our action. For freedom to be realized, (1) the institutions that enable the fulfillment of self-consciousness must be developed, and (2) we must become explicitly self-conscious within those institutions. It is in light of these instrinsic demands of freedom that we can see the necessity for freedom to be realized through posited law.

We inherit our political institutions, and our actions thus express ourselves in a language we do not understand, such that we are not self-conscious in the enactment of our self-consciousness. These historical, posited laws, however, have as their founding mandate *that they make sense*, that they be the appropriate and meaningful ways in which self-consciousness(es) is (are) to be integrated.[32] Such "human law" (in the language of Sophocles' *Antigone*) is explicitly a product of deliberation (as Aristotle makes clear in *Politics* 1.2), and is thus open to criticism and to further deliberation. It is because it thus defines itself as answerable to the demands of self-consciousness that posited law is the essential form through which self-consciousness as such can find itself fulfilled. Posited law has as its principle that it addresses intelligence, it speaks to us as self-conscious beings, and we are thus within our rights to demand of our posited laws that they be intelligent and that they be answerable to the demands of our intelligence. This definitive character of posited, "human" law has two implications that are important to us here.

The first implication of the fact that posited law is "for" individual self-consciousness is that this law has an inherent trajectory to universality. In being defined by its answerability to the "I," posited law is such that it can only live up to its own concept, its own founding imperative, by being universal: it must speak to any I qua I. This is the historical trajectory Hegel follows out in his discussion of "Culture." Kant, in his "Idea for a Universal History from a Cosmopolitan Perspective," had already made substantially this same point.[33] Roughly, tribal groups—essentially extended families—initially offered the freedom of shared living. Subsequently, city-states enabled a freedom beyond the simple struggle for subsistence, at the same time introducing the distinctive domain of "the political," that is, the domain in which individuals participate in deliberation about the direction of the community (the making of human law), but participate as "citizens," as representatives of the community rather than as representatives of their respective tribes or families.[34] Nation-states, again, and, beyond them, international organizations such as the United Nations and the International Criminal Court open up the possibilities for a universal equality of all persons, beyond the particularity and exclusivity of specific cultural allegiances and privileges. Basically, in each of these developments, from family to *polis* to nation-state to internationalism, there is, first, the establishment of a community that offers new possibilities for freedom and shared living, and, second, the establishment of a domain beyond that particular community in which the limitations of the determinateness and exclusivity of that community can be transcended, ultimately resulting in a community whose extent is the whole of humanity.[35]

The second implication of the fact that law is "for" individual self-consciousness is that its proclamations are not "sacred," but are recognized as attempts at just legislation that are required to be *understandable and criticizable*; that is, they are themselves answerable to the demands of self-conscious intelligence. Indeed, Kant in his "Cosmopolitanism" essay, again, makes the further point about this historical development that whereas each time a new "level" of political life is developed, the injustices of the "lower" level can be addressed in a way that was not possible before (one does not appeal to the head of the family to complain about the injustice of the head of the family, but appeals, rather, to the civil court, which stands outside the bias of the family and its leadership); at the same time, these higher level institutions will themselves always be enacted by persons, and so, just as each new level opens up new possibilities of justice, each also opens up new possibilities for injustice.[36] The history of our political institutions, in other words, can be seen as the history of injustice and the history of the development of institutions of exploitation (as Marx emphasizes) as readily as it can be seen as the history of justice.[37] For this reason, posited law, by its nature (that is, if it is to enable the integration of "I"s as such), must be permanently open to criticism and revision.

Law, as we saw above, is the medium for accomplishing the integration of self-consciousness. Because of its inherent ethicality and historicality, however, the significance—*viz*, the integrative character—of my law-governed action is opaque to me. In other words, I am not integrated with the other in my "I" (or in her "I"); that is, our *subjectivity* does not normally dwell at the level of our *substantial* integration. The strength of positive law, however, is precisely that it recognizes the necessity that this subjectivity be recognized. Our historical, posited law, then, should in principle be open to our self-consciousness: though we inherit our historical institutions without having insight into them, they are in principle open to our insight, and we can thus "own" our traditions. The identifying of the subjective side of our freedom with its substantiality demands that we do precisely this.

To live up to our own nature as self-conscious, we must understand the mediation inherent in our own action—we must ask ourselves, "Who am I?" "What am I doing?"—and, inasmuch as it is an internal demand upon self-consciousness that it realize itself in a situation of equal recognition, this self-interrogation needs to be a self-critical one; that is, I must equally ask myself, "Am I right to be doing this?" Inasmuch as we are thus driven to interrogate the institutional mediation inherent in our action, we must ultimately ask of our laws—and, indeed, of our whole history—"Are these laws good?" "Does this history make sense?" and so on. *The intelligent asking of this question* is mandated by the nature of freedom itself, and, thus, free laws must be such as to enable this very questioning. It is both a subjective demand upon us and a substantial demand upon laws that this critical self-interpretation be realized.

The history of our political institutions is the history of establishing the substantial reality of freedom. On its own, that is, *as* simply inherited, this historical context introduces an opacity into our attempt to realize our self-consciousness. Accomplishing the integration of self-consciousness *as* self-consciousness, then, will require that we "find ourselves" within our laws; that is, that we recognize the laws we live by *as* the appropriate medium for the fulfilment of the needs of our self-consciousness, of our freedom. To be free, then, we must see our history—the history of our laws, of our attempts to establish the institutions that allow for the realization of freedom, of equal recognition—as the history of freedom, as the process of freedom, the equal recognition between self-consciousnesses, bringing itself into being in the world.[38] It is the internal demand of self-consciousness, then, that it appropriate its history, and that it appropriate it precisely *as* its own, as the history of self-consciousness, as the history of freedom.

Freedom is realized in the integration of self-consciousness, and law is the essential medium for this realization. We can see in self-consciousness's "owning" of its own historicality a crucial carrying-out of this realization. But while positive law has this *self-conscious* integration as its goal, and in this "transparency" that it offers does, in fact, constitute an irreducibly essential dimension of a free integration of self-consciousnesses, it is not sufficient to define the domain of law and, hence, the domain of self-conscious integration. We can see this fundamental insufficiency if we consider further the necessary form of posited law.

Inasmuch as posited law is "for" individual self-consciousness, it must be universal, and it must address each self-consciousness as such, which means as equal to every other. Said otherwise, posited law has something like a doctrine of "universal, individual human rights" as its goal and its form. What is this as a form? It is the demand that laws take the form of formal rules—*procedures* of justice—that specify the same requirements for each and all without discrimination. This necessary formality of posited law, however, entails that *such law in principle cannot adequately address situations that are inherently characterized by non-universalizable particularity.* In fact, however, human life—the life of free self-consciousness—is always and necessarily characterized by such situations of irreducible particularity. Love, for example, whether familiar or romantic, is inherently a matter of "playing favorites," as is belonging to a community and as is, indeed, eating.[39] In all of these (and other similar) situations, any "I" will necessarily enact and realize itself in exclusive situations that cannot be shared at all (as in my partaking of the food I eat) or cannot be shared universally (as in my partaking of this love relationship with you). If posited law, then, is the demand that one enact one's "I" only in terms that could be enacted by any and every other "I," then it is the demand *that there be no actual I.*[40] It is inherent to the nature of the I, in other words, that it *cannot* be adequately captured in the terms of posited law.[41]

Posited law will always take the form of a *universal* rule, which means it will always demand that one take up a *specific* situation in a way that does not acknowledge the authoritative weight of that specificity. And yet, our situations are always *inherently* specific, and posited laws—rules for our integrative behavior—will always demand that we *mis*treat our specificities, that we deny the essentiality of essential dimensions of our situations. Posited laws, then, will always enact their "justice" through some form of one-sidedness, emphasizing this rather than that aspect of a situation as the essential one.[42] Derrida, writing about democracy, makes an analogous point in *Rogues*:

> [O]ne will never actually be able to "prove" that there is more democracy in granting or refusing the right to vote to immigrants, . . . nor that there is more or less democracy in a straight majority vote as opposed to proportional voting; both forms of voting are democratic, and yet both also protect their democratic character through exclusion. . . . One electoral law is thus always at the same time more and less democratic than another.[43]

Laws will always be enacted in particular ways by particular legislative bodies, emphasizing this one-sided justice rather than that. Such laws are, indeed, "justice," in that their embrace of the needs of self-conscious individuality makes them the irreplaceable medium for the enactment of self-conscious integration: it is right, in other words, that we should live under posited law. But, while we should thus live under law, it remains true that there is a fundamental injustice, a fundamental unfreedom, in the formality of posited law, and we can never be fully satisfied in this: posited law can never be the sufficient domain for self-conscious integration.

Conscience and Cosmopolitanism

From what we have seen about the nature of posited law, we can see that the domain of posited law can never be an unproblematic guarantor of justice, can never be a simple "machine" that automatically produces freedom as its output, for its rules are insufficient to integrate self-consciousness, insufficient to fulfill the needs of freedom.

> [W]ith the laws of right [as opposed to the laws of nature], the spirit of reflection comes into play and their very diversity draws attention to the fact that they are not absolute. The laws of right are something *posited*, something *derived from* human beings. . . . Thus a conflict may arise between what is and what ought to be, between the right which has being in and for itself, which remains unaltered, and the arbitrary determination of what is supposed to be accepted as right.[44]

Let us here consider three dimensions of reality not adequately accommodated by posited law: (1) the openness of freedom; (2) the determinate, ethical foundations of law outside the domain of historically posited rules and institutions; and (3) the demands of justice beyond the established terms of law.

The first and most basic reason that the "machine" of posited law can never be sufficient to freedom is that openness is the very nature of freedom. Though freedom, as we have seen, is only enacted *as* determinacy, it is not reducible to that determinacy. As we have noted before, Hegel describes this nature of freedom in the introduction to the *Philosophy of Right*:

> the will contains (α) the element of *pure indeterminacy* or of the 'I''s pure reflection into itself, in which every limitation . . . is dissolved;

> this is the limitless infinity of *absolute abstraction* or *universality*, the pure thinking of oneself . . . [and] (β) . . . the transition from undifferentiated indeterminacy to *differentiation, determination,* and the *positing* of a determinacy as a content and object . . . the absolute moment of the *finitude* or *particularization* of the 'I.'[45]

Freedom does indeed necessarily enact itself as particularity, but it is precisely the nature of freedom qua *freedom* to be "beyond" any determinacy. The laws that embody and facilitate freedom are precisely the laws that empower this "going beyond." The laws of freedom are the laws that sponsor creativity, the inclusion of what has been excluded, the embrace of the irreducible infinitude of the good. Free laws must precisely make room for situations of responsibility, interpretation, and judgment, make room, that is, for the forms of intelligent and meaningful behavior that are the unique province of freedom. Indeed, it is precisely the problem of modern societies that tend toward bureaucracy, surveillance, and security that, in the name of protecting freedom, they precisely rule it out. The institutions of freedom, on the contrary, must precisely sponsor a situation in which self-conscious individuals rise to situations of responsibility, which are always situations of interpretation, judgment, and risk—situations, that is, that precisely stand beyond the domain of "rules." The exclusion of self-responsible and self-transformative choice is the first insufficiency of posited law. Let us consider the second insufficiency of posited law.

We noted above that it would be question-begging to imagine that legislation could establish the compelling character of legislation. Human laws, in other words, will never *generate* communal bonds or a personal sense of morality, but will always presuppose this. Posited law, in other words, will always rest on a domain that does not operate from posited law. This founding domain of communal bonds is ethicality, which is precisely the domain of exclusivity and non-universalizability that we considered above, when we considered the dimensions of self-consciousness that cannot function according to a universal rule. Posited law, the domain of the universal and "transparent," will always have this domain of the particular and the opaque as its condition. Posited law is insufficient for our mutual integration, second, then, because to be integrated with each other will ultimately require that we integrate ourselves with each other *as* thus rooted in such (different) opaque exclusivities.

Third, the demand that I integrate with—that is, accommodate the reality of—the other requires that I recognize the constrictive character of law; that is, it requires that I recognize the ways in which the formality of law *as such* does not make room for the definitive particularity of others. *Justice*, in other words, demands ultimately that I acknowledge the inherent *injustice* of law, and that I take a stand on the needs of those who are oppressed by the Procrustean application of law, that I hold law accountable to the bias inherent to its unbiased application. Just as law's ethical roots exceed its terms, so does its goal of justice exceed its accomplishment.

We have been following out the logic of the integration of self-consciousness, and we have seen that law is both the essential domain of that integration and insufficient to that integration. Where, beyond law-governed subjectivity, is the integration of self-consciousness—freedom—accomplished? It is the stance of conscience that answers to the imperative to recognize the limits of law that we have so far diagnosed.

To act on conscience is to act from the demands of this situation *in its particularity*, and to experience oneself as called upon *in one's self-conscious singularity* to enact justice, to act on behalf of the good as such.

> The self-certain spirit rests, *qua* conscience, within itself, and its *real* universality or its duty lies in its pure *conviction* of duty. . . . [A]ction is called for, something must be *determined* by the individual, and the self-certain spirit in which the in-itself has attained the significance of the self-conscious "I," knows that it has this determination and content in the immediate *certainty* of itself.[46]

In conscience, I find that the needs of the one I face are my needs: my own answerability to justice will not allow me to disregard the appeal of the one who confronts me. The one confronting me, further, is not an abstract instance for the application of an already established law, but a unique individual calling for my unique and creative intervention.

> [Conscience] is . . . *concrete* moral spirit which, in the consciousness of pure duty, does not give itself an empty criterion to be used against actual consciousness. . . . It is, in its immediate unity, a *self-actualizing* being, and the action is immediately something *concretely* done.[47]

Conscience is the experience of the unique imperative of the concrete unity that is "this particular reality" with "my particularity subjectivity": "[consciousness], *qua* conscience, knows it [an objective actuality] in an immediate concrete manner; and it equally *is* only as conscience knows it."[48]

The call of conscience is the call to take responsibility, the call to experience answerability to this finite situation within one's inmost subjectivity. Typically, we experience conscience in a relative way, feeling ourselves called to take responsibility *within* the established terms of our world. Antigone in this respect can be seen as a figure of conscience, in that she experiences the perception of her unburied brother as an immediate imperative to right the wrong in this situation and bury him; the duty she experiences, though, is defined by the terms of the "divine law" that she has inherited, but never questioned.[49] We can also interpret the call of conscience absolutely, however, and this is the call to responsibility *for* the terms of the world. We saw above that it is constitutive of the fulfillment of self-consciousness to enact a philosophical reflection on its own history that critically assesses the functioning of the human institutions that structure its practice. To take responsibility for the terms of one's situation will require such a cultural critique, which will require that one take on oneself the norm of universality and inclusiveness both as a standard by which to assess one's cultural institutions and as an imperative upon one's own practice that one enact a welcoming of others beyond the established terms of one's situation. I am called to make a place for that other, beyond the established terms of integration.[50] The call of conscience, in other words, is the call to hospitality, the call to be open, beyond the established terms of recognition, to an otherwise unrecognizable other.

And beyond the recognition of the sense of its own historicality, the stance of absolute conscience must, further, recognize its own rootedness in ethicality, which means it must acknowledge the fundamental way in which it is not and cannot be transparent to itself, the way in which its very stance of openness is rooted in the particularities of its own personal, familial, and cultural roots.[51] The stance of absolute conscience, then, in "owning" the mediation implicit in its stance of recognizing others, must own its own finitude, its own self-opacity, its own exclusivity. It must, that is, see that its very openness depends on a closedness and an exclusivity that it cannot see, and turn to the other with a request for forgiveness for its own inability to *be* infinite and infinitely welcoming.[52] And this recognition by conscience of the inescapable opacity integral to self-consciousness entails that the very forgiveness that it seeks from the other for its own closedness is something that it must extend to the other.

Conscience, then, as the stance that fulfills the logic of self-consciousness, completes itself in a dialogue of mutual forgiveness in which the closedness of our ethical roots are thus enacted as sites of openness.[53]

> The word of reconciliation is the objectively existent Spirit, which beholds the pure knowledge of itself qua universal essence, in its opposite, in the pure knowledge of itself qua absolutely self-contained and exclusive individuality—a reciprocal recognition which is absolute Spirit.[54]

Conscience, the stance that fulfills the project of self-conscious integration, is itself completed in a stance of forgiveness, a stance of finding itself only through the alien ethicality of another.[55] Conscience is thus ultimately enacted in a stance of cosmopolitanism or multicultural dialogue. This unity-to-be-enacted is not the application of a pre-established rule to an indifferent recipient, but is the *inauguration* of an unprecedented unity between and within the terms of otherwise alien particularities.[56] It is a unity that is performed in a way that demonstrates through its enactment an otherwise unanticipated plasticity in our ethical roots.[57]

Whereas law *starts from* the universal (starts from, that is, the reality that is to be shared, the principle of integration), conscience, in recognizing the demands for justice that emanate from particularity, starts from the position of the as-yet-unreconciled and acts *so as to accomplish* a situation of integration. In recognizing the weight of particularity, conscience acknowledges the necessity and the legitimacy of the exclusive and the local; in answering to justice, conscience acknowledges the imperative to integration and inclusiveness; in experiencing itself as called in its singularity, conscience "owns" the terms of its action.

When one acts from law, one acts from the terms of an already established world, terms, we have noticed, that are inherently insufficient to house the full needs of self-conscious integration. In conscience, however, I live my freedom as the imperative to accomplish the integration of self-consciousness; that is, I experience myself as *living from* the unity-to-be of self-consciousness, and act as its representative in challenging the limits of the law. In conscience, I still act as a citizen, but a citizen, we might say, of a "republic to be" or, as Derrida might say, a "republic to come," a free world of universal hospitality that exists only in my performance of its actualization.[58] Because my action transcends/transgresses the law, however, it can, of course, never be sufficiently justified by the law, and I thus have only my singular subjectivity—my faith—to rely upon. Because of this, I can never be guaranteed to be in the right rather than to be simply a criminal: conscientious action as such will always involve and enact such a risk.[59] This citizenship in the "republic to be," then, is always presumptive, and must in fact wait upon the confirmation of others, to acknowledge that my action was what I took it to be.[60] The integration of the human world—and therewith the true freedom of action—is never simply given, but is always problematic; conscience is the ultimate stance of free self-consciousness for it "lives," so to speak, at this problematic level, trusting that its sense of itself—its subjective self-consciousness, its subjective freedom—is an accurate perception of its substantiality—its objective freedom.[61]

Conscience acts from its singularly held conviction regarding what is right in this particular situation, but its attempt to act on behalf of the universal-to-be can in fact be simply a self-important act of self-assertion. In conscience, which knows that it can be vindicated only through the recognition of its legitimacy by the forgiveness of others, self-consciousness most fully recognizes *for itself* the very terms we identified as characterizing it *in itself*, inasmuch as it understands itself in terms of the very demands of recognition and law that we have ourselves analyzed.[62]

Finally, it is with the stance of conscience, and its culmination in the relationship of forgiveness, that we see the final form of self-conscious integration, and, indeed, that we see the relationships that characterize self-consciousness enacting the logic of infinite and finite that we initially identified as defining the terms of the integration of being with itself.[63] It is in the cosmopolitan dialogue of mutually forgiving consciences that we have the universal enacted—a "we"—in and through the finite actions of individuals. The unity of the human world—the unity that is "spirit"—is not a given, and it is not accomplished simply by the fact of spatial coexistence nor by the "globalization" that is the machine-like application of the rules of capitalist uniformity around the planet. The unity of the human world, on the contrary, exists only through the hard work of meaningful reconciliation wherein particular human communities, *without effacing their differences of ethical origin and historical development*, find within the substance of their freedom the plasticity for welcoming each other in the establishment of new forms of co-habitation.[64] This, furthermore, is not simply a matter of the establishing of new cross-cultural institutions, but is ultimately a matter of finite individuals finding it incumbent upon themselves, in their self-conscious singularity, to be responsible to the demands of enacting this shared world. An individual is inevitably particular, incapable of adequately identifying with and bringing about the universal in the world. Yet at the same time the acting individual is the avenue through which the universal, expressed in and by particular communities, exists as such. The individual, through her actions, brings into being a particular way of being in community, a particular way of obeying and construing its universals. No particular individual can be adequate to the universal, but no universal can exist without being interpreted and carried out in precise ways by discrete agents.[65]

Said otherwise, the recognition of freedom in history is not a passive noticing of an alien fact, but is, instead, a *performance*: to recognize it is to take up an imperative, to act from a reality that can only exist in and through that action. The integration of self-consciousness—the unity of the human world—does not and cannot *exist* as a simply present fact.[66] Rather, the imperative of freedom is to enact our institutions *as* the institutions of freedom, and, indeed, to recognize that finite institutions as such can never "be" freedom—they can never efface the need for people to be responsible: on the contrary, that turn to self-consciousness must be precisely what our institutions facilitate and call for.

Conclusion

The norm of forgiveness, which Hegel studies in the *Phenomenology of Spirit* as the culmination of spirit, that is, the ultimate character of the situation in which self-conscious selfhood can be fulfilled, operates on the logic of "the infinite" as articulated by Hegel in the *Science of Logic*. Far from being an effacing of singularity and difference in "a night in which all cows are black," the infinite as construed by Hegel defines a relationship that simultaneously insists on the autonomy of finite individuality while also holding that individuality accountable to reconciliation with other finite individuals.[67] The playing out of this logic in forgiveness suggests a political vision that offers a powerful challenge to the cultural uniformity of modern, bureaucratic liberalism, and points instead to a heterogeneous political arena that must be responsive to the unanticipated forms of otherness appearing within it. The Hegelian conception of the norm of forgiveness points to a conception of justice that is not a matter of applying an already established standard to new situations, but that is an openness to the redefinition of the very terms in which political identity is articulated.

13

The Phenomenology of Religion: Freedom as Exposure to the Absolute

The Phenomenon and Concept of Religion

What is religion? Whenever we want to understand one of Hegel's analyses in the *Phenomenology of Spirit*, we must first remember that this book is a phenomenology—a description of phenomena—and we must secure for ourselves a clear sense of the phenomenon under description. To understand Hegel's phenomenology of religion, we must first have the relevant phenomenon in front of ourselves. What is religion as a phenomenon? What is the appearance in our world to which we attach the name "religion"?

The first point to notice is that Hegel is affirming that indeed there is such a thing as religion. Contemporary anthropologists and scholars of religion have often argued that the experiences and practices we often call "religious" in fact serve a varied range of social and personal functions, and that this varied array of human practices should not be construed as a single reality; indeed, it has become common to deny that there is a single reality properly called "religion." While Hegel has no reason to challenge the complexity of our human practices—indeed, his philosophy is a primary resource for identifying the unacknowledged personal, interpersonal, and social purposes served by our practices—he nonetheless has a reason for maintaining that there is a unique and irreducible human experience that attaches to the notion of "religion."

Most definitively, religion is the affirmation of what I will call "the infinite object." Throughout the *Phenomenology of Spirit*, we have studied forms of experience all of which are ways of relating to an object. The phenomenology itself began (in the introduction) with the familiar epistemological question of scepticism: how can we know that the object of our experience is the way reality really is?[1] We subsequently studied the object for consciousness, the object for self-consciousness, the object for reason, the object for spirit.[2] In each case, we precisely discovered the object as the "object for," that is, we discovered that the object was correlative with the subject. Most definitively, what religion affirms is that the object, ultimately, is not to be equated with any of those correlative formulations: "the object is saved from being degraded to pure objectivity, to the form of negativity for self-consciousness."[3] Indeed, for this reason we should, properly, not call it "object" at all, and that is why Hegel, instead, refers to it as "absolute reality, in and for itself." I will, nonetheless, refer to it as the infinite "object" precisely to mark out its relationship to this phenomenological history of "objects."

Religion is the affirmation that its object—"the" object—is ultimate and that it does not answer to the limitations of experience: it is not a function of or derivative of a more fundamental subjectivity, but is itself the absolute, self-defined and infinite.

> In the forms so far considered, which are distinguished generally as *consciousness, self-consciousness, reason,* and *spirit,* religion, too, as consciousness of *absolute being* as such, has indeed made its appearance, although only from the *standpoint of consciousness* that is conscious of absolute reality [*Wesen*]; but absolute reality in and for itself, the self-consciousness of spirit, has not appeared in these shapes.[4]

Religion is the affirmation that the ultimate reality is, and is beyond the limited forms that respond to it; indeed, it is beyond them as their source. Religion is the affirmation of the infinitude of reality and the reality of the infinite.

As source, the infinite object—"absolute reality in and for itself"—is implicit in everything: in everything we are and do, it is the infinite that is appearing. Religion is thus an affirmation about the nature of truth, about the inherent truth of all our existence. At the same time, however, religion—this affirmation of the infinite—is also a human practice: it is something we do, that is, it is a particular practice, one practice among many. Religion, that is, also appears as a particular part of our existence.

> [S]pirit's *existence* [*Dasein*] is distinct from its *self-consciousness* . . . . There is indeed one spirit of both, but its consciousness does not embrace both together, and religion appears as a part of existence, of conduct and activity, whose other part is the life lived in its real world.[5]

Religion is that special set of practices within a culture that are the practices of affirming this infinite. Religious practices indeed mark themselves out as the specific practices of affirming the infinite, and they thus distinguish the sacred from the profane, the religious from the secular.

Here then we have the phenomenon of religion, a phenomenon with which we are all, presumably, quite familiar. Religion is the determinate sphere of practices within a culture that mark themselves out as the explicit form of affirming the reality of the infinite object. Though the vast array of human practices that are commonly called "religious" can in fact serve many different functions, in this definitive function of affirming the reality of the absolute object religion is a unique phenomenon not reducible to any other form of human practice.

Let us consider the nature of this affirmation: what is involved in asserting that the absolute object exists? The absolute object is self-defined; if it were other-defined, it would be only a relative object: "absolute reality would be but an empty name if in truth there were for it an 'other.'"[6] The absolute object is not other-defined and especially not defined by "consciousness," or in general by our human perspective. This is why religion can legitimately say, "our claims exceed any of your arguments." One can make any objections one likes about what is or is not rational, plausible, etc., but these claims will always be claims about the terms and parameters of our perspective; *ex hypothesi* however, such claims have no bearing on the absolute object. Religion asserts that ultimate reality is determined by the form that ultimate reality *in fact* takes: it is only what the infinite object itself shows itself to be that has final authority.

This logical character of the religious claim—its character of being in principle beyond answerability to the terms of consciousness, self-consciousness, reason, or spirit—supplies the methodological reason that the phenomenology of religion appears after these earlier chapters of the *Phenomenology of Spirit.* The earlier chapters lead us to the point of the "absolute" human perspective: "spirit" is the comprehensive context within which all other human activities are contained, and is itself the "absolute" or self-defining human domain. "Spirit," Hegel writes, "is thus self-supporting, absolute, real being. All previous shapes of consciousness are abstract forms of it."[7] That domain—"spirit"—is the comprehensive whole that the absolute object—"God"—is defined as in principle exceeding. Religion, which is the way a culture says this "beyond," appears later in the *Phenomenology of Spirit* because it makes a claim that is in principle not adequately analyzable in the terms of any of the standpoints contained within the phenomenon of spirit. The object of the religious perspective is the object *defined* as that which is "beyond" any possible human perspective, "that than which a greater cannot be conceived." Religion is the affirmation of *the* absolute. Just as Descartes is led to acknowledge the omnipotence of God as a possible challenge to all self-evident truths of understanding in the first of his *Meditations on First Philosophy,* Hegel's *Phenomenology of Spirit* recognizes religion as a possible challenge to all the terms of finite experience, all the terms of "subjectivity."[8]

In identifying the way in which the absolute as such necessarily exceeds "subjectivity," we have begun the project of articulating what *is* in principle, what is inherently entailed in asserting the existence of the absolute. Hegel's *Science of Logic* is the explicit embrace of this project, and the working out of this "logic" of the absolute in detail; religion itself is the affirmation of this transcendence of the absolute, but, unlike Hegel's *Science of Logic*, it makes this affirmation in and through the specific images, practices, and narratives ["*Vorstellungen*"] that make up the phenomena we familiarly recognize as "religion," rather than in conceptual prose explicitly recognized as such. As Hegel says, religion appears as just one of the parts of existence, that is, it is a particular set of images, practices, and narratives; specifically, it is that part that identifies itself as advancing the distinctive images, practices, and narratives that affirm the transcendence of the absolute.

Religion is thus one determinate part of experience, one sphere of human practices and products. This very determinacy—this limitation of religion to one particular set of human practices rather than another—is a problem, though. Religion is precisely an affirmation about the nature of the whole of experience, which can properly neither privilege one part (since "all is *vanity*" [*Ecclesiastes* 1:2], so to speak) nor exclude another (since "*all* is vanity"). *Religious* practices are, for example, going to Christian church on Sunday and singing Christian hymns. It is not only Sunday and not only these songs that should be sacred, however. The truth is not "this human practice" as opposed to "that human practice," but the infinite beyond to which each and every human practice is subordinate. The absolute beyond is true everywhere and always, and thus should be recognized everywhere and always. Thus the religious message is always "take Sunday into the whole week." From the start, the religious imperative is to go beyond the limitations of its determinacy.

The religious message is that *God* is the ultimate authority. Religious practices are validated by God, and not the opposite, which is the core idea behind the iconoclastic anti-idolatry that is characteristic of the Abrahamic religions. The point of the finite religious practices is *to point*, to bring to appearance the inexhaustible infinite that gives them their meaning and validity, *not* to set themselves up as "the absolute." It is the infinite object that demands adherence, not the finite practice—this is the definitive "premise" of religious practices.

And yet, these practices are always determinate: religion is always a determinate piece of life that takes determinate cultural shape. As Jeremiah complains, "According to the number of thy cities are thy gods,

O Judah" (*Jeremiah* 2:28). Religion is enacted in *Vorstellungen,* in specific, established determinacies. All these determinacies, qua religious determinacies, point to the need that *they be transcended*: it is precisely the imperative of a *religious* determinacy that *its very determinacy* is "to be transcended": as Hegel might say, "here is your cross, here is your sacrifice."[9]

> [T]he reality enclosed within religion is the shape and the guise of its *Vorstellung*. But, in this *Vorstellung,* reality does not receive its perfect due, viz. to be not merely a guise but an independent free existence; and conversely, it is a *specific* shape, which does not attain to what it ought to show forth.[10]

Every religion is thus the uniting of these two sides: it is a commitment to a set of determinacies, and it is the very nature of those determinacies to point to their own transcendence, that is, they point to the effacing of their own exclusivity and primacy.

It is therefore the inherent trajectory of religion to enact itself in a form in which its *Vorstellungen* are "vanishing moments," practices that perform the effacement of their own essentiality in their showing forth of reality:

> The totality of . . . the spirit of religion is . . . the movement away from its immediacy towards the attainment of the *knowledge* of what it is *in itself* or immediately, the movement in which, finally, the *shape* in which it appears for its consciousness will be perfectly identical with its essence, and it will behold itself as such.[11]

But because religion inherently exists in the non-identity of the *Vorstellung* and the reality to which it points, it is not immediately the case that the taking up of this religious reality is such that what is shown forth in it is its truth. Indeed, because a religion is determinate—is enacted in and as a determinacy—it invites three basic appropriations of this its determinate reality. (1) Religion can be enacted as blind adherence to the "image," to the determinate *Vorstellung* in its exclusive determinacy. (2) A more developed religious consciousness is enacted in thinking from the "image" (which can itself take myriad forms), that is, embracing the *Vorstellung* as a route to a deeper, essential reality. This, presumably, is where most religious consciousness exists, whether in the everyday experience of "living from" the richness of meaning that religious images and practices make available to cultures and individuals, or in the explicit reflection on these images that is the practice of "theology," broadly construed. In this second form, though, as in the first, "the shape itself and the *Vorstellung* are still the unvanquished aspect from which spirit must pass over into the concept [*Begriff*]."[12] Finally, (3) religion can be enacted in a thinking beyond the "image," that is, experiencing the *Vorstellung* from the point of view of what it reveals, such that the inessentiality of the specific *Vorstellung* is recognized. "It is then that [the religious] spirit has grasped the concept of itself, just as we now have first grasped it."[13]

In other words, though the real point of the religion is to point to the absolute beyond, its manners of thus pointing can easily become what is taken up as if they were the goal. Indeed, the necessary determinateness of religion entails that commitment to the religion is ambiguously commitment to the "message" and commitment to the "medium." There is thus a dogmatism, an idolatry, inherent to any religious tradition. Islam, for example, insists on five daily prayers, and the particular manner of prayer, that is, adopting a "humbling" stance. Yet Islam itself insists that it is God who by "his" nature must be worshipped, and to give anything else this "divine" status is "*shirk*"; these very practices of prayer, in other words—practices necessarily enacted in the terms of human life—must be only relatively important, not absolutely important; relative, that is, to the absolute purpose of recognizing God. They are proper, in other words, *exactly to the extent that* they in fact participate in the accomplishment of that divine recognition. But in that case, they are necessarily not necessary, and to insist that they are necessary is to worship an idol. Some version of this recognition is made explicit, for example, in the Sufi tradition of Islam. According to the Sufi scholar Al-Hujwiri, the true *hajj* (pilgrimage), for example, is not found in the fact of bodily moving oneself to Mecca, but in the inner journey of the soul to Allah, or, again, "It is the inner flame that makes the Sufi, not their religious garb."[14] Hinduism (a name I use as a convenient label for the long tradition of religious development in the Indian sub-continent, though this name is at best controversial and at worst misrepresentative), similarly, for all the multiplicity of its religious practices, can be seen to be ultimately monotheistic, ultimately recognizing all practices as ways of relating to the gods "with qualities" (*sa-guna*) as a means of turning to the ultimate truth that is the god without qualities (*nir-guna*), a point nicely made by the great eleventh-century Muslim scholar al-Biruni (Abū al-Rayhān Muhammad ibn Ahmad al-Bīrūnī):

> The Hindus believe with regard to God that he is one, eternal, without beginning and end, acting by free-will, almighty, all-wise, living, giving life, ruling, preserving; one who in his sovereignty is unique, beyond all likeness and unlikeness, and that he does not resemble anything nor does anything resemble him.[15]

So-called "fundamentalism" is precisely the failure to recognize this, and to insist on the necessity and the adequacy of specific practices, thereby venerating certain determinate features of the human world as divine.

St. Augustine, in book 7 of his *Confessions*, effectively articulates this very point. The world of experience is ordered, Augustine says, to the soul, which is in turn ordered to God.[16] The ultimate reality—"God"—he says, is experienced as a call, a point of light, to which one must respond.[17] God is experienced as the absolute imperative, and the soul is called to care for the world that is ordered to it in such a way as to respond to that call. But the response will always be from "this world," and therefore will always necessarily *not* be the given terms of that call itself, but will already be a *particular* human answering to the call. There is in principle no "this worldly" behavior that *can* be adequate to the call, for the call is by definition the imperative to recognize the insufficiency of any this-worldly determinacy to claim absolute status. Thus all religious ritual, and, indeed, *Augustine's own words* must be understood as *exhortations*, as calls to the reader to *read through them*, so to speak, rather than as strict "reproductions" of the truth. In this sense, then, religious images are always "metaphoric," not in the sense of being a less-perfect-than-literal language, but in the sense that they have religious meaning precisely to the extent that they communicate that there is no truly "literal" language: the notion of literal language is based on the idea that words are adequate to truth when they correspond to the actual divisions of reality, but, in fact (according to the vision of the absolute object), the actual divisions of reality *are not the truth*, but are themselves metaphysically derivative of a reality that *in principle* cannot be *adequately* representative in *any* determinate images, words or otherwise.

Augustine's words, though, like Muslim prayer and Hindu devotions (*bhakti*), can, in fact, precipitate the desired end, and exhort one to "turn around" (*periagōgē*), as Socrates puts it, experiencing one's own finite answerability to the infinite beyond.[18] We can and do *live in* the world of meaning opened up for us by these "exhortations," these "pointers." Indeed, in the absence of some such determinate pointer, there is no such experience. It is only *in* and *by* the setting up of these routes—these *Vorstellungen*—that we enact the context within which the whole domain of meaningful answerability to the infinite object becomes possible. Recognizing, therefore, the inadequacy of determinate forms of "worship" and recognition of the divine is not the same as rejecting them in favor of some other supposed route of access, some other means of recognition. On the contrary, it is precisely the imperative of the divine call that it be recognized, realized, and answered to in necessarily inadequate forms.

The true import of the call, then, is the *validation* of the realm of "this worldly" finitude, not the call for its renunciation.

The Determinate Forms of Religion

Any religion *is* only insofar as it is the affirmation of a specific set of practices, images, and narratives. Though its intent may be to point to the infinite, it must nonetheless *actually* point, and must, thus, embrace the various determinate forms of affirming this infinity. Religions are practices *by* a culture, by a "we," which defines itself by the very gestures through which it affirms its relation to the absolute. The embrace of the specific "how" is as essential to it as the fact of the pointing to the absolute, for it *is* this religious community only in and as the enactment of its collective "how."[19] For this reason, religions are necessarily committed to their forms—this, as we saw above, is the truth behind fundamentalism, and why it is necessarily a dimension of the attitude always involved in religion, namely, that we must be committed to *some* form to do any recognizing—and Hegel himself is (or we ourselves, as phenomenologists are) called similarly to recognize the *truth* of all "scripture": in other words, we appreciate the phenomenon of religion for what it is only when we see the culture's embrace of the necessity of various images and practices *as telling the truth*, as an enactment of witnessing to the absolute.

Our challenge as phenomenologists of religion is thus to hear what is specifically affirmed in the determinacies of a religion's "*Vorstellungen*," to hear how they speak to us of the absolute, how they offer an essential message not reducible to a "worldly" communication, but always necessarily a "revelation." While all these religions are ultimately exhortations to acknowledgment of the absolute, the determinacies in which they accomplish this exhortation all offer determinately different resources—for better or for worse—for speaking to us. "For better or for worse" in the sense that different, determinate modes of address will have strengths and weaknesses for engaging with the domains of human meaningfulness—the domains, that is, within which we *can be* addressed. A tall person must crouch to get through the lower door but can reach the top shelf easily, whereas a short person must work harder to reach the shelf but can pass through the door without a second thought; similarly, the determinacies of a religion make it more or less of a challenge to address different dimensions of human experience. Buddhism, for example, speaks more easily to the demands of individuality than Islam, while Islam more easily addresses our sense of the social needs of a community; Hinduism, again, speaks more easily to the vast multiplicity of the forms of localized cultural life than Christianity, which speaks more easily to the culture of global, secular modernity. As Hegel says, all religions ultimately offer all religious possibilities:

> The series of different religions which will come to view, just as much sets forth again only the different aspects of a *single* religion, and, moreover, of every single religion, and the ideas which seem to distinguish one actual religion from another occur in each one.[20]

This means, in other words, that Islam has the resources to validate and address individuality, Hinduism has the resources to address global modernity, and so on; nonetheless, the determinacies of different religions more immediately address some aspects of human experience—some aspects of "spirit"—than others. "At the same time," that is, "the difference must also be viewed as a difference of religion," and showing how this is so is the main focus of Hegel's description of religion in chapter VII of the *Phenomenology of Spirit*.[21] I will outline this only very briefly, in order to see only the overall shape of the development, and to extract the point of the discussion; rather than working through all the details of Hegel's account, I will emphasize only the most important structural moments, which are the use of *nature, art,* and *revelation* as figures of the divine.

Religion of Nature

To what could we more immediately turn than to those forms of reality that are naturally given to us, in order to point to the divine? What Hegel refers to as the "religions of nature" are precisely those religions whose religious *Vorstellungen* are rooted in natural figures.[22] And within this world of nature, which reality better reveals the relationship of "source" than the light? As Socrates makes clear in book 6 of the *Republic,* our vision depends upon the light which is itself not one of the objects perceived but the illumination which brings them to visibility.[23] The clarity of vision—the quality of vision that is its manifestness—is itself the contribution of light that "makes clear" what can be seen. Itself perceivable only as the clarity of the visible—perceivable, that is, only through what it illuminates—the light is the condition of the possibility of the experience of vision; itself not one of the objects of perception but the illuminating that exceeds the entire field of the illuminated, the light is the source that gives vision, that to which the entire visible realm owes its reality as visible. As such, the light is a part of the natural world that is a powerful figure for that which, exceeding the domain of beings, gives all beings to be: the relation of visible objects to light within experience is a powerful analogy for the relation between the entire domain of the world of experience and its ultimate source. The "religion of light" is the original communal recognition of this point.

The ancient Zoroastrian worship of Ahura Mazda sees in the light the essential figure of the divine;[24] "God," that is, the infinite object, is especially seen in the experience of illumination of the sun, the light and heat that is the nurturance of our natural reality.[25] The infinite object is beyond any finite reality, and yet we need to assert its existence; how better to make clear what it is that we are acknowledging than in the figure of light? Indeed, Augustine's own "conceptual" discussion of these relations uses exactly this language of "illumination" to exhort us to the recognition of the divine. Again, as we exhort another to make this recognition, we might precisely say, "Can't you *see* . . . ?," drawing again upon the image of vision to characterize the situation we have in mind. The infinite object can never be equated with any finite reality, yet our recognition of it, our articulation of our acknowledgment of it, must always come through finitude, and what better finite figure than the figure that is vision itself, the figure "illuminated/illuminating" as illuminative of the divine illumination?

On the one hand, light is specially privileged for drawing our attention to the absolute object—this is the basic thesis of the light-religion. On the other hand, this religion, while turning to the light, must also insist that it does not worship the physical light—the light with which we are all immediately, experientially familiar—but the divine light, *das Lichtwesen.* "Spirit," Hegel says, "beholds itself in the form of *being,* though not of the non-spiritual being that is filled with the contingent determinations of sensation, the being that belongs to sense-certainty; on the contrary, it is being that is filled with spirit."[26] In short, physical light is but a metaphor. But in that case, it is no more essential an image than any other, for, in fact, it is just one of the illuminated realities, *exactly equal* with respect to its failure to be appropriately illuminative of the nature of the divine. The light religion is thus—like all religion—caught in the ambivalence of its essential commitment to a determinacy the inessentiality of which it is essentially committed to. Here, then, we see the light religion as a straightforward instantiation of the concept of religion.

The light religion also offers something specific, though, and this is equally its strength and its weakness as a determinate religion. Its determinacy—its preferential commitment to the finite determinacy of light—is specially powerful as a route for recognizing the singularity and the ultimacy of God, and for recognizing the character of "beyond" that characterizes the infinite object: indeed, it is a determinacy that is specially good at recognizing the need to go beyond determinacy. Something similar is true of Islam, with its unbending, anti-idolatrous focus on the "mono" of monotheism: there is no God except God (and it is perhaps more than a mere historical coincidence that Islam itself grew up in a cultural world with roots in the Zoroastrian religion).[27] The weakness of this figure of the divine, however, is simply the "flip-side" of its strength: in effectively saying that God is "not" any determinate thing, no determinate thing is empowered to communicate anything about God and, indeed, no determinacy is any more or less like the divine.

> The movements of its own externalization, its creations in the unresisting element of its otherness, are torrents of light; in their simplicity, they are at the same time the genesis of its being-for-self and the return from its being-there [*Dasein*], streams of fire destructive of structured form. . . . The determinations of this substance are only attributes that do not attain to self-subsistence, but remain merely names of the many-named One.[28]

The purity of its articulation is thus equally the emptiness of its articulation. Politically or practically, the one-sided emphasis on the irreducible singularity of divine transcendence—"this substance which merely *ascends*, without *descending* into its depths to become a subject and through the self to consolidate its distinct moments"[29]—can encourage an equally one-sided renunciation of all finitude, producing a simple denunciation or even hatred of the world.

The light-religion drew on an essential relationship within our experience of nature—the relation of light/sun to other natural things—and the other nature religions draw upon other sides of this same relationship. In its imagery, the long religious tradition that developed in the Indian sub-continent—"Hinduism"—comes close to being the opposite of this religion of light, in that this Hindu religious tradition can see in almost any determinacy a figure of the divine. The very absoluteness of the divine transcendence points to an equalizing of all finite determinacies in their capacity to reflect the divine—"Pure light disperses its unitary nature into an infinity of forms, and offers up itself as a sacrifice to being-for-self, so that from its substance the individual may take an enduring existence for itself"[30]—and it is this recognition that is more easily brought out by religions like Hinduism that effectively find infinite routes to the divine through the world of finitude. Such religions, however, while multiplying the routes to recognition, also risk obscuring the singularity of divine transcendence. What such a religion risks, politically and practically, is either a one-sided or an indiscriminate embrace of finitude. Hegel makes essentially this point in his discussion of the "plant-" and "animal-religions." Accepting a determinate bit of nature—this animal as opposed to that animal—as manifesting the divine is—or risks—investing the exclusiveness of that specificity with divine sanction. Different animals characteristically oppose each other—dog versus cat or lion versus lamb, for example—and the recognition of various divinities (themselves associated with specific animal natures) can encourage a sectarianism such that a community develops a loyalty to a specific divinity *as opposed to* another:

> The *actual* self-consciousness of this dispersed spirit is a host of separate, antagonistic national spirits who hate and fight each other to the death and become conscious of specific forms of animals as their essence.[31]

Further, whether or not animals are explicitly taken as images of the divine, the divine can be construed *as if it were an animal*. Here, rather than recognizing "no god except God," there is perceived to be a multiplicity of divinities, one of which is "ours." As Harris notes in *Hegel's Ladder*, this situation describes primitive Judaism, which construed Yahweh effectively as its "champion," and perhaps resonates as well with contemporary Malaysian Muslims who opposed Christian usage of the term "Allah," maintaining that it was well-known that Allah was the Muslim's god.[32] When natural species are taken as expressive of the divine, determinacy is introduced that allows meaningful access to the divine, but this determinacy also introduces an exclusivity and a relativity that risks debasing the absoluteness of the "infinite object." And though Hegel does not here note this himself, it seems that this "polytheism" also risks a sort of ultimate secularism; that is, it risks precisely a failure to recognize the divine in a *confusion* of the divine and the mundane that parallels the indiscriminate renunciation of finitude risked by the light-religion.

In his description of the different forms of cultural religious experience, Hegel tries to demonstrate that the different forms of historical religions have embraced *Vorstellungen* that reflect the systematic range of forms of possible experience that he has himself so far documented in the *Phenomenology of Spirit* (the Zoroastrian light-religion having an object comparable to the object of sense-certainty, Hindu plant- and animal-religions having an object comparable to the object of perception, the Egyptian artificer-religion having an object comparable to the object of understanding, and so on), but it is not my intention here to work through or defend the identifications Hegel makes.[33] My goal, rather, is simply to make clear the basic sense (a) that determinate religions are "differently abled" by the determinate forms of their *Vorstellungen*, and (b) that there is an important distinction between the *Vorstellungen* of the nature-, art-, and revealed religions. With the austere light-religion and with the exuberant plant- and animal-religions, we have seen some of both the rationale for, and the problems associated with, relying on natural realities as *Vorstellungen* for God. With the religion of the Greeks, there is a different form of *Vorstellung* altogether. For the Greek religion, it is art (*Kunst*), rather than nature, that offers an expression of the divine.

Religion of Art

In his discussion of religion, Hegel tries to show that specific approaches to religion correspond to particular approaches to political life: "the specific religion has likewise a specific actual spirit."[34] In the *Encyclopaedia*, Hegel writes:

> [T]he nature of a nation's moral life, the principle of its law, of its actual liberty, and of its constitution, as well as of its art and science, corresponds to the principle which constitutes the substance of a religion. That all these elements of a nation's actuality constitute one systematic totality, that one spirit creates and informs them, is a truth on which follows the further truth that the history of religions coincides with the world-history.[35]

In other words, the political order and the religious practice both reflect the same fundamental commitment of a society.[36] The discussion of the art-religion is particularly striking and important in this regard, for it is the religion that Hegel understands to be uniquely related to the basic form of free political life; indeed, inasmuch as the "political" precisely designates the situation of free, collective deliberation about "the just and the unjust, the expedient and the inexpedient" for a community, it would be truer to say that the art-religion is integral to the original establishment of a political community.[37]

This original free community is what Hegel calls "the ethical substance": it is "the free nation in which hallowed custom constitutes the substance of all, whose actuality and existence each and everyone knows to be his own will and deed."[38] Hegel describes this political community at a few different spots in the *Phenomenology of Spirit*: though the "phenomenology" of the ethical spirit is taken up in chapter VI, "Spirit," part A, sections a and b, there are also substantial discussions of ethicality at the beginning of the section called "The Actualization of Rational Self-Consciousness through its Own Activity" (M350–352, W/C 234–236), in the final paragraphs of chapter V, "Reason" (M436–437, W/C 285–287), and here in the discussion of the "Art Religion" (especially paragraphs M700–701, 727, W/C 458–460, 474–475). The ethical community understands its commitment to the good to be equally a commitment to human flourishing—freedom—and is oriented to establishing a culture of excellence, in which natural human potential is brought to actualization. The community itself is charged with this responsibility of fostering the good, and the community exists as a kind of trust: individuals trust that the structure of society looks out for their interests; the society trusts that individuals are inherently good; people trust that reality—divinity and nature—has providently established a world in which human action will fit harmoniously with the nature of things.

> The reality of the ethical substance rests partly on its passive unchangeableness . . . and consequently on the fact that [self-consciousness] has not yet withdrawn into itself from its contented acceptance of custom and its firm trust therein. Partly, too, on its organization into a multiplicity of rights and duties, as also on its distribution into the spheres of the various classes and their particular activities which co-operate to form the whole; and hence on the fact that the individual is content with the limitation of his existence.[39]

In short, this society lives in the presumption of harmony, the "happy state" in which the received form of human social life is itself presumed to be natural—indeed, presumed to be the very fulfillment of human nature.[40]

This ethical society is a society that is both committed to the maintenance of its religious and cultural traditions—the "divine law"—and committed to the legitimacy of institutions of self-governance—the "human law."[41] The ethical substance is the original democracy in the sense of the community that understands itself to be self-governing, rather than, say, simply blindly following traditional rules, and it sees this commitment to human, communal self-governance to be of a piece with its religious worship. This is, in other words, what Aristotle defines as the "political" society, characterized by collective deliberation about value and policy, about what is "just and unjust, expedient and inexpedient." It is the happy society that believes human deliberation to be compatible with "natural law," and thus different both from the oppressive, pre-democratic, "theocratic" regimes that do not hold the liberating of human deliberation to be a goal, and from modern democracies that recognize the liberation of human deliberation to be incompatible with presumptions of a normative human essence. It is this presumption of the harmony of the divine order and the human order that is fundamentally reflected in the religion of art.

Inasmuch as this society is premised on the harmony of the human and the divine, it is enactments of this harmony that provide its proper *Vorstellungen*. Now, whereas this religious culture is identifying the validation of human deliberation—of "being-for-self" in Hegel's language—within the godhead, this was precisely what was occluded by the perspective of the light-essence, "the divine Light which, being devoid of a self, does not contain within it the self-certainty of the individuals, but is only their universal essence and the lordly power in which they disappear."[42] Indeed, any natural form, inasmuch as it is natural—that is, self-emergent—reflects no essential role for human being-for-self. For this reason, the perspective of the ethical substance is not found in a religion of nature, but in a religion that finds the divine presented in distinctly human works.[43] This is the culture, that is, in which religion and art are essentially identified, the culture in which worship is enacted in human gestures of accomplishing the perfect union of human and divine.[44] This is the culture in which art is the highest achievement of human endeavor—"In such an epoch, absolute art makes its appearance"[45]—the very route to the acknowledgment of the divine.

The "dialectic" of the religion of art is the changing way in which art accomplishes—the changing form of art that accomplishes—religious need. Inasmuch as it is the inclusion of human being-for-self in the divine that is ultimately to be expressed, it will be this being-for-self that must ultimately define the form of art. Hegel writes:

> The first work of art, as immediate, is abstract and individual. As for itself, it has to move away from this immediate and objective mode towards self-consciousness, while self-consciousness, on the other hand, in the cult aims at getting rid of the distinction by which it distinguishes itself at first from its Spirit, and by so doing to produce a work of art which is its own self and animate.[46]

In fact Hegel identifies three distinct ways in which the religion/art of the ethical society reflects and expresses humanity—or, rather, the unity of the divine and the human—which he refers to as the "abstract," the "living," and the "spiritual" work of art. These changing approaches to the artistic expression of divinity correspond to different forms of the political development of the community, and the fullest development of the art-religion is in fact correlated with the self-transcendence of the political community; that is, the fullest development of the art-religion corresponds to a recognition of the nature of humanity that calls for a transformation in the political realization of human freedom.[47]

Initially, temples and statues—works of architecture and sculpture—celebrate the divine. As Hegel says, "[t]he nation that approaches its god in the Cult of the religion of art is the ethical nation that knows its state and the actions of the state to be the will and the achievement of its own self,"[48] and these works of moulded stone, unlike sunlight, are essentially works of culture, that is, "it is essential to the statue to be the work of human hands."[49] But though their creation reflects an essential humanity, they are otherwise only static, alien objects.[50] Statues of the gods as "ideal" humans go furthest in this domain in portraying the identity of human and divine within the artwork, but even here what is portrayed is the human as "looked at," as a "body for others," as Sartre would say.[51] In other *practices*, however, the unity of divine and human is *lived* rather than "looked at": one witnesses in the *performance* of the athlete, for example, a truer image of the divine humanity than that presented in the inanimate statue, and, beyond this, in the feast one's celebration of the divine is also one's own experience of satisfaction.[52] But even beyond these "living" works of art, there is a deeper expression of humanity in works of literature, "spiritual" works of art, because these portray, beyond external appearance and beyond action, the inwardness of humanity (and, indeed, these poetic works operate within the medium of imagination—subjectivity—rather than in stone or sound as such).[53] And whereas tragedy captures the substantiality of ethical life in presenting the *pathos*—the identity of human and divine enacted in and as the suffering of the dramatic protagonist and repeated cathartically in the experienced mood of the witness—comedy "ends" the religion of art—ends it in both the sense of fulfilling it and terminating it—in recognizing the ultimate character of humanity in the very "first person" perspective that phenomenology itself calls us to recognize.[54]

Especially in the living work of art, the harmony of divine and human practice is powerfully manifest, and so this stage of the art-religion is in many ways the most emblematic of the mature flourishing of the Greek democracy. Just as the self-determining community confidently undertakes the charting of its own course, the religious festivals are simultaneously a celebration of the human participants and of human excellence in general. With the spiritual work of art, however, we see a significant development beyond this. In the changing conceptions of the artwork (from abstract to living to spiritual), we are effectively seeing a changing conception/vision of the human, moving from an external to a behavioral to an internal interpretation of the essential "locus" of humanity, and the change to the "spiritual" vision entails a critique of the sense of communal self-determination that defines the Greek democracy.

Hegel identifies comedy as the culmination of the spiritual artworks, for here the notion of human inwardness is most fully developed.

> The consummation of the ethical sphere in free self-consciousness, and the fate of the ethical world, are therefore the individuality that has withdrawn into itself, the absolute levity of the ethical spirit which has dissolved within itself all the firmly established distinctions of its stable existence and the spheres of its organically ordered world and, being perfectly sure of itself, has attained to unrestrained joyfulness and the freest enjoyment of itself.[55]

In comedy—the works of writers such as Aristophanes, which were performed at religious festivals such as the Lenaia—the substantial institutions of society, which are the very embodiment of the free community, are subjected to criticism from the perspective of the individual: comedy portrays individuals who experience their singular self-interests beyond the demands of the institutions of society and in so doing comedy demonstrates that human freedom is not exhausted by institutional life. It is this same perspective that is enacted by Socrates, who demands of the institutions of freedom that they be answerable to the internal norms of his personal powers of self-critical reasoning. Comedy is a recognition at the level of the artwork of the same dimension of humanity that Socrates gives voice to in his historical practice. As the story of Socrates' trial makes clear, the interpretation of what is essential about humanity that is expressed in Socrates' vision is fundamentally in tension with the interpretation of humanity that is definitive of Greek politics, and thus the culminating, "spiritual" form of the art-religion corresponds to the dissolution of the ethical, political community.[56]

Greek democracy is a reality—a "concept"—that is not realized in a moment, but is realized, rather, in a process—an historical process spanning a few centuries. This society, premised on the "divinity" of human flourishing and committed to enabling this has, as its result, its ultimate product, the cultivating of the experience of singular human freedom. The coming into being of a figure like Socrates, and all the corresponding practices and attitudes of which his life is emblematic, is a great accomplishment of this society. And yet, in thus coming to inwardness, the culture has actually transcended itself, for in a figure like Socrates the fundamental sense of human freedom has shifted from that upon which the Greek society was founded.

Greek society had rightly recognized that there are *institutions* of freedom, and that freedom is realized in participation in these institutions. This is the perspective, in fact, that Socrates himself explains in the *Crito* when he explains the formative role of the laws in establishing the substantial identities of persons.[57] The institutions of social life provide the essential formative education for citizens, allowing them to grow into the role of participant members of the political community, and this social participation allows a richness of human life that is fundamentally fulfilling of our human capacities. The institutions of social life offer us a substantial freedom; the "comedic" standpoint of Socratic philosophy, however, points to a different sense of human fulfillment, namely, the freedom of singular subjectivity. The comedic, Socratic standpoint turns inward to the self-determining domain of human inwardness, for which the institutions of social life are external: no longer *substantial,* but simply *objective.*[58] The very effectiveness of the social institutions in facilitating a human flourishing has resulted in their being transcended by a freedom that now defines itself in terms opposed to the terms upon which the institutions were founded.

> Through the religion of Art, Spirit has advanced from the form of *Substance* to assume that of *Subject*. . . . This incarnation of the divine Being starts from the statue which wears only the *outer* shape of the Self, the *inwardness,* the Self's activity, falling outside of it. But in the Cult the two sides have become one; and in the outcome of the religion of Art this unity, in its consummation, has even gone right over at the same time to the extreme of the Self. In Spirit that is completely certain of itself in the individuality of consciousness, all essentiality is submerged. The proposition that expresses this levity is 'The Self is Absolute Being.' The essence, the Substance, for which the Self was an accident, has sunk to the level of a predicate.[59]

Freedom and human flourishing is now recognized as fundamentally a reality of individuals rather than a reality of communities.

Religion of Revelation

The inwardness displayed by the comic spirit points to the inherent nonimmediacy of human subjectivity. Subjectivity is "appeared to," that is, any being is "for" it. To be a subject is to be involved in a determinate situation—"thrown," as Heidegger says—but to *be aware of* that situation, rather than simply to "be" it. As Sartre says, I "am" my situation, but "in the mode of not-being it"; in Hegel's language, subjectivity is a "negative self-relation," a reality that exists only as a negation of itself, a not-being itself.[60] Indeed, this is the fundamental character of freedom, namely, to be inherently beyond any determinacy, to be "free" of, or "free" in, what it determinately is. Freedom—subjectivity—is thus inherently non-immediate; that is, it immediately exists as a negative, a mediation, a relation.[61] Subjectivity always *is not* whatever it immediately is.

It is this notion of the negative self-relation that is captured in the central presentation of the divine that defines the revealed religion, namely, the crucifixion of Christ. The dialectic of religion is captured in the changing shape in which the "ultimate object" is presented, from light to art to crucifixion. Whereas light emphasizes the divine illumination and art emphasizes the unity of the infinite and the finite, the crucifixion emphasizes the way in which finitude or determinacy *from within itself* gives itself over to the appearing of the infinite, the revealing of the divine.[62] The crucifixion is an image of a determinacy that is itself only as not-being itself, it is itself only *as* already from or for a beyond.

This "beyond," however, is not another presence: rather, the image of the crucifixion announces a fundamentally different kind of reality. A negative self-relation is not the juxtaposing of one determinate being, one positivity, against another, but is the happening of a fundamentally different kind of reality—a *negativity*—that is not itself a present being, but is a reality revealed through that presence. The *meaning of* words, for example, is not a different set of letters or sounds juxtaposed to the letters or sounds that compose the words, but is a sense revealed *in* and *through* those letters or sounds. It is the meaning *of* them, but not reducible to them; and, indeed, it is *what is really appearing* on the page or through the voice—it is why those letters or sounds *are there. They* are *its* "being there"—the words are the *Dasein of* the meaning. And this meaning can only be apprehended by an intelligence, by an act of understanding that looks to the present letters or sounds to see what, beyond themselves—beyond their immediacy—they reveal. Such an understanding will precisely look, not to what is present *as such,* but to what is presented through that immediate presence: it will look for that meaning that, qua meaning, can never be a simple presence—in that sense cannot "be present"—but can only be presented through a presence. The meaning as such is not a present being beside other present beings, but is the essentially non-present that is revealed through a presence that sacrifices itself to allowing that non-present to appear. In this same sense, then, the crucifixion is an image of finitude—of determinacy—that is the making present of another reality that can never be finite, can never be a determinate being, but is precisely that which, beyond the finite, is made apparent in and through the finite as the truth of the finite. The crucifixion is the image of the finite that is as the self-appearing of the infinite. It is precisely an image of the finite as always in fact the presenting of the "absolute object," the presenting of "God."

The divine—God, the absolute object—cannot "exist," in the sense that by its nature it cannot have simple *Dasein*, cannot be a determinate being, for then it would be a finite presence. Instead, God can only *be revealed*, that is, can only be presented *through* that which is "there" *as* the ultimate, as the "real as such" that can itself never be present.[63] The crucifixion is the image of the present as the presenting of what cannot be present, the presenting of the essential unpresentable that can only be revealed, and, indeed, can only be revealed *to* one who looks beyond the finite *for* the infinite that is there revealed. The present—the finite, the determinate—will thus always be the presenting of that which cannot be present as such, and, inasmuch as that non-presentable is the truth—the "absolute object" itself—the present will be seen in its truth only when it is seen as not true as such, but as the revelation of the absolute. The crucifixion, then, as the image of the self-transcendence of the finite, is the expression of the imperative to "look beyond." The image presents the imperative to go beyond the present. The revealed religion, then, is the religion that advocates the need to answer only and ultimately to the absolute, and not to worship the finite—not to be idolatrous, as it were. Inasmuch as religions themselves are finite, determinate practices and their images finite, determinate images, the image of the crucifixion is equally the imperative to go beyond this very image itself: "The *content* of this imagining [*des Vorstellens*] is absolute spirit; and all that now remains is to supersede this mere form."[64] The revealed religion, with its constitutive image of crucifixion, is the final religion in the dialectic of religion because it is the self-transcending of religion—it is the religion that says about religion, "go beyond religion."

Indeed, the definitive *Vorstellung* of the revealed religion is the entire story of "the incarnation": of God becoming a man, fully human and fully divine, who is crucified, such that through his death the entirety of finitude is "saved," all transgression is forgiven. The story of the incarnation is the story of the divine penetrating to the depths of finitude, leaving nothing outside its proper domain; forgiveness, the definitive norm of the revealed religion, is again the concept of the vindication of finitude, the recognition that transgression is not excluded from the domain of the absolute, but is the very medium of its existence.[65] This is, indeed, precisely how we have defined the notion of revelation, namely, as that which has self-consciousness as its *Dasein*; that is, the absolute is that which cannot exist as such but can exist only as the existing of the relative, of the non-absolute. The finite transcends itself, that is, self-consciousness completes itself (becomes truly conscious of the nature of its self) when it recognizes its constitutive answerability to the revelation of sense that is the divine; the absolute, similarly, is truly absolute only when it is limited by no other, when it embraces finitude as its very own. The story of God and the story of self-consciousness are the same story told from two sides, and this is the sense of the *Vorstellungen* of the revealed religion.

> This incarnation of the divine reality [*des göttlichen Wesens*], or the fact that it essentially and directly has the shape of self-consciousness, is the simple content of the absolute religion.[66]

"The resurrection" is precisely the image of this mutuality of divine and human accomplishment: God is realized in his revelation, which is equally the experience of the faithful.[67] The community of faith is the self-presenting of the absolute: the reality of each is the same.

> This concept of the transcended individual self that is absolute reality immediately expresses, therefore, the establishing of a community which, tarrying hitherto in the sphere of *Vorstellen*, now returns into itself as the self; and in doing this, spirit passes over . . . from *Vorstellen* into . . . self-consciousness as such.[68]

The community is resurrected in recognizing itself as the self-appearing of the absolute, the spirit conscious of itself as spirit.

Probably the most important point about the community of the revealed religion is that it is a community based on *conversion*. Often, we use the term "convert" simply to mean "change," and in this sense we have all "converted" many times over, in changing jobs, in changing relationships, and so on; often one speaks of "conversion" to Judaism or "conversion" to Hinduism, and here too "conversion" has the sense of exchanging one for another. In the context of the religion of revelation, however, "conversion" means something more singular. To convert in the sense of the revealed religion—in the sense of Paul's call to conversion in his letters—is precisely to recognize that the one and only absolute calls to one from within one's singular subjectivity, within the "inwardness" revealed by the comic spirit. This is the recognition of the "inner light" that Augustine identified and the "submission" called for by Mohammed: it is the turning inward that discovers itself to be an exposure to a new "outside," a "beyond" to which one is intrinsically answerable and which calls to one in one's inmost, non-transferable, undeniable singularity. It is the recognition of an absolute that itself can only be found within this inward turning, an absolute that appears as such only to the one who has turned toward this revelation. The revealed religion, in other words, is a religion into which one cannot be "born," as one might be born into a Greek or Vedic religion/culture; rather, one must be "born again," that is, one must *through one's own singular initiative* recognize and commit oneself to this inner truth.

The religion of revelation, like the religions of nature and art, is also the religion of a particular society; that is, the conception of divinity reflected in its *Vorstellungen* reflects a principle that has equally determined an historical form of social life. Hegel distinguishes different stages in the history of this community of the revealed religion. The initial community—the community associated in the writings of the Christian *New Testament* with the leadership of Peter, the apostle, in contrast to the community Paul fostered that did not valorize membership in the initial company of Jesus—understands the import of the story of the incarnation to be found in being in the living presence of the living person Jesus.[69] This community understands itself to be formed around a "real event," and thereby misses the central import of conversion, confusing an external, worldly reality with inner transformation.[70] In general, the writings in the *New Testament* seem to anticipate a "second coming" of Jesus that will be a "real event" only a few calendar days in the future. The community of the revealed religion developed beyond this point, however, in the centuries that in fact passed. Here, *a community of memory* developed, a community for which neither the incarnation nor the "second coming" was a "real event" within their experience: in other words, *in fact* this community enacted a wholly "inward" self-transformation, though *in its self-interpretation* this community still understood itself to be responding ultimately to an external reality.[71] The community of the revealed religion completes itself in the community that recognizes that the memory itself—the recognition—and not what is remembered is what is important.[72] This last community, in other words, is the one that recognizes that the *anastasis nekrōn*, the "resurrection of the dead" of which Paul writes, is enacted *in and as the community of the revealed religion*:

> Death becomes transfigured from its immediate meaning, viz. the non-being of *this singular* individual, into the *universality* of the spirit who dwells in his community, dies in it every day, and is daily resurrected.[73]

This, the third phase of the historical community of the religion of revelation, is the community that recognizes its own recognizing of the divine—the living church—to be the living presence of that divinity.[74]

> Spirit is thus posited in the third element, in *universal self-consciousness*; it is its *community*. The movement of the community as self-consciousness that has distinguished itself from its *Vorstellung* is to make explicit what has been implicitly established. The dead divine man or human god is *in himself* the universal self-consciousness; this he has to become explicitly *for this self-consciousness*.[75]

This is the community that completes the revealed religion in transcending it, for it has precisely heeded the call of the *Vorstellungen* to go beyond *Vorstellungen* and to enact the living presence of the absolute in and through its own finite self-transcendence.

In fact, the second phase of the society of the revealed religion, like the second phase of the "ethical" society of the art-religion, most corresponds to our familiar sense of the distinctive character of that society. This is the form of social life that Hegel calls "culture" (*Bildung*), the society of Christian Europe from the fall of Rome to the French Revolution.[76] The notion of self-transcending inwardness[77]—"conversion"—entails a new sense of freedom compared to that realized in the ethical society, and its institutionalization leads to a new form of social, cultural, and political life. The essentiality of self-transcendence involves the idea that the natural state is insufficient in itself: "although here the self knows itself as *this* self, yet its actuality consists solely in the setting-aside of its natural self."[78]

> [Self-consciousness] has *actuality* only in so far as it alienates itself from itself; by so doing, it gives itself the character of a universal, and this its universality is its worth and actuality.[79]

Hence nature and persons need to be "cultivated" to attain their proper form: "It is therefore through *culture* that the individual acquires worth and actuality."[80] Hegel identifies the principle of this Christian world as the idea that "all are free," for the essentiality of inwardness involves the idea that each individual singly is responsible to this higher truth, and therefore each is in principle equally worthy to each other.[81]

> This *equality* with everyone is, therefore, not . . . that immediate recognition and validity of self-consciousness simply because it *is*; on the contrary, to be valid it must have conformed itself to the universal by the mediating process of alienation.[82]

The individual self-conscious person—*any* person—is called to turn inward and to recognize his higher calling. But also, "the process in which the individuality moulds itself by culture is . . . at the same time . . . the development of the actual world."[83] Actually answering to this calling involves acting in the world to bring it into conformity with this higher truth and this means establishing the world as a culture in which the freedom of all individuals is equally recognized. In his discussion of "Culture," Hegel works through the history of social and political developments that defined the culture of the Christian West throughout the medieval and early modern period. I will not retrace that path here, but will emphasize only the ultimate development of this movement of "culture," which is the emergence of modern democracy, epitomized in the emergence of the French republic in the revolution of 1789.

Whereas Greek democracy had recognized the freedom of the human *community*, Christian democracy recognizes the freedom of the human *individual*.[84] The freedom of that individual, however, as we saw in chapter 11, is not a freedom that accrues to it naturally, just by virtue of being a singular self, but is the freedom *of conversion*. This is the freedom of the individual who has within herself the capacity to apprehend the absolute, which ultimately comes to mean the *rational* individual. This has led to the interpretation of the political sphere as a domain for individual self-determination, a domain of "civil society" in which rational individuals are protected in their freedom to pursue their own individual ends, provided they do not undermine the freedom of other rational individuals to do the same.[85] The French Revolution is a paradigmatic and, indeed, original enactment of this modern democratic politics.

The French Revolution is also paradigmatic of the problem of this political vision, and Hegel lays out the reasons for this in his analysis of "the Terror" into which the French Revolution developed in 1793.[86] As we saw in chapter 11, the problem with the principle of modern democratic politics—the principle of "universally equal, free, rational individuality"—is that no person can actually be the person who is validated in that political regime. Persons are inherently finite, inherently communal, inherently biased: though each of us has the capacity to transcend ourselves in the inward recognition of the absolute, *we necessarily do this from a non-absolute position*, that is, *we are as much defined by our ineffaceable finitude as we are defined by our inherent infinitude.* No person can live from the standpoint of universal, disinterested impartiality; instead, we will always necessarily be involved in violent, transgressive, partial activity that trespasses against others, just as they will necessarily trespass against us, and a political regime that renounces this *implicitly renounces humanity*. In other words, the democracy that intends to be universally *inclusive* by recognizing precisely the legitimacy of all rational individuals as such is in fact universally *exclusive*, for in rejecting all partiality it in fact rejects all persons.

None of us can ever be the self-determining, rational individual demanded by the principle of modern democracy. First, we are never fully individual nor fully "rational," (in the sense understood by modernity). Instead, we can achieve such an identity only on the basis of partialities—commitments to human bonds, locations, habits of behavior, particular resources—that necessarily exclude others.[87] Unlike the "universal human rights of the rational individual" whose abstract inclusiveness is in fact universally equal only in its failure to recognize the definitive particularities of anyone, the stance of *forgiveness* of our inherent partiality is the only attitude that could be universally, concretely inclusive.[88] Second, our definitive "rationality"—the "higher" self that is the justification for our "individual rights"—is precisely a site of a *calling*, of our *receiving* our determination from without. Our engagement with our higher self, in other words, is *an exposure*, not a *choosing*. We already saw that in principle the second phase of the history of the revealed religion was insufficient to its own principle and that the completion of the community of the revealed religion only comes in a transformation of the very nature of its relationship to "religion."[89] Similarly, we here see that the political community that emerges out of this second phase of the society of the revealed religion is also inherently inadequate and points to the need for a new vision of politics, beyond both the ancient and the modern conceptions of democracy. Let us conclude, now, with a consideration of this transformed shape of "spirit," a spirit beyond religion and beyond politics.

Conclusion: Community as the Self-Showing of the Absolute—beyond "Human" Sovereignty

Religion, as we have seen from the start, settles on the necessity and essentiality of finite determinacies—of rituals and myths, that is, *Vorstellungen*—to present the absolute, when in fact the absolute cannot be limited to an exclusive finitude. From the start, then, the very concept of religion is the call to go beyond religion. The revealed religion is the religion that recognizes this necessity of religious self-transcendence within its very *Vorstellungen*. The fixity of finite rituals and myths allows the comfort of a rule, a comfort that is satisfied with the adequacy of the image: in other words, the inherently conservative tendency of ritual practice is to treat the image as absolute. This is the inherent idolatry of religion, and it is precisely the imperative of the revealed religion to renounce such idolatry. The imperative of the revealed religion is the imperative to go beyond the image, to go beyond the established parameters of religious practice, overcoming the alienation between oneself and the essence of religion in recognizing one's personal answerability to accomplishing the appearing of the absolute here and now, which is the imperative to recognize the absolute in *and as* a performatively enacted reality in which one participates.[90] The notion of revelation, and its corresponding notion of conversion, is its singling out of the individual self-consciousness as the essential site of the appearing of the absolute. Indeed, it is the very imperative to *be* the site of the appearing of the absolute. In this way, the enactment of the definitive imperative of the revealed religion is in principle a stand beyond religion. It is analogously a stand beyond politics.

The domain of politics has been the domain of human self-determination, the essential difference between the Greek ("ethical") and the Christian ("cultural") forms of this being whether "the human" is understood communally or individually. In fact, both orientations recognize something essential about the human, in that it is true both that we are essentially communal and that we are essentially individual. Consequently, it is incumbent upon a just politics to recognize legally both the essential rights of individuality and the essential need for community. This dual need for recognition already points to a politics different both from the repressive conservatism of the Greek polis and from the alienated liberalism of early modern democracy, and its descendents in market-driven, global capitalism.[91] Yet even with revised institutions that recognize these dual needs, as opposed to institutions rooted simply in one or the other of these one-sided political conceptions, there is a fundamental inadequacy in principle in the whole conception of the political domain.

Whether Greek or Christian, these conceptions of politics display a fundamental "humanism," inasmuch as both rely on a conception (either communal or individual) of human self-determination. In fact, the real insight of the revealed religion in particular is that humanity is realized only insofar as it is the enactment of *the self-showing of the absolute.*[92] The human is, indeed, the essential domain for the happening of the absolute, but it *is not* the absolute as such: this is the profound recognition of the Unhappy Consciousness—the culminating form of the "Freedom" of self-consciousness—namely, that its own reality is received; that is, self-consciousness *participates in* its own reality, but it does not bring itself into being. The unhappy consciousness is the recognition that, ultimately, freedom does not take the form of stoic self-control, but takes, rather, the form of abandoning oneself to exposure to the absolute.

This recognition that freedom is a matter of passivity has political implications: as Derrida argues in *Rogues*, the history of democracy has been the history of equating humanism and freedom, but the future of freedom will be found in the severing of these two terms.[93] Of course it will always remain the case that we need to make our own laws, and therefore to protect the notion of human, communal self-determination in that sense, and of course it will always remain the case that we must protect individual rights, since the individual is the site for the appearing of the absolute: these political interpretations of the human are not "opinions," but *recognitions* of irreducible dimensions of our reality—irreducible dimensions of freedom. These dimensions of our experience, however, while irreducible, are not exhaustive of the reality of freedom. Beyond interpersonal "recognition" and "stoicism" (to use the terms of Hegel's categories of self-consciousness), freedom is the openness to being enlightened, the openness to the gift of transformative insight. As dimensions of freedom, the community and the individual self-consciousness assume their identity *only as self-transcending finites*, that is, only insofar as they are involved in *collaboratively undergoing* the process of the absolute.

The completion of the religion of revelation, then, is ultimately "beyond politics" in that (1) the imperative of the revealed religion is that we re-envisage the domain of freedom beyond humanism, "a freedom," as Derrida says, "that would no longer be the power of a subject," a freedom that does not accept the already established identity of the human subject as the sufficient basis for determining the terms of reality and the terms of our living together.[94] The demand on politics, in this context, is that it provide a supportive environment for the reception of transformative insight. In this light, the visionary work of such writers as André Breton, with the call for the "rights of the imagination" in his first surrealist manifesto, or Gaston Bachelard, who calls, in *The Poetics of Space*, for the cultivation of a space for dreaming, may well be among the most progressive political writings.[95] The space of imagination is precisely the space in which the established terms of the world are put into question, and cultivating the space for imagination may well be cultivating our greatest "post-political" resource. This call for a post-humanist vision of the political may very well also point to a special significance to the culture of Islam. In *Rogues*, Derrida writes of the contemporary historical significance of the Islamic world as the "other" of democracy:[96] historically, it was largely the Muslim world that was colonized by the Christian West;[97] at least since the time of the attacks on the World Trade Center in New York City in 2001 the Islamic world has been popularly identified in America, which identifies itself as "democratic," as its greatest potential threat; at the time of the writing of *Rogues* (2002), the only significant national regimes that defined themselves as statutorily non-democratic were Muslim. Inasmuch as the definitive notion of Islam is submission to the will of God, Islam, this "other" of democracy, may very well speak on behalf of a conceptual orientation that holds the future for democracy. Both politically and conceptually, in other words, it may be a mutually transformative dialogue between the culture of the Christian West and the world of Islam that holds the future for freedom.

The completion of the religion of revelation is also "beyond politics" in that (2) the very necessity to recognize a truth beyond humanism to which freedom is answerable—the need, that is, to answer to what *justice* demands of us—means that it will never be sufficient to point to conformity with political institutions in order to justify one's actions. The comfort of obedience to laws will always be inadequate to the demands of exposure to justice. In that sense, the imperative of the revealed religion inherently calls one beyond the domain of institutions—the domain of politics—analogously to the way in which it calls one beyond the idolatrous comfort in established myth and ritual.

Both of these ways in which the completion of the religion of revelation is "beyond politics" point to the way in which it is incumbent upon us to submit our established ways of enacting our political and religious realities to the imperatives of intercultural dialogue, demanding of our religious *Vorstellungen* and our political institutions of social recognition that they be self-transcending, that is, that they, in their finitude, evince a fundamental plasticity, such that they can accommodate the lives of others who live within different religious *Vorstellungen* and different institutions of political recognition. This is a freedom that is ultimately a stance of hospitality, an openness to the self-showing of the absolute that is enacted as the reconciliation of otherwise opposed finitudes.

Epilogue

Subjectivity and Objectivity in Hegel's *Science of Logic*

The project of the *Phenomenology of Spirit* is explicitly articulated by Hegel in terms of the notion of "Science": the *Phenomology of Spirit* is presented as completing itself in the accomplishment of the scientific attitude. This is what Hegel calls "Absolute Knowing."[1] The completion of the *Phenomenology of Spirit* is thus the point of transition into the project of science as such, and it is the project that is carried out in Hegel's second great work, the *Science of Logic.*

> With this, the phenomenology of spirit is concluded. What spirit prepares for itself in it, is the element of knowing. In this element the moments of spirit now spread themselves out in that *form of simplicity* which knows its object as its own self. . . . Their movement, which organizes itself in this element into a whole, is *logic* or *speculative philosophy.*[2]

Because the *Phenomenology of Spirit* intrinsically points to its immanent connection to this other work, an understanding of this other work is important to the understanding of the *Phenomenology of Spirit.* As a conclusion to our reading of the *Phenomenology of Spirit,* I will thus turn to the *Science of Logic* to clarify where the phenomenological study of experience ends. A thorough study of the *Science of Logic* would require another book, so what I will offer in this chapter is instead a concise encapsulation of the accomplishment of that work as a whole.

Like Plato's *Laws,* Hegel's *Science of Logic,* though a work of profound philosophical significance, is rarely studied except by specialists in the field. One consequence of this is that its most basic parameters are typically not understood.[3] This final chapter will clarify the basic tripartite division that organizes Hegel's *Science of Logic*—the division into the "Doctrine of Being," the "Doctrine of Essence," and the "Doctrine of the Concept"—emphasizing in particular what is definitive of the third section, the "Doctrine of the Concept." To accomplish this, I will show how Hegel is responding to central arguments from the Transcendental Analytic of Kant's *Critique of Pure Reason,* particularly in the section on the "System of All Principles of Pure Understanding" (Anticipations of

Perception, Axioms of Intuition, Analogies of Experience, Postulates of Empirical Thought), and with the Transcendental Deduction in general. The first half of the chapter will focus mostly on a general discussion of some Kantian themes from the *Critique of Pure Reason*, and I will show how the basic tripartite division of Hegel's text is visible in Kant's work and its development in Fichte.[4] Roughly, I will here be telling the story of the logical build-up of an object (which complements the logical build-up of the subject that we carried out through the discussion of mood in chapter 5). I will then turn to Hegel's text, in an effort to understand what the nature of a "conceptual" determination is. Throughout we will be attending to the inherent demands of the objectivity and intersubjectivity that characterize our experience.

Kant and the Logic of the Object

In the *Critique of Pure Reason*, Kant identifies what he calls "categories" or "pure concepts of the understanding," which are the *a priori* dimensions necessarily at play in our grasping the object of our experience—appearance—*as* "real." Within the table of twelve categories that he articulates, Kant draws a basic distinction. The six categories of quantity and quality he calls "mathematical," those of relation and modality, "dynamical."[5] The mathematical, he says, pertain to intuition, the dynamical to the "existence" of an appearance in general. What this means, essentially, is that the categories of quantity and quality are the basis of the very *constitution* of an "is." They are what Hegel would call categories of "immediacy," the subject matter of the "Doctrine of Being." The dynamical categories of relation and modality are about the relations that pertain *to* or hold *between* such immediacies; these categories are regulative—they are the rules that govern their relation—not constitutive, and they pertain, he says, to what admits of discursive, rather than intuitive, certainty.[6] These are what Hegel would call categories of "reflection," the subject mater of the "Doctrine of Essence." In the analyses of the categorical syntheses that follow this discussion, Kant effectively "builds up" an object, by showing what the necessary parameters are for anything to be an object.[7]

In the "Axioms of Intuition," Kant argues that for anything to have, so to speak, a purchase on reality, it must have some *extent*—it must be situated in space and time: it must be a quantitative magnitude. In the "Anticipations of Perception," he argues that whatever is to be must have some intrinsicality, a qualitative or intensive magnitude. This is just what we mean by calling something "something." It is by virtue of being thus constituted that something "has" *immediacy*, that it can be *intuited*. These are the characteristics by virtue of which something can enter into relation with something else—specifically, can enter into relation with sensibility.

In the "Analogies of Experience," Kant argues about the relations that must hold among these immediacies for them to be able to be objects of a coherent experience. Basically, they must one and all be modifications of a single, enduring, coherent field of the real as such—substance. They must have their own integrity that explains their order, such that our experience can be said to be of a real object, and not just of a figment of fantasy—they must be involved in relations of cause and effect. And, finally, the multiple, individual causal histories that hold amongst things must fit coherently together—they must form a system. In short, for something to assume the status of "real object," it must be the coherent world of independent nature. These are the necessary parameters that define relations internal to the immediacies that constitute the world of experience; as they are themselves not immediacies but relations of immediacies, they are the dimensions of the real that demand to be apprehended by understanding.

Through these analyses, Kant is able to show both what the "logic" must be of anything that can bear the title of "reality," and also why reality itself can only be comprehended by the coordinated efforts of both sensibility and understanding: reality itself is both immediate and reflected (in Hegel's terms) and therefore can only be apprehended by a cognition that is both intuitive and discursive.

Hegel's analysis of the categories of immediacy and reflection in the "Doctrine of Being" and the "Doctrine of Essence," respectively, is more complex, more thorough, and more dialectical than Kant's (though it should be noted that, despite Hegel's generally insulting tone toward Kant here, [a] Kant does not arbitrarily grab a bunch of categories that he thoughtlessly takes over from the tradition, but, on the contrary, has quite a rigorous argument in these sections to show why these categories are the necessary ones, and [b] Kant's mode of argumentation is explicitly dialectical in the sense of showing that the categories work as triads in which the third unites the opposed first two while offering a qualitative advance that is not reducible to those first two; and, further, the argument he makes about substance, cause, and reciprocity is very much the archetype for all the German Idealist arguments that centrally use these notions, including Hegel's own)—Hegel's analysis is more complex, but its basic orientation is the same, in its distinguishing of immediacy and reflection.

Kant and the Transcendental Logic of the Subject

This reflection on Kant's discussion of the categories allows us to grasp the basic meaning of "being" and "essence" in Hegel's *Science of Logic.* What, though, is "concept"? I want to approach this by drawing on the idea above that in his analyses of the mathematical and the dynamical categories, Kant effectively establishes why cognition must be both intuitive and discursive—he establishes, in other words, why knowing takes the dual form of sensation and understanding. To establish what "concept" is as the third missing triplet to "being" and "essence," we can ask, "what mode of cognition is necessary but not recognized in the dyad of sensibility and understanding?" As I said above, I think for our answer to this question we can again turn to Kant. Quite simply, what is missing is the cognition accomplished in transcendental analysis.

In his transcendental argumentation, Kant takes up subjectivity on its own terms. This comprehension of subjectivity is not adequately characterized by the terms laid out in his bi-partite table of categories and its corresponding duality of sensation and understanding. The categories, recall, were explicitly the categories of *objectivity*: they are derived in the course of answering the question "how can subjectivity be objective?" His analysis of these categories in the section to which we have just been referring precisely shows how they are necessary to explain the constitution of the object. But Kant's transcendental argument itself is a study of *subjectivity.* His categories have given us, as Hegel says of the first two books of the *Science of Logic,* an objective logic. What Kant's table is missing is the logic of subjectivity, the "subjective logic," as Hegel refers to the doctrine of the concept.[8] If we reflect upon Kant's discussion of transcendental subjectivity, we can see why this presents a field of "the real" that is not comprehended by his table of objective categories.

If we think of what Kant is discerning in his transcendental analysis, we can see that the dimensions of experience that he uncovers do not strictly belong either to the side of the empirical subject or the side of the empirical object. The transcendental dimensions are both structures of subjectivity and structures of objectivity. They do not, for example, belong in the world of nature—the proper object of experience on Kant's conception[9]—for nature contains only the system of sensible bodies subject to the laws of physical causality. The transcendental unity of apperception—the "I think" that is the necessary context and structure of any experience[10]—for example, is not an immediate object of sense and it is not a regulative structure for the participation of such a sensible object in nature. The transcendental unity of apperception, rather, and, indeed, the whole of the transcendental, is the articulation of *the very field of appearing*, the articulation of the medium within which all sensing and all understanding happens. This dimension is not an alien other to the world of experience: it is realized only as that world. Rather as understanding discovers the "inner" of sense—*what* it is—transcendental analysis reveals something like the "inner" of all objects. In so doing, it does not just take a given immediacy (sense) and identify its identity (as understanding does), but, in finding this new "inner," transcendental analysis also recognizes a different immediacy from that of sense: whereas sense recognizes spatial bodies as the immediate, transcendental analysis reveals experience itself—the identity of subject and object—as the immediate. The logic of the transcendental thus does not fit within the logic of sensible immediacy or of the reflectivity of understanding: it explains and redefines them both, while being explicable in terms of neither. Let us now think further about the "categories," so to speak, of the transcendental; that is, let us consider the characteristics of a determination of the transcendental, and see how these differ from the characteristics of a sensible object or an object of understanding.

The most important characteristic of a determination of the transcendental is that it is a relation—not, however, a relation of cause and effect, which is more or less the exemplary relation within understanding. In cause and effect, the two related elements are outside each other, and *both are objects*: we look on at two things within the world that produce a change in each other. The relation within the transcendental, on the contrary, is a relation of *subject* and object, rather than a relation of two objects. The transcendental structure is a structure of *appearing*, a "for" structure or an intentionality. In such a structure, the one term is realized only *as* the other term: the appearing does not happen to some separate entity called a subject, for the subject is just the "being aware" that pervades the experience; equally, what appears is not something other than the fact of appearing. At the same time, however, the subject and object are not conflated. Subject and object are "the same" in relation to itself, but relating to itself as differing from itself: this is, at a minimum, what Hegel calls a negative self-relation, or a determination of reflection. But beyond the relations of reflection that populate the doctrine of essence, the relation that is a transcendental determination is not "blind": this is what it means to say that the appearing is "for." In other words, the starting, definitive dimension of a transcendental structure is that it is "for." Indeed, we could say that this is not just a structure of reflection in itself, but it is reflective for itself, or, it is self-reflective.

What we can already see in Kant, then, is that the very transcendental analysis in which Kant works out the "objective" logic of immediacy and reflection enacts a "subjective" logic that exceeds and grounds these two, that is, the logics of immediacy and reflection depend on the logic of subjectivity, but it is not itself reducible to their terms. Behind the logic of sense and understanding, we need a logic of the transcendental ego. Most simply, this is the logic of concept, which grounds the logics of being and essence in Hegel's *Science of Logic.* Let me turn, now, to a further consideration of the transcendental ego before turning, finally, to Hegel's *Science of Logic* itself.

Fichte and the Transcendental Ego

Fichte's "Fundamental Principles for the Entire Science of Knowledge" is a helpful place to turn to allow us to make the transition from Kant's *Critique of Pure Reason* to Hegel's "Doctrine of the Concept." Fichte begins from Kant's transcendental unity of apperception—the transcendental "I"—which means he takes up the logic of the transcendental on its own terms, rather than approaching it through the logic of sense and understanding. Let us look briefly at Fichte's version of this "logic of the concept."

As we noted in our brief discussion of Fichte in chapter 5, experience always has as its object some identity: A = A. The recognition of that identity requires an act of experience that holds on to the sense of the first A throughout the experience of asserting its identity with the second A. In other words, to assert "A = A" is not the same as simply saying A: we acknowledge something about it, integral to it. That means that the one doing the recognizing must know what she was saying at the beginning in order to meaningfully assert what she claims at the end. To recognize that A = A, then, requires that I who do the recognizing hold on to the coherence of my experience throughout this assertion: I must still retain my initial recognition, and I must recognize it as my own. To assert that A = A, then, always tacitly involves recognizing that I am I, that I who assert the first A am also the I that completes the recognition of self-identity. Since the recognition of A = A is the logical form implicit in the recognition of any self-identical object, it follows that "I am I" is the logical form of any recognition of an object. At the most general level, then, in all experience I am recognizing myself. This self-recognition is the *universal* form of all experience. Fichte's first principle, the ego positing itself, is the absolute or ultimate context, the presupposed field within which the notion of "object" makes sense at all.[11]

But, there would be no experience, no "I am I" happening, if there were no recognition of an object. In the absence of the recognition of an object, an "other" to me, there would be no asserting, and therefore no self-experience. For there to be experience, for there to be an "I am I," there must be a determinate positing, which means an op-positing, an opposing of myself as recognizer to something I recognize. This is Fichte's second principle: the ego op-poses to itself a not-self. This opposing, though, is still a positing; it is, that is to stay, still a recognition. The I must say "it," but that is still a saying. This means that the opposition of self to not-self itself occurs within the form of the ego's self-positing. The op-posing of self to not-self is the *determinate* form that self-positing takes, and there is no self-positing—the *universal* form of all experience—except insofar as it is *determinate*.[12]

There are thus two opposed demands that experience embraces: experience is founded on the demand that I only ever experience myself, and on the demand that I always experience what is not myself. The ultimate form, then, the absolute, is both universal and determinate, and this, its own immanent nature, is a self-opposition, that is, these two demands, inherent to its very character, contradict each other. And thus, experience is inherently characterized by a third demand, namely, that this contradiction be reconciled, and that this unresolved duality be a coherent singularity. It is this demand that is realized as the dynamism of experience.[13]

In place, then, of Kant's transcendental unity of apperception, Fichte has developed what we might call a transcendental trinity. This trinity is the logic of subjectivity; not, however, the subjectivity of empirical life that is only one side of the domain of worldly objects; this, rather, is the transcendental subjectivity that precedes and makes possible the very opposition of subject and object. Here, then, we see Fichte's version of the logic of "the concept," and its logical dynamism is precisely the ground for ultimately explaining why the world of objects takes the form of a logic of immediacy and a logic of reflection. Hegel's own preliminary discussion of the concept is highly reminiscent of this.

Hegel explicitly compares the concept to Kant's transcendental unity of apperception, and he goes on to describe the character of this "I":

> [T]he *I* is, *first,* this pure self-related unity, and it is so not immediately but only as making abstraction from all determinateness and content and withdrawing into the freedom of unrestricted equality with itself. As such it is *universality*; a unity that is unity with itself only through its *negative* attitude, which appears as a process of abstraction, and that consequently contains all determinedness dissolved in it.[14]

The I is self-equal as a negative relation to all determinacy, and thus is implicitly defined by that determinateness that it op-poses to itself. As does Fichte, Hegel emphasizes that the opposition to an other is not an alien imposition: it is not as if an other were simply "there" and forced itself upon the I; on the contrary, the "I" can be an "I" only if it is defined in relation to (more exactly, in opposition to) an other. Describing, like Fichte, what is under consideration here as "the absolute form," Hegel emphasizes that this is not a form that is "applied" to an independently defined content; rather, the content of which it is the form must emerge from the immanent demands of the form itself:

> This absolute form has in its own self its content or reality; the concept, not being a trivial, empty identity, possesses in its moment of negativity or of absolute determining, the differentiated determinations; the content is simply and solely these determinations of the absolute form and nothing else—a content posited by the absolute form itself and consequently also adequate to it.[15]

Indeed, the topic of the Doctrine of the Concept is precisely "how the concept builds up in and from itself the reality that has vanished in it." The I as absolute form is thus the universal, but it is also simultaneously defined by the determinateness to which it is opposed and, as thus definitively opposed to that determinateness, that "content," the I is thus also an exclusive individual:

> *Secondly*, the *I* as self-related *negativity* is no less immediately *individuality* or is *absolutely determined*, opposing itself to all that is other and excluding it—*individual personality*.[16]

The "I" is simultaneously the form of the whole and the determinate stance of opposition to the determinacy in relationship to which each of these two moments is defined.

Hegel explicitly identifies this structure of the "I" as the distinctive logic—the very "concept"—of the concept:

> This absolute *universality* which is also immediately an absolute *individualization*, and an absolutely determined being, which is a pure positedness and is this *absolutely determined* being only through its unity with the *positedness*, this constitutes the nature of the *I* as well as of the concept.[17]

The concept is the universal that is self-sundering: its determinacy is an opposition that calls for reconciliation. "[T]he absolute concept," Hegel writes in the *Phenomenology of Spirit,* "alone grasps otherness as such, or its absolute opposite, as its own self."[18] A concept has its determinacy *as* the appearance of an other, where in principle that other is to-be-oneself, or equally, oneself is to-be-that-other. What is distinctive of conceptual relations, as contrasted with relations of being and essence, is that they take the form of a self-consciousness realized as an opposition.

In this section, I have, like Hegel, articulated the "concept of 'the concept'" through considering its most exemplary realization in the general logic of the ego. Now I want to turn more broadly to thinking about Hegel's *Science of Logic* in general, and about the doctrine of the concept in particular.

Concept and Absolute Idea: Being through Another

Hegel's *Science of Logic* initially asks the question, "what is it 'to be'?" and the progress of the book is the rigorous development of ever more sophisticated answers to this question. Later answers—later categories—reveal the insufficiency of earlier answers, and in that sense the book can be thought of as a series of refutations, in which insufficient interpretations of the nature of reality have their limitations demonstrated. As Hegel makes clear, however, the earlier categories of the *Science of Logic* are not "lost" in the later; instead, one-sided definitions of reality—of "the absolute"—are shown to be essential, but relative to something more basic.[19] We will, for example, always think in terms of things, even though the logic of the thing (from the "Doctrine of Essence") is not the ultimate category of the *Science of Logic.* Said otherwise, reality will always be articulated in terms of things. Things are not the absolute, though; that is, they do not exhaustively realize the nature of the real, and they are not the ultimate concepts needed to understand the real. Things will always be situated in a larger context of a reality that has its own autonomous principles. Things, therefore, are not metaphysically absolute, but metaphysically relative: they always exist relative to a larger whole, and must be understood in terms of that. The same is true of forces, of chemical relations, of finitude, of the distinction between quality and quantity, and of identity and difference. All of these determinations are necessary dimensions of reality and necessary dimensions of thought, but none is the absolute.[20]

At the broadest level, there are three basic dimensions of reality or characteristics of thought that must be distinguished. These irreducibly necessary determinations are being, essence, and concept. First, reality as a whole and anything real within it will always necessarily be immediate; that is, it will be the first, that before which there could be no other. This, most basically, is what it means to "be" at all. This immediacy takes a variety of forms—catalogued in the Doctrine of Being—and these forms are all the forms of single-term concepts that identify something like the simplicity of the fact of being. Second, reality will always be mediated (reflected) in itself, which means it will have an identity, a meaningful "itself-ness" that pervades and permeates the entire range of its determinacy. This is essence, the realm of two-term relations of, basically, a self and its appearance (such as thing and property, force and expression, substance and accident) or generally essence and show. Third, reality will ultimately always be realized only through intrinsic relations to an opposed other. This is reality as concept, reality as intrinsically having the form of being-through-another, a three-term relation of an identity accomplished through a self-opposition. Let us say a bit more about this last sort of determination.

The doctrine of the concept is the study of the forms of reality that can only be insofar as they are self-identities realized only as a relation of opposition, that is, identities that are only through another. Hegel writes:

> The universal [i.e., the immediate concept], on the contrary, even when it posits itself in a determination, *remains* therein what it is. It is the soul [*Seele*] of the concrete which it indwells, unimpeded and equal to itself in the manifoldness and diversity of the concrete. It is not dragged into the process of becoming, but *continues* itself through that process undisturbed and possesses the power of unalterable, undying self-preservation.[21]

In the relations of reflection studied in the Doctrine of Essence, it might look like we have this, inasmuch as essence and show stand in negative relation; that is, for example, the thinghood and the property are *not* the same. This *not,* however, is insufficiently strong for the concept.[22] At an obvious level, the properties, inasmuch as they are *of* the thing, are the same as the thing; that is, thinghood and properties are two ways of talking about the same thing, and the relationship of dependency between them is significantly asymmetrical, in that the properties do not have an autonomous identity apart from the thing. The being-through-another of conceptual determinations is characterized, on the contrary, by a relation of *opposition* between the two elements; that is, the other for the self must be inherently expelled from the self, and must itself inherently expel the self from itself. The universal is precisely realized through the opposed particularities—the "species"—through which it is realized and which, in their opposition, form a complete or closed totality. "The genus," Hegel writes, "is *unaltered* in its species, and the species are not different from the universal but only *from one another.*"[23]

> [B]y virtue of the identity of the particulars with the universal, their diversity is, *as such*, universal; it is *totality*. The particular, therefore, not only *contains* the universal but *through its determinateness* also exhibits it; consequently, the universal constitutes a *sphere* that must exhaust the particular. The totality appears, in so far as the determinateness of the particular is taken as mere *diversity*, as *completeness* . . . . But diversity passes over into *opposition*, into an *immanent relation* of the diverse moments.[24]

A concept, then, is a reality that exists precisely as its expression as a relationship of opposition where that opposition constitutes and defines the totality of a field.

A paradigmatic example of such a "conceptual" reality is the relation of an organism and its environment.[25] In *Biology as Ideology*, R. C. Lewontin argues that there is no organism without *its* environment, and equally no environment without *its* organism; that is, each is defined in terms of the other (what J. J. Gibson calls a relation of "complementarity").[26] But the "otherness" of environment and organism is not like that of property and thing. The relationship of organism and environment is a relationship of *opposed things*: the thrush, for example, eats the snail, which snail itself opposes this ingression and hides from the thrush. To get the snail, the thrush will have to smash the snail against a rock, and oppose the snail's self-seclusion behind its protective wall of shell. That same rock on which the thrush does the smashing could also hurt or kill the thrush if the thrush were to smash its beak or wing against it too sharply, or if the thrush were to be under it when someone stepped upon it. Or again, the same sun that supplies life-sustaining warmth to the healthy gazelle will kill it when the gazelle with broken legs lies exposed on the plain. And of course the mosquito that takes my blood will die when I express my opposition to it with my hand. In each situation, the organism is able to be itself only by virtue of active relations of dependence upon the other determinations of its environment, but these other determinations are oppositional, which means they inherently resist the organism's assimilation of them, and equally must be resisted by the organism or their own oppositional natural activity will destroy the organism. In the being-for-other of conceptual relations, the relation to other must be one of opposition.

What I have been describing here under the heading of "organism and environment" corresponds to the category of "Life" from the *Science of Logic* (which Hegel also discusses in the *Phenomenology of Spirit* at the beginning of chapter IV, "Self-Consciousness," and in his discussion of the observation of organic nature in chapter V, "Reason"). In my earlier discussion of Fichte, I discussed this conceptual logic of being-through-another inherent to the self-positing of the ego, or to the concept as such. I want to conclude simply by identifying three other essential realizations of the concept, namely spirit (the central concept of the *Phenomenology of Spirit*), the absolute (the central concept of the *Science of Logic*), and philosophy itself as dialectical phenomenology. These, like the logic of the ego or the ecosystem, are again examples of aspects of reality that could not be conceptualized simply with a logic of immediacy or a logic of reflection. They are realities that can only be self-identities as relations to an opposed other.[27]

After the ego or ecosystem, the next most obvious conceptual reality is what Hegel calls "spirit," that is, the reality of a "we." Whether in the unity formed by a romantic couple or in a historically continuous political community, there is an intersubjective reality established that exceeds and redefines the individuals who enter into it. The identity each and all have is a shared one, but it is one that, far from effacing, is essentially premised on the opposed autonomous identities of the members. This is perhaps clearest in the spiritual (therefore conceptual) reality of language.

Communication requires something to communicate; that is, there must be something emanating from me that you cannot have on your own without the mediation of language, hence the existence of opposed, alienated realities, but, equally, I can communicate it to you only because the language is neither mine exclusively, nor yours, but inherently ours. Language is premised on both the essentiality of subjective alienation and the essentiality of intersubjective union. This also means, incidentally, that the reality of spirit is not settled in advance: it is real, but inasmuch as it is realized through autonomous individuals, it is uniquely realized through what we do. The universal, as we argued in earlier chapters, is given as an inherent imperative, but not as an already accomplished fact.[28] It is, however, mostly the task of the *Phenomenology of Spirit* to articulate the reality of spirit, and it is not explicitly present in the *Science of Logic*, so I will not dwell on it further.[29] I mention it, rather, only to help make clear how we must think in the sphere of the concept.[30]

A closely analogous conceptual logic is required to understand reality itself, or the nature of being as such—the absolute. I mentioned above that the logic of thinghood is ineffaceable, meaning that things are real. At the same time, the participation of things in a single selfsame reality—substance—is also real. In the logic of the absolute relation—which is the absolute understood as a relation between itself qua substance and itself qua things, or itself qua universal and itself qua determinate—this relation that maintains the reality and autonomy of both the universal and the particular, both things and substance, is called, in Hegel as in Kant, "reciprocity," or the recognition of reality as a system. But what is the inner logic of this system?

For each thing *both* to retain its autonomy *and* to be a member of a system that itself is real and autonomous, and not just an epiphenomenon, the reality *of the system* must be the reality *of the member*, which means the whole must be internal to the member. Each member must then be unique, but a reflection of the whole; it must be, in Leibniz's language, a monad. But this monad, qua unique thing, must be intrinsically opposed to the other things, which means it can live up to the demand to embody the system only inasmuch as it is a unique individual that carries in itself the intrinsic imperative to reconcile with its others. This means the ultimate terms in which the reality of things (and of the whole) is to be understood are expressive terms, i.e., the reality of the thing is how it articulates the nature of other things, and the reality of the system is how a common reality is spoken—accomplished—through the reciprocal action of things. Reality itself, then, as reciprocity, is really in Hegel's sense a concept—or, rather, *the* concept—in that it exists only as a being-through-another, an identity accomplished as a communication between intrinsically opposed members.

Reality, then, the absolute, is no separate entity over and above the actual things, but is the immanent demand within things themselves that they reconcile. Things, then, are not effaced or surpassed, but they are also not metaphysically self-sufficient, for their very nature can only be understood out of the cooperative and self-definitive reality they interactively constitute. This again means that *what it is to be* cannot be settled in advance, but must be accomplished uniquely on the basis of the life of things. This is the idea of dialectic, or the absolute idea—namely, that reality is what is worked out immanently through the life of things, of the determinateness of reality.

Note finally that these notions of spirit and the absolute are not indifferent to each other. Indeed, Hegel specifically affirms this identity of the absolute concept and infinite spirit:

> Insofar as life, ego, finite spirit are, as they certainly are, also only determinate concepts, their absolute resolution is in that universal which as truly absolute concept is to be grasped as the Idea of infinite spirit,

> whose *posited* being is infinite, transparent reality wherein it contemplates its *creation*, and in this creation its own self.[31]

If the absolute is the universality realized internally to the real individuals, then it is only as spirit that the absolute can be, inasmuch as those individuals include us, and, indeed, include us preeminently: it is only in the context of the communication of the we that the unity of reality is accomplished. The need for spirit is thus internal to the absolute. And equally the immanent demand *to reconcile* that we saw must be internal to things is precisely the lived demand of the I as a self-consciousness: we precisely saw above that the nature of self-consciousness is to experience itself as realizing itself only through the comprehension of its other; that is, the need to accomplish the realization of the absolute is internal to the logic of self-consciousness. Indeed, self-consciousness and being, subject and substance, name the ultimate opposition—the very opposition of mind and body, consciousness and reality—that plagues the history of philosophy.

The *Science of Logic* ends with the category of "the absolute idea," which Hegel explains as "the *self-knowing concept that has itself,* as the absolute, both subjective and objective, *for its subject matter,*" and, if our analysis of reality as concept, as absolute idea, announces that the reconciliation of subject and object is thus inherent to reality as such, then this means that reality is *significance*—it is *meaning,* "for."[32] It exists only as the event of happening, the event of appearing. What this means in the end is that reality itself is not, as James-inspired philosophers like to say, a "brick" universe: reality is not some immediate stuff. The accomplishment of reality is not given—it is not "a" given in the sense of an immediacy, and it is not given "how" it will be realized. The accomplishment of reality is the task that defines us—that is what it means to be spirit.

Conclusion

Finally, what is the name for the reality that is accomplished precisely through this opposition—that is, the conceptual reality whose being-through-another is this reconciliation of subject and substance? This is philosophy. Of philosophy, Hegel writes in the *Phenomenology of Spirit,* "its element and content is not the abstract or non-actual, but the actual, that which posits itself and is alive within itself—existence within its own concept."[33] Hegel writes in the *Science of Logic*:

> It [the absolute idea] is the sole subject matter and content of philosophy. Since it contains *all* determinations within it, and its essential nature is to return to itself through its self-determination or particularization, it has various shapes, and the business of philosophy is to cognize it in these. Nature and spirit are in general different modes of presenting *its existence*, art and religion its different modes of apprehending itself and giving itself an adequate existence. Philosophy has the same content and the same end as art and religion; but it is the highest mode of apprehending the Absolute Idea, because its mode is the highest mode, the concept.[34]

Philosophy is thus the absolute idea—reality itself—comprehending itself as absolute idea. Philosophy is precisely self-consciousness living as the need to allow reality to show itself. And, inasmuch as this dynamic of being is integral to one's own self, it is the stance of resolute openness to a kind of bearing witness, a facilitation or shepherding of being, where that revelation of being is as much a redefinition of oneself.

Appendix

The Reception of Hegel in French Philosophy

Hegel in France

There have been a number of occasions in history when the (re)discovery of something from the past by a culture or a community has had a remarkably stimulating and revitalizing effect on the work of that community. The discovery of Aristotle's texts in the Christian West in the thirteenth century led to a sort of philosophical revolution in the works of Albertus Magnus and St. Thomas Aquinas. The works of Plato provided a seemingly inexhaustible source of nourishment and inspiration for the cultural imagination of the Italian Renaissance. Though never lost, St. Paul's writings from the New Testament were in a sense "rediscovered" by Luther, leading to a revolutionary reformation of the Christian church. Winckelmann's experience of the art of the Hellenistic and Hellenic world led to an explosive "classicism" in German writers. The unearthing of the works in Lascaux, and related "discoveries" of "primitive" art around the world, led to a revolution in twentieth-century European art. In each of these cases, the revolutionary developments are new; nonetheless, there is an important sense in which they are—and are seen to be—a kind of belated reception of the force of those "original" works. There is a profound sense in which the rediscovered works motivate and shape the original and revolutionary cultural developments, even as those developments themselves give new life and new meaning to those older documents or artifacts.

Something similar could be said about the role of the texts of G. W. F. Hegel in French intellectual culture of the 1930s and 40s.[1] In particular, Hegel's *Phenomenology of Spirit* of 1807 demonstrated some of its incredible potency through the huge impact it had on original work in many different areas of intellectual culture. Before the late 1920s, Hegel's philosophy was known almost exclusively through his *Encyclopaedia of the Philosophical Sciences*. The *Encyclopaedia*, though vast and rich in its content, is opaque and schematic, written by Hegel as a handbook to accompany his lectures. Careful reading of the *Encyclopaedia*, especially by those highly conversant with his central works (the *Phenomenology of Spirit* and the *Science of Logic*), reveals it to be a powerful and exciting work of philosophy; when it was read in isolation from his other texts and without a strong understanding of the principles of Hegel's philosophy, however, the work appeared dry and, indeed, machine-like in its attempt to categorize systematically the full range of reality. The introduction of Hegel's *Phenomenology of Spirit* to French readers—especially through the work of Jean Wahl and Alexandre Koyré—suddenly presented a new Hegel, vibrant, provocative, and revolutionary. Initially through these writers, and subsequently through a multi-year seminar on Hegel's *Phenomenology of Spirit* led by Alexandre Kojève from 1933 to 1939, a new Hegel was discovered who spoke powerfully to the existential contradictions of personal and interpersonal life, to the motor and meaning of historical and political development, to the stifling and alienating conditions of modern social life, to the transformative power of artistic creation, to the dynamism and life of the mind, and to the "irrationality" of reason. In Hegel's text, vital new resources were discovered for engaging with many of the most pressing concerns of contemporary life.

The reception of Hegel flowed down many different channels. Jean Wahl, Alexandre Koyré, Alexandre Kojève, Jean Hyppolite, and Eric Weil were engaged in the scholarly interpretation of Hegel. In Jacques Lacan, Hegel's ideas intersected with the tradition of psychoanalysis. Hegel's philosophy had a significant impact on the artistic world through André Breton and the Surrealists, a trajectory that, in the work of Georges Bataille, also intersects with the work of Claude Lévi-Strauss and structuralist anthropology. Indeed, this line of structuralism, with its roots in the structural linguistics of Ferdinand de Saussure, also intersects with Lacan and the psychoanalytic stream, and later flows into the deconstruction of Jacques Derrida. Hegel's work had a direct and powerful impact on existentialism, through Jean-Paul Sartre and Simone de Beauvoir, a trajectory itself interwoven, in the works of Maurice Merleau-Ponty and Jacques Derrida, with the mainstream trajectory of phenomenology that had been developing through the works of Edmund Husserl and Martin Heidegger. Many of these thinkers, too, can also be understood to be continuing the tradition of Marxism, and, through the work of de Beauvoir, Hegel's text was involved in some of the most influential work in the founding of contemporary feminism. The explosive influence of Hegel's thought and texts is thus implicated in, and significantly contributed to, the interweaving of surrealism, existentialism, Marxism, structural linguistics, structural anthropology, psychoanalysis, feminism, phenomenology, deconstruction, and the discipline of the history of philosophy. Indeed, as Merleau-Ponty rightly says, "all the great philosophical ideas of the last century—the philosophies of Marx and Nietzsche, phenomenology, German existentialism, and psychoanalysis—had their beginnings in Hegel," and "there would be no paradox involved in saying that interpreting Hegel means taking a stand on all the philosophical, political, and religious problems of our century."[2]

Like Hellenistic sculpture, the works of Aristotle, and the epistles of St. Paul, Hegel's *Phenomenology of Spirit* offers inexhaustible resources. The critical appropriations of this philosophy, however, typically involved various expressions of critical dissatisfaction. These dissatifactions, too, were interwoven with interpretations of Hegel that ranged from sensitive but imperfect to highly incompetent, and along with a recognition of many of his great insights came a legacy of outrageous misrepresentations that have themselves influentially colored subsequent developments in French philosophy. The "meaning" of a text or a philosophy—Hegel's or any other—will always be open-ended, for its meaning will always be its significance as defined by the living parameters of the world in which it is apprehended, and thus the "reading" of Hegel's text is not simply a matter of reconstituting like a dehydrated fruit an already fully accomplished sense but will always be interpretation, will always be transformative.[3] This undecidability of the authoritative meaning of the text does not, however, change the fact that Hegel's text is itself very determinate, and the text itself thus still offers itself as a standard for judging the adequacy of any "reading," and the history of the reception of Hegel in French philosophy must be recognized to be as much a history of misrepresentation (significantly because of the incredible difficulty of Hegel's text) as it is the *Wirkungsgeschichte* of that text, which defines retroactively what it was able to mean. Nonetheless, through the embrace of Hegelian ideas in response to and within the phenomenological movement, the reading of Hegel grew progressively more substantial and more rigorous, reaching a kind of culmination in the works of Merleau-Ponty and Derrida from the late 1940s through the early 1960s. In what follows, I will address the reception of Hegel as a response to the phenomenological philosophy that had been developing in the works of Edmund Husserl and Martin Heidegger. My primary orientation will not be toward the claims about Hegel made by the various figures involved, but toward how they can be seen to be deploying Hegelian themes as those are understood by the best contemporary scholarship on Hegel.[4]

The New Hegel of the 1920s and 30s: Reason as Open Sense

Hegel's philosophy is the project of being rigorously committed to allowing *whatever appears* to show itself on its own terms, and philosophy is thus a project of bearing witness to the dynamism by which the phenomenon transforms itself for its own reasons. This is what Hegel calls "phenomenology" or "the science of the experience of consciousness."[5] Hegel's philosophy was revolutionary in the history of philosophy for introducing this new method of philosophy—the method of adopting a stance of descriptive receptivity to the self-motion of the object. Hegel's philosophy is unique—at least prior to parallel developments in twentieth-century phenomenology—in being rigorously and by definition without a thesis or an author. Hegel's philosophy is true exactly insofar as it does not present views attributable to the author "Hegel," but instead is only a site for the self-presentation of the phenomenon itself according to its own standards. This rigorous demand that the philosopher not import a point of view of her own equally means that the process of description cannot presume in advance to know what rules to follow or what principles to use in interpretation. Hegel's method, in other words, is the abrogation of method, and his bearing witness to the *sense* of the phenomenon itself (which Hegel calls variously *die Vernunft, der Geist,* and *der Begriff*) is precisely a renunciation of all conceptions of an independent reason that could define in advance the terms of meaningfulness.[6] It is the phenomena themselves, in their own self-manifestation, that must be the very *Darstellung* (presentation) of sense, or rationality.

That the sense of things must emerge from their own dynamism, and cannot be measured by some alien, pre-defined, static "reason," is probably the single most salient idea in Hegel's phenomenology. Merleau-Ponty writes,

> It was [Hegel] who started the attempt to explore the irrational and integrate it into an expanded reason that remains the task of our century. He is the inventor of that Reason, broader than the understanding, which can respect the variety and singularity of individual consciousnesses, civilizations, ways of thinking, and historical contingency but which nevertheless does not give up the attempt to master them in order to guide them to their own truths.[7]

Hegel's *Phenomenology of Spirit* studies violent struggles for personal recognition and glory, slavery, religious ecstasy, Hellenic funerary practices, the Roman emperor, sun worship, and Dionysiac processions. Hegel's philosophy teaches one not to look "up" to universal principles, but to look "into" the specificities and singularities of determinate realities, and to find sense within things, events, and practices that are pointedly non-universal. This conception of reason as immanent sense leads to the prominence of the theme of the philosophical interpretation of history as the phenomenon of freedom realizing itself; as thus self-creative, history is a process that actually accomplishes meaning rather than being a vehicle for an already established sense. This notion is paralleled by Hegel's emphasis on the primacy of the practical in general, seen especially in his analysis of the distinctive form of self-consciousness—namely, the consciousness of oneself as a competent agent and a participant in the real—that is accomplished through the experience of work.[8] These aspects of the Hegelian conception of meaning resonated with a number of emerging cultural movements in France in the 1920s.

The Hegelian themes of the inherent meaningfulness of history and work characterize the writings of Marx that self-consciously drew on these Hegelian ideas and that made their own explosive entry into French culture at roughly the same time as the discovery of Hegel, through the discovery of the *Economic and Philosophic Manuscripts of 1844*, and many of Hegel's ideas were thus obviously significant to the intellectual and political traditions of French Marxism. The demand of Hegel's "method" that one find an immanent sense within phenomena rather than defining them in terms of a pre-established standard of rationality or normalcy also had a natural affinity with psychoanalysis and its recognition of "illness" as autonomously meaningful. And Hegel's notion of sense as something that is not established in advance and held in reserve but is realized in giving oneself over to the self-defining life of the particular is what appealed to the Surrealists in their enthusiasm for Hegel in the early 1930s.

The Surrealist movement aligned itself with the Communist Party, and thus was already in the political ambit of Marx and Hegel, but the connection with Hegel was more significant and more explicit in the definitive "method" of Surrealism. André Breton (1896–1966), in his Surrealist Manifestos, called for a commitment to a vibrant pursuit of meaning through the rejection of the rule of alien reason. Along with an invocation, in the First Manifesto (1925), of Freud as a path-breaker for "recovering the rights" of imagination against convention and conformity, Hegel's dialectical method was imagined, in the Second Manifesto (1929), to offer a resource for overcoming the strictures of a bureaucratizing and normalizing "rationality."[9] In the First Manifesto's definition of surrealism as an "automatism . . . by which one proposes to express . . . the actual functioning of thought . . . in the absence of any control exercised by reason," Breton's words clearly resonate with Hegel's "method" of abandoning oneself to the immanent rationality of what appears.[10] A similar resonance is apparent in Breton's notion of "objective chance," according to which one gives oneself over in desire to what unexpectedly arrives through the unpredictable development of the object of desire.[11] Finally, the surrealist notion of the generation of novel "syntheses" through the conjoining of seeming aliens clearly drew on a notion of synthesis that was seen to be at work in Hegel's dialectic. Though his relation with the Surrealists was always strained, Georges Bataille's thought in the 1930s and 40s is strongly resonant with this movement. Perhaps the strongest connection between Bataille and the Surrealists, and also his strongest connection with Hegel, is found in his idea that the regularized relations of normal social life (which he later called a "restricted economy") do not present the original or ultimate form of meaning, but rather depend upon a more fundamental flow of energy ("general economy") that does not itself answer to the terms of normalized life. This Hegelian idea of a more basic *sens* that is both the condition of and the source for the undermining of the conformist rationality of social systems was subsequently highly influential on Derrida, Lacan, and others for shaping their own engagement with phenomenology.[12]

Breton and Bataille were not Hegel scholars, but the contemporaneous commentaries on Hegel's philosophy written by Jean Wahl and Alexandre Koyré are straightforward works of Hegel scholarship. Wahl, who was Professor at the Sorbonne from 1936 to 1967 (except for a period during World War II, when he fled to the United States after escaping from a German prison camp), was highly influenced by the philosophical ideas of Henri Bergson and William James. He was himself highly influential on both Sartre and Levinas, and on French philosophy in general, especially through his early works on Hegel and Kierkegaard. The work on Hegel was a self-conscious attempt to introduce French readers to the perspective of the young Hegel whose works had been published by Wilhelm Dilthey and Hermann Nohl in Germany in 1905 and 1907.[13] What distinguished Wahl's work on Hegel was its emphasis on the existential concreteness behind the logical forms of Hegel's *Phenomenology of Spirit.* Wahl, strongly influenced by Kierkegaard, showed Hegel to be of compelling existential importance by rightly recognizing the centrality for Hegel's philosophy of the figure Hegel calls "the Unhappy Consciousness." As we saw in chapter 7, "the Unhappy Consciousness" is Hegel's name for the ultimate condition of self-consciousness, which is, namely, that we are never fully self-possessed but are always at a distance from our own selves, waiting to receive our own sense of meaning and identity.[14] As Wahl puts it, "consciousness is too small for itself, because greater than itself."[15] Wahl found in Hegel's study of unhappy consciousness the "tragic, religious, and romantic" context of meaning—the "fear and trembling"—that so prominently shapes Kierkegaard's thought.[16] Unhappy consciousness is the experience of a self torn between its being embedded in the finite, and its being drawn to an infinite beyond: it both is and is not itself, is and is not its object, such that its unity is its dismemberment, its duplicity its unity.[17] Philosophy, religion, and the search for meaning that is the motor of human history all begin in the affectivity of this divided consciousness, and Wahl understands Hegel's *Phenomenology of Spirit* to be the history of the attempts by unhappy consciousness to fill its inner void, its inability ever to fully "be" itself. Wahl's interpretation of Hegel is distinguished primarily by this idea that the dialectic of the *Phenomenology of Spirit* is to be understood as the working through of this existential situation, an interpretation that privileges affectivity and existentiality over abstract rationality or systematicity. Wahl (who took himself ultimately to disagree with Hegel) construed the ultimate force of this insight to be the need to reinvest the contingent with the force of the infinite, the initial experience of transcendence being thus folded back into immanence.[18] Wahl's insight into Hegel's figure of the "Unhappy Consciousness," that we must always be in a stance of waiting for ourselves, fit well with Koyré's writings on Hegel's understanding of time. Koyré, himself explicitly operating in the phenomenological tradition of Husserl and Heidegger, correctly recognized (*pace* Heidegger) that Hegel's philosophy operates with a conception of temporality that is essentially characterized by futurity.[19]

These two interpretations of Hegel, like the work of the Surrealists and Bataille, draw from Hegel the notion of the openness of sense, and, correspondingly, of the way in which our existential condition is one of being necessarily both excluded from participation in a fully established rational system and responsible for engaging with the issue of meaning. These themes obviously resonate powerfully with the existential movement in French philosophy in the 1940s, and the Hegel-inspired works of these intellectuals had a direct influence on that movement. In fact, though, because of the work of Alexandre Kojève, the Hegel-interpretation begun in Wahl and Koyré was temporarily eclipsed by the less competent but much more influential Hegel-interpretation of Kojève, a situation that was not corrected until the work of Jean Hyppolite.

Existentialism and Phenomenology in the 1940s: Sense and the Other

The most manifest impact of Hegel on French philosophy is found in the writings of the existentialist philosophers of the 1940s. In 1927, Heidegger, in *Being and Time,* launched an "existential analytic of *Dasein.*" This study argued that we are always already "in-the-world" and that experience cannot be understood as a "product" of a pre-existent and independently defined, transcendental meaning-giving power. Whether the transcendental ego, as that is understood by Husserl, ultimately is such a detached, autonomous meaning-giving power is by no means obvious, but the effect of Heidegger's work was to inaugurate an "existential" approach to phenomenology that challenged such a "transcendental" phenomenology that was identified with Husserl. The existentialist philosophers, in advancing this "anti-transcendental" orientation, found Hegel's phenomenology a welcome ally, partially because of the Hegelian-Marxist focus on engagement, but especially because of Hegel's emphasis on the experience of others and the "dialectic of recognition."[20]

Hegel's phenomenology aims to describe accurately the various forms experience takes, and one of its central studies is the description of the experience of self-consciousness. In the sections of the *Phenomenology of Spirit* entitled "the Struggle to the Death" and "Lordship and Bondage," Hegel shows that the definitive desire of explicitly self-conscious beings is a "desire of the other"; that is, we desire to be the object of the other's desire, and we are inherently responsive to the experience of being subjected to the gaze of other explicitly self-conscious beings.[21] His description captures the various strategies we live out in response to this experience that run from (i) trying to obliterate our "outside" as embodied in the perspective of the other upon us so as to maintain an experience of total self-possession (the struggle to the death), through (ii) trying to subordinate and control that outside/other (lordship and bondage), to (iii) embracing the shared intersubjectivity of our self-identity (the reciprocal recognition of "spirit," the "I that is We and We that is I"[22]). These latter two developments are interpersonal relations that are only possible through a kind of institutionalization, which means they are relations that are inherently mediated by law and language. The half dozen pages of the *Phenomenology of Spirit* in which Hegel describes this dialectical development were perhaps the most influential pages for French philosophy of the 1940s.

These pages made their entry into French thought primarily through Alexandre Kojève's seminar on Hegel's *Phenomenology of Spirit* at the École Pratique des Hautes Études from 1933 to 1939.[23] Kojève worked through the entirety of Hegel's text with seminar participants who included Raymond Queneau, Georges Bataille, Jacques Lacan, Eric Weil, and Maurice Merleau-Ponty. As Wahl before him had seen the power of Hegel's figure of "the Unhappy Consciousness" for interpreting a wide range of human affairs, so Kojève found in the figures of "the Struggle to the Death" and "Lordship and Bondage" powerful keys for unlocking the significance of the whole range of human experience. Through

Kojève's direct or indirect influence, an entire generation of French intellectuals saw the importance of the idea that self-consciousness is the desire of the other and that this definitive structure naturally ushers in a dialectic of interpersonal struggle that weaves together the psychological and the political, and that situates law and language at the heart of human identity.

Sartre apparently did not himself attend Kojève's seminar, but his *Being and Nothingness* (1943) is nonetheless highly alive to these ideas from Hegel that were popularized by Kojève. Sartre argues that all experience must be characterized by a pre-reflective *cogito,* a tacit awareness of oneself as an experiencing subject that must be constitutive of any experience, and he makes a parallel argument for what he describes as a sort of "*cogito* of the other."[24] Just as I always necessarily experience myself tacitly as an "I" or subject, I also tacitly experience myself as a "me," that is, an object for another. "The look" of the other to which I am subjected is also a constitutive feature of all experience, and my self-consciousness is thus (irremediably) divided between a sense that I am what I take myself to be and a sense that I am what others take me to be. What I am, in other words, is from the start not in my possession but is determined by others, and thus "the original meaning of being-with-others is conflict" because my own reality is inherently a site of contestation between the definitive authority of myself and the definitive authority of others.[25] In a manner highly reminiscent of Hegel's discussion of "Lordship and Bondage," Sartre argues that we become trapped in unsuccessful strategies for embracing our own subjectivity in a way that also embraces the subjectivity of others such that our strategies typically result in some form of relationship of domination and subordination.

In these sections of *Being and Nothingness,* Sartre draws upon Heidegger's discussion in *Being and Time* of the constitutive being-with-others that characterizes our being-in-the-world, and the discussion of the experience of the alter-ego in the fifth of Husserl's *Cartesian Meditations,* but uses the resources of Hegel's phenonomenology of self-consciousness to bring to this theme a richness and a dynamism unexplored in these other texts. His deploying of this Hegelian theme of "the Other" is especially powerful for challenging what critics imagined to be the excessively "immanentist" theme of Husserl's transcendental phenomenology. One of the main perceived problems of the "transcendental" approach to phenomenology is that Husserl's conception of a "sense-giving" transcendental ego, that is, a "constituting power," is the conception of an agent that is actually constructing experience which, in one form or another, ends up making experience into a kind of representation of the other.[26] If there can be sense only within the purview of the transcendental ego, then both the forms of meaning brought to experiential material and the very materials with which the forming power works must be within the domain of that transcendental ego, so in a profound way the "I" will only ever deal with itself. Transcendental phenomenology is thus accused of being ultimately solipsistic, and providing only a model for a self-absorbed subjectivity. Heidegger's existential analytic, Levinas's writings on phenomenology throughout the 1930s and 40s (which seem to have been highly influential on Sartre), and Sartre's existentialism all emphasize a primary realm of sense that cannot be understood on the "representational" model of a self-absorbed subject. Ek-sistent or ek-static *Dasein* (in Heidegger's language) is outside itself, engaged with what is other. *Dasein* is not "consciousness" but engagement, being-in-the-world. Sartre's emphasis on the experience of the other underscores the essentiality of this point. For it to count as experience of the other, that experience must *necessarily not* be immanent, must not be a representation, but must be precisely what cannot be found within the internal horizons of my ego.[27] The experience of the other is precisely, on Sartre's account, the experience of the insufficiency of "my own" constitutive powers to be adequate to the sense of world in which I find myself. Here, then, Sartre draws upon a powerful Hegelian insight in order to highlight the way in which phenomenology must always recognize an unclosable gap in the experience of meaning.

Closely related developments are found in the works of Simone de Beauvoir. In both *The Ethics of Ambiguity* (1947) and *The Second Sex* (1949), the influence of Hegel is prominent and explicit. In studying the inherently situated character of freedom, de Beauvoir brings together explicitly the rich themes of being-with-others developed by Sartre and his notion of "bad faith" in what is roughly a systematic model of the forms of bad faith in attitudes of taking up our intersubjective freedom. Sartre in his notion of "bad faith" and Heidegger before him in his notion of "*das Man*" had both emphasized the way in which our freedom (in Sartre's vocabulary) can be lived authentically or inauthentically; that is, we can live in a way that owns up to our free nature (authenticity) or in such a way that the image we present of our nature through our actions contradicts the freedom that is the true condition of those actions (bad faith).[28] This idea that a form of behavior can be at odds with itself such that its manifest character contradicts its inherent nature is one of the primary characteristics of the dialectical self-transformations of experience as described by Hegel. Sartre had already begun to make something like this link manifest inasmuch as he demonstrated the ways in which our attitudes toward our being-with-others contradict themselves and transform themselves in accordance with those contradictions. This structure is at the core of de Beauvoir's *Ethics of Ambiguity*, the second chapter of which shows both how our attitudes are rooted in the dynamic development of free self-consciousness from childhood and how the different adult attitudes we adopt themselves can each be understood to respond to tensions generated by the contradictions in other attitudes. The attitudes de Beauvoir addresses are all one-sided in actively or passively embracing the inherent duality of freedom that is both transcendence (that is, we are always faced with defining anew the significance of what we have done) and facticity (that is, through the choices we make we are always defining who we are).[29] De Beauvoir portrays this work as significantly Hegelian, and it is strongly Hegelian in its emphasis on our essential intersubjectivity, in its emphasis on the dynamism within and between attitudes, and, in general, in its emphasis on the self-contradictory character of forms of behavior. *The Second Sex* is even more direct in its appropriation of Hegel because of its wholesale taking over of Hegel's dialectic of the relationship of "Lordship and Bondage" to explain the formation of women's and men's identities in Western culture.[30]

Though neither *The Second Sex* nor *The Ethics of Ambiguity* presented itself expressly as a response to phenomenology, they both operate within the tradition of the existentialist appropriation of phenomenological philosophy so prominently and powerfully introduced by Sartre, and demonstrate the importance of the reception of Hegelian ideas to the history and vicissitudes of the phenomenological tradition. Just as we have already noted that the reception of Hegel ran along many avenues that coalesced and intersected with each other in various ways, so here do we see in de Beauvoir's work how the Hegelianized existential phenomenology itself grew into a cultural significance far behind the exclusive field of official, intra-disciplinary philosophical discourse. *The Second Sex* in particular stands out not only for its impact in a larger field but indeed for its virtual inauguration of the field of contemporary feminism. In the roughly contemporary work of Jacques Lacan, we can also see the impact of Hegel outside intra-disciplinary philosophical discourse.

We noted above a certain natural affinity between the project of psychoanalysis and the results of Hegel's phenomenological inquiry into human experience. This connection was powerfully developed by Lacan, who used the parameters of the development of self-consciousness mapped out by Hegel (and interpreted by Kojève) as the model for understanding the child's psychological development through the Oedipus Complex that Freud had outlined. Freud's own psychological writings certainly presumed the important place of the experience of the other in psychological development, but they never justified the idea that desire is inherently motivated to care about the other *as* a self-consciousness;[31]

Lacan's insight was to see that Hegel's description of the desire of self-consciousness as the desire of the other supplied the understanding of desire that would complete the Freudian model. And, following Hegel, Lacan, too, saw that the dialectic of self-consciousness depends on the mediation of desire through the establishing of law and language.[32] Because desire defines itself through the other, growing up into the world requires social integration, which is the insertion of oneself into a system of normalizing relations ("the law of the father") that effectively constitute a universal language. This very system of universal interpretation, however, draws its resources for meaning from the originary propulsion of desire, which will itself never be fully assimilated by or adequately articulated in the terms of this universal order. Through and behind the regularized, "literal" language of culture, desire—the unconscious—speaks in its own language of metaphor/condensation and metonymy/displacement. The interest in an immanent "reason" beneath the surface of regularized rationality that initially defined the common terrain of Hegel, psychoanalysis, and surrealism is hereby shown by Lacan to be translatable into a matter of signs, with the result that the central existential and humanistic questions of meaning are displaced into the domain of linguistics and semiology.[33] Lacan's early work was initially influential among the Surrealists, but it was in the 1950s that the trajectory of these developments intersected with the main development of phenomenological philosophy in the work of Maurice Merleau-Ponty and Jacques Derrida.

From Existentialism to Deconstruction through the 1950s: Method and Difference

The central place of Hegel's dialectic of recognition in the existentialism of Sartre and de Beauvoir is reproduced in Merleau-Ponty's *Phenomenology of Perception* (1945), especially in his discussion of the "metaphysical" dimension of sexuality and in his discussion of the role of expression as "confirmation."[34] Merleau-Ponty's engagement with Hegel, however, goes far deeper than this. The first and most obvious "Hegelianism" of the *Phenomenology of Perception* is found in its structure and method.

Like Hegel's *Phenomenology of Spirit,* which describes the dialectical development of experience from its most immediate form ("Sense-Certainty") to its most developed form ("Absolute Knowing"), the *Phenomenology of Perception* is a phenomenological description of experience that runs from the most immediate form ("The Sensation as a Unit of Experience") to its richest development ("Freedom"). Merleau-Ponty's work is also organized around a triadic structure of subject (part 1: "The Body"), object (part 2: "The World as Perceived"), and their relation (part 3: "Being-for-itself and Being-in-the-World"). In these respects, there is a strong mirroring of Hegel's work in Merleau-Ponty's own.

The most striking and important parallel, however, is in the method Merleau-Ponty follows in his phenomenological description. Merleau-Ponty's manner of proceeding in his description and analysis of each successive topic in his work is not to assert and defend the position he advocates, but rather to take up familiar approaches to the phenomenon in question and, through careful attention to their responsiveness to the phenomenon they purport to explain, to allow them to demonstrate their own insufficiencies. More or less with respect to each topic, Merleau-Ponty first describes an empiricist interpretation (that is, one that interprets the subject as inherently passive), which description typically reveals an insufficient account of agency, and then turns to a rationalist interpretation (that is, one that interprets the subject as inherently active) as an alternative, which description typically reveals an insufficient account of passivity; the positive characteristics of the phenomenon revealed through these accounts together with their mutual insufficiencies are shown to point to the need for a third form of accounting for the phenomenon that reveals the subject (and *mutatis mutandis* the object) to be being-in-the-world, a condition that, indeed, necessarily underlies and makes possible the sorts of attitudes empiricism and rationalism presume to be primary. Though somewhat more formulaic than Hegel's approach in the *Phenomenology of Spirit* (indeed, in external form it resembles more closely the method of Bergson in *Matter and Memory* in particular, which work is organized around the idea that neither idealism [rationalism] nor realism [empiricism] can adequately account for experience, and which proceeds, like Merleau-Ponty, by considering in turn the errors of each method in order to make possible the articulation of Bergson's own account), this method of allowing one-sided accounts (1) separately to demonstrate their own need for supplementation by what they exclude as opposite and (2) mutually to demonstrate their reliance on a more basic form of experience that is not itself defined in terms of the antithesis that characterizes the two opposites is very much the method of dialectical observation demanded by Hegel. The *Phenomenology of Perception* can, with equal legitimacy, be called a book of Hegelian or Husserlian (or, for that matter, Heideggerian) phenomenology.

Merleau-Ponty thus represents the strongest version of the reception of Hegel's phenomenology as a response to Husserl's phenomenology inasmuch as his work is effectively an argument for the identity of those two phenomenologies. Merleau-Ponty, too, reproduces the comprehensiveness of Hegel's philosophy—which is a call to openness—inasmuch as he similarly calls for an identification of phenomenology with linguistics, psychoanalysis, and art. Indeed, all the streams of "Hegel-interpretation" that we identified in French culture themselves come together explicitly in Merleau-Ponty's work. The very openness of phenomenology—its very comprehensiveness—ultimately erases its unique and distinctive status as an exclusive discipline.

Merleau-Ponty's writings from the 1940s resemble very much the writings of Sartre and de Beauvoir in that they are very much occupied with the "human drama" of existence. Like Heidegger, however, Merleau-Ponty's emphasis on experience is not "anthropological" or "humanistic" but rather provides an opening for engaging with the "question of being," and Merleau-Ponty's writings of the 1950s and early 60s explicitly emphasize this "ontological" dimension. If, as Merleau-Ponty and Heidegger argue, we are essentially being-in-the-world and if, therefore, the very opposition of "self and world" is a meaning that occurs *within* being-in-the-world, then the terms of that opposition cannot explain the source of meaning—indeed, they cannot explain themselves. Just as the oppositions of rationalism and empiricism are shown in the *Phenomenology of Perception* to point to a more fundamental source from which they derive their meaning but that they cannot explain, so does this "ultimate" opposition point to a more basic source that gives it meaning and that it is inadequate to explain. Like Heidegger's, Merleau-Ponty's philosophy ultimately points to something like being as the ultimate sense-giver.

This development within the French existential response to phenomenology from a focus on human experience as the site of meaning to a focus on the human as responsive to being is paralleled in the development in Hegel-interpretation manifest in Jean Hyppolite's *Logic and Existence* (1952). Hyppolite was important in the tradition of French Hegelianism initially because of his translation of Hegel's *Phenomenology of Spirit* into French in 1939 and 1941, and subsequently because of his commentary on the same book, *Genesis and Structure of Hegel's Phenomenology of Spirit* (1946). This book was particularly notable because of its continuation of the line of interpretation developed by Wahl, which rightly recognized the figure of "the Unhappy Consciousness" as the essential form of self-consciousness in Hegel's understanding. In this respect, Hyppolite's book was an important corrective to the exciting and provocative, but substantially misrepresentative, interpretation developed by Kojève in his lectures (which Hyppolite apparently avoided). Kojève drew powerful lessons from the analysis of Hegel's description of the relation of Lordship and Bondage, but he failed to understand the logic and organization of Hegel's argument in his description of self-consciousness, and wrongly presented the relationship of Lordship and Bondage as the completed form of self-consciousness.

In *Genesis and Structure*, Hyppolite continues Wahl's emphasis on the tragedy and division that inherently characterize human experience, and he understands the movements of the dialectic as our attempts to deal with the questions of meaning within this context, drawing this especially from the analysis of "Unhappy Consciousness."[35] This book, which is primarily a careful and detailed commentary on Hegel's text, emphasizes the permanent dilemmas that characterize our human situation, rather than finding in the text a fundamental drive toward "systematization" or the "overcoming" of tensions. Elsewhere Hyppolite writes, "Hegel maintains the tension of opposition within the heart of mediation, [with the result that] . . . he would reject the possible disappearance of the 'tragedy of the human situation.' . . . It is in the *existential tragedy* of history that Hegel apprehended the Idea."[36] It is this tragedy that points to the essentiality of forgiveness for human life, and Hyppolite's work stands out for its emphasis on this topic from Hegel's *Phenomenology of Spirit*: the violence and the tensions of human life are not erased, but we become reconciled with them and, through this, we become reconciled with each other. Finally, the figure of Unhappy Consciousness points to the ultimate goal of our existence, and hence of Hegel's philosophy, in a reconciliation between the here-and-now and the beyond; such a reconciliation, however, must neither deny our permanent experience of self-division nor reduce either side of the opposition to the other. Because there is no "other world" beyond human history, history is the domain invested with ultimate meaning; at the same time, history itself—the empirical reality of humanity—is not a self-defining realm of meaning (as Kojève might ultimately have it),[37] but is itself the site for the revelation of God (in the language of religion) or of the self-showing of the absolute (in the language of philosophy).[38] Hyppolite thus interprets Hegel's philosophy as a site for uniting existentialist themes of meaningfulness with the Marxist theme of the dialectic of history, and, ultimately, with the Heideggerian theme of Being.

Genesis and Structure was an important corrective to Kojève, but it was with *Logic and Existence* that Hyppolite developed the interpretation of Hegel's philosophy that showed how it could contribute to the "ontological" approach to phenomenology developing in the works of Merleau-Ponty and Heidegger. The strength of Hyppolite's analysis in *Logic and Existence* is that it argues for the essentiality of the *Science of Logic* and its engagement with the problematic of "being" for Hegel's philosophy, as a corrective to the "humanistic" views that saw the *Phenomenology of Spirit* as the definitive work and as a work whose value was found in separating it from the *Science of Logic.* Whereas earlier interpreters had made of the *Science of Logic* an otherworldly importation of reason, Hyppolite rightly recognized that what Hegel calls the concept (*der Begriff*) is the immanent *sense* (*sens*) of whatever is. Hyppolite argues, in *Logic and Existence,* that the *Science of Logic* and the *Phenomenology of Spirit* form a pair, each of which presupposes the other and neither of which can be reduced to the other. Against the "anthropological" approach of Kojève, Hyppolite's argument is that the human experience that is the subject of the *Phenomenology of Spirit* is not itself "the absolute," but is rather the site for the self-showing of the absolute (that is, being).[39] In this way, humanity is not the ultimate subject of history; rather, history, language, and human practice are the contingent, determinate modes of articulation through which this self-showing of being accomplishes itself. In this interpretation of Hegel, Hyppolite is clearly drawing on Heidegger's discussion of language as "the house of being" in his "Letter on Humanism," itself recognized as an important gesture of distancing phenomenology from anthropology and humanism. While it is not at all clear that it is correct to call the existentialism of the 1940s "anthropological," it is certainly correct to describe Kojève, and his interpretation of Hegel, in this way. In addition to his (misrepresentative) emphasis on the dialectic of Lordship and Bondage, Kojève's interpretation of Hegel was also specially significant for its interpretation of Hegel's notion of the "end of history" from Hegel's lectures on the philosophy of history. Kojève presented Hegel as maintaining that history had reached an end, meaning there was fundamentally nothing further to be accomplished politically. Hyppolite's much more accurate interpretation of Hegel comes closer to recognizing that Hegel's references to the "closure" of history are precisely a demand for infinite openness, and that, far from claiming the accomplishment of human happiness, it is the condition of "unhappy consciousness" that is the permanent and final condition of humanity. The openness of "the Concept" and, likewise, the "unhappiness" of self-consciousness are both situations of an unclosable divide between reality and its own meaning, the permanent condition of a humanity defined as a site for the self-disclosure of being and a reality, as Koyré noted two decades earlier, defined as inherently futural. Hyppolite's interpretation is important in the tradition of the French reception of Hegel primarily because it begins to come to terms with Hegel's understanding of being as an originary self-differing, a notion very similar to what Merleau-Ponty had been developing in his own "ontological" writings of the 1950s under such headings as "interrogation," "flesh," and "écart."

Hyppolite's *Logic and Existence* was highly influential on the developments of French philosophy in the 1960s. Inasmuch as this work (like his *Genesis and Structure*) is a massive improvement over the interpretation offered by Kojève, this influence had a salutary effect on the reception of Hegel. Inasmuch, however, as engagement with Hyppolite's interpretation seems often to have functioned as a substitute for the actual engagement with Hegel (much as engagement with Kojève played such a role for an earlier generation of French intellectuals), Hyppolite, who is by no means a perfect interpreter of Hegel, is also responsible for the perpetuation of many unfortunate misrepresentations of Hegel's philosophy. Much of the focus upon language in such writers from the 1960s as Jacques Derrida, Gilles Deleuze, and Michel Foucault (all of whom were students of Hyppolite[40]) seems directly inspired by their studies of and with Hyppolite, and this is perhaps even truer of the focus upon difference. The recognition of the notion of constitutive and irreducible differing discussed above marked a significant advance in the interpretation of Hegel's *Science of Logic* and of Hegel's philosophy in general. Hyppolite, however, also put his authority behind the perpetuation of more familiar cartoons of Hegel's engagement with the themes of dialectic, synthesis, and contradiction, with the result that Hegel's own profound reflections on the relationship between difference, opposition, and contradiction have largely been lost on a generation of philosophers who made a point of distancing themselves from a notion of difference-as-contradiction that they attributed to Hegel but that has very little connection with anything in Hegel's actual philosophy.

Derrida in his "deconstruction" is obviously and explicitly influenced by Hegel in many ways. Though Derrida at a number of points avows a distancing of himself from Hegel, it is to his actual works that one must turn to determine the relationship of deconstruction and Hegel's dialectical phenomenology.[41] It is particularly in *Glas* (1974) that Derrida demonstrates most effectively his appreciation of Hegel's philosophy, but the Hegelianism of Derrida's thinking is already manifest in his writings on phenomenology from the 1950s and early 60s.[42] Most definitively he, like Merleau-Ponty, embraces Hegel's method, and the ontology of difference.

Hyppolite's discussion of Hegel rightly showed that "the absolute" both can never appear as such and yet nevertheless must always be appearing in and as something or other. This is the relation between the ontological and the anthropological, between the "origin" and the site that conditions the origination of that origin. This description conforms almost exactly to the notion of *différance* that Derrida introduced in his discussion of Husserl in *Speech and Phenomena* in

1967, and these notions were already present in his writings on Husserl between 1954 and 1962. Especially in *The Problem of Genesis in Husserl's Phenomenology* (1954) and the introduction to Husserl's *Origin of Geometry* (1962), Derrida grapples with this theme of the emergence of the ontological within the phenomenological, or of the ideal within the historical.[43]

In "The Problem of Genesis," Derrida looks at Husserl's works from the *Philosophy of Arithmetic* through the *Crisis* to note the abiding tension between, on the one hand, the ideal value of universal and necessary truths (mathematics), "transcendental" ideas such as "the thing in general," and essences, and, on the other hand, the empirical genesis of meaning within experience. Derrida's argument is analogous to Merleau-Ponty's in the *Phenomenology of Perception,* which sees each philosophical *topos* as motivating both a rationalist account that begins from the necessary pre-givenness of ideal truths (in order to account for the apodicticity) and an empiricist account that begins from the necessary historical accomplishment of meanings (in order to account for the relevance to experience). Following out Husserl's own analyses of the origin of sense, Derrida shows that this "original" must already be characterized by an irreducible alterity. In his working-through of Husserl's *Lectures on Internal Time Consciousness,* Derrida shows that Husserl shows that the "original" "absolute" must be an engagement with the real that is a temporally thick moment, a duration, which means that the experience of meaning is already characterized by a relationship to—a retaining of—the past (and future), and thus, by its own terms, is already not first: it is itself delayed with respect to itself, self-differing. Husserl's own search for an entirely immanent, self-constituting/constituted meaning thus completes itself in the discovery of a moment that transcends itself, an immanence that is already inherently characterized on its own terms as a relation to outside.[44] Sense is thus irreducibly characterized by what Derrida came to refer to as "*différance,*" here understood through the irreducible temporality of sense.[45]

In the "Introduction" of 1962, these same themes are replayed with special attention to the nature of writing (a theme introduced in Husserl's text on the origin of geometry), and this provides the occasion for Derrida to develop a further understanding of this notion of *différance* through the irreducible role of signs in sense. Basically, any "moment" of sense can function only by being determinate—having a meaning of its own—and by serving as a pointer to other sense—having its meaning outside itself. Determinacy is thus a sign inasmuch as it embeds itself/is embedded in a contextualizing system of reference. A sign is a mark, a contingent, historical, empirical specificity that, by invoking a transcending meaning, inaugurates the engagement with an inexhaustible sense that can be universally repeated. Meaning is thus founded in the sign, always second to a graphic difference (as de Saussure argued), which itself has its character as sign only on condition of its revelation of an inexhaustible sense.[46] The universal and the determinate, the ideal and the empirical are thus intertwined, each the origin of the other, irreducibly different but mutually implicated: "contaminated." The "original" is always already delayed, a meaning always interpreted by the very sense it inaugurates, always thus a "representation" of an infinitely repeatable sense that exceeds this trace, and thus always already available to others, and thus always inherently in dispute.

The phenomenological tradition, which began with Husserl as the imperative to describe what presents itself, thus concludes, in Derrida, with the recognition that "what presents itself" is the unpresentable, that is, appearing is always the disappearing of the writing that is its condition (a theme that brings us back to the Hegelianized psychoanalysis of Lacan). Descriptive phenomenology will never be present at the origin of meaning, but will always be instead the revelation of its own condition in a givenness for which it can never account but to which it must respond and from which it is given its resources.

Derrida's taking up of Husserl in these early works is highly influenced by Hegel. *The Problem of Genesis in Husserl's Phenomenology* and "'Genesis and Structure' and Phenomenology" (1959) both draw explicitly on Hegel, though the sense of Hegel that Derrida deploys is not highly refined. In the "Introduction to Husserl's *Origin of Geometry*," however, Derrida's relationship to Hegel is signficantly more refined, apparently through the direct influence of Hyppolite. In this work, Derrida remarks that *Logic and Existence* "lets the profound convergence of Hegelian and Husserlian thought appear."[47] We saw above that Hegel's notion of an originary differing—the core of Derrida's notion of *différance*—is a prominent theme in *Logic and Existence,* and the importance of this for the development of Derrida's appropriation of phenomenology is made clear in a note in his 1964 "Violence and Metaphysics."

> Hegel's critique of the concept of pure difference is for us here, doubtless, the most uncircumventable theme. Hegel thought absolute difference, and showed that it can be pure only by being impure.[48]

Presumably through the direct influence of Hyppolite, Derrida was able to recognize in Hegel the very terms of his own most central philosophical (non-)concept.

These early works of Derrida from the 1950s and 60s parallel very closely in time and in content the work done by Merleau-Ponty himself on the theme of the origin of geometry, both in the "Cogito" chapter of the *Phenomenology of Perception* and in his lecture course on Husserl's "Origin of Geometry" from 1959–60 entitled "Husserl at the Limits of Phenomenology." In these works of Derrida, as in the work of Merleau-Ponty generally, the philosophy that emerges is not a criticism of Husserlian phenomenology but rather stays with Husserl to the point that phenomenology shows its own limits, shows its own reliance upon what exceeds it. This method of staying with the phenomenon and allowing it to demonstrate its own nature without external imposition is, of course, the method called for by Hegel, and, indeed, with both philosophers, their resulting philosophy can with equal legitimacy be called Hegelian or Husserlian, though both of these philosophers rhetorically identify themselves more primarily with Husserl.

But though Derrida and Merleau-Ponty are remarkably similar in their philosophical projects (and, indeed, are remarkably close to Hegel) the works ultimately have a rather different style. In his earlier works especially (as opposed to late works such as *Aporias*, for example), Derrida uses the fundamental insights about writing as a motivation to work from the themes of language and to focus on the character of written texts (in the familiar sense of that designation), whereas Merleau-Ponty works much more from the phenomena of human engagement. The result of this is that Derrida's work links him much more with the traditions and trajectories of structural linguistics and literary criticism, while Merleau-Ponty's work intersects more obviously with "humanist" phenomenology and existentialism and with psychology. Structuralism in linguistics had already been embraced as a response to "humanism," as a way to displace the human subject's centrality by showing the embeddedness of meaning in "inhuman" systems (a tradition for which the Hegelianized psychoanalysis of Lacan was already significant). While Merleau-Ponty, in "Indirect Language and the Voices of Silence," had already established a connection with de Saussure's linguistics, it was much more the work of Derrida that had the transformative force of allowing the seemingly more humanistic tradition of existential phenomenology to be displaced from the center of French thought by the tradition of structural linguistics in the later 1960s.

Throughout each of the stages of its development from the 1920s to the 1960s, French philosophy took powerful and productive inspiration from Hegel's philosophy. This intellectual world also produced, in Jean Wahl, Alexandre Koyré, and Jean Hyppolite, three of the most sympathetic and insightful of Hegel's interpreters. The engagement with Hegel was hearty: it was enthusiastic and polemical, and it was rooted in a real sense of the power of Hegel as an interlocutor, and of the importance of grappling with the specifics of his text. The generation of French thinkers that followed this period, however, seems in many cases to have accepted a "received" Hegel, which as much carries on the misrepresentations and inadequacies of these earlier Hegel interpreters as it carries on their insights. It is unfortunate that the work of Hegel, which was so consistently essential to this very development, has suffered from continuous misrepresentation, with the result that these later French thinkers have consistently adopted an anti-Hegelian rhetoric in their philosophizing, rather than generating their own, reinvigorated Hegel. It is worth remembering that Wahl, Koyré, and Hyppolite produced their Hegel-interpretations in large measure to correct existing misrepresentations, and it is this spirit, rather than the imperfect letter of their interpretations, that should be carried on.

Notes

Introduction

1. M81–89, W/C 63–68.

2. M685, W/C 452: "das schöpferische Geheimnis seiner Geburt." Compare Maurice Merleau-Ponty's reference, in *Phenomenology of Perception*, p. 214, to "the primordial silence" that is "behind the chatter of words" and to "all who transform a certain kind of silence into speech."

3. See M97, W/C 71–72.

4. "Du mußt dein Leben ändern," *Selected Poetry of Rainer Maria Rilke*, pp. 60–61.

5. M134, W/C 94. See John Russon, "The Metaphysics of Consciousness and the Hermeneutics of Social Life," pp. 87–90.

6. Hegel develops these points in detail in M135–44, W/C 94–102.

7. *Reading Hegel's Phenomenology* takes up this dialectic of recognition as its central interpretive tool. For that reason, I have given it considerably less emphasis in this work. The reader interested in my more detailed studies of the "struggle to the death" and the relationship of "lordship and bondage" should consult especially chapters 4 through 7 of *Reading Hegel's Phenomenology*. Chapter 9, "Spirit and Method," below, discusses explicitly the "lesson" of Hegel's description of lordship and bondage.

8. M197, W/C 137. This material is well studied in the unpublished M.A. thesis of Timothy Fitzjohn, *From Desire Through Thought To Conscience*, chapter 2.

9. I have discussed aspects of the chapters on "Reason" and "Absolute Knowing" throughout the chapters of this book, and I have offered focused interpretations of these chapters in "Hegel's Phenomenology of Reason and Dualism," and "Absolute Knowing: The Structure and Project of Hegel's System of Science," chapter 15 of *Reading Hegel's Phenomenology*.

10. Beyond the discussions in the prologue and chapter 7, I have not included a separate chapter studying the chapter on absolute knowing. The reader should consult the final chapter of *Reading Hegel's Phenomenology* for my discussion of this chapter and its relationship to the argument and structure of the *Phenomenology* as a whole.

11. See M805, W/C 528–29.

12. Jon Stewart, *The Hegel Myths and Legends*, is a good place to start for identifying some of the standard misrepresentations of Hegel that circulate in a context of otherwise responsible scholarship.

Prologue

1. On Hegel as completing Kant's "Copernican Revolution," see Hans-Georg Gadamer, "Hegel's Inverted World" in *Hegel's Dialectic: Five Hermeneutical Studies*, and Robert C. Solomon, "Hegel's *Phenomenology of Spirit*," p. 181. See also H. S. Harris, *Hegel's Ladder*, vol. 1, pp. 3–4, on the relationship between Kant's philosophy and the emergence of the project of the *Phenomenology of Spirit*. See especially p. 4: "The *Phenomenology* begins with a justification of the Kantian theoretical philosophy of Understanding; then, after a critical destruction of Kant's practical standpoint (in *Phenomenology* IV–V), we come to a 'history of mankind' (in Chapter VI) which establishes the absolute (or 'divine') standpoint." This interpretation resonates strongly with what I will say below.

2. M88, 36, W/C 68, 28.

3. See M71, W/C 52–53.

4. Compare the definitive sense of "Islam": "The word *Islam* means 'the willing and active recognition of and submission to the Command of the One, Allah'" (David Waines, *An Introduction to Islam*, p. 3). Compare also the notion of "bhakti"—devotional self-surrender—in the Shvetashvatara Upanishad, and of central importance to the Bhagavad-Gita. Karen Armstrong, in *The Great Transformation*, helpfully discusses the etymology of this word in a way that underlines the logic of this relation to the absolute: "The word *bhakti* is complex. Some scholars believe that it comes from *bharij*, 'separation': people become aware of a gulf between them and the divine, and yet, at the same time, the god of their choice slowly detached himself from the cosmos he created and confronted them person to person. Other scholars believe that the word relates to *bhaj*—to share, participate in—as the yogin in Shvetashvatara becomes one with Lord Rudra" (p. 430). The ambiguity in the etymology nicely captures the different dimensions that characterize one's adopting the position—as artist, religious person, or philosopher—of giving voice to the absolute. Hegel's explicit study of this relationship is found in the section of the *Phenomenology* entitled "The Unhappy Consciousness"; see especially M210 for the discussion of the threefold logic of this relationship.

5. The quotation may be apocryphal, but it is consistent with much that Michelangelo did write. For a rich and extensive account of Michelangelo's life and letters, see the texts collected in Charles Holroyd, *Michael Angelo Buonarroti*.

6. M1, W/C 3.

7. For the theme of art, religion, and philosophy as the forms of consciousness of the absolute, see Hegel, *Philosophy of Mind*, sections 553–77, especially section 572.

8. Hegel's phenomenology is thus a form of empiricism. Compare Tom Rockmore's discussion of Hegel's "tertiary empiricism," in *Cognition*, p. 197.

9. M90, W/C 69.

10. M106–7, W/C 75.

11. M3, W/C 5.

12. When a disdain for rigorous thinking is put forth as an attempt "to phi-

losophize in a true and holy manner," "when [such minds] give themselves up to the uncontrolled ferment of substance [and] imagine that by drawing a veil over self-consciousness and surrendering understanding they become the beloved of God to whom He gives wisdom in sleep, . . . what they in fact receive, and bring to birth in their sleep, is nothing but dreams" (M10). Giving oneself over to the subject matter is not as easy as simply abandoning oneself, for this lack of rigor produces only what is arbitrary.

13. See M83, W/C 64 for the idea that we already possess the object of our investigation. See also M26–27, W/C 19–22: "[T]he individual has the right to demand that science should at least provide him with the ladder to this [scientific] standpoint, should show him this standpoint within himself. . . . Science must therefore unite this element of self-certainty with itself, or rather show *that* and *how* this element belongs to it. . . . It is this coming to be of *Science as such* or of *knowledge*, that is described in this *Phenomenology* of Spirit."

14. M5, W/C 6.

15. M1–29, W/C 3–24 basically articulate the project of the phenomenology from the point of view of science. See also M17, W/C 13–14 on the insufficiency of the individual standpoint: "In my view [Es kömmt nach meiner Einsicht], which can be justified only by the exposition of the system itself . . . [welche sich durch die Darstellung des Systems selbst rechtfertigen muß . . .]."

16. M53, W/C 39.

17. On the theme of the openness integral to Hegel's project, compare Catherine Malabou's discussion of Hegel's concept of "plasticity" throughout *The Future of Hegel*. See also the review of this book by William Dudley.

18. M134–35, 145, W/C 94–95, 102.

19. M113–14, W/C 80–81.

20. On the logic of immediacy or being, see Stephen Houlgate, *The Opening of Hegel's Logic*. For the logic of immediacy as it first emerges in Hegel's *Logic*, see Dieter Henrich, "Anfang und Methode der Logik"; for the logic of reflexion as it first emerges in Hegel's *Science of Logic*, see Henrich, "Hegels Logik der Reflexion. Neue Fassung," and see Houlgate's helpful analysis of this section in "Essence, Reflexion, and Immediacy in Hegel's *Science of Logic*." M37 and 48 (W/C 28–29, 35–36) discuss the nature of logic in relation to the *Phenomenology of Spirit*.

21. As we will see in chapter 5 and the epilogue, this is what Fichte identifies as the first principle of experience; see *Science of Knowledge*, part 1, "Fundamental Principles of the Entire Science of Knowledge," section 1, "First, Absolutely Unconditioned Principle," pp. 94–102.

22. M17, W/C 13–14 and M37, W/C 28–29 discuss the project of the *Phenomenology of Spirit* in terms of the recognition of truth as both substance and subject. See also M26, W/C 19 for the notion of "pure self-recognition in absolute otherness," and the discussion in M54, W/C 41 of "pure self-identity in otherness." On the logic of the concept, see Jean Hyppolite, *Logic and Existence*. Hyppolite's construal of the concept as "*sens*" and "love" (pp. 4–5, 19) is accurate and helpful. Note, too, his claim (pp. 170–71) that the Doctrine of Being corresponds to the Transcendental Aesthetic, the Doctrine of Essence to the Transcendental Analytic, and the Doctrine of the Concept to the Transcendental Dialectic. Com-

pare also Hyppolite, *Genèse et Structure*, vol. 1, pp. 142–48. For an introduction to Hegel's logic in general, see John Burbidge, *The Logic of Hegel's Logic.*

23. See Hegel, *The Philosophy of History*, pp. 9–11, especially p. 11: "To him who looks upon the world rationally, the world in its turn presents a rational aspect."

24. See M87, W/C 67–68 on phenomenology as the perspective that recognizes the transitions between different stances of consciousness. See M796–98, W/C 521–23 on the completion of the project in the stance of the phenomenologist who recognizes the lesson *of the path of description* undertaken in the *Phenomenology of Spirit.*

25. This is the substance of Kant's discussion of the importance of the "mathematical" categories in the "Axioms of Intuition" and the "Anticipations of Perception" in *Critique of Pure Reason*, A160 / B199, A162–76 / B202–18. The mathematical categories basically correspond to what Hegel calls a logic of immediacy or "being."

26. This is the substance of Kant's discussion of the importance of the "dynamical" categories in the "Analogies of Experience" and in the "Postulates of Empirical Thought" in *Critique of Pure Reason*, A160 / B199, A176–235 / B218–94. The dynamical categories basically correspond to what Hegel calls a logic of reflection or "essence."

27. *Critique of Pure Reason*, A25 / B39–40.

28. *Critique of Pure Reason*, A20–22, 26 / B34–36, 42.

29. *Critique of Pure Reason*, A28 / B24.

30. *Critique of Pure Reason*, A23 / B38 (my emphasis).

31. *Critique of Pure Reason*, A106–8, 116 and B131–2. This is also Fichte's "first principle"; see note 21.

32. Because the transcendental "I" is accessible only to thought and has no empirical presentation, Kant himself refuses to designate this an "intuition." Fichte, on the contrary, describes this recognition as precisely an "intellectual intuition" because its significance has the character of something *found*, rather than something constructed. Like Fichte, I will use the language of "intuition" to describe the recognition of the transcendental "I."

33. This is the focus of the "Paralogisms of Pure Reason."

34. My language of "substance" and "subject" here is drawn from Hegel, not Kant. While Kant explicitly associates "infinity" with space, this is not his language in his own discussion of what he calls "substance," and it is not obvious that he would choose this term as a description of the pure "I."

35. Compare Fichte's second principle of all experience: *Science of Knowledge*, "Second Principle, Conditioned as to Content," pp. 102–5.

36. M160–5, W/C 114–9. For a sustained study of the relationship of Hegel's philosophy to Kant's epistemology, see Robert B. Pippin, *Hegel's Idealism.*

37. *Critique of Pure Reason*, A444–53, B472–81.

38. M166–67, W/C 120–22. On the nature of desire, see David Ciavatta, "Hegel on Desire's Knowledge."

39. See M174, W/C 125–26. This language is how Schelling describes the

situation in *System of Transcendental Idealism* (1800), introduction, section 3, "Preliminary Deduction of Transcendental Philosophy."

40. I have given an overview of this theme of "exposure" as it pertains to chapter IV, "Self-Consciousness" in "Self and Other in Hegel's Phenomenology of Spirit."

41. See M178–85, W/C 127–29 for the definitiveness of recognition for the dialectic of self-consciousness. On the primacy of the theme of recognition (*Anerkennung*) for Hegel's *Phenomenology of Spirit*, see Robert R. Williams, *Recognition*, and Andreas Wildt, *Autonomie und Anerkennung*.

42. Compare Richard Dien Winfield, "Commentary on Hegel's Concept of *Geist*," p. 22: "Hegel understands consciousness to be the very concrete structure that can only be conceived as the embodied awareness of a living individual inhabiting a world of nature common to others."

43. M177, 351, 439, W/C 127, 235–36, 288–89. See also M69, W/C 50–51.

44. M440, 352, W/C 289–90, 236. J. N. Findlay, *Hegel: A Re-Examination*, pp. 39–47, helpfully interprets Hegel's notion of *Geist* as a descendent of Kant's transcendental ego, as I am arguing here; while I think Findlay's account is imperfect, it nonetheless contains considerable insight. For "the infinity realizing itself in self-consciousness," ("der sich im Selbstbewußtsein realisierenden Unendlichkeit"), see W/C 127; this phrase is left out of Miller's translation of M178.

45. Hegel, *Science of Logic*, G II.13, E389: "The truth of *being* is *essence*."

46. See Jean Wahl, *Le malheur de la conscience*, on the ultimacy of unhappy consciousness, and also H. S. Harris's comprehensive discussion of this section of the *Phenomenology of Spirit* in *Hegel's Ladder*, vol. 1, pp. 395–436. For a useful discussion of this history of the interpretation of Unhappy Consciousness in French philosophy that is misrepresentative of Hegel but helpful in its understanding of the French interpreters of Hegel, see Bruce Baugh, *French Hegel*.

47. M354, W/C 236–37.

48. See M355, 441, W/C 237, 290.

49. These figures appear, respectively, in M360–66, 381–93, 397–418, 464–76, 500–526, 531–37, 661–69, W/C 240–44, 251–59, 261–77, 304–16, 331–48, 352–55, 434–40.

50. M107, 113, W/C 75, 80–81.

51. M134–35, W/C 94–95.

52. M192–93, W/C 133–34.

53. See M89, W/C 68.

54. Compare the idea, discussed in M24, W/C 18, that the method of dialectic is such that the "refutation" of a position is the same as its "development" into its own truth.

55. M669–71, W/C 440–42. For the interpretation of Hegel's descriptions of conscience and forgiveness, see Jay Bernstein, "Confession and Forgiveness" and "Conscience and Transgression," and Shannon Hoff, "Law, Right and Forgiveness," chapter 5 of *The Laws of the Spirit*. See also Kym Maclaren, "The Role of Emotion in an Existential Education."

56. M793–98, W/C 519–23. For an interpretation of Hegel's conception

of absolute knowledge, see John Burbidge, "Hegel's Absolutes." On the theme of the self-showing of the absolute, compare Hyppolite, *Logic and Existence,* p. 74. On the theme of enacting the absolute here and now, compare the discussion of "Here is your Rhodes, here is your jump" in Hegel, *Elements of the Philosophy of Right,* p. 21.

57. Compare Fichte, *Science of Knowledge,* p. 91: "The Science of Knowledge should in no way *force* itself upon the reader, but should *become a necessity* for him, as it has for the author himself." Compare William Maker, "Does Hegel Have a Dialectical Method?"

58. He contributes the recognition that the next phenomenon lives up to the logic of the last; we must do the same, recognizing in our own experience that we already have an intuition of the phenomenon Hegel points to that resolves the contradiction of the preceding shape of consciousness. Hegel cannot supply this recognition for us; what he can do is educate our expectations, preparing us for this recognition, exhorting us to acknowledge what is already appearing, and inspiring us to be open to self-transformation.

59. That phenomenology must be a rigorous method of attending to intuitions is what Husserl calls the "principle of all principles." See Edmund Husserl, *Ideas,* §24; see also §20.

60. Compare Fichte's third principle of all experience: *Science of Knowledge,* "Third Principle, Conditioned as to Form," pp. 105–19.

Chapter 1

1. M107, W/C 75: "Ein Itzt, welches absolut viele Itzt ist."

2. See Immanuel Kant, *Critique of Pure Reason,* A138–39 / B177–78, A142–47 / B182–87.

3. M90, W/C 69: "Wir haben uns ebenso *unmittelbar* oder *aufnehmend* zu verhalten, also nichts an ihm, wie es sich darbietet, zu verändern, und von dem Auffassen das Begreifen abzuhalten."

4. M90, W/C 69: "Das Wissen, welches zuerst oder unmittelbar unser Gegenstand ist, kann kein anderes sein, als dasjenige, welches selbst unmittelbares Wissen, Wissen des *Unmittelbaren* oder *Seienden* ist."

5. Immanuel Kant, *Critique of Pure Reason,* A19 / B33, A50–52 / B74–76.

6. M95, W/C 71.

7. M106, W/C 75 describes the experience of the passing of the moment. The opening lines of M107, W/C 75 describe the difference between (1) the now that passed and (3) the now that witnesses the passing.

8. M107, W/C 75: "1) Ich zeige das Itzt auf, es ist als das Wahre behauptet; ich zeige es aber als Gewesenes, oder als ein Aufgehobenes, hebe die erste Wahrheit auf, und 2) Itzt behaupte Ich als die zweite Wahrheit, daß es *gewesen,* aufgehoben ist. 3) Aber das Gewesene ist nicht; Ich hebe das Gewesen- oder Aufgehobensein, die zweite Wahrheit auf, negiere damit die Negation des Itzt, und kehre so zur ersten Behauptung zurück; das *Itzt* ist. . . . Aber dieses in sich reflektierte Erste ist nicht ganz genau dasselbe, was es zuerst, nämlich ein *Unmittel-*

bares, war; sondern es ist eben *ein in sich Reflektiertes,* oder *Einfaches,* welches im Anderssein bleibt, was es ist; ein Itzt, welches absolut viele Itzt ist."

9. "The present is, only because the past is not: the being of the now has the determination of not-being, and the not-being of its being is the future; the present is this negative unity. . . . [T]he concrete present is the result of the past and is pregnant with the future." *Philosophy of Nature,* §259, *Zusatz,* p. 39 (*Enz* 2, pp. 54–55). Compare M642, W/C 421–22. On the theme of the future, see Dennis J. Schmidt, "Circles—Hermeneutic and Otherwise: On Various Senses of the Future as 'Not Yet'"; as my own paper implies, I am dissatisfied with Schmidt's interpretation of Hegel. For a fuller dialectic of the "Sense-Certainty" chapter, see John Russon, "Sense, Time and My Meaning," chap. 1 of *Reading Hegel's Phenomenology.* For an especially rich discussion of the "now," see Jay Lampert, *Deleuze and Guattari's Philosophy of History,* pp. 27–28 and especially pp. 152–54.

10. I have developed this theme of the exemplary temporality of music more fully in chapters 1 and 5 of *Bearing Witness to Epiphany,* and chapter 1 of *Human Experience.*

11. M108, W/C 75–76: "Es ist eine einfache Komplexion vieler Hier . . . welches wie der Tag eine einfache Vielheit der Itzt, so eine einfache Vielheit der Hier ist." Compare also M169, W/C 122–23: "das einfache Wesen der Zeit, das in dieser Sichselbstgleichheit die gediegene Gestalt des Raumes hat."

12. "I were but 14 1/2 yr. old no razor had yet touched my upper lip but as I cantered after Harry Power my pockets crammed with marbles I were already travelling full tilt towards the man I would become." Peter Carey, *True History of the Kelly Gang,* p. 77. See also William Faulkner, quoted as an epigraph to *True History of the Kelly Gang*: "The past is not dead. It is not even past."

13. Reflected determinations are the subject of book 2 of the *Science of Logic.*

14. M111, W/C 79: "Die unmittelbare Gewißheit nimmt sich nicht das Wahre, denn ihre Wahrheit ist das Allgemeine, sie aber will das *Diese* nehmen"; and M112, W/C 79–80: "Da sein Prinzip, das Allgemeine, in seiner Einfachheit ein *vermitteltes* ist, so muß er dies als seine Natur an ihm ausdrücken; er zeigt sich dadurch als *das Ding von vielen Eigenschaften.* Der Reichtum des sinnlichen Wissens gehört der Wahrnehmung, nicht der unmittelbaren Gewißheit an, . . . denn nur jene hat die *Negation,* den Unterschied oder die Mannigfaltigkeit an ihrem Wesen."

15. The analysis of temporal experience in terms of anticipation and fulfillment or protention and retention is richly developed in Edmund Husserl, *The Phenomenology of Internal Time-Consciousness,* section 2. The notion of "horizon" is articulated in Edmund Husserl, *Cartesian Meditations,* section 14. For discussion of these themes, see Jay Lampert, "Husserl's Account of Syncategorematic Terms."

16. Aristotle, *On the Soul,* bk. 2, chap. 1, 412a22–28.

17. See Catherine Malabou, *The Future of Hegel,* p. 55 for an analogous argument.

18. *On the Soul,* bk. 2, chap. 1, 412a22–28, 412b11–22, bk. 2, chap. 5, 417a22–b2.

19. M291, W/C 196: "Das Fürsichsein des Organisch-lebendigen aber tritt

nicht so auf die Seite gegen sein Äußeres, sondern hat das Prinzip des *Andersseins* an ihm selbst. Bestimmen wir das Fürsichsein als *einfache sich erhaltende Beziehung auf sich selbst,* so ist sein Anderssein die einfache *Negativität,* und die organische Einheit ist die Einheit des sichselbstgleichen sich auf sich Beziehens, und der reinen Negativität."

20. This is the lesson of the "struggle to the death," M189, W/C 132: "In dieser Erfahrung wird es dem Selbstbewußtsein, daß ihm das Leben so wesentlich als das reine Selbstbewußtsein ist."

21. This is one aspect of the significance of the dialectic of being and nothing that begins book 1 of the *Science of Logic.*

22. Compare Hegel's description (M169, W/C 122–23) of "the simple essence of time which, in this equality with itself, has the stable shape of space," in his discussion of the concept of life; "das einfache Wesen der Zeit, das in dieser Sichselbstgleichheit die gediegene Gestalt des Raumes hat."

23. M113, W/C 80–81: "Dies abstrakte allgemeine Medium, das die Dingheit überhaupt oder das reine Wesen genannt werden kann, ist nichts anderes als das Hier und Itzt, wie es sich erwiesen hat, nämlich als ein einfaches Zusammen von vielen . . . ." "Alle diese vielen Eigenschaften sind in einem einfachen Hier."

24. I am alluding to the logic of thinghood as "also" that Hegel develops in M113, W/C 80–81, emphasizing the differentiated successive moments (properties) rather than the differentiated simultaneous moments (properties) that Hegel emphasizes.

25. This notion of *ousia* corresponds to the logic of thinghood as "one" that Hegel develops in M114, W/C 81. For the relevant discussion in Aristotle, see *Metaphysics* Z, on the notion of *ousia* as *eidos.* For discussion, see Joseph J. Owens, *The Doctrine of Being,* passim. John McCumber develops an excellent critique of the notion of *ousia* that is directly pertinent to the themes discussed in this chapter in *Reshaping Reason,* chapter 3.

26. Hegel uses Antigone, from Sophocles' tragedy *Antigone,* to exemplify the logic of *Sittlichkeit* (*ethos*), in chapter 6 of the *Phenomenology of Spirit.* See M465–66, W/C 305–6 and compare M447, W/C 292–93, M457, W/C 299–300, for the idea that in the individual's action the identity of the ethical substance is present.

27. M437, W/C 286–87.

28. M437, W/C 287: "Daß das Rechte mir *an und für sich* ist, dadurch bin ich in der sittlichen Substanz; so ist sie das *Wesen* des Selbstbewußtseins; dieses . . . ist *ihre Wirklichkeit* und *Dasein,* ihr *Selbst* und *Willen.*"

29. M436, W/C 286: "Jenes Bewußtsein . . . hat sich als einzelnes aufgehoben."

30. See John Russon, *The Self and Its Body,* chap. 4, especially pp. 81–100, and "The Ritual Basis of Self-Identity," chap. 12 of *Reading Hegel's Phenomenology,* especially pp. 173–77.

31. This is the central point in Hegel's analysis of "Ethical Action," M464–76, W/C 304–16, especially M467–68, W/C 306–9: Antigone's actions in fact involve initiative, but her self-portrayal requires her to interpret herself as being driven from without.

32. This notion of habit as grasp provides a link to contemporary theories of "enactive cognition." See particularly Alva Noë, *Action in Perception*, and compare the notion of "kinetic melodies" in the work of Maxine Sheets-Johnstone.

33. This translation was suggested to me by David Hitchcock.

34. Aristotle himself, in the *Nicomachean Ethics*, book 2, chapter 1, and in *Politics*, book 1, chapters 1 and 2, gives us one of the best accounts of this story of the entry into culture. See Plato, *Alcibiades I*, 111a, where Alcibiades identifies his cultural education into language use; this passage is powerfully discussed in Patricia Fagan, *Plato and Tradition*, chapter 1.

35. Compare M97, W/C 71–72, for the idea that it is only in and with language that the meaning of our own experience becomes available to us.

36. M171, W/C 125: "das sich entwickelnde, und seine Entwicklung auflösende und in dieser Bewegung sich einfach erhaltende Ganze."

37. For the non-historical character of nature, see M295, W/C 199: "But organic nature has no history; it falls from the universal, from life, directly into the singleness of existence, and the moments of simple determinateness, and the single organic life united in this actuality, produce the process of becoming merely as a contingent movement, in which each is active in its own part and the whole is preserved; but this activity is restricted, so far as *itself* is concerned, merely to its centre, because the whole is not present in it, and is not present in it because here it is not *qua* whole *for* itself." ["Aber die organische Natur hat keine Geschichte; sie fällt von ihrem Allgemeinen, dem Leben, unmittelbar in die Einzelheit des Daseins herunter, und die in dieser Wirklichkeit vereinigten Momente der einfachen Bestimmtheit und der einzelnen Lebendigkeit bringen das Werden nur als die zufällige Bewegung hervor, worin jedes an seinem Teile tätig ist und das Ganze erhalten wird, aber diese Regsamkeit ist *für sich* selbst nur auf ihren Punkt beschränkt, weil das Ganze nicht in ihm vorhanden ist, und dies ist nicht darin vorhanden, weil es nicht als Ganzes hier *für sich* ist."] See also M168–70, W/C 122–23.

38. Compare Hegel, *Reason in History*: "We must bring to history the belief and conviction that the realm of the will is not at the mercy of contingency. That world history is governed by an ultimate design, that it is a rational process—whose rationality is not that of a particular subject, but a divine and absolute reason—this is a proposition whose truth we must assume; its proof lies in the study of world history itself, which is the image and enactment of reason." The ideas involved in this text are helpfully discussed in Réal Fillion, *Multicultural Dynamics and the Ends of Reason*, chapter 4. These ideas are further explored in chapter 12.

39. M77, W/C 60.

40. M84, W/C 64–65: "Das Bewußtsein gibt seinen Maßstab an ihm selbst, und die Untersuchung wird dadurch eine Vergleichung seiner mit sich selbst sein. . . . und hiemit wir nicht nötig haben, Maßstäbe mitzubringen, und *unsere* Einfälle und Gedanken bei der Untersuchung zu applizieren; dadurch, daß wir diese weglassen, erreichen wir es, die Sache, wie sie *an und für sich* selbst ist, zu betrachten." Hegel discusses the "method" of the *Phenomenology* in M81–89, W/C 63–68.

41. This is discussed in more detail in "The Absolute Idea," in the *Science of Logic.*

42. *Encyclopaedia Logic* section 78 (p. 124, *Enz* 1, 167–68). Compare M78, W/C: "The scepticism that is directed against the whole range of phenomenal consciousness . . . renders the spirit for the first time competent to examine what truth is"; ["Der sich auf den ganzen Umfang des erscheinenden Bewußtseins richtende Skeptizismus macht dagegen den Geist erst geschickt zu prüfen, was Wahrheit ist."]

43. For the "resolve," see *Science of Logic,* p. 70. On this notion that Hegel's philosophy can have no pre-established method, see William Maker, *Philosophy Without Foundations,* pp. 99–100.

44. M10, W/C 9: "Die Kraft des Geistes ist nur so groß als ihre Äußerung, seine Tiefe nur so tief, als er in seiner Auslegung sich auszubreiten und sich zu verlieren getraut."

45. M53, W/C 40: "Das wissenschaftliche Erkennen erfordert aber vielmehr, sich dem Leben des Gegenstandes zu übergeben."

46. Quentin Lauer, *A Reading of Hegel's Phenomenology of Spirit,* p. 56, helpfully comments upon how the reader should understand the finished form of Hegel's presentation: "[Hegel] is describing a journey which he has already made, whose tortuous windings have already been traversed. Nevertheless, he does not take his stand at the goal and then write a book to tell us what we must do to join him at the goal. Rather, he invites us to join him as he retraces the journey step by step and, in the process, discovers that there are aspects of the journey which take on an importance and an amplitude of which he need not have been aware in making the journey for the first time."

47. M78, W/C 61: "Indem es aber unmittelbar sich vielmehr für das reale Wissen hält, so hat dieser Weg für es negative Bedeutung, und ihm gilt das vielmehr für Verlust seiner selbst, was die Realisierung des Begriffs ist; denn es verliert auf diesem Wege seine Wahrheit. Er kann deswegen als der Weg des *Zweifels* angesehen werden, oder eigentlicher als Weg der Verzweiflung." This distinctive character of Hegel's philosophical project is studied in detail in the prologue.

48. See, for example, Aristotle, *Parts of Animals,* bk. 1, chap. 1, 639b25–640a8.

49. M701: "this [self-consciousness] has not yet withdrawn into itself from its staid custom and its firm trust therein"; W/C 459: "dieses noch nicht aus seiner ruhigen Sitte und seinem festen Vertrauen in sich gegangen ist."

50. These points are very helpfully developed in Shannon Hoff, "Restoring Antigone to Ethical Life."

Chapter 2

1. René Descartes, *Meditations on First Philosophy,* pp. 144–49.

2. *Meditations,* p. 145.

3. M 78, W/C 61: "Der sich auf den ganzen Umfang des erscheinenden

Bewußtseins richtende Skeptizismus macht dagegen den Geist erst geschickt zu prüfen, was Wahrheit ist."

4. M79, W/C 62.

5. M80, W/C 63: "Das Bewußtsein leidet also diese Gewalt . . . von ihm selbst."

6. M86, W/C 66: "*ihm der neue wahre Gegenstand* daraus *entspringt*."

7. See Jean Hyppolite, *Genesis and Structure*, p. 100: "The point of view of perception is that of common consciousness and, more or less, of the various empirical sciences which raise the sensuous to the universal and mingle sensuous determinations with determinations of thought, while remaining unaware of the contradictions which thus arise."

8. See *Categories*, chapter 5. "Substance, in the truest and primary and most definite sense of the word, is that which is neither predicable of a subject nor present in a subject; for instance, the individual man or horse. . . . Everything except primary substances is either predicable of a primary substance or present in a a primary substance. . . . 'Animal' is predicated of the species 'man,' therefore of the individual man, for if there were no individual man of whom it could be predicated, it could not be predicated of the species 'man' at all. Again, colour is present in a body, therefore in individual bodies, for if there were no individual body in which it was present, it could not be present in body at all. Thus everything except primary substances is either predicated of primary substances, or is present in them, and if these last did not exist, it would be impossible for anything else to exist. . . . The most distinctive mark of substance appears to be that, while remaining numerically one and the same, it is capable of admitting contrary qualities." See Aryeh Kosman, *The Activity of Being*, for a precise account of the meaning of "*ousia*" and its relationship to individual beings.

9. Compare Fichte, *The Vocation of Man*, part 1.

10. M116, W/C 82: "es hat ihn *nur zu nehmen*, und sich als reines Auffassen zu verhalten; was sich ihm dadurch ergibt, ist das Wahre. Wenn es selbst bei diesem Nehmen etwas täte, würde es durch solches Hinzusetzen oder Weglassen die Wahrheit verändern."

11. M143, W/C 100: "Dieses wahrhafte Wesen der Dinge hat sich itzt so bestimmt, daß es nicht unmittelbar für das Bewußtsein ist, sondern daß dieses ein mittelbares Verhältnis zu dem Innern hat, und als Verstand *durch diese Mitte des Spiels der Kräfte in den wahren Hintergrund der Dinge blickt*."

12. Compare Aristotle on arguments "hoti" and "dioti."

13. M144, W/C 101: "schließt sich erst über der *sinnlichen* als der *erscheinenden* Welt nunmehr eine *übersinnliche* als die *wahre* Welt auf, über dem verschwindenden *Diesseits* das bleibende *Jenseits*."

14. Merleau-Ponty, *Phenomenology of Perception*, p. 62.

15. Compare Hyppolite, *Genesis and Structure*, p. 110.

16. M134, W/C 94 is the essential logical statement of this transition.

17. M117, W/C 83–84.

18. See M114, W/C 81 for the language of "one."

19. M114, W/C 81: "Das Eins is das *Moment der Negation*, wie es selbst auf eine einfache Weise sich auf sich bezieht, und Anderes ausschließt; und wodurch

die *Dingheit*, als *Ding* bestimmt ist. An der Eigenschaft ist die Negation als *Bestimmtheit*, die unmittelbar eins ist mit der Unmittelbarkeit des Seins, welche durch diese Einheit mit der Negation Allgemeinheit ist; als *Eins* aber ist sie, wie sie von dieser Einheit mit dem Gegenteil befreit, und an und für sich selbst ist."

20. Compare Hyppolite, *Genesis and Structure*, p. 106: "But we do not perceive only the thingness, the simple medium of the properties; we also claim to perceive a determinate thing in-and-for-itself, *this* crystal of salt." Lauer, *A Reading of Hegel's Phenomenology of Spirit*, pp. 60–61 and 64, discusses some aspects of the tension between the singularity of the thing and the universality of the properties.

21. The language of "present in" is Aristotle's. See *Categories*, 1.

22. M121, W/C 86.

23. M113, 121, W/C 80–81, 86.

24. M114, W/C 81: "[W]enn die vielen bestimmten Eigenschaften schlechterdings gleichgültig wären, und sich durchaus nur auf sich selbst bezögen, so wären sie keine *bestimmte*; denn sie sind dies nur, insofern sie sich *unterscheiden*, und sich *auf andere* als entgegengesetzte *beziehen*. Nach dieser Entgegensetzung aber können sie nicht in der einfachen Einheit ihres Mediums zusammen sein, die ihnen eben so wesentlich ist als die Negation; die Unterscheidung derselben, insofern sie nich eine gleichgültige, sondern ausschließende, anderes negierende ist, fällt also außer diesem einfachen Medium; und dieses ist daher nicht nur ein *Auch*, gleichgültige Einheit, sondern auch *Eins, ausschließende Einheit*."

25. See Lauer, *A Reading of Hegel's Phenomenology of Spirit*, p. 57: "We begin to differentiate perception from sensation when we recognize that the objects of sensation, insofar as it is 'immediate,' are unrelated sense data—if they were related they would be mediated—whereas perception grasps these same sense data as related to one and the same object, or 'thing,' and thus as determining it." Again (p. 60), "perception puts the sensible qualities present to sense where they *belong*, in the percept, since properties are essentially properties of *something*."

26. Hegel lays out this inherent contradiction in the opening paragraphs of the chapter on perception (M111–16, W/C 79–83), and then describes the basic experience of the perceptual process in which these contradictions are encountered (M117, W/C 83–84). The subsequent paragraphs describe the characteristic ways in which we try to make sense of these contradictions without leaving the logical terms of perception (M118–28, W/C 84–89). I want to draw attention to one particular part of this latter process. We have seen that the thing must be both "one" and "also," but cannot in fact be both. Perception also involves the distinction of perceiving and perceived, however, and so one (ultimately unsuccessful) strategy for reconciling the contradiction is to posit the thing as inherently an "also" while positing the unity of subjective experience as supplying the significance of it as a "one," or to posit the thing as inherently a "one" while positing the multiplicity of subjective experience as supplying the significance as "also"; (these "subjective" impositions would thus be the "deceptions," alluded to in Hegel's title to the chapter, "Perception, or, the Thing and Deception"). This strategy is unsuccessful, however, because the necessity to be both "one" and "also" now simply shifts to the subject, and, indeed, there is a process to working through this contradiction that parallels the initial process of working through

the contradiction inherent to thinghood (described initially in M118–22, and then with a further complication in 123–28). Hyppolite, *Genesis and Structure*, discusses the contradiction of "one" and "also" in the experience of subjectivity on pp. 113–15; see also p. 107: "What we have said about the perceived thing can also be said about the perceiving thing."

27. At M177, W/C 127, Hegel defines "spirit" as "'I' that is 'we' and 'we' that is 'I.'" ["Ich, das *Wir*, und *Wir*, das *Ich* ist."] On the topic of "joint attention," see C. Moore and P. J. Denham, *Joint Attention*, and N. Eilan (ed.), *Joint Attention*; see also Daniel D. Hutto, "Elementary Mind Minding, Enactivist Style."

28. Indeed, the same point can be made about the relation between thing and property: to perceive the thing is to treat the thing as the ground of the property, but perceptually the property is the finitude that releases its own grounding infinite.

29. Hegel himself invokes the logic of perception at various other points in the *Phenomenology*, most importantly, perhaps, in his discussion of morality. Here he argues that the (roughly Kantian) moral point of view implicitly depends on the presumption of a God whose perspective will guarantee the "one" of duty that corresponds to the "also" of the many dimensions of a situation that might otherwise give rise to a multiplicity of conflicting duties. See M626, W/C 411–12.

30. *Lectures on Natural Right and Political Science*, section 73, p. 138.

31. Jean-Paul Sartre, *Being and Nothingness*, p. 481.

32. *Being and Nothingness*, p. 481.

33. M425, W/C 280: "Die tätige Liebe—denn eine untätige hat kein Sein, und ist darum wohl nicht gemeint,—geht darauf, Übel von einem Menschen abzusondern, und ihm Gutes zuzufügen. Zu diesem Behuf muß unterschieden werden, was an ihm das Übel, was gegen dies Übel das zweckmäßige Gute, und was überhaupt sein Wohl ist; das heißt, ich muß ihn mit *Verstand* lieben."

34. Hegel presents the concept of reciprocal recognition in M178–84, W/C 127–29. The ensuing discussions of the "Struggle to the Death" and "Lordship and Bondage" bring out various aspects of the problems associated with inadequate approaches to dealing with the singularity, universality, and particularity of our identities.

35. Compare the continuation of the passage quoted above concerning active love from M425, W/C 280: "Intelligent, substantial beneficence is, however, in its richest and most important form the intelligent universal action of the state." ["Das verständige wesentliche Wohltun ist aber in seiner reichsten und wichtigsten Gestalt, das verständige allgemeine Tun des Staats."]

36. This ideal of singularity that would be an inability to articulate itself to itself—simplicity being precisely non-articulation—is first introduced in the dialectic of "meaning/mineness" in chapter I, "Sense-Certainty," and its problem as an intersubjective stance is the subject of the description of "the beautiful soul" in the section on "Conscience."

37. G. W. F. Hegel, *Elements of the Philosophy of Right*, §5: "Der Wille enthält α) das Element der *reinen Unbestimmtheit* oder der reinen Reflexion des Ich in sich, in welcher jede Beschränkung . . . aufgelöst ist; die schrankenlose Unendlichkeit der *absoluten Abstraktion*"; and §6: "β) . . . das Übergehen aus unterschiedsloser

Unbestimmtheit zur . . . *Setzen* einer Bestimmtheit als eines Inhalts und Gegenstands . . .—das absolute Moment der *Endlichkeit* oder *Besonderung* des Ich."

38. On this notion that being led is a loss of oneself, compare M78, W/C 61: "But since [natural consciousness] directly takes itself to be real knowledge, this path has a negative significance for it, and what is in fact the realization of its concept counts for it rather as the loss of its own self; for it does lose its truth on this path. It can therefore be regarded as the pathway of *doubt*, or more precisely as the way of despair"; ["Indem es aber unmittelbar sich vielmehr für das reale Wissen hält, so hat dieser Weg für es negative Bedeutung, und ihm gilt das vielmehr für Verlust seiner selbst, was die Realisierung des Begriffs ist; denn es verliert auf diesem Wege seine Wahrheit. Er kann deswegen als der Weg des *Zweifels* angesehen werden, oder eigentlicher als Weg der Verzweiflung."]. On the idea that it is in this process of self-abandonment that self-consciousness finds its fulfillment, compare M10, W/C 9: "The power of spirit," Hegel writes, "is only as great as its expression, its depth only as deep as it dares to spread out and lose itself in its exposition"; ["Die Kraft des Geistes ist nur so groß als ihre Äußerung, seine Tiefe nur so tief, als er in seiner Auslegung sich auszubreiten und sich zu verlieren getraut."]

Chapter 3

1. M32, W/C 25: "The activity of dissolution is the power and work of the *Understanding*, the most astonishing and mightiest of powers, or rather the absolute power." ["Die Tätigkeit des Scheidens ist die Kraft und Arbeit *des Verstandes*, der verwundersamsten und größten, oder vielmehr der absoluten Macht."]

2. M53, W/C 40: "Der tabellarische Verstand behält für sich die Notwendigkeit und den Begriff des Inhalts, das, was das Konkrete, die Wirklichkeit und lebendige Bewegung der Sache ausmacht, die er rangiert, oder vielmehr behält er dies nicht für sich, sondern kennt es nicht; denn wenn er diese Einsicht hätte, würde er sie wohl zeigen. Er kennt nicht einmal das Bedürfnis derselben; sonst würde er sein Schematisieren unterlassen oder wenigstens sich nicht mehr damit wissen, als mit einer Inhaltsanzeige; er gibt nur die Inhaltsanzeige, den Inhalt selbst aber liefert er nicht."

3. Compare Walter Abish, "In So Many Words." This work, in which each paragraph is preceded by an alphabetical list of the words that will appear in it, demonstrates clearly the distance between the list and reading. On the other hand, it is interesting to note that, even *in reading through* the alphabetical list, significations and intimations begin to emerge through the unguided couplings of the words. See below, note 23.

4. For the notion of the "one," see M114, W/C 81. For Aristotle's conception of *ousia*, see *Categories* 5, and *Metaphysics* Z (VII), 1.

5. For the notion of the "also," see M113, W/C 80–81. For Locke's conception of substance, see *An Essay Concerning Human Understanding*, bk. 2, chap. 23, especially section 6.

6. For Hume, see *An Enquiry Concerning Human Understanding*, section 4.

7. M113, W/C 80–81.

8. M114, W/C 81, M117, W/C 83–84.

9. M106–7, W/C 75.

10. And, indeed, I must live each as the expectation of its replacement by a new "definition" of "this." I can be in the moment, in other words, only by being *temporal,* that is, by being *simultaneously* engaged with past, present, and future. The "comparison" and "conclusion" identified here are also not discursive, temporally separate processes, but are rather the very immanent logical structure of apprehension itself. It is such immanent functions of experience that Kant discusses as the "synthesis of apprehension in intuition," the "synthesis of reproduction in imagination," and the "synthesis of recognition in a concept" (*Critique of Pure Reason,* A98–110). Compare Aristotle, *On the Soul,* bk. 3, chaps. 1–2, on the "common power of sensing," and Plato, *Theaetetus* 186–9.

11. For Kant, see *Critique of Pure Reason,* A77–78/B103–4, B129–31. Synthesis is a central theme throughout Husserl's *Logical Investigations*; for an interpretation, see Jay Lampert, *Synthesis and Backwards Reference.*

12. In reading, we presume that what we encounter is an "it"; that is, we treat a multiplicity of text *as* a unit, and then look to see what the character of this unity is. In so doing, we treat the object according to a logic of reflection (the subject of book 2 of Hegel's *Science of Logic*). See *Science of Logic,* G II.24–35, E399–408.

13. See M150, W/C 105–6.

14. M149, W/C 104–5: "Er ist im *Gesetze* ausgedrückt, als dem *beständigen Bilde* der unsteten Erscheinung. Die *übersinnliche* Welt ist hiemit ein *ruhiges Reich von Gesetzen,* zwar jenseits der wahrgenommenen Welt, denn diese stellt das Gesetz nur durch beständige Veränderung dar, aber in ihr ebenso *gegenwärtig,* und ihr unmittelbares stilles Abbild." The designation "first" supersensible world is from M157, W/C 111.

15. On the idea that the proper object of understanding is the "inner," see M143–7, W/C 100–103.

16. M143, W/C 100: "Dieses wahrhafte Wesen der Dinge hat sich itzt so bestimmt, daß es nicht unmittelbar für sich das Bewußtsein ist, sondern daß dieses ein mittelbares Verhältnis zu dem Innern hat."

17. This is the emptiness of the cycle of "explanation" that Hegel discusses in M154–55, W/C 108–10.

18. In *Posterior Analytics,* bk. 2, chap. 19, and *Metaphysics,* bk. A (1), chaps. 1–2.

19. The *archē* is what Aristotle identifies as the object of insight; *Posterior Analytics* II.19, 100a11–13.

20. This transition from necessity to freedom marks the transition from the objective to the subjective logic in Hegel's *Science of Logic.* See G vol. 2.216–17, 245–51, E 553, 577–82.

21. This is what Hegel means by "the infinite": M160–4, W/C 114–18.

22. See Aristotle, *Posterior Analytics,* bk. 2, chap. 19, 100b8, *Metaphysics,* bk. Theta (9) chap. 10, and *On the Soul,* bk. 3, chap. 6.

23. Regarding the sufficiently interchangeable character of words in everyday situations, compare Maurice Merleau-Ponty's notion of "second order"

speech, *Phenomenology of Perception*, pp. 213–14. This is contrasted with the "first order" speech in which words are not indifferent "carriers" of meaning, but have, in their "materiality," their own irreducible sense (p. 208, n. 1). This is furthermore a sense that can never be rendered in terms of the world of signification they enable. See Jacques Derrida, "Différance," p. 5. This character of the word that is not exhausted in the conceptual meaning it makes present is manifest, for example, in the irreducible significance of the rhyme. See Jacques Derrida, *Glas*, pp. 43, 45, 46, 79, 119, left hand columns; see also Julia Kristeva, *The Revolution in Poetic Language*, part 1, chapter 12, "Genotext and Phenotext," on the notion of "genotext." Compare note 3, above.

24. It is because of its definitive character of transforming the self-identity of the "reader" that Hegel refers to the movements in the *Phenomenology* as "the way of despair," M78, W/C 60–62. Compare Jacques Derrida, *Of Grammatology*, p. 5: "The future can only be anticipated in the form of an absolute danger."

25. *Glas* p. 8 (left column): Derrida describes Genet reading the Gospel of John as "like a miner who is not sure of getting out from the depths of the earth alive."

26. Rainer Maria Rilke, "Archaischer Torso Apollos," translated as "Archaic Torso of Apollo," in *Selected Poetry of Rainer Maria Rilke*, pp. 60–61.

27. M157, W/C 111: "Durch dies Prinzip wird das erste Übersinnliche, das ruhige Reich der Gesetze, das unmittelbare Abbild der wahrgenommenen Welt in sein Gegenteil umgekehrt; das Gesetz war überhaupt das sich *Gleichbleibende*, wie seine Unterschiede; itzt aber ist gesetzt, daß beides vielmehr das Gegenteil seiner selbst ist; . . . *Diese zweite übersinnliche Welt* ist auf diese Weise die *verkehrte* Welt; . . . Das Innere ist damit als Erscheinung vollendet." For the "simple infinite" ["die einfache Unendlichkeit"], see M162, W/C 115.

28. This is the central theme behind John Sallis's discussion of the *chora* of Plato's *Timaeus* in *Chorology*.

29. "*Einfaches Unterschied*": see M149, 160, W/C 104–5, 114, and *Science of Logic*, G vol. 2.46–47, 148–49; E, 417–18, 501–2.

30. On the theme of the negative (and its relationship to understanding), see M32, W/C 25–26.

31. On this idea that understanding must turn on its self and develop an insight into its own character, compare Hegel's description of his own phenomenological observation as an "insight [*Einsicht*] into this process [of understanding]": M140, W/C 139.

32. Jacques Derrida, "Différance," p. 6. For the idea of exceeding the opposition of sensible and intelligible, see p. 5. Compare *Glas*, pp. 31–33 (left column), on the notion of a giving of sense that is not captured by the sense it gives. See also Karin de Boer, "Tragedy, Dialectics, and Différance," p. 334, for a helpful discussion of the notion of *différance*.

33. See de Boer, "Tragedy, Dialectics, and Différance," p. 334: "Différance is one of the many names that Derrida chooses for the differencing force by virtue of which nothing can remain identical to itself or be present to itself, yet without which nothing could even begin to take shape or accomplish itself."

34. Compare M148, W/C 104.

35. *Différance* is both more and less than the differences, which in turn are both more and less than *différance.* See Rodolphe Gasché, *The Tain of the Mirror,* pp. 142–54, on the "infrastructure" that shows itself as the differences, but never shows up as such.

36. For the distinction between first and second actuality, see Aristotle, *On the Soul,* bk. 2, chap. 1; this is illustrated by the example of the grammarian (or "the literate person," depending on how one understands *he grammatikē*) in book 3, chapter 4.

37. Compare Merleau-Ponty's notion of "first order" or "authentic" speech, *Phenomenology of Perception,* p. 208, n. 1.

38. Compare Aquinas, *Summa Theologica,* I q.3, a.4 resp., and I q.75, a.2, resp. See also Jean-Paul Sartre, *Nausea,* p. 2. Sartre's narrator here discusses the way music enacts an immanent necessity in its own movement that cannot be interrupted, though a recording may be stopped or broken: "nothing can interrupt it, yet all can break it."

39. *Science of Logic,* G I.82–83, E 82–83. The remainder of the paragraph explicates the dialectic of being, which is the basic argument of these pages.

40. Compare Aristotle's description of passive *nous* in *On the Soul,* bk. 3, chap. 4, and Timaeus's description of the *chora* in Plato's *Timaeus.*

41. The ushering of the dialectic of being into determinate being is studied in the *Science of Logic,* G I.113–15, E 106–9.

42. For Hegel's concept of the infinite, including the distinction between the good and the bad infinite, see *Science of Logic,* G. I.149–66, E 137–56. This material is expertly analyzed and explained by Stephen Houlgate in *The Opening of Hegel's Logic,* pp. 394–435. Compare also Houlgate, "World History as the Progress of Consciousness," pp. 79–80: "What will happen, we cannot predict. However, that future cannot confront us with anything which we are not equipped to understand."

43. For the concept of the "horizon," see Edmund Husserl, *Cartesian Meditations,* pp. 44–45.

44. "Homeric Hymn to Earth, Mother of All," in *Hesiod, the Homeric Hymns, and Homerica,* p. 457. See also the discussion of Earth in the second choral ode of Sophocles, *Antigone.*

45. For this conception of earth, see especially Martin Heidegger, "The Origin of the Work of Art." Compare Derrida, *Glas,* pp. 151, 162 (right column): "What if what cannot be assimilated, the absolutely indigestible, played a fundamental role within the system, abyssal rather, the abyssal playing . . . a quasi transcendental role and letting be formed above it, like a sort of effluvium, a dream of appeasement? Is there not always an element excluded from the system which assures the space of the system's possibility?"; and "Tympan," in *Margins of Philosophy,* p. xxiii. Compare M162, W/C 115.

46. Derrida would himself resist the word "itself" here, precisely because this self-deconstruction is the way "the" text reveals itself to be non-unitary, non-self-identical.

47. *Positions,* p. 82. Compare *Glas,* p. 25. Note that this means that "deconstruction" must work through the determinacies of the given sense, and is

therefore not abandoning meaning, but going through meaning to the singular "beyond" it makes possible.

48. See Jacques Derrida, "Tympan," p. xi.

49. For the idea that deconstruction is the deconstruction of method, see Gasché, *The Tain of the Mirror*, pp. 123, 171.

50. This is the central idea in Hegel's discussion of "The Absolute Idea," which concludes the *Science of Logic*. For an excellent discussion of Hegel's notion of the absolute, which distinguishes Hegel's view from many common misrepresentations of it, see Burbidge, "Hegel's Absolutes."

51. Theodor W. Adorno, *Negative Dialectics*, p. 5.

52. In this sense, Hegel's reading is a deconstructive "incision," in the sense defined above. (See note 47).

53. For a standard interpretation of Derrida as a critic of Hegel, see Simon Critchley, "A Commentary Upon Derrida's Reading of Hegel in *Glas*." De Boer, "Tragedy, Dialectics, and Différance," gives a clear and helpful statement of the grounds for criticism of Hegel. See also Derrida, "Tympan," p. xi: "I shall be examining the *relevance* of the limit. And therefore relaunching in every sense the reading of the Hegelian *Aufhebung*, eventually beyond what Hegel, inscribing it, understood himself to say or intended to mean"; see also *Positions*, p. 55: *différance* is "the limit, the interruption, the destruction of the Hegelian sublation wherever it operates." On the theme of what it takes to read Hegel, see *Glas*, pp. 5–6, 76, 198–99, and 227–28 (right column).

54. Compare *Glas*, pp. 229 (right column).

55. See, for example, de Boer, "Tragedy, Dialectics, and Différance," p. 335.

56. This is the notion of the "primacy of perception" that Merleau-Ponty introduces in *Phenomenology of Perception*, introduction, chapter 4.

57. See Jay Lampert, "Leaving the System as Is," for an interpretation of Hegel and Derrida that I take to be compatible with my own. On the relationship between Hegel and Derrida, see also Rocío Zambrana, "Hegel's Logic of Finitude." Catherine Malabou, *L'Avenir de Hegel*, and Jim Vernon, *Hegel's Philosophy of Language*, offer helpful avenues for rethinking the relation between Hegel and Derrida.

58. I have taken up related themes to those of this chapter throughout *Reading Hegel's Phenomenology*, especially in chapters 3 and 14.

Chapter 4

1. Immanuel Kant, *Critique of Pure Reason*, A97–110. See also A76–80 / B102–5.

2. This is the argument of the "Transcendental Aesthetic" of the *Critique of Pure Reason*, A22–49 / B37–73. Compare A98–100.

3. A100–2. See B151: "Imagination is the power of presenting an object in intuition even without the object's being present."

4. A103–10. See also A50–52 / B74–76, and A67–69 / B92–94.

5. See A110–14 and A125–30. Substance and Accident, Cause and Effect,

and Reciprocity are the categories of relation. They are centrally discussed under the heading "Analogies of Experience." See A80/B106 and A176–218/B218–65. The study of the categories is the general subject of the "Transcendental Analytic" as a whole.

6. For a detailed and thorough analysis of Kant's argument, see Beatrice Longuenesse, *Kant and the Capacity to Judge.*

7. This is the subject of the "Transcendental Dialectic." See A293–98/B349–55 and A321–32/B377–89. On transcendent vs. transcendental/immanent, see A295–96/B352. On the cognitive value of the categories as limited to the realm of possible experience, see B146–50.

8. Maurice Merleau-Ponty, *Phenomenology of Perception,* p. 5.

9. Gilles Deleuze, *Pourparlers,* p. 13.

10. See Gilles Deleuze and Félix Guattari, *L'Anti-Oedipe,* p. 88, *Anti-Oedipus,* p. 75: "In what he termed the critical revolution, Kant intended to discover criteria immanent to understanding so as to distinguish the legitimate and the illegitimate uses of the syntheses of consciousness. In the name of *transcendental* philosophy (immanence of criteria), he therefore denounced the transcendent use of syntheses such as appeared in metaphysics. In like fashion we are compelled to say that psychoanalysis has its metaphysics—its name is Oedipus. And that a revolution—this time materialist—can proceed only by way of a critique of Oedipus, by denouncing the illegitimate use of the syntheses of the unconscious as found in Oedipal psychoanalysis, so as to rediscover a transcendental unconscious defined by the immanence of its criteria, and a corresponding practice that we shall call schizoanalysis." Further references to this work will give the French pagination first (F), followed by the English pagination (E); all quotations are from the English translation. See also Gilles Deleuze, *Two Regimes of Madness,* p. 309: "The ambition of *Anti-Oedipus* was Kantian in spirit. We attempted a kind of *Critique of Pure Reason* for the unconscious: hence the determination of those syntheses proper to the unconscious; the unfolding of history as the functioning of these syntheses; and the denunciation of Oedipus as the 'inevitable illusion' falsifying all historical production." Compare Eugene W. Holland, "The Anti-Oedipus," p. 293. On interpreting this work in relationship to Kant's philosophy, see also Andrew Cutrofello, *Continental Philosophy,* pp. 189–91.

11. *Anti-Oedipus,* pp. F7–15, 80–89/E1–8, 68–75. On the "connective synthesis," see Brian Massumi, *A User's Guide to Capitalism and Schizophrenia,* pp. 47–48, and also pp. 5–6. On the notion of the machine (and the significance of Deleuze and Guattari's analysis in *Anti-Oedipus* in general), see Todd May, *Gilles Deleuze,* pp. 121–29.

12. *Anti-Oedipus,* pp. F15–22 89–100/E9–16, 75–84. On the recording synthesis, see Massumi, *Capitalism and Schizophrenia,* pp. 49–50; on the "body without organs," see pp. 70–71. For the notion of the "virtual," see May, *Gilles Deleuze,* pp. 46–55.

13. *Anti-Oedipus,* pp. F22–29 100–126/E16–22, 84–105. On the synthesis of consumption, see Massumi, *A User's Guide to Capitalism and Schizophrenia,* pp. 50–51. On the nature of the "subject," see Massumi's excellent summary discussion on pp. 80–81, and compare also pp. 33–34.

14. Gilles Deleuze, *Kant's Critical Philosophy*, pp. 15–16. The "transcendental object = x" and the "transcendental unity of apperception," are both introduced in the discussion of the "synthesis of recognition in a concept," A103–10.

15. See *Civilization and Its Discontents*, pp. 66–68. The logic of condensation and displacement is central to Freud's analysis of dreams throughout *The Interpretation of Dreams*.

16. *Anti-Oedipus*, pp. F85, 86–87/E71, 73, emphasis in original.

17. Gilles Deleuze, *Logic of Sense*, pp. 102, 103.

18. Martin Heidegger, *Being and Time*, sections 15–16, especially pp. 102–103.

19. M166–67, 173–77, W/C 120–22, 125–27. The best analysis of Hegel's account of the dialectic of desire with which I am familiar is David Ciavatta, "Hegel on Desire's Knowledge." My own analysis of desire closely parallels Ciavatta's.

20. M167, W/C 121–22. See Ciavatta, "Hegel on Desire's Knowledge," pp. 529–30.

21. M167, W/C 121–22: "[E]s ist *Begierde* überhaupt. Das Bewußtsein hat als Selbstbewußtsein nunmehr einen gedoppelten Gegenstand, den einen, den unmittelbaren, den Gegenstand der sinnlichen Gewißheit und des Wahrnehmens, der aber *für es* mit dem *Charakter des Negativen* bezeichnet ist, und den zweiten, nämlich *sich selbst*, welcher das wahre *Wesen*, und zunächst nur erst im Gegensätze des ersten vorhanden ist. Das Selbstbewußtsein stellt sich hierin als die Bewegung dar, worin dieser Gegensatz aufgehoben, und ihm die Gleichheit seiner selbst mit sich wird."

22. M174, W/C 125: "Der Nichtigkeit dieses Andern gewiß, setzt es *für sich* dieselbe als seine Wahrheit, vernichtet den selbstständigen Gegenstand und gibt sich dadurch die Gewißheit seiner selbst."

23. See Ciavatta, "Hegel on Desire's Knowledge," pp. 543–44.

24. M168, W/C 122: "Das Selbstbewußtsein, welches schlechthin *für sich* ist, und seinen Gegenstand unmittelbar mit dem Charakter des Negativen bezeichnet, oder zunächst *Begierde* ist, wird daher vielmehr die Erfahrung der Selbstständigkeit desselben machen."

25. See Ciavatta, "Hegel on Desire's Knowledge," pp. 534 and 546, for the notion of desire as a lived, performative refutation of realism.

26. Hegel identifies the self-related negativity of desire, such that it relates to itself in relating to what is not itself, in M167 and M175, W/C 121–22, 126; for the logic of negative self-relation in general, see *Science of Logic*, vol. 1, bk. 2, sect. 1, chap. 1, part C, "Reflection" (*Reflexion*). For the logic of reflection as it first emerges in Hegel's *Science of Logic*, see Henrich, "Hegels Logik der Reflexion."

27. M174, W/C 125: "Das einfache Ich ist diese Gattung oder das einfache Allgemeine, für welches die Unterschiede keine sind, nur indem es *negatives Wesen* der gestalteten selbstständigen Momente ist."

28. M174, W/C 126: ". . . Gewißheit, als solche, welche ihm selbst auf *gegenständliche Weise* geworden ist."

29. M176, W/C 126–27: "Aber die Wahrheit derselben ist vielmehr die gedoppelte Reflexion, die Verdopplung des Selbstbewußtseins. Es ist ein Gegen-

stand für das Bewußtsein, welcher an sich selbst sein Anderssein oder den Unterschied als einen nichtigen setzt, und darin selbstständig ist. . . . [D]er Gegenstand des Selbstbewußtseins ist . . . selbstständig in dieser Negativität seiner selbst; und damit ist er für sich selbst Gattung, allgemeine Flüssigkeit in der Eigenheit seiner Absonderung; er ist lebendiges Selbstbewußtsein."

30. M177, W/C 127: "Es ist ein *Selbstbewußtsein für ein Selbstbewußtsein.*"

31. M177, W/C 127: "Indem ein Selbstbewußtsein der Gegenstand ist, ist er ebensowohl Ich, wie Gegenstand."

32. M175, W/C 126: "But this universal independent nature in which negation is present as absolute negation is the genus as such or the genus as *self-consciousness*"; ["Diese allgemeine selbstständige Natur aber, an der die Negation als absolute ist, ist die Gattung als solche, oder als Selbstbewußtsein."].

33. M179, W/C 128: "Es ist für das Selbstbewußtsein ein anderes Selbstbewußtsein; es is *außer sich* gekommen. . . . [E]s hat sich selbst verloren, denn es findet sich als ein *anderes* Wesen."

34. M175, W/C 126: "Die Begierde und die in ihrer Befriedigung erreichte Gewißheit seiner selbst ist bedingt durch ihn, denn sie ist durch Aufheben dieses Andern; daß dies Aufheben sei, muß dies Andere sein."

35. M179, W/C 128: "Es ist für das Selbstbewußtsein ein anderes Selbstbewußtsein; es is *außer sich* gekommen. Dies hat die gedoppelte Bedeutung; *erstlich*, es hat sich selbst verloren, denn es findet sich als ein *anderes* Wesen; *zweitens*, es hat damit das Andere aufgehoben, denn es sieht auch nicht das Andere als Wesen, sondern sich *selbst* im Andern."

36. M182, W/C 129: "Jedes sieht *das Andre* dasselbe tun, was *es* tut; jedes tut Selbst, was es an das Andre fodert; und tut darum, was es tut, auch *nur* insofern, als das Andre dasselbe tut; das einseitige Tun wäre unnütz; weil, was geschehen soll, nur durch beide zu Stande kommen kann."

37. M184, W/C 129: "Sie *anerkennen* sich, als *gegenseitig* sich *anerkennend.*"

38. The scenario of the baby at the breast is itself discussed (very well) by Massumi, *A User's Guide to Capitalism and Schizophrenia*, pp. 71–73. Massumi's entire discussion of "personal" development (pp. 68–80) should be compared with my discussion in this final section. Massumi offers a compelling and subtle "schizoanalytic" account of the development of a person, which addresses at many levels the conflictual experience of other selves, which is my topic in this final section. Excellent as this analysis is, however, it still presumes rather than explains the fundamental meaning of "other person" with which we contend in our experience. Note especially the initial discussion (pp. 73–74) of the "inconsistent availability" of the mother's breast; I am arguing that the terms offered by Deleuze and Guattari for explaining our experience of experiencing another *as* another person always falls short of explaining that meaning fully. Such an objection is not answered by identifying the process by which a sense of self is developed in the "mirror stage," for such an account still requires a justification *in principle* for how it is that we are able to engage with such a sense. (Demonstrating such conditions of possibility is, of course, precisely Kant's transcendental project, the project that Deleuze and Guattari commit themselves to in *Anti-Oedipus.*) On the significance of the mirror stage, see Holland, "The Anti-

Oedipus," pp. 293–4. Compare Jacques Lacan, *The Seminar Book XI*, pp. 207, 214, 221, and 235, and Luke Caldwell, "Schizophrenizing Lacan."

39. Massumi, *A User's Guide to Capitalism and Schizophrenia*, p. 68. See also p. 69: "The supermolecule [baby] sees its father and the smile is translated into a curl of the toes; it sees its mother and kicks."

40. In this respect, Deleuze and Guattari stay within the domain of Kant's epistemology, which similarly does not account for the distinctive experience of other persons; on this theme, see Kant's brief but provocative discussion in the "Paralogisms" of "viewing myself from the standpoint of another person," at A362–63, and the idea of "putting oneself in the place" of another, at A346–47 and A353. In "The Bodily Unconscious in Freud's 'Three Essays,'" I have made a parallel argument to show that Freud's psychoanalytic categories similarly fall short in principle of being able to explain the sense "other person" upon which his analyses in fact rely.

41. M176–84, W/C 126–29.

42. The goal of mutual recognition is identified in M184, W/C 129; M177, W/C 127 identifies this as "spirit."

Chapter 5

1. The primary texts in which Hegel's analysis of mood are contained are the "Anthropology" section of the *Philosophy of Mind*, especially the *Zusätze* to §§399–402, but there are also significant treatments in §§446–50 and §§471–80 (*Enz* 3, pp. 95–122, 246–57, 290–300). The discussion of the emergence of consciousness (§§413–19) is also relevant, and seems to be referred to in the *Zusatz* to §446 (*Enz* 3, 199–208, 246–47).

2. The distinction of sleeping and waking is the preceding step in the *Philosophy of Mind*, §398 (*Enz* 3, 87–95). Sensibility (*Empfindung*) is discussed in §399 (*Enz* 3, pp. 95–97). Mood as a species of *Empfindung* is discussed in the *Zusatz* to §401 (*Enz* 3, pp. 102–17).

3. §399, *Zusatz*, p. 72: "On waking, we find ourselves at first only quite vaguely distinguished from the outer world generally. . . . In order to become fully awake and certain of it, we open our eyes, take hold of ourselves, in short, examine ourselves to find out whether something is, for us, a definite Other, is definitely distinct from us" (*Enz*, p. 97).

4. *Phenomenology of Perception*, p. 3.

5. *Science of Logic*, G II.477–78, E 767–68. The terms "Empfindung" and "Sensibilität" should not be confused, though the fact that both can properly be translated as "sensibility" rightly suggests the proximity of their meanings. Murray Greene's rendering of *Empfindung* as "sentience" might offer a helpful way to mark the difference in an English translation. In the *Zusatz* to §401, p. 85, Hegel defines *Sensibilität* as "the simple general inwardness of the sentient (*empfindenden*) subject" (*Enz* 3, p. 113). Hegel also discusses sensibility and irritability briefly in the *Zusatz* to §398 (*Enz* 3, pp. 89–95). The confusion of sensibility with

irritability plagues David Krell's (mis-)description of Hegel in *Contagion: Sexuality, Disease and Death in German Idealism and Romanticism.*

6. Compare the *Zusatz* to §396, p. 58: "The completeness of the bodily structure which is lacking in the plant and is first accomplished in the animal organism, this leading back of all members to the negative, simple unity of life, is the ground of the origin of self-feeling in the animal, and therefore also in the child" (*Enz* 3, p. 79). Compare also *Lectures on the Philosophy of Spirit: 1827–8,* pp. 75–76: "as sentient soul, the I is omnipresent in the body, and it exists only as a unity. <I am constantly conscious of this unity. When feeling the tip of my finger, I [also] feel [myself] there. There the feeling soul exists, the capacity of feeling, sensation. . . .>"

7. The *Philosophy of Mind* explicitly refers to Aristotle's *De Anima,* but, more than that, Hegel's work is clearly deeply responsive to that text. This analysis of sensibility should be compared with Aristotle's definition of soul, his definition of *aisthesis,* and especially his notion that sensation is characterized by a "mean" (*De Anima,* 2.12).

8. *Being and Nothingness,* pp. 11–17, especially p. 13.

9. *Zusatz* to §399, p. 72 (*Enz* 3, p. 96).

10. This is the structure of "positing reflection," *Science of Logic,* G II.25–28, E 400–402.

11. Compare the *Zusatz* to §387, p. 27: "We must start, therefore, from mind which is still in the grip of Nature and connected with its corporeity, mind which is not as yet in communion with itself, not yet free" (*Enz* 3, p. 40). On feeling as an arena of non-distinction of subject and object, see Willem de Vries, *Hegel's Theory of Mental Activity,* p. 76, and Murray Greene, *Hegel on the Soul,* pp. 82 and 104; though Greene's book covers this whole section of Hegel's text (pp. 81–102), he tends more to repeat than to explain Hegel's claims.

12. Hegel's central discussion of mood (*Stimmung*) is in the *Zusatz* to §401, pp. 80–88 (*Enz* 3, pp. 107–16), and this is the text with which our study is primarily concerned.

13. On the theme of "finding" oneself in mood, note Hegel's use of this language in §399 and *Zusatz,* p. 71 (*Enz* 3, pp. 95, 96); compare the *Zusatz* to §398, p. 67: "Here in Anthropology we are contemplating waking only in so far as it is a happening and, too, a still quite indeterminate happening such that mind simply finds a world confronting it; a *finding of itself* [*ein Sichfinden*] which, to begin with, only gets as far as sensation [*Empfindung*], but still remains quite remote from the concrete determinations of intelligence and will. It is just in this fact that the soul on waking merely *finds* itself and the world . . . that the natural life of mind consists" (*Enz* 3, p. 90; italics in original).

14. See §400, p. 73: "*Everything is in sensation (feeling)* [*Alles ist in der Empfindung*]" (*Enz* 3, p. 97, italics in original). In the hands of the British Empiricists, this Aristotelian slogan was given a reductive meaning, and led to a sceptical isolation of the mind and its contents from the world; see, for example, Hobbes, *Leviathan,* part 1, chapter 1, and its consequence in chapter 3—all "knowledge" of the world is only presumption. In Hegel, on the contrary, this *Empfindung* is

the original identity of self and world, a founding context *within which* any further differentiation will develop. For the language of "being at home in determinacy," see the *Zusatz* to §401, p. 82: "When we speak of the inner determination of the sentient subject without reference to its corporealization, we are considering only how this subject is for us, not how it is for itself and at home with itself in its determination, how it feels itself in the latter" (*Enz* 3, p. 109).

15. *Phenomenology of Perception*, p. 178.

16. The Id never learns this lesson. It is interesting that (in "The Dissection of the Psychical Personality," p. 106) Freud says of the Id that it is characterized by no negation. In this way, Freud effectively identifies the Id with Fichte's first principle ("the ego posits itself") (*Science of Knowledge*, pp. 93–105), itself basically the equivalent of Sartre's pre-reflective cogito. The universally self-same versus the particularly (negatively) distinguished again reflects the difference between sensibility and irritability. Hegel identifies the original self-positing as already *inherently negative*; see *Science of Logic*, G II.253, E 583, which is discussed in the epilogue. This implicit negativity is the ground of subsequent dialectical development. For the basic distinction between the pleasure principle and the reality principle, see Freud, *Civilization and Its Discontents*, chapter 2. Others have considered different aspects in which Hegel's work parallels Freud's; see, for example, Daniel Berthold-Bond, *Hegel's Theory of Madness*, pp. 77 and 101, and Jon Mills, *The Unconscious Abyss*, passim.

17. §401 and *Zusatz*, primarily pp. 77–83 (*Enz* 3, pp. 102–10); for the language of "substantial" and "subjective," see the *Zusatz* to §399, p. 72 (*Enz* 3, p. 96).

18. Hegel discusses colors in the *Zusatz* to §401, pp. 81–82 (*Enz* 3, pp. 108–9).

19. See *Zusatz* to §401, p. 82: "It is only by the corporealization of its inner determinations that the subject is enabled to feel them" (*Enz* 3, pp. 109–10).

20. *Zusatz* to §401, p. 85 (*Enz* 3, p. 113).

21. This point itself is very important, I think, for two reasons. First, it draws our attention to the need to use the right sorts of categories for understanding emotions: emotions will be inherently characterized by dynamism and negation—that is, they will be processes and not simple positivities. Second, this, I take it, is a phenomenological claim. It is a description of the form of our experience, and something that we can understand and argue about only from the inside.

22. On the theme of freedom, see *Zusatz* to §401, p. 83 (*Enz* 3, pp. 110–11), and also the *Zusatz* to §387, p. 27 (*Enz* 3, p. 40).

23. *Zusatz* to §401, p. 83 (*Enz* 3, p. 111).

24. *Zusatz* to §401, p. 87 (*Enz* 3, p. 116).

25. *Zusatz* to §398, p. 69 (*Enz* 3, p. 92).

26. On the theme of the soul's becoming equal to itself by "outing" itself, compare Plotinus 3.8.6, and also the theme of work in Hegel's discussion of "Lordship and Bondage." Work is also central to Hegel's understanding of the cure for mental illness, for related reasons; see *Zusatz* to §408, p. 138 (*Enz* 3, p. 181).

27. *Critique of Pure Reason*, B131–32.

28. *Science of Knowledge*, pp. 94–102.

29. *Science of Knowledge*, pp. 102–5.

30. This is helpfully discussed in *Science of Knowledge*, pp. 185–87.

31. *Science of Knowledge*, p. 189. For a fuller discussion of Fichte's position, see John Russon, "The Body as Site of Action and Intersubjectivity."

32. On the need for the gesture to be recognized, see Jennifer Bates, *Hegel's Theory of Imagination*, pp. 49–50, and also her general discussion of Hegel's systematic treatment of language in the 1805 *Philosophy of Mind* (pp.72–75) and the 1830 *Philosophy of Mind* (pp. 93–96). The need for the gesture to be recognized is also a central theme in Jim Vernon, *Hegel's Philosophy of Language*.

33. The dialectic of intersubjective recognition and its relation to Fichte's principles is helpfully addressed in Paul Redding, *Hegel's Hermeneutics*, pp. 101–4, and in John Russon, *Reading Hegel's Phenomenology*, chapter 6.

34. For the "thing" upon which each imposes her own interpretation, see Hegel's analysis of "The Spiritual Animal Kingdom and Deceit, or *die Sache selbst*," chapter V, part 3, section A, in the *Phenomenology of Spirit*. On the universality of language, compare *Encyclopaedia Logic*, section 20 (*Enz* 1, pp. 71–75), and *Philosophy of Mind*, *Zusatz* to §457 (*Enz* 3, p. 269). Analogous themes of having "one's own" in a public context are excellently studied by David Ciavatta in "Hegel on Owning One's Own Body." See also Jay Lampert, "Locke, Fichte and Hegel on the Right to Property"; though in my judgment this paper is ultimately quite misrepresentative of the positions of Locke and Fichte, it does a very effective job of working through many of the philosophical themes involved in the notion of ownership.

35. *Zusatz* to §401, p. 87 (*Enz* 3, p. 111); §459 (*Enz* 3, pp. 271–77). See the *Zusatz* to §462 (*Enz* 3, pp. 279–80) for a discussion of language that anticipates the distinction between first-order and second-order speech that Merleau-Ponty draws in part 1, chapter 6, of his *Phenomenology of Perception*. This theme also runs prominently throughout Hegel's *Aesthetics*; see, for example, Hegel, *Aesthetics*, vol. 1, p. 282.

36. See Berthold-Bond, *Hegel's Theory of Madness*, pp. 43: "Only in the publicity of language, in which the particular, isolated 'I' vanishes and becomes for others in a common world, can spirit find its true element." See also p. 131.

Chapter 6

1. *The Divided Self*, p. 106.

2. M177, W/C 127.

3. *The Divided Self*, chapter 3. Compare also Gregory Bateson, "Towards a Theory of Schizophrenia."

4. Henri Bergson, *Matter and Memory*, p. 36.

5. Compare the parallel discussion in Simone de Beauvoir, *The Ethics of Ambiguity*, chap. 2, pp. 34 ff.

6. I have discussed related issues of childhood development in "The Virtues of Agency."

7. I have pursued these themes more fully in *Human Experience*, especially chapters 4 and 5.

8. Hegel outlines the concept of recognition in M178–85, W/C 127–29, and gives a phenomenological description of inadequate approaches to recognition in M186–96, W/C 129–36.

9. M178, W/C 127: "Das Selbstbewußtsein ist *an und für sich*, indem, und dadurch, daß es für ein Anderes an und für sich ist; d. h. es ist nur als ein Anerkanntes."

10. See John Russon, "Self and Other in Hegel's Phenomenology of Spirit."

11. M174–77, W/C 125–27.

12. M186–96, W/C 129–36.

13. I have studied Hegel's analyses of these forms of experience in chapters 4 through 7 of *Reading Hegel's Phenomenology*.

14. M177, W/C 127: "Hiemit ist . . . der Begriff *des Geistes* für uns vorhanden: . . . diese absolute Substanz, welche in der vollkommenen Freiheit und Selbstständigkeit ihres Gegensatzes, nämlich verschiedener für sich seiender Selbstbewußtsein, die Einheit derselben ist: Ich, *das Wir, und Wir, das Ich* ist." Compare M351, W/C 236: "In the universal spirit, therefore, each has only the certainty of himself, of finding in the actual world nothing but himself; he is as certain of the others as he is of himself"; ["In dem allgemeinen Geiste hat daher jeder nur die Gewißheit seiner selbst, nichts anders in der seienden Wirklichkeit zu finden, als sich selbst; er is der andern so gewiß als seiner."].

15. See Peg Hutson-Nechkash, *Narrative Toolbox*. Compare Piaget and Inhelder, *The Child's Conception of Space*.

16. For related themes regarding childhood development, particularly in relationship to stories, see Kirsten Jacobson, "Heidegger, Winnicott, and *The Velveteen Rabbit*." See also John Dewey, *Democracy and Education*, Chapter 2.

17. *Nicomachean Ethics*, bk. 1, chap. 7; see also *Politics*, bk. 1, chap. 2.

18. Discussions of narrative in contemporary psychological work tend to focus on the theoretical comprehension of explicit, spoken narrative, rather than on the practical and implicit sense I am discussing here; what I am calling lived narrative is more commonly studied under the heading of "play." For an introduction to this literature, see Ageliki Nicolopoulou, "Play and Narrative in the Process of Development," Judith A. Eckler and Otto Weininger, "Structural Parallels between Pretend Play and Narrative," Susan Engler, "The Narrative Worlds of What Is and What If," and Carol Fleisher Feldman, "Mimesis: Where Play and Narrative Meet." For a rich concept of play that could be a helpful corrective to much of this literature, see Hans-Georg Gadamer, *Truth and Method*, pp. 102–10. See also Daniel D. Hutto (ed.), *Narrative and Understanding Persons*.

19. M729, W/C 475: "die erste Sprache, das *Epos* als solches." Just as we might imagine conceptuality as beginning in narrative, so should we imagine language as beginning with story rather than with vocabulary and grammar. In short, *logos* begins as *muthos*. On the pan-Hellenism of epic, see Gregory Nagy, *The Best of the Achaeans*.

20. M733, W/C 478: "Diese höhere Sprache, die *Tragödie*, faßt also die Zerstreuung der Momente der wesentlichen und handelnden Welt näher zusam-

men; . . . In Ansehung der Form, hört die Sprache, dadurch, daß sie in den Inhalt hereintritt, auf, erzählend zu sein, wie der Inhalt ein vorgestellter. Der Held ist selbst der Sprechende, und die Vorstellung zeigt . . . *selbstbewußte* Menschen." On the history of the development of Greek literature, see John Herington, *Poetry into Drama.* The philosophical and cultural significance of the "first-person" character of tragic poetry is studied in Plato, *Republic,* bk. 3.

21. In referring to families, here, I intend to point to the domain of intimate, particular others within whose company one grows up, whether or not this is a "family" in the familiar sense.

22. M437, W/C 286–87.

23. *Reason in History,* p. 64. Compare *Philosophy of Mind,* section 552, p. 283: "[R]eligion . . . is the consciousness of *'absolute' truth*"; it implicitly enacts that community's self-consciousness [M677, W/C 444–45]. On the idea that a pretheoretical embrace of values is the condition of "theoretical thought," compare Herman Dooyeweerd, *A New Critique of Theoretical Thought.*

24. On the theme of gossip, see John Russon, "The (Childish) Nature of the Soul in Plato's *Apology.*"

25. Religious practices are how a community says "we": they are in fact the community's self-consciousness, but, as Hegel says, it is self-consciousness in the form of consciousness, that is, in engaging with these practices we do not recognize these practices *as* our attempt to make sense of ourselves [M677, W/C 444–45].

26. I have done so in chapter 13 below. Hegel wrote about world religions without the depth of anthropological knowledge that we possess today, with the result that various aspects of his descriptions and interpretations of world religions need correction. His overall insight into the logic and history of religion is nonetheless brilliant, and his insight into the ancient Greek and Christian religions remains particularly provocative.

27. *Philosophy of Mind,* p. 284.

28. *Philosophy of Mind,* section 562, p. 296.

29. *Philosophy of Mind,* p. 289: "[I]t is in fact necessary that in point of time the consciousness of the absolute Idea should be first reached and apprehended in this form: in other words, it must exist in its immediate reality as religion, earlier than it does as philosophy. Philosophy is a later development from this basis . . . and in fact reaches its completion by catching and comprehending in all its definite essentiality that principle of spirit which first manifests itself in religion." And note p. 290: "Political power, which is developed similarly, but earlier than philosophy, from religion . . ."

30. The stoic is the first figure of "the Freedom of Self-Consciousness," M197–201, W/C 136–40, and the political recognition of such stoic individuals is the "Condition of Right" (*Rechtszustand,* Miller's "legal status") (M477–83, W/C 316–20).

31. M527–73, W/C 348–78.

32. I have developed this theme in "Heidegger, Hegel and Ethnicity: The Ritual Basis of Self-Identity."

33. M69, W/C 51: "Denn die Natur dieser [Humanität] ist, auf die Über-

einkunft mit andern zu dringen, und ihre Existenz nur in der zu Stande gebrachten Gemeinsamkeit der Bewußtsein."

Chapter 7

1. M167–77, W/C 120–27 describes desire and life.

2. M175–77, W/C 126–27.

3. M185–96, W/C 129–36. (M178–84, W/C 127–29 presents the concept of mutual recognition.)

4. M197–201, W/C 136–40.

5. M202–5, W/C 140–43.

6. M206–31, W/C 143–57. Note that I include the first paragraph of chapter V, "Reason," here; this is because (as will become clear below) it is in this paragraph that Hegel completes his argument about Unhappy Consciousness.

7. One of the most important (of the many) corrections that Harris's *Hegel's Ladder* makes to the familiar views that have become standard in Hegel-interpretation pertains to this figure of "Unhappy Consciousness." Harris, who interprets the *Phenomenology* as a "logic" book (in Hegel's sense of that term), is carefully attentive to the argumentative structure of the whole book, and has recognized the "logical" structure of the "Self-Consciousness" chapter in a way that his been missed by most other commentators. He has shown that the "Independence and Dependence of Self-Consciousness" operates according to the (insufficient) logic of the "Judgment," whereas the "Freedom of Self-Consciousness" plays out a logic of "Syllogism," and that it is the "Unhappy Consciousness" that is the culminating form of the syllogistic logic inherent to self-consciousness. Harris has demonstrated, that is, that the Unhappy Consciousness is the completed form of self-consciousness, i.e., a form never to be surpassed by the single self-consciousness. In this way, he continues (in a more rigorous and accurate fashion) the line of interpretation begun in Jean Wahl's *La malheur de la conscience* (1929) and Jean Hyppolite's *Genèse et Structure dans le phénoménologie de Hegel* (1946), an interpretation that recognizes the Unhappy Consciousness to be the central figure in the *Phenomenology*. Though my use of the figure of Unhappy Consciousness will differ from Harris's, I will use his insight about Unhappy Consciousness to understand the broad structure of the later parts of the book in a way that corresponds with his understanding of the project and structure of the *Phenomenology* as a whole. As I will go on to discuss, it is the normal (and sensible) practice to use the expression "Unhappy Consciousness" to refer to the second form of unhappy consciousness, since the bulk of Hegel's chapter is devoted to the discussion of this form. In fact, though (according to M210, W/C 145–46), "unhappy consciousness" properly refers to a structure that comprehends a broader range of phenomena, including especially the experiences of reconciliation, which will be my central focus in this book. I will, therefore, use the expression "unhappy consciousness" to refer to this logical structure of self-conscious selfhood in all its forms, rather than simply in its second form. On the "transportability" of the logic of unhappy consciousness outside the "Catholic"

model Hegel alludes to in his discussion of the second form, see also John Burbidge, "Unhappy Consciousness in Hegel."

8. M197–230, W/C 136–56.

9. M197, W/C 137: "ein Bewußtsein, welches sich als die Unendlichkeit, oder reine Bewegung des Bewußtseins das Wesen ist."

10. M197, W/C 137: "*bin* Ich *frei,* weil ich nicht in einem Andern bin, sondern schlechthin bei mir selbst bleibe, und der Gegenstand, der mir das Wesen ist, in ungetrennter Einheit mein Fürmichsein ist."

11. M204–5, W/C 141: "*Skeptizismus* . . . verschwinden läßt; nicht nur das Gegenständliche als solches, sondern sein eignes Verhalten zu ihm. . . . Was verschwindet, ist das Bestimmte, oder der Unterschied, der, auf welche Weise und woher es sei, als fester und unwandelbarer sich aufstellt"; and 142: "Dies Bewußtsein ist aber eben hierin in der Tat, statt sichselbstgleiches Bewußtsein zu sein, nur eine schlechthin zufällige Verwirrung, der Schwindel einer sich immer erzeugenden Unordnung."

12. M205, W/C 142: "*Es ist dies für sich selbst*; denn es selbst erhält und bringt diese sich bewegende Verwirrung hervor. Es bekennt sich darum auch dazu, es bekennt, ein ganz *zufälliges, einzelnes* Bewußtsein zu sein,—ein Bewußtsein, das *empirisch* ist, sich nach dem richtet, was keine Realität für es hat, dem gehorcht, was ihm kein Wesen ist, das tut and zur Wirklichkeit bringt, was ihm keine Wahrheit hat."

13. *Ecclesiastes* 1:2. Jean Wahl, *Le malheur de la conscience,* an excerpt of which is translated in *G.W.F. Hegel: Critical Assessments*; see p. 287: "Scepticism destroyed one of the terms of consciousness, namely, the external world. But at the very moment when it suppressed one term, it made another dualism appear within the remaining term. From this arises the sceptic's unhappiness. Hegel's sceptic therefore is less Montaigne than Pascal; or he is Ecclesiastes, relating the infinite essence of God to the nothingness of creatures and unable to reconcile these two ideas."

14. Harris, *Hegel's Ladder,* vol. 1, p. 397. This situation here outlined by Hegel under the name "Unhappy Consciousness" might be described as "Kierkegaard before Kierkegaard," which is roughly what Jean Wahl recognized in his interpretation, which was largely responsible for the French enthusiasm for Hegel in the 1930s. For a useful discussion of this history of interpretation that is weak in its understanding of Hegel but rich and complex in its understanding of the French interpreters of Hegel, see Bruce Baugh, *French Hegel.*

15. Harris, *Hegel's Ladder,* p. 396, regarding M206, W/C 143–44. Compare Jean Wahl, in *G.W.F. Hegel: Critical Assessments,* p. 295: "[this] phenomenological theory is analogous to a theory of grace in which we cannot separate what comes from God and what comes from free will."

16. Jean Wahl, *Le malheur de la conscience,* p. 155.

17. Harris, *Hegel's Ladder,* vol. 1, p. 396.

18. M207–8, W/C 144: "Dieses *unglückliche, in sich entzweite* Bewußtsein muß also, weil dieser Widerspruch seines Wesens sich *ein* Bewußtsein ist, in dem einen Bewußtsein immer auch das andere haben"; and "so ist ihm das eine, nämlich das einfache unwandelbare, als das *Wesen*; das andere aber, das vielfache wandelbare,

als das *Unwesentliche* . . . . [Es] ist sich das Unwesentliche . . . und das Unwandelbare ihm ein Fremdes ist."

19. It is for this reason that Hegel calls this highest form of self-consciousness "consciousness," i.e., experience of an other.

20. M208, W/C 144: "[Die Stellung kann] nicht eine Gleichgültigkeit seiner selbst gegen das Unwandelbare sein."

21. Asserting the essential apartness (the first stance of Unhappy Consciousness) makes the definitive power of the universal impossible—there is no ground for communion. The second stance (the focus of most of Hegel's discussion) is a self-contradictory attempt at preserving itself while eliminating itself, and these strategies all fail, for they are premised on denying the necessary terms of the situation. The third stance is the one that recognizes that the reconciliation is not *yet to be* achieved but is *already* definitive *of each.* (Note that, in principle, this calls for a reality that is simultaneously the "absolute" and historical singularity, which is a reality that cannot exist as something already accomplished, i.e., it is a reality that is essentially open.)

22. M189, W/C 132.

23. For the bonds that hold the slave to the master, see M190, W/C 132: "The lord relates himself mediately to the bondsman through a thing that is independent, for it is just this which holds the bondsman in bondage; it is his chain from which he could not break free in the struggle, thus proving himself to be dependent, to possess his independence in thinghood"; ["Der Herr bezieht sich *auf den Knecht mittelbar durch das selbstständige Sein*; denn eben hieran ist der Knecht gehalten; es ist seine Kette, von der er im Kampfe nicht abstrahieren konnte, und darum sich als unselbstständig, seine Selbstständigkeit in der Dingheit zu haben, erwies."] For the experience by the unhappy consciousness of its own particular embodiment as an impediment to its identification with the universal, see M223–30, W/C 152–56.

24. Harris, *Hegel's Ladder,* vol. 1, p. 383.

25. Harris, *Hegel's Ladder,* vol. 1, p. 14, italics in original.

26. M353–54, W/C 236. Harris calls this the "Eden of spirit," and he particularly argues against Judith Shklar's characterization of Hegel's project as a "lament for Hellas."

27. See M26, W/C 20: "Conversely, the individual has the right to demand that Science should at least provide him with the ladder to this standpoint [of science], should show him this standpoint within himself. His right is based on his absolute independence, which he is conscious of possessing in every phase of his knowledge; for in each one, whether recognized by science or not, and whatever the content may be, the individual is the absolute form, i.e., he is the *immediate certainty* of himself"; "Umgekehrt hat das Individuum das Recht zu fodern, daß die Wissenschaft ihm die Leiter wenigstens zu diesem Standpunkte reiche. Sein Recht gründet sich auf seine absolute Selbstständigkeit, die es in jeder Gestalt seines Wissens zu besitzen weiß, denn in jeder, sei sie von der Wissenschaft anerkannt oder nicht, und der Inhalt sei welcher er wolle, ist es die absolute Form zugleich oder hat die *unmittelbare Gewißheit* seiner selbst."

28. M353–55, W/C 236–37: "Aus diesem Glücke aber, seine Bestimmung erreicht zu haben, und in ihr zu leben, ist das Selbstbewußtsein, welches zunächst

nur *unmittelbar* und dem *Begriffe nach* Geist ist, herausgetreten. . . . Die Vernunft *muß aus diesem Glücke heraustreten* . . . . [D]as *einzelne* Bewußtsein, wie es unmittelbar seine Existenz in der realen Sittlichkeit . . . hat, . . . sich . . . auch nicht als reine *Einzelnheit für sich zu sein* weiß. Ist es aber zu diesem Gedanken gekommen, wie es muß, so ist diese *unmittelbare* Einheit mit dem Geiste . . . verloren."

29. This movement from "true spirit" to "self-certain spirit" is the content of chapter VI of the *Phenomenology*, "Spirit."

30. Harris, *Hegel's Ladder*, vol. 1, p. 14, italics in original.

31. Jean Hyppolite, *Logic and Existence*. The quotations are from pp. 74 and 187, respectively.

32. See M73, W/C 58: ". . . wenn es [das Absolute] nicht an und für sich schon bei uns wäre."

33. M26, W/C 20: "die absolute Form." Compare M208, W/C 144: "it [the unhappy consciousness] is *itself* a simple, hence unchangeable, consciousness, and hence is aware that this consciousness is its essence"; "so *ist es selbst* einfaches, und hiemit unwandelbares Bewußtsein, dessen hiemit als *seines* Wesens sich bewußt."

34. See M231, W/C 157: "Für das unglückliche Bewußtsein ist das *Ansichsein* das *Jenseits* seiner selbst," that is, the "in itself" is, for the unhappy consciousness, "its" beyond.

35. M210, W/C 149.29–39, my translation. Italics in original: "Es ist dadurch die dreifache Weise für dasselbe vorhanden, wie die Einzelnheit mit dem Unwandelbaren verknüpft ist; *einmal* geht es selbst sich wieder hervor als entgegengesetzt dem unwandelbaren Wesen; und es ist in den Anfang des Kampfs zurückgeworfen, welcher das Element des ganzen Verhältnisses bleibt. Das *andremal* aber hat das *Unwandelbare* selbst *an ihm* die *Einzelnheit* für es; so daß sie Gestalt des Unwandelbaren ist, an welches hiemit die ganze Weise der Existenz hinübertritt. Das *drittemal* findet *es sich selbst* als dieses Einzelne im Unwandelbaren." Wahl discusses the three forms on pp. 291–94 of *G.W.F. Hegel: Critical Assessments*. Wahl is unlike most commentators in (correctly) recognizing that there are three forms, and recognizes the experience of spirit as the realization of the third form (p. 294).

36. M207–8, W/C 144–45 discuss the initial misapprehension by unhappy consciousness of its own nature, such that it imagines the unchangeable as an alien *being*.

37. M214–30, W/C 147–56. For "Absolute Freedom and Terror," see M582–95, W/C 385–94.

38. Kant's *Groundwork for the Metaphysics of Morals* is the classic articulation of this perspective; Hegel's phenomenological description of this experience of morality is found in the sections on "Law-giving Reason" and "Law-Testing Reason" (M419–37, W/C 277–87) and in the sections of "Self-Certain Spirit" called "The Moral View of the World" and "Dissemblence or Duplicity" (M599–631, W/C 395–415). I have discussed Hegel's phenomenology of moral experience in chapter 10 of *Reading Hegel's Phenomenology*.

39. M231, W/C 157, my trans.: "das *einzelne* Bewußtsein *an sich* absolutes Wesen ist."

40. M231, W/C 157, my trans.: "Seine Wahrheit ist dasjenige, welches in

dem Schlusse, worin die Extreme absolut auseinandergehalten auftraten, als die Mitte erscheint, welche es dem unwandelbaren Bewußtsein ausspricht, daß das Einzelne auf sich Verzicht getan, und dem Einzelnen daß das Unwandelbare kein Extrem mehr für es, sondern mit ihm versöhnt ist. Diese Mitte ist die beide unmittelbar wissende und sie beziehende Einheit, und das Bewußtsein ihrer Einheit, welche sie dem Bewußtsein und damit *sich selbst* ausspricht, die Gewißheit, alle Wahrheit zu sein."

41. I will not rehearse the parameters of the argument here. I have traced out the argument of the chapter in these terms in "Hegel's Phenomenology of Reason and Dualism." For an excellent discussion of the first section of this chapter, see Daniel Dahlstrom, "Challenges to the Rational Observation of Nature in the Phenomenology of Spirit."

42. M235, W/C 160: "Die Vernunft is die Gewißheit, alle *Realität* zu sein."

43. M235, W/C 160: "Dieses *Ansich* oder diese *Realität* ist aber noch ein durchaus allgemeines, die reine *Abstraktion* der Realität."

44. M28, 808, W/C 22–23, 530–31.

45. Hegel discusses ethicality in three spots in the *Phenomenology*: M349–56, M441–76 (the central discussion), and M700–701, W/C 234–38, 290–316, and 458–60. The character of Antigone is implied throughout Hegel's analysis of ethicality (*Sittlichkeit*); see especially M437, M457–60, M464–70, M473–74, W/C 286–87, 299–301, 304–10, 311–3. For an excellent interpretation and appraisal of Hegel's interpretation of *Antigone* that corrects many common misunderstandings, see Shannon Hoff, "Restoring Antigone to Ethical Life."

46. M439, W/C 289: "gegenständliche wirkliche *Welt* . . . welche aber ebenso für das Selbst alle Bedeutung eines Fremden, so wie das Selbst alle Bedeutung eines von ihr getrennten . . . Fürsichseins verloren hat." Compare M436, W/C 285–86: "the 'I' which is immediately a reality, and the world *is* only this reality"; ["das . . . Ich . . . , das unmittelbar die Wirklichkeit ist, und die Welt ist nur diese Wirklichkeit."].

47. M436, W/C 286: "Sondern die Gesetze sind Gedanken seines eignen absoluten Bewußtseins, welche es selbst unmittelbar *hat. Es glaubt* auch nicht an sie. . . . Das sittliche *Selbst*bewußtsein ist durch die *Allgemeinheit* seines *Selbsts unmittelbar* mit dem Wesen eins."

48. See M465, 468, 470, W/C 305, 307–9, 309–10.

49. M354, W/C 236–37: "dieser allgemeine Geist selbst ein einzelner [ist], das Ganze der Sitten und Gesetze, eine *bestimmte* sittliche Substanz, welche erst in dem höhern Momente, nämlich im *Bewußtsein über ihr Wesen*, die Beschränkung auszieht, und nur in diesem Erkennen ihre absolute Wahrheit hat, nicht aber unmittelbar in ihrem *Sein*."

50. Chapter VI, part C, "Spirit that is Certain of Itself: Morality."

51. M670, W/C 440: "Dies, das . . . sich zum *aufgehobnen Diesen* macht, stellt sich dadurch in der Tat als Allgemeines dar. . . . Die Verzeihung, die es dem ersten widerfahren läßt, . . . Böses genannt wurde, als gut anerkennt. . . . Das Wort der Versöhnung ist der *daseiende* Geist, . . .—ein gegenseitiges Anerkennen, welches *der absolute Geist* ist." Compare M793, W/C 519, which draws out the implications of the discussion of conscience and forgiveness. On the themes of

conscience and forgiveness, see Jay Bernstein, "Conscience and Transgression" and "Confession and Forgiveness"; see also Shannon Hoff, *The Laws of the Spirit*, chapters 1 and 5. On ethicality as language, compare David Ciavatta, *Spirit, the Family, and the Unconscious in Hegel's Philosophy*, chapter 1.

52. M780, W/C 508: "Die *Versöhnung* des göttlichen Wesens mit dem *Andern* überhaupt und bestimmt mit dem *Gedanken* desselben, dem *Bösen*, ist also hierin vorgestellt."

53. That "universal reconciliation" is the definitive concept of the revealed religion is the subject of M759 and M779–87, W/C 494–95, 506–15.

54. M794, W/C 519: "Diese Versöhnung des Bewußtseins mit dem Selbstbewußtsein zeigt sich hiemit von der gedoppelten Seite zu Stande gebracht, das einemal im religiösen Geiste, das andremal im Bewußtsein selbst als solchem."

55. M796, W/C 426: "Seine Erfüllung gab sich dieser Begriff, einesteils *im handelnden* seiner selbst gewissen Geist, andernteils in der *Religion*: in der letztern gewann er den absoluten *Inhalt als Inhalt* oder in der Form . . . des Andersseins für das Bewußtsein; hingegen in jener Gestalt ist die Form das Selbst selber, denn sie enthält den *handelnden* seiner selbst gewissen Geist, das Selbst führt das Leben des absoluten Geistes durch."

56. M797, W/C 522: "Was also in der Religion *Inhalt* oder Form des Vorstellens eines *andern* war, dasselbe ist hier eignes *Tun* des *Selbsts*; der Begriff verbindet es, daß der *Inhalt* eignes *Tun* des *Selbsts* ist;—denn dieser Begriff ist, wie wir sehen, das Wissen des Tuns des Selbsts in sich als aller Wesenheit und alles Daseins, das Wissen von *diesem Subjekte* als der *Substanz*, und von der Substanz als diesem Wissen seines Tuns."

57. M798, W/C 523: "Diese letzte Gestalt des Geistes, der Geist, der seinem vollständigen und wahren Inhalte zugleich die Form des Selbsts gibt, und dadurch seinen Begriff ebenso realisiert, als er in dieser Realisierung in seinem Begriffe bleibt, ist das absolute Wissen; es ist der sich in Geistsgestalt wissende Geist oder das *begreifende Wissen* . . . . Der Geist in diesem Elemente dem Bewußtsein *erscheinend . . . ist die Wissenschaft*."

58. M71, W/C 53: "Wir müssen überzeugt sein, daß das Wahre die Natur hat, durchzudringen, wenn seine Zeit gekommen, und daß es nur erscheint, wenn diese gekommen, und deswegen nie zu früh erscheint noch ein unreifes Publikum findet; auch daß das Individuum dieses Effekts bedarf, um das, was noch seine einsame Sache ist, daran sich zu bewähren und die Überzeugung, die nur erst der Besonderheit angehört, als etwas Allgemeines zu erfahren."

Chapter 8

1. The argument of this first section roughly parallels the path traveled in much greater detail in Stephen Houlgate, *The Opening of Hegel's Logic*.

2. Compare M780: "The absolute reality would be but an empty name if in truth there were for it an 'other.'" [W/C 506: "das absolute Wesen hätte nur diesen leeren Namen, wenn es in Wahrheit ein ihm *Anderes*."]

3. Compare Houlgate, *The Opening of Hegel's Logic*, p. 399: "Since infinite

being is inseparable from the *process* of the world, such being cannot simply *be* infinite. It must constantly prove to be infinite and unending in the process whereby finite things themselves end. . . . Infinite being *is* what it is and never ends, but this is only because it always *proves itself* to be infinite and never ending."

4. Compare Paul Guyer, "Hegel, Leibniz und der Widerspruch des Endlichen," p. 258.

5. M149, 156–57, 160–64, W/ C 104, 110–11, 114–18.

6. Houlgate, *The Opening of Hegel's Logic*, p. 399: "Being can turn out to be infinite, however, only insofar as it remains as finite things cease to be. In other words, being proves to be infinite only by grace of the finite. Indeed, as we have seen, it is the unending being that finitude *itself* comes to constitute as it ceases to be mere ceasing-to-be."

7. Compare Houlgate, *The Opening of Hegel's Logic*, on ontological tragedy: "Ontological tragedy for Hegel is not the brutal incursion of nothingness into being but the conversion or slippage of being and nothing into one another through their own nature and 'action'" (p. 282); and "It is also clear, however, that for Hegel tragedy is unavoidable at a deeper level: for however broadminded or virtuous one may be, every finite thing ultimately consigns *itself* to death or destruction simply by being what it is" (p. 374). See also p. 380 on the "sadness" (*Trauer*) that attaches to the thought of finitude.

8. Compare Houlgate, *The Opening of Hegel's Logic*, p. 388: "Finitude, or bringing oneself to an end, is the *tragic* quality at the heart of all being. . . . The fundamental paradox, for Hegel, is thus that what finite things actually *are* entails *failing* to be what they are in various ways. . . . [W]hereas their intrinsic nature and determination—namely, *simply being what they are*—is what *should* characterize them but (because of their limitation) does *not* characterize them in fact."

9. See Houlgate, *The Opening of Hegel's Logic*, p. 399: "[T]he infinite . . . does not consist in the endless generation of new finite things but is rather the selfsame being that continues and relates only to itself in all such othering. Hegel is adamant that there is no such infinite being apart from, before, or outside the process of change and death undergone by finite things." On the relation of the infinite and the finite, see also Rocío Zambrana, "Hegel's Logic of Finitude."

10. *Science of Logic* G I.140, E129; *Philosophy of Nature*, §375, p. 441 (*Enz* 2, p. 535).

11. M255: The inorganic is "no more than the freedom—a freedom opposed to the simple notion of organic Nature—of the *loosely connected* determinatenesses in which the individual forms of Nature are *dissolved* and which, at the same time, breaking away from their continuity, exist on their own account. Air, water, earth, zones, and climate are universal elements of this sort, which constitute the indeterminate simple essense of individualities, and in which these are at the same time reflected into themselves"; W/ C 175: "eben die ihrem einfachen Begriffe entgegengesetzte Freiheit der *losgebundenen* Bestimmtheiten, in welchen die individuelle Natur *zugleich aufgelöst*, und aus deren Kontinuität sie *zugleich* sich absondert und *für sich* ist."

12. M171, W/ C 123–24: "Im ersten Momente ist die bestehende Gestalt; als *fürsichseiend* . . . tritt sie gegen die *allgemeine* Substanz auf, verleugnet diese

Flüssigkeit und Kontinuität mit ihr und behauptet sich als nicht in diesem Allgemeinen aufgelöst, sondern vielmehr als durch die Absonderung von dieser ihrer unorganischen Natur, und durch das Aufzehren derselben sich erhaltend."

13. M171, W/C 124: "Die einfache allgemeine Flüssigkeit ist das *Ansich*, und der Unterschied der Gestalten das *Andere*. Aber diese Flüssigkeit wird selbst durch diesen Unterschied *das Andere*; denn sie ist itzt *für den Unterschied*, welcher an und für sich selbst, und daher die unendliche Bewegung ist, von welcher jenes ruhige Medium aufgezehrt wird."

14. For Hegel's discussion of the organism, see M254, 265–78, W/C 173, 180–87.

15. Hans Jonas, *The Phenomenon of Life*, p. 83.

16. Hegel uses language like this when describing the emergence of the living individual: M171: "Life in the universal fluid medium, a *passive* separating-out of the shapes becomes, just by so doing, a movement of these shapes or Life as a *process*"; W/C 125: "Das Leben in dem allgemeinen flüssigen Medium, ein *ruhiges* Auseinanderlegen der Gestalten wird eben dadurch zur Bewegung derselben, oder zum Leben als *Prozeß*."

17. M136, W/C 95: "[T]he 'matters' posited as independent directly pass over into their unity, and their unity directly unfolds its diversity, and this once again reduces itself to unity. But this movement is what is called *force*. . . . [F]orce is the unconditioned universal which is equally in its own self what it is *for an other*"; ["die selbstständig gesetzten gehen unmittelbar in ihre Einheit, und ihre Einheit unmittelbar in die Entfaltung über, und diese wieder zurück in die Reduktion. Diese Bewegung ist aber dasjenige, was *Kraft* gennant wird. . . . [D]ie Kraft das unbedingt Allgemeine [ist], welches, was es *für ein Anderes*, ebenso an sich selbst ist."].

18. M149, W/C 104–5. I have discussed Hegel's chapter "Force and Understanding" in relationship to natural science in "The Metaphysics of Consciousness and the Hermeneutics of Social Life."

19. M143, W/C 100: "Dieses wahrhafte Wesen der Dinge hat sich itzt so bestimmt, daß es nicht unmittelbar für das Bewußtsein ist, sondern daß dieses ein mittelbares Verhältnis zu dem Innern hat, und als Verstand *durch diese Mitte des Spiels der Kräfte in den wahren Hintergrund der Dinge blickt*."

20. See M163, W/C 116: "im *Innern* erst ist sie selbst frei hervorgetreten. Die Erscheinung oder das Spiel der Kräfte stellt sie selbst schon dar, aber als *Erklären* tritt sie zunächst frei hervor."

21. M152, W/C 107: "So ist, zum Beispiel, die *einfache* Elektrizität die *Kraft*; der Ausdruck des Unterschieds aber fällt in *das Gesetz*; dieser Unterschied ist positive und negative Elektrizität. . . . Die Elektrizität selbst ist nicht der Unterschied an sich oder in ihrem Wesen das Doppelwesen von positiver und negativer Elektrizität; daher man zu sagen pflegt, sie *habe* das Gesetz, auf diese Weise *zu sein*, auch wohl, sie *habe die Eigenschaft*, so sich zu äußern. Diese Eigenschaft ist zwar wesentliche und einzige Eigenschaft dieser Kraft, oder sie ist ihr *notwendig*. Aber die Notwendigkeit ist hier ein leeres Wort; die Kraft *muß* eben, *weil* sie *muß*, so sich verdoppeln."

22. *Philosophy of Right*, *Zusatz* to section 268 [H], p. 289.

23. Compare Houlgate, *The Opening of Hegel's Logic*, p. 391: "Inanimate things are, of course, unaware that they are restricted in any way or that they should be anything other than they are. Human beings, by contrast, are often acutely conscious that they have an obligation to improve themselves—for example, that they should be fully and explicitly free—and can feel pain in the knowledge that they fall short of what they should be." "The animal that takes account of itself" (*zōion logon echon*) is Aristotle's definition of the human being; see especially *Politics*, bk. 1, chap. 3 and *Nicomachean Ethics*, bk. 1, chap. 7. Heidegger's extended analysis of animality and *logos* in *The Fundamental Concepts of Metaphysics* is a helpful complementary study.

24. M28, W/C 22–23: "[I]n dem pädagogischen Fortschreiten die wie im Schattenrisse nachgezeichnete Geschichte der Bildung der Welt erkennen werden. Dies vergangne Dasein ist schon erworbnes Eigentum des allgemeinen Geistes, der die Substanz des Individuums oder seine unorganische Natur ausgemacht.—Die Bildung des Individuums in dieser Rücksicht besteht von seiner Seite aus betrachtet, darin, daß es dies Vorhandne erwerbe, seine unorganische Natur in sich zehre und für sich in Besitz nehme."

25. *Philosophy of Right*, section 151.

26. See M351, 354, W/C 235–37. These themes are given substantial discussion through David V. Ciavatta, *Spirit, the Family and the Unconscious in Hegel's Philosophy*.

27. Compare *Philosophy of Right*, section 175: "[Children's] *upbringing* has the *positive* determination that, in them, the ethical is given the form of immediate *feeling* [*Empfindung*] which is still without opposition, so that their early emotional life may be lived in this [context], as the *basis* of ethical life, in love, trust, and obedience."

28. M437, W/C 286: "So gelten sie der Antigone des Sophokles als der Götter *ungeschriebnes und untrügliches* Recht: 'nicht etwa jetzt und gestern, sondern immerdar / lebt es, und keiner weiß, von wannen es erschein.'"

29. M436, W/C 287–88.

30. Of course, as I argued in the preceding chapter, the attitude of morality is itself a (different) form of "unhappy consciousness."

31. M475, W/C 314: "Das Gemeinwesen kann sich aber nur durch Unterdrückung dieses Geistes der Einzelnheit erhalten, und, weil er wesentliches Moment ist, erzeugt es ihm zwar ebenso, und zwar durch die unterdrückende Haltung gegen denselben als ein feindseliges Prinzip."

32. See M424–25, W/C 278–80, M621, W/C 408. I have developed this theme more fully in "The Contradictions of Moral Life," chapter 10 of *Reading Hegel's Phenomenology*.

33. See *Philosophy of Right*, Remark (e) to section 140 (p. 178): "But *the law does not act*; only an actual human being acts"; and compare M464, W/C 304.

34. See M16, W/C 12–13.

35. Compare *Philosophy of Right*, remark to section 187 (p. 224): "Spirit attains its actuality only through internal division, by imposing this limitation and finitude upon itself in natural needs and the continuum of this external necessity, and, *in the very process of adapting itself to these* limitations, by overcoming them and gaining its *objective* existence within them."

36. M189–96, W/C 132–36.

37. M295, W/C 199: "Aber die organische Natur hat keine Geschichte; sie fällt von ihrem Allgemeinen, dem Leben, unmittelbar in die Einzelnheit des Daseins herunter . . . . [D]as Ganze nicht in ihm vorhanden ist, und dies ist nicht darin vorhanden, weil es nicht als Ganzes hier *für sich* ist."

38. M171–72, W/C 125: ". . . das sich entwickelnde, und seine Entwicklung auflösende und in dieser Bewegung sich einfach erhaltende Ganze. . . . Sie ist die *einfache Gattung*, welche in der Bewegung des Lebens selbst nicht für *sich als* dies *Einfache existiert*; sondern . . . verweist das Leben auf ein anderes, als es ist, nämlich auf das Bewußtsein, für welches es als diese Einheit, oder als Gattung, ist."

39. M196, W/C 135: "[I]n dem Bilden des Dinges wird ihm die eigne Negativität, sein Fürsichsein, . . . dadurch zum Gegenstande. . . . [Es] setzt *sich* als ein solches in das Element des Bleibens; und wird hiedurch *für sich selbst*, ein *für sich Seiendes*."

40. M188–90, W/C 131–33.

41. M194, W/C 134: "Dies Bewußtsein hat nämlich nicht um dieses oder jenes, noch für diesen oder jenen Augenblick Angst gehabt, sondern um sein ganzes Wesen; denn es hat die Furcht des Todes . . . empfunden."

42. M189, W/C 132: "In dieser Erfahrung wird es dem Selbstbewußtsein, daß ihm das Leben so wesentlich als das reine Selbstbewußtsein ist."

43. M193–94, W/C 134.

44. M196, W/C 135–36.

45. I have taken up this theme in more detail in "Hermeneutical Pressure and the Space of Dialectic."

46. *Science of Logic* G II.551, E826.

47. W72, W/C 53: ". . . so muß dieses [das Individuum], wie die Natur der Wissenschaft schon es mit sich bringt, sich um so mehr vergessen, und zwar werden und tun, was es kann, aber es muß ebenso weniger von ihm gefordert werden, wie es selbst weniger von sich erwarten und für sich fordern darf."

Chapter 9

1. G. W. F. Hegel, *Reason in History*, pp. 22–25. For discussion of this theme, see Réal Fillion, *Multicultural Dynamics and the Ends of History*, chapter 4.

2. *Reason in History*, pp. 22 and 25.

3. See *Reason in History*, pp. 23–24. "Ethicality" and "Culture" are, respectively, parts A and B of chapter VI of the *Phenomenology*, "Spirit."

4. *Reason in History*, p. 23.

5. M455, W/C 297: "Das *Gemeinwesen*, das obere und offenbar an der Sonne geltende Gesetz, hat seine wirkliche Lebendigkeit in der *Regierung*, als worin es Individuum ist. Sie ist der *in sich reflektierte wirkliche* Geist, das einfache *Selbst* der ganzen sittlichen Substanz."

6. On behalf of the community, rather than on behalf of their independent (e.g., familial) interests; see M455: "The spirit of universal assembly and association is the simple and negative essence of those systems which tend to isolate themselves. In order not to let them become rooted and set in this isolation,

thereby breaking up the whole and letting the spirit evaporate . . ."; W/C 298: "Der Geist der allgemeinen Zusammenkunft ist die *Einfachheit* und das *negative* Wesen dieser sich isolierenden Systeme. Um sie nicht in dieses Isolieren einwurzeln und festwerden, hiedurch das Ganze auseinanderfallen und den Geist verfliegen zu lassen. . . ." Compare Aristotle, *Politics,* bk. 1, chaps. 1–2.

7. Aristotle, *Physics,* bk. 2, chap. 1; *Categories,* chap. 5; *History of Animals,* bk. 1, chap. 1.

8. *Nicomachean Ethics,* bk. 1, chap. 7.

9. For the meaning of Aristotle's definition of human nature, see Francis Sparshott, *Taking Life Seriously.*

10. M464, W/C 304: "die ruhige Organisation und Bewegung der sittlichen Welt . . . [die] Ordnung und Übereinstimmung ihrer beiden Wesen . . . deren eins das andere bewährt und vervollständigt." Compare M463: "The ethical realm is in this way in its enduring existence an immaculate world, a world unsullied by any internal dissension. Similarly, its process is a tranquil transition of one of its powers into the other, in such a way that each preserves and brings forth the other"; W/C 303: ["Das sittliche Reich ist auf diese Weise in seinem *Bestehen* eine unbefleckte durch keinen Zwiespalt verunreinigte Welt. Ebenso ist seine Bewegung ein ruhiges Werden der einen Macht desselben zur andern, so daß jede die andere selbst erhält und hervorbringt."].

11. See M473: "But that [the youth] still belongs to the nature from which he wrenched himself free is evidenced by the fact that he emerges in the contingent form of two brothers, each of whom with equal rights takes possession of the community"; W/C 311: "daß er [der Jüngling] aber der Natur, der er sich entriß, noch angehöre, erweist sich so, daß er in der Zufälligkeit zweier Brüder heraustritt, welche mit gleichem Rechte sich desselben [des Gemeinswesens] bemächtigen."

12. M473, W/C 311: "[Es] bietet sich . . . nach seiner formellen Seite, als der Widerstreit der Sittlichkeit und des Selbstbewußtseins mit der bewußtlosen Natur und einer durch sie vorhandenen Zufälligkeit . . . und seinem Inhalte nach als der Zwiespalt des göttlichen und menschlichen Gesetzes dar."

13. M475, W/C 314: "Das Gemeinwesen kann sich aber nur durch Unterdrückung dieses Geist der Einzelnheit erhalten."

14. On the conflation of nature and freedom in ethicality, see M451 and 465, W/C 294–95 and 305. On the interpretation of Hegel's text here, see Shannon Hoff, "Restoring Antigone to Ethical Life."

15. This latter is the (Roman) "Condition of Right" (Miller's "Legal Status"), which Hegel describes in M477–83, W/C 316–20. For a helpful discussion and defence of Hegel's position, see Patricia Fagan, "Philosophical History and the Roman Empire."

16. *Philosophy of Right,* remark to section 124: "The right of *subjective freedom* is the pivotal and focal point in the difference between *antiquity* and the *modern* age."

17. *Reason in History,* p. 24.

18. For a helpful introduction to St. Paul, see Alain Badiou, *Saint Paul: The Foundation of Universalism.*

19. M488, W/C 324: "das Selbstbewußtsein . . . hat nur *Realitat,* insofern es sich selbst entfremdet; hiedurch setzt es sich als allgemeines, und diese seine Allgemeinheit ist sein Gelten und Wirklichkeit. Diese *Gleichheit* mit allen ist daher nicht . . . jenes unmittelbare Anerkanntsein und Gelten des Selbstbewußtseins, darum weil *es ist;* sondern daß es gelte, ist durch die entfremdende Vermittlung, sich dem Allgemeinen gemäß gemacht zu haben."

20. M485, W/C 321: "diesem Bewußtsein . . . steht jene Einheit des Selbst und des Wesens gegenüber, dem *wirklichen* das *reine Bewußtsein.*" This is a structure of "unhappy consciousness," which is discussed in chapter 7.

21. M491, W/C 326: "Das Selbst ist sich nur als *aufgehobenes* wirklich."

22. M489, W/C 324: "Wodurch also das Individuum hier Gelten und Wirklichkeit hat, ist die *Bildung.* Seine wahre *ursprüngliche Natur* und Substanz ist der Geist der *Entfremdung* des *natürlichen* Seins. . . . Diese Individualität *bildet* sich zu dem, was sie *an sich* ist, und erst dadurch *ist sie an sich* und hat wirkliches Dasein."

23. M490, W/C 325: "Was in Beziehung auf das einzelne *Individuum* als seine Bildung erscheint, ist das wesentliche Moment der *Substanz* selbst. . . . Die Bewegung der sich bildenden Individualität ist daher unmittelbar das Werden derselben als des allgemeinen gegenständlichen Wesens, d. h. das Werden der wirklichen Welt."

24. M486, W/C 321–23 summarizes the entire path of "culture."

25. *Discipline and Punish,* p. 189.

26. *Discipline and Punish,* p. 199.

27. On this point, see Kirsten Jacobson, "The Experience of Home and the Space of Citizenship."

28. M587, W/C 388: "Es ist nach Aufhebung der unterschiedenen geistigen Massen, und des beschränkten Lebens der Individuen . . . nur die Bewegung des allgemeinen Selbstbewußtseins in sich selbst vorhanden, als eine Wechselwirkung desselben in der Form *der Allgemeinheit* und des *persönlichen* Bewußtseins. . . . [D]ies *einzelne* Bewußtsein ist sich seiner ebenso unmittelbar als allgemeinen Willens bewußt. . . . [I]n Tätigkeit übergehend und Gegenständlichkeit erschaffend, macht es also nicht Einzelnes, sondern nur Gesetze und Staatsaktionen."

29. M588, W/C 388–89: "Es folgt daraus, daß es zu keinem positiven Werke . . . kommen kann. . . . Das Werk, zu welchem die sich *Bewußtsein* gebende Freiheit sich machen könnte, würde darin bestehen, daß sie . . . sich zum *Gegenstande* und *bleibenden Sein* machte. . . . in das Element des *Seins* gesetzt, erhielte sie die Bedeutung einer *bestimmten;* sie hörte auf, in Wahrheit allgemeines Selbstbewußtsein zu sein."

30. M588–91, W/C 388–91.

31. M592, W/C 391: "In diesem ihrem eigentümlichen *Werke* wird die absolute Freiheit sich zum Gegenstande, und das Selbstbewußtsein erfährt, was sie ist. *An sich* ist sie eben dies *abstrakte Selbstbewußtsein,* welches allen Unterschied und alles Bestehen des Unterschiedes in sich vertilgt. Als dieses ist sie sich der Gegenstand; der *Schrecken* des Todes ist die Anschauung dieses ihres negativen Wesens."

32. *Reason in History,* p. 22.

33. M780, W/C 506: "das absolute Wesen hätte nur diesen leeren Namen, wenn es in Wahrheit ein ihm *Anderes . . . gäbe*."

34. For a substantially different approach to the theme of democracy in Hegel's philosophy of history, see Mark Tunick, "Hegel's Claim About Democracy and his Philosophy of History." On the topic of democracy in general, see Humberto Schettino, "The Notion of Politics in Marx's Early Writings."

35. For a parallel argument, see "Spirit and Scepticism," chapter 9 of *Reading Hegel's Phenomenology*.

36. This is the central thesis of Réal Fillion, *Multicultural Dynamics and the Ends of History*.

Chapter 10

1. Merleau-Ponty, *Phenomenology of Perception*, introduction, chapter 1, and passim. Hegel restricts the term "perception" [*Wahrnemung*] to the specific experience of the apprehension of things-with-properties; though this has substantial overlap with Merleau-Ponty's use of "perception," the broad range of experience Merleau-Ponty includes under this designation would more closely correspond with what Hegel calls "consciousness" [*Bewußtsein*] or "experience" [*Erfahrung*]. See Russon, *Reading Hegel's Phenomenology*, chapters 1–3 for the continuity of this twentieth-century phenomenological position with Hegel's position in the *Phenomenology of Spirit*.

2. *Phenomenology of Perception*, p. 10.

3. Chapter 4, part A, "Independence and Dependence of Self-Consciousness: Lordship and Bondage," M178–96, W/C 111–19. The tensions and transformations that characterize the dialectic in which the attitude of desire confronts the self-determination of the free other are studied in Russon, *Reading Hegel's Phenomenology*, chapters 5 and 6. The themes in this section very closely parallel Fichte's discussion of the intersubjective and bodily conditions of freedom in his *Foundations of Natural Right*; on this topic, see Russon, "The Body as Site of Action and Intersubjectivity."

4. M176 and 182, W/C 126: "Es ist ein Gegenstand für das Bewußtsein, welcher an sich selbst sein Anderssein oder den Unterschied als einen nichtigen setzt, und darin selbstständig ist"; and 128–29: "[Es] hat den Gegenstand nicht vor sich, wie er nur für die Begierde zunächst ist, sondern einen für sich seienden selbstständigen, über welchen es darum nichts für sich vermag, wenn er nicht an sich selbst dies tut, was es an ihm tut."

5. Compare Merleau-Ponty's discussion of the "phantom limb" and the "habit body," *Phenomenology of Perception*, part 1, chapter 1, especially p. 95. Merleau-Ponty's analysis of the phantom limb is helpfully discussed by Maria Talero, "Merleau-Ponty and the Bodily Subject of Learning," and by Kirsten Jacobson, *Being at Home: A Phenomenological Analysis of the Experience of Space*, pp. 104–7 and 126–36. See also Russon, "Haunted by History."

6. Compare Heidegger, *Being and Time*, pp. 116–17.

7. M182, W/C 128: "das Andere ist . . . selbstständig, in sich beschlossen, und es ist nichts in ihm, was nicht durch es selbst ist."

8. Compare Sartre's discussion of the perceptual changes that characterize encountering another person in a park in *Being and Nothingness*, pp. 341–43.

9. In chapter 2, we investigated the experience to which Hegel gives the technical name "perception" ["*Wahrnemung*"], and ultimately came to the same conclusion.

10. *Philosophy of Right, Zusatz* (G) to section 10, p. 45. Compare Houlgate, *An Introduction to Hegel*, p. 17: "For Hegel, the absolute truth of humanity is that human beings have no fixed, given identity, but rather determine and produce their identity and their world in history, and that they gradually come to the recognition of this fact in history." Compare also Pippin, *Idealism as Modernism*, p. 227: "this is the original meaning of the Hegelian doctrine of negation: Only by losing or 'negating' my natural self can I become a genuine self, or self-conscious subject."

11. See Merleau-Ponty, *Phenomenology of Perception*, p. 159.

12. See *Philosophy of Right*, section 47, and compare sections 12–13, including *Zusatz* (H) to section 13, p. 47: "A will which resolves on nothing is not an actual will."

13. *Philosophy of Right*, section 6, p. 39, *Grundlinien*, p. 52.

14. *Philosophy of Right*, section 41, p. 73, *Grundlinien*, p. 102, and compare the *Zusatz* (H) to section 41. See also section 48, and the idea that one must take possession of one's own body. On the theme of taking possession of one's own body, see David Ciavatta, "Hegel on Owning One's Own Body."

15. See *Philosophy of Right*, section 149, on the notion of freedom through binds, and compare *Philosophy of Mind*, §539, p. 266: "In fact, every true law is a freedom" (*Enz* 3, p. 353). As Dieter Henrich notes, the account of "Objective Spirit" in the *Encyclopaedia* is often more helpful than the *Philosophy of Right* is for grasping the systematic character of the argument. See Henrich, "Logical Form and Real Totality," p. 263; for the possible differences between these accounts, see pp. 257–263.

16. *Lectures on Natural Right and Political Science*, section 4, pp. 53–54. See also *Lectures on Natural Right and Political Science*, sections 21–22, on the theme of work. "Idea," in Hegel's vocabulary, refers to a reality that is a self-expression or a self-manifestation, such that its actual existence is adequate to its nature. See *Science of Logic*, E 755–60, G II.462–69.

17. For "negative self-relation," see *Science of Logic*, E 398–99, G II.22–24. In general, the theme of the relation of the universal and the determinate that runs throughout the analysis of freedom in the *Philosophy of Right* is a working out of the logic of the "concept" as that is articulated in the *Science of Logic*. On the relation of the logic of the concept (and, more specifically, the logic of the syllogism) as it relates to the *Philosophy of Right*, see Henrich, "Logical Form and Real Totality," pp. 241–67. The relation of Hegel's *Science of Logic* to his *Philosophy of Right* is also discussed throughout Kolb, *The Critique of Pure Modernity*.

18. Compare M178: "The twofold significance of the distinct moments has

in the nature of self-consciousness to be infinite, or directly the opposite of the determinateness in which it is posited"; W/C 128: "Die Doppelsinnigkeit des Unterschiedenen liegt in dem Wesen des Selbstbewußtseins, unendlich oder unmittelbar das Gegenteil der Bestimmtheit, in der es gesetzt ist, zu sein."

19. *Lectures on Natural Right and Political Science,* section 4, p. 53.

20. See Michael Wolff, "Hegel's Organicist Theory of the State," p. 299.

21. See *Philosophy of Mind,* section 538, p. 264: "Laws express the content-determinations [*Inhalts-Bestimmungen*] for objective freedom" (*Enz* 3, p. 331).

22. See *Philosophy of Right,* section 164, p. 204, *Grundlinien,* p. 315, for language as "the most spiritual existence of the spiritual."

23. See *Philosophy of Mind,* section 502, p. 248, and compare §539, pp. 265–68; (*Enz* 3, pp. 311–12, 331–35).

24. See especially *Philosophy of Mind,* sections 552, 540, and 548, on the state as a natural individual (*Enz* 3, pp. 353–65, 336, 347); see especially section 540, pp. 268–69: "It is the indwelling spirit and history—and indeed the history is only *its* history—by which constitutions have been and are made" (*Enz* 3, p. 336). See also sections 529 on contingency and 536 on history (*Enz* 3, pp. 323–26, 350).

25. See *Lectures on Natural Right and Political Science,* section 71: "The ethical substance is absolute foundation." Compare *Philosophy of Mind,* section 486, p. 242: "This 'reality,' in general, where free will has *existence,* is *Recht*—the term being taken in a comprehensive sense not merely as the limited juristic law, but as the actual body of all the conditions of freedom" (*Enz* 3, p. 304).

26. See *Philosophy of Right,* section 153, for the idea that it is only within ethical actuality that the rights-bearing individual can exist (and compare the *Zusatz* [H]). For the idea that laws appear as restrictions to individuals but are actually their ground, see *Philosophy of Mind* sections 538 and 539 (*Enz* 3, pp. 331–35). See also *Philosophy of Mind* section 544, pp. 272–73, on the distinction of *vulgus* and *populus*: "The aggregate of private persons is often spoken of as the *nation*: but as such an aggregate it is *vulgus,* not *populus* . . . . Such a condition of a nation is a condition of lawlessness, demoralization, brutishness: in it the nation would only be a shapeless, wild, blind force. . . . If there is to be any sense in embarking upon the question of the participation of private persons in public affairs, it is not a brutish mass, but an already organized nation—one in which a governmental power exists—which should be presupposed" (*Enz* 3, pp. 341–42). Compare "System of Ethical Life" in *System of Ethical Life (1802/03) and First Philosophy of Spirit,* pp. 144, *Jenaer Systementwürfe I,* p. 462: "Since the people is a living indifference, and all natural difference is nullified, the individual intuits himself as himself in every other individual; he reaches supreme subject-objectivity; and this identity of all is just for this reason not an abstract one, not an equality of citizenship, but an absolute one and one that is intuited, displaying itself in empirical consciousness, in the consciousness of the particular. The universal, the spirit, is in each man and for the apprehension of each man, even so far as he is a single individual."

27. *Phenomenology,* M469, W/C316.22; compare the "hidden divine law," M477, W/C316.12–13.

28. Compare F. W. J. Schelling, *System of Transcendental Idealism,* pp. 166–67.

29. On these points, see *Philosophy of Mind,* sections 490–491 (*Enz* 3, p. 307).

30. This again is the idea developed in the *Phenomenology of Spirit* that self-consciousness is realized in a dialectic of mutual recognition; for relevant texts, see note 5, above. For law as the context in which mutual recognition is accomplished, see in particular Russon, *Reading Hegel's Phenomenology*, chapter 6, pp. 91–92, and chapter 12, pp. 173–74. See *Philosophy of Mind*, section 541 (*Enz* 3, pp. 336–38) on the idea that it is the articulateness of laws that allows differences to be recognized, and compare *Philosophy of Mind*, section 515 (*Enz* 3, 318–19), on the idea that it is in the experience of ethicality that one accomplishes one's sense of self-identity.

31. *Philosophy of Mind*, section 487 (*Enz* 3, p. 306), *Philosophy of Right*, section 142.

32. See *Phenomenology*, M349–55, and M441, W/C 234–37, 290.

33. *Philosophy of Mind*, section 535 (*Enz* 3, p. 330); *Philosophy of Right*, section 257.

34. *Philosophy of Mind*, section 549, p. 279 (*Enz* 3, p. 350), translation modified.

35. *Philosophy of Mind*, section 541 (*Enz* 3, 336–38). Compare *Philosophy of Right*, section 255, p. 272: "The *family* is the first *ethical* root of the state; the *corporation* is the second, and it is based in civil society," *Grundlinien*, p. 396. Compare also *Lectures on Natural Right and Political Science*, section 69 on the "right of substance" and the "right of individuals" as the essential moments of ethicality; compare also section 122. According to the categories of Hegel's *Science of Logic*, such a reality that exists as a unity only in and as an opposition of its constituent species operates according to the logic of "the concept." See *Science of Logic*, E 583, 600–5, especially 603, G II.253, 273–79, especially 277.

36. *Phenomenology*, M450, W/C 293–94. The family is thus the "real" beginning of the *Philosophy of Right* in that it provides the context within which all the other determinations of right emerge; see *Philosophy of Right*, sections 158 and 256.

37. *Philosophy of Right*, section 157, *Lectures on Natural Right and Political Science*, sections 89, 91.

38. See *Lectures on Natural Right and Political Science*, section 137, *Philosophy of Right*, section 256, p. 274: "In the development of civil society, the ethical substance takes on its *infinite form*" (*Grundlinien*, p. 398).

39. *Lectures on Natural Right and Political Science*, remark to section 86, p. 157. This discipline is not just an external imposition however: "What sets children on the upward path is their impulse to grow or mature, dissatisfaction with their present self."

40. For a rich, thorough, and highly insightful study of the experience of family membership, see Ciavatta, *Spirit, the Family, and the Unconscious in Hegel's Philosophy*.

41. *Lectures on Natural Right and Political Science*, section 73, p. 138.

42. See *Philosophy of Right*, section 158, *Zusatz* (H,G). On the nature of family membership, see Ciavatta, "The Unreflective Bonds of Intimacy."

43. *Lectures on Natural Right and Political Science*, remark to section 73, p. 138.

44. In the marriage bond, the individuals involved achieve their identity

through their shared accomplishment of single identity: "With their exclusive individualities these personalities combine to form a *single person*" (*Philosophy of Mind*, section 519, *Enz* 3, p. 320).

45. *Philosophy of Mind*, section 521 (*Enz* 3, p. 320).

46. *Lectures on Natural Right and Political Science*, remark to section 86, p. 156.

47. *Lectures on Natural Right and Political Science*, remark to section 86, p. 158.

48. Aristotle, *Poetics*, chap. 4.1448b4–8. See *Philosophy of Right*, section 175, p. 212, regarding children: "[T]heir *upbringing* has the *positive* determination that, in them, the ethical is given the form of immediate *feeling* [*Empfindung*], *which is still without opposition* [my emphasis], so that their early emotional life may be lived in this [context], as the *basis* of ethical life, in love, trust and obedience"; *Grundlinien*, p. 327.

49. *Philosophy of Mind*, section 521 (*Enz* 3, p. 320); *Philosophy of Right*, section 158 *Zusatz* (H,G).

50. Compare M451, 455, W/C 294–95, 297–98.

51. It is worth noting that the membership in civil society is *identical* to the membership in family life: civil society and family are two different *ways* that the same body of individuals structures its practices of mutual recognition. On the insufficiency of the family to adequately realize freedom and its opposition to the other essential domains of freedom (civil society and state), compare *Phenomenology*, M450, W/C 294.

52. See for example Stephen B. Smith, *Hegel's Critique of Liberalism*.

53. Critics of liberalism are legion; those oriented to our "embeddedness" include Michael Sandel, Alisdair MacIntyre, Charles Taylor, David Hollenbach, Michael Walzer, Patricia Williams, Charles W. Mills, Will Kymlicka, Alison Jaggar, Iris Young, Drucilla Cornell, Nancy Fraser, and Lisa Schwartzman.

54. See "Hegel's First Philosophy of Spirit," in *System of Ethical Life (1802/03) and First Philosophy of Spirit*, pp. 248–49, *Jenaer Systementwürfe I*, p. 230. On the role of the state in resisting this, see also *Natural Law*, p. 94, *Gesammelte Werke* Bd. 4, p. 451: "But the ethical whole must on the contrary preserve in this [commercial] system the awareness of its inner nullity, and impede both its burgeoning in point of quantity, and the development of ever greater difference and inequality for which its nature strives."

55. *Philosophy of Mind*, sections 538–39 (*Enz* 3, pp. 331–35).

56. *Philosophy of Right*, section 164.

57. *Philosophy of Right*, remark to section 256. On this inversion of the notion of "belonging," see Michael Wolff, "Hegel's Organicist Theory of the State," p. 296.

58. The (conceptual) logic of social life is complete in our seeing the essential opposition of these institutions and the demand to accomplish a social unity through this *as* constituting the "reality" of freedom, a reality to which the "internal" logics of family and civil society are inadequate. It has been the task of the *Philosophy of Right* to articulate the essential dimensions of this structure; see *Philosophy of Mind*, section 486 (*Enz* 3, pp. 304–5). For interpretation of Hegel's conception of the "end of history," see Richard Dien Winfield, "The Theory and Practice of the History of Freedom," Stephen Houlgate, "World History as

Progress of Consciousness," and Will Dudley, "Freedom In and Through Hegel's Philosophy."

59. See *Philosophy of Mind*, sections 529 and 542 (*Enz* 3, pp. 323–26, 338–39) on the necessity and arbitrariness of the decisive finitude that characterizes the explicit positedness that is essential to the domain of the state. Compare sections 531 (*Enz* 3, p. 328) on the "barbaric origins of the jury." On these topics, see William Conklin, *Hegel's Laws: The Legitimacy of a Modern Legal Order.*

60. That they can be taken up in a "closed" way is the reason that any institution within the society can work against the good of society, whether, for example, in the repressive conservatism of family values and traditionalism or in the exploitative instrumentalism of the free market. On these themes, see T. E. Wartenburg, "Poverty and Class Struggle in Hegel's Theory of Civil Society," and Karin de Boer, "Hegel's Account of the Present." For an excellent discussion of the problem of the free market as that is portrayed in Hegel's early writings, see Nathan Ross, "The Mechanization of Labor and the Birth of Modern Ethicality in Hegel's Jena Writings."

61. *Philosophy of Mind*, section 483 (*Enz* 3, p. 303).

62. *Philosophy of Mind*, section 484 (*Enz* 3, p. 303).

63. *Philosophy of Mind*, section 513 (*Enz* 3, pp. 317–18).

64. See *Philosophy of Mind*, sections 548 and 549 (*Enz* 3, pp. 347–52), on the idea that states have a tendency, parallel to that of the individual, to become a center [*Zentrum*]; that is, to close in self-interestedly on the terms of their limited, finite identities; it is the process of history that demonstrates the insufficiency of these finite identities to the infinite demands of freedom. Compare also *Philosophy of Mind*, section 552, especially p. 283 (*Enz* 3, p. 354), on the idea that the finitude ethical spirit with which the reality of freedom is itself "freed" in the overcoming of its finitude.

65. See *Philosophy of Mind*, section 536 (*Enz* 3, p. 530), regarding our definedness by inner law, outer law, and history.

66. *Philosophy of Mind*, section 550, p. 481 (translation modified): "The freeing of spirit, in which it proceeds to come to itself and to realize its truth, and the business of so doing, is the supreme right, the absolute law." (And therefore that to which all particular laws answer.) "Against this absolute will the other particular national wills have no right" (*Enz* 3, pp. 353–4).

67. In this sense, we can say that right is completed in the recognition of it—the practical recognition of it, that is, the enactment of it—as language.

68. See Réal Fillion, *Multicultural Dynamics and the Ends of History*, and John Russon, "Hegel, Heidegger and Ethnicity." See also Andrew Buchwalter, "Is Hegel's Philosophy of History Eurocentric?" and "Hegel's Concept of an International 'We.'"

69. Compare Hegel's reference to the "infinite elasticity [*die unendliche Elastizität*] of the absolute form," *Philosophy of Mind*, section 552, p. 291 (*Enz* 3, p. 439).

70. Compare Ermanno Bencivenga, *Hegel's Dialectical Logic*, p. 70: "Hegel wants to understand *his own* time, the time in which he is living, the one that is contemporaneous with him. He also says, however, that the only data relevant to

his rationalizing task concerns what has *already* happened. The conjunction of these two statements leaves one with the strange conclusion that Hegel would have to be seeing his own present as past—that in some way he would have to have a *future* position with respect to it. This strange conclusion is exactly right."

71. See *Philosophy of Mind,* section 552, pp. 283, 286, 290 (*Enz* 3, pp. 431, 434, 438). Compare *Lectures on Natural Right and Political Science,* section 123, p. 222.

72. Preface to the *Philosophy of Right,* p. 21, *Grundlinien,* p. 26.

Chapter 11

1. M477–83, W/ C 316–20, especially M480: "[W]hat counts as absolute, essential being is self-consciousness as the sheer *empty unit* of the person"; W/ C 317: "[W]as als das absolute Wesen gilt, ist das Selbstbewußtsein als das reine *leere Eins* der Person"; and M479: "Stoicism is nothing else but the consciousness which reduces to abstract form the principle of legal status"; W/ C 317: "Er [Stoizismus] ist nichts anderes als das Bewußtsein, welches das Prinzip des Rechtszustands . . . auf seine abstrakte Form bringt." For the interpretation of this section, see Patricia Fagan, "Philosophical History and the Roman Empire," and Shannon Hoff, "The Rights of Personhood," chapter 3 of *The Laws of the Spirit.* I have discussed this section in *The Self and Its Body in Hegel's Phenomenology of Spirit,* pp. 87, 92.

2. M488, W/ C 324: "setzt es sich als allgemeines, und diese seine Allgemeinheit ist sein Gelten und Wirklichkeit. Diese *Gleichheit* mit allen ist daher nicht jene Gleichheit des Rechts, nicht jenes unmittelbare Anerkanntsein und Gelten des Selbstbewußtseins, darum weil *es ist;* sondern daß es gelte, ist durch die entfremdende Vermittlung, sich dem Allgemeinen gemäß gemacht zu haben."

3. Immanuel Kant, *Groundwork for the Metaphysics of Morals;* on the political vision associated with this point of view see "The Idea of a Universal History from a Cosmopolitan Perspective."

4. For the Christian principle that "all are free," see *Reason in History,* p. 24.

5. M582–95, W/ C 385–94. For an excellent and detailed study of Hegel's interpretation of the French Revolution, see Rebecca Comay, *Mourning Sickness.* See also David Ciavatta, "The Event of Absolute Freedom."

6. M587, W/ C 388: "der allgemeine Willen geht *in sich,* und ist *einzelner* Willen. . . . [Das] einzelne Bewußtsein ist sich seiner ebenso unmittelbar als allgemeinen Willens bewußt."

7. M586, W/ C 387: "das Einzelne ist sich unmittelbar selbst . . . allgemeines Bewußtsein und Willen"; and M587, W/ C 388: "in Tätigkeit übergehend und Gegenständlichkeit erschaffend, macht es also nichts Einzelnes, sondern nur Gesetze und Staatsaktionen."

8. M588, W/ C 389: "in das Element des *Seins* gesetzt, erhielte sie [die Persönlichkeit] die Bedeutung einer *bestimmten;* sie hörte auf, in Wahrheit allgemeines Selbstbewußtsein zu sein."

9. M590, W/ C 389: "Aber die höchste und der allgemeinen Freiheit entgegengesetzteste Wirklichkeit oder vielmehr der einzige Gegenstand, der für sie noch wird, ist die Freiheit und Einzelnheit des wirklichen Selbstbewußtseins selbst."

10. M590, W/C 389–90: [N]un . . . ist dies ihr einziger Gegenstand;—ein Gegenstand, der keinen andern Inhalt, Besitz, Dasein und äußerliche Ausdehnung mehr hat, sondern er is nur dies Wissen von sich als absolut reinem und freiem einzelnem Selbst."

11. M590, W/C: "An was er erfaßt werden kann, ist allein sein *abstraktes* Dasein überhaupt."

12. M588, W/C 388–89. Aspects of the problem of translating the notion of a "people's revolution" into a determinate government can be seen in the recent example of the Egyptian revolution of 2011 and the subsequent attempts to establish a new government.

13. M589, W/C 389.

14. M591, W/C 390–91.

15. M590 and 591, W/C 390: "Das einzige Werk und Tat der allgemeinen Freiheit ist daher der *Tod* . . . [worin] was negiert wird, ist der unerfüllte Punkt des absolut freien Selbsts" and W/C 391: "[Es besteht in] dem trocknen Vertilgen dieses seienden Selbsts, an dem nichts sonst wegzunehmen ist, als nur sein Sein selbst." This theme is further developed in M592–93, W/C 391–92. See Rebecca Comay, "Dead Right."

16. See M591, W/C 390–91.

17. For the general history of the French Revolution, see Georges Rudé, *The French Revolution.*

18. See the Decree on Emergency Government (October 1793), and especially the "Law of Prairial" (June 10, 1794), reducing the import of evidence and facilitating the application of the death penalty. For Carl Schmitt, see *The Concept of the Political,* p. 71. The notion of the "state of exception" is prominently discussed in Jacques Derrida, *Rogues,* and in Giorgio Agamben, *State of Exception.*

19. The quotation is from the "Law of Suspects."

20. In principle, the Committee of Public Safety and the Committee of General Security, which were the directors of the Terror, were answerable to the National Convention, but this did not have a real impact during the year of the Terror.

21. In a comparable way, the "year of the four emperors" (A.D. 69) already showed forth the contradiction of the Roman Empire, even though that regime lasted another four hundred years. See Fagan, "Philosophical History and the Roman Empire."

22. On the interpretation of the Constitution of the United States, see Charles Beard, *An Economic Interpretation of the Constitution of the United States.*

23. See for example Karl Marx, *The Holy Family,* excerpted in *Karl Marx: Selected Writings,* p. 155. Compare Albert Soboul, *A Short History of the French Revolution 1789–1799,* p. 1: "The Revolution marks the advent of bourgeois, capitalist society in French history. Its essential achievement was the creation of national unity through the destruction of the seigneurial system and the privileged orders of feudal society. . . . Its final outcome, the establishment of liberal democracy, provides a further clue to its historical meaning. From this double point of view, and considered within the perspective of world history, it may be regarded as the definitive model of all bourgeois revolutions."

24. See, for example, Karl Marx, "Wage-Labour and Capital," in *Karl Marx:*

Selected Writings, pp. 273–93, especially pp. 291–93. Compare *The Civil War in France* (drafts), in *Karl Marx: Selected Writings*, p. 597: "The first French Revolution with its task to found national unity (to create a nation) had to break down all local, territorial, townish, and provincial independence. It was, therefore, forced to develop what absolute monarchy had commenced, the centralization and organization of state power, and to expand the circumference and the attributes of state power, the number of its tools, [and] its independence. . . . Every minor solitary interest engendered by the relations of social groups was separated from society itself, fixed and made independent of it and opposed to it in the form of state interest."

25. See Marx, "Wage-Labour and Capital," p. 291. For "growth" as definitive of capitalist economics in principle and in practice, see Max Weber, *The Protestant Ethic and the Spirit of Capitalism.*

26. See Marx, *The Communist Manifesto,* part 1, in *Karl Marx: Selected Writings,* p. 248.

27. See Marx, *The Communist Manifesto,* part 1, p. 251.

28. See Marx, "Alienated Labour," in *Economic and Philosophical Manuscripts (1844),* in *Karl Marx: Selected Writings,* pp. 85–95. Hegel (and, in an earlier form, Locke) emphasizes that freedom only exists in its self-externalization, in its self-objectifying which, in part, involves property. This is the essential "making itself at home"—in its body, in things, in a community, in history—that is essential to any free being. Capitalist labor practices—themselves legitimated by the modern revolutions, etc.—in fact install the "abstract individual" in practice, that is, they undermine the essential "home-making" dimension of our engagement and produce alienated labor. Here we see the "practical" equivalent of the conceptual problem Hegel diagnosed in the French Revolution. In an analogous way, modern representational democracy offers people an equivalently alienated relationship to their government/social substance, in contrast to the sense of being at home in a community/state in which one is a participant/member. For these issues in Hegel and Locke, see Jay Lampert, "Locke, Fichte and Hegel on the Right to Property"; for a more subtle interpretation of Locke, see Shannon Hoff, "Locke and the Nature of Political Authority."

29. Compare Weber on the Protestant ethic, according to which the individual is essentially defined by non-fulfillment (thus abandoning the notion of "enjoyment," which is essentially an embrace of the "finality" of our particularity), and essentially defined as a means for realizing something else (which is defined as the higher good). Compare Heidegger's conception of modern technology as governed by the notion of "reserve": see Martin Heidegger, "The Question Concerning Technology"; I have discussed this theme in "On Secrets and Sharing: Hegel, Heidegger and Derrida on the Economics of the Public Sphere."

30. This is the principle of utility that Hegel identifies as the "Truth of Enlightenment": M579–80, W/C 382–84.

31. M589, W/C 389.

32. The modern, as opposed to the ancient, world, from its rise in the Christian Middle Ages.

33. M599–631, W/C 395–415.

34. I have discussed the analogous inhuman anti-humanism in relation to the Kantian moral position in "The Contradictions of Moral Life," chapter 10 of *Reading Hegel's Phenomenology.*

35. I have discussed Hegel's treatment of conscience in *The Self and Its Body in Hegel's Phenomenology of Spirit,* pp. 100–6. See also "Selfhood, Conscience and Dialectic," chapter 11 of *Reading Hegel's Phenomenology.*

36. My emphasis. M635, W/C 417–18: "Das Gewissen sondert ferner die Umstände des Falles nicht in verschiedene Pflichten ab. . . . [E]s ist einfaches pflichtmäßiges Handeln, das nicht diese oder jene Pflicht erfüllt, sondern das konkrete Rechte weiß und tut." Compare also M643, W/C 422–23.

37. M637, W/C 419: "Diese *unmittelbare* konkrete Gewißheit seiner selbst ist das Wesen; . . . die eigne unmittelbare *Einzelnheit* der Inhalt des moralischen Tuns [ist]; und die *Form* desselben ist eben dieses Selbst als reine Bewegung, nämlich . . . die *eigne Überzeugung.*"

38. M647–53, W/C 426–29. Compare M640, W/C 421: conscience's conviction is "*implicity universal* self-*consciousness,* or the *state of being recognized,* and hence reality." ["Es ist das *an sich allgemeine* Selbst*bewußtsein,* oder das *Anerkanntsein* und hiemit die Wirklichkeit"].

39. M666–70, W/C 438–41.

40. M184–85, W/C 129. Compare M177, W/C 127: the "Concept of Spirit" ["der Begriff des Geistes"] as the "I that is We and We that is I" ["Ich, das *Wir,* und *Wir,* das *Ich* ist"]. See also M671, W/C 442: "The reconciling *Yea,* in which the two 'I's let go their antithetical *existence,* is the *existence* of the 'I' which has expanded into a duality and thereby remains identical with itself, and, in its complete externalization and opposite, possesses the certainty of itself" ["Das versöhnende *JA,* worin beide Ich von ihrem entgegengesetzten *Dasein* ablassen, ist das *Dasein* des zur Zweiheit ausgedehnten *Ichs,* das darin sich gleich bleibt, und in seiner vollkommnen Entäußerung und Gegenteile die Gewißheit seiner selbst hat."].

41. M670, W/C 441: "Das Wort der Versöhnung" and "ein gegenseitiges Anerkennen, welches der *absolute Geist* ist."

42. As Hegel shows in the *Science of Logic,* being is always determinate being.

43. See Jacques Derrida and Anne Dufourmantelle, *Of Hospitality.* See also *Rogues,* pp. 149–51, 126.

44. On the politics of "home," see Kirsten Jacobson, "The Experience of Home and the Space of Citizenship," *Southern Journal of Philosophy.*

45. Jacques Derrida, *Specters of Marx,* e.g., pp. 59, 65, 181. See also Caputo, *Deconstruction in a Nutshell,* pp. 22–25.

46. Michael Naas, "A Last Call for Europe," chapter 4 of *Derrida From Now On,* p. 84.

47. This is the fundamental significance of the progress, in Hegel's account of the dialectic of spirit, from "true spirit" to "self-certain spirit": this is a development from a situation in which the "natural" form of the human community is taken to be fixed and given ("truth") to a situation in which the "universal" is only provisional, and stands in permanent need of interactive confirmation ("certainty").

48. Preface to the *Elements of the Philosophy of Right*, p. 21.

49. See Derrida, *Rogues*, pp. 120–24, 154–57, 18, 85.

50. *Rogues*, p. 155.

51. *Rogues*, p. 121.

52. Compare Derrida's notion of "altermondialisation" in "A Europe of Hope." On the ways in which Hegel's philosophy is both European and beyond European, see Andrew Buchwalter, "Is Hegel's Philosophy of History Eurocentric?"

53. *Rogues*, pp. 28–29.

54. For an excellent introduction to this topic, see Tamim Ansary, *Destiny Disrupted.*

55. See *Rogues*, pp. 31–33.

56. This the subject of part A, "The True Spirit: Ethicality," of chapter VI, "Spirit." For a clear discussion of the "happy" state of ethicality, see M349–53, W/C 234–36; for its insuffiency see M354–55, W/C 236–37. For the insufficiency of "ethicality" to fulfill the needs of freedom, see "Spirit and Scepticism," chapter 9 of *Reading Hegel's Phenomenology*, pp. 138–40.

57. For an excellent overview, see David Waines, *An Introduction to Islam*, pp. 211–64.

58. Quoted in Naas, "A Last Call for Europe," p. 91.

59. *Rogues*, pp. 98–99.

60. Compare Derrida's idea of "democracy to come" in *Rogues*, pp. 80–86.

61. See Réal Fillion, *Multicultural Dynamics and the Ends of History*, introduction and chapter 3.

Chapter 12

1. Compare Merleau-Ponty, *Phenomenology of Perception*, p. 62: "The tacit thesis of perception is that at every instant experience can be coordinated with that of the previous instant and that of the following, and my perspective with that of other consciousnesses." Compare also Bergson, *Matter and Memory*, p. 36: "that which distinguishes it as a *present* image, as an objective reality . . . is the necessity which obliges it to act through every one of its points upon all the points of all other images, to transmit the whole of what it receives, to oppose to every action an equal and contrary reaction, to be, in short, merely a road by which pass, in every direction, the modifications propagated throughout the immensity of the universe."

2. The richness of the relation between being as such and determinate beings is thoroughly articulated by Heidegger in *Basic Concepts.*

3. The logic of finite and infinite is precisely explained by Houlgate in *The Opening of Hegel's Logic.* See also Burbidge, *The Logic of Hegel's Logic.* See also chapter 3.

4. Compare Houlgate, *The Opening of Hegel's Logic*, p. 395: "The disappearance of one finite thing must, therefore, result in the presence of another *finite* thing"; and p. 397: "[I]n ceasing to be, something does not just violate but also

fulfills its determination. . . . This means, however, that, in ceasing to be, a finite thing is actually revealing a previously hidden dimension of its own being and so is in fact coming to be *itself* in another guise. Its being continues beyond its demise—albeit in a radically transformed mode."

5. See Houlgate, *The Opening of Hegel's Logic,* p. 397: "We do not need to look beyond finitude itself for this new infinity. We simply need to look more closely at what occurs when one finite thing gives way to another." See *Science of Logic,* G I.148–49, E136–37.

6. See *Science of Logic,* G I.82–83, E82–83. Compare Houlgate, *The Opening of Hegel's Logic,* p. 277: "Being vanishes into nothing, according to Hegel, because it is so indeterminate in itself that logically *it is not even the pure being that it is* and so is in fact the absence of being."

7. Compare Houlgate, *The Opening of Hegel's Logic,* p. 399: "[T]he [genuine] infinite to which Hegel draws attention at this point does not consist in the endless generation of new finite things but is rather the self-same being that continues and relates only to itself in all such othering. Hegel is adamant that there is no such infinite being apart from, before, or outside the process of change and death undergone by finite things. Since infinite being is inseparable from the *process* of the world, such being cannot simply *be* infinite. It must constantly prove to be infinite and unending in the process whereby finite things themselves end. Indeed, it must constantly *constitute* itself as infinite. Infinite being *is* what it is and never ends, but this is only because it always *proves itself* to be infinite and never ending." See Hegel, *Encyclopaedia Logic,* §95, pp. 150–51 (*Enz* 1 pp. 200–1).

8. Hegel's discussion of the infinite is found in the *Science of Logic,* E 137–56, G I.49–166. Compare Plato, *Phaedo,* 99b.

9. M174, W/C 125–26.

10. For a rich discussion of the nature of action see David Ciavatta, "Hegel on Desire's Knowledge," and chapter 2 of *Spirit, the Family, and the Unconscious in Hegel's Philosophy.*

11. Schelling, *System of Transcendental Idealism,* pp. 212–13. Compare Kant, "The Idea of a Universal History," p. 29: "Whatever concept one may form of *freedom of the will* in a metaphysical context, its *appearances,* human actions, like all other natural events, are certainly determined in conformity with universal natural laws."

12. *System of Transcendental Idealism,* p. 213.

13. *System of Transcendental Idealism,* p. 213.

14. These themes are studied in the opening sections of the *Philosophy of Right.* Compare David Ciavatta, "Hegel on Owning One's Own Body."

15. M417, W/C 274–75: "Eine Individualität geht also, etwas auszuführen; sie scheint damit etwas *zur Sache* gemacht zu haben; sie handelt, wird darin für andere, und es scheint ihr um die *Wirklichkeit* zu tun zu sein. Die anderen nehmen also das Tun derselben für ein Interesse an der Sache als solcher . . . [Aber] es ist *sein* Tun und Treiben, was es bei der Sache interessiert, und indem sie innewerden, daß dies *die Sache selbst* war, finden sie sich also getäuscht." This is the problem that is at the center of "The Spiritual Animal Kingdom," M397–418, W/C 261–77. Compare also the problem of conviction and the beautiful soul,

M648–66, W/C 426–38. See M648, where virtually the same point is made: "Once fulfilled, set in the medium of *being*, this identity [of the acting self-consciousness with itself in its action] is . . . no longer this process of differentiation in which its differences are at the same time immediately superseded; on the contrary, in *being*, the difference is established as an *enduring* difference, and the action is a *specific* action, not identical with the element of everyone's self-consciousness, and therefore not necessarily acknowledged. Both sides, the conscience that acts and the universal consciousness that acknowledges this action as duty, are equally free from the specificity of this action. On account of this freedom, their relationship in the common medium of their connection is really a relation of complete disparity"; W/C 426–27: "Aber vollbracht, in das allgemeine Medium *des Seins* gestellt, ist diese Gleichheit . . . nicht mehr dieses Unterscheiden, welches seine Unterschiede ebenso unmittelbar aufhebt; sondern im *Sein* ist der Unterschied bestehend gesetzt, und die Handlung eine *bestimmte*, ungleich mit dem Elemente des Selbstbewußtseins Aller, also nicht notwendig anerkannt. Beide Seiten, das handelnde Gewissen und das allgemeine, diese Handlung als Pflicht anerkennende Bewußtsein, sind gleich *frei* von der Bestimmtheit dieses Tuns. Um dieser Freiheit willen ist die Beziehung in dem gemeinschaftlichen Medium des Zusammenhangs vielmehr ein Verhältnis der vollkommnen Ungleichheit." On the notorious difficulty of finding good English translations of the word "Sache" in this section of Hegel's text, see Daniel E. Shannon, *The Question Concerning the Factum of Experience*, passim. H. S. Harris, *Hegel's Ladder*, volume 2, pp. 97–108, offers a very helpful discussion of "die Sache selbst."

16. M417, W/C 275: "die Verwirklichung ist . . . eine Ausstellung des Seinigen in das allgemeine Element, wodurch es zur *Sache* Aller wird, und werden soll."

17. The points made here are the essential argument of chapter 4, "Self-Consciousness," from its opening discussion of desire to the end of the discussion of the "Independence and Dependence of Self-Consciousness." For Hegel's description of the dialectic of recognition specifically, see *Phenomenology* M177–84, W/C 127–29.

18. M436, W/C 285–86: "Es [das Gesetz] ist . . . ein ewiges Gesetz, welches nicht in dem *Willen dieses Individuums* seinen Grund hat, sondern es ist an und für sich. . . . Es *glaubt* auch nicht an sie, denn der Glauben schaut wohl auch das Wesen, aber ein fremdes an. Das sittliche *Selbst*bewußtsein ist . . . *unmittelbar* mit dem Wesen eins."

19. M418, W/C 276: "ein Wesen, dessen *Sein* das *Tun* des *einzelnen* Individuums und aller Individuen [ist]."

20. M351, W/C 235: "Wie der Einzelne in seiner *einzelnen* Arbeit schon eine *allgemeine* Arbeit *bewußtlos* vollbringt, so vollbringt er auch wieder die allgemeine als seinen *bewußten* Gegenstand; das Ganze wird *als Ganzes* sein Werk, für das er sich aufopfert, und ebendadurch sich selbst von ihm zurückerhält.—Es ist hier nichts, das nicht gegenseitig wäre."

21. Compare *Philosophy of Mind*, §552, p. 283: "If religion then is the consciousness of *'absolute' truth*, then whatever is to rank as right and justice, as law and duty, i.e., as *true* in the world of free will, can be so esteemed only as it is participant in that truth, as it is subsumed under it and is its sequel" (*Enz* 3, p. 355).

22. M351, W/C 235: "Diese Einheit des Seins für Anderes oder des sich zum Dinge Machens, und des Fürsichseins, diese allgemeine Substanz redet ihre *allgemeine Sprache* in den Sitten und Gesetzen seines Volks."

23. I have discussed this theme in "For Now We See as Through a Glass Darkly." See also David Ciavatta, "On Burying the Dead."

24. Compare *Reason in History*, pp. 51–52: "The spiritual individual, the people, insofar as it is organized in itself, an organic whole, is what we call the State. This designation is ambiguous in that by 'state' and 'constitutional law' one usually means the simple political aspect as distinct from religion, science, and art. But when we speak of the manifestation of the spiritual we understand the term 'state' in a more comprehensive sense, similar to the term *Reich* [empire, realm]."

25. M351, W/C 235: "der Einzelne in seiner *einzelnen* Arbeit . . . eine *allgemeine* Arbeit *bewußtlos* vollbringt."

26. M475, W/C 314: "Das Gemeinwesen kann sich aber nur durch Unterdrückung dieses Geistes der Einzelnheit erhalten, und, weil er wesentliches Moment ist, erzeugt es ihn zwar ebenso, und zwar durch die unterdrückende Haltung gegen denselben als ein feindseliges Prinzip."

27. M448, W/C 293: "Dieser Geist kann das menschliche Gesetz genannt werden, weil er wesentlich in der Form der *ihrer selbst bewußten Wirklichkeit* ist." Compare also the transition from "ethical action" to "legal status," M477–80, W/C 316–18. See also *Philosophy of Right*, remark to section 124: "The right of *subjective freedom* is the pivotal and focal point in the difference between *antiquity* and the *modern* age"; Kenneth Westphal, in "The Basic Context and Structure of Hegel's *Philosophy of Right*," writes: "Hegel regarded the demand for rational understanding and justification of norms and institutions as the hallmark of modern times, and he sought an account of society and government that met that demand" (p. 237). See also Adriaan Peperzak, *Modern Freedom*, pp. 176–83.

28. Compare *Philosophy of Right*, preface, p. 13, addition [H]: "To know what a law of nature is, we must familiarize ourselves with nature, for these laws are correct and it is only our notions concerning them which may be false. . . . We get to know the laws of right in just the same way, simply as they are; the citizen knows them more or less in this way, and the positive jurist also stops short at what is given."

29. See *Philosophy of Right*, sections 124, 149, 275, 276, and *Philosophy of History*, p. 104.

30. See *Philosophy of Right*, remark to section 187.

31. This is the general situation of "Observing Reason" in its relationship to nature (M244–97, W/C 166–200). The terms that "reason" is prepared to recognize self-consciously are inferior to the "reason" that actually animates the world of inorganic and organic nature upon which reason depends (both for its having an object and for its very existence). I have discussed this material in "Hegel's Phenomenology of Reason and Dualism," especially pp. 75–80; see also Joseph C. Flay, *Hegel's Quest for Certainty*, pp. 122–36.

32. This theme is richly discussed in Timothy Brownlee, "Freedom of Conscience and Subjective Right in Hegel's Political Philosophy," and "Conscience

and Recognition," and in Frederick Neuhouser, *Foundations of Hegel's Social Theory*. As Allen Wood writes in "The Right of Insight," in *Hegel's Ethical Thought*, "Hegel holds that as modern agents we need to live in a society that can give a rational account of itself. Freedom, the harmony of our inner subjectivity with our outward life, is possible only where reflection of the best minds on social norms and institutions can result in their rational confirmation" (p. 191).

33. Immanuel Kant, "The Idea of a Universal History." Rèal Fillion, *Multicultural Dynamics and the Ends of History* offers a very helpful interpretation of the philosophies of history developed in this Kantian essay, in Hegel's introduction to his *Lectures on the Philosophy of History*, and in Marx and Engel's *Communist Manifesto.*

34. See Aristotle, *Politics*, bk. 1, chap. 1.

35. Compare also Schelling, *System of Transcendental Idealism*, p. 198, on the notion of a universal constitution.

36. Kant, "The Idea of a Universal History," p. 34: Law's effectiveness requires a guarantor to assure that coercive force will be used justly, but this guarantor must always be a person. Compare Schelling, *System of Transcendental Idealism*, p. 197, on the preponderance of executive branch of government. See also Jacques Derrida, *Rogues*, p. 102: "Abuse of power is constitutive of sovereignty itself."

37. See Marx and Engels, *The Communist Manifesto*, part 1, in *Karl Marx: Selected Writings*, p. 246: "The history of all hitherto existing societies is the history of class struggle."

38. See Hegel, *Reason in History*, p. 11: "The sole thought which philosophy brings to the treatment of history is the simple concept of *Reason*: that Reason is the law of the world and that, therefore, in world history, things have come about rationally. This conviction and insight is a presupposition of history as such." He continues, "We must bring to history the belief and conviction that the realm of the will is not at the mercy of contingency." For the interpretation of these passages, see Fillion, *Multicultural Dynamics and the Ends of History*, pp. 90–100.

39. And, indeed, we always belong to a particular generation, which means we must always favor our time over the past and the future; similarly, we are always bodily located in a particular space, and we will always have to favor that location for the deployment of our agency.

40. This is the point of Hegel's analysis of "Absolute Freedom and Terror," M582–95, W/C 385–94.

41. For a rich development of this idea, see Shannon Hoff, "Themes from 'The Spirit of Christianity and Its Fate,'" chapter 1 of *The Laws of the Spirit: A Hegelian Theory of Justice.*

42. Compare Hegel's discussion of the multiplicity of moral duties that emerge from any ("perceptual") situation; the abstract moral point of view must presume a "God's-eye view" in which these are unified (M605–6, 626, W/C 400–401, 411–12), whereas the concrete moral point of view of "conscience" takes responsibility itself for being this "negative One" that decides what is the unique imperative in any particular situation (M635, W/C 417–18).

43. Jacques Derrida, *Rogues*, p. 36. Compare H. S. Harris, *Hegel's Ladder*,

vol. 2, pp. 771–72: "In the sphere of 'objective Spirit' (i.e. the sphere of 'Law' in all its forms, positive, natural and moral) disagreements are formulated in terms of conflicting 'rights'; but quite apart from conflicts between levels of social life (e.g. family and civil) Hegel's analysis of the concept of justice (par. 430) shows why a consistent and universally recognized system of 'rights' is impossible. So in our dealings with socially contentious questions such as abortion (for instance) we are doomed to go on making compromises that satisfy neither side, unless and until the conflicting attitudes move towards reconciliation at the immediate level of feeling (or 'insight')."

44. *Philosophy of Right,* preface, p. 13, *Zusatz* [Hotho].

45. *Elements of the Philosophy of Right,* section 5: "Der Wille enthält α) das Element der *reinen Unbestimmtheit* oder der reinen Reflexion des Ich in sich, in welcher jede Beschränkung . . . aufgelöst ist; die schrankenlose Unendlichkeit der *absoluten Abstraktion* oder *Allgemeinheit,* das reine *Denken* seiner selbst"; and §6: "β) . . . das Übergehen aus unterschiedsloser Unbestimmtheit zur *Unterscheidung, Bestimmen* und *Setzen* einer Bestimmtheit als eines Inhalts und Gegenstands . . .—das absolute Moment der *Endlichkeit* oder *Besonderung* des Ich."

46. M643, W/C 422–423: "Der seiner selbst gewisse Geist ruht als Gewissen in sich, und seine *reale* Allgemeinheit, oder seine Pflicht, liegt in seiner reinen *Überzeugung* von der Pflicht. . . . Es soll . . . gehandelt, es muß von dem Individuum *bestimmt* werden; und der seiner selbst gewisse Geist, in dem das Ansich die Bedeutung des selbstbewußten Ich erlangt hat, weiß diese Bestimmung und Inhalt in der unmittelbaren *Gewißheit* seiner selbst zu haben."

47. M634, W/C 417: "Est ist . . . *konkreter* moralischer Geist, der nicht am Bewußtsein der reinen Pflicht sich einen leeren Maßstab gibt, welcher dem wirklichen Bewußtsein entgegengesetzt wäre. . . . [E]r ist in unmittelbarer Einheit sich *verwicklichendes moralisches* Wesen, und die Handlung unmittelbar *konkrete* moralische Gestalt."

48. M635, W/C 417: "Dieses als Gewissen weiß ihn [eine gegenständliche Wirklichkeit] auf unmittelbare konkrete Weise, und er ist zugleich nur, wie es ihn weiß."

49. Sophocles, *Antigone,* ll. 1–117. See M465–66, W/C 305–6. I have discussed this facet of Antigone's perception in "For Now We See Through a Glass Darkly," pp. 209–10, and "Reading and the Body in Hegel," pp. 330–31.

50. For the idea that reliance on a procedure amounts to not having to take responsibility, see Bernstein, "Conscience and Transgression," p. 63. This theme runs throughout Jacques Derrida, "Force of Law."

51. On the essentiality for identity of the religious ethicality that liberal individualism treats as a "private" matter, and the challenge this essentiality poses to standard forms of liberal politics, see John Russon, "Heidegger, Hegel and Ethnicity" and Réal Fillion, *Multicultural Dynamics and the Ends of History.* See also Herman Dooyeweerd, *Roots of Western Culture,* pp. 7–9, on the relation between "theory" and its religious root, and H. Evan Runner, *The Relation of the Bible to Learning,* pp. 154–55, on the idea that "life is religion"; Runner's idea is discussed throughout Henry Vander Goot, *Life as Religion.*

52. See H. S. Harris, *Phenomenology and System,* p. 78: "Forgiveness is the

only moral duty that is truly *absolute,* for the willingness to enter even into the standpoint of the coward who saved his own life in the battle is the condition of truly human communication. This is the reality of moral respect. The coward must, of course, confess that he was a coward and that he needs forgiveness if the communication is to become perfect." Compare also Jay Bernstein, "Confession and Forgiveness," p. 56. For the culmination of the logic of conscience in the stance of forgiveness, see M669–71, W/C 440–42. The logic of forgiveness is powerfully articulated in Jacques Derrida, "On Forgiveness." See also Shannon Hoff, "Law, Right and Forgiveness," chapter 5 of *The Laws of the Spirit.*

53. On the theme of conscience completing the logic of self-consciousness, see M795–96, W/C 520–22.

54. M670, W/C 441.

55. Compare Vladimir Jankélévitch, *Forgiveness,* p. 161: "the person who forgives abstains from denying his essential similarity with the guilty person. . . . [H]e does not keep for himself the privilege of alone being infallible, impeccable, and irreproachable, and he rejects any monopoly that he may have on this position."

56. As Bernstein says, "the generality of mutual recognition of one another as conscientious individuals displaces the universality of principles, choices, and acts," "Conscience and Transgression," p. 64.

57. See H. S. Harris, *Hegel's Ladder,* vol. 2, p. 771: "We must not expect too much, of course. The principal virtue of Hegel's science in its practical bearing is negative. It shows us why disagreement and conflict are bound to persist, and how creatively imaginative the task of conceptual reconciliation is bound to be even when the will is there."

58. M640, W/C 421: Conscience rests on the commitment to being "the *implicitly universal* self-*consciousness*" ["das *an sich allgemeine* Selbst*bewußtsein*"]. One must always, therefore, be acting from an assurance of the reality of "morality," the assurance of human reconciliation *in a context in which it is not actual:* one must act toward non-reconciled others from the view that they are "to be reconciled" in principle, i.e., in acting for reconciliation one is acting for them—for the future them, the them-to-come. This is the unity of the world that can never "be": see Schelling, *System of Transcendental Idealism,* pp. 205–7 on the moral world-order, and compare Kant, *Critique of Pure Reason,* A684–85/B712–13 on "world" as a regulative idea.

59. See Shannon Hoff, "Criminal Action," chapter 7 of *The Laws of the Spirit.*

60. Compare H. S. Harris, *Hegel's Ladder,* vol. 2, pp. 772–73: "It is, of course, the public law that sets the bounds within which all consciences are effectively 'free.' A conscience that is in conscious opposition to the universally recognized authority of the law—one that sees itself, or would like to see itself, as the 'Law of the Heart'—must choose between the public sanction (which may go as far as the guillotine) and self-incarceration in the Stoic thought-world. But the religion of loving forgiveness sets up 'the Law of the Heart' in its only demonstrably rational guise, as the regulative ideal for our system of public law. The final object of the legal system must be to bring everyone (offenders and offended, agents and observers alike) into the community of rational reconciliation, and to maintain

them there. Thus, if it is the law of someone's Heart to execute a *fatwa* against Salman Rushdie, they will certainly learn that this cannot rationally be the 'law of all hearts.' But if someone aids a fugitive from political persecution (generally recognized *as* a victim of persecution) then the appeal to the 'law of the heart' will be allowed as *rational*, however ineffective it may prove in the immediate circumstances of the moment."

61. In this way, it is a figure of "unhappy consciousness," which Hegel sees as the completed form of free self-consciousness. I have discussed the nature of "unhappy consciousness" in *The Self and Its Body in Hegel's Phenomenology of Spirit*, chapter 1.

62. Indeed, we see in conscience the ultimate "truth" of the "struggle to the death" with which Hegel's description of the dialectic of self-consciousness began, for in conscience one stakes oneself absolutely on a justice beyond finite justification, a justice for which one would risk one's life based on one's self-certainty. For the "struggle to the death," see M186–88, W/C 129–31.

63. Compare Houlgate, *The Opening of Hegel's Logic*, p. 425: "True infinity thus proves to be not just the endless series of occurrences in space and time but the process whereby being brings itself to self-consciousness (and to life) and so becomes *spirit*."

64. M69: "It is the nature of humanity to press onward to agreement with others; human nature only really exists in an achieved community of consciousness." [W/C 51: "Denn die Natur dieser [Humanität] ist, auf die Übereinkunft mit andern zu dringen, und ihre Existenz nur in der zu Stande gebrachten Gemeinsamkeit der Bewußtsein."]

65. See Shannon Hoff, "Law, Right, and Forgiveness," chapter 5 of *The Laws of the Spirit*.

66. Compare Schelling, *System of Transcendental Idealism*, p. 211: "For God never *exists*, if the existent *is* that which presents itself in the objective world; if *He existed* thus, then *we* should not; but He continually *reveals* himself."

67. For the "night in which all cows are black" see M16, W/C 12–13.

Chapter 13

1. See M73–79, W/C 57–62.

2. On the relation of religion to these earlier shapes of spirit, see M679–81, W/C 446–48.

3. M682, W/C 449: "der Gegenstand zur reinen Gegenständlichkeit, zur Form der Negativität des Selbstbewußtseins herabsänke."

4. Compare M672, W/C 443: "In den bisherigen Gestaltungen, die sich im allgemeinen als *Bewußtsein*, *Selbstbewußtsein*, *Vernunft* und *Geist* unterscheiden, ist zwar auch die Religion, *als Bewußtsein* des *absoluten Wesens* überhaupt vorgekommen; allein vom *Standpunkte des Bewußtseins* aus, das sich des absoluten Wesens bewußt ist; nicht aber ist das absolute Wesen *an und für sich* selbst, nicht das Selbstbewußtsein des Geistes in jenen Formen erschienen."

5. See M678, W/C 445: "[S]ein *Dasein* von seinem *Selbstbewußtsein* unterschieden [ist]. . . . [E]s ist wohl *ein Geist* beider, aber sein Bewußtsein umfaßt nicht beide zumal, und die Religion erscheint als ein Teil des Daseins."

6. See M780, W/C 507: "das absolute Wesen hätte nur diesen leeren Namen, wenn es in Wahrheit ein ihm *Anderes* . . . gäbe." On this "absolute reality," see Lauer, *A Reading of Hegel's Phenomenology of Spirit* (New York: Fordham University Press, 1993 [second edition]), p. 258.

7. See M440, W/C 289: "Der Geist ist hiemit das sich selbst tragende absolute reale Wesen. Alle bisherigen Gestalten des Bewußtseins sind Abstraktionen desselben."

8. René Descartes, *Meditations on First Philosophy*, pp. 147–48. Religion thus stands as a challenge to the results of the phenomenological study up to this point. The dialectic of spirit had concluded with the stance of conscientious "self-certainty" as the "absolute form"; the phenomenology concludes (in "Absolute knowing") in the demonstration by religion itself, with its "absolute content," that it confirms this result. See M794, 797–98, W/C 519–20, 522–23.

9. Jesus says, "Take up your cross and follow me." Matthew 16:24, Mark 8:34, Luke 9:23. Compare M807: "to know one's limit is to know how to sacrifice oneself"; W/C 529: "Seine Grenze wissen heißt sich aufzuopfern wissen." In the preface to the *Philosophy of Right*, Hegel quotes Aesop: "Here is your Rhodes, here is your jump."

10. M678, W/C 445: "[D]ie in ihr eingeschloßne Wirklichkeit ist die Gestalt und das Kleid seiner Vorstellung. Der Wirklichkeit widerfährt aber in dieser Vorstellung nicht ihr vollkommnes Recht, nämlich nicht nur Kleid zu sein, sondern selbstständiges freies Dasein; und umgekehrt ist sie, . . . eine *bestimmte* Gestalt, die nicht dasjenige erreicht was sie darstellen soll."

11. M680, W/C 447: "Der ganze . . . Geist der Religion, ist . . . die Bewegung, aus seiner Unmittelbarkeit zum *Wissen* dessen zu gelangen, was er *an sich* oder unmittelbar ist, und es zu erreichen, daß die *Gestalt*, in welcher er für sein Bewußtsein erscheint, seinem Wesen vollkommen gleiche, und er sich anschaue, wie er ist."

12. M683, W/C 450, "die *Gestalt* selbst und die *Vorstellung* [sind] noch die unüberwundne Seite, von der er in den *Begriff* übergehen muß.

13. M683, W/C 450: "Alsdann hat der Geist den Begriff seiner selbst erfaßt, wie wir nur erst ihn erfaßt haben."

14. David Waines, *An Introduction to Islam*, pp. 137–41.

15. *Alberuni's India*, chap. 2, p. 27. On god with and god without qualities, see also Wendy Doniger, *The Hindus*, p. 283.

16. Augustine, *Confessions*, bk.7, chap. 11, p. 145: "I was a higher creature than any physical place, though a lower thing than you, and my joy is to be subordinate to you while subordinating to me the creatures lower than I am."

17. Augustine, *Confessions*, bk. 7, chap. 16, p. 149: "You guiding, I entered my own recesses, though only you, helping me, made that possible. Entered there, I could see, so far as I could see anything with my poor soul's vision, something beyond my soul's vision, and beyond my mind, an always-unfailing light—not the light common to all our physical vision, nor simply like that but on a grander

scale, as if it just got brighter and brighter, till nothing else could be seen. Nothing of that sort was it. No, of some other, some far different sort it was—not a thing layered above my mind, as oil floats above water, or heaven above earth, but something higher than I am because it made me, who am lower because made by it. To know truth is to know this light, and to know this light is to know eternity. It is the light love knows."

18. Plato, *Republic*, bk. 7.518d.

19. See Lauer, *A Reading of Hegel's Phenomenology*, p. 264, on the communal character of religion: "As Hegel sees it, religious experience is from the beginning a corporate experience, whether of human society as a whole at a given stage or of a segment of that society which is taken as paradigmatic of a stage in the overall development."

20. M684, W/C 451: "Die Reihe der verschiednen Religionen, die sich ergeben werden, stellt ebensosehr wieder nur die verschiednen Seiten einer einzigen, und zwar *jeder einzelnen* dar, und die Vorstellungen, welche eine wirkliche Religion vor einer andern auszuzeichnen scheinen, kommen in jeder vor."

21. M684, W/C 451: "Allein zugleich muß die Verschiedenheit auch als eine Verschiedenheit der Religion betrachtet werden."

22. As Lauer, *A Reading of Hegel's Phenomenology* notes (p. 264), Hegel identifies the religions of nature with Asian religions. In fact, Hegel's text in the *Phenomenology* does not always give sufficient detail to make these identifications unambiguously clear. Though I have made some such identifications here, nothing hangs on these identifications; indeed, the anthropology of Asian religions is one area in which modern scholarship can clearly do a better job than Hegel was able to do in 1807, and in general the *logic* of his description is of more value than his attempts at empirical interpretation of these religions and at the correlation of these religious *Vorstellungen* with the logical features of his analysis. H. S. Harris, *Hegel's Ladder*, vol. 2, p. 555, challenges the empirical associations with "Plant and Animal Religions" in particular.

23. *Republic*, bk. 6.507d–e.

24. Lauer, *A Reading of Hegel's Phenomenology*, p. 265, explains that the description of the light-religion is about "the vague deification of any one cosmic force, such as 'light,' not about the nuances which may have attached historically to this phenomenon in Zoroastrianism." Presumably, any worship of a sun-god belongs here, though the sun is itself something made visible to us by the light, that is, the attribution of "causality" to the sun already *presupposes* the revelation of the sun to us by the light.

25. M686, W/C 453.

26. M686, W/C 452–53: "Er schaut sich in der Form des *Seins* an, jedoch nicht des geistlosen mit zufälligen Bestimmungen der Empfindung erfüllten *Seins*, das der sinnlichen Gewißheit angehört, sondern es ist das mit dem Geiste erfüllte Sein"; see also M684: "For since spirit lives in the difference of its consciousness and its self-consciousness, the aim of the movement is to supersede this cardinal distinction and to give the form of self-consciousness to the 'shape' that is the object of consciousness. . . . [I]t must, on the one hand, be posited in the 'shape' by the act of self-consciousness, and, on the other hand, the lower

determination must show itself to be reduced to a moment of the higher and be comprehended by it"; W/C 451: "Denn indem der Geist sich im Unterschiede seines Bewußtseins und seines Selbstbewußtseins befindet, so hat die Bewegung das Ziel, diesen Hauptunterschied aufzuheben, und der Gestalt, die Gegenstand des Bewußtseins ist, die Form des Selbstbewußtseins zu geben. . . . [M]uß es teils durch das Tun des Selbstbewußtseins in sie gesetzt werden, teils muß die niedrige Bestimmung von der höhern aufgehoben und begriffen zu sein sich zeigen."

27. For some discussion of this theme, see Marianna Stepaniants, "The Encounter of Zoroastrianism with Islam."

28. M686, W/C 453: "die Bewegungen seiner eignen Entäußerung, seine Schöpfungen in dem widerstandslosen Elemente seines Andersseins sind Lichtgüsse, sie sind in ihrer Einfachheit zugleich sein Fürsichwerden und Rückkehr aus seinem Dasein, die Gestaltung verzehrende Feuerströme"; and M687, W/C 453: "Ihre Bestimmungen sind nur Attribute, die nicht zur Selbstständigkeit gedeihen, sondern nur Namen des vielnamigen Einen bleiben."

29. M687, W/C 453.

30. M688, W/C 453–54: "Das reine Licht wirft seine Einfachheit als eine Unendlichkeit von Formen auseinander und gibt sich dem Fürsichsein zum Opfer dar, daß das Einzelne das Bestehen an seiner Substanz sich nehme."

31. M689, W/C 454: "Das *wirkliche* Selbstbewußtsein dieses zerstreuten Geistes ist eine Menge vereinzelnter ungeselliger Völkergeister, die in ihrem Hasse sich auf den Tod bekämpfen, und bestimmter Tiergestalten als ihres Wesens sich bewußt werden."

32. See H. S. Harris, *Hegel's Ladder*, vol. 2, p. 556. Harris argues that "animal religion" really means militant tribalism, and corresponds to any society that acts as if it had "its own" gods, as with the early Jewish claim that Yahweh was one of many gods, and stronger than the others. Harris writes, "In this perspective, primitive Judaism is an "animal religion"; and Yahweh is bound to be a warrior-God precisely because he has chosen just this one 'people' for Himself. Yahweh, of course, must not be called a 'lion'; but that is the appropriate name for the human leader whom He chooses." On early Judaism, see Karen Armstrong, *The Great Transformation*. On the Malaysian dispute about usage of the term "Allah," see for example, Seth Mydans, "Churches Attacked in Malaysian 'Allah' Dispute." Lauer, *A Reading of Hegel's Phenomenology*, interprets plant and animal religion as referring to totemism, a view that Harris rejects (p. 555).

33. M680, W/C 447.

34. M680, W/C 447: "damit die bestimmte Religion ebenso einen *bestimmten wirklichen* Geist [hat]."

35. *Philosophy of Mind*, section 562, p. 296 (*Enz* 3, pp. 370–71).

36. See *Reason in History*, p. 64: "The Idea of God thus is the general fundament of a people."

37. This definition of "the political" is from Aristotle, *Politics* bk. 1, 1–2. For the development of this idea, see Hannah Arendt, *The Human Condition*, chapter 2, "The Public and the Private Realm," and chapter 5, "Action."

38. M700, W/C 458: "[E]r ist das freie Volk, worin die Sitte die Substanz aller ausmacht, deren Wirklichkeit und Dasein alle und jeder einzelne als seinen

Willen und Tat weiß." See Lauer, p. 267, on the nature of the ethical community to which the religion of art corresponds.

39. M701, W/C 459: "[D]ie *Wirklichkeit* der sittlichen Substanz beruht teils auf ihrer ruhigen *Unwandelbarkeit* . . . und hiemit darauf, daß dieses noch nicht aus seiner ruhigen Sitte und seinem festen Vertrauen in sich gegangen ist;—teils auf seiner Organisation in eine Vielheit von Rechten und Pflichten, sowie in die Verteilung in die Massen der Stände und ihres besondern Tuns, das zum Ganzen zusammenwirkt;—hiemit darauf, daß der Einzelne mit der Bschränkung seines Daseins zufrieden ist." This self-consciousness "has not yet grasped the unrestricted thought of his free self"; "den schrankenlosen Gedanken seines freien Selbsts noch nicht erfaßt hat."

40. M353, W/C 236; compare M441, W/C 290.

41. M448–49, 463, W/C 293, 303–4.

42. M720, W/C 470: "das Lichtwesen, das selbstlos nicht die Gewißheit der Einzelnen in sich enthält, sondern vielmehr nur ihr allgemeines Wesen und die herrische Macht ist, worin sie verschwinden."

43. See M733, W/C 478–79. In the religion of the artificer [Egypt], human power was indeed acknowledged, but in its formal instrumentality, not in its creativity as a self-governing act that gives itself its own content; indeed, not as "self-certain," or self-conscious. As Lauer, *A Reading of Hegel's Phenomenology,* p. 267, writes: "Having traced the movement of the divine presence from a formless cosmic force, through differentiated forms of life, to the work of men's hands, he now turns to that creative work which is most clearly infused with man's creative spirit, the works through which both the divine and the human spirit speak—more authentically than in the works of nature alone."

44. See Lauer, *A Reading of Hegel's Phenomenology,* pp. 267–68: "It is important to note that what Hegel is engaged in here is not a philosophy of art—in particular, classical Greek art. Rather he is engaged in a phenomenology of the religious consciousness which expresses itself in classical art." For a discussion of Hegel's parallel treatment of the Greeks in the context of his *Aesthetics,* see John Russon, "Expressing Dwelling."

45. M702, W/C 460: "In solcher Epoche tritt die absolute Kunst hervor."

46. M705, W/C 461: "Das erste Kunstwerk ist, als das unmittelbare, das abstrakte und einzelne. Seinerseits hat es sich aus der unmittelbaren und gegenständlichen Weise dem Selbstbewußtsein entgegen zu bewegen, wie andererseits dieses für sich im Kultus darauf geht, die Unterscheidung aufzuheben, die es sich zuerst gegen seinen Geist gibt, und hiedurch das an ihm selbst belebte Kunstwerk hervorzubringen."

47. M703–4, W/C 460–61 give a condensed discussion of the transformations of the ethical substance that ultimately gives rise to the recognition of the primacy of the individual subjectivity who has the absolute in herself. This is the "pure form" [*reine Form*] that is "the night in which substance was betrayed and made itself into subject," "die Nacht, worin die Substanz verraten ward, und sich zum Subjekte machte" (M703, W/C 460–61). Harris, *Hegel's Ladder,* vol. 2, pp. 581–84, helpfully traces out the process to which the images of these two paragraphs allude.

48. M720, W/C 470: “Das Volk, das in dem Kultus der Kunstreligion sich seinem Gotte naht, ist das sittliche Volk, das seinen Staat und die Handlungen desselben als den Willen und das Vollbringen seiner selbst weiß.”

49. M733, W/C 479: “wesentlich es der Bildsäule ist, von Menschenhänden gemacht zu sein.” It is their character *as artworks* that is important, as opposed to a religious attitude in which statues of, for example, animal divinities, are important because of the animal; M707: “But the indwelling god is the black stone drawn forth from its animal covering and pervaded with the light of consciousness”; W/C 462: “Der inwohnende Gott aber ist der aus dem Tiergehäuse hervorgezogne schwarze Stein, der mit dem Lichte des Bewußtseins durchdrungen ist.” With Harris (*Hegel's Ladder*, vol. 2, p. 588), I believe that Baillie was mistaken to take this to be a reference to the “Black Stone” of Mecca.

50. See Lauer, *A Reading of Hegel's Phenomenology*, pp. 268–69.

51. On the human form as the paradigm for beauty—the notion that Hegel identifies as the essence of the Greek art-religion—compare Kant's discussion of the “Ideal of Beauty” in §17 of the *Critique of Judgment.* See Hegel, *Aesthetics,* I.153–57, 433–34.

52. M720–26, W/C 470–74.

53. M727–47, W/C 474–88. On imagination as the medium of poetry, see Hegel, *Aesthetics,* II.962–63.

54. M733, 744, and 747, W/C 478–79, 485, and 487–88.

55. M701, W/C 459–60: “Die Vollendung der Sittlichkeit zum freien Selbstbewußtsein und das Schicksal der sittlichen Welt ist daher die in sich gegangene Individualität, der absolute Leichtsinn des sittlichen Geistes, der alle festen Unterschiede seines Bestehens und die Massen seiner organischen Gegliederung in sich aufgelöst, und vollkommen seiner sicher zur schrankenlosen Freudigkeit und zum freisten Genusse seiner selbst gelangt ist.” Compare M747, W/C 487–88.

56. Plato, *Apology.*

57. Plato, *Crito.*

58. M750–53, W/C 489–91; compare M477–80, W/C 316–18.

59. M748, W/C 488: “Durch die Religion der Kunst ist der Geist aus der Form der *Substanz* in die des *Subjekts* getreten. . . . Diese Menschwerdung des göttlichen Wesens geht von der Bildsäule aus, die nur die *äußere* Gestalt des Selbsts an ihr hat, das *innre* aber, ihre Tätigkeit, fällt außer ihr; im Kultus aber sind beide Seiten eins geworden, in dem Resultate der Religion der Kunst ist diese Einheit in ihrer Vollendung zugleich auch auf das Extrem des Selbsts herübergegangen; in dem Geiste, der in der Einzelnheit des Bewußtseins seiner vollkommen gewiß ist, ist alle Wesenheit versunken. Der Satz, der diesen Leichtsinn ausspricht, lautet so: *das Selbst ist das absolute Wesen*; das Wesen, das Substanz und an dem das Selbst die Akzidentalität war, ist zum Prädikate heruntergesunken.”

60. On the notion of the “negative self-relation,” see Hegel's discussion of “Reflection” in the *Science of Logic,* G II.24–35, E399–408, and Dieter Henrich, “Hegels Logik der Reflexion.” See M775, W/C 503–4, on the essential selfothering both from the side of self-consciousness and from the side of the divine.

61. See Hegel, *Lectures on Natural Right and Political Science,* pp. 53–4: “The science of right has the free will as its principle and starting point. . . . The will con-

tains (1) the element as absolute negativity—the pure *indeterminacy* [*Unbestimmtheit*] of the ego consisting in its pure reflection into itself, having within itself no limitation, no immediately present content determined by nature, needs, desires and instincts, or in any other way. . . . (2) As absolute negativity the ego is at the same time the *passing over to determinacy* and the positing of a determinacy or of a distinction as an inner content. . . . and it is only through positing itself as something determinate that the ego enters into *determinate existence* [*Dasein*]—the *absolute finitude* or infinitude of its *individuality*."

62. These three figures of the divine correspond to the three figures of unhappy consciousness, in M210, W/C 145–46, the dialectic of "the unchangeable" corresponding through its own self-development to the dialectic of the "changeable."

63. On translating "*die offenbare Religion*" as "the religion of revelation," see Lauer, *A Reading of Hegel's Phenomenology*, p. 262, n.4. On the notion of revelation, compare Schelling, *System of Transcendental Idealism*, p. 211: "For God never *exists* [*ist nie*], if the existent *is* that which presents itself [*sich darstellt*] in the objective world; . . . but he continually *reveals* [*offenbart*] himself." Compare Plato, *Timaeus*, 52a–d on *chora*.

64. M788, W/C 516: "Der *Inhalt* des Vorstellens ist der absolute Geist; und es ist allein noch um das Aufheben dieser bloßen Form zu tun."

65. See M780, W/C 507–9 for the idea that all the images of the religion of revelation point to self-othering as opposed to dualism.

66. M759, W/C 494: "Diese Menschwerdung des göttlichen Wesens, oder daß es wesentlich und unmittelbar die Gestalt des Selbstbewußtseins hat, ist der einfache Inhalt der absoluten Religion."

67. See M779, W/C 506–7 on the image of resurrection. Harris, *Hegel's Ladder*, vol. 2, pp. 687–90, has a helpful discussion of this and the following two paragraphs (M780–81, W/C 507–10) in which the image of resurrection is identified with the shared self-consciousness of the spiritual community.

68. M780, W/C 507: "Die aufgehobne unmittelbare Gegenwart des selbstbewußten Wesens ist es als allgemeines Selbstbewußtsein; dieser Begriff des aufgehobnen einzelnen Selbsts, das absolutes Wesen ist, drückt daher unmittelbar die Konstituierung einer Gemeinde aus, die bisher im Vorstellen verweilend itzt in sich als in das Selbst zurückkehrt; und der Geist geht somit aus . . . dem Vorstellen, in . . . das Selbstbewußtsein als solches über."

69. See M762–63, 782, W/C 497–98, W/C 510. On the relation of Peter and Paul and on the historical setting of the New Testament writings in general, see Julie Galambush, *The Reluctant Parting*. Compare Badiou's discussion in *St Paul: The Foundation of Universalism*.

70. M782, W/C 510.

71. M764–65, W/C 498–99.

72. M780, W/C 507–9.

73. M784, W/C 511: "der Tod wird von dem, was er unmittelbar bedeutet, von dem Nichtsein *dieses Einzelnen* verklärt zur *Allgemeinheit* des Geistes, der in seiner Gemeine lebt, in ihr täglich stirbt und aufersteht."

74. Matthew 18:19–20: "For where two or more are gathered in My Name,

I am there in the midst of them." Compare Colossians 1:24, ". . . the afflictions of Christ, for the sake of His Body, which is the church," 1 Corinthians 12:27: "Now you are the body of Christ, and members individually," and Ephesians 5:30: "For we are members of His Body, of His flesh and His bones." Compare also 1 Peter 2:5.

75. M781, W/C 509: "Der Geist ist also in dem dritten Elemente, im *allgemeinen Selbstbewußtsein* gesetzt; er ist seine *Gemeinde.* Die Bewegung der Gemeinde als des Selbstbewußtseins, das sich von seiner Vorstellung unterscheidet, ist, das *hervorzubringen,* was *an sich* geworden ist. Der gestorbne göttliche Mensch oder menschliche Gott ist *an sich* das allgemeine Selbstbewußtsein; er hat dies *für dies Selbstbewußtsein* zu werden."

76. "Self-Alienated Spirit; Culture," part B of chapter VI, "Spirit," M484–595, W/C 320–94.

77. M491: "the self is actual to itself only as *transcended*"; W/C 326: "Das Selbst ist sich nur als *aufgehobnes* wirklich."

78. M489, W/C 324: "Obwohl das Selbst als *dieses* sich hier wirklich weiß, so besteht doch seine Wirklichkeit allein in dem Aufheben des natürlichen Selbsts." See also M485, W/C 321.

79. M488, W/C 324: "es hat nur *Realität,* insofern es sich selbst entfremdet; hiedurch setzt es sich als allgemeines, und diese seine Allgemeinheit ist sein Gelten und Wirklichkeit."

80. M489, W/C 324: "Wodurch also das Individuum hier Gelten und Wirklichkeit hat, ist die *Bildung.*"

81. *Reason in History,* p. 24.

82. M488, W/C 324: "Diese *Gleichheit* mit allen ist daher nicht . . . jenes unmittelbare Anerkanntsein und Gelten des Selbstbewußtseins, darun weil *es ist*; sondern daß es gelte, ist durch die entfremdende Vermittlung, sich dem Allgemeinen gemäß gemacht zu haben."

83. M490, W/C 325: "Die Bewegung der sich bildenden Individualität ist . . . unmittelbar . . . das Werden der wirklichen Welt."

84. Mohammad's Islamic revolution in the early seventh century (by the Christian calendar) is an interesting hybrid of these two notions in being a religion calling for individual conversion and for universal equality while being a social order—the *ummah*—that exemplifies something like the Greek ideal of communal freedom. The infinite richness of the Islamic revelation, of course, offers possibilities for contemporary Islamic culture that are not defined by the terms in which the *dar al Islam* established itself in its "Golden Age." On the character of early Islamic culture, see Ira M. Lapidus, *A History of Islamic Societies,* pp. 10–30.

85. See especially Kant, "On the Idea of a Universal History," for an argument about why the nature of human freedom can only be fulfilled through the establishing of a universal civil society. Fichte's *Foundations of Natural Right* and Schelling's *System of Transcendental Idealism* both develop this same basic argument in the context of a systematic science of human freedom in a way that is very helpful for understanding Hegel's own treatment of these matters in his *Philosophy of Right* and his *Philosophy of History.*

86. M589–92, W/C 389–91. On Hegel's analysis of the Terror, see Rebecca Comay, "Dead Right: Hegel and the Terror."

87. This is the notion of the essentiality of *property*. On this theme, see Hegel, *Philosophy of Right*, sections 41–71; compare Fichte, *Foundations of Natural Right*, pp. 101–23.

88. I have developed this point at greater length in *The Self and Its Body in Hegel's Phenomenology of Spirit*, pp. 100–107.

89. Compare M787: "The spirit of the community is thus in its immediate consciousness divided from its religious consciousness, which declares, it is true, that *in themselves* they are not divided, but this merely *implicit* unity is not realized, or has not yet become an equally absolute being-for-self"; W/C 515: "Der Geist der Gemeinde ist so in seinem unmittelbaren Bewußtsein getrennt von seinem religiösen, das zwar es ausspricht, daß sie *an sich* nicht getrennt seien, aber ein *Ansich*, das nicht realisiert, oder noch nicht ebenso absolutes Fürsichsein geworden."

90. This is in contrast to the not-yet-fully-reconciled religious consciousness, whose "own reconciliation enters its consciousness as something *distant*, as something in the distant *future*" (M787); W/C 514: "Seine eigne Versöhnung tritt . . . als ein *Fernes* in sein Bewußtsein ein, als ein Fernes der *Zukunft*."

91. A fuller articulation of the needs of self-consciousness to which politics must answer is found in the *Philosophy of Right*.

92. See Jean Hyppolite, *Logic and Existence*, p. 74: "Man is the house of the Logos, of the being which reflects on itself and thinks itself"; and p. 187: "Through this freedom, which Hegel says is the absolute Idea of history . . . man does not conquer himself as man, but becomes the house of the Universal, of the Logos of Being, and becomes capable of Truth."

93. See especially *Rogues*, p. 18–27, and compare p. 41: if democracy means that power (*kratos*) belongs to "the people" (the *demos*), then "if one values freedom in general . . . then one should no longer be afraid to speak without or against democracy."

94. *Rogues*, p. 152.

95. André Breton, *First Surrealist Manifesto*; Gaston Bachelard, *The Poetics of Space*. See also Drucilla Cornell, "The Philosophy of the Limit: Systems Theory and Feminist Legal Reform," and John Russon, *Bearing Witness to Epiphany*, p. 127.

96. *Rogues*, pp. 28–41: "The Other of Democracy, the 'By Turns': Alternative and Alternation."

97. An excellent account of this basic history is Tamim Ansary, *Destiny Disrupted*. See also Karen Armstrong, *Islam: A Short History*.

Epilogue

1. See, for example, M26–7, 35–7, 53, W/C 19–22, 27–9, 39–40.

2. M37, W/C 29.

3. Misunderstandings typically take the form of claiming that "absolute knowing" marks a (supposed) kind of knowledge that is discontinuous with the

rest of the dialectic of experience in the *Phenomenology of Spirit* and that this absolute knowledge—in which everything is comprehended, and all opposition overcome—is presupposed by the *Science of Logic* (and, indeed, even by the *Phenomenology* itself). This form of knowledge, it is then asserted, does not exist, and so the very project of the *Logic* is vitiated (along with the conclusion of the *Phenomenology*). For a corrective to this view of absolute knowledge, see John Burbidge, "Hegel's Absolutes," and John Russon, "Absolute Knowing: The Structure and Project of Hegel's System of Science," chapter 15 of *Reading Hegel's Phenomenology*. For the project of Hegel's *Logic* in general, see chapter 3 of John Burbidge, *The Logic of Hegel's Logic*, and chapters 1, 2, and 6 of Stephen Houlgate, *The Opening of Hegel's Logic*. On the subtle relationship between these two works, compare Jean Hyppolite, *Logic and Existence*, pp. 3, 34: "Absolute knowledge means the in principle elimination of . . . non-knowledge, that is, the elimination of a transcendence essentially irreducible to our knowledge. . . . If we just stayed with the *Phenomenology*, by separating it from its conclusion as well as from its preface, we would remain at a humanism, at a philosophical anthropology, and the Logic, the Logos of Being, which is of such importance to Hegel, would be incomprehensible."

4. Burbidge, in chapter 3 of *The Logic of Hegel's Logic*, has a helpful discussion of ways in which Hegel's *Science of Logic* emerges from the themes at work in Kant's *Critique of Pure Reason*, and makes a similar link to the work of Fichte that I make in this chapter (see pp. 23–24). A helpful explanation of Hegel's project in the *Science of Logic* in terms of Kant's agenda in the *Critique of Pure Reason* is given by Houlgate, *The Opening of Hegel's Logic*, pp. 9–28.

5. A160 / B199.

6. A161–2 / B201.

7. A162–235 / B202–94. Compare Hyppolite, *Logic and Existence*, 170–71, who argues that the Doctrine of Being corresponds to the Transcendental Aesthetic, the Doctrine of Essence to the Transcendental Analytic, and the Doctrine of the Concept to the Transcendental Dialectic. This association of the Doctrine of the Concept with Kant's Transcendental Dialectic is hasty, for the correlation is not as direct as is the case with the former two parts of each philosopher's work; my argument in this chapter would suggest that the closer correlation is between the Doctrine of the Concept and the "Paralogisms" section of the Transcendental Dialectic (see next note). For the language of "immediacy" (*Unmittelbarkeit*), see *Science of Logic*, volume 1, book 1, section 1, chapter 1, part A, "Being"; for the language of "reflexion" (*Reflexion*), see *Science of Logic*, volume 1, book 2, section 1, chapter 1, part C, "Reflection." For the logic of immediacy as it first emerges in Hegel's *Science of Logic*, see Dieter Henrich, "Anfang und Methode der Logik"; for the logic of reflexion as it first emerges in Hegel's *Science of Logic*, see Henrich, "Hegels Logik der Reflexion."

8. Compare Kant's own remark at the beginning of the discussion of the "Paralogisms of Pure Reason": "We have now come to a concept that was not entered in the above general list of the transcendental concepts, and that must yet be classed with them, but without in the least changing the table and declaring it deficient. This is the concept, or, if one prefers, the judgment: *I think* . . . . [T]his

concept is the vehicle of all concepts as such and hence also of transcendental concepts. . . . [H]owever pure of the empirical (the impressions of the senses) this concept may be, it still serves to distinguish two kinds of objects taken from the nature of our power of representation. *I*, as thinking, am an object of inner sense and am called soul; what is an object of the outer senses is called body" (A341–42 / B399–400, trans. Werner S. Pluhar, emphasis in original). Kant is concerned to show that we cannot have knowledge of the "I" as a worldly substance; what he effectively establishes is that the logic of the "I" is not defined according to the terms of the opposition of subject and object that characterizes empirical life, but is, instead, what makes that opposition possible. As we will see, this is remarkably close to Hegel's logic of the concept.

9. On Hegel's view, nature is not the proper object. As we saw in the discussion of mood in chapter 5, we need an object that adequately reflects back to us our own nature. For that reason, our ultimate object is spirit. Nature does demonstrate a logic of the concept, but in too immediate a form. I have discussed this point in *The Self and Its Body in Hegel's Phenomenology of Spirit*, chap. 2, pp. 39–41. Compare also Giambattista Vico's argument that, whereas historical acts are acts by self-conscious agents like ourselves with whom we can identify, natural processes are the result of a non-self-conscious agency with which in principle we can never identify; therefore, it is only history, and not nature, which can offer to us a proper object for knowledge: "Whoever reflects on this cannot but marvel that the philosophers should have bent all their energies to the study of the world of nature, which, since God made it, He alone knows; and that they should have neglected the study of the world of nations, or civil world, which, since men had made it, men could come to know," *The New Science of Giambattista Vico*, §331, p. 96.

10. Transcendental apperception is introduced at A106–7. It is the central subject of the Transcendental Deduction. See especially B131–32: "The *I think* must be *capable* of accompanying all my presentations. For otherwise something would be presented to me that could not be thought at all—which is equivalent to saying that the presentation either would be impossible, or at least would be nothing to me. . . . I call it *pure apperception*, in order to distinguish it from *empirical* apperception. Or, again, I call it *original apperception*; for it is the self-consciousness which, because it produces the presentation *I think* that must be capable of accompanying all other presentation[s], and [because it] is one and the same in all consciousness, cannot be accompanied by any further presentation. I also call the *unity* of this appreception the *transcendental* unity of self-consciousness, in order to indicate that a priori cognition can be obtained from it" (trans. Pluhar, emphasis in original). This notion will be discussed further in relation to Fichte's philosophy. Hegel introduces his own discussion of the concept through discussion of the transcendental unity of apperception (*Science of Logic*, G II.254–55, E584–85); note especially, "Thus we are justified by a cardinal principle of the Kantian philosophy in referring to the nature of the *I* in order to learn what the *Concept* is" (G II.255, E 585).

11. Fichte, *Science of Knowledge*, part 1, "Fundamental Principles of the Entire Science of Knowledge," section 1, "First, Absolutely Unconditioned Principle," pp. 94–102, especially p. 99.

12. *Science of Knowledge*, "Second Principle, Conditioned as to Content," pp. 102–5. I am taking the language of "universal" and "determinate" from Hegel's discussion of the logic of the concept in *Science of Logic*, volume 2, section 1, chapter 1, "The Concept": the relation of universality and determinateness is the central issue in the dialectic of the first two moments of the concept, "the universal concept" (*der allgemeine Begriff*) and "the particular concept" (*der besondere Begriff*).

13. *Science of Knowledge*, "Third Principle, Conditioned as to Form," pp. 105–19.

14. *Science of Logic*, G II.253, E583.

15. *Science of Logic*, G II.265, E592.

16. *Science of Logic*, G II.253, E583.

17. *Science of Logic*, G II.253, E583.

18. M611, W/C: 403: ". . . der absolute Begriff, der allein das *Anderssein* als solches, oder sein absolutes Gegenteil als sich selbst erfaßt."

19. Hegel discusses this idea on G II.249–50, E 580. Again, I here take myself to be in agreement with Burbidge's analysis.

20. The dialectic of things, forces, and substance is at the heart of the "Doctrine of Essence," book 2 of the *Science of Logic*. It also provides the central structure to the dialectic of "Consciousness" in Hegel's *Phenomenology of Spirit.*

21. *Science of Logic*, G II.276, E 602.

22. On the developing nature of "the negative" throughout the *Logic*, see Dieter Henrich, "Formen der Negation in Hegels Logik."

23. *Science of Logic*, G II.280, E 606.

24. *Science of Logic*, G II.280, E 606.

25. Compare *Science of Logic*, G II.257, E 586: "Life, or organic nature, is the stage of nature at which the concept emerges."

26. R. C. Lewontin, *Biology as Ideology*, chap. 5; James J. Gibson, *The Ecological Approach to Visual Perception.*

27. Compare Heidegger's notion that we exist as being-in-the-world: we are at home in our world in such a way that we live out our life as a relationship of opposition between subject and object; *Being and Time*, division 1, chap. 2, §13.

28. See my discussion of morality in "Spirit and Scepticism," chapter 9 of *Reading Hegel's Phenomenology.*

29. *Science of Logic*, G II.264–5, E 592: "Since it is primarily logic and not science generally with whose relation to truth we are here concerned, it must further be conceded that logic as the *formal science* cannot and should not contain the reality which is the content of the further parts of philosophy, namely, the philosophical sciences of nature and of spirit."

30. On the relation of spirit and logic, see Kenneth L. Schmitz, "Hegel's Attempt to Forge a Logic for Spirit." On the general theme of the relationship between Hegel's *Science of Logic* and language, see Jim Vernon, *Hegel's Philosophy of Language*, and chapter 4 of Houlgate, *The Opening of Hegel's Logic*, especially pp. 75–79; see also Wolfgang Wieland, "Bemerkungen zum Anfang von Hegels Logik."

31. *Science of Logic*, G II.279, E 605.

32. *Science of Logic,* G II.551, E 826: Hyppolite's construal of the concept as "sens" and "love" (*Logic and Existence,* pp. 4–5, 19) is thus quite accurate. Hegel refers to the concept as "free love" on G II.277, E 603.

33. M47, W/C 34–35.

34. *Science of Logic,* G II.549, E 824.

Appendix

1. The reception of Hegel in France is discussed in Judith Butler, *Subjects of Desire,* Michael S. Roth, *Knowing and History,* and Bruce Baugh, *French Hegel.* Helpful discussions of these works are Marcel Stoetzler, "Subject Trouble: Judith Butler and Dialectics," Judith Butler, "Review of Michal S. Roth, *Knowing and History,*" and Stefanos Geroulanos, "Review of Bruce Baugh, *French Hegel.*" On Butler's interpretation of Hegel, see also Shannon Hoff, "Restoring Antigone to Ethical Life." For a brief discussion that parallels my own of the significance of Wahl, Kojève, and Hyppolite, see Terry Pinkard, "Hegel in the Twentieth Century."

2. "Hegel's Existentialism," pp. 63–64.

3. As Merleau-Ponty says, "A man cannot receive a heritage of ideas without transforming it by the very fact that he comes to know it, without injecting his own and always different way of being into it." "Man and Adversity," p. 224.

4. The quality of scholarship on Hegel underwent a great qualitative improvement in the 1960s and 70s, largely in tandem with the publication of high quality research in the journal *Hegel-Studien.* Since the 1970s many outstanding interpreters have distinguished themselves, and one cannot claim to be working competently in the domain of Hegel-interpretation without engaging with the work of these scholars. The best contemporary English-language commentary on the *Phenomenology of Spirit* (and possibly the best in any language) is H. S. Harris, *Hegel's Ladder*; Harris addresses in detail modern scholarship on the *Phenomenology of Spirit* up to the mid-1990s. For the *Science of Logic,* the best modern work is Stephen Houlgate, *The Opening of Hegel's Logic*; Houlgate discusses in detail the whole range of current scholarship on the *Science of Logic.* Unfortunately, Houlgate's discussion only goes as far as Hegel's category of "the infinite"; for an excellent interpretation of the *Science of Logic* as a whole, see John W. Burbidge, *The Logic of Hegel's Logic.*

5. M27, 26, 88, W/C 21–22, 28, 68.

6. On this point, see William Maker, "Does Hegel Have a 'Dialectical Method'?"

7. "Hegel's Existentialism," p. 63.

8. The discussion of work is at M194–96, W/C 134–36. For contemporary interpretation of these passages, see Harris, *Hegel's Ladder,* vol. 1, pp. 363–70, and John Russon, *Reading Hegel's Phenomenology,* chap. 6. Themes pertinent to history are found in chapter VI, "Spirit," of the *Phenomenology of Spirit*; these claims are more directly found in the introduction to Hegel's *Philosophy of History.*

9. André Breton, *Manifestoes of Surrealism,* pp. 117–94.

10. Breton, *Manifestoes of Surrealism,* p. 26.

11. André Breton, *L'Amour fou*, p. 46. Compare Jacques Derrida, "The Theatre of Cruelty and the Closure of Representation," p. 248: "dialectics is the indefinite movement of finitude."

12. For Bataille's notions of "restricted" and "general" economy, see *The Accursed Share*. The significance of this for Derrida is explicit in "From Restricted to General Economy: An Hegelianism Without Reserve."

13. Wilhelm Dilthey, "Die Jugendgeschichte Hegels," and Hermann Nohl (ed.), *Theologische Jugendschriften*.

14. M206–31, W/C 142–57. For contemporary interpretations of the Unhappy Consciousness, see Harris, *Hegel's Ladder*, volume 1, chapter 9, and John Russon, *The Self and Its Body in Hegel's Phenomenology of Spirit*, chapter 1.

15. Jean Wahl, *Le malheur de la conscience*, p. 155.

16. The language is from Alexandre Koyré's review of *Le malheur de la conscience*.

17. See Jean Wahl, "Commentaire d'une passage de la Phénomenologie de Hegel."

18. See Jean Wahl, *Existence humain et transcendence*, pp. 37–38.

19. Alexandre Koyré, "Hegel à Iéna"; see especially pp. 160, 170, 176–77.

20. This opposition of Husserl and Heidegger is expressly discussed in Tran-Duc-Thâo, "Existentialisme et matérialisme dialectique," according to which Husserl's *epoché* puts the transcendental ego "outside the world" whereas Heidegger recognizes that there must be "a concrete and temporal self"; Tran-Duc-Thâo rejects "Hegelianism," but nonetheless draws substantially on Marx and on notions derived from Hegel.

21. M178–96, W/C 127–36. For contemporary commentary, see Harris, *Hegel's Ladder*, volume 1, chapter 8, and Russon, *Reading Hegel's Phenomenology*, chapters 5 and 6.

22. Hegel defines spirit (*Geist*) as the "I that is We and We that is I" in M177, W/C 127.

23. These lectures were published as *Introduction à la lecture de Hegel*, with selections translated in English as *Introduction to the Reading of Hegel*.

24. Jean-Paul Sartre, *Being and Nothingness*, pp. 11–14, and 301–3, 338.

25. *Being and Nothingness*, p. 475.

26. This basic orientation is captured in these remarks by Paul Ricouer: "Thus Husserl . . . conceives of phenomenology not only as a method of description . . . but also as a radical self-grounding. . . . [But] in its effective practice phenomenology already displays its distance from rather than its realization of the dream of such a radical grounding in the transparence of the subject to itself. . . . It is because we find ourselves first of all in a world to which we belong in which we cannot but participate, that we are then able, in a second movement, to set up objects . . . that we can claim to constitute. . . . The subject-object link—on which Husserl continues to depend—is thus subordinated to the testimony of an ontological link more basic than any relation of knowledge" ("On Interpretation," pp. 188–90). Basically, this "transcendental I," this constituting power, is a position that "I," as an engaged, perspectival being-in-the-world, can never occupy.

In the 1930s (in *The Transcendence of the Ego* [1936] and "Une Idée Fondamentale de la Phénoménologie de Husserl: l'Intentionnalité" [1939]), Sartre himself defends Husserl against a "representational" view, which he attributes to Descartes and neo-Kantianism, though he does criticize Husserl for an analogous problem of reifying reflecting consciousness.

27. Sartre also emphasizes the practical and situated character of the self, both in *Being and Nothingness* and in his later *Critique of Dialectical Reason*. Like the emphasis on the experience of the gaze of the other, this notion of the engaged subject brings out the way that subjectivity is something in-the-world rather than in consciousness. Hegel's and Marx's analyses of work are highly influential on Sartre's notions of situatedness, action, and history. In "Merleau-Ponty vivant," Sartre credits Merleau-Ponty with teaching him about the importance of this theme of the "action that since Marx and Hegel has been called praxis" (p. 582). These themes of engagement and history in Sartre's philosophy are helpfully discussed in Baugh, *French Hegel*, pp. 101–17. For other thinkers, Hegel and Marx also provided the basis for a philosophy of nature and history that seemed missing in Husserl's phenomenology. See Tran-Duc-Thâo, *Phénoménologie et matérialisme dialectique*, p. 5: "Marxism imposed itself on us as the only conceivable solution to the problems posed by phenomenology itself." Compare also Jay Lampert, "Husserl and Hegel on the Logic of Subjectivity."

28. *Being and Nothingness*, pp. 86–116; *Being and Time*, division I, chap. 4.

29. This is the subject of chapter 2 of *The Ethics of Ambiguity*.

30. This is the subject of the concluding section of *The Second Sex*.

31. For relevant texts and discussion, see John Russon, "The Bodily Unconscious in Freud's 'Three Essays.'" See also Rosi Braidotti and Alan D. Schrift, "Psychoanalysis and Desire."

32. See in particular the so-called "Rome lecture," "The Function and Field of Speech and Language in Psychoanalysis," published as chapter 3 of *Écrits: A Selection*. On the relation of Hegel and Lacan, see Slavoj Žižek, *Tarrying with the Negative: Kant, Hegel and the Critique of Ideology*.

33. A helpful presentation of these ideas is part 1, "The Semiotic and the Symbolic," of Julia Kristeva, *The Revolution in Poetic Language*.

34. Maurice Merleau-Ponty, *Phenomenology of Perception*, pp. 193–94, and 215; see also "Metaphysics and the Novel." In his discussion in the "Sexuality" chapter of "existence" as the coming together of necessity and contingency, Merleau-Ponty effectively equates the definitive notion of existentialism with Hegel's notion of "spirit" (which is likewise the coming together of reason and history). See *Phenomenology of Perception*, pp. 196–98.

35. *Genèse et structure*, pp. 187–88, *Genesis and Structure*, pp. 190–91.

36. "La conception hégélienne de l'état et sa critique par Karl Marx," pp. 152–53.

37. Like Hyppolite, Eric Weil also rejected Kojève's claim that the end of history had arrived, instead arguing, in *Hegel et l'état*, that our world has reached a point where in principle the goal of history can be articulated, but it has not been accomplished (pp. 77–79, 102). In this work Weil also challenged the view

that Hegel was a defender of the Prussian State, seeing, on the contrary, ways in which Hegel's philosophy was precisely a critique of that state, a point ultimately made most powerfully by Jacques d'Hondt in *Hegel en son temps.*

38. *Genèse et structure,* pp. 509–10, 514, *Genesis and Structure,* pp. 524, 528.

39. See *Logic and Existence,* p. 74: "Man is the house of the Logos, of the being which reflects on itself and thinks itself," and p. 187, "Through this freedom, which Hegel says is the absolute Idea of history . . . man does not conquer himself as man, but becomes the house of the Universal, of the Logos of Being, and becomes capable of Truth."

40. Deleuze dedicated his first book, *Empiricism and Subjectivity* (1953), to Hyppolite; and Foucault, who succeeded him at the Collège de France, acknowledged his importance on several occasions, including at his memorial at the École Normale Supérieure, where, noting Hyppolite's influence as a teacher, said: "All the problems which are ours—we his former students or his students of today—all these problems are ones that he has established for us" ("Jean Hyppolite. 1907–1968," p. 785).

41. Jacques Derrida, *Positions,* p. 44. These remarks from the 1970s should be read in relation to his introductory remarks to Catherine Malabou, *The Future of Hegel: Plasticity, Temporality, Dialectic.* This latter work aims to correct misportrayals of Hegel that too easily distance him from the work of Derrida and other contemporary French philosophers. See also the review of this book by William Dudley. On the relation of Derrida and Hegel, see John Russon, *Reading Hegel's Phenomenology,* chapter 14.

42. Excellent treatments of these texts are Leonard Lawlor, *Derrida and Husserl,* and Joshua Kates, *Essential History.*

43. *Le problème de la genèse dans la philosophie de Husserl*; "'Genèse et structure' et la phénoménologie"; Edmund Husserl, *L'Origine de la géometrie,* translation and introduction by Jacques Derrida.

44. *Le problème de la genèse,* pp. 110–29.

45. In some respects this work, like that of Tran-Duc-Thâo, may be functioning primarily to establish the necessity to reinterpret Husserl's transcendental ego in terms of Heidegger's being-in-the-world, thus reflecting more the emphasis of the "humanist" appropriations of phenomenology from the 1940s.

46. *Edmund Husserl's Origin of Geometry,* pp. 87–93.

47. *Edmund Husserl's Origin of Geometry,* 67n62.

48. "Violence and Metaphysics," 320n91.

Bibliography

Primary Texts

German Texts

Hegel, G. W. F. *Enzyklopädie der philosophischen Wissenschaften im Grundrisse.* Teile I, II, and III. *Werke in zwanzig Bänden,* Bde. 9, 10, 11, ed. Eva Moldenhauer and Karl Markus Michel. Frankfurt am Main: Suhrkamp, 1970.

———. *Grundlinien der Philosophie des Rechts. Werke in zwanzig Bänden.* Bd. 7, ed. Eva Moldenhauer and Karl Markus Michel. Frankfurt am Main: Suhrkamp, 1986.

———. *Jenaer Schriften, 1801–1807, Werke.* Bd. 4, ed. Eva Moldenhauer and Karl Markus Michel. Frankfurt am Main; Suhrkamp, 1986.

———. *Hegels Philosophie des subjektiven Geistes/Hegel's Philosophy of Subjective Spirit.* Bde. 1 and 2. Text, translation, and notes by M. J. Petry. Dordrecht, Holland: D. Reidel, 1978.

———. *Jenaer Systementwürfe I.* Edited by K. Düsing and H. Kimmerle. Hamburg: Felix Meiner, 1986.

———. *Phänomenologie des Geistes.* Edited by Hans-Friedrich Wessels und Heinrich Clairmont. Hamburg: Felix Meiner, 1988.

———. *Theologische Jugendschriften.* Edited by Hermann Nohl. Tübingen: Mohr, 1907.

———. *Vorlesungen über die Philosophie der Geschichte. Werke.* Bd. 12. Edited by Eva Moldenhauer and Karl Markus Michel. Frankfurt am Main; Suhrkamp, 1986.

———. *Vorlesungen über die Philosophie der Religion.* Teil 3. *Vorlesungen: Ausgewählte Nachschriften und Manuskripte.* Bd. 5. Edited by Walter Jaeschke. Hamburg: Felix Meiner, 1984.

———. *Wissenschaft der Logik.* Bde. I and II. *Werke in zwanzig Bänden.* Bde. 5, 6. Edited by Eva Moldenhauer and Karl Markus Michel. Frankfurt am Main: Suhrkamp, 1986.

English Translations

———. *Aesthetics.* Translated by T. M. Knox. 2 vols. Oxford: Clarendon, 1975.

———. *The Difference Between Fichte's and Schelling's System of Philosophy.* Translated by H. S. Harris and Walter Cerf. Albany: State University of New York Press, 1977.

———. *The Encyclopaedia Logic, with the Zusätze.* Translated by T. F. Geraets, W. A. Suchting, and H. S. Harris. Indianapolis/Cambridge: Hackett, 1991.

———. *Elements of the Philosophy of Right.* Translated by Allen W. Wood. Cambridge: Cambridge University Press, 1991.

———. *Lectures on Natural Right and Political Science: The First Philosophy of Right.* Translated by J. Michael Stewart and Peter C. Hodgson. Berkeley: University of California Press, 1995.

———. *Lectures on the Philosophy of Spirit: 1827–8.* Translated by Robert R. Williams. Oxford: Oxford University Press, 2007.

———. *Lectures on the Philosophy of Religion.* Vol.3. Translated by R. F. Brown, P. C. Hodgson, and J. M. Stewart, with the assistance of H. S. Harris. Berkeley: University of California Press, 1985.

———. *Natural Law.* Translated by T. M. Knox. Philadelphia: University of Pennsylvania Press, 1975.

———. *Phenomenology of Spirit.* Translated by A. V. Miller. Oxford: Oxford University Press, 1977.

———. *The Philosophy of History.* Translated by J. Sibree. New York: Dover, 1956.

———. *Philosophy of Mind, being Part III of the Encyclopaedia of the Philosophical Sciences.* Translated by William Wallace and A. V. Miller. Oxford: Clarendon, 1971.

———. *Philosophy of Nature, being Part II of the Encyclopaedia of the Philosophical Sciences.* Translated by A. V. Miller. Oxford: Clarendon, 1970.

———. *Philosophy of Right.* Translated by T. M. Knox. Oxford: Oxford University Press, 1967.

———. *Reason in History.* Translated by Robert S. Hartman. New York: Bobbs-Merrill, 1953.

———. "Relationship of Skepticism to Philosophy, Exposition of its Different Modifications and Comparison to the Latest Form with the Ancient One." Translated by H. S. Harris. In *Between Kant and Hegel: Texts in the Development of Post-Kantian Idealism,* edited by George di Giovanni and H. S. Harris. Albany: State University of New York Press, 1985. pp. 313–62.

———. *Science of Logic.* Translated by A. V. Miller. New York: Humanities Press, 1976.

———. *System of Ethical Life (1802/03) and First Philosophy of Spirit.* Translated by H. S. Harris and T. M. Knox. Albany: State University of New York Press, 1979.

Commentaries

Abish, Walter. "In So Many Words." In *In the Future Perfect,* pp. 74–97. New York: New Directions, 1977.

Adelman, Howard. "Hegel's *Phenomenology*: Facing the Preface." *Idealistic Studies,* 14 (1984): 159–70.

Adorno, Theodor W. *Negative Dialektik.* Frankfurt am Main: Suhrkamp, 1966. Translated by E. B. Ashton as *Negative Dialectics.* New York: Seabury, 1973.

Agamben, Giorgio. *State of Exception.* Translated by Kevin Attell. Chicago: University of Chicago Press, 2005.

Al-Biruni, *Alberuni's India,* abridged edition. Edited by Ainslie Embree, translated by Edward C. Sachau. New York: Norton, 1971.

Aquinas, Saint Thomas. *Summa Theologica.* Translated by Fathers of the English Dominican Province, 5 vols. Brewster, Mass.: Christian Classics, 1981.

———. *de Ente et Essentia.* Translated by Peter King as *On Being and Essence.* Indianapolis: Hackett, 2007.

Ansary, Tamim. *Destiny Disrupted: A History of the World Through Islamic Eyes.* New York: Public Affairs, 2009.

Arendt, Hannah. *The Human Condition.* Chicago: University of Chicago Press, 1998.

Aristotle. *The Complete Works of Aristotle.* Edited by Jonathan Barnes. 2 vols. Princeton, N.J.: Princeton University Press, 1984.

Armstrong, Karen. *The Great Transformation: The Beginning of Our Religious Traditions.* Toronto: Vintage Canada, 2007.

———. *Islam: A Short History.* New York: Random House, 2002.

Augustine. *Confessions.* Translated by Garry Wills. New York: Penguin, 2002.

Bachelard, Gaston. *The Poetics of Space.* Boston: Beacon Press, 1994.

Badiou, Alain. *Saint Paul: The Foundation of Universalism.* Translated by Ray Brassier. Stanford: Stanford University Press, 2003.

Bates, Jennifer. *Hegel's Theory of Imagination.* Albany: State University of New York Press, 2004.

Bateson, Gregory. "Towards a Theory of Schizophrenia." Chapter 4.4 of *Steps to an Ecology of Mind: Collected Essays in Anthropology, Psychiatry, Evolution, and Epistemology.* Chicago: University of Chicago Press, 2000.

Bataille, Georges. *The Accursed Share.* Vol. 1. New York: Zone Books, 1991.

Baugh, Bruce. *French Hegel: From Surrealism to Postmodernism.* New York: Routledge, 2003.

———. "Sartre and James on the Role of the Body in Emotion." *Dialogue* 29 (1990): 357–373.

Baur, Michael, and John Russon (eds.). *Hegel and the Tradition: Essays in Honour of H. S. Harris.* Toronto: University of Toronto Press, 1997.

Beard, Charles. *An Economic Interpretation of the Constitution of the United States.* New York: Macmillan, 1965.

Bencivenga, Ermanno. *Hegel's Dialectical Logic.* New York: Oxford University Press, 2000.

Bergson, Henri. *Matter and Memory.* Translated by Nancy Margaret Paul and W. Scott Palmer. New York: Zone Books, 1991.

Berlin, Isaiah. *Vico and Herder: Two Studies in the History of Ideas.* New York: Vintage, 1976.

Bernstein, Jay. "Confession and Forgiveness: Hegel's Poetics of Action." In *Beyond Representation: Philosophy and Poetic Imagination,* edited by Richard Eldridge. New York: Cambridge University Press, 1996.

———. "Conscience and Transgression: The Exemplarity of Tragic Action." In *Hegel's Phenomenology of Spirit: A Reappraisal,* edited by G. K. Browning. London: Kluwer, 1997. pp. 79–97.

———. "Conscience and Transgression: The Persistence of Misrecognition." *The Bulletin of the Hegel Society of Great Britain,* 29 (1994): 55–70.

Berthold-Bond, Daniel. *Hegel's Grand Synthesis: A Study of Being, Thought, and History.* Albany: State University of New York Press, 1989.

———. *Hegel's Theory of Madness.* Albany: State University of New York Press, 1995.

Bowman, Brady. *Hegel and the Metaphysics of Absolute Negativity.* Cambridge: Cambridge University Press, 2013.

Braidotti, Rosi, and Alan D. Schrift. "Psychoanalysis and Desire." In *History of Continental Philosophy. Volume 6: Poststructuralism and Second Generation Critical Theory,* edited by Alan D. Schrift. Durham: Acumen, 2010, pp. 311–336.

Breton, André. *Manifestoes of Surrealism.* Translated by Richard Seaver and Helen R. Lane. Ann Arbor: University of Michigan Press, 1969.

———. *L'Amour fou.* Paris: Gallimard, 1937.

Brownlee, Timothy. "Freedom of Conscience and Subjective Right in Hegel's Political Philosophy." Boston University: Unpublished Doctoral Dissertation, 2007.

———. "Conscience and Recognition." Unpublished.

Buchwalter, Andrew. "Is Hegel's Philosophy of History Eurocentric?" Chapter 5 of Dudley, *Hegel and History.*

———. "Hegel's Concept of an International 'We,'" in *Identity and Difference in Hegel's Logic, Philosophy of Spirit and Politics,* ed. Philip Grier. Albany: State University of New York Press, 2007.

Burbidge, John. *The Logic of Hegel's Logic: An Introduction.* Ottawa: Broadview, 2006.

———. "Hegel's Open Future." Baur and Russon (eds.), *Hegel and the Tradition.*

———. "Hegel's Absolutes." *Owl of Minerva,* 29 (1997): 23–37.

———. "Language and Recognition," in Westphal (ed.), *Method and Speculation in Hegel's Phenomenology,* 85–94.

———."Unhappy Consciousness in Hegel—An Analysis of Medieval Catholicism?" *Mosaic,* 11, 4 (1977–78), 67–80.

Butler, Judith. *Subjects of Desire: Hegelian Reflections in Twentieth-Century France.* New York: Columbia University Press, 1987.

———. "Review of Michal S. Roth, *Knowing and History.*" *History and Theory* 29 (1990): 248–58.

Caldwell, Luke. "Schizophrenizing Lacan: Deleuze, [Guattari], and *Anti-Oedipus.*" *intersections* 10 (2009): 18–27.

Caputo, John D. (ed.) *Deconstruction in a Nutshell: A Conversation with Jacques Derrida.* New York: Fordham University Press, 1997.

Carey, Peter. *True History of the Kelly Gang.* New York: Vintage International, 2002.

Ciavatta, David. *Spirit, the Family and the Unconscious in Hegel's Philosophy.* Albany: State University of New York Press, 2009.

———. "Hegel on Desire's Knowledge." *The Review of Metaphysics* 61 (2008): 527–54.

———. "Hegel on Owning One's Own Body." *Southern Journal of Philosophy* 43 (2005).

———. "On Burying the Dead: Funerary Rites and the Dialectic of Freedom and Nature in Hegel's *Phenomenology of Spirit.*" *International Philosophical Quarterly*, 47 (2007): 279–96.

———. "The Event of Absolute Freedom: Hegel on the French Revolution and its Calendar." *Philosophy and Social Criticism* 40 (2014): 577–605.

———. "The Unreflective Bonds of Intimacy: Hegel on Family Ties and the Modern Person." *The Philosophical Forum* 37 (2006): 153–81.

Comay, Rebecca. "Dead Right: Hegel and the Terror." *The South Atlantic Quarterly*, 103 (2004): 375–95.

———. *Mourning Sickness: Hegel and the French Revolution.* Stanford: Stanford University Press, 2010.

Conklin, William. *Hegel's Laws: The Legitimacy of a Modern Legal Order.* Stanford: Stanford University Press, 2008.

Cook, Daniel J. *Language in the Philosophy of Hegel.* The Hague: Mouton and Co. 1973.

Cooper, Barry. *The End of History: An essay on modern Hegelianism.* Toronto: University of Toronto Press, 1984.

Copleston, Frederick. *A History of Philosophy*, vol. 7, "Fichte to Hegel." Garden City, N.Y.: Image Books, 1965.

Cornell, Drucilla. "The Philosophy of the Limit: Systems Theory and Feminist Legal Reform." In Drucilla Cornell, Michael Rosenfeld, David Gray Carlson (eds.), *Deconstruction and the Possibility of Justice.* New York: Routledge, 1992.

Critchley, Simon. "A Commentary Upon Derrida's Reading of Hegel in *Glas.*" *Bulletin of the Hegel Society of Great Britain*, 18 (1988): 6–32.

Cutrofello, Andrew. *Continental Philosophy: A Contemporary Introduction.* New York: Routledge, 2005.

Dahlstrom, Daniel. "The Dialectic of Conscience and the Necessity of Morality in Hegel's *Philosophy of Spirit.*" *Owl of Minerva*, 24 (1993): 181–89.

———. "Challenges to the Rational Observation of Nature in the Phenomenology of Spirit." *Owl of Minerva* 38 (2006–2007).

de Beauvoir, Simone. *Pour une morale de l'ambiguïté.* Paris: Gallimard, 1947; translated into English by Bernard Frechtman as *The Ethics of Ambiguity.* New York: Citadel, 1948.

———. *La deuxième sexe.* Paris: Gallimard, 1949; partially translated into English by H. M. Parshley as *The Second Sex.* Harmondsworth: Penguin, 1972.

Debrock, Guy. "The Silence of Language in Hegel's Dialectic." *Cultural Hermeneutics*, 3 (1973), 285–304.

de Boer, Karin. "Tragedy, Dialectics, and Différance: On Hegel and Derrida." *Southern Journal of Philosophy*, 39 (2001): 331–57.

———. "Hegel's Account of the Present: An Open-Ended History." Chapter 3 of Dudley (ed.), *Hegel and History.*

Deleuze, Gilles. *Empiricism and Subjectivity.* Translated by Constantin V. Boundas. New York: Columbia University Press, 1991.

———. *Pourparlers: 1972–1990.* Paris: Éditions de Minuit, 1990.

———. *Two Regimes of Madness.* Translated by Ames Hodges and Mike Taormina. New York: Semiotext(e), 2006.

———. *Kant's Critical Philosophy: The Doctrine of the Faculties.* Translated by Hugh Tomlinson and Barbara Habberjam. Minneapolis: University of Minnesota Press, 1984.

———. *Logic of Sense.* Translated by Mark Lester and Charles Stivale. New York: Columbia University Press, 1990.

———. and Félix Guattari. *L'Anti-Oedipe. Capitalisme et Schizophrénie 1,* Nouvelle Édition Augmentée. Paris: Les Éditions de Minuit, 1972/1973. Translated by Robert Hurley, Mark Seem, and Helen R. Lane as *Anti-Oedipus: Capitalism and Schizophrenia.* New York: Viking, 1977.

de Nys, Martin J. "Force and Understanding: The Unity of the Object of Consciousness." In Westphal (ed.), *Method and Speculation in Hegel's Phenomenology,* pp. 57–70.

Derrida, Jacques. *Glas.* Paris: Galilée, 1974. Translated by John P. Leavey Jr. and Richard Rand as *Glas.* Lincoln and London: University of Nebraska Press, 1986.

———. *Of Grammatology.* Translated by Gayatri Chakravorty Spivak. Baltimore and London: Johns Hopkins University Press, 1976.

———. *Rogues: Two Essays on Reason,* trans. Pascale-Anne Brault and Michael Naas. Stanford: Stanford University Press, 2005.

———. *Specters of Marx: The State of the Debt, the Work of Mourning, and the New International.* Translated by Peggy Kamuf. New York: Routledge, 1994.

———. "A Europe of Hope." Translated by Pleshette DeArmitt, Kas Saghafi, and Justine Malle, in *Epoché* 10 (2006): 407–12.

———. "Différance," in *Margins of Philosophy.* Translated by Alan Bass. Chicago: University of Chicago, 1982.

———. Edmund Husserl, *L'Origine de la géometrie,* translation and introduction by Jacques Derrida. Paris: Presses Universitaires de France, 1974. Translated by John P. Leavey Jr. as *Edmund Husserl's Origin of Geometry: An Introduction.* Lincoln: University of Nebraska Press, 1989.

———. "Force of Law: The Mystical Foundation of Authority." In Gil Anidjar (ed.), *Acts of Religion.* New York: Routledge, 2002, pp. 230–98.

———. "From Restricted to General Economy: An Hegelianism Without Reserve." In *Writing and Difference,* pp 251-77.

———. " 'Genèse et structure' et la phénoménologie." In *Entretiens sur les notions de genèse et de structure,* Maurice de Gandillac (ed.). Paris: Mouton, 1965, pp. 243–68. Revised version translated as " 'Genesis and Structure' and Phenomenology," in *Writing and Difference,* pp. 154–68.

———. *Le problème de la genèse dans la philosophie de Husserl.* Paris: Presses Universitaires de France, 1990.

———. *Margins of Philosophy.* Translated by Alan Bass. Chicago: University of Chicago Press, 1982.

———. "On Forgiveness." Translated by Michael Hughes, in *On Cosmopolitanism and Forgiveness.* New York: Routledge, 2001.

———. *Positions.* Translated by Alan Bass. Chicago: University of Chicago Press, 1971.

———. "The Theatre of Cruelty and the Closure of Representation." In *Writing and Difference,* pp 232-50.

———. "The Pit and the Pyramid: Introduction to Hegel's Semiology." In *Margins of Philosophy,* pp. 69–108.

———. "Tympan," in *Margins of Philosophy,* pp ix-xxix.

———. "Violence et métaphysique: Essai sur la pensée d'Emmanuel Levinas." In *L'écriture et la différence.* Paris: Éditions du Seuil, 1967. Translated as "Violence and Metaphysics: An Essay on the Thought of Emmanuel Levinas," in *Writing and Difference,* pp 79-153.

———. *Writing and Difference.* Translated by Alan Bass. Chicago: University of Chicago Press, 1978.

———, and Anne Dufourmantelle. *Of Hospitality.* Translated by Rachel Bowlby. Stanford: Stanford University Press, 2000.

Descartes, René. *Meditations on the First Philosophy in which the Existence of God and the Distinction between Mind and Body are Demonstrated,* in *The Philosophical Works of Descartes,* vol. 1. Translated by Elizabeth S. Haldane and G. R. T. Ross. Cambridge: Cambridge University Press, 1931.

de Vries, Willem. *Hegel's Theory of Mental Activity: An Introduction to Theoretical Spirit.* Ithaca and London: Cornell University Press, 1988.

Dewey, John. *Art as Experience.* New York: Perigree (Penguin), 1980.

———. *Democracy and Education: An Introduction to the Philosophy of Education.* New York: The Free Press, 1944.

d'Hondt, Jacques. *Hegel en son temps.* Paris: Éditions Sociales, 1968.

Dilthey, Wilhelm. "Die Jugendgeschichte Hegels," *Abhandlung der königlichen preussischen Akademie der Wissenschaften.* Berlin: Reimer, 1905.

Dodd, James. "The Body as 'Sign and Tool' in Hegel's *Encyclopaedia.*" *International Studies in Philosophy* 27 (1995): 21–32.

Doniger, Wendy. *The Hindus: An Alternative History.* New York: Penguin, 2009.

Donougho, Martin. "The Woman in White: On the Reception of Hegel's Antigone." *Owl of Minerva,* 21 (1988): 65–89.

Dooyeweerd, Herman. *A New Critique of Theoretical Thought.* 4 vols. Lewiston, N.Y.: Edwin Mellen, 1997.

———. *Roots of Western Culture: Pagan, Secular and Christian Options.* Toronto: Wedge, 1979.

Dove, Kenley. "Phenomenology and Systematic Philosophy." In Westphal (ed.), *Method and Speculation in Hegel's Phenomenology,* pp. 27–39.

Dudley, William. Review of Malabou, *The Future of Hegel, Notre Dame Philosophical Reviews,* October 5, 2006.

———. (ed.). *Hegel and History.* Albany: State University of New York Press, 2009.

———. "Freedom In and Through Hegel's Philosophy." *Dialogue* 39 (2000): 683–704.

Düsing, Klaus. "Hegels Theorie der Einbildungskraft." In *Psychologie und Anthropologie oder Philosophie des Geistes: Beiträge zu einer Hegel-Tagung in Marburg*

1989, ed. Franz Hespe and Burkhard Tuschling. Frommann-Holzboog, 1991, pp. 297–320.

Eckler, Judith A., and Otto Weininger. "Structural Parallels between Pretend Play and Narrative." *Developmental Psychology* 25 (1989): 736–43.

Eilan, N. (ed.). *Joint Attention: Communication and Other Minds: Issues in Philosophy and Psychology.* Oxford: Clarendon, 2005.

Elder, Crawford L. "Hegel's Teleology and the Relation Between Mind and Brain." *Southern Journal of Philosophy* 17 (1979): 27–45.

Engler, Susan. "The Narrative Worlds of What Is and What If." *Cognitive Development* 20 (2005): 514–25.

Fackenheim, Emil L. *The Religious Dimension in Hegel's Thought.* Chicago: University of Chicago Press, 1982.

Fagan, Patricia. "Philosophical History and the Roman Empire." In Baur and Russon (eds.), *Hegel and the Tradition.*

———. *Plato and Tradition: The Poetic and Cultural Context of Philosophy.* Evanston, Northwestern University Press, 2013.

———, and John Russon (eds.). *Reexamining Socrates in the Apology.* Evanston: Northwestern University Press, 2009.

Fichte, Johann Gottlieb. *Foundations of Natural Right.* Translated by Michael Baur. Cambridge: Cambridge University Press, 2000.

———. *Science of Knowledge.* Edited and translated by Peter Heath and John Lachs. Cambridge: Cambridge University Press, 1982.

———. *The Vocation of Man.* Translated by Peter Preuss. Indianapolis: Hackett, 1987.

Fillion, Réal. *Multicultural Dynamics and the Ends of History: Exploring Kant, Hegel, and Marx.* Ottawa: University of Ottawa Press, 2008.

Findlay, J. N. *Hegel: A Re-Examination.* London: George Allen and Unwin, 1958.

Fitzjohn, Timothy. *From Desire Through Thought to Conscience: Hegel on the Fulfillment of Self-Consciousness.* University of Guelph: Unpublished MA thesis, 2010.

Flay, Joseph C. *Hegel's Quest for Certainty.* Albany: State University of New York Press, 1987.

———. "The Dialectic of Irony and the Irony of Dialectic." *Owl of Minerva* 25 (1994): 209–14.

———. "Essence and Time in Hegel." *Owl of Minerva* 20 (1989): 183–92.

———. "Hegel and Merleau-Ponty: Radical Essentialism." In Galen A. Johnson and Michael B. Smith (eds.), *Ontology and Alterity in Merleau-Ponty.* Evanston: Northwestern University Press, 1990, pp. 142–57.

———. "Hegel's *Science of Logic*: Ironies of the Understanding." In di Giovanni (ed.), *Essays on Hegel's Logic.* Albany: State University of New York Press, pp. 153–69.

———. "Pragmatic Presuppositions and the Dialectics of Hegel's *Phenomenology.*" In Westphal (ed.), *Method and Speculation in Hegel's Phenomenology,* pp. 15–26.

———. "Time in Hegel's *Phenomenology of Spirit.*" *International Philosophical Quarterly,* 31 (1991): 259–73.

Fleisher Feldman, Carol. "Mimesis: Where Play and Narrative Meet." *Cognitive Development* 20 (2005): 503–13.

Forster, Michael N. *Hegel and Skepticism.* Cambridge, Mass.: Harvard University Press, 1989.

Foucault, Michel. *Discipline and Punish: The Birth of the Prison.* Translated by Alan Sheridan. New York: Vintage, 1977.

———. "Jean Hyppolite. 1907–1968." In *Dits et Écrits I: 1954–1975.* Paris: Gallimard, 2001.

Freud, Sigmund. *Civilization and Its Discontents.* Vol. 21 of *The Standard Edition of the Complete Psychological Works of Sigmund Freud,* edited by James Strachey. London: The Hogarth Press and the Institute of Psycho-Analysis, 1953.

———. "The Dissection of the Psychical Personality." Lecture 31 of *New Introductory Lectures.* Translated by James Strachey. Hammondsworth: Penguin, 1964.

———. *The Interpretation of Dreams.* Vol. 5 of *The Standard Edition.*

Friedman, R. Z. "Hypocrisy and the Highest Good: Hegel on Kant's Transition from Morality to Religion." *Journal of the History of Philosophy,* 24 (1986): 503–22.

Fulda, Hans Friedrich. "Zur Logik der *Phänomenologie* von 1807." *Hegel-Studien,* Beiheft 3 (1966): 75–101.

Gadamer, Hans-Georg. *Truth and Method.* Second, revised edition. Translated by Joel Weinsheimer and Donald G. Marshall. New York: Continuum, 2004.

———. *Hegels Dialektik: Sechs Hermeneutische Studien.* Tübingen: Mohr, 1980. Translated (excluding one essay) by P. Christopher Smith as *Hegel's Dialectic: Five Hermeneutical Studies.* New Haven: Yale University Press, 1976.

Galambush, Julie. *The Reluctant Parting: How the New Testament's Jewish Writers Created a Christian Book.* New York: HarperCollins, 2005.

Gasché, Rodolphe. *The Tain of the Mirror: Derrida and the Philosophy of Reflection.* Cambridge, Mass.: Harvard University Press, 1986.

Geroulanos, Stephanos. "Review of Bruce Baugh, *French Hegel.*" *MLN* 118 (2003): 1332–336.

Gibson, James J. *The Ecological Approach to Visual Perception.* New York: Houghton Mifflin, 1979.

Greene, Murray. *Hegel on the Soul: A Speculative Anthropology.* The Hague: Martinus Nijhoff, 1972.

———. "Natural Life and Subjectivity." In Stillman (ed.), *Hegel's Philosophy of Spirit,* pp. 94–117.

Grimmlinger, Friedrich. "Zum Begriff des Absoluten Wissens in Hegels Phänomenologie." In *Geschichte und System,* edited by Hans-Dieter Klein and Erhard Oeser. Vienna and Munich: R. Oldenbourg, 1972, pp. 279–300.

Guyer, Paul. "Hegel, Leibniz und der Widerspruch des Endlichen." In *Seminar: Dialektic in der Philosophie Hegels,* edited by R.-P. Horstmann. Frankfurt: Suhrkamp, 1978, pp. 230–60.

Hanna, Robert. Review of Michael N. Forster, *Hegel and Skepticism. Review of Metaphysics,* 43 (1990): 630–31.

Harris, H. S. *Hegel's Development: Toward the Sunlight (1770–1801)*. Oxford: Clarendon, 1972.

———. *Hegel's Development: Night Thoughts (Jena 1801–1806)*. Oxford: Clarendon, 1983.

———. *Hegel's Ladder*. 2 vols. Indianapolis: Hackett, 1998.

———. *Hegel: Phenomenology and System*. Indianapolis: Hackett, 1995.

———. "Comment on Phenomenology as Systematic Philosophy." In Westphal (ed.), *Method and Speculation in Hegel's Phenomenology*, pp. 41–46.

———. "The Concept of Recognition in Hegel's Jena Manuscripts." *Hegel-Studien Beiheft* 20 (1979), pp. 229–48.

———. "Hegel and Antigone's Unwritten Laws." Lecture 1 of *Literature and Religion in Hegel's Phenomenology*. Unpublished.

———. "Skepticism, Dogmatism and Speculation in the Critical Journal." In di Giovanni and Harris (eds.), *Between Kant and Hegel: Texts in the Development of Post-Kantian Idealism*, pp. 252–71.

Heidegger, Martin. *Hegels Phänomenologie des Geistes, Gesamtausgabe*, Bd. 32. Frankfurt am Main: Vittorio Klosterman, 1980. Translated by Parvis Emad and Kenneth Maly as *Hegel's Phenomenology of Spirit*. Bloomington and Indianapolis: Indiana University Press, 1988.

———. *Being and Time*. Translated by John Macquarrie and Edward Robinson. New York: Harper and Row, 1962.

———. *The Fundamental Concepts of Metaphysics: World, Finitude, Solitude*. Translated by William McNeill and Nicholas Walker. Bloomington and Indianapolis: Indiana University Press, 2001.

———. *Grundbegriffe, Gesamtausgabe*. Vol. 51. Frankfurt am Main: Vittorio Klostermann, 1981. Translated by Gary E. Aylesworth as *Basic Concepts*. Bloomington: Indiana University Press, 1993.

———. "The Origin of the Work of Art." Translated by Albert Hofstadter, in *Poetry, Language, Thought*. New York: Harper and Row, 1971, pp. 17–87.

———. "The Question Concerning Technology." In Krell (ed), *Basic Writings*. New York: HarperCollins, 1993, pp. 311–41.

Heidegren, Carl-Göran. "Hegels Nürnberger Propädeutik—eine wichtige Phase in der Entstehung der 'Rechtsphilosophie'." *Archiv für Geschichte der Philosophie* 70 (1988): 179–211.

Henrich, Dieter. *Aesthetic Judgment and the Moral Image of the World: Studies in Kant*. Stanford: Stanford University Press, 1992.

———. (ed). *Hegels Philosophische Psychologie. Hegel-Studien*, Beiheft 19, 1979.

———. "Hegels Logik der Reflexion: Neue Fassung," *Hegel-Studien*, Beiheft 18, 1978. Bonn: Bouvier, 1978, pp. 203–324.

———. "Anfang und Methode der Logik." *Hegel-Studien* Beiheft 1 (1964): 19–35. Reprinted in *Hegel im Kontext*, edited by Dieter Henrich. Frankfurt am Main: Suhrkamp, 1971, pp. 73–94.

———. "Fichte's Original Insight." Translated by David R. Lachterman, in *Contemporary German Philosophy*, vol. 1., ed. Darrell E. Christensen, Manfred Reidel, Robert Spaemann, Reiner Wiehl, and Wolfgang Wieland. University Park and London: Pennsylvania State University Press, 1982, pp. 15–53.

———. "Formen der Negation in Hegels Logik." In *Seminar: Dialektik in der Philosophie Hegels*, edited by R.-P. Horstmann. Frankfurt am Main: Suhrkamp, 1978, pp. 213–29.

———. "Logical Form and Real Totality: The Authentic Conceptual Form of Hegel's Concept of the State." Chapter 10 of *Hegel on Ethics and Politics*, edited by Robert B. Pippin and Otfried Höffe. Cambridge: Cambridge University Press, 2004.

Herbenick, Raymond M. "Hegel's Concept of Embodiment." *Philosophical Studies* (Dublin) 20 (1972): 109–12.

Herington, Jon. *Poetry into Drama: Early Tragedy and the Greek Poetic Tradition.* Berkeley: University of California Press, 1985.

Hesiod, the Homeric Hymns, and Homerica. Translated by Hugh G. Evelyn-White. Loeb Classical Library. Cambridge, Mass.: Harvard University Press, 1914.

Hinchman, Lewis P. *Hegel's Critique of the Enlightenment.* Gainesville and Tampa: University of Florida / University of South Florida Press, 1984.

Hobbes, Thomas. *Leviathan.* Ottawa: Broadview Press, 2010.

Hoff, Shannon. "Restoring Antigone to Ethical Life: Nature and Sexual Difference in Hegel's *Phenomenology of Spirit.*" *Owl of Minerva* 38 (2006–2007): 77–99.

———. *The Laws of the Spirit: A Hegelian Theory of Justice.* Albany: State University of New York Press, 2014.

———. "Locke and the Nature of Political Authority." *The Review of Politics* 77 (2015): 1–22.

Holland, Eugene W. "The Anti-Oedipus: Postmodernism in Theory; or the post-Lacanian historical contextualization of psychoanalysis." *Boundary 2,* 14 (1985): 291–307.

Holroyd, Charles. *Michael Angelo Buonarroti.* London: Duckworth and Company, 1903.

Hösle, Vittorio. *Hegels System. Der Idealismus der Subjektivität und das Problem der Intersubjektivität,* Bd. 2. Hamburg: Felix Meiner, 1987.

Houlgate, Steven. "Essence, Reflexion, and Immediacy in Hegel's *Science of Logic.*" In Stephen Houlgate and Michael Baur (ed), *A Companion to Hegel.* Chichester: Blackwell, 2011, pp. 139–58.

———. *Freedom, Truth and History: An Introduction to Hegel's Philosophy.* London and New York: Routledge, 1991.

———. *The Opening of Hegel's Logic: From Being to Infinity.* Purdue University Press, 2005.

———. "World History as the Progress of Consciousness: An Interpretation of Hegel's Philosophy of History." *Owl of Minerva* 22 (1990): 69–80.

Hume, David. *An Enquiry Concerning Human Understanding.* Oxford: Oxford University Press, 1999.

Husserl, Edmund. *The Phenomenology of Internal Time-Consciousness.* Translated by James S. Churchill. Bloomington: Indiana University Press, 1966.

———. *Cartesian Meditations.* Translated by Dorion Cairns. The Hague: Martinus Nijhoff, 1960.

———. *Ideas Pertaining to a Pure Phenomenology and to a Phenomenological Philosophy*, First Book. Translated by Fred Kersten. Dordrecht: Kluwer, 1982.

———. *Logical Investigations.* Translated by J. N. Findlay. 2 vols. London: Routledge, 2001.

Hutson-Nechkash, Peg. *Narrative Toolbox: Blueprint for Storybuilding.* Eau Claire, Wisc.: Thinking Publications, 2001.

Hutto, Daniel D. (ed.). *Narrative and Understanding Persons.* Cambridge: Cambridge University Press, 2007.

———. "Elementary Mind Minding, Enactivist Style." In *Joint Attention: New Developments in Philosophy, Psychology and Neuroscience*, edited by Axel Seemann. Cambridge, Mass.: MIT Press, 2011.

Hyppolite, Jean. *Genèse et Structure de la Phénoménologie de l'Esprit de Hegel.* Paris: Éditions Montaigne, 1946. Translated by Samuel Cherniak and John Heckman as *Genesis and Structure of Hegel's Phenomenology.* Evanston: Northwestern University Press, 1974.

———. "La conception hégélienne de l'état et sa critique par Karl Marx." *Cahiers internationaux de sociologie* 2 (1946): 142–159.

———. *Logique et Existence.* Paris: Presses Universitaires de France, 1952. Translated by Leonard Lawlor and Amit Sen as *Logic and Existence.* Albany: State University of New York Press, 1997.

Jacobson, Kirsten. *Being at Home: A Phenomenological Analysis of the Experience of Space.* Unpublished doctoral dissertation, Pennsylvania State University, 2006.

———. "Heidegger, Winnicott, and *The Velveteen Rabbit*: Anxiety, Toys, and the Drama of Metaphysics." Chapter 1 of Peter Costello (ed.), *Philosophy in Children's Literature.* Lanham, MD: Lexington Books, 2011.

———. "The Experience of Home and the Space of Citizenship." *Southern Journal of Philosophy*, 48 (2010): 219–245.

Jankélévitch, Vladimir. *Forgiveness.* Translated by Andrew Kelley. Chicago: University of Chicago Press, 2005.

Jonas, Hans. *The Phenomenon of Life: Towards a Philosophical Biology.* Evanston: Northwestern University Press, 2001.

Kalenberg, Thomas. *Die Befreiung der Natur. Natur und Selbstbewusstsein in der Philosophie Hegels.* Hamburg: Felix Meiner, 1997.

Kant, Immanuel. *Critique of Pure Reason.* Translated by Werner S. Pluhar. Indianapolis: Hackett, 1996.

———. *Critique of Judgment.* Translated by Werner S. Pluhar. Indianapolis: Hackett, 1987.

———. *Groundwork for the Metaphysics of Morals.* Edited by Lara Denis (revised Thomas Abbott translation). Ottawa: Broadview Press, 2005.

———. "The Idea of a Universal History from a Cosmopolitan Perspective." In *Perpetual Peace and Other Essays.* Translated by Ted Humphrey. Indianapolis: Hackett, 1983.

Kates, Joshua. *Essential History: Jacques Derrida and the Development of Deconstruction.* Evanston: Northwestern University Press, 2005.

Kelly, George Armstrong. *Hegel's Retreat from Eleusis: Studies in Political Thought.* Princeton, N.J.: Princeton University Press, 1978.

Kline, George L. "The Dialectic of Action and Passion in Hegel's *Phenomenology of Spirit.*" *Review of Metaphysics,* 23 (1969–70): 679–89.

Knox, T. M. "Hegel's Attitude to Kant's Ethics." *Kant-Studien,* 49 (1957–58): 70–81.

Kojève, Alexandre. *Introduction à la Lecture de Hegel.* Paris: Gallimard, 1947. Partially translated by James H. Nichols Jr. and edited by Allan Bloom as *Introduction to the Reading of Hegel.* New York: Basic Books, 1969.

Kolb, David. *The Critique of Pure Modernity: Hegel, Heidegger and After.* Chicago: University of Chicago Press, 1986.

———. "The Final Name of God." In Baur and Russon (eds.), *Hegel and the Tradition.*

Kosman, Aryeh. *The Activity of Being: An Essay on Aristotle's Ontology.* Cambridge, Mass.: Harvard University Press, 2013.

Koyré, Alexandre. "Hegel à Iéna." In *Etudes d'histoire de la pensée philosophique.* Paris: Gallimard, 1981, pp. 147–89.

———. Review of *Le Malheur de la conscience* in *Revue philosophique de la France et de l'étranger,* 110 (1930): 136–43.

Krell, David. *Contagion: Sexuality, Disease and Death in German Idealism and Romanticism.* Bloomington: Indiana University Press, 1998.

Kristeva, Julia. *La révolution de langage poétique.* Paris: Éditions du Seuil, 1974. Abridged and translated by Margaret Waller as *The Revolution in Poetic Language.* New York: Columbia University Press, 1984.

Labarriere, Pierre-Jean. "La *Phénoménologie de l'Esprit* comme Discours Systématique: Histoire, Religion et Science." *Hegel-Studien,* 9 (1974): 131–53.

Lacan, Jacques. *The Seminar Book XI: Four Fundamental Concepts of Psychoanalysis.* Translated by Jacques-Alain Miller and Alan Sheridan. London: Hogarth, 1977.

———. *Écrits: A Selection.* Translated by Alan Sheridan. New York: Norton, 1977.

Laing, R. D. *The Divided Self: An Existential Study in Sanity and Madness.* Harmondsworth: Penguin, 1990.

Lampert, Jay. *Synthesis and Backwards Reference in Husserl's Logical Investigations.* Dordrecht: Kluwer, 1995.

———. *Deleuze and Guattari's Philosophy of History.* London and New York: Continuum, 2006.

———. "Hegel and Ancient Egypt: History and Becoming." *International Philosophical Quarterly* 35 (1995): 43–58.

———. "Hegel in the Future." Unpublished.

———. "Husserl and Hegel on the logic of subjectivity." *Man and World,* 21 (1988): 363–93.

———. "Husserl's Account of Syncategorematic Terms: The Problem of Representing the Synthetic Connections That Underlie Meaning." *Southern Journal of Philosophy,* 30 (1992): 67–94.

———. "Leaving the System as is—Derrida and Hegel." In David Goicoechea and Marko Zlomislic (eds.), *Joyful Wisdom* 6 (1997): 187–206.

———. "Locke, Fichte and Hegel on the Right to Property." Chapter 2 of Baur and Russon (eds.), *Hegel and the Tradition.*

Lapidus, Ira M. *A History of Islamic Societies.* 2nd ed. Cambridge: Cambridge University Press, 2002.

Lawlor, Leonard. *Derrida and Husserl: The Basic Problem of Phenomenology.* Bloomington: Indiana University Press, 2002.

Lauer, Quentin. *A Reading of Hegel's Phenomenology of Spirit.* 2nd ed. New York: Fordham University Press, 1993.

———. "Commentary on 'The Birth of Spirit for Hegel out of the Travesty of Medicine'." In Stillman (ed.), *Hegel's Philosophy of Spirit,* pp. 43–46.

Lewontin, R. C. *Biology as Ideology: The Doctrine of DNA.* San Francisco: Harper Perennial, 1993.

Locke, John. *An Essay Concerning Human Understanding.* Harmondsworth: Penguin Classics, 1998.

Longuenesse, Beatrice. *Kant and the Capacity to Judge: Sensibility and Discursivity in the Transcendental Analytic of the Critique of Pure Reason.* Translated by Charles T. Wolfe. Princeton, N.J.: Princeton University Press, 1998.

Löwith, Karl. *From Hegel to Nietzsche: The Revolution in Nineteenth-Century Thought.* Translated by David. E. Green. Garden City: Anchor Books, 1967.

Ludwig, Walter D. "Hegel's Conception of Absolute Knowing." *Owl of Minerva,* 21 (1989): 5–19.

MacGregor, David. "The State at Dusk." *Owl of Minerva,* 21 (1989): 51–64.

MacIntyre, Alasdair (ed.). *Hegel: A Collection of Critical Essays.* Notre Dame: University of Notre Dame Press, 1976.

———. "Hegel on Faces and Skulls." MacIntyre (ed), *Hegel: A Collection of Critical Essays,* pp. 219–36.

Maclaren, Kym. "The Role of Emotion in an Existential Education: Insights from Hegel and Plato." *International Philosophical Quarterly,* 48 (2008): 471–92.

Maker, William. *Philosophy Without Foundations: Rethinking Hegel.* Albany: State University of New York Press, 1994.

———. "Does Hegel Have a 'Dialectical Method'?" *Southern Journal of Philosophy* 20 (1982): 75–96.

Malabou, Catherine. *L'Avenir de Hegel: Plasticité, temporalité, dialectique.* Paris: Vrin, 1996. Translated by Lisabeth During as *The Future of Hegel: Plasticity, Temporality, Dialectic.* New York: Routledge, 2005.

Marx, Karl. *Selected Writings,* 2nd ed. Edited by David McClellan. Oxford: Oxford University Press, 2000.

Massumi, Brian. *A User's Guide to Capitalism and Schizophrenia: Deviations from Deleuze and Guattari.* Cambridge, Mass.: MIT Press, 1992.

May, Todd. *Gilles Deleuze: An Introduction.* Cambridge: Cambridge University Press, 2005.

McCarthy, Vincent A. *Quest for a Philosophical Jesus: Christianity and Philosophy in Rousseau, Kant, Hegel, and Schelling.* Macon, Georgia: Mercer University Press, 1986.

McCumber, John. *The Company of Words: Hegel, Language and Systematic Philosophy.* Evanston: Northwestern University Press, 1993.

———. *Reshaping Reason: Towards a New Philosophy.* Bloomington: Indiana University Press, 2005.

———. “Hegel and Hamann: Ideas and Life.” In Baur and Russon (eds.), *Hegel and the Tradition.*

———. “Hegel on Habit.” *Owl of Minerva,* 21 (1990): 155–65.

Merleau-Ponty, Maurice. “Hegel's Existentialism.” In *Sense and Non-Sense,* pp. 63–70.

———. *Husserl at the Limits of Phenomenology.* Edited by Leonard Lawlor and Bettina Bergo. Evanston: Northwestern University Press, 2002.

———. “Indirect Language and the Voices of Silence.” In *Signs,* pp. 39–83.

———. “Man and Adversity,” in *Signs,* pp. 224–43.

———. “Metaphysics and the Novel.” In *Sense and Non-sense,* pp. 26–40.

———. *Phenomenology of Perception.* Translated by Colin Smith. London and New York: Routledge, 2002.

———. *Sense and Non-Sense.* Translated by Hubert L. Dreyfus and Patricia Allen Dreyfus. Evanston: Northwestern University Press, 1964.

———. *Signs.* Translated by Richard C. McCleary. Evanston: Northwestern University Press, 1964.

Mills, Jon. *The Unconscious Abyss.* Albany: State University of New York Press, 2002.

Moore, C., and P. J. Denham, eds. *Joint Attention: Its Origins and Role in Development.* Hillsdale, N.J.: Lawrence Erlbaum Associates, 1995.

Mure, G. R. G. *A Study of Hegel's Logic.* Oxford: Oxford University Press, 1950.

Mydans, Seth. “Churches Attacked in Malaysian ‘Allah’ Dispute.” *New York Times,* January 8, 2010, accessed online: http://www.nytimes.com/2010/01/09/world/asia/09malaysia.html.

Naas, Michael. *Derrida From Now On.* New York: Fordham University Press, 2008.

Nagy, Gregory. *The Best of the Achaeans: Concepts of the Hero in Archaic Greek Literature.* Baltimore: Johns Hopkins University Press, 1979.

Nancy, Jean-Luc. *Hegel: The Restlessness of the Negative.* Translated by Jason E. Smith and Steven Miller. Minneapolis: University of Minnesota Press, 2002.

Neuhouser, Frederick. *Foundations of Hegel's Social Theory.* Cambridge, Mass.: Harvard University Press, 2000.

Nicolin, Friedhelm. “Zum Titelproblem der *Phänomenologie des Geistes.*” *Hegel-Studien,* 4 (1967): 113–23.

Nicolopoulou, Ageliki. “Play and Narrative in the Process of Development: Commonalities, differences and interrelations.” *Cognitive Development* 20 (2005): 495–502.

Noë, Alva. *Action in Perception.* Cambridge, Mass.: MIT Press, 2004.

Owens, Joseph J. *The Doctrine of Being in the Aristotelian Metaphysics.* Toronto: Pontifical Institute of Medieval Studies, 1978.

Peperzak, Adriaan. *Autoconoscenza dell'assoluto: Lineamenti della filosofia dello spirito hegeliana.* Napoli: Istituto Italiano per gli Studi Filosofici, 1988.

———. *Modern Freedom.* Boston: Kluwer, 2001.

Petry, M. J. Review of Murray Greene, *Hegel on the Soul: A Speculative Anthropology. Hegel-Studien,* 9 (1974): 290–95.

Piaget, Jean, and Bärbel Inhelder. *The Child's Conception of Space,* F. J. Langden and J. L. Lunzer (trans). London: Routledge and Kegan Paul, 1956.

Pinkard, Terry. "Freedom and Social Categories in Hegel's Ethics." *Philosophy and Phenomenological Research*, 47 (1986–87): 209–32.

———. *Hegel's Phenomenology: The Sociality of Reason.* Cambridge: Cambridge University Press, 1996.

———. "Hegel in the Twentieth Century." Chapter 4 of Dermot Moran (ed), *The Routledge Companion to Twentieth Century Philosophy.* New York: Routledge, 2008, pp. 127–32.

Pippin, Robert B. *Hegel's Idealism: the Satisfactions of Self-Consciousness.* Cambridge: Cambridge University Press, 1989.

———. *Idealism as Modernism: Hegelian Variations.* New York: Cambridge University Press, 1997.

———, and Otfried Höffe (eds.). *Hegel on Ethics and Politics.* Cambridge: Cambridge University Press, 2004.

Plato. *Collected Dialogues.* Edited by Edith Hamilton and Huntingdon Cairns. Princeton, N.J.: Princeton University Press, 1963.

Plotinus. *Enneads.* Translated by A. H. Armstrong. 7 vols. Loeb Classical Library. Cambridge, Mass.: Harvard University Press, 1969–88.

Pöggeler, Otto. "Die Komposition der *Phänomenologie des Geistes.*" *Hegel-Studien*, Beiheft 3 (1966): 27–74.

———. "Zur Deutung der *Phänomenologie des Geistes.*" *Hegel-Studien*, 1 (1961): 255–94.

Redding, Paul. *Hegel's Hermeneutics.* Ithaca and London: Cornell University Press, 1996.

Reyburn, Hugh A. *The Ethical Theory of Hegel.* Oxford: Clarendon Press, 1921.

Ricouer, Paul. "On Interpretation." Translated by Kathleen McLaughlin, in Montefiore (ed), *Philosophy in France Today.* Cambridge: Cambridge University Press, 1983, pp. 175–97.

Rilke, Rainer Maria. *Selected Poetry of Rainer Maria Rilke.* Translated by Stephen Mitchell. New York: Random House, 1982.

Ripstein, Arthur. "Universal and General Wills: Hegel and Rousseau." *Political Theory* 22 (1994): 444–67.

Ritter, Joachim. *Hegel and the French Revolution: Essays on the Philosophy of Right.* Translated by Richard Dien Winfield. Cambridge, Mass.: MIT Press, 1982.

Robinson, Jonathan. *Duty and Hypocrisy in Hegel's Phenomenology of Mind: An Essay in the Real and Ideal.* Toronto and Buffalo, N.Y.: University of Toronto Press, 1977.

Rockmore, Tom. *Cognition: An Introduction to Hegel's Phenomenology of Spirit.* Berkeley: University of California Press, 1997.

———. "Foundationalism and Hegelian Logic." *Owl of Minerva*, 21 (1989): 41–50.

Rosen, Michael. *Hegel's Dialectic and its Criticism.* Cambridge: Cambridge University Press, 1982.

Rosen, Stanley. "*Sophrosune* and *Selbstbewusstsein.*" *Review of Metaphysics*, 26 (1972–73): 617–42.

Ross, Nathan. "The Mechanization of Labor and the Birth of Modern Ethicality in Hegel's Jena Writings." Chapter 9 of Dudley (ed.), *Hegel and History.*

Roth, Michael S. *Knowing and History: Appropriations of Hegel in Twentieth-Century France.* Ithaca: Cornell University Press, 1988.

Rudé, George. *The French Revolution: Its Causes, Its History, and Its Legacy after 200 Years.* New York: Grove Press, 1991.

Runner, H. Evan. *The Relation of the Bible to Learning.* Jordan Station, Ontario: Paideia Press, 1982.

Russon, John. "Aristotle's Animative Epistemology." *Idealistic Studies* 25 (1995): 241–53.

———. *Bearing Witness to Epiphany: Persons, Things, and the Nature of Erotic Life.* Albany: State University of New York Press, 2009.

———. "The (Childish) Nature of the Soul in Plato's *Apology.*" In Fagan and Russon (eds.), *Reexamining Socrates in the Apology.*

———. "Embodiment and Responsibility: Merleau-Ponty and the Ontology of Nature." *Man and World* 27 (1994): 291–308.

———. "Expressing Dwelling: Dewey and Hegel on Art as Cultural Self-Articulation." *Contemporary Pragmatism* 12 (2015): 37–57.

———. "'For Now We See as Through a Glass Darkly': The Systematics of Hegel's Visual Imagery." In David Levin (ed.), *Sites of Vision: The Discursive Construction of Sight in the History of Philosophy.* Cambridge, Mass.: MIT Press, 1997, pp. 197–239.

———. "Haunted by History: Merleau-Ponty, Hegel and the Phenomenology of Pain." *Journal of Contemporary Thought* 37 (2013): 81–94.

———. "Hegel's Phenomenology of Reason and Dualism." *Southern Journal of Philosophy* 31 (1993): 71–96.

———. "Heidegger, Hegel and Ethnicity: The Ritual Basis of Self-Identity." *Southern Journal of Philosophy* 33 (1995): 509–32.

———. "Hermeneutical Pressure and the Space of Dialectic: What Hegel Means by 'Spirit'." In Charles E. Scott and John Sallis (eds.), *Interrogating the Tradition: Hermeneutics and the History of Philosophy.* Albany: State University of New York Press, 2000, pp. 235–53.

———. *Human Experience: Philosophy, Neurosis, and the Elements of Everyday Life.* Albany: State University of New York Press, 2003.

———. "On Secrets and Sharing: Hegel, Heidegger and Derrida on the Economics of the Public Sphere." In Divya Diwedi and Sanil V. (eds.), *The Public Sphere from Outside the West.* New Delhi: Bloomsbury, 2015, pp. 41–57.

———. "Reading and the Body in Hegel." *Clio* 22 (1993): 321–36.

———. *Reading Hegel's Phenomenology.* Bloomington: Indiana University Press, 2004.

———. Review of Steven Houlgate, *Freedom Truth and History: An Introduction to Hegel's Philosophy. Hegel-Studien* 27 (1992): 192–95.

———. "Self and Other in Hegel's Phenomenology of Spirit." *Journal of Indian Council of Philosophical Research* 18 (2011): 1–18.

———. "Self-Consciousness and the Tradition in Aristotle's Psychology." *Laval Théologique et Philosophique* 52 (1996): 777–803.

———. "The Bodily Unconscious in Freud's 'Three Essays'." In Jon Mills (ed),

Rereading Freud: Psychoanalysis Through Philosophy. Albany: State University of New York Press, 2004, pp. 33–50.

———. "The Body as Site of Action and Intersubjectivity in Fichte's *Foundations of Natural Right.*" In Gabriel Gottlieb (ed), *The Cambridge Companion to Fichte's Foundations of Natural Right.* Cambridge: Cambridge University Press, 2016.

———. "The Metaphysics of Consciousness and the Hermeneutics of Social Life: Hegel's Phenomenological System." *Southern Journal of Philosophy* 36 (1998): 81–101.

———. *The Self and Its Body in Hegel's Phenomenology of Spirit.* Toronto: University of Toronto Press, 1997.

———. "The Virtues of Agency: Phenomenological Reflections on Confidence, Courage, and Creativity." Chapter 10 of Kevin Hermberg and Paul Gyllenhammer (eds.), *Phenomenology and Virtue Ethics.* London and New York: Bloomsbury, 2013.

Sallis, John. *Chorology: On Beginning in Plato's Timaeus.* Bloomington: Indiana University Press, 1999.

———. "Hegel's Concept of Presentation: Its Determination in the Preface to the Phenomenology of Spirit." *Hegel-Studien* 12 (1977): 129–56.

———. "Imagination and Presentation in Hegel's Philosophy of Spirit." In Peter Stillman (ed.), *Hegel's Philosophy of Spirit.* Albany: State University of New York Press, 1987, pp. 66–88.

Sartre, Jean-Paul. *Critique of Dialectical Reason.* 2 vols. Translated by Alan Sheridan-Smith (vol. 1) and Quintin Hoare (vol. 2). New York: Verso, 2004 (vol. 1) and 2006 (vol. 2).

———. *Nausea.* Translated by Hayden Carruth. New York: New Directions, 1964.

———. *L'Être et le néant.* Paris: Gallimard, 1943. Translated by Hazel E. Barnes as *Being and Nothingness.* New York: Washington Square Press, 1992.

———. "Une Idée Fondamentale de la Phénoménologie de Husserl: l'Intentionnalité." In *Situations* I. Paris: Gallimard, 1947.

———. "Merleau-Ponty vivant." In *Situations* vol 4. Paris: Gallimard, 1964. Translated and reprinted in *The Debate Between Sartre and Merleau-Ponty,* Jon Steward (ed). Evanston: Northwestern University Press, 1998.

———. *The Transcendence of the Ego: An Existentialist Theory of Consciousness.* Translated by Forrest Williams and Robert Kirkpatrick. New York: Noonday Press, 1960.

Sax, Benjamin C. "Active Individuality and the Language of Confession: The Figure of the Beautiful Soul in the *Lehrjahre* and the *Phänomenologie.*" *Journal of the History of Philosophy* 21 (1983): 437–66.

Scheiber, Wolfgang. "'Habitus' als Schlüssel zu Hegels Daseinslogik." *Hegel-Studien,* 20 (1985): 125–44.

Schelling, F. W. J. *System of Transcendental Idealism (1800).* Translated by Peter Heath. Charlottesville: University Press of Virginia, 1978.

Schettino, Humberto. "The Notion of Politics in Marx's Early Writings." *Crítica. Revista Hispanoamericana de Filosophia* 36 (2004): 3–38.

Schmidt, Dennis J. "Circles—Hermeneutic and Otherwise: On Various Senses of the Future as 'Not Yet'." In David Wood (ed.), *Writing the Future.* London: Routledge, 1990, pp. 67–77.

Schmitt, Carl. *The Concept of the Political.* Translated by Georges Schwab. Chicago: University of Chicago Press, 1996.

Schmitz, Kenneth L. "Enriching the Copula." *Review of Metaphysics* 27 (1973–74): 492–512.

———. "Hegel's Assessment of Spinoza." In Richard Kennington (ed.), *Studies in Philosophy and the History of Philosophy,* vol. 7. Washington, D.C.: Catholic University of America Press, 1980.

———. "Hegel on Kant: Being-in-itself and the Thing-in-itself." In Richard Kennington (ed), *Studies in Philosophy and the History of Philosophy,* vol. 12. Washington, D.C.: Catholic University of America Press, 1985.

———. "Hegel's Attempt to Forge a Logic for Spirit." *Dialogue* 10 (1971): 653–72.

———. "Hegel's Philosophy of Religion: Typology and Strategy." *Review of Metaphysics,* 23 (1969–70): 717–36.

———. "Metaphysics: Radical, Comprehensive, Determinate Discourse." *Review of Metaphysics,* 39 (1986): 675–94.

———. "Philosophy of Religion and the Redefinition of Philosophy." *Man and World* 3,2 (1970): 54–82.

———. "Purity of Soul and Immortality." *Monist,* 69 (1986): 396–415.

Schrader, George A. "Hegel's Contribution to Phenomenology." *Monist* 48 (1964): 18–33.

Shannon, Daniel Edward. *The Question Concerning the Factum of Experience: The Ontological Dimensions of Hegel's Thought.* Toronto: University of Toronto, Unpublished Doctoral Dissertation, 1989.

———. "Hegel's Criticism of Analogical Procedure and the Search for Final Purpose." *Owl of Minerva* 19 (1988): 169–82.

Sheets-Johnstone, Maxine. *The Primacy of Movement.* Philadelphia: John Benjamins Publishing, 1999.

Shklar, Judith N. *Freedom and Independence: A Study of the Political Ideas of Hegel's Phenomenology of Mind.* Cambridge: Cambridge University Press, 1976.

Siep, Ludwig. "The 'Aufhebung' of Morality in Ethical Life." Lawrence S. Stepelevich and David Lamb (eds.), *Hegel's Philosophy of Action,* pp. 137–55.

———. "Zur Dialectik der Anerkennung bei Hegel." *Hegel-Jahrbuch* 1975, pp. 366–73.

Simpson, Peter. *Hegel's Transcendental Induction.* Albany: State University of New York Press, 1998.

Smith, Stephen B. *Hegel's Critique of Liberalism.* Chicago: University of Chicago Press, 1989.

Soboul, Albert. *A Short History of the French Revolution 1789–1799.* Translated by Geoffrey Symcox. Berkeley: University of California Press, 1977.

Solomon, Robert C. "Hegel's Epistemology." *American Philosophical Quarterly,* 2 (1974): 277–89.

———. "Hegel's Concept of *Geist.*" In MacIntyre (ed.), *Hegel: A Collection of Critical Essays,* pp. 125–49.

———. "Hegel's *Phenomenology of Spirit.*" Chapter 6 of Robert C. Solomon and

Kathleen M. Higgins (eds.), *The Age of German Idealism*. London and New York: Routledge, 1993.

Sophocles. *Antigone*. Translated by Richmond Lattimore, in David Grene (ed.), *Greek Tragedies* vol. 1, 2nd edition. Chicago: University of Chicago Press, 1991.

Sparshott, Francis. *Taking Life Seriously*. Toronto: University of Toronto Press, 1996.

Stegmaier, Werner. "Leib und Leben: zum Hegel-Nietzsche-Problem." *Hegel-Studien*, 20 (1985): 173–98.

Stepaniants, Marianna. "The Encounter of Zoroastrianism with Islam." *Philosophy East and West*, 52 (2002): 159–72.

Stepelevich, Lawrence, and David Lamb (eds.). *Hegel's Philosophy of Action*. Atlantic Highlands, N.J.: Humanities Press, 1983.

Stern, David S. Review of David Kolb, *The Critique of Pure Modernity: Hegel, Heidegger and After*. *Owl of Minerva* 21 (1990): 185–90.

Stern, Robert (ed.). *G.W.F. Hegel: Critical Assessments*. New York: Routledge, 1993.

Stewart, Jon. *The Hegel Myths and Legends*. Evanston: Northwestern University Press, 1996.

Stillman, Peter G. (ed). *Hegel's Philosophy of Spirit*. Albany: State University of New York Press, 1987.

Stoetzler, Marcel. "Subject Trouble: Judith Butler and Dialectics." *Philosophy and Social Criticism* 31 (2005): 343–68.

Talero, Maria. "Merleau-Ponty and the Bodily Subject of Learning." *International Philosophical Quarterly*, 46 (2006): 191–203.

Taylor, Charles. *Hegel*. Cambridge: Cambridge University Press, 1975.

———. "Hegel and the Philosophy of Action." In Stepelevich and Lamb (eds.), *Hegel's Philosophy of Action*, pp. 1–18.

———. "Understanding and Ethnocentricity." Chapter 4 of *Philosophy and the Human Sciences*. Cambridge: Cambridge University Press, 1985.

Tran-Duc-Thâo. "Existentialisme et matérialisme dialectique." *Revue de métaphysique et de morale* 54 (1949): 317–29.

———. *Phénoménologie et matérialisme dialectique*. Paris: Éditions Minh-Tan, 1951.

Tunick, Mark. "Hegel's Claim About Democracy and his Philosophy of History." Chapter 10 of Dudley (ed.), *Hegel and History*.

Vander Goot, Henry (ed.). *Life as Religion: Essays in Honor of H. Evan Runner*. Jordan Station, Ontario: Paideia Press, 1981.

van der Meulen, Jan. "Hegels Lehre von Leib, Seele und Geist." *Hegel-Studien*, 2 (1963): 251–74.

van Roden Allen, Robert. "Hegelian Beginning and Resolve: A View of the Relationship between the *Phenomenology* and the *Logic*." *Idealistic Studies*, 13 (1983): 249–65.

Verene, Donald Phillip. *Hegel's Recollection: A Study of Images in the Phenomenology of Spirit*. Albany: State University of New York Press, 1985.

Vernon, Jim. *Hegel's Philosophy of Language*. New York: Continuum, 2007.

Vico, Giambattista. *The New Science of Giambattista Vico*. Translated by Thomas

Goddard Bergin and Max Harold Fisch. Ithaca: Cornell University Press, 1984.

von der Luft, Eric. "Would Hegel have liked to burn down all the churches and replace them with philosophical academies?" *Modern Schoolman* 68 (Nov. 1990): 41–56.

Wahl, Jean. *Le malheur de la conscience dans le philosophie de Hegel.* Paris: Riedel, 1929.

———. *Existence humain et transcendence.* Neuchâtel: Editions de la Baconnière, 1944.

———. "Commentaire d'une passage de la Phénomenologie de Hegel." *Revue de métaphysique et de morale* 34 (1927): 441–71.

Waines, David. *An Introduction to Islam.* Cambridge: Cambridge University Press, 1995.

Warminski, Andrej. "Reading for Example: 'Sense-Certainty' in Hegel's *Phenomenology of Spirit.*" *Diacritics,* 11 (1981): 83–94.

Wartenburg, T. E. "Poverty and Class Struggle in Hegel's Theory of Civil Society." *Philosophy and Social Criticism* 8 (1981): 169–82.

Weber, Max. *The Protestant Ethic and the Spirit of Capitalism.* Translated by Peter Baehr and Gordon C. Wells. London: Penguin, 2002.

Weil, Eric. *Hegel et l'État: Cinq Conférences.* Paris: Vrin, 1985.

Westphal, Kenneth. "The Basic Context and Structure of Hegel's *Philosophy of Right.*" In Frederick C. Beiser (ed.), *The Cambridge Companion to Hegel.* New York: Cambridge University Press, 1993.

Westphal, Merold (ed.). *Method and Speculation in Hegel's Phenomenology.* Atlantic Highlands, N.J.: Humanities Press, 1982.

Wieland, Wolfgang. "Bemerkungen zum Anfang von Hegels Logik," in *Seminar: Dialektik in der Philosophie Hegels,* ed. R.-P. Horstmann. Frankfurt am Main: Suhrkamp Verlag, 1978, pp. 194–212.

Wilcocks, R. W. *Zur Erkenntnistheorie Hegels in der Phänomenologie des Geistes.* Hildesheim: Georg Olms Verlag, 1917, reprinted 1981.

Wildt, Andreas. *Autonomie und Anerkennung: Hegels Moralitätskritik im Lichte seiner Fichte-Rezeption.* Stuttgart: Klett-Cotta, 1982.

Williams, Robert R. *Recogniton: Fichte and Hegel on the Other.* Albany: State University of New York Press, 1992.

———. "Hegel and Skepticism." *Owl of Minerva* 24 (1992): 71–82.

———. "Hegel's Concept of *Geist.*" In Stillman (ed.), *Hegel's Philosophy of Spirit,* pp. 1–20.

———. Review of Michael Forster, *Hegel and Skepticism. Owl of Minerva* 25 (1993): 84–88.

Winfield, Richard Dien. "Commentary on 'Hegel's Concept of *Geist*'." In Stillman (ed.), *Hegel's Philosophy of Spirit,* pp. 21–24.

———. "The Theory and Practice of the History of Freedom: The Right of History in Hegel's Philosophy of Right." In *Overcoming Foundations.* New York: Columbia University Press, 1989.

Wolff, Michael. "Hegel's Organicist Theory of the State: On the Concept and

Method of Hegel's 'Science of the State.'" Chapter 12 of Pippin and Höffe, *Hegel on Ethics and Politics.*

Wood, Allen W. *Hegel's Ethical Thought.* Cambridge: Cambridge University Press, 1990.

Zambrana, Rocío. "Hegel's Logic of Finitude." *Continental Philosophy Review* 45 (2012): 213–33.

Žižek, Slavoj. *Tarrying with the Negative: Kant, Hegel and the Critique of Ideology.* Durham: Duke University Press, 1993.

Index of Passages

Discussions of and references to passages in Hegel's text are identified here according to the paragraph number in Miller's translation of the *Phenomenology of Spirit.*

Index of Subjects